# THE NIV®
# STANDARD LESSON
# COMMENTARY
# 2004-2005

edited by

## RONALD L. NICKELSON

published by
**Standard Publishing**

Jonathan Underwood, Senior Editor

Douglas Redford,
Contributing Editor

Carla J. Crane,
Production Manager

*Eleventh Annual Volume*

**Standard**
PUBLISHING
CINCINNATI, OHIO

# CD-ROM AVAILABLE

The *Standard Lesson Commentary*® is available separately in an electronic format. This compact disk contains the full text of the King James *Standard Lesson Commentary*® and *The NIV Standard Lesson Commentary*®, a variety of preparation resources powered by the Libronix Digital Library System, and a collection of presentation helps that can be projected or reproduced as handouts. Ask for the *Standard Lesson eCommentary* (#06005) at your local Christian bookstore or directly from Standard Publishing.

*System Requirements: Windows XP/2000/ME/98/95; Pentium 133 MHz processor (300MHz recommended), 64 Meg RAM (128 recommended); 60 Meg Available Hard Drive Space; 2x or better CD-ROM drive.*

If you have any questions regarding the installation, registration, or activation of this CD-ROM, please contact Logos **Customer Service** at **(800) 875-6467.**

If you have problems with the CD, *Technical Support* is available by telephone at *(360) 679-4496,* by e-mail at *tech@logos.com,* or online at *www.logos.com/support.*

© 2004
STANDARD PUBLISHING
a division of STANDEX INTERNATIONAL Corporation
8121 Hamilton Avenue, Cincinnati, Ohio 45231
Printed in U.S.A.

# In This Volume

## Special Features

## Fall Quarter, 2004
### *The God of Continuing Creation*

#### Writers

**Lesson Development**..........................Orrin Root
**Verbal Illustrations** ...............Charles R. Boatman
**Why Teach This Lesson?** ......Ronald L. Nickelson

**Discovery Learning** ..............J. David Lang (1-4),
................Alan Weber (5-13)
**What Do You Think?**....A. Eugene Andrews (1-6),
Jonathan Underwood (7-13)

## Winter Quarter, 2004-2005
### *Called to Be God's People*

#### Writers

**Lesson Development** .............Lloyd Pelfrey (1, 2),
Mark Krause (3, 4), Thomas D. Thurman (5-9),
Douglas Redford (10, 11), Jim Lloyd (12, 13)
**Verbal Illustrations** .......Robert C. Shannon (1-6),
................John Russell (7-13)

**Why Teach This Lesson?** .......A. Eugene Andrews
**Discovery Learning**..............John Conaway (1-4),
....Jonathan Underwood (5-13)
**What Do You Think?** ....Thomas Claibourne (1-9)
..A. Eugene Andrews (10-13)

## Spring Quarter, 2005
### *God's Project: Effective Christians*

#### Writers

**Lesson Development** .......Marshall Hayden (1-8),
J. Michael Shannon (9-13),
**Verbal Illustrations** ...............Charles R. Boatman
**Why Teach This Lesson?** ...............Vicki Edwards

**Discovery Learning** ...........Ronald G. Davis (1-8),
Alan Weber (9-13)
**What Do You Think?**........................David Marvin

## Summer Quarter, 2005
### *Jesus' Life, Teachings, and Ministry*

#### Writers

**Lesson Development** ...............Jon Weatherly (1),
Mark Krause (2-4), Kenny Boles (5-9),
..............Blair Yaeger (10-13)
**Verbal Illustrations** ........Robert C. Shannon (1-8)
..............Terry A. Clark (9-13)

**Discovery Learning** ...........Ronald G. Davis (1-4),
.....Thomas Hutchison (5-13)
**What Do You Think?** .........Jonathan Underwood
**Why Teach This Lesson?**.............Ronald G. Davis

# Index of Printed Texts, 2004-2005

The printed texts for 2004-2005 are arranged here in the order in which they appear in the Bible. Opposite each reference is the page number on which the lesson that treats the passage begins in this volume.

# A Tribute to Orrin Root

*by Shawn McMullen, Editor of* The Lookout

*Orrin Root, 1905-2003*

Standard Publishing employees, Sunday school teachers, and Bible students around the world recently lost a dear friend, teacher, writer, editor, and mentor. Orrin Root died May 13, 2003 at the age of 98.

Mr. Root began his ministry with Standard Publishing in 1945. His early responsibilities included editing *Bible Teacher and Leader, the* adult Sunday school curriculum, and three age levels of youth curriculum.

From June 26, 1949, through October of 2003 Mr. Root wrote Sunday school lesson commentary for *The Lookout* magazine. If my calculations are correct, this means that Mr. Root wrote 2,826 consecutive weekly Scripture commentaries. First under the title, "Untying Some Knots," and later, "Background and Commentary," his insightful commentary and polished writing have helped Bible students around the world understand and apply God's Word to their lives. His mastery of the English language combined with a concise and accurate writing style made him an "editor's editor." Mr. Root worked ahead and never missed a deadline.

In 1953 Mr. Root, as editor-in-chief of Standard Publishing's Sunday school materials, oversaw the production of the first STANDARD LESSON COMMENTARY. As editor and as writer, he has been instrumental in the production of the COMMENTARY each year. His name appears in every issue except one as either editor or writer. This year marks the thirty-third consecutive issue in which he was writer or co-writer of one full quarter of verse-by-verse exposition of the Scripture text.

Mr. Root left his post as Standard Publishing's editor-in-chief to retire in 1970. When editor Jay Sheffield died, Mr. Root was called out of retirement to serve as editor "pro tempore" of *The Lookout* from August of 1975 to September of 1976.

Even in retirement, Mr. Root's influence at Standard Publishing continued to be felt through his ministry as a freelance writer and editor. His regular visits to the office to deliver manuscripts and receive new assignments were welcomed by everyone. His gentle spirit, quick wit, charm, and humility endeared him to us all.

I know few people who have served God with greater purpose, passion, and steadfastness. *Christian Standard* editor Mark Taylor and I visited Mr. Root in the hospital a few days before his death. Weakened physically but still focused and thoughtful, he told us he had informed the hospital staff that he needed to get home right away because he had a great deal of writing to do.

I had been editing only a few months when I paid a visit to Mr. Root at the Mt. Healthy Christian Home in Cincinnati, Ohio. We talked about writing, editing, and ministry. Among the many helpful things he said to me, I fondly remember two. I asked what advice he could give me as a new editor. He said, "Write and edit not only to be understood, but also not to be misunderstood." Near the conclusion of our visit he said, "I read your material. You're a good writer." I'll hold onto those words as long as I live.

Upon hearing of Mr. Root's death, I thought, *What does an editor like Mr. Root do in Heaven?* He worked so long and hard and faithfully in this life to help men and women understand and apply God's Word. Now he lives where there are no mistakes to correct, no misunderstandings to set right, no puzzling thoughts to clarify. Then it occurred to me. Whatever else Mr. Root is doing in Heaven, he is enjoying a well-deserved rest.

*Then I heard a voice from heaven saying to me, "Write: 'Blessed are the dead who die in the Lord from now on.'" "Yes," says the Spirit, "that they may rest from their labors, and their works follow them" (Revelation 14:13, NKJV).*

# How to Say It

The following pages list some of the names and other hard-to-pronounce words used in the lessons of this edition of *The NIV® Standard Lesson Commentary®* along with a phonetic pronunciation guide for each. In each lesson is an abridged version of this list that includes only the words used in that lesson.

**A**bana. AB-uh-nuh or Uh-BAN-uh.
Abba. AB-buh.
Abinadab. Uh-BIN-uh-dab.
Abraham. AY-bruh-ham.
Abram. AY-brum.
Absalom. AB-suh-lum.
Achaia. Uh-kay-uh.
Adam (*Hebrew*). uh-DAHM.
Ahab. AY-hab.
Ahaz. AY-haz.
Ai. AY-eye.
Alphaeus. AL-fee-us.
Ammonite. AM-un-ite.
Amorites. AM-uh-rites.
Amos. AY-mus.
Amoz. AY-mahz.
anathema. uh-NATH-uh-muh.
Annas. AN-nus.
Antioch. AN-tee-ock.
Aphrodite. Af-ruh-DITE-ee.
Arabia. Uh-RAY-bee-uh.
Aram. AIR-um.
Aramaic. AIR-uh-MAY-ik.
Aramean. AR-uh-ME-un (strong accent on me).
Arimathea. AIR-uh-muh-THEE-uh (TH as in THIN).
Aristophanes. A-ris-TOF-a-neez.
Artemis. AR-teh-miss.
Asaph. AY-saff.
Asher. ASH-er.
Assyrian. Uh-SEAR-e-un.
Assyrians. Uh-SEAR-e-unz.
Athena. Uh-THEE-nuh.
Athens. ATH-unz.
Augustine. A W-gus-TEEN or Aw-GUS-tin.

**B**aal. BAY-ul.
Babylon. BAB-uh-lun.
Babylonians. Bab-ih-LOW-nee-unz.
Barnabas. BAR-nuh-bus.
Bar-Tholami. Bar THAL-uh-me.
Bartholomew. Bar-THAHL-uh-mew.
Bartimaeus. BAR-tih-ME-us.
Bashan. BAY-shan.
Bathsheba. Bath-SHE-buh.
Benedictus. BEN-eh-DIK-tus.

Ben-Hadad. Ben-HAY-dad.
Bethel. BETH-ul.
Bethlehem. BETH-lih-hem.
Bethsaida. Beth-SAY-uh-duh.
Bethuel. Be-THU-ul.
Bezalel. Bih-ZAL-ih-el.
blasphemer. BLAS-feem-er.
blasphemy. BLAS-fuh-me.
Bolshevik. BOL-shuh-vik.
Buddha. BOO-duh.

**C**aesarea Philippi. Sess-uh-REE-uh Fih-LIP-pie or FIL-ih-pie.
Caesarea. Sess-uh-REE-uh.
Caiaphas. KAY-uh-fus or KYE-uh-fus.
Cana. KAY-nuh.
Canaan. KAY-nun.
Canaanites. KAY-nun-ites.
Capernaum. Kuh-PER-nay-um.
carpe diem (*Latin*). kar-pay DEE-um.
centurion. sen-TURE-ee-un.
Cephas. SEE-fus.
Chaldeans. Kal-DEE-unz.
Chemosh. KEE-mosh.
Colossians. Kuh-LOSH-unz.
Corinth. KOR-inth.
Corinthians. Ko-RIN-thee-unz (th as in thin).
Cornelius. Cor-NEEL-yus.
Cyrus. SIGH-russ.
Czarist. TSAR-ist.

**D**almanutha. Dal-muh-NEW-thuh.
Damascus. Duh-MASS-kus.
Decapolis. Dee-CAP-uh-lis.
denarii. dih-NAIR-ee or dih-NAIR-eye.
denarius. dih-NAIR-ee-us.
Derbe. DER-be.
Deuteronomy. Due-ter-AHN-uh-me.
Didymus. DID-uh-mus.
dissimulation. dis-SIM-you-LAY-shun.

**E**bal. EE-bull.
Ecclesiastes. Ik-LEEZ-ee-AS-teez.
eczema. EK-zuh-muh.
Eden. EE-den.
Egypt. EE-jipt.
Eliab. Ee-LYE-ab.

Elijah. Ee-LYE-juh.
Elimelech. Ee-LIM-eh-leck.
Elisha. E-LYE-shuh.
elohim (*Hebrew*). el-o-HEEM.
Emmaus. Em-MAY-us.
Ephesians. Ee-FEE-zhunz.
Ephesus. EF-uh-sus.
Esau. EE-saw.
Essenes. EH-seenz.
Ethiopian. E-thee-O-pee-un.
Euphrates. You-FRAY-teez.
Eusebius. You-SEE-be-us.
Ezekiel. Ee-ZEEK-ee-ul or Ee-ZEEK-yul.
Ezra. EZ-ruh.

**G**adarenes. GAD-uh-reens.
Gadites. GAD-ites.
Gaius. GAY-us.
Galatians. Guh-LAY-shunz.
Galilean. Gal-uh-LEE-un.
Galilee. GAL-uh-lee.
Gauls. Gawlz.
Gennesaret. Geh-NESS-uh-ret.
Gentiles. JEN-tilez.
Gerasenes. GUR-uh-seenz.
Gerizim. GAIR-ih-zeem or Guh-RYE-zim.
Gethsemane. Geth-SEM-uh-nee (G as in get).
Gibeah. GIB-ee-uh (G as in get).
Giuliani. Joo-lee-AHN-ee.
Golgotha. GAHL-guh-thuh.
Goliath. Go-LYE-uth.
Guyana. Guy-AH-nuh.

**H**abakkuk. Huh-BACK-kuk.
Hagar. HAY-gar.
Hannah. HAN-uh.
Haran. HAIR-un.
Hercules. HER-kew-leez.
Herod Agrippa. HAIR-ud Uh-GRIP-puh.
Herod Antipas. HAIR-ud AN-tih-pus.
Herod. HAIR-ud.
Hezekiah. Hez-ih-KYE-uh.
Hittites. HIT-ites or HIT-tites.
Hivites. HI-vites.
Horeb. HO-reb.
Hosea. Ho-ZAY-uh.
Hoshea. Ho-SHAY-uh.

Iconium. Eye-KO-nee-um.
Isaac. EYE-zuk.
Isaiah. Eye-ZAY-uh.
Iscah. IS-ka.
ish (*Hebrew*). ish.
Ishmael. ISH-may-el.
ishshah (*Hebrew*). ish-SHAW.
Isis. EYE-sis.
Israel. IZ-ray-el.

Jacob. JAY-kub.
Jairus. JYE-rus or JAY-ih-rus.
Jebusites. JEB-yuh-sites.
Jehoiachin. Jeh-HOY-uh-kin.
Jehoiakim. Jeh-HOY-uh-kim.
Jehoram. Jeh-HO-rum.
Jeremiah. Jair-uh-MY-uh.
Jericho. JAIR-ih-co.
Jerusalem. Juh-ROO-suh-lem.
Jesse. JESS-ee.
Jethro. JETH-ro.
Jezebel. JEZ-uh-bel.
Joram. JO-ram.
Jordan. JOR-dun.
Josephus. Jo-SEE-fus.
Joses. JO-sez.
Joshua. JOSH-yew-uh.
Jotham. JO-thum.
Judah. JOO-duh.
Judaism. JOO-day-iz-um.
Judaizers. JOO-day-ize-ers.
Judas Iscariot. JOO-dus Iss-CARE-e-ut.
Judea. Joo-DEE-uh.

Kebar. KEE-bar.
Kerioth. KEE-rih-oath.
Keturah. Keh-TOO-ruh.
Kilion. KIL-ee-on.
Kinnereth. KIN-e-reth.
korinthiazesthai (*Greek*). ko-rin-thee-
    ADZ-ess-thai.

Lamentations. Lam-en-TAY-shunz.
Lazarus. LAZ-uh-rus.
Levi. LEE-vye.
Levite. LEE-vite.
Leviticus. Leh-VIT-ih-kus.
lex talionis (*Latin*). leks tal-ee-OH-niss.
Lystra. LISS-truh.

Maccabees. MACK-uh-bees.
Macedonia. Mass-eh-DOE-nee-uh.
Magdalene. MAG-duh-leen or Mag-
    duh-LEE-nee.

Magnificat. Mag-NIF-ih-cot.
Mahlon. MAH-lon.
Malachi. MAL-uh-kye.
Manasseh. Muh-NASS-uh.
martyrs. MAR-turz.
Melchizedek. Mel-KIZ-eh-dek.
Mesopotamia. MES-uh-puh-TAY-me-uh.
Messiah. Meh-SIGH-uh.
messianic. Mess-ee-AN-ick.
Micah. MY-kuh.
Midian. MID-ee-un.
Milcah. MIL-kuh.
Moab. MO-ab.
Moabites. MO-ub-ites.
Mojave. Moh-HAH-vee.
Moreh. MOE-reh.
Moses. MO-zes or MO-zez.

Naaman. NAY-uh-mun.
Nahor. NAY-hor.
Naomi. Nay-OH-me.
Nathan. NAY-thun (th as in thin).
Nathanael. Nuh-THAN-yull (th as in
    thin).
Nazareth. NAZ-uh-reth.
Nazareth. NAZ-uh-reth.
Nebuchadnezzar. NEB-yuh-kud-NEZ-er.
Nehemiah. NEE-huh-MY-uh.
Nicodemus. NICK-uh-DEE-mus.
Nun. None.
Nunc Dimittis (*Latin*). Nunk Dih-MIT-
    us.

Omri. AHM-rye.
Orpah. OR-pah.

Parthenon. PAR-thuh-non.
parthenos (*Greek*). par-THEN-ahss.
Perea. Peh-REE-uh.
Perizzites. PAIR-ih-zites.
Phanuel. Fuh-NYOO-el.
pharaoh. FAIR-o or FAY-roe.
Pharisees. FAIR-ih-seez.
Pharpar. FAR-par.
Philippi. Fih-LIP-pie or FIL-ih-pie.
Philippians. Fih-LIP-ee-unz.
Philistines. Fuh-LISS-teens
    or FILL-us-teenz.
Phoenicia. Fuh-NISH-uh.
Pilate. PIE-lut.
Pisgah. PIZ-guh.
Pisidian. Pih-SID-ee-un.
Pontius Pilate. PON-shus or PON-ti-us
    PIE-lut.

proselyte. PRAHSS-uh-light.
psoriasis. suh-RYE-uh-sis.

Rabbi. RAB-eye.
Raca. RAY-kuh or Ray-KAH.
Ramah. RAY-muh.
Rebekah. Reh-BEK-uh.
Reubenites. ROO-ben-ites.
ruah (*Hebrew*). RUE-ah.

Sadducees. SAD-you-seez.
Salome. Suh-LO-me.
Samaria. Suh-MARE-ee-uh.
Samaritans. Suh-MARE-uh-tunz.
Sanhedrin. SAN-huh-drun or
    San-HEED-run.
Sarai. SEH-rye.
Sarapis. Suh-RAP-is.
Satan. SAY-tun.
Septuagint. Sep-TOO-ih-jent.
Sergio Gutierrez. SAIR-jyo Goo-TAR-ez.
Shechem. SHEE-kem or SHEK-em.
shema (*Hebrew*). shih-MAH.
Sierra Leone. See-AIR-uh Lay-OWN.
Sihon. SIGH-hun.
Silas. SIGH-luss.
Silvanus. Sil-VAY-nus.
Simeon. SIM-ee-un.
Sinai. SIGH-nye or SIGH-nay-eye.
Sirach. SIGH-rak.
Solomon. SOL-o-mun.
Strabo. STRAY-bow (bow as in rainbow).
Sychar. SIGH-kar.
synagogue. SIN-uh-gog.
Syria. SEAR-ee-uh.

Terah. TAIR-uh.
tetrarch. TEH-trark or TEE-trark.
Thaddaeus. Tha-DEE-us.
Tiberias. Tie-BEER-ee-us.
Tigris. TIE-griss.
Timothy. TIM-o-thee.
Titus. TY-tus.
Tyre. Tire.

Ur. Er.
Uzziah. Uh-ZYE-uh.

Zacchaeus. Zack-KEY-us.
Zarephath. ZAIR-uh-fath
Zebedee. ZEB-eh-dee.
Zechariah. Zek-uh-RYE-uh.
Zedekiah. Zed-uh-KYE-uh.
Zeus. Zoose.

# Fall Quarter, 2004

## *The God of Continuing Creation*

## About These Lessons

Is there anyone who isn't fascinated by "newness"? New cars, new careers, new babies, and new houses signify important changes to our lives and to the lives of those closest to us. Such changes cause excitement! But are we as excited about the "newness" that comes from God? This quarter's lessons teach us why we should be.

Sep 5

Sep 12

Sep 19

Sep 26

Oct 3

Oct 10

Oct 17

Oct 24

Oct 31

Nov 7

Nov 14

Nov 21

Nov 28

# Starting Again, for the First Time

Those who have experienced the entire six-year cycle of International Sunday School Lessons that just ended are in for a treat: it's time to start over! This observation is not meant to be flippant, but recognizes the fact that there's always more to learn. Each time we work through our Bibles, we do so with "new eyes" because our life situations are always changing. For instance, those who have come to Christ only recently will relate to the idea of being a "new creation" somewhat differently than will the long-time Christians.

Our "new eyes" should notice something else as well: the six-year cycle of the past is now a three-year cycle, as the chart below reveals. We begin with two surveys. The two surveys then give way to considerations of specific themes in specific books. Some will challenge our thinking about doctrine. Others will move us to change our behavior. Still others will convict us in our hearts and spirits. All will draw us closer to God.

A feature continued from the old six-year cycle is the high value placed on both Old and New Testaments. Neither Testament can be fully understood without reference to the other. God's Word forms a unity that must not be broken.

As we work through our new three-year plan, may we never forget that both Testaments ultimately point to Jesus. From the very beginning, Jesus was involved in our creation (Colossians 1:16). From the very beginning, he was part of the plan of our redemption (Genesis 3:15b). He is the One who promises to return for us (Revelation 22:20).

When Jesus does return, will he find us serving and ready as he expects? (See Matthew 24:36-51.) This new cycle of lessons will help ensure that he does.

## International Sunday School Lesson Cycle
## September, 2004—August, 2007

| YEAR | FALL QUARTER (Sept., Oct., Nov.) | WINTER QUARTER (Dec., Jan., Feb.) | SPRING QUARTER (Mar., Apr., May) | SUMMER QUARTER (June, July, Aug.) |
|---|---|---|---|---|
| 2004-2005 | The God of Continuing Creation (Bible Survey) | Called to Be God's People (Bible Survey) | God's Project: Effective Christians (Romans, Galatians) | Jesus' Life, Teachings, and Ministry (Matthew, Mark, Luke) |
| 2005-2006 | "You Will Be My Witnesses" (Acts) | God's Commitment— Our Response (Isaiah; 1 and 2 Timothy) | Living in and as God's Creation (Psalms, Job, Ecclesiastes, Proverbs) | Called to Be a Christian Community (1 and 2 Corinthians) |
| 2006-2007 | God's Living Covenant (Old Testament Survey) | Jesus Christ: A Portrait of God (John, Philippians, Colossians, Hebrews, 1 John) | Our Community Now and in God's Future (1 John, Revelation) | Committed to Doing Right (Various Prophets, 2 Kings, 2 Chronicles) |

| "Creation" | "Call" | "Covenant" | "Christ" | "Community" | "Commitment" |

# God's Continuing Creation

## *by Orrin Root*

September, October, and November of 2004 bring us a new cycle in the International Sunday School Lesson series. This cycle is an innovative one, including only three years instead of the customary six; but this three-month introduction follows the usual pattern. By considering events widely separated in time, it creates an awareness of the whole scope of Bible history in which all the lessons of the three-year cycle will find their places.

This time our introductory series of thirteen lessons follows the theme of creation through the Bible. Beginning with the creation of man, it leaps to the new beginning after the great flood, then to the creation of a chosen nation, Israel, to maintain faith in God in a pagan world.

Along the way we shall be led to think of the creation of intangible things like hope and trust. Later we shall consider the importance of being new creatures in Christ Jesus and to anticipate the new spiritual bodies that will be ours when we are raised from the dead. The thirteen lessons of this quarter fall into three units corresponding to the months of September, October, and November.

### UNIT 1. CREATED FOR A PURPOSE

SEPTEMBER

The unit title suggests that we look for God's purposes. Why did he make us in his own image? When human behavior proved to be unsatisfactory, why did he start again with the same kind of people? Perhaps the lesson texts will not state God's purpose as plainly as we would like to see it all along the way, but the question does make us think.

**Lesson 1: From the Dust of the Ground.** Our first lesson comes from the second chapter of Genesis and centers attention on the creation of Adam and Eve. When we read of a new man with a new wife at home in a garden newly created from God's hand, we see a wonderful opportunity to live happily ever after. But there is a touch of foreboding here. The mention of one prohibition indicates that from the beginning there was the possibility of disobedience and disaster.

**Lesson 2: Beginning Again.** It is a long leap from the creation to Noah's new beginning after the flood, but Genesis itself provides a three-and-a-half chapter background for lesson 2. Adam and Eve did disobey the only prohibition in the world and lost their home in the garden. Generation after generation then became worse and worse. Looking at the human race, God saw that "every inclination of the thoughts of his heart was only evil at all times" (Genesis 6:5). So God cleansed the earth with a great flood.

But God didn't overlook the glimmer of righteousness. He saw one good family in an evil world, and so eight people survived the flood in the ark.

**Lesson 3: God Raises Up a Deliverer.** Like Adam's descendants, Noah's descendants kept getting worse and worse in their character and action. This time God did not destroy the evil people, but instead chose one man of faith, Abraham, to be the father of a good nation.

Abraham's family numbered about seventy people when it moved to Egypt to escape a famine in Palestine. In Egypt it prospered and increased, perhaps until it numbered in the millions. Eventually a new king made slaves of Abraham's people and tried to work them to death, but still they increased. So the hostile king ordered that all their boy babies must be put in the river.

Moses was one of those babies, but his thoughtful mother put him in a tiny boat that floated among the reeds near the bank. There the king's daughter found him. Moved by sympathy, she reared him as her own son, a prince of Egypt.

At the age of forty, this prince killed a slave driver who was abusing a Hebrew slave. Moses escaped retribution by fleeing to Midian. Lesson 3 takes up the story forty years later. God sent this eighty-year-old man back to Egypt to lead the Hebrew slaves to freedom.

**Lesson 4: Becoming God's People.** This time the gap between lessons is only about forty years. God and Moses did lead the Hebrew slaves to freedom; but because they lacked faith and refused to obey, the older generation had to die off during forty years in the desert before the younger generation could have the promised land. Lesson 4 brings us some of what Moses said to them as they stood ready to go forward as God's people and take that promised land as their own.

OCTOBER

## UNIT 2. GOD'S CREATIVITY CONTINUES

Again we leap across a gap of centuries. The people of Israel captured the promised land and lived there for hundreds of years. Then, for reasons that seemed good to them, leaders decided to make their country into a monarchy. God consented without approving. Saul became the first king, and David the second.

**Lesson 5: Creating a New Dynasty.** David was Israel's great empire-builder. He captured Jerusalem from the pagans and made it his capital. He brought the ark of the covenant there and proposed to house it in a magnificent temple.

David wanted to build a splendid house for God, but God sent a prophet to dissuade him. God said his house should be built by David's son; but God would build for David a house: that is, a household, a family, a dynasty of kings that would rule forever. The text of lesson 5 records David's prayer in response to that surprising promise.

**Lesson 6: Creating a Redeemed People.** Again we leap across a wide span of time between lessons. David's son Solomon built a temple as God had predicted. He also brought Israel to the peak of power and glory.

After Solomon's death, Israel split into two weaker nations that swiftly lost their power and glory. Isaiah was a prophet in Judah, the south part of divided Israel. He wrote of events to come as if they were past, for already they were determined in the mind of God. Clearly the prophet foretold Judah's captivity in Babylon (Isaiah 39:5-7). In lesson 6 we shall see that he foretold the end of that captivity just as clearly. God would redeem his captive people and send them home.

**Lesson 7: Creating a New Covenant.** Jeremiah was God's prophet in Judah before and during Judah's captivity in Babylon. He predicted that Babylon's rule of Judah would end after seventy years. Then he looked further into the future and predicted a new covenant that would feature the forgiveness of sins. That is the Christian covenant under which we live today.

**Lesson 8: Creating a New Hope.** Ezekiel was one of the captives in Babylon. God gave him a fantastic vision to create new hope in the minds and hearts of his fellow captives.

**Lesson 9: Creating a Renewed Trust.** Now we turn back through centuries to the time of David. Asaph, a psalmist and musician, found his faltering trust in God renewed by a time of worship. Anyone whose trust is faltering may find a like renewal in a time of sincere worship.

## UNIT 3. A NEW CREATION

November brings us to the New Testament part of these studies that introduce our new cycle of lessons. We are now at the time of the new covenant foretold by Jeremiah (lesson 7), the time when God's plan allows us to become new creations (2 Corinthians 5:17).

**Lesson 10: A New Approach.** Jesus fulfilled the Old Testament laws. He reaffirmed their original meaning by reasserting their application to thoughts and motives as well as to actions. What a guide for every Christian's self-control!

**Lesson 11: A New Body.** This lesson moves us to anticipate the trumpet that will call the dead to be raised incorruptible. When that happens, we will enjoy a change from natural bodies to spiritual bodies that are fitted for eternity. What joy!

**Lesson 12: A New Creature in Christ.** Even while we wear our natural bodies we are new creatures. What an incentive to guide these natural bodies in spiritual ways!

**Lesson 13: A New Relationship.** When we are children of God we are brothers and sisters of all of God's children. Aren't we glad we are part of the family of God?

From our hearts we sing with the psalmist, "Your word is a lamp to my feet and a light for my path" (Psalm 119:105). At the end of the stanza, we sing also the resolution of each heart: "My heart is set on keeping your decrees to the very end" (v. 112). As we study the thirteen lessons of this introductory series, we shall find in each some guidance on life's pathway. If we give attention also to the long periods of time between the lessons, we shall refresh our concept of the whole scope of Bible history. As we go on through the three-year cycle of lessons, we shall be able to fit each one into that concept of the whole. Happy learning!

# Lesson Planning Page

*List the aims here, either directly from the lesson or revised to suit your individual needs.*

**LESSON AIMS**

*Begin with an opening activity like the illustration from the beginning of the lesson, "Into the Lesson" from the Discovery Learning page, a discussion question, or some other appropriate opener.*

**GETTING STARTED**

*List in order the activities you will use. These include discussion questions, activities from the discovery learning page and the reproducible page—as well as key points from the commentary section.*

**LESSON DEVELOPMENT**

    I.

    II.

    III.

*How will you bring the lesson to a climax, stressing the key point and desired action steps?*

**CONCLUSION & APPLICATION**

*Dismiss the class with an activity that reinforces the Bible lesson.*

**CLOSING ACTIVITY**

The World of Moses

MEDITERRANEAN SEA

Salt Sea

MOAB

EDOM

MIDIAN

GOSHEN

EGYPT

SINAI

RED SEA (Gulf of Suez)

Nile River

# The God of Continuing Creation

| Created for a Purpose | God's Creativity Continues | A New Creation |
|---|---|---|
| From the Dust of the Ground: Adam and Eve<br><br>Genesis 2 | Creating a New Dynasty: King David<br><br>2 Samuel 7 | A New Approach: Attitudes and Actions<br><br>Matthew 5 |
| Beginning Again: The Flood<br><br>Genesis 6–9 | Creating a Redeemed People: Israel's Savior<br><br>Isaiah 43 | A New Body: Our Resurrection<br><br>1 Corinthians 15 |
| God Raises Up a Deliverer: Moses and the Exodus<br>Exodus 3 | Creating a New Covenant: Looking Toward Jesus<br>Jeremiah 29, 31 | A New Creature in Christ: Reconciled to God<br>2 Corinthians 5 |
| Becoming God's People: Covenant Promise<br><br>Deuteronomy 29 | Creating a New Hope: Life From Death<br><br>Ezekiel 37 | A New Relationship: Community in Christ<br><br>Ephesians 2 |
| | Creating a Renewed Trust: Looking Upward<br><br>Psalm 73 | |

# FROM THE DUST OF THE GROUND

## LESSON 1

## WHY TEACH THIS LESSON?

As you undoubtedly have noticed, scientific probing into the issue of human origin is never ending. It seems as if every five years or so another mummified corpse or ancient skeleton is discovered, resulting in a new flurry of carbon dating, giddy speculation, and revision of current theory. Those researchers who bow the knee to God Almighty will ensure that their conclusions do not conflict with Genesis 1 and 2. Unfortunately, such scientists seem to be rather few in number these days!

Today's lesson offers your learners an opportunity to avoid the siren song of ungodly conclusions on the issues of human origin and human accountability to God. When we realize that our Redeemer was first our Creator, we will discover —or rediscover—our value to him. Then our worship of him will take on a new intensity and depth.

## INTRODUCTION

Where do babies come from? Parents are likely to be challenged by that question from their firstborn when a second child is born into the family. It is not easy to frame an accurate answer for a three-year-old, so parents improvise.

### A. VARIOUS ANSWERS

From a land where storks perch on rooftops beside wide chimneys has come a tradition that storks bring new babies by way of those chimneys. That, of course, is patently preposterous. If even a two-year-old accepts it, he or she probably will abandon it before age six. But the fiction is so charming that it has a firm place in popular culture—even in places where no stork has been seen since the creation of the world.

More sober minds explain our origin via rational theories of evolution. Through countless millennia, we are told, microscopic living things developed into fish, and fish developed into birds, etc., etc., until monkeys finally became human.

But if that theory is true, then why aren't people developing into something else? We are, we are told; but the change is too slow to be observed in a lifetime, or even by the techniques of modern science. Again, we are left to wonder.

When the question of origin is broadened to include all the things we see in earth and sky, it engages the attention of not only our greatest scientists but also that of the average person on the street. Where did everything come from? All the power of human intellect is engaged in the search for rational answers that do not include God, for God is not seen even with our most powerful telescope.

The authentic answer is written in the first two chapters of Genesis: God made them. He created the basic stuff of which stars and planets are made. With

DEVOTIONAL READING:
PSALM 150
BACKGROUND SCRIPTURE:
GENESIS 2
PRINTED TEXT:
GENESIS 2:4-7, 15-25

LESSON AIMS

After participating in this lesson, each student will be able to:

1. Tell briefly about the origin of life on earth, especially human life.

2. Explain how the Genesis 2 account reveals the special place men and women have in God's creation.

3. Suggest a way to live consistent with that special place in some specific area.

KEY VERSE

The LORD God formed the man from the dust of the ground and breathed into his nostrils the breath of life, and the man became a living being.

—Genesis 2:7

or without a "big bang," he put each where he wanted it to be. He shaped each one according to his will. He fashioned all living things and gave them life.

How did the ancient writer know so many facts that modern researchers seem unable to discover? God revealed those facts—sometimes directly to the ancient writer and sometimes through creation itself (Psalm 19:1-6). In the first two chapters of Genesis we have God's own report of his own creation. Nothing can be more authentic than that.

## B. LESSON BACKGROUND

Easily we see that in Genesis 1 and 2 we have two reports of creation. Some students conclude that those two reports were written by different authors, but that is not a necessary conclusion.

Chapter one may be called a diary of creation. The days are counted one by one, and there is a brief summary of what God did each day. Then it seems most probable that the same author (Moses) wrote chapter two, adding some interesting and important details.

This week we take our lesson from Genesis 2. Naturally its background is seen in Genesis 1. Learners will find this lesson more meaningful if they first read Genesis 1 and the first three verses of Genesis 2.

## I. HOME FOR MAN (GENESIS 2:4-7)

We begin with two things of importance to us. First, the new earth of our text is the same earth (now grown old) upon which we live and move and have our being. Second, the new man of our text is the father of us all, the primary provider of the genes that make us who and what we are. We are not only investigating the origin of things, we are investigating the origin of ourselves.

## A. HABITATION (vv. 4-6)

**4. This is the account of the heavens and the earth when they were created. When the LORD God made the earth and the heavens—**

This *account* or record tells us that there was a day *when the Lord God made the earth and the heavens.* This brief statement of fact draws our attention back to the fuller account in Genesis 1:1-5.

**5. . . . and no shrub of the field had yet appeared on the earth and no plant of the field had yet sprung up, for the LORD God had not sent rain on the earth and there was no man to work the ground,**

There was not a single *plant* on the *earth* on that first day of creation. The word *for* in the middle of the verse, which means "because," directs us to look for explanations as to why this was so. Two reasons are given: a lack of *rain* and a lack of manpower. The next two verses tell how these two issues were resolved, thus opening the way for vegetation to flourish.

**6. . . . but streams came up from the earth and watered the whole surface of the ground—**

*Streams* bubble up from below the earth's surface to provide the needed water. The Hebrew word for "streams" could also be translated "mist," however, as a footnote to your *New International Version* may indicate. If this is the intent, then the description is that of the weather cycle producing rainfall. The idea would be that as water evaporated there went up a mist from the earth (especially that part of the earth that was covered with expanses of water) into the cooler temperature of the upper atmosphere. There the mist or vapor condensed into clouds, then into rain, and watered the whole face of the ground. In either case, it is God causing the natural irrigation so that the earth will be ready for vegetation.

## WHAT DO YOU THINK?

What does the recognition that God is the Maker of Heaven and earth mean for us? How should Christians order their lives, thinking, and worship to reflect this fact?

## B. Inhabitant (v. 7)

**7. . . . the Lord God formed the man from the dust of the ground and breathed into his nostrils the breath of life, and the man became a living being.**

The second reason for the absence of plants was that there was not a *man* to till the ground (v. 5). Now there is a man. True, God made the plants before he made the man, but only three days before (Genesis 1:11-13). The man was there in plenty of time to do the needed tillage.

Although man's body is formed of *the dust of the ground,* it is the very breath of God that transforms that dust into living flesh. At this point in our Bible text we should not think that the phrase *a living being* means that man is a being different from the animals and above them. Genesis 1:30 translates the same Hebrew phrase as "life" and indicates that all the animals have it. Genesis 1:26-28 makes it plain that humans are indeed different from the animals and superior to them. But in the text at hand the phrase *a living being* asserts man's similarity to the animals, not his difference from them.

### Reproducing Creation

You can be in touch with a celebrity! How about owning Edgar Allen Poe's hackberry tree or Orville and Wilbur Wright's red cedar tree or, for a real historical contact, how about owning George Washington's tulip poplar tree?

You can't actually own those specific trees, of course, but you can own a seedling started from them. American Forests is an organization that collects seeds from trees owned by famous people and grows them as seedlings to sell for the historical interest and also as a way of promoting the planting of trees for ecological reasons.

But how about owning a really historic tree? Actually, every tree or plant we have in our yards and gardens can in some way trace its lineage back to those trees God created in the beginning. Within those plants God placed the reproductive power that would perpetuate the image of his creation for millennia to come.

And, of course, the same is true of humans. We continue to reproduce the image of our first ancestors, Adam and Eve. More important, since they were created in God's image we also continue to reproduce that image. The question for each of us is whether we are striving to replicate the untarnished image of the God who made us, or are we satisfied merely to reflect the sin-blemished image of the first parents of our race?

—C. R. B.

## II. INSTRUCTIONS FOR MAN (GENESIS 2:15-17)

When a boy is born, those around him do not think of him as a man until he reaches a certain age (depending on the culture). Through his pre-adult years he is taught, guided, and disciplined by his parents, teachers, and other authority figures. After becoming a man in the sense of being an adult, he has more freedoms.

It seems that the first man was an adult as soon as he was animated by the breath of life, but he had no more experience than a newborn baby. Almost immediately "God commanded the man" (v. 16). Then did God give him the gift of language in a miraculous way, or did it take two years for the man to learn to talk? We have no information about that, but some items of God's instruction are suggested.

### A. Location and Occupation (v. 15)

**15. The Lord God took the man and put him in the Garden of Eden to work it and take care of it.**

Gardening can truly be called "the world's oldest profession," since man's first job was the care of the *garden* that God had prepared as man's home (vv. 8, 9,

---

*What Do You Think?*

*How would you answer someone who sees no real difference between people and animals? How would you stress the importance of the evidence of intelligent design?*

*Visuals for These Lessons*

*The visual pictured in each lesson (e.g., page 22) is a small reproduction of a large, full-color poster included in the Adult Visuals packet for the Fall Quarter. The packet is available from your supplier. Order No. 192.*

*DAILY BIBLE READINGS*

*Monday, Aug. 30—Praise the Lord (Psalm 148:1-6)*

*Tuesday, Aug. 31—Let All the Earth Praise God (Psalm 148:7-13)*

*Wednesday, Sept. 1—God's Creation Is Good (Genesis 1: 26-31)*

*Thursday, Sept. 2—God Created Man (Genesis 2:4b-9)*

*Friday, Sept. 3—The Garden Is Watered by Rivers (Genesis 2: 10-14)*

*Saturday, Sept. 4—Man Is Placed in the Garden (Genesis 2:15-20)*

*Sunday, Sept. 5—God Creates a Helper for Man (Genesis 2:21-25)*

*HOW TO SAY IT*

*Adam (Hebrew). uh-DAHM.*
*Corinthians. Ko-RIN-thee-unz*
  *(th as in thin).*
*Eden. EE-den.*
*Euphrates. You-FRAY-teez.*
*ish (Hebrew). ish.*
*ishshah (Hebrew). ish-SHAW.*
*Tigris. TIE-griss.*

not in today's text). We are left to wonder about how much instruction God gave to *the man* in this regard. Did he tell the man to plant wheat in the autumn, or did the man learn that by experience? Did God say grapevines should be pruned? And how did the man or his descendants ever learn to make a pruning knife?

For such questions we have no answers. What is important is the bigger picture: God is our Creator. It was in this garden that the first humans were to have fellowship with him (Genesis 3:8).

### B. PERMISSION AND PROHIBITION (vv. 16, 17)

**16. And the LORD God commanded the man, "You are free to eat from any tree in the garden;**

Man's food is described more completely in Genesis 1:29. There, seed-bearing plants and trees that have fruit with seed in them are noted, but there is no mention of meat. It seems that God prescribed a vegetarian diet in the beginning. But when there was a new beginning of mankind after the great flood, the Lord authorized the eating of meat as well (Genesis 9:3). Permission *to eat* of the fruit of every *tree* of the *garden* is mentioned to prepare us for the one exception in the next verse.

**17. " . . . but you must not eat from the tree of the knowledge of good and evil, for when you eat of it you will surely die."**

In the description of the Garden of Eden, two trees are given special mention: the tree of life and the tree of the knowledge of good and evil (Genesis 2:9). Dwellers in that garden can live as long as they continue to eat from the tree of life, but they *must not eat from the tree of the knowledge of good and evil.* To eat from that tree, God says, will bring death.

We wonder what the word *die* means to the man at this point. Is it possible that a predator-prey relationship exists among the animals in the Garden of Eden, so that man can see firsthand what death is? In any case, man begins to learn about death all too soon.

Genesis 3 records that the man and his wife ignore God's one prohibition and eat from the forbidden tree. Thus by personal experience the first two people gain the knowledge of evil and its consequences. For this disobedience the man and his wife will be banished from the garden, with the tree of life "off limits" (Genesis 3:22, 23; Revelation 22:2). In that day the process of dying will set in, and in the course of years it will be complete. (See Romans 5:12.)

### III. COMPANION FOR MAN (GENESIS 2:18-25)

Wherever the man looks there is beauty, "trees that were pleasing to the eye" (Genesis 2:9). Abundant food is in the reach of his hand. He is in the Garden of Eden, and the word Eden means delight! What more could a man need?

If you have ever been desperately lonely, you know what that solitary person needed. In the midst of delight he was alone, all alone, the only one of his kind.

### A. MAN'S CONDITION (v. 18)

**18. The LORD God said, "It is not good for the man to be alone. I will make a helper suitable for him."**

Perhaps the man does not know what he needs, but *the Lord God* knows! The Creator himself has built into that man the need for companionship and now the Creator determines to supply that need. This companion or *helper* will be *suitable for him.*

In all the new world there is no suitable companion for that lonely man. But that situation is about to change. Centuries later the apostle Paul will offer some important reflections on why some people should remain unmarried (1 Corinthians 7). Those cases, however, are the exception rather than the rule. *It is not good for . . . man to be alone.*

## B. GOD'S CREATURES (vv. 19, 20)

**19. Now the LORD God had formed out of the ground all the beasts of the field and all the birds of the air. He brought them to the man to see what he would name them; and whatever the man called each living creature, that was its name.**

The Lord God had made the animals before he made man. Now God brings to *the man* the animals he had previously created, and the man gives them their names.

**20. So the man gave names to all the livestock, the birds of the air and all the beasts of the field.**

**But for Adam no suitable helper was found.**

All kinds of animals and *birds* are viewed and named, but not one of them is fit to be man's companion. Speaking of names, here for the first time we see the name *Adam*. In the original Hebrew, the same word appears in 2:5, 7, 8, 15, 16, and 18, where it is translated as the general term "man." Thus *the man* is literally "Adam."

The process of naming seems also to involve a process of searching for such a companion. Man is a special creation. He is unique. But that uniqueness makes him alone. Today we may keep dogs, cats, birds, ferrets, and hamsters as pets. But none of these can come close to substituting for human companionship. The person who wears a T-shirt that says, "The more people I meet, the more I prefer my cat" needs some biblical counseling!

## C. MAN'S COMPANION (vv. 21, 22)

**21. So the LORD God caused the man to fall into a deep sleep; and while he was sleeping, he took one of the man's ribs and closed up the place with flesh.**

Humorists like to describe this as the world's first surgery with anesthesia. Perhaps it was, but the surgeon was the almighty Creator performing a slight alteration on one of his own creatures. It seems that our popular English versions agree that God took a rib from Adam. The Hebrew word that is translated *ribs* is much more often translated "side" in the Old Testament, but this difference scarcely affects the meaning here.

**22. Then the LORD God made a woman from the rib he had taken out of the man, and he brought her to the man.**

Whatever it is that God takes from Adam—a *rib* in particular or part of his side in general—the companion he fashions for *the man* is not only suitable, but fascinating as well. We may safely conclude that when Adam opens his eyes, he opens them wide!

## D. MAN'S COMMENT (v. 23)

**23. The man said,**

> **"This is now bone of my bones**
> **and flesh of my flesh;**
> **she shall be called 'woman,'**
> **for she was taken out of man."**

Adam had been in deep sleep during the surgery, but he knows what has happened. Perhaps God tells him, either before or after the operation. Now Adam realizes that what he is seeing is a part of himself. Obviously she is more like him than any animal is, but how delightfully she is different from him as well!

---

**WHAT DO YOU THINK?**

*The marriage of one man to one woman for life is God's ordained plan. How can the church lead people back to God's plan for marriage? How do we avoid treating divorce as an "unpardonable sin"?*

**WHAT DO YOU THINK?**

*God, in a sense, chose to make himself "dependent" on man when calling upon Adam to name the animals. What are some other ways God has made himself dependent on us, and how can we fulfill our role in this partnership?*

*[Hint: make sure you consider Matthew 22:37-39; 28:19, 20; and Ephesians 3:10.]*

**WHAT DO YOU THINK?**

*Adam saw in his newly formed wife a part of himself. When Paul spoke of the church, he used the imagery of husband and wife (Ephesians 5:22-24). How can our church do a better job of reflecting this imagery of the bride of Christ to her Groom?*

Visual for Lesson 1. *Use these images to remind your learners of God's unchanging design for marriage.*

PRAYER

*Father in Heaven, holy and mighty, hallowed be your name! Thank you for making the pleasant and productive world we live in. Thank you for stretching around it the ever-changing and always beautiful sky. Thank you for giving Adam firm guidelines in the beginning. Thank you for giving us firm guidelines in your written Word. Today we pledge ourselves anew to do your will, and we look to you for wisdom and strength to keep our pledge. In Jesus' name, amen.*

THOUGHT TO REMEMBER

*Remember your Creator. Know his goodness.*

The word at the very end of the verse translated *man* is not the Hebrew *adam* that we have seen before, but rather is the word *ish*. In designating his new companion, Adam simply adds the feminine suffix to this word and we translate the resulting *ishshah* as *woman*. The word *ishshah* is the generic name of all the female members of humanity. To his own personal companion Adam will gave the name Eve, which means life, "because she was the mother of all living" (Genesis 3:20).

### PROOF OF THE DESIGNER'S SKILL

In the summer of 1908 at the Brooklands racetrack near London, England, three Cadillacs were disassembled into their more than six thousand separate parts. Royal Automobile Club officials intermixed the parts, then selected eighty-nine of those pieces and locked them away so they could not be used. The replacements were taken from standard spare parts stock.

The cars were then reassembled from this jumble of pieces, so that the "new" vehicles were a combination of parts from the three original cars. Mechanics were not allowed to change or manipulate any of the pieces to make them fit together in their new environments. Following this reassembly, each car was driven five hundred miles on the racetrack. All three cars passed the test, proving that precision mass production had become a reality.

The creation narrative of today's text tells us that after God had made one "model" of a human being, he took a part of it and created another whole new being. Although this new person was slightly different from the original, she was similar enough to him that she and the man from whom she had been made would each portray the image of God. Upon seeing his new companion Adam could exclaim, "At last, here is someone like me!" These two specimens of the Creator's skill were so perfectly matched that the human race still thrives thousands of years and "millions of miles" later!     —C. R. B.

### E. GOD'S COMMENT (v. 24)

**24. For this reason a man will leave his father and mother and be united to his wife, and they will become one flesh.**

This cannot be a continuation of Adam's comment in verse 23. What did Adam know about father and mother? He was just beginning to know about wife! Furthermore, Jesus attributed the comment in verse 24 to God and regarded it as God's statement against divorce (Matthew 19:4-6).

### F. COMFORTABLE NAKEDNESS (v. 25)

**25. The man and his wife were both naked, and they felt no shame.**

In their innocence the new man and his wife are unclothed and unashamed. Too soon that innocence will be gone, with the two gripped by shame and fear and an urgent need to hide from the God who created them (Genesis 3). But that issue belongs to the Background of next week's lesson.

## CONCLUSION

This series of lessons deals with God's beginning and his new beginnings, his creation and his re-creations. So the drama of his first recorded creation ends on a high note of triumph. God set the stage and provided the persons for a drama that ought to end "they lived happily ever after." When unhappiness invaded the drama, it was the fault of the creatures, not the Creator.

Today's lesson reminds us that God is Creator and that all good things come from him. Living in the shadow of our Creator means that we should bow in humble submission, realizing in wonder the special place we have in his creation. This week, how will you live in a way that is consistent with these facts?

# Discovery Learning

*This page contains an alternative lesson plan emphasizing learning activities. Classes desiring such student involvement will find these suggestions helpful. The next page is a reproducible activity page to further enhance discovery learning.*

## LEARNING GOALS

After participating in this lesson, each student will be able to:

1. Tell briefly about the origin of life on earth, especially human life.

2. Explain how the Genesis 2 account reveals the special place men and women have in God's creation.

3. Suggest a way to live consistent with that special place in some specific area.

## INTO THE LESSON

Prepare a large balloon filled with bits of paper, flat and rolled into small balls. Inflate the balloon to capacity. As class begins, take a sharp object and puncture it. As the class reacts, say, "This is a picture of the Big Bang theory of the origin of the universe."

Ask, "What is wrong with this theory?" Ask these questions: (1) "From where did the balloon—that is, original substance—come?" (2) "From where did the energy for the explosion come?" (3) "How did new substances find direction, speed, revolutions, and order?"

Note that the popular "Big Bang theory" of the creation of the universe creates as many difficulties as it resolves. It is even more improbable to think that out of these "balls" or suns or planets that human, animal, and plant life could suddenly appear from cold pieces of space rocks.

While the Bible has given us a clear record of the creation, much detail is accepted by faith and intelligent logic.

## INTO THE WORD

The first chapter of Genesis must be reviewed, if only briefly, before the verses in our text in chapter two. Consider an oral reading of the entire chapter by one of your outstanding readers (or a professionally recorded version).

Remind the class, "Our task is not to explain God's method. Surely it is sufficient to trust his word and accept the fact that God created in his own way. It is enough to believe that God created in his own timelessness and in his own omniscient, omnipotent way."

From a map showing the courses of the Tigris and Euphrates rivers, identify what is generally believed to have been the approximate location of the Garden of Eden—in the southern valley of modern Iraq. Note,

"Some suggest that the cataclysmic changes at the flood obliterated the possibility of knowing certain exact locations and indeed made precise dating for the earth an impossibility."

Make copies of today's text and give one to each learner. Provide highlighters or pens to each. Assign the following words/phrases to three groups, respectively: *Lord God* to those born in the first ten days of a month; *created, made, formed* to those born from the eleventh to the twentieth; *man* to those born the twenty-first and following. Direct the groups to highlight/circle their word(s) in the text and count how many times each appears. (The count is 9, 6, 16, respectively.)

Note that, "This count reflects the significant characters and acts in the text, the relationship between God and man. No other creature 'gets as much press'; no other creature gets the face-to-face interaction with God nor receives God's special attention. Man is special." Give the class this list (without the references) and ask them to identify a verse or verses in chapters one or two of Genesis that reveal and confirm each: (1) man is given moral choice—2:16, 17; (2) man is given dominion over the earth—1:26; (3) man is assigned specific responsibility—2:15; (4) man is given a privilege that is by all rights God's: naming creatures—2:19b; (5) humans have the possibility of shame—2:25; (6) man is created in God's image—1:26, 27.

## INTO LIFE

Give your learners a copy of the reproducible page. Discuss collectively an answer to "What is God's purpose for humanity in general?" Then give each person a time to answer the "Me" question.

Say, "God gave Adam the task of naming the animals and tending the garden." Suggest they write a statement to answer, "What is your task or purpose in this life?"

Finally, direct them to respond to the other stimulus headings, either in class or at home in their own study and devotional times: "Make a list of all the things you believe God has created you to do. You may include things you have done in the past as well as what you are doing now and what you might do in the future."

Be certain the learners see the last activity on the reproducible. Suggest that the question, "How do your accomplishments and your interests help you determine your spiritual gifts?" is a critical one for every Christian.

# Created for What?

Briefly describe God's intention (purpose) for mankind in general and for you specifically.

MANKIND                                                                    ME

Make a list of the things God has created you to do. Include things you have done in the past as well as what you are doing now and what you might do in the future.

THINGS I HAVE DONE FOR GOD IN THE PAST

THINGS I AM DOING NOW FOR GOD

THINGS I COULD DO IN THE FUTURE FOR GOD

# Spiritual Gifts

If what God has enabled you to do in the past and present is an indication of your spiritual gifts, how would you describe those gifts?

# BEGINNING AGAIN

**LESSON 2**

Sep
12

## WHY TEACH THIS LESSON?

Many years ago a late-night talk-show host related some difficulties that he had been having with his son. At one point during an argument the son had exclaimed in anguish, "I didn't ask to be born!" To this the father retorted, "It's a good thing you didn't, because I might have said, 'No!'"

As we consider the sad, sinful state of humanity today—with more than six billion people in the world—we can easily imagine having this same interchange with our heavenly father. Indeed, there was a time when God's regret at having created us was so profound that, in computer terminology, he decided to "reboot" the world (see Genesis 6:6).

But God offers new beginnings. Rainbows remind us of this (Genesis 9:12-17). The coming of Christ is a reminder as well. As your learners discover God's mercy in this regard, they will also realize that a day is coming when "second chances" will be no more. The time to "begin again"—for the last time—is now.

## INTRODUCTION

### A. "THE DEVIL MADE ME DO IT!"

In the early 1970s, comedian Flip Wilson (1933–1998) became known for his line, "The devil made me do it!" People began to pick up that line and quote it to excuse certain behaviors. Of course no one really believed it, not even the comedian who originally said it. It was a quip, a joke. The devil cannot make us do anything unless we cooperate with him. He does not compel, he persuades. And it is not very hard to persuade people to do wrong if they have a heart that is inclined toward evil.

By the power of God you can beat the devil every time (1 Corinthians 10:13). James urges us to "Resist the devil, and he will flee from you" (James 4:7). It is your own fault if you give in to the devil and do wrong. It will be because you have not done your best to resist him.

### B. LESSON BACKGROUND

Last week's lesson reminded us that God made earth, sky, plants, and animals. God crowned his creation with human beings who would be in charge over the things on earth. For the home of the humans, God planted the Garden of Eden, which may be translated "the garden of delight." Beauty was everywhere, food was abundant, and only one kind of fruit was forbidden.

But there was a snake in the garden. To Eve the snake praised that forbidden fruit. Since you and I have never heard a snake talking, we easily conclude that the devil was making this one his mouthpiece. Poor Eve! She had never heard anything but truth before. Too easily she was fooled. Rashly she ate some of the forbidden fruit, and rashly her husband shared it with her.

The results were tragic. Suddenly the two were ashamed of their nakedness and tried to cover themselves in crude garments of leaves. When they heard the voice of God, they tried to hide from him. Worse yet, they were banished from the garden and had to battle weeds to produce food from the ground. Worst of

**DEVOTIONAL READING:**
*GENESIS 9:8-17*
**BACKGROUND SCRIPTURE:**
*GENESIS 6:5–9:17*
**PRINTED TEXT:**
*GENESIS 6:5-8, 13, 14; 7:1-5, 17, 23; 8:14-16; 9:1*

### LESSON AIMS

*After participating in this lesson, each student will be able to:*

*1. Recite the account of God's punishment of sin and giving the world a new start in the time of Noah.*

*2. Express confidence in God's willingness to give second chances today.*

*3. Identify a personal area of sin and ask for God's help in making a fresh start.*

### KEY VERSE

*Whenever the rainbow appears in the clouds, I will see it and remember the everlasting covenant between God and all living creatures of every kind on the earth.* —Genesis 9:16

all, they could not eat from the tree of life, so they had to die. You can read all of this in Genesis 3.

After the tragic loss of the garden, you might think that the growing race of humanity would be careful to do what was pleasing to God. But no—one of Adam's sons killed his brother "because his own actions were evil and his brother's were righteous" (1 John 3:12). See Genesis 4.

Then in the opening verses of Genesis 6 we read what happened as the human race continued to multiply: "The sons of God saw that the daughters of men were beautiful, and they married any of them they chose." This tells us about what may be called the normal state of affairs between the time of Adam and Eve's sin and the great flood that was to come. Perhaps it indicates that people didn't have much of a clue about God's coming wrath. "For in the days before the flood, people were eating and drinking, marrying and giving in marriage, up to the day Noah entered the ark; and they knew nothing about what would happen until the flood came and took them all away" (Matthew 24:38, 39).

## I. SITUATION AND GRIEF (GENESIS 6:5-8)

Many centuries after the time of creation, the people of the world had come to the sorry state described in the opening verse of our text.

### A. CONTINUAL EVIL (v. 5)

5. *The LORD saw how great man's wickedness on the earth had become, and that every inclination of the thoughts of his heart was only evil all the time.*

What a world! Most of the people had not even one good thought to brighten the darkness of sin. And just as Adam had been unable to hide his sin from the Lord, now not one sin of multiplied thousands can be hidden from his sight. We may be certain that God is just as able to see all sins today.

#### A BAND-AID® REMEDY

The close of the twentieth century brought significant advances in our understanding of the human body. In December 1999 scientists announced that they had broken the genetic code of human chromosome number twenty-two. This chromosome is thought to contain genetic information that affects immunity, heart disease, and several cancers and types of mental illness. The project was able to discover the order in which the thirty-three million chemical components are put together in the DNA that makes up the chromosome. It would take a very large telephone book to hold the information!

Scientists think that this knowledge may enable us to predict illnesses such as cancer, arthritis, and heart disease. The next step, of course, would be to find ways to prevent such problems. Whether that day will ever come we do not know.

What we do know from Scripture is that these imperfections are the result of sin. Even God's drastic action in the flood could not change the human heart, so we should not expect our modern genetic manipulations to do much more than put a Band-Aid® on a problem requiring an even greater solution. The spiritual problem was much harder to solve and would have to wait until Christ came to redeem us.         —C. R. B.

### B. GOD'S GRIEF (v. 6)

6. *The LORD was grieved that he had made man on the earth, and his heart was filled with pain.*

Imagine God's grief, if you can. He had made a bright new world with new plants and animals and people, and "God saw all *that he had made,* and it was very good" (Genesis 1:31). But over the course of hundreds of years God has

HOW TO SAY IT

*Abraham.* AY-bruh-ham.

*Abram.* AY-brum.

*Corinthians.* Ko-RIN-thee-unz
   (th *as in* thin).

*Haran.* HAIR-un.

*Hebrews.* HEE-brews.

*Ur.* Er.

seen that same world with its multitudes of people grow progressively bad. God is at the point of regretting that he had created humanity in the first place.

## C. GOD'S REMEDY (v. 7)

**7. So the LORD said, "I will wipe mankind, whom I have created, from the face of the earth—men and animals, and creatures that move along the ground, and birds of the air—for I am grieved that I have made them."**

What a disappointment! God had *made* man in his own image and appointed humanity to have dominion over the lesser creatures. Now, centuries later, God is looking at vast numbers of that man's descendants. They look more like images of the devil than images of God. They are not even fit to rule themselves with decency and honor. What is there to do but destroy them all! So the Lord proposes to *wipe* them out, along with all the rest of the living *creatures*.

## D. GOD'S EXCEPTION (v. 8)

**8. But Noah found favor in the eyes of the LORD.**

In a world of wicked people there is one exception. "*Noah* was a righteous man, blameless among the people of his time, and he walked with God" (v. 9). With incredible strength of character, Noah continues that walk when no one else walks by his side. Noah is "a preacher of righteousness" (2 Peter 2:5). In him the image of God is bright in a world of darkness, and he keeps it so for hundreds of years (Genesis 7:6; 9:29).

No less remarkable, he married a woman of his own kind. Or perhaps he taught an unrighteous woman to be holy. And, wonder of wonders, this peerless pair has brought up three sons who are worth saving when others on earth are fit only for destruction. Here is a family worthy of starting to repopulate the world, a good family toughened by long years of godly living in a godless world.

## II. PLAN AND INSTRUCTION (GENESIS 6:13, 14)

Of course God does not intend to destroy that one good family along with the wicked. He means to preserve it for a new start, but Noah will have a big part in saving himself and his extended family.

## A. ANNOUNCEMENT OF DISASTER (v. 13)

**13. So God said to Noah, "I am going to put an end to all people, for the earth is filled with violence because of them. I am surely going to destroy both them and the earth.**

First, the Lord tells Noah what is going to happen: God will destroy the people of earth because they are so wicked. Apparently there is no hope of reclaiming them. The wicked are determined to remain wicked. The Lord also says that the means of destruction will be a great flood (v. 17).

It may be surprising and puzzling to see the words *and the earth* at the end of verse 13, for the earth itself is going to survive the coming disaster. Perhaps we should understand this to mean that the earth as people know it for their habitation will be destroyed. Noah and his family will survive, but they will find no house to live in, no growing crop, no flock of sheep. They will have to "start from scratch" to make a home on the renewed earth.

### CARRIERS OF A DREAD DISEASE

"Typhoid Mary" is a name many of us recognize, but most people probably don't know why the woman was famous. She was Mary Mallon (1869–1938), an immigrant from Ireland who found work in America as a cook.

WHAT DO YOU THINK?

One of the saddest comments in all of Scripture is that God was filled with pain. How do we keep from causing God pain today?

[Passages such as Zechariah 4:6; 2 Corinthians 5:7; Philippians 4:6; and 1 Peter 1:16 can start your thinking.]

## DAILY BIBLE READINGS

Visual for Lesson 2. *Use this interesting visual as you discuss the various ways that God uses to remind us of his covenants.*

Although Mary was immune to typhoid herself, she was a carrier of the disease—eventually infecting about fifty people (and killing at least three) through the food she prepared. An investigator traced several typhoid outbreaks over seven years to Ms. Mallon. In 1907 she was quarantined for three years. After promising never to work as a cook again, she was released in 1910. But eventually a 1915 epidemic was also traced to her. This time she was isolated until her death.

The people of Noah's time did not realize how deadly was the disease that afflicted them. They went on sinning, unaware of the terrible fate that awaited—"infecting" others with the spiritual malady that would soon destroy almost everyone. It would remain for God to "quarantine" the disease by means of the flood.

Unfortunately, Noah and his family members, even though they were comparatively righteous people themselves, would turn out to be "carriers" of the dread disease of sin, and the process of infection would begin again. May we never forget that even though we as Christians are relatively healthy spiritually, we also carry the disease.
—C. R. B.

### B. WAY OF ESCAPE (v. 14)

*14. So make yourself an ark of cypress wood; make rooms in it and coat it with pitch inside and out.*

*An ark* is a box, a chest. Our translators tell us that it is made of *cypress wood,* but the original Hebrew is a bit vague on the actual type of wood used.

The ark is described further in verses 15 and 16 (not in today's text). The next part of our text takes up the story when the *ark* is complete.

## III. COMMAND AND OBEDIENCE (GENESIS 7:1-5)

Every reader who is accustomed to handling animals must have wondered how Noah got all of those beasts aboard the ark. The domestic animals would have been difficult enough, but there were wild animals, too.

Do you suppose the assembling and loading of those animals was one of the most spectacular miracles ever done? Do you suppose that each beast obeyed the unspoken will of God as if it were instinct? Do you suppose that all those creatures actually paraded into the ark in orderly pairs, as our artists like to picture them? We can only conjecture. The record gives no information—but it gives no hint of difficulty, either.

### A. INVITATION OFFERED (vv. 1-3)

*1. The LORD then said to Noah, "Go into the ark, you and your whole family, because I have found you righteous in this generation.*

This *ark* is the haven of life in the presence of death. Noah and his family are invited to enter because they are *righteous.* This may be seen as an analogy to our own future entrance into Heaven. Christians will be able to enter that place of eternal security because they have been counted righteous through the blood of Christ. God will have nothing to do with unrighteousness.

*2. "Take with you seven of every kind of clean animal, a male and its mate, and two of every kind of unclean animal, a male and its mate,*

*Clean* animals are suitable as food for people on earth and as sacrifices to God in Heaven (Genesis 8:20, 21); *unclean* animals are not. For example, cattle and sheep are clean, but rabbits and camels aren't. Obviously the distinction is well known in Noah's time. Centuries later it will be recognized in the law given at Sinai (Leviticus 11). When Jesus comes, he will declare all foods to be clean (Mark 7:19).

*3. "... and also seven of every kind of bird, male and female, to keep their various kinds alive throughout the earth.*

The law to be given at Sinai will make a distinction between clean and unclean birds (Leviticus 11:13-19). But we see no such distinction in our text, and no explanation is given.

### B. INVITATION EXPLAINED (v. 4)

4. *"Seven days from now I will send rain on the earth for forty days and forty nights, and I will wipe from the face of the earth every living creature I have made."*

The invitation is given a week before the *rain* starts. This advance notice is probably necessary because it will take most of that time for all the animals and birds to come aboard, find their places, and get settled for a long stay.

### C. INVITATION ACCEPTED (v. 5)

5. *And Noah did all that the LORD commanded him.*

Noah counts the animals as they board the ark. Ample food already has been loaded (Genesis 6:21). The ark, its cargo, and its passengers are ready for the coming storm as Noah continues his pattern of obedience (Genesis 6:22; Hebrews 11:7).

## IV. THE OLD AND THE NEW (GENESIS 7:17, 23; 8:14-16; 9:1)

The ark rests on solid ground before the flood. Outside, the people go about their business and their pleasures (Luke 17:27). No doubt they are loud in their ridicule of Noah and his big box. The time frame is given precisely: It was "in the six hundredth year of Noah's life, on the seventeenth day of the second month" (Genesis 7:11). Then comes the deluge!

### A. END OF THE OLD (7:17, 23)

17. *For forty days the flood kept coming on the earth, and as the waters increased they lifted the ark high above the earth.*

*Forty days* is not the entire time of *the flood*—rather, it is the duration of the rainfall (Genesis 7:12). The rain is so heavy that it is described as "the floodgates of the heavens" being opened (7:11). Still, the flood is not due to rain alone since "the springs of the great deep burst forth" (again, 7:11). Vast quantities of ocean water must be flowing out onto the land.

23. *Every living thing on the face of the earth was wiped out; men and animals and the creatures that move along the ground and the birds of the air were wiped from the earth. Only Noah was left, and those with him in the ark.*

The flood accomplishes God's purpose. The wicked people of earth die, one and all. With them die the living creatures that walk or crawl on the ground. The birds can fly above the flood, of course, but they cannot fly continually without food for five months (7:24). Utterly exhausted, they sink one by one from air to water, where they die. Ducks and geese can swim, but they cannot dive to the bottom of that flood for food (v. 20). Noah *only* remains alive, and they that are *with him in the ark.*

### B. BEGINNING OF THE NEW (8:14-16; 9:1)

14. *By the twenty-seventh day of the second month the earth was completely dry.*

It was also in *the second month* that the rain began (Genesis 7:11), but that was the six hundredth year of Noah's life. Now we are reading of the following year (8:13), and of a time just a year and ten days after "the floodgates of the heavens were opened" for forty days of torrential rain. Inside the ark is the entire population of the world: eight people. For more than a year, not one of the eight has been able to go out for a walk.

*WHAT DO YOU THINK?*

*Just as Noah did everything according to God's plan, God desires similar obedience from his people now. What are some specific things your church can do to accomplish God's will today?*

*[Matthew 28:19, 20; Ephesians 3:10; Colossians 3:1-17; and 1 Peter 1:16 can provide a general backdrop for your specific answers.]*

*WHAT DO YOU THINK?*

*Some people ask how a loving God could destroy people in the wholesale manner seen in our text. How would you answer this very real concern—a concern that hinders some from coming to faith in God and Christ?*

## WHAT DO YOU THINK?

*How can we do a better job at going forth and being fruitful in a spiritual sense today?*

## THOUGHT TO REMEMBER

*"Be faithful, even to the point of death, and I will give you the crown of life" (Revelation 2:10).*

## WHAT DO YOU THINK?

*The water of Christian baptism is a dividing line—it is a point in time when we move from lost to saved, from death to life, from life without the Spirit to life filled with the Spirit. How does (or should) this new nature affect the life of the Christian?*

But now once again the ark rests on solid earth (8:4). Now again one can look out the window and see *dry* ground. The eight must be impatient, but God has shut them in (7:16). No one moves to open the door until God gives the word. **15, 16. Then God said to Noah, "Come out of the ark, you and your wife and your sons and their wives."**

*God* now gives the welcome order! It is time for the people to leave *the ark*, and to take the animals with them (8:17). The order is obeyed promptly (8:18, 19). Once outside, the first act of the grateful people is to build an altar and worship the Lord (8:20). The Lord responds with a promise that he will never again punish the evil of earth as he has done (8:21, 22).

There will be other beginnings, as we shall see in future lessons, but never an ending like the one just past. The rainbow becomes the symbol of that promise (9:8-17). Even so, unrepentant people will be caught off guard as in the days of Noah when the Son of Man returns (Matthew 24:38, 39). **9:1. Then God blessed Noah and his sons, saying to them, "Be fruitful and increase in number and fill the earth."**

Like Adam and Eve many centuries before (Genesis 1:27, 28), the survivors of the flood receive God's blessing along with instructions to produce children. Those children, in turn, will produce other children in numbers increasing in generation after generation until the earth has a suitable population. Like Adam and Eve, the survivors are given dominance over the animal creatures (9:2).

## CONCLUSION

On the basis of this week's Scripture text and other passages, some have described the Lord as "the God of second chances." What a chance for happiness our original parents had! Faced with opportunity for joy, they chose the one slim chance of misery. Warned that disobedience meant death, they defied the only prohibition in the world, and humanity's chance for perfect happiness was gone.

Instead of learning from their parents' experience, the children of Adam and Eve followed their parents' example of wrong. Century after century, people wandered in the way of unrighteousness. To a God of absolute holiness, that was intolerable. Evil had to be cleansed. Yet one family was an island of decency in a world of corruption. So in the family of Noah God gave humanity a second chance.

As water flows downhill, the natural course of humanity seems to be downward, away from God and goodness. Through centuries the descendants of Noah followed that course until most of them had forgotten God and were worshiping gods of their own invention.

But in Ur, and later in Haran, lived a man whose faith in God was steadfast. God chose Abram (later known as Abraham) to be the father of a nation to be faithful to God, a nation to show the world that it is good and profitable to serve God alone. But that chosen nation followed the downward course of willful sin until its leaders contrived to have God's Son crucified. Soon after that, the nation of Abraham's people was crushed under the Roman boot and scattered.

While the nation of Abraham's children was crumbling, God's ambassadors were sounding his call to the kingdom of Heaven. Today that call still sounds in a world of sinners, and sinners are still responding. Men and women are repenting and being baptized for the remission of sins, and are receiving the gift of the Holy Spirit (Acts 2:38). In something of a parallel, the waters of baptism form a dividing line between saved and unsaved, as did the floodwaters of Noah's day (see 1 Peter 3:18-21). This, however, is the last chance.

Like the rest of humanity, we Christians have felt the pull of the downward way. But in Christ our sins have been forgiven. Praise the Lord!

# Discovery Learning

*This page contains an alternative lesson plan emphasizing learning activities. Classes desiring such student involvement will find these suggestions helpful. The next page is a reproducible activity page to further enhance discovery learning.*

## LEARNING GOALS

After participating in this lesson, each student will be able to:

1. Recite the account of God's punishment of sin and giving the world a new start in the time of Noah.

2. Express confidence in God's willingness to give second chances today.

3. Identify a personal area of sin and ask for God's help in making a fresh start.

## INTO THE LESSON

Bring in some borrowed children's building blocks for this brief statement and demonstration. Say, "Many preschoolers love to play with building blocks. They work diligently to erect whatever structure is in their minds, and then at one fell swoop they knock them down with a squeal of delight." (*Demonstrate by building some kind of structure with blocks and suddenly knock them over with a yell of delight.*)

"Then they are unhappy. With some encouragement they begin a reconstruction project." (*Demonstrate again by building up the structure again.*)

"Today's lesson is a dramatic story of beginning again. This is a story of God's disappointment with his perfect creation that succumbed to the temptation offered by Satan. Sins continued and multiplied. There were apparently no written instructions about worshiping God or avoiding sin and wickedness. How did the people know what was right and wrong?" Let the class suggest answers.

"In God's holiness and sorrow, he set about to destroy his creation as it centered on planet Earth—with the exception of one man and his family. Noah found favor with God because of his righteousness."

## INTO THE WORD

Display two large flash cards: one with the word *GOD* and one with the word *HUMANS*. Say, "The Bible answers the two most significant questions that can be asked: one, 'Who is God and what is he like?' and two, 'Who are humans and what are they like?'"

Provide blank paper and pens to each class member and ask them to fold the sheet lengthwise, putting "God" at the top of one half, "Humans" at the top of the other. (Perhaps use the back of the reproducible page.) Direct the class to examine today's text for answers to the basic questions above. For example, "God is a God who sees" (6:5); "God is a God of grace" (6:8); "Humans are capable of evil," (6:5); "Humans can choose righteousness even in a wicked time and place" (6:9). Note to the class that it is possible to develop a substantial "theology" from today's texts and story.

Give the class a few minutes, then collectively make a list of truths for both God and Man. If no one suggests this truth, add it at the end: "God gives second chances."

Say, "The flood was a catharsis or cleansing of the earth of its evil. As in the beginning, when Adam sinned, the animals and the plant life suffered from human guilt. All of God's creation is interrelated. When God destroyed the earth for human wickedness in the flood, all nature suffered as well.

"The New Testament uses the figure that as in Christian baptism the old man dies and a new man arises in Christ. The flood brought death to the old life on the earth and in Noah a new life began." Have someone read 1 Peter 3:18-21 and Romans 6:1-4. "God gave the earth and humanity a second chance, as he still will."

## INTO LIFE

God gave the world a second chance, beginning with the life of Noah and his family, who were charged with repopulating the earth. Would people now be pure or once again return to wickedness? Of course, the latter was true. That is the reason God sent his Son to rectify our awful plight. Jesus became "the last Adam."

Direct your learners to the reproducible page. Ask, "What are the steps one must go through to achieve a second chance at rebuilding life?" On the simple stairway graphic, refer to the words from the earlier flashcards that are also on the stairway—HUMANS at the bottom and GOD at the top, and ask, "What are the steps one must climb to achieve a second chance at rebuilding life? What can you do to help a person 'get back on top'?"

Have copied and ready to distribute as class ends pieces of paper with two words, one atop the other: CHANCE over CHANCE. Draw an arrow toward the lower one. When all have a copy, ask if anyone can identify the symbolism (each has a "second chance"). Suggest that they carry this slip for a time as a ready reminder that all who are in Christ are living God's life of "a second chance."

# A Second Chance

Perhaps you know of someone who is trying to make a renewal of his or her life. Instead of criticizing or kicking them further down, how can you help that person get back on top?

What are the steps one must go through to achieve a second chance at rebuilding his or her life?

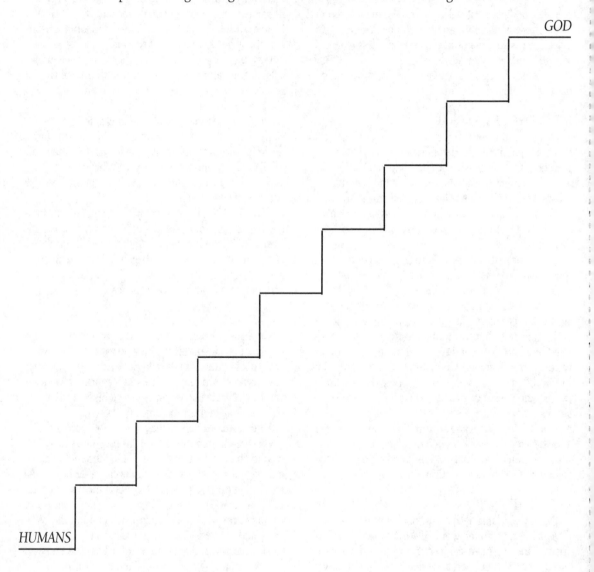

*GOD*

*HUMANS*

# GOD RAISES UP A DELIVERER

**LESSON 3**

Sep
19

## WHY TEACH THIS LESSON?

People seem to love stories about "underdogs" who rise up to challenge the status quo. The 1995 movie *Braveheart* was just such a story. In that production actor Mel Gibson played the part of the legendary William Wallace, the thirteenth-century warrior who led the Scots in defeating the English in several battles. People were enthralled, and the movie was a big hit (despite historical inaccuracies).

A much more unlikely "deliverer" in the pages of history is Moses. His reluctance to assume a leadership role in delivering his people from bondage is quite clear (see Exodus 4:13). After all, he was a shepherd by profession, not a diplomat or army general! And we don't often think of great leaders as being especially humble (see Numbers 12:3).

But perhaps the fact of Moses' great humility was what led God to choose him for leadership. Today will be a time for each of your learners to examine his or her own heart and ask, "What does God see in my heart that would cause him to select me—or reject me—for a leadership role in his church?"

## INTRODUCTION

### A. THE MAKING OF A LEADER

In reviewing the book *Leadership* by Rudolph "Rudy" Giuliani, Stephen Wolter poses an age-old question: "Does the man make the times, or do the times make the man?" Giuliani was elected mayor of New York City in 1993 and 1997.

During his tenure as mayor, Giuliani seemed destined to be remembered by history as an effective administrator, as one who dramatically lowered his city's crime rate, and as someone whose style and politics polarized his constituents. But then came the terrorist attacks of September 11, 2001, and Giuliani's true leadership skills became obvious to the entire world.

We often pause to wonder about what we do not know. As we read our Bibles, do we see God finding people naturally fitted to lead and shape their times, or does God design and create such leaders through the trials they undergo? Or is it a little of both? Noah, Abraham, Joseph, Moses, David, John the Baptist, Paul— so many great leaders, so many unanswered questions about them! We meet one of these leaders today.

### B. LESSON BACKGROUND

Many centuries after Noah's descendants were wandering away from God, the Lord called Abraham to be the father of a great nation. That nation would show the rest of the world what it means to be holy. All this must have seemed very mysterious to Abraham, for "he did not know where he was going" (Hebrews 11:8). As a result the chosen family was planted in the land of Canaan, or Palestine as it came to be called.

DEVOTIONAL READING:
EXODUS 3:13-17
BACKGROUND SCRIPTURE:
EXODUS 3–4
PRINTED TEXT:
EXODUS 3:1-12

LESSON AIMS

*After participating in this lesson, each student will be able to:*

*1. Retell, in his or her own words, the story of God's call to Moses.*

*2. Estimate honestly his or her own abilities and how they can be used in Christian service.*

*3. Engage in service suited to his or her abilities.*

KEY VERSE

*I am sending you to Pharaoh to bring my people the Israelites out of Egypt.* —*Exodus 3:10*

*LESSON 3 NOTES*

Jacob, grandson of Abraham, had twelve sons. One was Joseph, who became a ruler in Egypt through an interesting series of events (Genesis 37, 39–41). God worked through human weakness (Jacob's foolish favoritism toward Joseph and the jealousy of Joseph's brothers) to save a people from famine.

Then came disaster. After Joseph's death, a new Egyptian king became frightened when he saw all those foreigners living in his land (Exodus 1:1-10). What if they joined forces with a foreign country against Egypt? So the new king made slaves of the Hebrews and worked them under brutal overseers. When the Hebrew people continued to increase in number, the king decreed that every boy born among them should be thrown in the river (Exodus 1:22). This is the situation in which God moved to prepare his people to leave Egypt for the land that he had promised long before (Genesis 28:10-14).

Moses was one of the babies born in the days when the king was insisting that every baby boy of the Hebrews must be thrown into the river. Moses' mother did indeed put him there, but she protected him with a watertight basket.

The princess found the floating baby, and her motherly instincts were stirred. She took him home and reared him as her own. So the Hebrew baby became a prince of Egypt, trained in all the wisdom of that culture (Exodus 2:1-10).

When Moses was forty years old, he happened to see a merciless overseer beating one of the Hebrew slaves. Angered by that treatment, Moses killed the overseer. Such behavior was not to be tolerated, even in a prince. The king meant to have Moses executed, but Moses fled eastward across the desert to Midian.

There Moses joined the retinue of a priest and sheep grower named Jethro, married one of Jethro's daughters, and settled down to be a shepherd for the rest of his life (Exodus 2:11-22; Acts 7:23-29). For the next forty years (Acts 7:30) Moses enriched his wisdom of Egyptian culture with the lore of nomadic tribes and knowledge of desert living. Thus he was about eighty years old when God interrupted his life in a profound way.

## I. STRANGE FIRE (EXODUS 3:1-3)

### A. SHEPHERD (v. 1)

**1. Now Moses was tending the flock of Jethro his father-in-law, the priest of Midian, and he led the flock to the far side of the desert and came to Horeb, the mountain of God.**

The land *of Midian* is named after one of Abraham's sons (Genesis 25:1-6). It is a large area without definite boundaries, perhaps one hundred fifty miles to the southeast of Egypt. Moving his *flock to the far side of the desert* likely means that Moses is traveling into *Horeb* or *Sinai,* toward Egypt. Pasture is so scarce that the sheep have to move far and wide to get enough to eat.

A certain mountain in Horeb is known as *the mountain of God,* as this record is written many years after the fact. We do not know whether or not it has that name when Moses first goes there. We do know, however, that this is not the last time that Moses will visit this place (Exodus 17:6; 33:6).

### B. SURPRISE! (v. 2)

**2. There the angel of the LORD appeared to him in flames of fire from within a bush. Moses saw that though the bush was on fire it did not burn up.**

It is very strange to see a *fire* in that remote place, and as Moses stares at the flame he sees something stranger still: the *bush* is not consumed. No branches are vanishing in the fire. What kind of fire could this be?

Moses has forty years of experience in desert environments—he knows what is out of the ordinary when he sees it. But this event is not just out of the ordi-

---

## HOW TO SAY IT

*Abraham. AY-bruh-ham.*

*Amorites. AM-uh-rites.*

*Canaan. KAY-nun.*

*Canaanites. KAY-nun-ites.*

*Corinthians. Ko-RIN-thee-unz* (th *as in* thin).

*Egypt. EE-jipt.*

*Giuliani. Joo-lee-AHN-ee.*

*Hittites. HIT-ites or HIT-tites.*

*Hivites. HI-vites.*

*Horeb. HO-reb.*

*Jebusites. JEB-yuh-sites.*

*Jethro. JETH-ro.*

*Joshua. JOSH-yew-uh.*

*Midian. MID-ee-un.*

*Mojave. Moh-HAH-vee.*

*Perizzites. PAIR-ih-zites.*

*pharaoh. FAIR-o or FAY-roe.*

*Sinai. SIGH-nye or SIGH-nay-eye.*

nary, it is a miracle. The God who is "a consuming fire" (Hebrews 12:29) has created a fire that does not consume!

## C. SCRUTINY (v. 3)

**3. So Moses thought, "I will go over and see this strange sight—why the bush does not burn up."**

Probably Moses says these words to himself; it is unlikely that anyone is with him. We might conclude that natural human curiosity "gets the best of him" and he can't resist stepping aside from his normal tasks to investigate what he sees.

## II. HOLY GROUND (EXODUS 3:4-8)

### A. AWE-INSPIRING IDENTIFICATION (vv. 4-6)

**4. When the LORD saw that he had gone over to look, God called to him from within the bush, "Moses! Moses!"**

**And Moses said, "Here I am."**

If Moses is moving toward the burning *bush,* the sound of a voice in the desert stillness stops him short. Or perhaps he has not yet started toward the bush. Perhaps the audible voice replies to his private thoughts, riveting him to the spot where he stands.

If the fire is surprising, this voice must be doubly so. Moses may be trembling, but nonetheless he answers *Here I am.*

### A VOICE IN THE DESERT

The "Mojave Phone Booth" stood for years in the desert between Los Angeles and Las Vegas. It had been installed in that lonely place in the 1960s for the benefit of miners in the area. Much later it became famous when information about its existence and location was put on a Web site. Soon callers from around the world were dialing its number.

As a result the phone booth became something of a shrine. People came from long distances just to experience the uniqueness of hearing a human voice in the midst of a desert. People camped out by the phone for days, answering each call as it came in. One person reported taking seventy-two calls in one four-and-a-half-hour period.

Moses' experience in the desert was rather different from this! The voice he heard was that of God himself. And to receive a "call" through a burning bush is unusual, to say the least. Moses responded as he should have; the rest, as they say, is history.

On May 17, 2000, Pacific Bell removed the "Mojave Phone Booth" that had been in service for more than thirty years; the voice in the desert disappeared. After thousands of years, the original bush that Moses saw is long gone. But that doesn't mean that God's voice is silenced! God still issues calls to repentance, forgiveness, and service today. Those calls come through his written Word as that Word is read and preached. As you hear God's call through that Word, are you ready to "pick up the phone"?                    —C. R. B.

**5. "Do not come any closer," God said. "Take off your sandals, for the place where you are standing is holy ground."**

The command not to *come any closer* puts a quick stop to Moses' thought of stepping up for a closer look at that incredible fire. We may assume that when he hears the command to bare his feet he does so—and quickly!

Moses is looking at holy fire, fire so holy that even at this distance he is *standing* on *holy ground.* A place where sheep and goats walk is now holy because of the presence of God.

WHAT DO YOU THINK?

What "burning bushes" are there in your life or church today where God demonstrates his presence and his power?

WHAT DO YOU THINK?

When God is present, holiness abounds. How can you show the proper respect due to God as you "stand on holy ground"?

## AWARE OF GOD'S PRESENCE

September brings with it the reds and golds of autumn leaves in many parts of the world. This is particularly so in southern Canada and the northern tier of American states from New England west to the Rocky Mountains. In these places the terrain comes alive with the fiery hues of autumn foliage. For many people, autumn's beauty makes it their favorite season, even though the frigid days of winter are sure to follow quickly.

A wonderful image of earth's autumnal beauty (as well as the human tendency to use God's creation without recognizing him in it) is summoned up by Elizabeth Barrett Browning (1806–1861) in her poem "Aurora Leigh":

> Earth's crammed with heaven,
> And every common bush afire with God;
> But only he who sees, takes off his shoes;
> The rest sit round it, and pluck blackberries.

At the burning bush Moses finally took notice of the presence of God that seemed suddenly to have entered his life. (God had been there all along, but he had to use this extraordinary means to arrest Moses' attention!) How many of us are oblivious to God's presence in our daily lives? Surely the beauty of changing seasons (wherever we may live) should awaken our souls to the evidence all around us of God's loving care. And how sad is our soul's plight if we ignore him—except, of course, to eat the "blackberries" he has provided!　　　　—C. R. B.

**6. Then he said, "I am the God of your father, the God of Abraham, the God of Isaac and the God of Jacob." At this, Moses hid his face, because he was afraid to look at God.**

Now *Moses* knows: it is *God* who is speaking—God the Creator, God the Keeper, God the Almighty. Perhaps Moses drops to his knees as he buries his face in his hands. Surely he knows that God is more than any fire, but he is afraid even to look at the symbol of God. (See also Acts 7:30-33.)

### B. AWE-INSPIRING MISSION (vv. 7, 8)

**7. The LORD said, "I have indeed seen the misery of my people in Egypt. I have heard them crying out because of their slave drivers, and I am concerned about their suffering.**

Moses has been away from *Egypt* for forty years, apparently content with his life as a shepherd. But who knows how much his heart is burdened with the memory of his people's *misery*? Does he feel a nagging frustration because he can do nothing to help them? We are not told, but the Lord speaks as if Moses is well aware of his people's distress. The Lord himself is even more keenly aware of the situation. No affliction escapes his notice (cf. Matthew 10:29; Acts 7:34).

**8. "So I have come down to rescue them from the hand of the Egyptians and to bring them up out of that land into a good and spacious land, a land flowing with milk and honey—the home of the Canaanites, Hittites, Amorites, Perizzites, Hivites and Jebusites.**

How the heart of Moses must leap! Already the Lord has come down; already God's campaign is in operation. The Lord is going to rescue his people from the terrible slavery and cruelty that has oppressed them all through the eighty years of Moses' life, and for some years before that.

The Lord is going to lead his people out of Egypt to a good land—a land so large that it is currently occupied by at least six other nations. Its description as being *a land flowing with milk and honey* is so profound that that phrase almost becomes a proverb (Exodus 3:17; 13:5; 33:3; etc.).

*Visual for Lesson 3. Use this visual all quarter long to help your learners "get their bearings" from lesson to lesson.*

When God keeps this promise, he will be fulfilling a prophecy that is hundreds of years old. And the heart of Moses must be saying, "Amen."

## III. BREATHTAKING CALL (EXODUS 3:9-12)

### A. MOSES' MISSION (vv. 9, 10)

**9, 10. "And now the cry of the Israelites has reached me, and I have seen the way the Egyptians are oppressing them. So now, go. I am sending you to Pharaoh to bring my people the Israelites out of Egypt."**

From the future triumph declared in verse 8, God turns to face again the depressing present. God's people in Egypt are suffering terribly and crying for help.

How many of us feel our hearts leaping when we read the triumphant announcement that in the end "The kingdom of the world has become the kingdom of our Lord and of his Christ, and he will reign for ever and ever" (Revelation 11:15)? But then how many of us feel our hearts sinking when we read what God expects us to do in the meantime: "Go and make disciples of all nations, baptizing them in the name of the Father and of the Son and of the Holy Spirit" (Matthew 28:19)? So likewise Moses' heart probably sinks at God's personal call to him. No wonder Moses protests (v. 11, next).

### B. MOSES' PROTEST (v. 11)

**11. But Moses said to God, "Who am I, that I should go to Pharaoh and bring the Israelites out of Egypt?"**

*Who am I?* is a natural question. Back in Egypt Moses is a murderer sentenced to death. He is alive only because he fled to another country. It would be dangerous even to go to Egypt, even secretly. But to go boldly *to Pharaoh* with an unwelcome demand—wouldn't that be a demand for Moses' own death?

On top of all that, Moses may be thinking, "I'm eighty years old and have spent the last half of my life herding sheep." But Moses will discover as events unfold that he will need some herding skills to guide and push an obstinate people forward.

### C. GOD'S ANSWER (v. 12)

**12. And God said, "I will be with you. And this will be the sign to you that it is I who have sent you: When you have brought the people out of Egypt, you will worship God on this mountain."**

What better promise can *God* give than *I will be with you?* It will not be humans alone who go to demand freedom for the Hebrews; God will be there as well. When Pharaoh says "no" to Moses, he will be saying "no" to God, too. But God has ways of enforcing his demands. Moses will not be able to mistake the hand of God in all of this when he serves God upon the very *mountain* where God is now speaking (again, Exodus 17:6; 33:6). Until then Moses must go in faith.

The rest of the story is well known to Bible readers. Pharaoh refuses to set God's people free, but God persuades that ruler with a series of plagues so terrible that at last both king and people urge the Hebrews to get *out of Egypt,* and get out quickly. Then for forty years Moses proves his skills as a leader as this people makes its way toward the promised land.

### WHAT TRUST CAN DO

Hulda Crooks began climbing mountains at the age of fifty-three. She climbed 11,502-foot Mount San Gorgonio in Southern California twenty times. At age sixty-six she made the first of twenty-four ascents of California's 14,495-foot Mount Whitney, the highest peak in America's forty-eight contiguous states. Her

---

**WHAT DO YOU THINK?**

*Being called by God to serve him is a humbling and awe-inspiring experience. How should we respond when we sense God calling us into his service?*

**WHAT DO YOU THINK?**

*God spent eighty years training Moses in "the school of life" to prepare him for the ministry he was to perform. How has God been training you for a particular ministry in the church? What ministry could you do in your church as a result?*

## PRAYER

*Dear Father of us all, we thank you for the witness of your leaders that speaks to us from the pages of the Bible. Noah, Abraham, Moses, Joshua, David, Nehemiah, Peter, and Paul all have something to teach us from both their successes and their failures. May all our leaders and all our followers be united in following you. In Jesus' name, amen.*

## THOUGHT TO REMEMBER

*The leader's call: "Follow my example, as I follow the example of Christ" (1 Corinthians 11:1).*

## WHAT DO YOU THINK?

*Realizing that the church is always one generation away from extinction, how can your church prepare leaders for the future?*

last ascent was at age ninety-one! She is also the oldest person to climb Mount Fuji, the highest mountain in Japan.

Hulda started jogging when she was seventy-two, saying, "it made climbing so much easier." She also backpacked the two hundred and twelve-mile John Muir Trail in the Sierra Nevada, set a Senior Olympics world record in her age group for fifteen hundred meters, and hiked to the bottom of the Grand Canyon.

Before she died in 1997 at age one hundred and one, Hulda—a Christian—expressed the guiding principle of her life: "When you have faith in a supreme power that you believe is love and kindness and justice and has a care for you, you're not under tensions [like other people]. You develop a habit of trusting."

Trusting: so easy to say, so hard to do. At first, Moses had trouble trusting God. He had questions about his own ability. In the end it was Moses' trust in God's promise, "I will be with you," that made the difference. When trust in God took hold in Moses' life, he began to accomplish things he never would have imagined doing before. Do you suppose the same could be true for the rest of us? —C. R. B.

## CONCLUSION

When we need someone to teach a Sunday school class, or sponsor a youth group, or manage the nursery, or be on the finance committee, we do not have the privilege of starting with an unborn baby to build the person we need. So we look for a person already qualified by nature, training, and/or experience. If we see no one as well qualified as God thought Moses to be, then perhaps we choose the best person available and pray that he or she will learn on the job.

Our search for leaders would be easier if we would take more care to have leaders in training. Mary Weber is known as the best teacher in the Primary Department of her Sunday school. The children love her and the class. They are eager to learn. Mary likes to have an assistant in her class, not so much because she needs assistance but rather because the Sunday school needs to have teachers in training.

At first Mary's helper may do little more than check attendance, take care of the offering, and distribute crayons. But soon Mary asks her assistant to lead the children in their songs, or to prepare a simple object lesson.

Seldom does Mary keep an assistant for as much as a year. The assistant learns the teacher's skill and is requested for another class that needs a teacher. The kingdom of God moves forward as a result.

Mary Weber is a good mentor, but Mary isn't perfect. Even after all these years she still makes an occasional mistake. Moses was a great leader, but on one important occasion his leadership failed (Numbers 20:1-12; Deuteronomy 32:50, 51). That failure didn't stop him from being a good mentor to Joshua, however. Undoubtedly Joshua saw Moses' failure and learned something from it.

Joshua was an "aide" for Moses (Exodus 24:13). Joshua went along with Moses for a forty-day stay with the Lord in a cloud of glory on Mount Sinai, and Joshua came back with Moses as well (Exodus 32:15-17). Apparently Joshua was Moses' constant companion. When Moses died at the border of the promised land, it was Joshua who stepped into his place to lead Israel (Joshua 1:1-9). Years of wandering were followed by years of warfare. But when the wars were over, the influence of Joshua was still strong. The people were loyal to the Lord until the death of that great leader, and loyal even beyond that time (Joshua 24:31; Judges 2:7).

All this has something to say to us today about the importance of mentoring and cultivating new leaders. Pause right now to take a close look at the age of your church's leaders. Are they all in their fifties, sixties, and seventies? Are they mentoring others? If not, that could be a big problem! When those leaders pass on, who will take their places?

# Discovery Learning

*This page contains an alternative lesson plan emphasizing learning activities. Classes desiring such student involvement will find these suggestions helpful. The next page is a reproducible activity page to further enhance discovery learning.*

## LEARNING GOALS

After participating in this lesson, each student will be able to:

1. Retell, in his or her own words, the story of God's call to Moses.

2. Estimate honestly his or her own abilities and how they can be used in Christian service.

3. Engage in service suited to his or her abilities.

## INTO THE LESSON

Begin this class on the development of leaders (deliverers) with the following statement: "Adolf Hitler, who wanted to be the world's greatest leader, has gone down in history as one of the world's most wicked. One of his goals was to create a superior race.

"Others are now attempting to unite the sperm and eggs of brilliant scholars and leaders in order to raise up outstanding children of unique mental ability and physical appearance. Still others are studying the possibility of the cloning of people. The question is always, 'What does it require to develop outstanding leaders? What qualities are necessary? Do circumstances play a part? Which is more important: genetic heredity or the environment in which a person is reared? To what degree does God's input play in developing a leader?'"

Let your class members suggest their answers. Note that God is able to take someone seemingly insignificant and unknown and mold him or her into a mighty force. Gideon, Deborah, David, and Peter are examples.

## INTO THE WORD

Make this observation: "Occasionally we hear of some CEO who is tired of the commercial rat race deciding to move to the mountains or sail around the world to live a more serene life. Moses, the 'CEO of Egypt,' was reared from infancy in the palace of the pharaoh. Brought up as the adopted son of the princess of Egypt and trained by the greatest minds of Egypt, he may have been in line to become the next pharaoh himself.

"But God's training of Moses was incomplete. He needed to learn another lifestyle and another worldview. So by God's providence, Moses will end up in the nomadic desert."

Divide your class into three smaller groups and give them the discussion assignment that follows.

*Group 1:* Relate as much as you can about Abraham, Jacob, Joseph, and Moses relative to their leadership traits. What specific deeds testify to their leadership abilities? [A sharp Bible student will know that Joseph was raised in the desert to serve in a palace, while Moses was raised in a palace to serve in the desert.] (The first activity on the reproducible page involves this same material.)

*Group 2:* Summarize the outstanding events of the three forty-year phases of Moses' life. (First forty, in pharaoh's palace; second forty, as a shepherd in Midian; third forty, as a leader of the Israelites.)

*Group 3:* Describe how God shaped and developed Moses (1) from birth until he ran to Midian; (2) during his life in the desert; (3) during his leading the Israelites to the promised land.

Have each group give a brief summary.

## INTO LIFE

Display these scrambled words of several people who helped in Moses' development into the outstanding leader whom he became: CEINPRSS, EHOMRT, EHJORT, AAHHOPR. (The princess who rescued him and kept him in the royal palace; his own mother who was his early nursemaid; Jethro, his father-in-law, who was a priest of Midian; pharaoh, who gave him all the education Egypt could offer.)

Ask the students to identify significant people who played important roles in their own personal development. A teacher? A preacher? A parent? A grandparent? Others? (This activity is included in the second activity on the reproducible page.)

Ask, "Have you thanked those people?" Provide paper or note cards for each to write a short letter of thanks to one who helped him or her. If the one chosen has died, direct the class member to write as if the person were still alive.

Note to the class: "God provided the church as a leadership-training institution. How can we both as a class and as individuals help in the leadership development of young people and other adults in our church and community?"

Give each an index card with the following imprinted (or to be written on as you write it on the board):

"Believing that I can be used by God to help another grow in leadership ability in his kingdom, I will, with God's empowering Spirit, . . ."

# Leadership Qualities

List the qualities of leadership of the following men.

| ABRAHAM | JACOB | JOSEPH | MOSES |
|---------|-------|--------|-------|
|         |       |        |       |

What similarities do you discover?

# Leadership Mentors

Identify some of those who have provided leadership training in your own life. Use the categories given.

FAMILY MEMBERS          SCHOOL PERSONNEL          CHURCH LEADERS          EMPLOYERS

Who is one to whom you owe a thanks unexpressed until now? Write your commitment here:

With the Spirit's motivation I will address my thanks to _____
for his/her training and encouragement in my becoming who I am.

Signed _____

Date _____, 2004

# BECOMING GOD'S PEOPLE

**LESSON 4**

DEVOTIONAL READING:
*DEUTERONOMY 30:15-20*
BACKGROUND SCRIPTURE:
*DEUTERONOMY 29:1-29*
PRINTED TEXT:
*DEUTERONOMY 29:1-15*

Sep
26

## WHY TEACH THIS LESSON?

We've all experienced the challenge of trying to convince someone else of the truthfulness of a certain position or idea. Sometimes the skeptic will refuse to be persuaded no matter how much evidence we present. In those cases we may have given up in exasperation, declaring, "Well, your mind is made up so I won't confuse you with the facts!"

Much of today's lesson involves the unmistakable facts about God's providential and miraculous care for his covenant people during their exodus from Egypt and approach to the promised land. These facts should have resulted in certain thinking and behavior. But as century after century of history unfolds, we see that reminders of God's care and God's expectations often fall on deaf ears (e.g., Isaiah 42:20).

Christians today rightly identify themselves as God's people in the New Testament era. But will God agree with that identification if we fail to understand his expectations that are based on what his Son has accomplished? Today's lesson reminds us of the vital connection between *understanding* and *identity*.

## INTRODUCTION

### A. A THIRTY-YEAR WASTE

On March 10, 1974, World War II finally ended for Second Lieutenant Hiroo Onoda of the Imperial Japanese Army. Lieutenant Onoda had been drafted into his country's army in 1942 and, evading capture, had survived in a remote part of the Philippines since the war ended in 1945.

For the next three decades, Lieutenant Onoda refused to believe any evidence that the war was over. The authorities knew his general location, and tried dropping leaflets, magazines, and newspapers to convince him to give up. Nothing worked. Finally, Lieutenant Onoda's former commanding officer arrived on the scene and personally ordered him to surrender. What should have been two or three years of service to his country turned into a thirty-year waste of time. Onoda's pointless war was finally over.

Such blindness is nothing new, is it? Just after Jesus' resurrection, he chastised some disciples on the road to Emmaus when he said, "How foolish you are, and how slow of heart to believe all that the prophets have spoken!" (Luke 24:25). They had the prophecies, they had the fulfillments, they had the miracles, they had the evidence. Yet they still doubted—just like their forefathers in the desert (Numbers 14:11). Today's lesson is about a people struggling to establish an identity as they recover from forty years of blindness.

### B. LESSON BACKGROUND

Last week we saw God call Moses from the pastureland of Midian to go to Egypt and free the Hebrew slaves. God had a place for those slaves to be free and to be his own people. It was the very place to which God had led Abraham long before. It was "a land flowing with milk and honey" (Exodus 3:8). In that place God would prepare that nation to usher in the Messiah.

## LESSON AIMS

After participating in this lesson, each student will be able to:

1. Summarize the details of the covenant Moses rehearsed with the Israelites at the border of the promised land.

2. Explain how keeping God's covenant was best for Israel and is best for us.

3. Express a commitment to live within God's covenant.

## KEY VERSES

You are standing here in order to enter into a covenant with the LORD your God, . . . to confirm you this day as his people.
—Deuteronomy 29:12, 13

So Moses took his request to the king of Egypt. Brusquely the king refused, but he changed his mind when God sent a series of plagues. After the death of their firstborn, all of Egypt joined the king in urging the Hebrews to get out of the country. So after four hundred and thirty years (Exodus 12:40, 41), the Hebrews left the valley of the Nile to begin forty years of life in the wilderness.

Forty years was certainly a long time to make a trip that at most should have totaled no more than three hundred and fifty miles! The travelers actually came to the border of the promised land in a little less than two years, although they camped at Sinai for nearly a year while on the way (Exodus 19:1; Numbers 10:11-13).

Pausing at the edge of the promised land, the Hebrews sent twelve scouts to study the countryside and plan an invasion (Numbers 13:1-25). Ten of the twelve came back with a frightening report: the cities of that land were fortified, and the warriors who defended them were giants. The other two scouts disagreed. With God's help, they said, the land could surely be taken.

But the majority report prevailed and the people refused to go forward (Numbers 14:1-4). For that failure of faith, God said they must live in the desert for thirty-eight more years (Deuteronomy 2:14). During those years they were not travelers moving toward a goal; rather, they were herdsmen moving about the desert to find pasture for their livestock.

When God allowed those wilderness wanderers to approach the promised land again, they did so by way of the eastern side of the Dead Sea and the Jordan River. Then there was a pause, for that was the end of the road for Moses. Now one hundred and twenty years old (Deuteronomy 34:7), Moses was to die east of the Jordan, leaving Joshua to lead the people to cross the river and conquer the larger part of the promised land (34:9). This week our text brings us a bit of what Moses said to his people before he left them and climbed up Mount Pisgah, never to return.

## I. REMEMBER EGYPT (DEUTERONOMY 29:1-4)

Of those listening to Moses, only two had left Egypt as adults some forty years earlier. The rest of the adults who had begun the trip died in the desert (Numbers 14:29-35; Deuteronomy 2:14, 15). Many of Moses' hearers had left Egypt as teenagers and younger children; many others had been born during the desert wanderings.

Moses, therefore, is very wise to begin his address by recalling the last days of Israel's long stay in Egypt. A reminder of those days sets the context for what Moses says afterward.

### A. What the Lord Says (v. 1)

*1. These are the terms of the covenant the Lord commanded Moses to make with the Israelites in Moab, in addition to the covenant he had made with them at Horeb.*

This verse may be called a title of the part of Moses' discourse that follows. See how it resembles the title in Deuteronomy 1:1. Nearly forty years have passed since God *had made* a *covenant* (a contract, an agreement) with his people *at Horeb,* or Sinai (1:6; 4:10, 15). That former covenant fills large parts of Exodus, Leviticus, and Numbers.

Now, *in Moab,* which is east of the Jordan River (1:5), *the Lord* is commanding another covenant. Of course, this is not to replace the earlier covenant. Rather, it is a supplement, consisting largely of instructions to abide by the former agreement.

### How to Say It

Abraham. AY-bruh-ham.

Bashan. BAY-shan.

Emmaus. Em-MAY-us.

Gadites. GAD-ites.

Horeb. HO-reb.

Isaac. EYE-zuk.

Jacob. JAY-kub.

Jeremiah. Jair-uh-MY-uh.

Manasseh. Muh-NASS-uh.

Midian. MID-ee-un.

Moab. MO-ab.

Moabites. MO-ub-ites.

Moses. MO-zes or MO-zez.

Pisgah. PIZ-guh.

Reubenites. ROO-ben-ites.

Sierra Leone. See-AIR-uh Lay-OWN.

Sihon. SIGH-hun.

Sinai. SIGH-nye or SIGH-nay-eye.

## B. WHAT YOU SAW (vv. 2, 3)

**2. Moses summoned all the Israelites and said to them:**
*Your eyes have seen all that the LORD did in Egypt to Pharaoh, to all his officials and to all his land.*

Moses is referring to the famous ten plagues that God had used to persuade the Egyptians to release their Hebrew slaves. Among the hearers those under age forty had been born since their parents had left Egypt. Although they had not seen the plagues personally, the others in the assembly could well remember the furor in Egypt.

**3. With your own eyes you saw those great trials, those miraculous signs and great wonders.**

Moses continues to speak of the ten plagues. The plagues are also *signs* of God's power, and all of them, without doubt, were *great wonders*.

### CREATING A FAMILY IDENTITY

Joe Mountain and his family have a unique family reunion each year. Joe, a bus driver, takes the proverbial "busman's holiday" by chartering a bus to take his family on a vacation trip. Recently, the vacation included forty-one relatives who shared a twelve-day, twenty-eight-hundred-mile reunion through the American Southwest. Another year it was a three-thousand-mile trip to the Pacific Northwest.

One year the bus broke down; on another occasion a family member was left behind for a short while before he was missed. The mishaps add color to the story as they are remembered later. And remembering is a large part of what these trips are all about. The mishaps, the adventures shared, and the marvelous sights they've seen all contribute to the family identity passed on to the next generations.

Moses' speech to Israel in today's text serves somewhat the same purpose as the Mountain family vacations. Moses reminds Israel of the marvelous sights they have seen as God brought them freedom and provided sustenance on their journey from Egypt. He reminds them of the miracles and signs of God's power they saw, as well as the "mishaps" along the way in which some got "left behind"—permanently.

To Israel's experiences we can add our own. In so doing, we find a growing awareness of God's care and of our community with the family of God in every age.

—C. R. B.

## C. HOW YOU RESIST (v. 4)

**4. But to this day the LORD has not given you a mind that understands or eyes that see or ears that hear.**

The Israelites certainly have "head knowledge" about God's miraculous intervention, but such knowledge does not always convert easily into "heart knowledge." After all the signs and great miracles that God has done on their behalf, the people should be perceptive enough to realize that God is on their side and that he will give them success when they obey him. But at their first approach to the promised land, those people had turned back in terror instead of trusting God and going forward. Why hadn't they provided their own *ears that hear* and *eyes that see* and *mind that understands,* instead of waiting for God to provide them with perceptions as well as doing great miracles for them?

In Romans 11:8 Paul uses this passage (along with Isaiah 29:10) to criticize the people of his own day. Jesus makes a similar observation in Matthew 13:13-15. Human nature doesn't seem to change much, even across thousands of years!

## II. REMEMBER THE WILDERNESS (DEUTERONOMY 29:5-9)

Those who remember what great things God had done for them in Egypt ought to be ready to trust him and obey him without fear. But events in the

---

WHAT DO YOU THINK?

We often forget the many ways that God has blessed us. What are some things we need to do to remember what God has done for us? Why is this important?

WHAT DO YOU THINK?

The people of God seem to forget rather quickly God's gracious leading in the past. Why is this, and what can we do to keep in remembrance the leading of God?

*Enter into covenant with the Lord thy God.*

Visual for Lesson 4. *Use these three images to start a discussion on the importance of covenants, both God's and ours.*

DAILY BIBLE READINGS

Monday, Sept. 20—*Moses Reminds the Israelites (Deuteronomy 29:2-9)*

Tuesday, Sept. 21—*The Israelites Join the Covenant (Deuteronomy 29:10-15)*

Wednesday, Sept. 22—*Moses Warns the Israelites (Deuteronomy 29:16-21)*

Thursday, Sept. 23—*The Reason for Devastation (Deuteronomy 29:22-29)*

Friday, Sept. 24—*God Will Forgive Those Who Return (Deuteronomy 30:1-5)*

Saturday, Sept. 25—*God Will Prosper Those Who Believe (Deuteronomy 30:6-10)*

Sunday, Sept. 26—*Obey God and Choose Life (Deuteronomy 30:11-20)*

wilderness had been even more encouraging: God had led his people and provided for them all the way.

### A. DECADES OF CARE (vv. 5, 6)

*5. During the forty years that I led you through the desert, your clothes did not wear out, nor did the sandals on your feet.*

All through those *forty years* in the *desert* God *led* his people, going before them in a pillar of cloud by day and a pillar of fire by night (Exodus 40:38; Numbers 14:14). The miraculous preservation of their *clothes* and shoes shows us that God is concerned about the Israelites' physical needs on top of their spiritual welfare.

*6. You ate no bread and drank no wine or other fermented drink. I did this so that you might know that I am the LORD your God.*

For forty years God's people planted no seed, harvested no wheat, picked no grapes, pressed *no wine*, and made no beer. Rather, each day they picked up their food ("manna") from the desert floor, food such as was never seen before or since. For forty years they drank clear water (Exodus 15:22-27; 17:1-7). Every helpful favor and every benevolent miracle is evidence that the One who did it is *the Lord your God.*

### B. VICTORY OVER ENEMIES (vv. 7, 8)

*7. When you reached this place, Sihon king of Heshbon and Og king of Bashan came out to fight against us, but we defeated them.*

*Sihon* and *Og* had been kings of two small nations east of the Dead Sea and the Jordan River, the very area where God's people now have their camp. Each of those kings had come *out* with an army to drive the invading Israelites away; but God helped the invaders, and the defenders were *defeated* (Numbers 21:21-35).

*8. We took their land and gave it as an inheritance to the Reubenites, the Gadites and the half-tribe of Manasseh.*

The few enemies who survived the battles had to flee from their lands, leaving them to the victorious Israelites (Deuteronomy 2:24–3:11). That area is notable for the rich grass that makes it a splendid place for cattle. The tribes of *Reubenites* and *Gadites,* and part of the tribe *of Manasseh* have many cattle, so they had asked Moses to let them have that area as their share of the promised land.

Moses granted that request, with the provision that the men of those tribes would not settle down on their new land until they had crossed the Jordan River and helped the other tribes capture the land on the western side (Numbers 32).

### C. ADVICE TO HEED (v. 9)

*9. Carefully follow the terms of this covenant, so that you may prosper in everything you do.*

Now Moses offers advice based on the facts he has been reviewing: the people must be faithful to the *covenant* now being made. As indicated in the comments to verse 1 above, this is not a different covenant to replace the one made at Sinai nearly forty years earlier. Rather, it is a ratification and renewal of that former covenant.

With one voice, those present at Sinai had said, "We will do everything the Lord has said; we will obey" (Exodus 24:7). Now Moses invites his current audience to make the same pledge. Clearly, that is the way to be assured *that you may prosper in everything you do.* Every miracle of the past forty years is evidence that nothing is impossible with God. So how can God's people be intimidated by walled cities and tall men? "Trust and obey" is the advice of Moses. Forty years of history prove that it is good advice.

## III. HONOR THE COVENANT (DEUTERONOMY 29:10-15)

A covenant with God is not an alliance of equals. It recognizes that God is supreme and we are his servants. Our duty and our pleasure is to do his will, and that is for our good. Moses stresses that God's people must accept the fundamental principle that God is Number One in the covenant. They must shape their lives in accord with that principle.

### A. ASSEMBLED PEOPLE (vv. 10, 11)

10, 11. *All of you are standing today in the presence of the* LORD *your God—your leaders and chief men, your elders and officials, and all the other men of Israel, together with your children and your wives, and the aliens living in your camps who chop your wood and carry your water.*

Notice the wide spectrum of people who are present! God's covenant is not just for the leaders, but for everyone—oldest to youngest, male and female. *Aliens* refers to the non-Israelites within the assembly. The covenant is for them as well. Another designation for such "resident aliens" is those *who chop your wood and carry your water* (see Joshua 9:21, 23, 27). In the case at hand, these may be Moabites, since the Israelites are on the east side of the Jordan River.

It may seem a bit surprising that foreigners can be welcomed into the promises of the Jewish nation since the Jews are not commanded to "evangelize" such people. In fact *God* requires the Israelites to avoid intermingling with non-Jews (Deuteronomy 7:1-6). But foreigners can participate in the covenant if they wish (Exodus 12:48, 49; Numbers 15:26; 19:10). The Israelites are not to oppress these resident aliens because the Jews themselves know what it was like to be in that position (Exodus 23:9; Deuteronomy 10:19).

### B. AWE-INSPIRING PURPOSE (vv. 12, 13)

12. *You are standing here in order to enter into a covenant with the* LORD *your God, a covenant the* LORD *is making with you this day and sealing with an oath,*

The people meet for the purpose of entering into the *covenant* that is being offered. By that covenant the Israelites have the added assurance that they are God's people. *God* intends to keep his *oath*—will they keep theirs?

13. *. . . to confirm you this day as his people, that he may be your God as he promised you and as he swore to your fathers, Abraham, Isaac and Jacob.*

Here the provisions of the covenant are summarized very briefly. The people entering into the covenant are to be God's *people.* That means they agree to obey all the commandments of the lengthy covenant that had been made nearly forty years earlier. God, in turn, will give them the blessings promised to *Abraham, Isaac, and Jacob* (all three now having been dead for hundreds of years), and the blessings *promised* in the covenant made at Sinai. Deuteronomy 28:1-14 briefly describes those blessings, while 28:15-68 sets forth the sobering penalties for failure.

### C. ADDITIONAL PEOPLE (vv. 14, 15)

14, 15. *I am making this covenant, with its oath, not only with you who are standing here with us today in the presence of the* LORD *our God but also with those who are not here today.*

Here is another mild surprise: the *covenant* is to be made with others besides those to whom Moses is talking. Verses 10 and 11 make it plain that the meeting is intended to include everyone in the camp of Israel, including foreigners. But what about *those who are not here today?*

This sounds too important to refer merely to a few Hebrews who may be out hunting deer and are not in the meeting at the moment. The proper interpreta-

*WHAT DO YOU THINK?*

*God does not show preference toward one group of people over another. How should this attitude of God affect how we view others?*

*[Acts 10:9-15; Galatians 2:11-13; 3:28; and James 2:1-9 may stimulate your thinking.]*

*WHAT DO YOU THINK?*

*All of the covenants that God established with Abraham, with Moses and the nation of Israel, and with David find their ultimate fulfillment in the new covenant that God made in Christ (Acts 13:32, 33). How does the significance of God's new covenant affect you today?*

tion is that this covenant is for Israelites of future generations, not just the ones currently alive. Again we note that verses 10 and 11 offer us a hint that people who are not Hebrews may find a place in God's covenant.

Acts 2:39 also points to future generations that may be included in the new covenant. Since our lesson title is "Becoming God's People," will not our study of that topic be most helpful if it includes some thoughts on being God's people in our own time? We turn our minds in that direction as we conclude this lesson.

### BLESSINGS OF THE COVENANT

In March 2000, a replica of the schooner *Amistad* was launched in Mystic, Connecticut. The original ship had a sobering history. In 1839 this vessel was bringing slaves to the Americas from what is now Sierra Leone, Africa.

During the trip the slaves revolted and took control of the ship near Cuba. The vessel sailed north, to be eventually captured by the U.S. Navy near Long Island where the slaves were arrested. While the slaves were imprisoned, students from (then Christian) Yale University taught them the Christian faith.

Former President John Quincy Adams took up the cause of the slaves, and in 1841 a ruling by the U.S. Supreme Court freed them. A year later the surviving thirty-five freedmen returned to Africa, where they began schools and churches. The faith of the "Christian" nation that had imprisoned them became the means to better the lot of people in their homeland. Even so, another twenty-five years would have to pass before American slaves would be freed by a civil war and President Lincoln's "Emancipation Proclamation."

When God established the nation of Israel thousands of years ago, he told his people that the powerless—women, children, aliens, and even the unnamed people who were yet to be among them—were to be considered members of the covenant, with all the blessings that that promise brought with it. In the era of the new covenant, it has taken us far too long to realize that God's compassion and offer of salvation extends to all people, not just the powerful or "chosen few."          —C. R. B.

## CONCLUSION

The covenant mentioned in today's text is definitely according to the earlier covenant, the one made at Sinai just after God brought his people out of Egypt. But in Jeremiah 31:31-34 we read God's promise of a new covenant that is not according to that covenant made in Sinai. That new covenant is promised to the houses of Israel and Judah: those two houses made up the descendants of Abraham, and now faithful Christians have replaced them as Abraham's children (Galatians 3:7-9). Lesson 7 of this series will bring us more thoughts about that prophecy, and lessons 10 to 13 will be drawn from the New Testament itself.

For the present, however, let us take note of two principles that belong to all of the covenants that God has made with humanity. Our *first principle* is that God is Number One in every instance. He commands us, we do not command him. He instructs us, we do not instruct him. He leads, and we follow; he sends, and we go. He is the potter, we are the clay.

The *second principle* is that the covenant is for our good. Keeping it does us good; breaking it does us harm. The blessings and curses described in Deuteronomy 28 may seem extreme, but they are verified in centuries of Israel's experience.

Today we do well to ask ourselves, "For if the message spoken by angels was binding, and every violation and disobedience received its just punishment, how shall we escape if we ignore such a great salvation?" (Hebrews 2:2, 3). Sin promises to pay, and in the short term it may seem to be paying. May we never forget, however, that we have a covenant with God. Sin has no place in this covenant that leads us into life eternal.

# Discovery Learning

*This page contains an alternative lesson plan emphasizing learning activities. Classes*
*desiring such student involvement will find these suggestions helpful. The next page*
*is a reproducible activity page to further enhance discovery learning.*

## LEARNING GOALS

After participating in this lesson, each student will be able to:

1. Summarize the details of the covenant Moses rehearsed with the Israelites at the border of the promised land.

2. Explain how keeping God's covenant was best for Israel and is best for us.

3. Express a commitment to live within God's covenant.

## INTO THE LESSON

Say, "In 1620 Puritans landed at Plymouth Rock on the barren, cold coast of Massachusetts near Cape Cod Bay. They were in search of a new life and religious freedom. The journey had been perilous with several deaths and sickness on board. But their spirits were high and their hope outstanding. Their new beginning is similar to that of the Israelites who came to the Jordan River and were led by Joshua into the promised land."

Ask your class to list some of the factors the Puritans overcame in starting a colony in the New World. (Climate, food, medicine, houses to build, illness, native inhabitants, death, loneliness.) What allowed them to persevere? (Faith, determination, God's care.)

Note that Moses gave the children of Israel a huge challenge as he made his final instructions to them before he died and God buried him.

## INTO THE WORD

For a review of Israel's history from the exodus to the time of today's lesson—as Moses does in the text—ask the following questions to your class:

(1) How many years did Israel wander in the wilderness before going into the promised land? (*Forty, v. 5*) (2) Since it took only a short time to reach Canaan from Egypt (including a day to worship God), why did they not go in and take the land immediately? (*They sent in twelve spies who returned with a mixed report. Ten of the spies reported that an invasion would be impossible, for the giants in the land and walled cities would prevent their taking the land.*) (3) Which two spies recommended that they go in and take the land with God's help? (*Joshua and Caleb*) (4) Who died on the forty-year journey? (*All adults who left Egypt except two men.*) (5) Who were the exceptions? (*again, Joshua and Caleb*) (6) Why were they spared when the other adults died? (*They were the two spies who gave the good report that expressed confidence in God's presence and power.*) (7) What other benefits were the Israelites given on their wilderness trek? (*God provided good water as they needed it. Neither their clothes nor shoes wore out for the forty years. Also they went to battle and defeated two kings—Og, King of Bashan, and Sihon, King of Heshbon. Lands east of the Jordan ruled by pagan kings were given to the Reubenites, the Gadites, and half of the tribe of Manasseh; see vv. 5-8*). (8) When Moses gave this new covenant, what was the reaction of the people? (*Eager anticipation*)

## INTO LIFE

The reproducible page includes simple line drawings of a house under construction and of a traditional church building on a single sheet. Copy and distribute these sheets and say the following, "This house represents Israel" (*write in the spiritual foundation for the house; this is the Mosaic covenant, including the Ten Commandments*). "Walls are built of the continuous teaching of the Word of God" (*write the names of some of the prophets of the Old Testament on the studs of the walls*). "The windows provide light to the interior of the house. The windows represent God's message by prophecies as they looked forward to the time of the Messiah" (*write a Messianic prophecy in the windows*). "The roof is God's protection" (*write an incident when God protected them from enemies, such as at the Red Sea*).

Now turn to the simple drawing of a church building. Ask the group to identify the foundation (*Jesus Christ*), the walls (*Christians*), the windows (*light via the Word of God*), the roof (*the protection of God's Holy Spirit*).

Remind the class, "The church, of course, is not the building, but rather the people committed to Jesus Christ. This people (perhaps) worships in a building dedicated for that specific purpose." Then ask, "What is the one thing that holds the church together?" (*The key is the power and providence of God and the relationship between the members.*)

Also, ask, "What is the 'glue' that solidifies the church in relationship?" (*The Bible identifies that relationship as love for one another. This is a key for an effective church.*) Finally, ask, "How is the church's 'glue' different from the 'glue' of the Israelites?" (*Theirs was national and biological; the church's is emotional and volitional.*)

# The House of Israel

Consider the following drawing to be "the house of Israel." Label these various parts of the house—foundation, walls, windows, roof—with corresponding spiritual elements.

# The House of God

Consider the following drawing a representation of Christ's church. Label the various components with the corresponding spiritual realities.

# CREATING A NEW DYNASTY

**LESSON 5**

## WHY TEACH THIS LESSON?

As I write this, some of my former high school classmates are busy planning our thirty-year reunion. It's safe to assume that at our gathering many sentences will begin with the four words, "Do you remember when . . . ?" What follows those four words will either bring a smile or a grimace to the face, depending!

Such is the stuff of legacies. We become "known for" our actions and characteristics, for good or for ill. As you consider the week, month, and year that have just gone by, what personal accomplishments—what kind of legacy—are you leaving for eternity? Our master is away temporarily, but when he returns he will ask a similar question (Luke 19:11-27), so it may be a good idea to start thinking about the answer in advance! It is unlikely that any of us will leave a legacy on the magnitude of a King David, but God will hold us to account nonetheless. Today's lesson will help us evaluate the effect our lives are having in the sight of God.

## INTRODUCTION

### A. RISES AND FALLS

Sports fans seem to be always on the alert for the next "dynasty" to come along. Just a passing mention of the Green Bay Packers of the 1960s, the Pittsburgh Steelers of the 1970s, the San Francisco 49ers of the 1980s, or the Dallas Cowboys of the 1990s is guaranteed to start a conversation with someone who follows professional football closely. The existence of dynasties—whether in sports, politics, or business—causes us to envy, to admire, or to grimace in distaste.

The collapse of a dynasty can cause us to mourn or to breathe a sigh of relief, depending on our viewpoint. And human dynasties do indeed tend to collapse and disappear over time! In 1982 Forbes magazine began its annual list of the four hundred wealthiest Americans. By 2002, just twenty years later, only sixty-four (or 16 percent) of the original "Forbes 400" remained on the list.

The ancient dynasty of King David is unique, however. Just before today's text begins, Scripture notes that the Lord had promised that David's throne would be established forever (2 Samuel 7:13, 16). But before we consider what all this means, we need a brief review of how history has moved in the three hundred or so years since we saw the Israelites camped on the border of the promised land in last week's lesson.

### B. LESSON BACKGROUND

After the death of Moses, Joshua led the Israelites across the Jordan River into the promised land and into conflict. This conflict continued for years. When the men of Israel had as much land as they thought they needed, they disbanded the army and settled down to peacetime living. All this and more is recorded in the book of Joshua.

Grateful to God for his help in their campaign and guided by the strong hand of Joshua, the people were loyal to the Lord for years. But then Joshua passed away at the age of one hundred and ten (Joshua 24:29; Judges 2:8). One by one the leaders associated with him passed away as well. Israel became a nation of

DEVOTIONAL READING:
2 SAMUEL 7:10-17
BACKGROUND SCRIPTURE:
2 SAMUEL
PRINTED TEXT:
2 SAMUEL 7:18-29

Oct
3

## LESSON AIMS

After participating in this lesson, each student will be able to:

1. Describe, using David's prayer, the blessings that God had bestowed on David and his people.

2. Explain how one's relationship with God can affect future generations.

3. Evaluate the effect of his or her life on others in the family.

## KEY VERSE

Your house and your kingdom will endure forever before me; your throne will be established forever. —2 Samuel 7:16

people with no personal remembrance of the miracles that had given birth to the nation and had brought it to independence and prosperity (Judges 2:10).

Then a common human tendency set in: a tendency to drift away from God. His law was still the law of the land; but there was no strong national government to enforce it, and local enforcement was feeble or absent. Lying, cheating, and stealing increased, followed by mayhem and murder.

When Israel's sin became intolerable in the sight of God, punishment followed. God allowed pagan bands to invade the land, driving off livestock, stealing the grain of harvest, and killing anyone who got in the way. Now unarmed and unorganized, Israel was helpless.

In poverty and misery, Israel had enough memory of God to realize what was wrong. The people stopped their wickedness and begged God for help. God responded by raising up among them talented leaders who rallied them to defeat the oppressors and drive them away. So peace returned, and prosperity followed.

For about three hundred years that cycle was repeated over and over: prosperity was followed by sin, sin by punishment, punishment by repentance, and repentance by renewed prosperity. This is told briefly in Judges 2:6-19 and recorded in detail in the rest of that book.

Samuel was one of the greatest of Israel's judges. After freeing the country from oppressors, he established a circuit court to administer justice (1 Samuel 7:16). His decisions were respected, for they were according to the law. When Samuel was old, he appointed his two sons to be judges as well. Those young men turned out to be evil. Leading men of Israel could see that when Samuel died, justice would be dead, too. So they asked Samuel to appoint a king for Israel. Neither God nor Samuel was pleased with that idea, but God said to let the people have their way (1 Samuel 8:6-9).

As a result, Saul became the first king. He started his reign in a splendid way, but later became arrogant and disobedient to God. God rejected him and then sent Samuel to anoint David to be king (1 Samuel 9–15). When Saul ended his own life in battle, David took the throne (1 Samuel 31; 2 Samuel 5).

Instead of letting David build a house for him, God said he would build for David a house—that is, a household, a family, a ruling dynasty. God said that people of David's family would continue to rule forever if they kept God's law (1 Chronicles 28:7). To that message David responded with the prayer we have taken for the text of this lesson.

## I. THE KING AND HIS LORD (2 SAMUEL 7:18-22)

If David is disappointed because he is not allowed to build the temple, his disappointment is lost in the grandeur of what God has done for him. Greater still is the grandeur of what God promises to do in the future.

### A. MODEST KING (vv. 18-20)

18. Then King David went in and sat before the LORD, and he said:

"Who am I, O Sovereign LORD, and what is my family, that you have brought me this far?

The year is roughly 1000 B.C. The phrase *then King David went in and sat before the Lord* probably means that David is sitting before the ark of the covenant inside a tent (2 Samuel 6:17).

Over the course of the years, God has transformed David from being a young shepherd of the fields into being the king of a great nation. What was there in that shepherd to merit such a transformation? Certainly his *family* had not been prominent, influential, or wealthy enough to make their boy a king.

*WHAT DO YOU THINK?*

*The path Saul took is, unfortunately, the same that many others take as well. Why do some leaders who begin well seem to finish so poorly? How can we help them avoid failure?*

As a matter of fact, David himself had much to do with his own advancement. As a shepherd he showed daring and strength in hand-to-paw combat with wild animals (1 Samuel 17:34-37). He showed like courage and skill in his conflict with Goliath, the Philistine giant who intimidated the whole army of Israel.

David also showed restraint and respect for authority when he spared the life of King Saul when the king was trying to kill him (1 Samuel 24, 26). As an officer in Saul's army, David was so successful in war that he became a national hero (1 Samuel 18:5-7). David seems to be a natural leader. But this modest king gives all the credit to *the Lord.*

19. *"And as if this were not enough in your sight, O Sovereign LORD, you have also spoken about the future of the house of your servant. Is this your usual way of dealing with man, O Sovereign LORD?*

Most of us may think that making a king out of a shepherd is a pretty big thing. But David recognizes that this is a small thing compared with what God intends to do next: God promises that David's house will continue into the future, in fact, "forever" (vv. 16, 29).

In the Hebrew, the question translated *Is this your usual way of dealing with man, O Sovereign Lord?* is a puzzle to translators. If this translation is correct, then David's rhetorical question is intended to express amazement.

20. *"What more can David say to you? For you know your servant, O Sovereign LORD.*

The *Lord* knows David—knows what is in his mind and heart. Actually, there is no need for David to go on expressing his humble gratitude for the great things the Lord has done because the Lord knows David's heart thoroughly. Still, David cannot refrain from praising the Doer of those great things, as we see next.

### GRACE TO THE HUMBLE; DEATH TO THE PROUD

Jim Jones was a man who rose from obscurity to a position of influence over other people. Fame and power turned his head and heart, and evil took over his life. Jones ministered to a church in a poorer area of San Francisco. That church was meeting the needs of the people in a significant way. However, in 1977 reports of physical and sexual abuse came to the attention of civic authorities.

Jones ordered his church members to go with him to Jonestown, his jungle compound in Guyana, where he could continue to control their lives. Continuing reports of abuse prompted Congressman Leo Ryan and several reporters to fly to Jonestown. On November 18, 1978, the day they were to return to the United States, Ryan and three reporters were murdered. That same day more than nine hundred people in the cult were either killed or committed suicide by drinking a poisoned beverage. Jones was found shot to death, perhaps a suicide.

David also came from a humble background. It is true that he succumbed at one point to the lust connected with power, an all too common occurrence. But David had a penitent heart, and God promised him a dynasty that exists today, with Jesus, his Son, still reigning. If we are wise, we will heed the striking difference between David and the Jim Joneses of the world. God gives grace to those who remain humble (Proverbs 3:34).       —C. R. B.

### B. GLORIOUS LORD (vv. 21, 22)

21. *"For the sake of your word and according to your will, you have done this great thing and made it known to your servant.*

David's modesty is still evident. He knows God had *done this great thing* to make him king. (See also the parallel version of this passage in 1 Chronicles 17:16-27, as well as David's praise in Psalm 145:6.) It is God who has decreed David to be a ruler (1 Samuel 16:1-13).

---

WHAT DO YOU THINK?

*David knew that in and of himself he did not deserve to be king. Why do you think that God chooses to use those whom the world often sees as weak to accomplish his purposes? How should this affect our own thinking?*

WHAT DO YOU THINK?

*Often we take for granted so much of what God has done in us and through us and for us. Why are we so quick to forget the great things God has done? How can we make sure we remember these great things?*

## DAILY BIBLE READINGS

**Monday, Sept. 27**—God's Steadfast Love Is Great (Psalm 86:8-13)

**Tuesday, Sept. 28**—David Moves the Ark of God (2 Samuel 6:1-5)

**Wednesday, Sept. 29**—David Brings the Ark to Jerusalem (2 Samuel 6:11-15)

**Thursday, Sept. 30**—God Sends a Message to David (2 Samuel 7:1-9)

**Friday, Oct. 1**—God Makes a Covenant with David (2 Samuel 7:10-17)

**Saturday, Oct. 2**—David Prays to God (2 Samuel 7:18-22)

**Sunday, Oct. 3**—David Seeks God's Blessing (2 Samuel 7:23-29)

## HOW TO SAY IT

Abraham. AY-bruh-ham.
Deuteronomy. Due-ter-AHN-uh-me.
Egypt. EE-jipt.
Goliath. Go-LYE-uth.
Guyana. Guy-AH-nuh.
Israel. IZ-ray-el.
Jeremiah. Jair-uh-MY-uh.
Joshua. JOSH-yew-uh.
Moses. MO-zes or MO-zez.
Nathan. NAY-thun.
Nehemiah. NEE-huh-MY-uh.
Philistine. Fuh-LISS-teens or FILL-us-teen.
Ur. Er.

For the *sake* of God's own *word*, the Lord has done all that is needed to bring this kingship about. David adds that what God has done is according to God's *will*—it is just what God wanted to do. God did not do it reluctantly, as when he gave in to the people's request for a king in the first place (1 Samuel 8:7, 22).

The phrase *and made it known to your servant* is part of David's acknowledgment that there is no guesswork about how all this has come to be. The evidence is clear: God's hand is behind everything. Realizing that, David will try very hard to make sure that God is not disappointed with his kingship.

22. *"How great you are, O Sovereign LORD! There is no one like you, and there is no God but you, as we have heard with our own ears.*

The great things that *God* has done show that God himself is *sovereign*. Not only is there no other God *like* him, there is no other God besides him. He is the one and only real and living God. When David reflects on all that *we have heard with our own ears,* he is undoubtedly thinking about God's mighty acts in Israel's history, as passed from generation to generation.

## II. THE LORD AND HIS NATION (2 SAMUEL 7:23, 24)

Thinking about the greatness of God leads to thinking about the greatness of the nation that God claims as his own. God has chosen that populous nation to emerge from only two people, namely Abraham and his wife.

God had taken those two away from the moon worshipers in Ur and planted them in the very land where David is now king. God has given that growing nation his providential and miraculous care through centuries, and now its people number in the millions.

### A. THE REDEEMED NATION (v. 23)

23. *"And who is like your people Israel—the one nation on earth that God went out to redeem as a people for himself, and to make a name for himself, and to perform great and awesome wonders by driving out nations and their gods from before your people, whom you redeemed from Egypt?*

God is incomparable: there is no other like him. Likewise, his *nation* is incomparable: there is not another like it. When it fell into slavery in Egypt, God did not abandon it. He rescued it *from Egypt,* protected it from other nations, and took it back to the promised land where he had first taken Abraham. The "redemption" of God's people is an important Old Testament theme (see Deuteronomy 7:8; 9:26; 13:5; 15:15; 21:8; 24:18; Nehemiah 1:10; and Jeremiah 31:11).

Just previously in 2 Samuel 7:9, the Lord promised that David's name would be great. Now, in abject humility, David recognizes the greatness of the Lord's *name.* By his mighty acts, God has made for himself that name through having a reputation for possessing irresistible power. The *great and awesome* things that the Lord has done include, of course, the ten plagues in Egypt and the defeat of pagan nations in the promised land. Israel is not the biggest of nations or the richest, but it is God's own nation. It is ruled by David, the king of God's own choosing.

### MANIFEST DESTINY

In 1845 journalist John L. O'Sullivan coined the phrase *manifest destiny* to describe a concept that has existed throughout history. From time immemorial kings who wished to expand their borders claimed it to be God's will (or the will of the gods, as the case may be). In Western civilization—from the Crusades of the Middle Ages (with their motto *deus lo vult* or "God wills it"), to the great empires of Europe of the sixteenth through the nineteenth centuries (Portugal, Spain, and England)—it was the same.

In the nineteenth and twentieth centuries—and this is what O'Sullivan was referring to—the United States developed this same sense that God had destined its expansion from the Atlantic to the Pacific. As many see it, manifest destiny *created* American history.

David saw the same principle at work in ancient Israel, but with this vital difference: through miraculous events there was *no doubt* that God indeed had played an active and intimate role in the history of Israel, his own people under the old covenant. It was a unique role in all of human history. Occurring in one era and in one place, it is a role never to be repeated with any other nation.

Today, God has covenant people in every nation. They are called Christians. Manifest destiny now calls for the continuous expansion of Christ's realm until he returns. —C. R. B.

## B. THE CONFIRMED NATION (v. 24)

**24. "You have established your people Israel as your very own forever, and you, O LORD, have become their God.**

*Israel* is God's nation because he is the one who created it. The one who creates is the one who has ownership rights! God *established* that ownership by redeeming Israel from Egypt, by defending it against other countries, by giving it the promised land, and by making David its king.

## III. PRAYER FOR THE FUTURE (2 SAMUEL 7:25-29)

The first verse of our printed text begins, "Then King David went in and sat before the LORD." All the rest of the text records what David said to the Lord. Now we come to the part of his prayer that makes requests for the future. It is notable that this modest king asks only for what God already has promised. Truly David is a man after God's own heart (1 Samuel 13:13, 14).

## A. FOR DAVID'S HOUSE (v. 25)

**25. "And now, LORD God, keep forever the promise you have made concerning your servant and his house. Do as you promised,**

See God's *promise* in verse 16 of this chapter. David is now asking God to keep that promise, to *do as* he has said he will do.

This means that David's kingdom will be established and his descendants will continue to rule. That certainly is pleasing to David, but also of great concern is God's reputation, as the next verse shows.

## B. FOR GOD'S NAME (v. 26)

**26. " . . . so that your name will be great forever. Then men will say, 'The LORD Almighty is God over Israel!' And the house of your servant David will be established before you.**

Again the glory of God's *name* and the glory of David's *house* are tied together. Again *David* gives first place to the glory of God's name. In verses 25-29 of this prayer, David refers to himself as *servant* seven times.

## C. REVELATION AND PRAYER (v. 27)

**27. "O LORD Almighty, God of Israel, you have revealed this to your servant, saying, 'I will build a house for you.' So your servant has found courage to offer you this prayer.**

Countless nations have risen and fallen; some have been forgotten. Countless dynasties have had their years of power and have ceased to be. Is it presumptuous and arrogant for the king of Israel to pray that his own dynasty might rule forever? It could be, if eternal rule is the king's own idea.

PRAYER

*Heavenly Father, we are grateful for the example set before us by your noble people, ancient and modern. Along with the precepts of your Word, their godly lives guide us in godly ways. And if we see in their lives some things less than godly, may we realize that these too are for our learning. By your grace may we be led in ways that are right, and by your grace may our sins be forgiven. In Jesus' name, amen.*

Visual for lessons 5 and 10. *This visual can be a discussion starter for the question, "How is Jesus 'the fulfillment'?"*

To this king, however, the Lord himself has already *revealed* that this dynasty will continue forever. The grateful king is only saying, *"O Lord Almighty, your will be done."* As we labor in God's everlasting kingdom, may we say the same thing.

### D. PROMISE AND PLEA (vv. 28, 29)

**28. "O Sovereign LORD, you are God! Your words are trustworthy, and you have promised these good things to your servant.**

The phrase *you are God* seems intended to emphasize David's belief that the God to whom he prays is the one and only true God. There is no other god. What God says is true because there is no other god to contradict him.

And what *good things* has the truthful God promised to David? He has promised David a house—not a building of stone, but a household, a family. And God has promised that men of that family will continue to rule among God's people forever (2 Samuel 7:12-16).

**29. "Now be pleased to bless the house of your servant, that it may continue forever in your sight; for you, O Sovereign LORD, have spoken, and with your blessing the house of your servant will be blessed forever."**

Again we hear David asking God only to do what God already has promised to do. But if God is going to do what David knows that God will do, whether or not David asks for it, then is this request merely a waste of words? Far from it! With this request David is expressing his submission to God and gratitude for what God is going to do.

As he prays, does David understand that the last and greatest of his ruling descendants will be the Son of God as well as a son of David? Does David realize that there will be one King eternal, the crucified Savior, risen to die no more, enthroned at the right hand of God in Heaven? Probably not.

Perhaps instead King David envisions a long line of his descendants, one by one enthroned in Jerusalem and ruling the nation of Israel from that day forward, as long as they are "unswerving in carrying out" God's commands (again, 1 Chronicles 28:7). But on the other hand, we know the Spirit of the Lord is with David (1 Samuel 16:13). Perhaps the Spirit has revealed to David far more than he learned from God's message spoken by Nathan in 2 Samuel 7:5-16.

Whether David knew it or not, today we certainly know that the King eternal is the crucified Savior who gave his life to redeem us. No less than David, we can be grateful for the providence of the God who invites us to live eternally.

### CONCLUSION

David could have claimed credit for his rise to the throne, for all the reasons listed in the discussion of verse 18. But David chose to give all the credit to God. God had chosen him to be king; God had sent the prophet to anoint him; God had arranged the circumstances and events that had contributed to his rise.

David's modesty is part of the attraction of this biblical hero. He was a doer, not a boaster. Even so, he did not carry his modesty to a counterproductive extreme. It seems that he graciously accepted the plaudits of a multitude in victory celebration. He did not mar the joy of the occasion by frowning or shrinking away, even though King Saul was obviously annoyed (1 Samuel 18:8).

Our challenge is to have the same balance. To be a "glory grabber" in the church is distasteful and ungodly; it is a violation of Romans 12:3. Christ is our model of humility (Mark 10:45). Even so, there is also such a thing as being overly modest. We see this problem arise in people who have skills and talents but pretend that they don't. This is false humility. May God deliver us from both extremes.

---

*WHAT DO YOU THINK?*

God made promises to his people because he placed his trust in people to seek his face. We in turn make promises to God because of the faith we have in him. How can we make promises—to God and to others—that we can keep?

*WHAT DO YOU THINK?*

As Christians we often pray for God's blessing upon our lives and our church. How can we play a part in the answer to this prayer?

*THOUGHT TO REMEMBER*

Choose a good example, and make it better.

# Discovery Learning

*This page contains an alternative lesson plan emphasizing learning activities. Classes desiring such student involvement will find these suggestions helpful. The next page is a reproducible activity page to further enhance discovery learning.*

## LEARNING GOALS

After participating in this lesson, each student will be able to:

1. Describe, using David's prayer, the blessings that God had bestowed on David and his people.

2. Explain how one's relationship with God can affect future generations.

3. Evaluate the effect of his or her life on others in the family.

## INTO THE LESSON

During the week ask four people to prepare a short synopsis of a portion of the historical review in the lesson commentary. Provide each student a copy of the appropriate page of the commentary. Also prepare a visual with the following outline points that you will uncover or write in as each person reports.

FROM MOSES TO DAVID

A. Taking the Promised Land

B. Backsliding and Repentance

C. Becoming a Monarchy

D. David the King

Ask, "For what would you like to be remembered when you die?" Ask the class to jot down answers. They can share these in groups or with the entire class.

After the reports have been given, make the transition to Bible study by saying, "King David wished to build a house or temple for God. But God said that he would build David a house—that is, a household or family that would rule forever. David's response is today's text, a prayer that reveals how God would create a whole new dynasty that would change the world forever.

"We'll learn something about how to live as we see how God worked in David's life."

## INTO THE WORD

Hang signs from the ceiling, each with one of the following headings: "David's Prominent Descendants," "The Modest King," "A Redeemed Nation," "Praying for the Future." The signs should be separated enough for small groups to gather under. Add duplicate signs for larger classes. Ask class members to choose one and to move under that sign. Give the following assignments, poster board, and markers to each group.

*David's Prominent Descendants:* Read 2 Samuel 7:11b-16. (1) Where do you see a promise of Solomon in this passage? A promise of Jesus? (2) Also read Matthew 1:1-17 and tell how Jesus, the Messiah, is the Son of David. List your answers on the poster board.

*The Modest King:* Read 2 Samuel 7:18-29. Then focus on verses 18-21. (1) As David looks back, for what might he be thankful about God's work in his personal life? (2) What does this text imply about how God works in everyday life? List answers on the poster board.

*A Redeemed Nation:* Read 2 Samuel 7:18-29. Now, focus on verses 22-24. (1) Make a list of the special, and sometimes miraculous, ways God worked in Israel's history. (2) Discuss and list lessons any nation should learn from how God worked in the nation of Israel.

*Praying for the Future:* Read 2 Samuel 18-29. Focus on verses 25-29 and write answers to the following: (1) Why do you think David asks God to do what God has already promised to do? What does this say about David's heart? (2) List David's requests from God (see verses 25, 26, 29). (3) Would David have any idea that the last of his ruling descendants would be the Son of God as well as a son of David?

Ask the groups to report their conclusions.

## INTO LIFE

Bring the group back together. Prepare the following instructions and questions on paper. Use the following heading: "Stick-Man Art and Application." Instructions include, "Draw stick art to represent how you would answer or apply the following assignments":

1. David was a great man. Using him as an example, illustrate how one's relationship with God can affect future generations.

2. We live in an uncertain world. What assurance about God's dynasty or kingdom do we find in David's prayer? Illustrate with stick art.

3. Thankfulness is an important element in human relationships with God. Sketch one thing for which you are especially thankful to God.

4. Use stick art or a word picture to answer the following. For what would you like to be most remembered when you die? What would you like on your tombstone to represent your values or your contribution to society?

Ask your learners to share their answers with one person and to pray together for each other.

# Discovering David

There are wonderful qualities of our God revealed in David's prayer. Read through the prayer in 2 Samuel 7:18-29 and list these characteristics, actions, or descriptions of God in the puzzle below. In so doing you will discover a key word in David's prayer that is one of the most wonderful qualities of all.

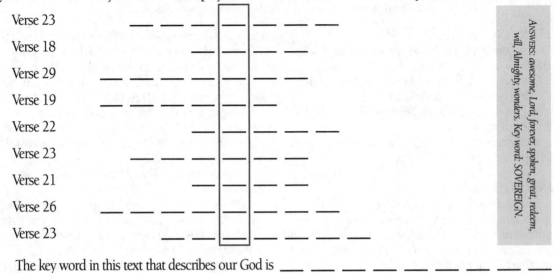

Verse 23 __ __ __ __ | __ __ __ __

Verse 18 __ __ __ | __ __ __

Verse 29 __ __ __ __ __ | __ __ __

Verse 19 __ __ __ __ | __ __ __

Verse 22 __ __ __ | __ __ __ __

Verse 23 __ __ __ __ | __ __ __ __

Verse 21 __ __ | __ __ __

Verse 26 __ __ __ __ __ | __ __ __ __ __

Verse 23 __ __ __ | __ __ __ __ __

The key word in this text that describes our God is __ __ __ __ __ __ __ __ __

# Getting to Know an Awesome God

David had a deep reverence and respect for his God. Look up each of the following Scripture passages and discover more qualities of our awesome God. Use the middle column to note God's character. In the right column, note an emotion, reaction, or action this characteristic brings to your mind.

| SCRIPTURE | GOD'S CHARACTER | MY RESPONSE |
| --- | --- | --- |
| Exodus 20:4 | | |
| Leviticus 19:2 | | |
| Deuteronomy 4:31 | | |
| 2 Samuel 22:31 | | |
| Psalm 47:2 | | |
| Matthew 19:17 | | |
| Luke 4:24 | | |
| Romans 1:25 | | |
| 1 Corinthians 10:13 | | |
| 1 John 3:1 | | |
| Revelation 19:6 | | |

# CREATING A REDEEMED PEOPLE

LESSON 6

## WHY TEACH THIS LESSON?

When the economy is strong and "times are good," people naturally seem to have a sense of well being, security, and hope. Part of this outlook frequently involves a sense of identity with a certain employer. But when the economy turns sour and the layoffs begin, this sense of "belonging" can evaporate quickly.

No matter the status of an earthly economy, however, Christians remain part of the covenant community known as the church. This is our eternal hope. Much of our inner peace comes through realizing that the God who kept his promises to Old Testament Israel is our God as well. Today's lesson should cause us once again to kneel in gratitude before the God who gives us our eternal security through Jesus, his Son, as we look back to that Old Testament history.

## INTRODUCTION

### A. "TWICE MINE!"

Jimmy's favorite toy was a little boat that he made himself. It started with a piece of driftwood that he found by the river. In Dad's workshop, he hollowed it out. In the little reflecting pool in Mom's garden, the little boat floated neatly, right side up. Jimmy fitted it with mast and sail. He brought the big fan from Dad's workshop, and it blew the boat all the way across the pool.

When the family had a picnic in the park by the river, Jimmy's boat went along. Near the bank the water was only a few inches deep and moving slowly. The little boat rode sedately down the stream for a hundred feet.

Then Jimmy peeled off his shoes and socks and waded in to get his boat for another trip. This time he let it go a little farther downstream. There a log in the edge of the water turned the current away from the bank. Before Jimmy realized what was happening, his boat was out in deep water and moving swiftly. Poor Jimmy! He could only watch the river carry his favorite toy out of sight.

The family went to town some time later. Mom liked to stop at the little store where the sign said, "Antiques and Oddities." There among other oddities Jimmy saw his little boat. "Look, Dad," he said. "That's my boat!" "Not anymore," Dad informed him. "Now it belongs to whoever got it out of the river."

The owner of the store was listening nearby. Jimmy asked him, "How much is the little boat?" The man rubbed his chin thoughtfully. "I guess I'd have to have a quarter for that."

So Jimmy paid a quarter and went home with his favorite toy. He hugged it tight before he put it in the reflecting pool. "Now you're twice mine," he told it. "You're mine because I made you and you're mine because I bought you."

This week we read about a nation that was like Jimmy's little boat. It belonged to God twice: first because God made it, and then because God bought it. We read about this nation in the book of Isaiah.

DEVOTIONAL READING:
ISAIAH 42:5-13
BACKGROUND SCRIPTURE:
ISAIAH 43
PRINTED TEXT:
ISAIAH 43:1-3a, 10-19

Oct
10

LESSON AIMS

After participating in this lesson, each student will be able to:

1. Recall some great nationwide movements that God predicted through Isaiah.

2. Understand what caused Israel's disaster and what caused its recovery.

3. Trust God and obey him.

KEY VERSE

"Fear not, for I have redeemed you; I have summoned you by name; you are mine."
—Isaiah 43:1

## B. LESSON BACKGROUND

As we open today's study from Isaiah 43, time has moved forward more than three hundred years since last week's lesson about King David. Various kings have come and gone, the nation of Israel sadly has split herself into two parts. The Jewish people have been through various cycles of sin and repentance.

The opening verse of the book of Isaiah tells us that what follows is a record of "the vision concerning Judah and Jerusalem that Isaiah son of Amoz saw during the reigns of Uzziah, Jotham, Ahaz and Hezekiah, kings of Judah." It is hard to be certain about many dates in Old Testament history, but we shall not be far off if we say that these four kings ruled from 790 to 695 B.C.

In chapter 39 of Isaiah we read a little of what Isaiah said to King Hezekiah. The prophet foretold captivity in Babylon, which would begin about a century later (Isaiah 39:5-7). Then chapter 40 begins what some call "The Book of Comfort." It promises the pardon of sinful Israel and the end of captivity (40:2). Less clear is the prophecy of John the Baptist (40:3), but its meaning is revealed when fulfilled (Matthew 3:1-3). To comfort the captives there is much more about the limitless power of God and his unfailing care for his people. Our text is part of it.

For the immediate background of the first part of our text, the last two verses of Isaiah 42 tell us that Israel's troubles were punishment imposed by the Lord because of Israel's sins. In Isaiah's own time the northern nation of Israel was defeated, and its people were scattered in foreign lands (2 Kings 17:5, 6). Isaiah foretold the captivity of Judah, the southern nation (Isaiah 39:5-7). Both of these disasters are punishment for the long-continued sins of the Jewish people.

Just so we don't get too confused by terminology, we should point out that sometimes the word *Israel* in Isaiah means only the northern kingdom of that name, as distinct from the southern kingdom of Judah. At other times, however, the word *Israel* refers to all the Jewish people in both northern and southern kingdoms together. The context will tell us what is meant at any one time.

## I. PRESERVATION BY GOD (ISAIAH 43:1-3a)

The last verses of Isaiah 42 speak of God's anger, the scattering of north Israel, and the coming captivity of Judah. Why, then, does anyone call this part of Isaiah "the Book of Comfort"? Read on! Even in his anger the Lord is merciful.

### A. REASSURANCE (v. 1)

1. But now, this is what the LORD says—
      he who created you, O Jacob,
      he who formed you, O Israel:
   "Fear not, for I have redeemed you;
      I have summoned you by name; you are mine.

The opening words *but now* create a link with chapter 42, but also signal a sharp contrast. Isaiah 42:25 speaks of anger and punishment, but we read of these no more. An opposite message is given, and notice how emphatic it is.

First, the Lord identifies himself as the Creator. He stresses that announcement by repeating it in different words after the fashion of Hebrew poetry. Notice that the statement *he who created you, O Jacob* is really the same as *he who formed you, O Israel.* The names *Jacob* and *Israel* are two designations of the same man (Genesis 32:28). In our text they are two names of the same nation, the nation descended from that one man. The words *created* and *formed* are synonyms, so the declaration that the Lord is the Creator is repeated with simplicity and power.

Next comes the substance of God's message: *Fear not.* These two words stand alone, clear and bright as a trumpet call. (See also v. 5, not in today's text.)

---

*HOW TO SAY IT*

*Ahaz. AY-haz.*

*Amoz. AY-mahz.*

*Babylon. BAB-uh-lun.*

*Chaldeans. Kal-DEE-unz.*

*Corinthians. Ko-RIN-thee-unz
(th as in thin).*

*Cyrus. SIGH-russ.*

*Hezekiah. Hez-ih-KYE-uh.*

*Isaiah. Eye-ZAY-uh.*

*Israel. IZ-ray-el.*

*Jordan. JOR-dun.*

*Jotham. JO-thum.*

*Judah. JOO-duh.*

*Uzziah. Uh-ZYE-uh.*

Then God explains why Israel should not fear. First, *I have redeemed you.* Israel had been captured and enslaved by her own sin, so the Lord bought her back. Although Babylonian captivity is still in the future, the Lord's rescue is so certain that he speaks of redemption in the past tense.

Second, God has *summoned you by name.* There could be no question about whom God redeemed. Third, God states the result, or effect, of his redemption: *You are mine.* How, then, can Israel be afraid of anything?

### WHAT'S IN A NAME?

It's a question dating back at least to the time of Shakespeare: "What's in a name?" The issue is philosophical. But it's also practical, as when a name helps us identify a person. When we hear our first name over the loudspeaker in a public place, our brain filters out all background noise and we pay attention—at least until the last name of the person being paged is spoken. Then we go back to ignoring it.

Another practical use of names has been discovered by the FBI. Its agents give nicknames to serial bank robbers, usually on the basis of the physical characteristics or habits of the criminals. For example, the "Gentleman Bandit" always said "please" and "thank you." The "Bourgeois Bandit" made his getaway in a limousine. The "Bad Breath Bandit" was noted for his halitosis. The nicknames give the public and the officers a "handle" by which to identify people on the wanted list.

God comforted Israel through Isaiah by noting that he called them by name. Their name means "he strives with God" or "God strives" (Genesis 32:28; 35:10). As we know, the nation of Israel did not often live up to its namesake! The question for us is whether the character we show the world merits the name Christian— "one who belongs to Christ." —C. R. B.

## B. SAFETY (v. 2)

2. "*When you pass through the waters,*
   *I will be with you;*
*and when you pass through the rivers,*
   *they will not sweep over you.*
*When you walk through the fire,*
   *you will not be burned;*
   *the flames will not set you ablaze.*

When Israel was young as a nation, God used miracles to bring his people through the Red Sea and the flooded Jordan River (Exodus 14; Joshua 3). It was not likely that they ever would need such miracles again, or a miracle to keep them safe in literal fire. God is using figurative language to promise to keep them safe in whatever dangers they may face.

But read carefully! This is not a promise to keep them from experiencing fire, whether literal or figurative. Rather, this is a promise to keep them safe as they *walk through the fire.* Also, God does not promise to keep them safe and unpunished if they again turn away from him and sell themselves to sin as they do prior to their captivity in Babylon.

## C. IDENTITY (v. 3a)

3. "*For I am the LORD, your God,*
   *the Holy One of Israel, your Savior;*
*I give Egypt for your ransom,*
   *Cush and Seba in your stead.*"

In verse 1 we saw that the Lord identified himself as the Creator and Redeemer and Owner of his people. In verse 3 he stresses that he is their *God*, their *Holy One*, their *Savior*. The message isn't new, but it does bear repeating.

---

*WHAT DO YOU THINK?*

*God is our Creator; God is our Redeemer. How should the knowledge of these two ideas affect our daily lives?*

---

*WHAT DO YOU THINK?*

*God is not only our Creator and Redeemer (Isaiah 43:1), he is also our Protector. Why is this knowledge important to you as you go through tough times?*

*[You can use Daniel 3:26, 27; 6:22; John 17:15; Acts 12:11, 12; and 2 Corinthians 11:23-28 in your reflections.]*

## II. WITNESSES FOR GOD (ISAIAH 43:10-13)

The assurance we saw in verses 1-3a is continued in verses 4-9, which are not included in our printed text. God affirms his love for his people; he promises to gather again those who are scattered; he challenges the pagan world to produce witnesses to prove that anyone among them has foretold future events as God has done. Then God names his own witnesses, as we see next.

### A. SERVANTS WHO KNOW (vv. 10, 11)

10. "You are my witnesses," declares the LORD,
    "and my servant whom I have chosen,
  so that you may know and believe me
    and understand that I am he.
  Before me no god was formed,
    nor will there be one after me.

The Lord's people are his *witnesses*. Both by his unfailing care and by fore-telling the future he gives them ample evidence that he alone is God.

The people of Israel are not only his witnesses, but their nation as a whole is also his servant. The behavior of the Israelites ought to demonstrate to the rest of the world that he is the only God. The devotion of the Jewish people should look back to the wonderful miracles and prophecies that prove he is God.

11. "I, even I, am the LORD,
    and apart from me there is no savior.

The pagan world is full of false gods (e.g., 2 Kings 23:13). Over and over, the Jewish people find themselves seduced by these idols, so God announces again that he is the Lord. And this time he adds that he is the one and only *savior* of his people. Long before Isaiah's time, God had saved them from Egypt, from starvation in the wilderness, and from strong nations in the promised land.

In Isaiah's time God saved the southern kingdom of Judah from the Assyrians, who defeated and scattered their kinsmen to the north in 722 B.C. After Isaiah's time God will save his people from the Babylonian exile that is to begin in 586 B.C. His witnesses should testify to all of these facts by their right behavior and worship.

### B. EVIDENCE THAT PROVES (v. 12)

12. "I have revealed and saved and proclaimed—
    I, and not some foreign god among you.
  You are my witnesses," declares the LORD, "that I am God.

Put the first and last phrases of this verse together: *I have revealed . . . that I am God*. Between those two phrases we see ample evidence that the Lord is indeed the only true God. Time after time he has saved his people from powerful forces.

In this way he has showed that he is God, more powerful than all pagan earthly forces or make-believe gods in Heaven. He did this when there was *not some foreign god among you*—when his people were giving him their undivided devotion. But when the people turned away from the Lord and looked to ficti-tious gods, they were defeated. The captivity of northern Israel proves it. God's people have seen the evidence: they are witnesses. Again, their right behavior and worship ought to be testifying to these facts.

### C. GOD WHO IS (v. 13)

13. "Yes, and from ancient days I am he.
  No one can deliver out of my hand.
    When I act, who can reverse it?"

Thus the Lord gives the conclusion drawn from the evidence presented. *From ancient days I am he* means that the Lord was God before the creation of the world and has been God ever since. No one can *deliver* anyone from his power, for he is all-powerful (cf. John 10:27-29). He will do what he ought to do, and no one can prevent it. He is God! His people are witnesses of this. May their actions testify!

## III. WORK OF GOD (ISAIAH 43:14-19)

The last part of verse 13 assures us that God will go on with his work, and no one will prevent it. Now the final part of today's text tells a little about what he will do. To assure us of his ability, he also reminds us of what he has done in the past.

### A. THE DOOM OF BABYLON (v. 14)

14. *This is what the LORD says—*
    *your Redeemer, the Holy One of Israel:*
    *"For your sake I will send to Babylon*
    *and bring down as fugitives all the Babylonians,*
    *in the ships in which they took pride.*

As in verses 1 and 10, the announcement begins by making it plain that it comes from God, not from Isaiah. God is going to bring down the haughty nobles of Babylon and end their oppression. God revealed this and Isaiah wrote it many years before the captivity even began! But God can put it in the past tense because in his mind it is already "a done deal." His plan is complete, and nothing is going to keep him from carrying it out.

### B. THE LORD AND HIS POWER (vv. 15-17)

15. *"I am the LORD, your Holy One,*
    *Israel's Creator, your King."*

Again comes the reminder of who is speaking. *Lord, Holy One, Creator, King—* such a list of titles! Can anyone in Israel be so foolish as to turn a deaf ear?

16, 17. *This is what the LORD says—*
    *he who made a way through the sea,*
    *a path through the mighty waters,*
    *who drew out the chariots and horses,*
    *the army and reinforcements together,*
    *and they lay there, never to rise again,*
    *extinguished, snuffed out like a wick:*

To anyone who knows Israel's history, this brief verse is a reminder both of God's power and of his favor to his people. As we noted with verse 2 above, he had made a road *through the* Red *Sea* for them to escape from Egypt; he had made a *path through* the raging Jordan for them to enter the promised land.

Egypt's army had charged into the dry bed of the Red Sea in pursuit of God's fleeing people, ignoring the walls of water on its right and left. That was the end of the army, as men and horses died together (Exodus 14:26-28). As the flame of *a wick* is extinguished by a puff of breath, so the life of Egypt's army was *extinguished* or *snuffed out* by the water of the sea as it returned to its usual place. How can Israel not know that God will protect them from every danger?

### C. THE COMING NEW THING (vv. 18, 19)

18. *"Forget the former things;*
    *do not dwell on the past.*

How's that again? Has the Lord used verses 16 and 17 to remind us of great events in the past, only to tell us to forget them? Not at all. The Jewish people are

WHAT DO YOU THINK?

*In what ways has God delivered you? In what areas do you still need God's deliverance?*

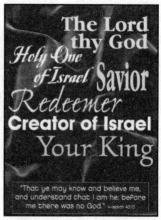

Visual for Lesson 6. *Ask your learners what these titles tell about the one who is really "in charge."*

to *forget* the old order of things such as their slavery in Egypt. What is important is to wake up and realize what God is doing now. See the next verse.

*19. "See, I am doing a new thing!*

*Now it springs up; do you not perceive it?*

*I am making a way in the desert*

*and streams in the wasteland.*

To dwell on the hardships of days gone by is pointless. To cherish the record of what God did in the ancient past to overcome those hardships is valuable, but is not a stopping point. What's most important is the *new thing* that God is *doing* and will be doing right before their very eyes.

God's ancient leadership of his people for forty years *in the desert* was no less remarkable than the spectacular crossings of the Red Sea and the Jordan River. But thinking ahead to the end of captivity in Babylon, God is laying the foundation for another journey to the ancient homeland. This future trip will lead the people there directly; they will not wander for a generation in a desert. God will keep them all the way.

## WHAT GOD IS DOING NOW

In 1633 Galileo "confessed" to being a heretic: he believed that the earth orbits the sun. The church prohibited him from discussing this Copernican view of the solar system. In 1874 John William Draper, a scientist and son of a Wesleyan clergyman, published his influential *History of the Conflict Between Religion and Science.* And so it went until the late twentieth century: science and religion (particularly Christianity) were thought to be mortal enemies.

But the times are changing, and scientists are "getting religion." The Massachusetts Institute of Technology offers Bible study courses; Carnegie Mellon Institute (whose engineering and computer science programs are rated in the top five in the country) offers a minor in religious studies; UC–Berkeley has a Center for Theology and Science; and Caltech now has a course in New Testament.

God urged Israel to look to the future, saying to Isaiah, "I am doing a new thing." God is doing a new thing in our time: he is helping a scientific world realize there is more to life than science. Some Christians are still living in the past, fighting old enemies. We would do better to help the world to see that "all truth is God's truth" and winsomely persuade it of the importance of the things of the spirit.    —C. R. B.

## CONCLUSION

What we have been reading in Isaiah was given as prophecy. It was given in the past tense because it was fully established in the mind of God. God promised captivity in Babylon for his people (Isaiah 39:5-7) as punishment for long-continued sin. But God also promised the defeat of Babylon (43:14). He named the Persian king, Cyrus, who would lead the conquerors (44:28). God even promised to redeem Israel by giving the Persians three countries in Africa as ransom (43:3b, 4).

After citing great things he has done in the past, God promised to provide a way by which his people would be able to return to their ancient homeland (Isaiah 43:15-19). Truly God can say that the Israelites are "twice mine" as he keeps all of these promises recorded by Isaiah.

Today, God can say that Christians are "twice mine" as well. This is true because he first created us, then he purchased our salvation through the blood of his Son. Because of those facts, our task is clear: we are to be "faithful, even to the point of death" so that we will receive "the crown of life" (Revelation 2:10).

We maintain our faithfulness when we trust him and obey him. We must listen to the Word of God. When we do, our obedience will be a natural outflow of our love for him (John 14:15, 23, 24). That is the way to be happy now and forever.

*WHAT DO YOU THINK?*

*God's desire is that we be made new, continually renewed, in our relationship with him. How will the knowledge of God's continuing work of renewal in your life cause you to face life differently this week?*

*PRAYER*

*Father in Heaven, while we stand in awe of your majesty and power and knowledge, we take delight in your love and goodness. Thank you for the Bible and the strong but gentle way it guides us in this confusing world. Give us understanding as we read, and give us courage to obey. In Jesus' name, amen.*

*THOUGHT TO REMEMBER*

*Only redeemed people have hope!*

*WHAT DO YOU THINK?*

*Like Israel, sometimes we are slow to hear and act. At other times we fail to learn from the past. What are some areas in your life where you need to be a better listener and learner?*

# Discovery Learning

*This page contains an alternative lesson plan emphasizing learning activities. Classes desiring such student involvement will find these suggestions helpful. The next page is a reproducible activity page to further enhance discovery learning.*

## LEARNING GOALS

After this lesson each student will be able to:

1. Recall some great nationwide movements that God predicted through Isaiah.

2. Understand what caused Israel's disaster and what caused its recovery.

3. Trust God and obey him.

## INTO THE LESSON

Give each of eleven students a sheet of copier paper with one word printed on it in large letters. Four students should receive one of the following four words printed on blue paper: *I have redeemed you.*

The remaining seven pieces of paper should be a different color from that of the first four. One of the following words should be printed on each: *"You are my witnesses," declares the Lord.* Distribute these sheets randomly to students as they enter the room.

Begin the class by having the four students with the blue paper stand in front of the class. Have them unscramble the words and stand in the correct order. After they have done so, ask them to remain in place while the second team does the same with their words.

Make the transition to Bible study by explaining, "These are two key statements by God to his people in the Old Testament. But these are certainly statements he could repeat to Christians. We'll find these concepts as we study today."

## INTO THE WORD

*Activity #1: Mini-lecture.* Prepare a short lecture introducing Isaiah's book and the lesson background by using the notes in the lesson commentary.

*Activity #2: Word Search.* Distribute copies of the reproducible activity "If I Were a Rich Man" from page 64. Ask a volunteer to read the text; then allow a few minutes for learners to complete the activity.

*Activity #3: Question and Answer.* Prepare a visual of the following outline to guide your Bible study. Ask the discussion questions that follow as you highlight or uncover each point of the outline. Use the notes in the lesson commentary to clarify concepts and answer questions the students may raise.

    I. God's Redemption (Isaiah 43:1-3a)

    II. Israel's Responsibility (Isaiah 43:10-13)

    III. God's Mercy (Isaiah 43:14-19)

I. *God's Redemption.* Have a student read verses 1-3. Then ask the following questions. (1) The word *but* is important in verse 1, since it signals a change. As you scan chapter 42, what is the stark contrast you see in today's printed text? (2) What are some of God's blessings that have or will come to Israel through their Redeemer? If this language could be figurative about future blessings, what may those blessings include? (3) Also scan verses 4-9, not in our printed text. What compliment(s) to Israel do you find?

II. *Israel's Responsibility.* Ask a student to read verses 10-13. Questions to ask include the following: (1) Notice the double call to be witnesses in verses 10 and 12. To what was Israel to be witness? What could or should be included in Israel's testimony? (2) Verse 11 echoes verse 3 and is later pronounced again in verse 15. Why do you think God placed a triple emphasis on this principle? (3) Notice the wonderful comfort to Israel in verse 13. How does this assurance give comfort to believers?

III. *God's Mercy.* Read verses 14-19 and ask: (1) Verses 18 and 19a are the key to this passage. Why did God make this statement? (2) How does it contrast with verses 16-18? (3) How will this encourage Israel?

## INTO LIFE

Introduce the following activity by reminding the class of God's infinite knowledge. He knows what will happen tomorrow and a hundred years to come. He not only *knows* the future, he *holds* the future in his hands.

Divide the class into small groups. Give each group one of the following assignments, a piece of poster board, and a marker pen.

*Task #1:* Remember how God declared "You are my witnesses" to Israel. Jesus echoed that command and brought it into Christian life when he said "You will be my witnesses" (Acts 1:8). List ways that Christians can fulfill this command in life today.

*Task #2:* Reread the assurances given in verses 13, 15, and 19. Discuss how this security brings hope to a Christian facing crisis.

*Task #3:* Read verses 13, 15, and 19 yet again. Discuss how this hope affects a believer's view of death and eternity. Then, write lines from hymns or songs that reflect this hope.

*Closing.* Distribute copies of the reproducible activity "Sharing My Riches." Use it as a closing challenge.

# "If I Were a Rich Man"

"If I Were a Rich Man" is the title of a wonderful song in the musical drama *Fiddler on the Roof.* Many of us dream of riches. We need to learn that we are rich—as one of God's children. Some of those riches are packed into today's text in Isaiah 43. Look for words that reveal or imply riches God gives to his children. Then, try to find these words in the word search grid below.

I have r_____ you (v. 1)

I have s_____ you (v. 1)

You are m_____ (v. 1)

I will be w_____ you (v. 2)

I am . . . your G_____ (v. 3)

I am . . . your S_____ (v. 3)

A n_____ thing (v. 19)

Your K_____ (v. 15)

You may k_____ . . . me (v. 10)

Whom I have c_____ (v. 10)

And my s_____ (v. 10)

You are my w_____ (v. 10)

```
M  V  K  F  W  J  C  O  T  X
K  I  N  G  E  L  G  E  X  Q
N  T  N  E  W  O  N  R  P  E
O  W  R  E  D  E  E  M  E  D
W  I  T  N  E  S  S  E  S  Z
L  I  S  U  M  M  O  N  E  D
M  B  T  A  L  Z  H  Q  R  J
J  L  S  H  V  M  C  B  V  M
Q  F  S  B  L  I  H  C  A  N
N  U  M  M  L  B  O  D  N  W
N  B  O  Q  M  V  L  R  T  F
```

ANSWERS/WORD LIST

redeemed, summoned, mine, with, God, Savior, new, King, know, chosen, servant, witnesses

# Sharing My Riches

"You are my witnesses!" That was God's pronouncement to Israel (Isaiah 43:10) and to believers today (see Acts 1:8). Here is one opportunity to complete Jesus' desire for you. In the space below, write a brief note to a friend who has yet to accept Christ. Let this note be a witness to your faith and a "practice run" for actually writing your friend such a note or sharing the same information in person.

Dear _____,

I want to tell you two things. First, I treasure our friendship. Second, as my friend you know that my faith is important to me. I want you to know that I have chosen to be a Christian because . . .

I am praying that you will also one day accept Jesus as your Lord. I hope that my experience and faith will help you in your decision.

Because I care,

Signed _____

# CREATING A NEW COVENANT

**LESSON 7**

## WHY TEACH THIS LESSON?

A few years ago I was listening to a woman on the radio who had called a talk show to discuss a family problem. It soon became apparent, however, that the caller had made up her mind in advance about what kind of answer she desired. When the talk-show host disagreed, the caller hung up! Apparently the caller was only interested in what she *wanted* to hear, not what she *needed* to hear.

People are like that, and human nature hasn't changed much in this regard across the millennia. A stark example is ancient Judah. The leaders and common folk of that country preferred to hear the soothing lies of false prophets to the "tough love" message of God's true prophets. But let us be grateful that we serve a God who always tells us what we need to hear for the long haul, no matter how much earthly difficulty results for us in the short term. It is God's "long-haul outlook" that has given us the new covenant, and the eternal life that it brings with it. Today's look into the distant past will renew our faith that looks forward.

## INTRODUCTION

### A. FORTUNE-TELLERS, THEN AND NOW

The fortune-teller's tent was a fascinating spot at our state fair. Unlike our camping tent of white canvas, this one was a riot of color. It rose to a lofty peak, from which a scarlet pennon fluttered in the fitful breeze. When the fortune-teller herself appeared in the doorway, her brunette beauty was enhanced by heavy makeup, big earrings, and a glittering tiara. Her long robe was solid black, but it, too, glittered as she moved.

A timid child at the age of nine, I watched from the other side of the midway. Fascinating as they were, that woman and her tent seemed somehow evil, dangerous, frightening. Bolder than I, a little bevy of high-school girls sat in the waiting area; yet they were prim and silent, and I knew they felt a bit of the fear that kept me on the other side of the busy midway.

Afterward I asked some of the girls about the fortune-teller. They said she promised each one a rosy future: every hope would be realized, every fear would prove to be unfounded.

Did ancient fortune-tellers also contrive to be mystical and half-frightening? No doubt some of them did. Why else would they "whisper" and "mutter" instead of speaking clearly (Isaiah 8:19)? And certainly they continued to say what the people wanted to hear, regardless of truth. Else why would they say Israel would not be subject to Babylonian rule (Jeremiah 27:9, 10)?

### B. LESSON BACKGROUND

God's real prophets spoke the truth that God gave them, whether anyone wanted to hear it or not. In last week's Lesson Background we noted that the

DEVOTIONAL READING:
JEREMIAH 30:18-22
BACKGROUND SCRIPTURE:
JEREMIAH 29–31
PRINTED TEXT:
JEREMIAH 29:10-14; 31:31-34

LESSON AIMS

After participating in this lesson, each student will be able to:

Oct 17

1. Tell what God promised for the future of the Jewish exiles, including a return to their homeland and the making of a new covenant.

2. Explain how the gospel of Jesus Christ fulfills Jeremiah's prophecy of a new covenant.

3. Describe the future that awaits those who enter into a covenant relationship with God.

KEY VERSE

"This is the covenant I will make with the house of Israel after that time," declares the Lord. "I will put my law in their minds and write it on their hearts. I will be their God, and they will be my people."
—Jeremiah 31:33

prophet Isaiah had foretold captivity in Babylon (Isaiah 39:5-7). But no one wanted to hear that message.

Jeremiah, prophesying many decades after Isaiah, said Jerusalem would be destroyed. The hearers wanted to kill him for bringing that message (Jeremiah 26:8-11). But the southern kingdom of Judah did indeed become captive in Babylon, and Jerusalem was indeed destroyed. These disasters could have been averted if God's people had listened to God's truth in time.

The Babylonian dominance over Judah occurred in three phases. **Phase 1** began about 605 B.C. when the Babylonian army approached Jerusalem. In short order King Jehoiakim (reigned 609–598 B.C.) gave up without a struggle. Daniel and a few others were taken captive (Daniel 1:1-6). In a few years Jehoiakim revolted. Babylon controlled several small nations near Judah, and those nations harassed Judah until Nebuchadnezzar returned with his army (2 Kings 23:36–24:2).

**Phase 2** began about 597 B.C. when the Babylonian army again arrived on the scene at Jerusalem. King Jehoiakim had died, and his son Jehoiachin had taken his place. Following his father's example, the new king surrendered to the enemy. This time the Babylonians took ten thousand captives, including civil and military leaders, blacksmiths skilled in making weapons, and probably the prophet Ezekiel. Zedekiah was left to rule Judah and pay tribute (2 Kings 24:8-17).

**Phase 3** began about 588 B.C. when Zedekiah revolted and the Babylonian army returned a third time. After besieging Jerusalem for a year and a half, that army captured the starving city in 586 B.C. The city and its temple were leveled, and most of the surviving people were taken to Babylon (2 Kings 25).

This week's lesson belongs in Phase 2 of the Babylonian domination. Ten thousand Jewish captives have been taken to Babylon, but this does not include the prophet Jeremiah. From Jerusalem he writes a letter to give God's message to his ten thousand countrymen who are being held against their will in Babylon.

## I. LONG-TERM PROMISE (JEREMIAH 29:10-14)

In Jeremiah's letter, the Lord advises the captives in Babylon to settle down and live normal lives. They are to work for the peace of Babylon so the captives, too, would be at peace. The Lord also warns them not to be fooled by self-proclaimed prophets who are not telling the truth (Jeremiah 29:1-9). The next part of the letter begins our text.

### A. THE LORD'S PLAN, PART 1 (vv. 10, 11)

**10. This is what the LORD says: "When seventy years are completed for Babylon, I will come to you and fulfill my gracious promise to bring you back to this place.**

*Seventy years*, a round number, is the time assigned for *Babylon* to rule Judah (Jeremiah 25:11). It includes all three phases listed in the Lesson Background.

Of the people of Judah, only Daniel and a few others are at Babylon all of that time (Daniel 1:3-7). Those who receive this letter from Jeremiah have nearly sixty years ahead of them to spend in Babylon. At the end of that time, and not before, the Lord will bring about their liberation and their return to *this place*, Jerusalem (cf. Jeremiah 27:22).

**11. "For I know the plans I have for you," declares the LORD, "plans to prosper you and not to harm you, plans to give you hope and a future.**

The Lord is quite sure about his thinking. He has planned captivity for his people because they have been sinning. But captivity is causing them to change their ways. Now the Lord is planning their liberation. False prophets are promising a quick end to the captivity (Jeremiah 28:1-4, 10, 11). The Lord's plan, however, is the one that offers the expected end of true *hope*.

**WHAT DO YOU THINK?**

*God promised that the captives in Babylon would be returned to their homeland after seventy years. Compare that promise with Jesus' promise to return at some future date. How does each promise inspire hope? What does each promise do to inspire faithfulness in the waiting period?*

## B. THE SPIRITUAL RESULT, PART 1 (vv. 12-14)

**12. "Then you will call upon me and come and pray to me, and I will listen to you.**

Before the captivity, the people and officials of Judah often ignore God's prophets. Sometimes the prophets are persecuted (e.g., Jeremiah 26:20-23). But, homesick in Babylon, many of the people and officials will have ample time to re-think their attitudes.

Perhaps while in captivity they will realize that the Lord is "the compassionate and gracious God, slow to anger, abounding in love and faithfulness" (Exodus 34:6). Perhaps while in captivity some wise teacher will remind them how important it is to pray.

God would rather pardon than punish the wayward. God ultimately will *listen to* the prayers of his penitent people. Even so, the most severe part of the captivity—including the destruction of Jerusalem—will make even Jeremiah wonder if God is listening (Lamentations 3:8, 44).

**13. "You will seek me and find me when you seek me with all your heart.**

God had not been hiding from his people in those years before the captivity. Rather, it is they who had been hiding from him. Happy with his gifts, they saw no need of the Giver. Now a precious gift—their liberty—is gone and in grief they will look for the Giver.

But there is a condition attached to being able to find the Lord: they must search for him with *all* their hearts. Only then will they *find* the Lord. When God restores their liberty, some hearts will rejoice at the gain while others will sorrow over what need not have been lost in the first place (Ezra 3:10-13).

**14. "I will be found by you," declares the LORD, "and will bring you back from captivity. I will gather you from all the nations and places where I have banished you," declares the LORD, "and will bring you back to the place from which I carried you into exile."**

What a striking list of events will happen when the captives seek the Lord with all their hearts! First, they will find him; they will really be his people. Second, he will *bring* them *back from captivity*—he will reverse it, setting them free. Third, he will *gather* them *from all the nations and places* to which he has driven them. As a result he will bring all those people *back to* the land from which they had been taken.

The forthcoming return will be to the ancient homeland, back to the promised land to which the Jewish people had gone from Egypt. It will be a return to the land promised to Abraham and his descendants centuries earlier.

### THE LONG ROAD HOME

Long-haul truckers have been called "road warriors" and "the last cowboys." They have a lonely job that takes them far from home for long periods at a time.

But temptations lurk at many stops along the road. That's why Truckstop Ministries began in the 1980s. The chapels are tractor-trailer rigs at some sixty locations in about one-half of the United States. Some of the volunteer ministers wish they could have been truckers themselves; some are former truckers. All want to share their faith.

A typical service may have a "crowd" ranging from none to several; an occasional motorist may even attend. A woman who had a flat tire in Hesperia, California, attended a trucker's service, saying, "I just wanted to talk to God." However, the primary goal is to help truckers find God and get their lives headed down the right road. No matter where their load of freight has to go, finding God is the most important thing.

Jeremiah told Judah that turning to God would bring their lonely captivity to an end. If they repented, God would put them on the long road home and bring them

*WHAT DO YOU THINK?*

Do you ever doubt that God hears your prayers? If so, when? Why? How can you reassure yourself or another that God truly does hear even when you are suffering?

*WHAT DO YOU THINK?*

Suppose a non-Christian neighbor has come to class with you this morning. As we read verse 13, he says, "I don't know how to find God. I searched for him when I was out of work, and I couldn't find him. It took me eighteen months to find work—and God had nothing to do with it." How would you respond?

safely there. We Christians are on the road to a heavenly home where temptation and loneliness will be banished forever. Although our destination is different from Judah's, God's promise to us is the same: our home awaits us if we let God take us there.

—C. R. B.

## II. LONGER-TERM PROMISE (JEREMIAH 31:31-34)

Chapters 30 and 31 of Jeremiah indicate that the promise of return is not made just to the captives in Babylon, but to all the scattered tribes of Israel (cf. 2 Kings 17:5, 6). The Lord specifies both "Israel and Judah" (Jeremiah 30:3) and "all the clans of Israel" (Jeremiah 31:1). As great as that will be, it is only preparatory for something better still: a new covenant.

### A. THE LORD'S PLAN, PART 2 (vv. 31, 32)

31. "The time is coming," declares the LORD,
    "when I will make a new covenant
with the house of Israel
    and with the house of Judah.

We notice three things in this verse. First, the Lord promises to *make a new covenant* to replace the old one he had made with Israel at Mount Sinai more than eight hundred years previously. For this reason, some consider Jeremiah 31:31-34 to be one of the most important sections in the entire Old Testament!

Second, the Lord promises to make it *with the house of Israel and with the house of Judah,* not just with the people of Judah who are captives in Babylon. The prophet Isaiah had earlier prophesied that the new covenant would be for the rest of the world, too (Isaiah 42:6; 49:6).

Third, the Lord does not make the new covenant at the time of this writing, but promises to make it later, or in the days to come. Historical hindsight tells us that the Lord is predicting something that will not occur for more than five hundred years. But it will indeed occur!

32. "It will not be like the covenant
    I made with their forefathers
when I took them by the hand
    to lead them out of Egypt,
because they broke my covenant,
    though I was a husband to them," declares the Lord.

In our lesson for September 26 we read that God spoke of making a *covenant* as his people ended their forty years of wandering in the desert (Deuteronomy 29:1, 9, 12). Evidently that covenant was mostly a reaffirmation of the one made forty years earlier at Mount Sinai. Now, however, we are reading God's promise of a new covenant that is very different from the one made at Mount Sinai.

It seems evident that a new covenant is needed, because the people have broken the old one so flagrantly and frequently. That is why north Israel has been scattered in foreign places and south Judah has suffered captivity in Babylon. Their breaking of the covenant is inexcusable, for God has been a husband unto them (cf. Jeremiah 3:14, 20). That means that he has generously provided all they needed, both in their wilderness wandering and in the promised land itself.

### B. THE SPIRITUAL RESULT, PART 2 (vv. 33, 34)

33. "This is the covenant I will make with the house of Israel
    after that time," declares the LORD.
"I will put my law in their minds
    and write it on their hearts.

*WHAT DO YOU THINK?*

*In verse 32 God uses the image of a loving husband to describe his relationship with his people. What other images describe this relationship? Which image is most significant to you? Why?*

*I will be their God,*
    *and they will be my people.*

We are startled to see the people of Israel breaking God's law in such an "in your face" way! Certainly one reason for this problem is that they do not know God's law by heart, so their hearts are not "in tune" with it.

In their defense we must note that the ancient Jews do not have Bibles in every home. How much of Leviticus would you know if your only way of learning were your parents' teaching by word of mouth? It would take persistent and consistent teaching to give children a working knowledge of Old Testament law, and incessant teaching was just what the law required (see Deuteronomy 6:6, 7).

The New Testament, for its part, is less than a third the length of the Old Testament, and we do have Bibles in every home today. We do tell Bible stories to our children and send them to Sunday school. Yet we are ashamed because neither we nor the children know Christian teaching as well as we should.

It takes effort on our part as well as on God's part to have his words really written in our *hearts* as they should be if we are God's *people*. And it should be obvious that he will write the new covenant only on willing hearts. To a person who stubbornly resists, that new covenant will be no more effective than was the old covenant when it was broken.

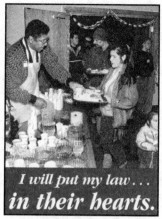

*I will put my law . . .*
## in their hearts.

Visual for Lesson 7. *The law of God in our hearts calls us to serve in many ways. How will you heed that call today?*

### ALL BRAIN AND NO HEART?

Parking meters came to town on July 16, 1935, in Oklahoma City. Today there are at least five million of them in the United States alone. Promoted as a way to discourage day-long parking in business districts, meters have proven to be good sources of municipal income—by one estimate $1,250,000 per day in the U.S.!

But the meters' original purpose was defeated when wily motorists began feeding the meter just before time ran out. This circumvented both the "Meter Maids" as well as the spirit and purpose of the law.

Now, electronic "smart" meters will not accept constant feeding. They will also reset to zero when a car moves away in order to deny any remaining time to the next car to park. As one report said of the new meters, they "have a brain, but no heart."

Spiritual scofflaws, who were all brain and no heart, thought that "feeding the meter" of the old covenant with sacrifices and offerings allowed them to keep just barely on "the right side of the law." Jeremiah says that there will be no doubt that the new covenant is to be based on the heart of the individual.

To stay technically on the right side of God's law is no longer an option (it never was, really). Instead, a true righteousness of the heart is fostered by our new relationship with God. Living for Christ involves our whole being: with the brain we affirm the covenant, with the heart we obey with right motives.   —C. R. B.

34. *"No longer will a man teach his neighbor,*
    *or a man his brother, saying, 'Know the LORD,'*
*because they will all know me,*
    *from the least of them to the greatest," declares the LORD.*
*"For I will forgive their wickedness*
    *and will remember their sins no more."*

According to the old covenant, descendants of Abraham enter the covenant at birth. According to the new covenant, a person does not become one of God's people by being born to parents who have a certain biological heritage. Rather, he or she becomes one of God's people by being born again (John 1:12, 13).

In the time of the new covenant, *no longer . . . teach* means that people will have direct access to God without needing to go through the human intermediaries—

### HOW TO SAY IT

*Abraham.* AY-bruh-ham.
*Babylonian.* Bab-ih-LOW-nee-un.
*Corinthians.* Ko-RIN-thee-unz (th *as in* thin).
*Egypt.* EE-jipt.
*Ezra.* EZ-ruh.
*Isaiah.* Eye-ZAY-uh.
*Jehoiachin.* Jeh-HOY-uh-kin.
*Jehoiakim.* Jeh-HOY-uh-kim.
*Jeremiah.* Jair-uh-MY-uh.
*Jerusalem.* Juh-ROO-suh-lem.
*Lamentations.* Lam-en-TAY-shunz.
*Nebuchadnezzar.* NEB-yuh-kud-NEZ-er.
*Thessalonians.* THESS-uh-LO-nee-unz.
*Zedekiah.* Zed-uh-KYE-uh.

the priests of the levitical system—that are a feature of the old covenant (cf. Isaiah 54:13; John 6:45; Hebrews 4:16; 10:19-22).

To remind us of these facts, the writer of Hebrews quotes from this section of Jeremiah in Hebrews 8:8-12 and 10:16, 17 (see also Romans 11:27 and 1 Thessalonians 4:9). Of course, a teaching function still exists under the new covenant as the New Testament makes clear (1 Corinthians 12:28, 29; Ephesians 4:11, 12). When Christ returns, all Christians will *know* him in the fullest sense of Jeremiah's prophecy.

An outstanding feature of this new covenant is God's permanent plan of forgiveness through the blood of Christ. Here is the Christian's hope! The Christian does not imagine that he or she is sinless. But forgiveness is certain nonetheless (see 1 John 1: 8, 9). Because Christ takes the sin penalty upon himself, God takes away the sins of his people. He forgives and forgets.

## CONCLUSION

Looking back at our seven lessons thus far, we see that God's good beginning is followed by the growth of evil again and again. In the beginning the Lord put Adam and Eve in a garden of delight, with light and easy chores to do and with an opportunity for unending happy life. But those two chose to do as they pleased instead of obeying God. They lost their garden home, they had to sweat to make a living, and death reared its ugly head.

Instead of learning from their parents' experience, the children and grandchildren of Adam and Eve also chose to do as they pleased. They became so evil in the course of centuries that God determined to wipe out sinners with a tremendous flood. Yet godly Noah and his family were saved to start a brave new world.

As more centuries passed, Noah's descendants learned to do as they pleased and the world grew wicked again. This time God did not wipe out the sinners, but chose to let them go their own way. The solution to sin this time was to come through the man Abraham. He was to be the father of a godly nation that would show the whole world what it meant to obey and fear the one true God.

When Abraham's family grew to be a nation, God sent Moses to lead it from Egypt to a country of its own, as we saw in two of our lessons. But through centuries the leaders and people ignored God's leading, and disaster came. The nation was divided. Both parts eventually ended up in exile, by God's decision.

We cannot conclude that God was like a scientist conducting experiments and hoping to learn by trial and error what to do. Rather, he was demonstrating his desires and his power for our learning. By Bible history and all other history, by our observation and experience, we are driven to the conclusion that Paul states so bluntly in Romans 3:23: "All have sinned and fall short of the glory of God."

What could be done about that? God knew before the world began. God's Son could give his life to pay the sin-penalty for humanity. Then forgiveness would be possible. So when God announced the coming of the new covenant he said, "I will forgive their wickedness and will remember their sins no more."

The new covenant is thus established through the birth, life, death, burial, and resurrection of Jesus Christ, the sinless Son of God. On the Day of Pentecost the apostle Peter stated firmly and simply what is required to enter into the new covenant and receive its blessings: "Repent and be baptized, every one of you, in the name of Jesus Christ for the forgiveness of your sins" (Acts 2:38). The apostle Paul explains the significance of the new covenant in Romans 3:21-26. May the Word of God guide us in understanding!

# Discovery Learning

*This page contains an alternative lesson plan emphasizing learning activities. Classes desiring such student involvement will find these suggestions helpful. The next page is a reproducible activity page to further enhance discovery learning.*

## LEARNING GOALS

After participating in this lesson, each student will be able to:

1. Tell what God promised for the future of the Jewish exiles, including a return to their homeland and the making of a new covenant.

2. Explain how the gospel of Jesus Christ fulfills Jeremiah's prophecy of a new covenant.

3. Describe the future that awaits those who enter into a covenant relationship with God.

## INTO THE LESSON

Prepare and display a poster reading "I enjoy going back home because. . . . " Ask where some of your class members were born and reared if not in your church's community. Then ask some to respond to the statement on the poster by completing the sentence.

Make the transition to Bible study by saying, "It is natural to have warm spots in our hearts for our homeland. History has seen peoples and nations that, when deported or exiled, struggled to return home. Being forced to be away brings heartache and a yearning for home. Such is true for the Israelites. Today, as God speaks to their longing for home, he makes a promise that will affect all of history and our very own lives."

## INTO THE WORD

*Mini-Lecture.* Early in the week ask a class member to use the Lesson Background material to prepare a five-minute summary of Israel's history, using this outline:

   I. Deterioration of Israel
  II. Babylonian Captivity
     A. Phase 1
     B. Phase 2
     C. Phase 3

Explain that today's text comes from Phase 2.

*Making Notes.* Distribute photocopies of Jeremiah 29:10-14; 31:31-34. Leave a wide margin for making notes. The class members may work in pairs or alone.

*Option.* Distribute copies of the reproducible activity "Oh, Israel" from the next page. Give the learners about ten minutes to complete the activity.

*Activity #1.* Ask the class to read Jeremiah 29:10-14 and circle every word or phrase that would offer hope or encouragement to this exiled people. After a few moments, ask class members to share findings as a "scribe"

jots their findings on the board under the heading "Hope." Then ask, "What was God's purpose for delay in completing this promise?" (v. 10)

*Activity #2*: Read Jeremiah 31:31-34 for the class. Then ask teams or individuals to locate and identify (1) The key verse that summarizes it all (v. 31) and (2) the eternal promise (v. 34b). Then ask the following questions: (1) "When and how will this promise be fulfilled?" (2) "How would the promised new covenant be different from the old covenant?" (vv. 32-34) See the lesson commentary for ideas to stimulate and supplement the discussion.

## INTO LIFE

*Activity #1*: Say, "Forgiveness is one of the outstanding and wonderful features of the new covenant." Ask the class to brainstorm and list some of the imagery God used in the Old Testament and New Testament to illustrate the depth and wonders of God's forgiveness. A great example is Jeremiah 31:34, which says that God "will remember their sins no more." Answers may include that sins are removed "as far as the east is from the west" (Psalm 103:12), our sins of scarlet will be made white as snow or wool (Isaiah 1:18), we are washed and sanctified (1 Corinthians 6:11). If the students need ideas, have them read the Scriptures noted.

*Activity #2*: Ask the question, "Why and how do these passages bring great peace to Christians today?" Expand this discussion by reminding the class that a person may sometimes feel he or she has a permanently broken relationship with God. Ask, "Is that possible? How does Israel's experience speak to this concern?"

*Concluding Activity*: Distribute copies of the activity "Relationships Restored" from the next page. Use it to help the students apply the message of today's text.

*Optional Concluding Activity*: The conclusion in the lesson commentary is an excellent summary of the last few lessons. Prepare and deliver another mini-lecture using material from that review.

Conclude with small-group prayers. Ask one person in each group to offer thanks for God's work in history. Another person should focus on forgiveness, praising God for having the authority and power to forgive. A third person may pray for the ability to accept and enjoy the peace that comes through knowing the Almighty God has chosen to forgive when we are not deserving of forgiveness.

# Oh, Israel!

As you read Jeremiah 29:10-14; 31:31-34, recall Israel's history. List a few specific examples of Israel's unfaithfulness and sins. Thumbing through Jeremiah's book will offer reminders of these sins.

A second chance for Israel was a wonderful opportunity. Why was God so eager to give unfaithful Israel a new covenant? What does this experience in Israel's history teach you about God's relationship with you?

| Israel: Sinful and Unfaithful | Israel: Loved and Chosen |
| --- | --- |
|  |  |

# Relationships Restored

God certainly gives a wonderful model on restoring relationships in this Scripture. The lesson is valuable in contemporary relationships with people we love—and a lesson on relationships with our heavenly Father. Read the following case studies and jot a few notes on the counsel you would give these persons.

*Case Study: Angry Offspring—A Broken Father/Son Relationship*

George's young adult son, Jordan, is away at college. While there, Jordan began breaking some of the family's Christian values and traditions. He has been arrested for DUI twice and is living with a female college student. They plan to marry in another eighteen months. George has expressed his disappointment in Jordan's choices. Because Jordan has not responded, George's anger led him to "disown" his son, even removing him from his will. Now George is sorry—but does not know how to mend the relationship. Jot a few of your notes of counsel to George.

*Case Study: A Sour Seduction—A Broken Relationship with God*

Greg was a Christian, married with two elementary age children, when he became infatuated with a single woman at the office. The relationship became sexual. He knew it was wrong, but continued in the relationship. Eventually he deserted his wife and children, crushing the youth group he was coaching. He moved in with his lover, eventually marrying her. Five years later he is wracked with guilt. He is sorry about what he has done to his family and is especially concerned about what this has done to his relationship with God. Suppose you sat down with Greg and read today's text together. From it what principles would you share with Greg?

## The God of Continuing Creation

### Unit 2: God's Creativity Continues
#### (Lessons 5-9)

# CREATING A NEW HOPE

## WHY TEACH THIS LESSON?

Being able to see a goal or an end result is an important part of having hope. A cancer patient receiving chemotherapy, for example, can have a great deal of hope if told, "We're giving you nine treatments over a period of eighteen weeks, then your chemotherapy will be finished." A patient who receives such a declaration can "count down" the treatments and anticipate a period of wellness at the end.

God knows of our need to have hope and he provides it. His message during the oppressive Babylonian domination and captivity was, "This will come to an end after seventy years." Even better than that, God promised a new day of restoration when his people would have a new spirit. For us, this fulfilled prophecy gives us hope for the glorious future that awaits us still.

## INTRODUCTION

### A. REVELATIONS—MEANINGFUL AND OTHERWISE

Carl was in love. He couldn't help it. Carla was so cute, so charming, and her smile was the most beautiful one on earth. Besides, her name was almost like his. Didn't that mean they were meant for each other?

Carl and Carla worked in the same big office. One day Carl went out to lunch. By chance, he entered a local restaurant just as Carla was seating herself at a little table for two. Putting a hand on the vacant chair, Carl asked, "Is this seat taken?"

"Not unless you're taking it," Carla responded with her dazzling smile. So Carl began watching Carla as lunchtime drew near. If she went out alone, he followed a few minutes later. Often they enjoyed delightful lunches at that same table for two.

One Saturday night, Carl had a vivid dream. He was sitting in a kitchen, and Carla was serving him breakfast. Carl believed in dreams because one had led him to the job he liked so well. So this dream meant it was time to push his courtship. The very next Monday he asked Carla for a Friday date. Carla looked straight across the table without her usual smile. "Thank you, Carl, but no."

Carl was surprised. Could his dream have misled him? "How about the next Friday?" he asked.

"That's no, too," Carla shook her pretty head.

Carl was crushed. "Does that mean you don't ever want a date with me?"

"I wouldn't put it that way," Carla said with half a smile. "It's my husband. He doesn't want me to date other men."

Now Carl doesn't believe in dreams anymore. He thinks that cozy kitchen dream deceived him cruelly. Perhaps you don't trust dreams to guide you either. I know I don't.

Still, there have been dreams full of meaning. God has used them as one way to present his messages to his people and to others. Pharaoh's dreams were a valuable warning of a famine (Genesis 41). Nebuchadnezzar's dreams revealed future world-history (Daniel 2). Dreams sent the wise men home by a secret way instead of giving information to Herod (Matthew 2:12). And the visions of the prophets, whether they can be called dreams or not, were used to give God's messages in picturesque ways, as we see today.

DEVOTIONAL READING:
EZEKIEL 37:24-28
BACKGROUND SCRIPTURE:
EZEKIEL 37
PRINTED TEXT:
EZEKIEL 37:1-14

### LESSON AIMS

After participating in this lesson, each student will be able to:

1. Describe the details of Ezekiel's vision and its application of hope to the captives from Judah.

2. Suggest some circumstances or situations of today in which a word of hope is needed.

3. Make a plan of action to inject the hope of Christ into one of those situations.

Oct
24

### KEY VERSE

I will put my Spirit in you and you will live, and I will settle you in your own land. Then you will know that I the LORD have spoken, and I have done it, declares the LORD. —Ezekiel 37:14

## B. LESSON BACKGROUND

Last week's Lesson Background discussed the three phases of the Babylonian captivity (see page 66). This week's lesson puts us into Phase 3 of that time of distress. The prophet Ezekiel, who was probably one of the ten thousand captives taken to Babylon in Phase 2, received messages from the Lord for his fellow captives. Some of the messages were given in visions (Ezekiel 1:1-3).

We take one of those visions as our text. As we begin our lesson from Ezekiel 37, we realize that we are now in Phase 3 of the exile because the city of Jerusalem has fallen (see Ezekiel 33:21).

## I. VISION AND QUESTION (EZEKIEL 37:1-3)

Ezekiel 1:1 indicates that Ezekiel's home while in captivity is with a colony of captives "by the Kebar River." Many think that that was not a natural river, but one of the big man-made canals used for irrigation and navigation. The "land of the Babylonians" (Ezekiel 1:3) is modern-day Iraq.

### A. DRY BONES REVEALED (v. 1)

1. The hand of the LORD was upon me, and he brought me out by the Spirit of the LORD and set me in the middle of a valley; it was full of bones.

The hand of the Lord, God's own power, takes control of Ezekiel and transports him to another place. The phrase by the Spirit of the Lord suggests that the Holy Spirit takes charge of Ezekiel's mind for the purpose of imparting some revelation to that prophet. Ezekiel seems to be saying that the Lord's hand carries him through the air and sets him down at his destination. Does Ezekiel's body go along on that trip, or only his mind and spirit?

We also have questions about the destination, a certain valley that is full of bones. Is this a real valley with bones visible to normal eyesight? Or is the whole scene a vision put into Ezekiel's mind by the Holy Spirit? As interesting as such questions are, we should not allow them to delay us in uncovering what message the Lord is giving to his prophet.

### B. DRY BONES EXAMINED (v. 2)

2. He led me back and forth among them, and I saw a great many bones on the floor of the valley, bones that were very dry.

The Lord leads the prophet about to inspect the entire floor of this open valley. It looks as if a terrific battle had been fought there in the long-ago time when Assyrians and Babylonians had battled for supremacy.

Apparently, thousands of dead bodies had been devoured by wild beasts and birds, or perhaps just reduced to dust by a century of decay. What Ezekiel sees is countless thousands of scattered bones, dried and bleached as if exposed to harsh rays of the sun for years and years.

### C. EZEKIEL QUESTIONED (v. 3)

3. He asked me, "Son of man, can these bones live?"

I said, "O Sovereign LORD, you alone know."

Perhaps we are surprised to see Ezekiel referred to as Son of man, since Jesus uses that phrase of himself many times in the Gospels. In the book of Ezekiel, however, this phrase points to that prophet's mortality. It is not a reference to deity here.

When God asks the question can these bones live?, it does not mean that he is seeking information. Rather, the question is designed to start a conversation and to gauge Ezekiel's outlook. Accustomed as we are to the ordinary course of

WHAT DO YOU THINK?

The valley of dry bones must have been a hopeless sight for the prophet. It may have caused a feeling of despair or anxiety. Have you ever been in a hopeless valley of "dry bones"? What did you do to maintain your faith?

events, we might answer God's question, "No way!" But Ezekiel is God's proph-et, and obviously God is setting the stage for something extraordinary. Wisely the prophet gives the answer he is sure of: *O Sovereign Lord, you alone know.*

### "FAREWELL, DEATH VALLEY"

Few North Americans set foot in Death Valley National Park in the summertime, but that's when many European tourists want to visit it. They are drawn to the ad-venture of going to the hottest, driest place on the continent! Much of the park is below sea level; "Badwater" is the lowest (at −282 feet) as well as the hottest.

The legend of how the valley got its name comes from the days of the gold-seek-ers who headed west in the mid-nineteenth century to find their fortune in the Sierra Nevada. One party of pioneers (including several families) sought to cross a very deep and wide valley in eastern California. Many in the party died from lack of fresh water. As the survivors finally made their way out of the valley—where the bodies and eventually the bones of those who died would lie—one of the fortunate ones is said to have remarked, "Farewell, Death Valley."

Ezekiel was transported in a dream to a place of death—a valley full of bones. In this place filled with symbols of death, the prophet is asked the question the human race has always asked: Can the dead live again? That question may explain in part the fascination that modern travelers have with Death Valley. Our technol-ogy can help us survive such a place; but even the most advanced technology can-not bring the dead back to life. Whether physically or spiritually, that can be accomplished only by God.                                    —C. R. B.

## II. DEATH AND LIFE (EZEKIEL 37:4-10)

In the first lesson of this series, we read that "the Lord God formed the man from the dust of the ground." The dust had no life in it, and neither did the man who was formed from it. But God "breathed into his nostrils the breath of life, and the man became a living being" (Genesis 2:7). Anyone who knows of that fact can hardly doubt that God can use dead bones and lifeless dust to create an-other person, or a multitude of people.

### A. INSTRUCTION (v. 4)

4. *Then he said to me, "Prophesy to these bones and say to them, 'Dry bones, hear the word of the LORD!*

God neither had nor needed a prophet to relay his word when he created Adam. But now God chooses to honor Ezekiel by having him speak the *word* for the *dry bones.* So God instructs, and his prophet obeys.

### B. PROMISE (vv. 5, 6)

5. *"'This is what the Sovereign LORD says to these bones: I will make breath enter you, and you will come to life.*

Just like the "mountains of Israel" that Ezekiel prophesies to in 36:1, the bones have neither ear to hear nor mind to understand. But God's prophet obe-diently gives them God's promise. Ezekiel himself can hear, understand, and be impressed when the promise is kept, and so can we.

6. *"'I will attach tendons to you and make flesh come upon you and cover you with skin; I will put breath in you, and you will come to life. Then you will know that I am the LORD.'"*

To those bare bones God intends to give sinews and flesh and skin—yes, and we may presume livers and lungs and brains as well. When God infuses breath into them, they will have all they need for new life. And with their new minds they will know that he is the Lord.

### DAILY BIBLE READINGS

**Monday, Oct. 18**—God's Name Was Profaned (Ezekiel 36:16-22)

**Tuesday, Oct. 19**—God Will Give a New Heart (Ezekiel 36: 23-32)

**Wednesday, Oct. 20**—The People Shall Know God (Ezekiel 36:33-38)

**Thursday, Oct. 21**—Ezekiel Sees the Dry Bones (Ezekiel 37: 1-6)

**Friday, Oct. 22**—The Dry Bones Live and Breathe (Ezekiel 37:7-14)

**Saturday, Oct. 23**—Two Nations Shall Become One (Eze-kiel 37:15-23)

**Sunday, Oct. 24**—God Will Bless the New Nation (Ezekiel 37:24-28)

## C. ACTION! (vv. 7-10)

**7. So I prophesied as I was commanded. And as I was prophesying, there was a noise, a rattling sound, and the bones came together, bone to bone.**

As Ezekiel begins to speak to *the bones* as the Lord had told him to do, the response is prompt. But it is hard for us to know exactly what the prophet hears and sees. The noise mentioned here of *a rattling sound* might be made by dry bones in motion, clicking against one another. Whatever details of sound and motion we choose to imagine, the result seems clear: countless disconnected bones join themselves together to form thousands of complete human skeletons.

**8. I looked, and tendons and flesh appeared on them and skin covered them, but there was no breath in them.**

Ezekiel watches as ligaments tie the bones together at every joint, as muscles appear and are joined by *tendons* to the proper bones. Easily we imagine what is not mentioned in the text: hearts, lungs, and other internal organs taking their proper places before *skin* is wrapped around a completed body. In other words, Ezekiel watches while thousands of complete human skeletons become complete human bodies. But they are bodies with *no breath* of life *in them*.

**9. Then he said to me, "Prophesy to the breath; prophesy, son of man, and say to it, 'This is what the Sovereign LORD says: Come from the four winds, O breath, and breathe into these slain, that they may live.'"**

In this verse and the next, we see some differences in our English versions. The Hebrew word *ruah* can mean wind or breath or spirit, depending on context. When we see the *breath* invited to come from *the four winds,* we have to understand that the four winds are the four directions—north, south, east, and west. When the *ruah* is invited to come from everywhere and blow on those lifeless bodies in the valley, we naturally translate it wind. But when the *ruah* enters those bodies, one version calls it breath and another calls it spirit—and who can say that either of them is wrong?

So we see Ezekiel, directed by God, calling the wind, or the breath, to come from all directions and blow or *breathe* on those lifeless bodies that they may live. Whatever of wind that enters those bodies will be breath or spirit or both, and with it God himself will supply life. The entire picture is one of God's great power.

**10. So I prophesied as he commanded me, and breath entered them; they came to life and stood up on their feet—a vast army.**

*Life* from death! Instead of a valley full of skeletal remains there is now *a vast army,* standing *on their feet.*

This imagery leaves us with some questions, however. Is it real and literal, this standing army suddenly raised from the bones of men long dead? Or is it just a vision given to the prophet? Is there actually a sudden army of the unemployed looking for jobs in a time when jobs are scarce and pay is low because all those captives from Judah have to take whatever work they can get? Are the dry bones and the living men seen only by Ezekiel? Look at chapter one of Ezekiel's book. Obviously it describes a fantastic vision. Perhaps we have been reading another.

In the final analysis, this lesson is not really about dead bones that come alive. Rather, it is about Jewish captives in a foreign land. The story of the dead bones that become living men is an illustration designed to show how great the change will be when those hopeless, despairing captives will be restored to liberty in their homeland. The last part of our text is part of God's message to those captives.

## III. EXPLANATION AND FUTURE (EZEKIEL 37:11-14)

The captives now have been in Babylon for between twelve and twenty-five years (compare Ezekiel 33:21 with 40:1). Homesickness grows worse instead of

### WHAT DO YOU THINK?

*It was an amazing sight! Dry bones had become human bodies, covered in flesh and skin. By itself, that would have been an awe-inspiring miracle. But of course, the miracle was not complete. Had the prophet left the valley right then, he would have missed the greater good God was doing. How do we sometimes miss out on God's blessings because we assume God is finished when he is not?*

better. Each morning the captives look out at the flat plain and long for the hills of home. Each evening their loneliness deepens as the sun sets behind a foreign horizon (e.g., Lamentations 2:11).

## A. SITUATION AS IS (v. 11)

*11. Then he said to me: "Son of man, these bones are the whole house of Israel. They say, 'Our bones are dried up and our hope is gone; we are cut off.'*

Now we have answers to the questions we raised in the commentary for verse 10. The Lord explains that the dry *bones* represent all captive Israelites (not just the Judeans in Babylon) as they see themselves. They are dead to family, friends, and country, as dead as those bleached bones in the valley (cf. Lamentations 3:6).

Even when they had been at home with their countrymen in Jerusalem, the Judeans had been too weak to resist the conquering army of Babylon. Now that Jerusalem has fallen, they see no *hope* of ever being released. Perhaps when the captives say *we are cut off* they are remembering the prophecy of 1 Kings 9:6-9.

The captives are out of contact with their homeland, their temple (now destroyed), and all that they hold dear. Undoubtedly, they think they will live and die in that condition (Lamentations 5:2, 3).

## B. SITUATION TO COME (vv. 12-14)

*12, 13. "Therefore prophesy and say to them: 'This is what the Sovereign LORD says: O my people, I am going to open your graves and bring you up from them; I will bring you back to the land of Israel. Then you, my people, will know that I am the LORD, when I open your graves and bring you up from them.*

The captives in Babylon think they are dead to home and country. But things are not really as they seem to be! The restoration to come will have two aspects. We see the first one mentioned in the verse before us: a physical renewal of Israel as a nation.

This renewal comes about when God brings the Persian army to defeat Babylon and free the captives (Ezra 1:1-4; Isaiah 44:28; 45:1, 13). When that happens, those former captives will know that it is God's doing because God's prophet has told them about it in advance. When it happens, the Jews will again give close attention to God and his law. This will inaugurate the second aspect of the renewal, as our next verse shows.

### GETTING OUT OF THE GRAVE

There's an old joke about a fellow who left a bar late one night after having spent the whole evening drinking. Although quite drunk, he still had enough awareness of his situation to know that he should walk home, rather than drive. However, home was a long way off, and his normal path would take him around the perimeter of a very large cemetery.

After contemplating this for a long time—his consumption of alcohol having slowed his thinking processes greatly—he decided to take a shortcut through the graveyard. Stumbling along in the dark, he fell into a new grave that had just been opened the previous afternoon. Little did he realize that another drunk had fallen into the grave and was lying there waiting for morning to come.

The subject of our story then started clambering for hand- and toeholds that would enable him to escape the grave. That's when the voice of the other man startled him from the darkness: "You'll never get out of here." But he did!

Israel's sin had placed many of them in graves in a foreign land. The graves were literal for those who died there, and figurative for those who felt themselves to be as good as dead. But as God spoke to the exiles through Ezekiel, his voice

Visual for Lesson 8. *Use this sobering visual to remind your learners of a question that each of us must answer.*

WHAT DO YOU THINK?

*The Jewish captives thought their situation was hopeless. Ezekiel was sent to tell them otherwise. What hopeless situation needs a word of comfort from you or your church?*

WHAT DO YOU THINK?

*What "grave" has God brought you out of? How did he do it? How can your story help to lift up someone else?*

*HOW TO SAY IT*

*Assyrians. Uh-SEAR-e-unz.*
*Babylon. BAB-uh-lun.*
*Babylonians. Bab-ih-LOW-nee-unz.*
*Kebar. KEE-bar.*
*Ezekiel. Ee-ZEEK-ee-ul or Ee-ZEEK-yul.*
*Ezra. EZ-ruh.*
*Isaiah. Eye-ZAY-uh.*
*ruah (Hebrew). RUE-ah.*

*PRAYER*

*Our Father and our God, we know that you are eternal and that your promises can never fail. Thank you for the bright hope they create to guide us and to energize us in the way everlasting. In Jesus' name, amen.*

*THOUGHT TO REMEMBER*
*God is dependable. Are you?*

was reassuring: "I'll bring you up out of your graves and you shall live again in the place I have given to you." God's promise through Christ to people of all nations is the same: "I'll raise you from the dead and bring you to the eternal place that I am preparing for you." Do we really have faith that this will happen as he promised? —C. R. B.

**14. "'I will put my Spirit in you and you will live, and I will settle you in your own land. Then you will know that I the LORD have spoken, and I have done it, declares the LORD.'"**

The second aspect of Israel's restoration is spiritual renewal. Free in their own country and knowing that it is *the Lord* who has made it so, the people will be ready to be led by his *Spirit*. Ezra 3 shows us the receptive attitude of the people upon their return.

## CONCLUSION

Never was there a people more hopeless than those held captive in Babylon. In their own estimation they were as good as dead—dead as bones that had been bleached by the harsh sunshine of many decades. But God did not want them to be captives forever. He wanted them to be free in their own land, serving him exclusively.

Yet God did not allow the captives to have hope in their own power. They were thoroughly intimidated by the might of Babylon's army. They could have no hope in the few remaining countrymen back home. Those folks had no more power than did the captives themselves. So for the captives God created hope in himself. He did it with a promise, a promise of liberty and of return to their homeland (also Jeremiah 30:3).

God had a long record of promises kept. To Adam he promised death for disobedience, and Adam died. To Noah he promised life for building an ark, and Noah lived. To Israelites enslaved in Egypt he had promised freedom and a land of their own, and they had lived in that land for centuries. To sinners in that land the Lord promised captivity in Babylon, and that promise was being kept in the lives of these captives. So when God promises a return to their own land, they can live in hope until they are home again.

Yet the captives do not pack their bags and set out for home as soon as they hear God's promise from Ezekiel. For several decades they will continue to live in Babylon, and in hope. We wonder how much their hope is dimmed when Phase 3 of the captivity begins, and Jerusalem and the temple are burned and battered to the ground. To the captives already living in Babylon, it must seem that there is no home to go back to.

But the holy hill of Zion is still there, and so is God's earlier promise. So hope has the potential of burning brightly in the hearts of the captives until the seventy years of Babylonian rule is complete. With love of God and love of country pushing them forward, God's people will go back to rebuild temple and town.

Hope in God is the best kind of hope! And to those of us who have put our trust in Jesus the Savior, Peter writes, "who raised him from the dead and glorified him, and so your faith and hope are in God" (1 Peter 1:21). Hope does not die easily when it rests in God. "In this world you will have trouble," said Jesus (John 16:33), and sometimes we have it year after weary year. "But take heart!" Jesus goes on, "I have overcome the world."

So we look forward, taking to ourselves Jesus' own promise: "Be faithful, even to the point of death, and I will give you the crown of life" (Revelation 2:10). Praise God for such a Savior!

# Discovery Learning

*This page contains an alternative lesson plan emphasizing learning activities. Classes desiring such student involvement will find these suggestions helpful. The next page is a reproducible activity page to further enhance discovery learning.*

## LEARNING GOALS

After this lesson each student will be able to:

1. Describe the details of Ezekiel's vision and its application of hope to the captives from Judah.

2. Suggest some circumstances or situations of today in which a word of hope is needed.

3. Make a plan of action to inject the hope of Christ into one of those situations.

## INTO THE LESSON

Have three or four unassembled simple models of human skeletons available on tables. As students enter, allow them to attempt to set up the skeletons. You may play the old spiritual "Dem Bones" during the activity.

Make the transition to Bible study by saying the following. "What opportunities for the future does a skeleton hold? Does it have any hope for the future? Today's study of the Old Testament includes an unusual vision or experience that tells how God used human bones to demonstrate hope in a hopeless and desperate world. Such is the hope he offers to believers who find themselves in desperate circumstances today."

If a model of a skeleton is not available, simply hold up a bone, ask the same questions, and make the same transition.

## INTO THE WORD

*Activity #1 Writing Newspaper Stories.* Ask groups of four or five to read Ezekiel 37:1-14 and outline a story suitable for newsletter publication. Their outline should include (1) a headline that captures attention, (2) facts to be included, (3) a section that emphasizes the unusual visual and audio scene Ezekiel witnessed. Give each team a sheet of poster board and a marker for notes. After the activity ask teams to share their headlines. Mention that most information is probably similar in each team's list. Make a transition to the next activity by mentioning the uniqueness and wonder of this vision. Say, "It could be helpful to have a firsthand impression from Ezekiel himself."

*Activity #2: Sense-sational.* Have the students use the reproducible activity on the following page to explore all the senses that Ezekiel employed in this vision.

*Activity #3: An Interview with Ezekiel.* Have a class member or guest portray Ezekiel. Give the person the following questions for the interview. Include the suggested items that he may choose to talk about under each question. Give this actor an article about Ezekiel from a Bible dictionary and one introducing the book of Ezekiel from a Bible handbook.

Ezekiel's costume may be as simple as wearing a name tag. However, a cloak and actor's beard may add flavor. Questions (and suggested material for answers) follow:

1. Tell us about yourself, Ezekiel. Who are you? Where did you come from? (*Mention his prophet and priest background, time that he lived, what was going on in his world at the time.*)

2. What was the occasion and purpose for writing your book? (*Offer a snapshot of Israel and Judah's captivities, what the Babylonians were like, how the book differs from and complements Jeremiah's, and what Ezekiel is communicating to Judah's captives with special emphasis on the hope God offers his people.*)

3. Your book is full of unearthly visions and vivid imagery. Tell us about some of these visions. Tell us how you felt when you saw the miracle in the valley of dry bones. (*Ezekiel may tell about several of his visions before focusing on the dry bones story.*)

4. What did you discover about the character and will of God in this unusual event? (*Note God's supernatural power, his yearning for peace for his people, his insistence on holy living, patience in waiting for his timing, and the hope that he offers to people feeling hopeless.*)

Thank your "Ezekiel" and make the transition to the lesson application by reminding the class of the hopeless feelings among the captives. Yet Ezekiel came offering hope, a lesson for people in hard circumstances.

## INTO LIFE

Ask the class to identify circumstances in today's world that bring some a sense of hopelessness. Examples: dysfunctional marriages, extreme financial hardships, terminal illnesses. List these on a visual during this brainstorming activity.

Ask the class members to imagine they are Judeans who lived through the captivity and heard Ezekiel's prophecies. Ask what advice they would give coming from their experience to people suffering hardships like those we listed. Again, list these answers.

Remind the class that there are Christian people in seemingly hopeless circumstances today. Challenge all to be ready to be God's encouraging word to them.

# An Unbelievable Scene You'd Better Believe!

This vision or event in Ezekiel's life has to be one of the most marvelous and mysterious in Scripture. It is a wonderful story to read. As you review this story again, let it assault your senses. Imagine you are Ezekiel in that valley described in Ezekiel 37. Give a first-person report of how the event affected your senses.

**Hearing**
What are the different sounds you heard as this vision unfolded?

**Smell**
How about your sense of Smell? What are the smells you experienced during this marvelous experience?

**Sight**
What a **Visual** treat this must have been. Describe the sights that made deep impressions on you.

**Touch**
Did you **Touch** anything? What would you have liked to touch—and why?

**Feelings**
What lessons about God or yourself have touched your heart as you experienced this unusual event? What would you tell people today about the lessons you have learned?

## The God of Continuing Creation
### Unit 2: God's Creativity Continues
(Lessons 5-9)

# CREATING A RENEWED TRUST

**LESSON 9**

## WHY TEACH THIS LESSON?

Every coin minted in the United States of America—even the newest "golden dollar" coin—is stamped with the words, "In God We Trust." But how many people who carry those coins around in their pockets each and every day really live their lives as if that statement were true? Many do not trust God because of all the injustice that they see in the world. They think that a just God would not allow such evil to exist.

Such a view does not properly grasp either the nature of God or of humanity. God gives us freewill; that's why evil exists. But God has promised that evil will not exist forever. He will bring this about on his timetable, not ours. This is where trust comes in. Casting our lot with evildoers ignores all that God has done and promises to do. Today's lesson prevents us from being so shortsighted.

## INTRODUCTION

### A. MYOPIC MIKE MURPHY

Mike Murphy made new friends quickly when he came to our town to be manager of the supermarket. Both the Rotary Club and the PTA eagerly welcomed him and his wife. But Mike's wife and children came to church without him. That was a surprise, for some knew Mike had been a leader in the church in his former town. To many invitations he answered, "I tried that. What does it get you?"

Mike was such a good friend that we didn't want to give up our efforts to get him back to church. With lots of information from him and his wife and other sources, we pieced together the story of his leaving the church. Mike had owned a store—not a very profitable one, but he had made a comfortable living. He was proud of being a successful merchant, and he gave God credit for his success. "If you're true to God, he will be true to you," he said frequently.

Then a chain of supermarkets had put a store in Mike's town. It dwarfed Mike's store. Its stock was vastly larger, and its prices were lower. Mike faced loss instead of profit, so he closed his store and sold the building. "If that's the way God takes care of his people," he thought, "I'm through with God."

The next day the very chain that had put Mike out of business looked him up to hire him and sent him to manage the store in our town. Strangely, it never occurred to Mike that God had anything to do with that. He never went to church again until his brother's family came for a weekend visit. Not going to church was unthinkable to that family, as it was to Mike's own wife and children.

Almost by force, the two families took Mike to church. Members of the choir later testified that Mike kept wiping his eyes through the whole service. At the front door the minister gripped Mike's hand and said, "I hope we'll see you again next Sunday." Struggling to find his voice, Mike managed to gulp, "You know, I had forgotten how good it is to worship."

DEVOTIONAL READING:
PSALM 91:1-10
BACKGROUND SCRIPTURE:
PSALM 73
PRINTED TEXT:
PSALM 73:1-3, 12, 13, 16-18, 21-26

LESSON AIMS

After participating in this lesson, each student will be able to:

1. Tell the reasons why Asaph's trust in God was lost and how it was restored.

2. Explain why we can trust God even when evil seems to prosper.

3. Identify a personal area of struggle and make a statement of trust in God to help him or her deal with it.

Oct 31

WHAT DO YOU THINK?

How would you have counseled Mike when he lost his store and his faith?

KEY VERSE

My flesh and my heart may fail, but God is the strength of my heart and my portion forever.
—Psalm 73:26

Mike has been seen in church every Sunday since that time. If a friend twits him about losing his store and being through with God, he says, "Only in December did my store make as much as my monthly pay is now. God will take care of you if you take care to do right."

## B. LESSON BACKGROUND

Asaph was a man who never stopped going to worship services, as Mike had. Indeed, Asaph's business *was* worship. But like Mike, Asaph inquired, "What's in it for me?"

For a time he was discontent with the remuneration he received. But Asaph did not have complete freedom in choosing his work, for he was born in the tribe of Levi. That means he was dedicated from his birth to help with the religious life of Israel. In the tribe of Levi, some were destined to be priests while others helped out in many ways, with duties ranging from janitor work to sacred music. (See Numbers 3:17-37; 4:4-15; 7:4-9; 1 Chronicles 6:1-48.)

Asaph was a musician, being one who sang psalms in the services of worship (1 Chronicles 15:16, 17). When the orchestra was performing, Asaph was one who handled cymbals (15:19). That may seem to be a minor part, but Asaph was made chief of the musicians (16:4, 5), so he must have been skilled.

Asaph was a songwriter, too. Psalms 50 and 73–83 are his work. Asaph's work was apparently so profound that he established what we might call a "school of music" that endured even after the return from exile (see Nehemiah 7:44). (Just so we don't get confused, three other Asaphs are mentioned in 2 Kings 18:18; 1 Chronicles 26:1; and Nehemiah 2:8.)

Last week we read how a new hope was created in despondent captives in Babylon. This week we look to a time several hundred years earlier to see how Asaph's trust was restored. King David was beginning to expand his empire. He had taken Jerusalem from the pagans, made it his capital city, and installed the ark of the covenant there in its special tent. Asaph was a leader among the musicians who served in ceremonies of worship there.

As David continued to press his campaign against the pagans, the wartime economy provided many businesses an opportunity to get rich quickly. Even so, Asaph and his fellow musicians found no corresponding increase in their income. Asaph was disturbed.

The line printed above Psalm 73 says, "A Psalm of Asaph." No doubt that simple byline names the writer of the song. But in this case it happens also to name the subject. This is a song about Asaph as well as by him.

## I. ASAPH'S ENVY (PSALM 73:1-3, 12, 13)

The first notes of the song sound a contrast between the beautiful harmony of God's goodness and the threatening peril of Asaph's nearly misguided walk.

## A. GOODNESS FROM ABOVE (v. 1)

1. *Surely God is good to Israel,*
    *to those who are pure in heart.*

*God* certainly *is good to* his people. Haven't all of us noticed that? A *pure* heart attracts God's favor as a magnet attracts steel (cf. Matthew 5:8). Matters of the *heart* are very important to Asaph (see Psalm 73:7, 13, 21, 26).

When we start to count our blessings, it's safe to say that the blessings we overlook are more than those we count. God is good. This essential truth stands like a rock at the beginning of the song. Beware of anything that seems to contradict it!

*WHAT DO YOU THINK?*

*Does this verse imply that those who are having a hard time must not be "pure in heart"? How would you convince someone otherwise who applied that reasoning to his or her own troubles or was pointing a finger at someone else?*

*[Make sure you look at John 9:1, 2; and James 1.]*

## B. Peril from Below (vv. 2, 3)

**2, 3. But as for me, my feet had almost slipped;**
   **I had nearly lost my foothold.**
 **For I envied the arrogant**
   **when I saw the prosperity of the wicked.**

The phrase *but as for me* signals a discord, something out of harmony with the fact of God's goodness that we saw in verse 1. What follows pictures a walker or hiker on a hazardous path. That unstable path for Asaph is to develop attitudes of envy and covetousness when seeing *the prosperity of the wicked.* So Asaph seems to speak of two "masters" who compete for his allegiance. Surely "God is good" (v. 1), but the path of the wicked seems to be very pleasant as well!

With refreshing candor, Asaph freely admits his error. But Asaph's problem brings up an age-old question: if God is good, how can he give prosperity to the wicked? (See also Job 21:7-15.) Verses 4-11 tell more about the wealthy wicked, but we can bypass that for this lesson. We already know enough about people who seem to prosper with impunity through less-than-ethical dealings, don't we?

## C. Error from Within (vv. 12, 13)

**12. This is what the wicked are like—**
   **always carefree, they increase in wealth.**

Thus the psalmist sums up what he has been saying about the wealthy *wicked.* The fact that they are ungodly is a commentary on their dishonesty and lack of ethics. This is a problem throughout Israel's history (e.g., 1 Samuel 8:1-3; Jeremiah 6:13; 22:17; Ezekiel 22:12, 23-31; Hosea 12:7; Amos 8:4-6). The temptation to join them is always there.

### Feeling Like Asaph

The final issue of *U.S. News & World Report* for 2002 had a ten-page article detailing—as it called them—the "actions of corporate honchos [that] horrified the nation." The lead page of the article mimicked another newsmagazine's red border and headline with the words, "Rogue of the Year," showing the picture of a former CEO of a large corporation who was charged in 2002 with stealing six hundred million dollars from his company.

The article also named other executives who had been charged variously with fraud, money laundering, conspiracy, insider trading, and—in at least one case— causing the bankruptcy of his firm with a loss of one hundred and forty billion dollars in market value! A few did some jail time, some were fined heavily; but most had protected themselves so that they could continue their lavish lifestyles even though thousands of their employees had lost jobs, health insurance, and pensions.

In the pages of the Psalms, Asaph reminds us that such behavior and outcome is nothing new. The world always has been full of selfish schemers who have no regard for others. We sometimes feel just like Asaph, don't we? Fortunately, there is another side to the story that our lesson makes clear. That's what we need to hear when we feel as Asaph did.              —C. R. B.

**13. Surely in vain have I kept my heart pure;**
 **in vain have I washed my hands in innocence.**

Asaph has been careful to keep himself clean and *pure,* both in the motives of his *heart* as well as what he has done with his *hands.* But at some point he came to think that such holiness was all *in vain.* His prosperity did not match that of the crooks. It wasn't fair! What was the use of being good and doing good? Asaph had indeed envied the wicked (v. 3). By the time he gets around to writing this song, he knows that that attitude was a mistake.

*What Do You Think?*

Have you ever felt envious of people who seemed to get ahead by unscrupulous means? Why? What helped you to get over such feelings?

*Daily Bible Readings*

**Monday, Oct. 25**—Sing for Joy to God (Psalm 84:1-7)

**Tuesday, Oct. 26**—Trust in God (Psalm 84:8-12)

**Wednesday, Oct. 27**—God Is Our Refuge (Psalm 91:1-10)

**Thursday, Oct. 28**—The Wicked People Prosper (Psalm 73:1-9)

**Friday, Oct. 29**—Is Our Faith in Vain? (Psalm 73:10-14)

**Saturday, Oct. 30**—The Prosperous Ones Are Destroyed (Psalm 73:15-20)

**Sunday, Oct. 31**—Faith in God Renewed (Psalm 73:21-28)

## II. ASAPH'S UNDERSTANDING (PSALM 73:16-18, 21, 22)

Asaph must have done a lot of thinking about the situation that troubles him. He will not think the Lord to be unfair, but he cannot think the situation itself to be fair, either. Why does God let his faithful servants be underpaid while every crooked businessman in Israel gets richer and richer?

### A. SUCCESS IN THE SANCTUARY (vv. 16, 17)

16. *When I tried to understand all this,*
    *it was oppressive to me*

The more Asaph thought about the apparent inconsistency, the more painful it became. Is God content with the unfair lot of his people? That seems incredible. Is he unable to do anything about it? That seems illogical. So Asaph agonizes, as have others (cf. Habakkuk 1:2-4.)

17. *. . . till I entered the sanctuary of God;*
    *then I understood their final destiny.*

Finally the musician carried his discord into *the sanctuary of God,* to worship with the assembled people. Perhaps he sang in the choir; perhaps he sounded his cymbals in the orchestra. No doubt the familiar forms of worship brought happiness to him as they brought it to Mike Murphy in the Introduction. No doubt the melody of well-known psalms was soothing to his troubled soul.

Perhaps special inspiration brought understanding to God's musician, and with understanding came peace. Specifically, says Asaph, *then I understood their final destiny.* He knows that the situation that troubles him is not permanent. The wealthy wicked are ecstatic now, but their end will be disaster (cf. Psalm 37).

### B. END OF ENVY (v. 18)

18. *Surely you place them on slippery ground;*
    *you cast them down to ruin.*

The wealthy wicked feel secure, but the ground under them is more *slippery* than they realize. At the proper time a nudge from the Lord will send them hurtling down into destruction. Asaph no longer envies them. Not for the world will he change places with one of those doomed souls. Asaph has more to say about the fate of the wicked in Psalm 75:8.

### NOT ALWAYS AS THEY SEEM

NASA's Viking I spacecraft was orbiting the planet Mars in 1976, taking photographs of possible landing sites. One of the pictures it relayed to earth showed what looked like a giant head rising from the Martian plain. NASA scientists jokingly called it the "Face on Mars," and released the picture to the media, hoping to increase public interest in America's space efforts.

Some people saw the "face" as evidence that the red planet had been inhabited by an intelligent civilization in the past. Some thought it to be like the Sphinx in Egypt, surrounded by other evidence of a lost civilization, including pyramids, cities, and even a sewage plant!

In 1998 NASA's Mars Global Surveyor took more pictures on two occasions, using improved technology that two decades had brought into existence. These pictures demonstrated that the "face" was nothing more than an eroded mesa on the planet's surface. But that didn't satisfy the operator of at least one Web site, who still claims to see "evidence" where few others see it.

As Asaph got a better look at things, he realized that his earlier view had been skewed by his envy of, and anger at, evil people. Things are not always as they seem, and we often need to take a clearer look at the situation. Looking through the eyes of God is often a cure for our mistaken perceptions of life.        —C. R. B.

*WHAT DO YOU THINK?*

*What is it about worship that helps you get a right perspective? What would you change—if you were in charge of the church's worship services—to make sure that that happened more regularly?*

Visual for lesson 9. *This visual shows one way to find God's strength. What other ways can your learners suggest?*

## C. VICTORY THROUGH SELF-EXAMINATION (vv. 21, 22)

**21. When my heart was grieved**
    **and my spirit embittered,**

Asaph's *heart was grieved,* not so much for the fate of the wicked as for his own recent envy of them. Now that understanding has come, Asaph is ashamed for ever allowing envy into his heart.

**22. I was senseless and ignorant;**
    **I was a brute beast before you.**

In the light of his new outlook, Asaph makes a sobering estimate of his previous understanding. He had been so foolish and ignorant that he was no better than a donkey or a dog. Such honesty!

## III. ASAPH'S APPRECIATION (PSALM 73:23-26)

When Asaph was foolish and ignorant enough to envy the wealthy wicked, that envy overshadowed his appreciation for the many blessings he already had. But when understanding comes and envy departs, Asaph can count his blessings with redoubled appreciation.

## A. PRESENCE AND GUIDANCE (v. 23)

**23. Yet I am always with you;**
    **you hold me by my right hand.**

What a privilege! To be continually with God is better than all the riches gathered by all the wicked through the ages. And God holds Asaph by his *right hand.* That implies God's constant guidance and support. Asaph is in good company!

## B. NOW AND LATER (v. 24)

**24. You guide me with your counsel,**
    **and afterward you will take me into glory.**

Divine guidance is emphasized again, and one who trusts God's *counsel* will never be led astray by it. To this singer of sacred songs, God's guidance no doubt includes inspiration of his writing. We wonder if inspiration makes him aware of future *glory* in Heaven that at the time of Asaph is not yet revealed to most of humanity. But God's counsel can lead one to have respect and honor even on this earth, and that, too, may be called glory.

## C. WEAKNESS AND STRENGTH (vv. 25, 26)

**25. Whom have I in heaven but you?**
    **And earth has nothing I desire besides you.**

Family and friends are good to have. They give encouragement, companionship, and practical help. But no one on *earth* can compare with our helper *in Heaven,* and in Heaven we have no helper but God.

**26. My flesh and my heart may fail,**
    **but God is the strength of my heart**
    **and my portion forever.**

Flesh is mere human tissue; *heart* is mere human courage. Neither is adequate for the needs of godly living in an ungodly world. But God supplies what we lack if what we have is truly committed to him. And he does it *forever!*

## CONCLUSION

### A. ANCIENT EXAMPLE

For Asaph trust faded with the coming of envy. Wicked people were getting richer and richer. That couldn't be right! If it is, why should anyone be good?

*WHAT DO YOU THINK?*

*How do people today react when they know they have been wrong? If they are not moved to sorrow for their sin, then what? Why?*

*WHAT DO YOU THINK?*

*How can we focus more on the truth that God will one day "take me into glory"? What difference will it make?*

## HOW TO SAY IT

*Amos.* AY-mus.

*Asaph.* AY-saff.

*Babylon.* BAB-uh-lun.

*Ezekiel.* Ee-ZEEK-ee-ul or Ee-ZEEK-yul.

*Habakkuk.* Huh-BACK-kuk.

*Hosea.* Ho-ZAY-uh.

*Jeremiah.* Jair-uh-MY-uh.

*Nehemiah.* NEE-huh-MY-uh.

## PRAYER

*We do trust you, Father—even when we are disappointed we trust you still. From a thousand evidences we know you love us and want us to have what is good for us. So forgive our misunderstanding and our selfish wishes, and love us still. We pray in Jesus' name, amen.*

## THOUGHT TO REMEMBER

*Come back to God; stay with him.*

At first glance we may think Asaph to be a mercenary wretch, greedy for gold. But the matter was not so simple. Didn't God's own honor and prestige demand that one of his chief musicians be rewarded more richly than some common crook? How could children be taught that honesty is the best policy if God's people plodded on weary feet while the wealthy wicked rode in gilded chariots?

So who can say what concerned Asaph most? Was it God's prestige or Asaph's income? His job was secure enough, and the people's tithes kept the Levites from poverty. Could it be that Asaph was merely coveting a gilded chariot of his own? Did Asaph's envy arise from simple greed, or was it based in his zeal for God? Probably it came from some combination of the two, for a human being is not a simple creature.

Whatever the cause of Asaph's envy and the fading of his trust in God, the cure was found in the sanctuary. Perhaps some godly teacher there reminded choir and audience that the destination is more important than the journey. Perhaps some Scripture reading emphasized the assurance that wickedness must lead to disaster and misery. Perhaps a song of the choir focused on God's eternity and reminded the singer that truth and righteousness are eternal, too.

For some reason or combination of reasons, Asaph rose above the shortsighted thinking that made him agitated with the status of the wealthy wicked. Taking the long view, he again rested secure with a steadfast trust in God's eternal goodness.

### B. MODERN EXAMPLE

Now think again of Mike Murphy, the genial fellow from the Introduction to this lesson. When he lost his business, he thought God had let him down. He retaliated by turning his back and refusing to speak to God.

As a matter of fact, the loss of Mike's business was no financial loss at all. He sold his building for twice as much as he had paid for it a few years earlier. An entrepreneur was eager to make it into an entertainment complex near the new supermarket. Mike had taken a small loss during the last few months of his operation, but the profit on the building more than compensated.

So what did Mike really lose? He lost some pride. He had been proud to be an independent, successful businessman in competition with larger stores. Now he was "only an employee." His employment was more profitable than his business had been, but he lost the pride in what he had been doing formerly. He felt humiliated and he blamed the Lord. Who else was there to blame?

Like Asaph, Mike found restoration in the sanctuary. He went there unwillingly at first; but once there, he knew he had long been homesick for that place and the people who met there and the God who was worshiped there. His full heart overflowed in tears, tears of mingled regret and joy. Then did Mike trust God again? You know he did.

### C. OUR DECISION

How is your trust in God? Has it faltered because God does not always do what you wish he would do? Have you stopped expecting help from Heaven because sometimes you do not get just the help you want in the way you want it? Are you a Mike Murphy? He wanted a business of his own. God gave him instead a position that brought him more money with less responsibility and less risk. Therefore Mike turned way from God, but kept the profitable position.

If we have followed Mike in turning away from God, let's be quick in following him back. Asaph, too, found truth and reason in the sanctuary, and so can we. Let us not neglect "meeting together" (Hebrews 10:25).

# Discovery Learning

*This page contains an alternative lesson plan emphasizing learning activities. Classes desiring such student involvement will find these suggestions helpful. The next page is a reproducible activity page to further enhance discovery learning.*

## LEARNING GOALS

After this lesson each student will be able to:

1. Tell the reasons why Asaph's trust in God was lost and how it was restored.

2. Explain why we can trust God even when evil seems to prosper.

3. Identify a personal area of struggle and make a statement of trust in God to help him or her deal with it.

## INTO THE LESSON

Prepare a huge poster by taping pieces of poster board together or by unrolling a long sheet of table paper and taping it to the wall. At the top print, "Why Do the Wicked Prosper?" Bring to class a large stack of newspapers and/or newsmagazines, several rolls of transparent tape, and numerous pairs of scissors. As students arrive, ask them to cut out articles or photos that illustrate unfair situations in the world today. These could include oppression, illegal monetary gains, profits from sin, courtroom injustice, and more. Ask them to tape the clippings to the poster.

Make the transition to Bible study by saying, "Many injustices in today's world may make us angry, even with God. Today's study is of one who will help us understand injustice, show us a model for handling unfairness, and teach us a lesson in trusting God."

## INTO THE WORD

*Mini-lecture*: Introduce Asaph by giving a brief lecture based on the Lesson Background on page 82. Prepare a poster as a visual aid; include the following notes: Musician (1 Chronicles 15:16, 17); Handled Cymbals (1 Chronicles 15:19); Chief of Musicians (1 Chronicles 16:4, 5); Songwriter (Psalms 50, 73-83); Asaph's Discontent; A Personal Song. Have each line covered with a piece of paper that you will remove as you lecture on that point.

*Scripture Search, Option 1:* Distribute copies of the reproducible activity page that follows. Students will use it to guide them in a study of today's text.

*Scripture Search, Option 2:* Give individuals or small groups handouts with the following headings: *Asaph's Discontent, Asaph Sees His Error,* and *Asaph's Trust Restored.* Students are to look for lines, phrases, or words that describe the heading's themes. They are to write these lines and the Scripture text under the appropriate headings. Here are some examples:

ASAPH'S DISCONTENT: Envied the arrogant (v. 3); Envied the prosperity of the wicked (v. 3); Saw the wicked prosper (v. 12); Considered his pure heart and clean hands to be in vain (v. 13); His heart was grieved (v. 21).

ASAPH SEES HIS ERROR: Feet had almost slipped (v. 2); Was senseless and ignorant (v. 22); Was dumb as a brute beast (v. 22).

ASAPH'S TRUST RESTORED (Where and how?): Entered the sanctuary (v. 17); Understood the final destiny of the wicked (v. 17); The wicked will slip down to ruin, v. 18; Is always with God (v. 23); God holds his right hand (v. 23); God's counsel and guidance (v. 24); God's strength (v. 26).

After the study ask groups or individuals to report what they found for each section.

## INTO LIFE

Ask the following two discussion questions to prepare for the group activity: (1) "How do you feel when an unjust or unfair situation continues over a long period?" (2) "What does Asaph's experience teach us about trusting God when evil seems to prosper?"

Ask the class to work in groups of three or four to prepare a worship service based on lessons from Psalm 73. Distribute a worksheet with the following guidelines for the worship service. Leave adequate space between segments.

A Worship Service Based on Psalm 73
(Theme: Trusting God While Evil Prospers)
Appropriate Songs to Sing:
New Testament Scripture Reading:
Prayer Theme:
Communion Theme/Scripture:
Sermon Title: "Learning to Trust Again"
Offertory Theme/Scripture:
Song of Commitment:

After the groups have completed their worship service, ask your learners to defend their choices. What Scripture readings were selected, and why? What songs were selected, and why? etc.

Conclude by asking class members to identify a personal struggle where this lesson of trust may apply. Pray for your class members' struggles, asking God to help them as he did Asaph in learning to trust him completely. After the prayer, sing one of the worship songs suggested by the class.

# Envy or Trust?

Asaph was troubled by his envy of wicked people who prospered while he did not. But he found peace for his envy and jealousy when he entered the sanctuary of God (Psalm 73:17). Read Psalm 73 and discover words that picture or describe the life of the wicked. Then look for words that describe how to trust God or the peace we find in that trust. Use each of the letters below as a prompt to enter descriptive words. The letters may begin, end, or merely appear in the words you write. (An example has been given for you.)

| | |
|---|---|
| W | T |
| I | R |
| C | GUIDE |
| K | S |
| E | T |
| D | |

# Slipping Feet

Asaph told how he found his feet slipping into sin because of his envy of the wicked who prosper. Use the space below to identify specific incidents of envy you experience, if applicable. Be honest with yourself.

My envy of prosperity (Psalm 73:3):

My envy of wicked and carefree lifestyles (Psalm 73:12):

# Trusting Again

Asaph learned to trust God, even when things were not going well (Psalm 73:23-26). Use this space to do one of two things. You may choose to look back in your life and note a time when you had difficulty trusting God, but time has proven that he was working in your life through that experience. Or you may choose to identify your present experience where you are having difficulty trusting him. Jot one word below that will remind you of this lesson in trusting God.

# The God of Continuing Creation

Unit 3: A New Creation
(Lessons 10-13)

# A NEW APPROACH

## WHY TEACH THIS LESSON?

Some people never seem to learn, do they? They just keep trying the same old approaches to life (and to God) that have failed in the past and are failing still. Just look at some of the people arrested on the reality-TV show *Cops.* Many are repeat offenders. They're headed back to jail yet again. One night a certain perpetrator tried to convince a police officer of the truthfulness of a statement with the oath "I swear to God." Without a moment's hesitation the officer responded, "Well, you're lying to God." An old, deceitful approach was recognized and exposed for what it was!

What we all need is the new approach that is only available through Jesus Christ. All of our old approaches that leave him out of the picture are bound to fail since only he has "the words of eternal life" (John 6:68). Today's lesson sets (or keeps) us on that path.

## INTRODUCTION

### A. THE GREATEST PREACHER

From my childhood I remember what a stir there was when a famous preacher came to town. The reason for his arrival was to address a meeting every night for two weeks. Most of the churches and both of the daily papers helped to spread the news in advance.

No auditorium in town was big enough for the expected crowd, so the baseball field was rented. Extra hitch racks were provided to tether the many horses that would arrive with carriages loaded with listeners. Most of the bicycle racks in town were borrowed and taken to the ball field. Extra streetcars were lined up because everyone wanted to hear the famous Gypsy Smith.

About eighty years later I witnessed a similar stir in a bigger town with a bigger grandstand. The name of Gypsy Smith was replaced by that of another famous preacher, the streetcars were replaced by buses, the hitch racks were replaced by parking lots, and no provision was made for bicycles. Otherwise the two campaigns were very much alike. Together they bear witness to the power of preaching.

By far the greatest preacher of all time is Jesus of Nazareth. He is the most famous, the most popular, the most influential. No newspapers heralded his coming, but word-of-mouth advertising was better. No rival churches joined forces to promote his program. Most of the hearers came on their own feet, and some came quite a distance (Matthew 4:25).

Jesus found no baseball field or grandstand to hold his listeners. Nowhere in town was there room for them (Mark 1:45). He led them to open spaces in the countryside, or to the beach by the Sea of Galilee, or to a sloping hillside that served as a grandstand.

Two things set Jesus apart from other teachers and attracted huge audiences. First, his miracles were amazing and obviously genuine (John 2:23; 6:2). Second, his teaching was also amazing, and strikingly different from that heard every Sabbath in the synagogues (Matthew 7:28, 29; Mark 1:22).

DEVOTIONAL READING:
MATTHEW 5:1-12
BACKGROUND SCRIPTURE:
MATTHEW 5
PRINTED TEXT:
MATTHEW 5:17, 18, 21, 22, 27, 28, 31-35, 38, 39, 43-45, 48

LESSON AIMS

After participating in this lesson, each student will be able to:

1. Give examples from the text of how Jesus corrected misunderstandings of the Old Testament law.

2. Explain why the law of love should be our guide in interactions with others.

3. Commit to Jesus one specific area in which he or she will choose to be more loving.

Nov
7

KEY VERSE

"Do not think that I have come to abolish the Law or the Prophets; I have not come to abolish them but to fulfill them."
—Matthew 5:17

## B. LESSON BACKGROUND

Jesus' famous Sermon on the Mount was spoken during the second year of his ministry, his "year of popularity." Great crowds gathered wherever he went.

It was a time to speak of the nearness of the kingdom of Heaven (Matthew 4:17). But so that there would be no misunderstanding, much of Jesus' Sermon on the Mount focused on the true nature of that kingdom. This was primarily for his disciples, but multitudes also were listening (Matthew 5:1, 2).

## I. RESPECT FOR GOD'S WORD (MATTHEW 5:17, 18)

As our printed text opens, Jesus is about to say some things that sound, on first impression, to be quite different from the bits he will quote from the Old Testament. But he does not want anyone in that Jewish audience to think he means to deny or contradict God's Word, so he begins by declaring his respect for the Scriptures and his relationship to them.

### A. JESUS' PURPOSE (v. 17)

**17. "Do not think that I have come to abolish the Law or the Prophets; I have not come to abolish them but to fulfill them.**

Many Old Testament *prophets* had predicted some of the things Jesus would do, but their messages are not complete until Jesus actually does those predicted things. Each prophecy and fulfillment demonstrates that God knows the future as well as the past. So many prophecies have been fulfilled that we ought to have complete confidence in those that are to be fulfilled in the future. The prophets point to Jesus!

Some of the events recorded in the Old Testament's five books of *law* (Genesis through Deuteronomy) function as prophecies, too. For example, the Passover law directed that a spotless lamb be sacrificed by each family of Israel. That was not only a memorial of the long-ago time when Israel was saved from slavery in Egypt; it also foreshadows the later time when Jesus, the spotless lamb of God, would be sacrificed to rescue God's people from slavery to sin (cf. 1 Corinthians 5:7, 8).

The apostle Paul acknowledges that the law and the prophets have always looked forward to something beyond themselves (Romans 3:21; Galatians 3, 4). That "something" is Jesus. This bears repeating!

### B. INDESTRUCTIBLE LAW (v. 18)

**18. "I tell you the truth, until heaven and earth disappear, not the smallest letter, not the least stroke of a pen, will by any means disappear from the Law until everything is accomplished."**

Jesus is saying that not even the tiniest part of the law will pass *until everything is accomplished.* In other words, *the law* will not fail to accomplish its purpose in pointing to the Christ, and in pointing people to the Christ. "The law was put in charge to lead us to Christ that we might be justified by faith" (Galatians 3:24).

When people are brought to Christ and justified by faith, part of the law is fulfilled when those new Christians "are no longer under the supervision of the law" (Galatians 3:25). The law will not reach its complete fulfillment until Christ returns. That will be the time when heaven and earth pass away (Revelation 6:12-14).

### WHAT DO YOU THINK?

Paul says we are to "keep the Festival, . . . with bread without yeast, the bread of sincerity and truth" (1 Corinthians 5:7, 8). Why is it difficult to live in consistent "sincerity and truth"? How can we get better at doing that?

### GOOD ADVICE, WHILE IT LASTED

"Wear sunscreen." Those were the opening words of an alleged commencement address that made the rounds on the Internet a few years ago. It was attributed to author Kurt Vonnegut, among others. Actually it was part of a newspaper column written by Mary Schmich for the *Chicago Tribune* and was never given as a commencement address.

Some of the other advice included "Sing. . . . Don't be reckless with other people's hearts. . . . Floss. . . . Remember compliments, forget insults. . . . Keep old love letters. Throw away old bank statements. . . . Be kind to your knees. You'll miss them when they're gone. . . . Get to know your parents. You never know when they'll be gone. . . . Be nice to your siblings. . . . Respect your elders. . . . Don't mess too much with your hair, or by the time you're forty it will look eighty-five." And the "speech" closed with the words, "But trust me on the sunscreen."

Some advice is timeless; some fits one time and place and may be irrelevant to another. Jesus said it was so even with the law. It was divinely inspired, but its purpose will be fully served when everything it points to has been accomplished. Christ is indeed that realization, and we look forward to the law's ultimate fulfillment when he returns. Until that time comes, it's still a good idea to remember the sunscreen!

—C. R. B.

The Fulfillment

*Use this visual as you ask how ancient prophecy establishes that Jesus is "the fulfillment."*

## II. EXAMPLES OF BEHAVIOR
### (MATTHEW 5:21, 22, 27, 28, 31-35, 38, 39, 43-45)

Now that Jesus has made his relationship to the law clear, he moves to a discussion of how the law actually should be applied. In what follows Jesus will not be "pouring additional meaning" into the Old Testament law. Rather, he will stress the true meaning that was there all along but had been lost over the centuries.

Those in Jesus' audience have a lot of misunderstandings that they must abandon! Jesus will clear up those misunderstandings with his "you have heard that it was said . . . but I tell you" technique.

### A. MURDER (vv. 21, 22)

**21. "You have heard that it was said to the people long ago, 'Do not murder, and anyone who murders will be subject to judgment.'**

This is the sixth of the Ten Commandments (Exodus 20:13). Everyone in Israel has heard of it. Some English versions have "kill" instead of *murder*. The latter, however, is closer to the real intent, for God prescribes capital punishment for various crimes (Genesis 9:6; Acts 25:11; Romans 13:4). This is indeed "killing," but it is not "murder." A murderer is in danger of being judged, condemned, and executed. A devout Jew in Jesus' day will not disagree with this.

**22. "But I tell you that anyone who is angry with his brother will be subject to judgment. Again, anyone who says to his brother, 'Raca,' is answerable to the Sanhedrin. But anyone who says, 'You fool!' will be in danger of the fire of hell.**

Jesus points to the fact that the action of murder (v. 21, above) has its roots in the attitude of anger. This has been true since the very first murder (Genesis 4:5-8). Why have the people apparently forgotten this?

There is such a thing as anger that results in righteous outrage. That is not sinful (cf. Matthew 21:12, 13; Mark 3:1-5). But *angry*, murderous attitudes that result from personal slights (real or imagined) are condemned (1 John 3:15).

Actually, an angry person is in some danger even if he or she has a good reason for being angry. Such a person still has to exercise self-control to be sure that the anger does not lead to personal vengeance. The angry person had better control his or her tongue as well, because contemptuous, insulting talk may feed the anger and lead to criminal acts. *Raca* is an insult comparable to "idiot" or "bonehead."

The word translated *you fool* in our text probably is even more malicious than that. Jesus referred to some people as fools on at least one occasion (Matthew

### WHAT DO YOU THINK?

Anger is altogether too common in our culture. Road rage, gang violence, political protests, spouse abuse—they all speak of anger in our society. How much of a problem is anger within the church? What can we do about it?

23:17). The fact that he did not sin in doing so shows us, again, the vital distinction between expressing righteous outrage and expressing personal offense. In any case, an expression of anger through labels, name-calling, and characterizations invites the same in return.

### B. Adultery (vv. 27, 28)

**27. "You have heard that it was said, 'Do not commit adultery.'**

This is the Seventh Commandment (Exodus 20:14). It forbids a physical act that is just as wrong in the New Testament era as it was in the Old Testament era. But in the next verse Jesus explains this commandment's true depth.

**28. "But I tell you that anyone who looks at a woman lustfully has already committed adultery with her in his heart.**

As murder has its roots in anger, so *adultery* has its roots in lustful thoughts. People who lived as far back as Job realized the nature of the lustful thought process (see Job 31:1), and Jesus brings this ancient knowledge back to life. People today who think they can drool over pornography and still be right with God just as long as they don't "actually" commit adultery are sadly mistaken! (See Psalm 101:3.)

*What Do You Think?*

How serious is the problem of lust in the church? What needs to be done to address it?

### C. Divorce (vv. 31, 32)

**31. "It has been said, 'Anyone who divorces his wife must give her a certificate of divorce.'**

The law allowed a man to divorce *his wife*. If she lost favor in his eyes because he found some uncleanness or indecency, all he had to do was to give her a written statement that he was divorcing her (Deuteronomy 24:1). But the requirement to find uncleanness or indecency apparently has been "lost" in Jesus' day.

**32. "But I tell you that anyone who divorces his wife, except for marital unfaithfulness, causes her to become an adulteress, and anyone who marries the divorced woman commits adultery.**

If we take a close look at Deuteronomy 24:1-4, we see Jesus reaffirming a part of the law that somehow has been ignored. The complicated conditions of that passage should have served to put the brakes on hasty divorces, and Jesus intends the same. Jesus will have more to say on this subject in Matthew 19:3-12.

*What Do You Think?*

Why is divorce such a problem in the church today? What can the church do to address this problem?

### D. Oath-taking (vv. 33-35)

**33. "Again, you have heard that it was said to the people long ago, 'Do not break your oath, but keep the oaths you have made to the Lord.'**

What the people have heard in regard to oath-taking is an accurate summary of Exodus 20:7; Leviticus 19:12; Numbers 30:2; and Deuteronomy 23:21-23. The problem is that the religious leaders of Jesus' day have developed very intricate rules regarding oaths that "counted" vs. oaths that "didn't count" (see Matthew 23:16-22). Jesus intends to put a stop to such quibbling.

**34, 35. "But I tell you, Do not swear at all: either by heaven, for it is God's throne; or by the earth, for it is his footstool; or by Jerusalem, for it is the city of the Great King."**

Jesus' plain instruction is *do not swear at all*. It is not fitting for us to swear (take oaths) by things that belong to God. We ought to be able to tell the truth and keep our promises without swearing oaths (Matthew 5:37; James 5:12). This straightforward plan affirms the intent of the Old Testament law that the Jewish leaders had set aside with their convoluted reasoning.

Even so, some students like to point out that Jesus himself, when on trial for his life, will be sworn in by the high priest to answer a question under oath (Matthew 26:63, 64). Therefore they think Jesus does not intend to forbid formal oath-taking in the most serious situations. (See also 2 Corinthians 11:31; Galatians 1:20; and Hebrews 6:16.) At least we can be sure that Jesus does not want us to join in uttering the frequent and reckless "I swear to God"-type of oaths that are so common today.

## E. VIOLENCE (vv. 38, 39)

**38. "You have heard that it was said, 'Eye for eye, and tooth for tooth.'**

If you want to know the Latin term for this kind of justice, it is *lex talionis*. This means, roughly, "law of equal and direct retribution." For physical injury the legal punishment is the same kind of injury in return, according to Exodus 21:24; Leviticus 24:19, 20; and Deuteronomy 19:21. That kind of justice, strictly speaking, is "fair." The prospect of such punishment might keep an angry person from injuring an opponent.

**39. "But I tell you, Do not resist an evil person. If someone strikes you on the right cheek, turn to him the other also.**

In Jesus' day a strike on the cheek is more of an insult than an outright attack. Jesus advises a nonviolent response, a response that goes against the natural wish to strike back. This is the quickest way to stop the confrontation from escalating.

This attitude speaks to what our hearts should look like in the kingdom of God. The ancient prophets had predicted a new heart for God's people (Jeremiah 31:31-34; 32:39; Ezekiel 36:26). This is all part of the fulfillment that Jesus brings.

## F. LOVE (vv. 43-45)

**43. "You have heard that it was said, 'Love your neighbor and hate your enemy.'**

*Love your neighbor* is plain in Leviticus 19:18. Jesus recognizes the importance of this command (Matthew 22:35-39), and so do Jewish students of the law (Luke 10:25-27).

But *hate your enemy* is not found anywhere in God's law. Even so, God's people sometimes were ordered to destroy whole nations of enemies, killing men, women, and children without mercy (Deuteronomy 7:2; 1 Samuel 15:3). It is not surprising that Jewish teachers interpreted such orders as orders to hate those enemies. The command to hate enemies is found in the Dead Sea Scrolls, written by a very conservative Jewish sect that existed just before the time of Christ.

**44. "But I tell you: Love your enemies and pray for those who persecute you,**

This is one of our Lord's more difficult commands. Quite naturally, we do not *love* our *enemies*. We do this only with diligent effort. Sternly we repress our inclinations to say or do anything to hurt an enemy.

Jesus requires that we look for opportunities to help an enemy. We even set about to create such opportunities. When we do, we fulfill Old Testament requirements found in Exodus 23:4, 5 and Proverbs 25:21. This really isn't anything new!

**45. "... that you may be sons of your Father in heaven. He causes his sun to rise on the evil and the good, and sends rain on the righteous and the unrighteous.**

It isn't easy to love our enemies. It takes thought, effort, and time. Sometimes it even costs money. Yet God sends the goodness of *sun* and *rain* on *evil* and *unrighteous* people, so why shouldn't we have a similar attitude?

It's our nature to be like God, and he is one who helps his enemies. They give him no thanks, no honor, no recognition; but still he helps them. Your duty, your pleasure, your desire is to be like *your Father in heaven.*

*WHAT DO YOU THINK?*

*When have you had occasion to return good to someone who deliberately did something to harm you or your reputation? What was the result?*

## How to Say It

Corinthians. Ko-RIN-thee-unz
(th *as in* thin).

Deuteronomy. Due-ter-AHN-uh-
me.

Ezekiel. Ee-ZEEK-ee-ul or Ee-
ZEEK-yul.

Galatians. Guh-LAY-shunz.

Jeremiah. Jair-uh-MY-uh.

Leviticus. Leh-VIT-ih-kus.

lex talionis (Latin). leks tal-ee-
OH-niss.

Raca. RAY-kuh or Ray-KAH.

## Prayer

*Father in Heaven, thank you for being perfect, and thank you for sending your Son, your perfect sacrifice for sin. Forgive our easy self-satisfaction, we pray, and help us to be better than we are in all the ways that glorify Jesus. In his name we pray, amen.*

## Thought to Remember

*May our obedience to Christ honor him.*

## An Untold Wealth of Information

A ninety-year-old man was talking with his son one day about the astounding leaps that technology has taken during the father's lifetime. He had been born two years after the first electric starter appeared on automobiles, in the same year that the head of the U.S. Patent Office is said to have proposed closing down the department because "everything has been invented"!

The man's son was explaining how computers work and was showing his father how one can access the Internet and find an untold wealth of information—some of which is actually true! They talked of how every eighteen months or so the power of computers doubles, or the price of the old computer is cut in half. In what became something of a litany, the father said with each succeeding revelation, "I was born thirty years too soon!"

Most of us who use computers for our living still don't completely understand them or take full advantage of their wealth of features. Jesus' explanation of the law said, in effect, "There is an untold wealth of information here; you don't completely understand it, so you can't take full advantage of its benefits."

Many in Jesus' audience saw the law only as an external force placing limits on their lives. They could not appreciate the freedoms God offers to those who let his words become an intrinsic motivator in their hearts! Are we repeating their error?

—C. R. B.

## III. CHALLENGE TO GROW (MATTHEW 5:48)

We now come to the conclusion of the matter. What follows next is Jesus' summary of all of his "you have heard that it was said . . . but I tell you" statements to this point.

**48. "Be perfect, therefore, as your heavenly Father is perfect."**

Now wait a minute, Jesus, please! I do want to be like God. I realize that I ought to be like him. But I'm only human. Isn't perfection too much to ask? "Nobody's perfect" is an axiom of our hearts; it is our excuse for all our imperfections. We are frightened by a blunt command to *be perfect,* and doubly frightened when the perfection demanded is like that of God himself.

Jesus knows, of course, that we can't be perfect in this life. But that fact should not keep us from trying. Jesus' command is nothing new, since Leviticus 19:2 says almost the very same thing, with "holy" instead of "perfect." (See also Deuteronomy 18:13.) As children of our Heavenly Father, we strive to be more and more like him every day. That's a vital part of our new heart that we have as members of the kingdom of God!

## CONCLUSION

Our lesson title directs our attention to "A New Approach." Readily we agree that we cannot be as great and good as God is; but just as readily we agree that we can be better than we are. Then why aren't we? With so many years of Christian living behind us, why aren't we closer to perfection? Some reasons (excuses, really!) are clearly seen.

First, when we notice some imperfection in our character or life, we shrug it off with the cliché, "Nobody's perfect." Often we just don't try very hard to be better than we are. Second, we often find that our time is fully occupied with things we like to do. It takes time and effort to do good to our enemies, for example. So we just don't get around to it.

Third, we never have done those good things that we are not doing now. A sense of inertia keeps us from improving. Maybe we should listen to the more mature Christians who say, "Try it—God commands it." If we can be a hundred-watt lamp, why be content with sixty watts?

# Discovery Learning

*This page contains an alternative lesson plan emphasizing learning activities. Classes desiring such student involvement will find these suggestions helpful. The next page is a reproducible activity page to further enhance discovery learning.*

## LEARNING GOALS

After participating in this lesson, each student will be able to:

1. Give examples from the text of how Jesus corrected misunderstandings of the Old Testament law.

2. Explain why the law of love should be our guide in interactions with others.

3. Commit to Jesus one specific area in which he or she will choose to be more loving.

## INTO THE LESSON

Prepare a handout with the following hidden message puzzle. (You may also include the activities suggested in "Into the Word" and "Into Life" in your handout.) The heading should read: "Changing our Thinking." Instructions should read: "Delete the letters of the words found in Matthew 5:17. The remaining letters will spell a theme from today's lesson, a guide for our lives. Enter those in the blanks below.

    D O N O A T T H N I N K T E H A T I H A V W
    E C O A M E T P O A B P O L I R S H T H E L A
    W O O R A T C H E H P R O P H E T S ; A I T T H
    A I T V E U N D E S O A T R E C A S O I M M E T
    P O A O R B O L T A N I T S H A T H E S M B A
    U T T O C F U L T F I L L I O T H E N M S.

    __ ___ _____ :
    _____ ___ __
    _____ __
    _____ .

(Answer: *A new approach: Attitudes are as important as actions.*)

Say, "We have been studying how God created a special people and offered them a new dynasty. Today's lesson begins a series that reminds us that we are new creations in Christ, bound to live within his will. Today's study addresses our attitudes as well as our actions. In the broad range of topics addressed, you will find Jesus touching a need in your life."

## INTO THE WORD

You may choose to do the following exercise as a whole class or in small groups. For this activity use the section of the reproducible page titled "Old Testament Law & Its Proper Meaning."

Ask the learners to identify and list in the first column the six subjects Jesus addressed (*Murder, Adultery, Divorce, Oath-taking, Violence, Love*).

Then they are to summarize misunderstanding of the Old Testament law for each in the second column and write Jesus' approach in the third column.

After completing the study of the first three columns, ask the following questions and write responses in the "Why Better?" column.

*Murder:* Explain the word *Raca* before asking (1) "Why would such name-calling bring one dangerously close to Hell?" and (2) "How is Jesus' approach a better approach?"

*Adultery:* Ask (1) "Why is Jesus' way a better approach?" (2) "What are some ways this temptation comes to us today?" (3) "What 'tips' can we list to help minimize the impact of such temptations in our lives?"

*Divorce:* See the lesson commentary to explain or clarify the meaning of this passage, and then ask why Jesus' way is a better way.

*Oath-taking:* (1) "If one phrase summarizes the teaching in verses 33-35, what would it be?" (*"Do not swear at all."*) "Why is this new approach better?"

*Violence:* "Why is a nonviolent response to violence better?" "On what everyday occasions are adults tempted to break this teaching?"

*Love:* "Why is this approach so difficult?" "How is this a better approach to life?"

## INTO LIFE

The second activity on the reproducible page is titled "Attitudes Are as Important as Actions." Ask students to read through the temptations that appear in the left column. These include the following: "Murder and Name-Calling," "Adultery and 'Just Looking,'" "Divorce and Remarriage," "To Swear Oaths or Not," "Violence and Retaliation," "Loving Our Enemies." Have them consider the level of temptation that they experience in each area, ranging from No Problem, Sometimes Tempted, At Risk, and I Need Help.

Invite students to circle the most appropriate answer for each of the six subjects. Afterward, ask each to select one area that needs attention. Ask each student to determine one immediate step to take to complete this commitment. Example: not to retaliate when someone cuts him or her off in traffic.

# Old Testament Law & Its Proper Meaning

Read today's printed text. In the first column list the six subjects Jesus discusses. Then summarize the misunderstanding of the Old Testament law in the second column, Jesus' approach to this law in the third column, and tell why Jesus' understanding results in a recovery of what the law meant all along.

| SUBJECT DISCUSSED | MISUNDERSTANDING | JESUS' APPROACH | WHY BETTER? |
|---|---|---|---|
| 1. | | | |
| 2. | | | |
| 3. | | | |
| 4. | | | |
| 5. | | | |
| 6. | | | |

# Attitudes Are as Important as Actions

The left-hand column raises the issues addressed in today's Scripture. Now is the time to do a self-evaluation. Circle the answer that best describes your life's compliance to Jesus' will.

| | | | | |
|---|---|---|---|---|
| MURDER AND NAME-CALLING | No Problem | Sometimes Tempted | At Risk | I Need Help |
| ADULTERY AND "JUST LOOKING" | No Problem | Sometimes Tempted | At Risk | I Need Help |
| DIVORCE AND REMARRIAGE | No Problem | Sometimes Tempted | At Risk | I Need Help |
| TO SWEAR OATHS OR NOT | No Problem | Sometimes Tempted | At Risk | I Need Help |
| VIOLENCE AND RETALIATION | No Problem | Sometimes Tempted | At Risk | I Need Help |
| LOVING MY ENEMIES | No Problem | Sometimes Tempted | At Risk | I Need Help |

# A NEW BODY

**LESSON 11**

## WHY TEACH THIS LESSON?

A few years ago, I sat in a certain Sunday school class for ten weeks and listened carefully to the prayer requests that were put forth. I discovered that there were three general types of requests: (1) for physical healing, (2) for healing of "situations" (broken marriages, job loss, etc.), and (3) for spiritual issues. At the end of the ten weeks, I tallied the results. To my astonishment and dismay, there had been ninety-seven requests for physical healing, thirty-three requests for healing of "situations," and only three requests involving spiritual matters!

Why such a focus on physical wellness? Aren't eternal, spiritual issues more important by far? Since we eventually die physically anyway, is the status of our earthly bodies really something that we should be preoccupied with? Today's lesson teaches us to say, after the apostle Paul, "Where, O death, is your victory?" When we learn that lesson, our prayer priorities (among other things) will be correct.

## INTRODUCTION

### A. OUR HOPE IS NOT LOST

Many years ago in a Western town there was a little congregation that irreverent neighbors called "the happy church." Its every meeting was a joyous celebration. Happiest of all was the preacher, though his health was frail. Cheerfully he told the congregation he would die soon, but would rise on the third day as Jesus had done. Members of the church trusted the preacher. He never had told them anything but truth, and no one thought of doubting his promise.

So there was no mourning when the preacher died, and no funeral. His body was laid on a couch on the speaker's platform in the little church building, and an honor guard attended him day and night. On the third day the congregation assembled before daylight and continued the meeting until midnight, but the preacher never stirred.

In the dark hours after midnight the disappointed congregation decided that their beloved preacher must have misunderstood the message. Perhaps he was to rise on the thirtieth day instead of the third. So he was left and guarded on his couch for a month, but still he never stirred.

Finally the county health officer obtained a court order, and the rotting corpse was buried without ceremony. Then there was a long period of mourning because a "godless" government had prevented the promised resurrection.

Every member of that long-ago congregation has passed away by now. Each in turn has been buried and mourned with genuine sorrow. But in every case the sorrow has been lightened by the steadfast hope that the dead will rise again (John 5:28, 29). That is the promise of Jesus.

### B. LESSON BACKGROUND

Worse than the belief that a dead friend will rise in three days is the belief that he or she will not rise at all—ever. That is the belief of millions of non-Christians today, and perhaps it is the belief of some members of your church. It was the

DEVOTIONAL READING:
*1 CORINTHIANS 15:1-11*
BACKGROUND SCRIPTURE:
*1 CORINTHIANS 15*
PRINTED TEXT:
*1 CORINTHIANS 15:42-57*

LESSON AIMS

After participating in this lesson, each student will be able to:

1. Describe the resurrection bodies in which believers will rise when Jesus returns to earth.

2. Explain why Jesus' resurrection gives us hope that we will receive a new eternal body.

3. Compose words of hope and encouragement to someone grieving the death of a Christian friend or family member.

Nov
14

KEY VERSE

"Where, O death, is your victory? Where, O death, is your sting?" —1 Corinthians 15:55

belief of some in the church at Corinth (1 Corinthians 15:12). This false belief was also held by some Jewish leaders of the day (Luke 20:27).

As proof that the dead do rise, Paul pointed to the resurrection of Christ. There can be no doubt that he really had been dead (cf. John 19:31-34). And Jesus really returned to life. That is proved in at least three ways: (1) an abundance of reliable witnesses (1 Corinthians 15:3-8), (2) the failure of Jewish authorities to produce a corpse to refute the claims of a resurrection, and (3) the willingness of the disciples to die martyrs' deaths for their belief in a risen Lord. It is Jesus' resurrection that sets the stage for our own.

## I. FOUR CHANGES (1 CORINTHIANS 15:42-44)

Since the fact of Jesus' resurrection was proven beyond doubt, some skeptics want to confuse the issue by quibbling about just how resurrection is accomplished and what the risen body looks like (1 Corinthians 15:35). Paul answers with an analogy. When you plant a grain of wheat, the plant that grows from it is very different from the seed itself (15:36-38). Likewise the body that rises from the dead may be very different from the body that died.

In verses 39-41 Paul goes on to point out the great variety of things in earth and sky: different kinds of flesh on earth, and sun and moon and many different stars in the sky. Then he moves to his summary or application.

### A. FROM CORRUPTION TO INCORRUPTION (v. 42)

42. *So will it be with the resurrection of the dead. The body that is sown is perishable, it is raised imperishable;*

The word *so* causes us to look back to the analogy in verses 37, 38. As a plant that grows is different from the seed that was planted, so also the body that rises from *the dead* is different from the body that died and was buried. The text goes on to point out some of the differences.

We marvel at the undertaker's art that makes our departed friend look so natural, as if he or she were sleeping and might wake and speak at any minute. But we know that the person's *body* is dead. That is why we bury it in the ground where it returns to dust. But the final trumpet (v. 52, below) will call from that grave or tomb a body forever alive, never again to be touched by decay or corruption (cf. 2 Timothy 1:10).

### A FUTILE PROJECT

Vladimir Lenin died in 1924. Most of us have seen pictures of his body lying interred in Moscow's Red Square, maintaining a fairly lifelike appearance. Throughout the Communist era in the old Soviet Union, the Communist leadership kept the body on view—with no apparent decomposition of the tissues—as a symbol of the supposed immortality of the Communist political and economic philosophy.

To accomplish this feat, embalming specialists inspect the body twice a week. From time to time, the face is treated with a solution that prevents breakdown of the tissues, and about every year-and-a-half the body is soaked in a bath of preservatives. (An irony of Lenin's fate is that since the fall of Communism the group entrusted with preserving his body has had to engage in capitalism: they have sold the secret embalming methods to the rest of the world in order to fund their work.)

How futile is this project in symbolizing a failed system of government! Even if Lenin's body could somehow retain its lifelike appearance for a millennium, it would still be a dead body, nothing more! How much better is the promise Paul makes to us that our natural bodies—physical, weak, and subject to decomposition—will someday be raised alive in the spiritual realm. Then we will live forevermore as symbols of a divine cause that shall never fail.      —C. R. B.

## B. FROM DISHONOR TO GLORY (v. 43a)

**43a. . . . it is sown in dishonor, it is raised in glory;**

We honor a departed friend with mounds of flowers, with glowing eulogies, and with words of honor carved in stone. But we know that the body we lay to rest is dishonored by death and will be dishonored by decay.

Even so, we know that *dishonor* to be only temporary. The "lowly" body (Philippians 3:21) will rise to *glory* grander than any seen on earth when the last trumpet sounds.

## C. FROM WEAKNESS TO POWER (v. 43b)

**43b. . . . it is sown in weakness, it is raised in power;**

What a sharp contrast! The effects of sin weaken our bodies as we live. At death the body is weaker still: utterly helpless and inert. But the coming resurrection will change all that. We cannot even imagine the *power* that will attend a body raised from the dead.

## D. FROM NATURAL TO SPIRITUAL (v. 44)

**44. . . . it is sown a natural body, it is raised a spiritual body.**
*If there is a natural body, there is also a spiritual body.*

We know much about *a natural body* since each of us lives in one and sees others. But what do we know about *a spiritual body?* This has been an area of many scholarly debates! From this lesson we know that the new body will be incorruptible, glorious, and powerful. We can also conclude that it will be a real, literal body; God intended from the beginning that humans should be a combination of body and spirit.

Much remains for us to learn about the nature of our new bodies. Our knowledge will be complete only when we are actually "in" them.

## II. TWO ADAMS (1 CORINTHIANS 15:45-49)

As we learn from Genesis, Adam became the father of the entire human race. Adam brought sin into the world very early in human history, and death followed. So death passed to the whole human race (Romans 5:12). Over the centuries all humanity has been burdened and handicapped by sin.

Then came Jesus, who never sinned. He suffered the agony of the cross to pay the sin price for others. Thus he became another Adam, the beginning of a new race of people, of people forgiven, and therefore not burdened and handicapped by sin. In the next part of our text, Paul compares and contrasts the first Adam, the Adam of Genesis, with the last Adam, namely Jesus Christ.

## A. STARK CONTRAST (v. 45)

**45. So it is written: "The first man Adam became a living being"; the last Adam, a life-giving spirit.**

In Genesis 2:7 it is written that *the first man Adam* was formed of lifeless dust and so was a lifeless being until God breathed into his nostrils the breath of life and made him *a living being.* By contrast Jesus, *the last Adam,* has existed from eternity past (John 1:1).

Not only has Jesus always lived, he is also *a life-giving spirit,* for all things were made by him, including all living things (John 1:3). But in another way he became a life-giving spirit when he gave his life to pay the price for our sins. Thus he won our forgiveness and gave life to those who were dead in trespasses and sins (Ephesians 2:1). Every Christmas we praise him as the "Second Adam from above" in the last stanza of "Hark! the Herald Angels Sing."

### WHAT DO YOU THINK?

Knowing the body will be raised imperishable in glory and power, why are we so distraught when we bury a loved one? What encouraging words do you say to the family of a departed believer?

## B. EVIDENT ORDER (vv. 46-49)

**46. The spiritual did not come first, but the natural, and after that the spiritual.**

It is plain to all that the first Adam lived his *natural* life in his natural body long before the last Adam arrived on the scene. That last Adam is Jesus Christ our Savior. He is the one who gives new *spiritual* life to people who are dead in their sins.

**47. The first man was of the dust of the earth, the second man from heaven.**

Now we see a contrast in origin, which tells us something about the order or hierarchy of creation. *The first man*, Adam, is the one who is *of the earth*. He was formed of dust, and lifeless as *dust* until God breathed into him the breath of life.

The second man, Jesus, is the one *from heaven*. There he lived with Father and Holy Spirit through countless millennia of unending time before the world was made.

In the order of appearance in visible form on earth, Adam is first and Jesus is second. But the phrases *of the earth* and *from heaven* reveal the true hierarchy. Also in our own experience the natural comes before the spiritual.

**48. As was the earthly man, so are those who are of the earth; and as is the man from heaven, so also are those who are of heaven.**

*Earthly* people are like Adam. You are, I am. Heavenly people are like Jesus (1 John 3:2). You will be, I will be—if we are Christians.

**49. And just as we have borne the likeness of the earthly man, so shall we bear the likeness of the man from heaven.**

*We have borne the likeness of the earthly man,* and we bear it still: we look very much like Adam (cf. Genesis 5:3). In our graves these natural bodies will come to look more like the dust from which Adam was formed. But the last trumpet will call us out, and we shall look neither like dust nor like Adam nor like our present natural bodies. We shall rise as spiritual bodies, and we shall look very much like Jesus in his glorified body (Philippians 3:20, 21). Wonderful!

We shall look something like Jesus, but that does not mean we shall be identical, like so many peas in a pod. In our natural bodies we all look much like Adam, but see how varied we are. Some are tall and some are short; some are thin and some are muscular. We cannot imagine what variety we will see in our spiritual bodies, but we can expect to be pleased.

## III. ONE MYSTERY (1 CORINTHIANS 15:50-53)

Only partly do we understand these natural bodies in which we are spending our lives on earth. Even with all our modern technology and diagnostic tools there is still much to learn!

Sometimes our bodies surprise us with their vigor and endurance; sometimes they frighten us with their weakness or illness. But the spiritual bodies that will be ours will be amazing; only dimly can we imagine them now. "What we will be has not yet been made known" (1 John 3:2).

## A. FLESH LIMITED (v. 50)

**50. I declare to you, brothers, that flesh and blood cannot inherit the kingdom of God, nor does the perishable inherit the imperishable.**

*Flesh and blood* are what our natural bodies are made of. In these bodies we do indeed experience a foretaste of *the kingdom of God* when we make God our King; but it is only a foretaste.

The fullness, the perfection, of that kingdom awaits our spiritual bodies. Immortal and forever incorruptible, we will be able to appreciate the perfection of God's rule when we have those new bodies.

---

*WHAT DO YOU THINK?*

*We share common features with Adam simply by virtue of our birth. Why is it that the traits we share with the second Adam depend on our faith?*

---

*HOW TO SAY IT*

*Corinth. KOR-inth.*

*Corinthians. Ko-RIN-thee-unz (th as in thin).*

*Hosea. Ho-ZAY-uh.*

*Isaiah. Eye-ZAY-uh.*

*martyrs. MAR-turz.*

*Philippians. Fih-LIP-ee-unz.*

*Vladimir Lenin. VLAD-ih-meer LEN-in.*

## B. Flesh Changes (vv. 51-53)

**51. Listen, I tell you a mystery: We will not all sleep, but we will all be changed—**

In the vocabulary of the New Testament, *a mystery* is not a puzzle that we can solve by clever detective work. A mystery is something we will never know unless someone tells us. Paul proposes to tell us this one.

Here the word *sleep* is a figure of speech, as it is in John 11:11-14. In literal English we would say, "We shall not all die." However, the word *sleep* is an appropriate figure, for Paul is about to emphasize the fact that literal death is not permanent. That is in the next verse; here in verse 51 we read that not everyone will die. Some will still be living in their natural bodies when the last trumpet sounds. Those natural bodies that have not died will *be changed* into spiritual bodies along with those who will be raised from the dead. See also 1 Thessalonians 4:13-17.

**52. . . . in a flash, in the twinkling of an eye, at the last trumpet. For the trumpet will sound, the dead will be raised imperishable, and we will be changed.**

The forthcoming change will not be a long, drawn-out process. It will be complete before the sound of the *trumpet* dies away. People long *dead* and people never dead will stand together, lost in the wonder of it all. See also Matthew 24:31 and Revelation 11:15.

**53. For the perishable must clothe itself with the imperishable, and the mortal with immortality.**

In a bit of a repeat from verse 42, Paul summarizes that which is best about the spiritual bodies: they are immortal, never to die. And they are *imperishable*—they will not even be sick or subject to weakness. Paul says nothing about how handsome, intelligent, strong, skillful, or useful they are. But we cannot imagine that any one of them is deficient in any way. See also 2 Corinthians 5:4.

## IV. FINAL VICTORY (1 CORINTHIANS 15:54-57)

"The last enemy to be destroyed is death" (1 Corinthians 15:26). When God's people rise triumphant over death, that will indeed be the final victory. The conflict between good and evil, wide as the world and long as human history, will be over. So our text ends with a brief song of victory.

## A. End of Death (v. 54)

**54. When the perishable has been clothed with the imperishable, and the mortal with immortality, then the saying that is written will come true: "Death has been swallowed up in victory."**

Paul is alluding to Isaiah 25:8. A glance at that passage shows us that the victory over death is God's doing, not our own: "He will swallow up death forever. The Sovereign Lord will wipe away the tears from all faces."

We think also of John 3:16: "For God so loved the world that he gave his one and only Son, that whoever believes in him shall not perish but have eternal life." God gave his Son, and his Son gave his life. His death paid the price for all our sins, and Christians have everlasting life. So the victory belongs to God, and we give him all the glory. But the benefits belong to us.

## B. End of Death's Power (vv. 55, 56)

**55. "Where, O death, is your victory?**
      **Where, O death, is your sting?"**

Now Paul draws his thoughts from Hosea 13:14. *Death* has been scaring people ever since Adam and Eve, but it should hold no terror for Christians. Why should we be afraid to turn loose of these frail bodies when we know we shall

*What Do You Think?*

*Do you expect the Lord to return before your own death? Why, or why not? How does your belief affect how you live your life?*

*Visual for lesson 11. Ask your learners what loved ones who have passed on are they most anticipating being united with at the resurrection.*

receive imperishable bodies in exchange? Death is an enemy, to be sure, but it is a defeated enemy.

**56. The sting of death is sin, and the power of sin is the law.**

What makes us afraid of *death*? Our sins do. We know we have earned eternal condemnation instead of everlasting life. And *the law* gives our sins the power to terrify us, because the law makes our sins so undeniable. Yet we are not terrified. We are Christians. We are forgiven. Our sins are taken away. We are not in line for the wages of sin, but for the gift of God. Eternal life is ours (Romans 6:23).

### REMOVING THE STING

Humans have long been fascinated with the idea of defying death. Some do it today by participating in the so-called "extreme sports." More traditionally, people have experienced the thrill of challenging death vicariously. Perhaps the most famous person to be connected with the concept is Harry Houdini (1874–1926). He was known for defying death by jumping into rivers while handcuffed or by being buried alive.

Many have imitated Houdini. For example, in 1999 David Blaine gained fame by spending seven days in a transparent coffin buried six feet into the ground in New York City. A three-ton tank of water covered his see-through coffin in which he had only six inches of headroom and two inches of room on either side. Like Houdini, Blaine survived this stunt and others, but also like Houdini (and the rest of us), Blaine will one day die.

But not being able to escape death through either technology or any amount of "magic" or trickery is only part of death's sting. The more significant part is, as Paul says, sin. It, too, is something we cannot avoid, and it is responsible for the fact of death. But we can thank God for the sacrifice of Christ. When he conquered death by his resurrection, he gave us hope and assurance of our own!    —C. R. B.

### C. ETERNAL GRATITUDE (v. 57)

**57. But thanks be to God! He gives us the victory through our Lord Jesus Christ.**

We have seen that *the victory* is God's, not ours (comments on v. 54). Now we see that it is ours, too—not in the sense that we won it, but because God gives it to us *through our Lord Jesus Christ*. So *thanks be to God!*

## CONCLUSION

With verse 57 our text ends in triumph. Thanks to God, victory is ours! But let us read one more verse, for verse 58 tells us what to be doing here and now in addition to speaking our thanks to God: "Therefore, my beloved brothers, stand firm. Let nothing move you. Always give yourselves fully to the work of the Lord, because you know that your labor in the Lord is not in vain." Verse 58 thus gives us our job assignment for this week, the one following, and all the weeks afterward. And as we work we constantly think forward to the day when Jesus will come back to earth, in person and visible (1 Thessalonians 4:16, 17).

Can you imagine that wonderful day when our own spiritual bodies will soar aloft along with those of all of God's saints? Yet the blessed saints are not the only dead ones who will return to life at the trumpet blast and Jesus' shout. A great many will be aroused to hear the sad sentence, "Depart from me, you who are cursed, into the eternal fire prepared for the devil and his angels" (Matthew 25:41). Their sins are noted in Revelation 21:8. Their lack of concern for others and failure to do anything good is stressed in Matthew 25:41-46. What a sobering thought!

So let our conclusion still be 1 Corinthians 15:58: "Stand firm. Let nothing move you. Always give yourselves fully to the work of the Lord."

# Discovery Learning

*This page contains an alternative lesson plan emphasizing learning activities. Classes desiring such student involvement will find these suggestions helpful. The next page is a reproducible activity page to further enhance discovery learning.*

## LEARNING GOALS

After this lesson each student will be able to:

1. Describe the resurrection bodies in which believers will rise when Jesus returns to earth.

2. Explain why Jesus' resurrection gives us hope that we will receive a new eternal body.

3. Compose words of hope and encouragement to someone grieving the death of a Christian friend or family member.

## INTO THE LESSON

Say, "Few people talk openly about death and dying. However, today we will face it head on." Ask the class to cite and define contemporary views of what happens to people after death. List the responses on a board under the heading "After Death?" The list may include reincarnation (Buddhism, Hinduism), various "New Age" views of becoming one with the universe, the idea that there is no life after death, and others.

Afterward, ask people to cite what they think happens after death. Of course, most of these responses will have a Christian perspective. List these in a second column on the board under the heading, "Our Beliefs." Make the transition to Bible study by reminding the class, "The Christian has strong evidence of life after death and a wonderful experience ahead for all believers."

## INTO THE WORD

*Option 1:* Distribute copies of the reproducible page that follows. Have learners complete the activities individually or in small groups. Then discuss their findings.

*Option 2:* This activity will require at least five small groups. (Larger classes having more than five groups can duplicate the group assignments.) Before class begins, have five different signs posted on the walls in different places in the classrooms, each with one of the following headings: "Death: Before and After—Part I," "Death: Before and After—Part II," "Unpacking a Mystery," "Happy Endings," and "Death's Dark Side."

Appoint a group leader for each discussion team. As these leaders move to sit or stand under the sign indicating the topic assigned, ask class members to choose and join them. (Each group must have at least three people.) Give each leader a marker, poster board, photocopies of the lesson commentary on the appropriate verses, and a piece of paper with the following instructions:

*Death: Before and After—Part I.* Your team is to study 1 Corinthians 15:42-44. Make a list with two columns, contrasting our present bodies with our resurrected bodies. Be ready to explain the significance of these contrasts. The lesson commentary attached may be helpful.

*Death: Before and After—Part II.* Your team is to study 1 Corinthians 15:45-49. Make a list with two columns, contrasting the first Adam with the second. Be ready to explain the significance of these contrasts. The lesson commentary attached may be helpful.

*Unpacking a Mystery.* Your team is to find and study 1 Corinthians 15:50-53. Make a list with two headings. The first will be the "limitations of the flesh" and the second will be "the process of change." Be ready to explain the significance of what is in your lists. The attached commentary may be helpful.

*Happy Endings.* Your group's task is to study 1 Corinthians 15:54-57. Make a list of key phrases and be ready to explain them. The attached commentary notes may be helpful.

*Death's Dark Side.* While the rest of the class reviews the wonderful joys of life beyond death for the believer, your task is to give a brief report of some of the things awaiting the unsaved. See Matthew 25:41-46, John 5:28, 29, and other passages. Attached notes from the conclusion of today's lesson commentary may be helpful in your discussion.

After the study groups have completed their work, ask the team leader from each group to report their findings to the whole class.

## INTO LIFE

Ask the class to help you pull these teachings into contemporary life. Ask them to imagine you are writing to a friend who is mourning the death of a Christian family member or Christian friend. What are the concepts and thoughts to include in the letter? Ask a class member to note these remarks on the board. After the exercise, remind the class that mourning is not limited to just a few months after the death of a loved one. Grief is especially strong at holidays. Thanksgiving Day is less than two weeks away. Ask them to consider sending a Thanksgiving card to someone this year who will be experiencing mourning. The card should mention why you are thankful for the deceased, as well as a reminder of our Christian hope.

# Lessons I've Learned

The verses in 1 Corinthians 15:42-56 contain one of the most encouraging and wonderful promises in God's Word. Read through this passage and note some of the lessons you've learned below.

1. What did you learn about the changes ahead for our perishable bodies?

2. What did you learn about an inheritance?

3. What did you learn about clothing?

# Hope Applied

Below are listed a few of the handicaps or difficulties we may experience in this perishable body. In the second column, note Christians you know (if any) who will lose this handicap when they are clothed with their new bodies.

| PERISHABLE BODIES | SOMEONE WHO WILL BE CHANGED<br>(In His/Her Resurrected Body) |
| --- | --- |
| Visually or Hearing Impaired | |
| Cancer or Other Life-threatening Disease | |
| Cerebral Palsy or Multiple Sclerosis | |
| Depression | |
| Extreme Poverty | |

# My Loss—and My Gain

Allow today's Scripture to become extremely personal. Jot a few notes of the things you are looking forward to having changed in Heaven.

# A NEW CREATURE IN CHRIST

**LESSON 12**

## WHY TEACH THIS LESSON?

Christian apologist Ravi Zacharias speaks to audiences all over the world—audiences that are often quite hostile to the Christian message. On one occasion a certain man brought his two atheist friends to one of Ravi's presentations. Afterward, the two atheists admitted to their friend that the logic they had heard in defense of the Christian faith was powerful and unshakable. Even so, these two men stated that they intended to remain atheists because "they preferred it"!

The apostle Paul was one who spent his Christian life trying to persuade others of the truthfulness of the Christian message. But some people, then as now, simply do not want a fresh start. No matter how much evidence and logic that Paul or any of us presents, some will not accept the message because they know that to become a Christian requires becoming a different person. Today's lesson will help us see that becoming a new creature in Christ is really "worth it"—it's worth *anything* that God expects us to give up.

## INTRODUCTION

### A. OLD REPUTATIONS

Bigtown and Smalltown are in such close proximity that they would be one and the same town if it were not for the state line that runs between them. Bigtown is an ordinary American city. It has a university, a symphony orchestra, an art museum, and many other embellishments of "culture." Smalltown is a typical suburb, with a new shopping center frightening the established businesses.

Back in the first half of the twentieth century, Smalltown was nicknamed Sin City. Its Palace Theatre changed its name to Sensation and began showing pornographic films.

The Bear Club opened its doors the same year. This was a showplace with a bar. There a cocktail was priced at thirty dollars, even during the Great Depression. A man who came in alone was greeted by a pretty hostess who asked him to buy a drink for her, too. Of course her drink sold elsewhere for a nickel in those days, but at the Bear Club it cost thirty dollars. The show itself was "free."

The Sensation and the Bear Club advertised in Bigtown and both promptly became popular with convention visitors wanting to "unwind," business visitors ready for a "holiday" after finishing their business, and hundreds of residents having plenty of money and looking for a "good time."

Reputations can be hard to live down! Yet both people and cities can change. But even if cities as a whole don't change, God still holds individuals accountable.

### B. LESSON BACKGROUND

Corinth in the first century A.D. was a city that combined the attractions of Bigtown with those of Sin City. It was a busy crossroads of culture and commerce. The streets were full of restless sailors on leave, thrill-seekers looking for excitement, and merchants willing to pander to all.

Writing about four hundred years before the time of Christ, the playwright Aristophanes used the Greek word *korinthiazesthai*—which means "to act like a

DEVOTIONAL READING:
*2 CORINTHIANS 4:16–5:5*

BACKGROUND SCRIPTURE:
*2 CORINTHIANS 5:11-21*

PRINTED TEXT:
*2 CORINTHIANS 5:11-21*

LESSON AIMS

*After participating in this lesson, each student will be able to:*

*1. Summarize the message of the "ministry of reconciliation" that Paul describes in the text.*

*2. Note specific evidence for the need of this ministry in his or her own community.*

*3. Suggest one specific way he or she can participate in this ministry of reconciliation in the coming week.*

Nov
21

KEY VERSE

*Therefore, if anyone is in Christ, he is a new creation; the old has gone, the new has come!*
—2 Corinthians 5:17

**LESSON 12 NOTES**

Corinthian"—as a reference to sexually immoral behavior. What a reputation Corinth had! The Romans destroyed the city in 146 B.C., but its reputation for immorality came back when it was reestablished in 44 B.C.

In Paul's day a popular place in Corinth was the great temple of Aphrodite, the goddess of love. The geographer Strabo, writing just before the time of Christ, claims that a thousand priestesses who doubled as prostitutes staffed this temple. In his first letter to the Corinthian church, Paul lists some of the sins that may well have given Corinth the reputation of being Sin City. But Paul also said that such things were not acceptable in the kingdom of God (see 1 Corinthians 6:9, 10).

When the Corinthians came out of such gross paganism to become Christians, it is not surprising that they were slow in learning Christian ways. Paul's first letter to them was unsparing in pointing out errors and urging correction. After sending such a critical letter, Paul naturally wondered how the Corinthians would receive it. Would they acknowledge their mistakes and correct them, or would they merely be resentful and angry? He had to wonder for a long time, but finally he reconnected with Timothy (2 Corinthians 1:1), who had been in Corinth to see how the letter was received (Acts 19:21, 22; 1 Corinthians 4:17; 16:10).

The news Timothy brought was encouraging, as the content of 2 Corinthians shows. Most of the Corinthians took the criticism seriously and were making improvements. Only a minority was resentful and angry. Even they acknowledged that Paul wrote a good letter, but they insisted that in person he was weak and his speech was contemptible (2 Corinthians 10:10).

With that information Paul wrote his second letter to the Corinthians. Grateful for the progress that was being made at Corinth, he made a modest defense of himself and, more importantly, a defense of the Christ whose ambassador he was. Paul declared that he himself was truthful (2 Corinthians 4:2), but said he proclaimed Christ, not himself (4:5). God had enlightened Paul with the knowledge of Jesus (4:6).

If Paul was unworthy to carry such a treasure, as a fragile clay jar is unworthy to hold a material treasure, that only served to emphasize the power of God that was in the message (4:7). Paul, the one who had persecuted the church (1 Corinthians 15:9), was now being persecuted for this message (2 Corinthians 4:9). His old reputation had given way to a new reputation because of that very message.

## I. PAUL'S EFFORT (2 CORINTHIANS 5:11-13)

Above all, Paul says, he is working to be acceptable to Christ, because Christ is the judge before whom all must appear to receive a just sentence for what they have done (2 Corinthians 5:9, 10). Now verses 11-13 continue the description and discussion of Paul's ongoing effort.

### A. OUTWARD AND INWARD (vv. 11, 12)

11. *Since, then, we know what it is to fear the Lord, we try to persuade men. What we are is plain to God, and I hope it is also plain to your conscience.*

Paul is thinking in terms of the final judgment (2 Corinthians 5:10, just previous). Such a thought should terrify anyone who is not obeying God. But Paul, as a Christian, faces the thought of judgment without *fear*. Instead, he has a deep reverence for God (e.g., 2 Corinthians 7:1).

It is in this light that Paul continually is trying *to persuade* people of certain things. These things include the truth of the gospel as it speaks of the need to be reconciled to God (v. 20, below).

*HOW TO SAY IT*

*Aphrodite. Af-ruh-DITE-ee.*

*Aristophanes. A-ris-TOF-a-neez.*

*Colossians. Kuh-LOSH-unz.*

*Corinth. KOR-inth.*

*Corinthians. Ko-RIN-thee-unz*
   (th *as in* thin).

*Galatians. Guh-LAY-shunz.*

*Hebrews. HEE-brews.*

*Isaiah. Eye-ZAY-uh.*

*korinthiazesthai (Greek). ko-rin-*
   *thee-ADZ-ess-thai.*

*Philippians. Fih-LIP-ee-unz.*

*Sergio Gutierrez. SAIR-jyo Goo-*
   *TAR-ez.*

*Strabo. STRAY-bow (bow as in*
   *rainbow).*

Paul also tries to persuade people of the purity of his own motives (2 Corinthians 1:12) and of the soundness of his credentials (4:1-6). Such facts are *plain* (evident, well known) to God, and Paul hopes they are equally manifest in the minds, hearts, and consciences of the Christians in Corinth.

**12. We are not trying to commend ourselves to you again, but are giving you an opportunity to take pride in us, so that you can answer those who take pride in what is seen rather than in what is in the heart.**

Paul may be thought of as commending himself when he declares his honesty and truthfulness (2 Corinthians 4:2) or when he speaks of his authority as an apostle (10:8; 11:5). But actually he is only trying to help the genuine Christians of Corinth. They want to defend him against the barbs of the critics who take pride in appearance rather than *what is in the heart.*

Such critics ridicule Paul's personal appearance and his speech (10:10). No doubt some of them are taller, handsomer, and more eloquent than he. But none is as honest and truthful, and none has been called by Jesus to be an apostolic witness for him. Paul is the one who had received such a calling (Acts 26:13-16). By this time the devout Corinthians should be able to defend Paul on their own against such critics (2 Corinthians 12:11).

WHAT DO YOU THINK?

How can we be sure our faithfulness is evident without "blowing our own horns"?

WHAT DO YOU THINK?

We all have known leaders or others who "take pride in what is seen." What is it that eventually gives them away? How can we be careful to spot them early so they do not lead us astray?

### BEAUTY ISN'T ONLY SKIN DEEP

We've all heard the saying, "Life begins at forty." Someone more cynical than most of us has rephrased it, "Life begins at forty . . . to start going downhill." By the time we have reached the end of our fourth decade we cannot deny that age (and gravity) are changing our appearance. One middle-ager said, "I weigh the same as I did when I was twenty; my weight's just shaped different now than it was then!"

To combat the effects of aging, cosmetic surgery has become a growth industry. In a recent year, 7.4 million cosmetic procedures were performed in America, up 198 percent from a decade earlier. Facelifts, eyelid lifts, chemical peels, cheek implants, hair transplants, and collagen injections are all used to get rid of the inevitable wrinkles and to disguise thinning tissue where we don't want to be thin.

Then there is liposuction, which takes away the fatty tissue where we don't want to be fat. Perhaps the strangest treatment is the injection of botulism toxin (botox) to counteract wrinkles. Some people even become addicted to cosmetic surgery!

It could be argued from all of this that modern culture is guilty of the sin that Paul alludes to: placing more emphasis on outward appearance than on character. There's nothing wrong with *looking* good—at least as good as we can! But our value to the world, and simply as persons, is far greater if we place our focus on *being* good.                                                    —C. R. B.

## B. INSANITY OR SANITY (v. 13)

**13. If we are out of our mind, it is for the sake of God; if we are in our right mind, it is for you.**

Paul received the gospel he preached from Jesus (Galatians 1:11, 12). And Paul received those things after Jesus died, rose, and ascended to Heaven.

Hearing of such things, opponents of Paul say that he is beside himself, *out of his mind,* crazy (e.g., Acts 26:24). In response, Paul points out that the things that cast doubt on his sanity are between him and *God.* When Paul talks with his fellow humans, his talk is sober, reasonable, with no indication of insanity. For example, when he tells of Jesus' resurrection he points to credible witnesses (1 Corinthians 15:1-8).

Paul's preaching is plain and direct. He simply presents the gospel, the good news, and urges the hearers to accept the opportunity it offers. That is what makes sense!

## II. LOVE'S CONTROL (2 CORINTHIANS 5:14, 15)

Jesus himself said to his disciples, "Greater love has no one than this, that he lay down his life for his friends" (John 15:13). Christ loved Paul with this kind of love, even when Paul was a bitter enemy trying to destroy the church.

When Paul realized his error, he knew he was obligated to do what he could for Christ. The following verses explain the reasoning that bring Paul to that conclusion.

### A. FACT OF DEATH (v. 14)

14. For Christ's love compels us, because we are convinced that one died for all, and therefore all died.

Christ indeed *died for all* sinners (cf. Romans 5:8). As a result, *all* people ought to have *died* to sin, separated from it forever, no longer sinning. But we know that not everyone will accept the meaning of Christ's death, and as a consequence not everyone will die to sin. Paul must preach this message!

### B. EFFECT OF DEATH (v. 15)

15. And he died for all, that those who live should no longer live for themselves but for him who died for them and was raised again.

Sinners are enslaved and controlled by sin (John 8:34). When they respond to Christ's love by dying to sin, they should not think themselves free to do whatever they please. In gratitude they should live for Jesus, *who died for them* (cf. Romans 14:7, 8). Paul must preach this message!

## III. RECONCILIATION'S RESULTS (2 CORINTHIANS 5:16-21)

To become a Christian is to become a different person. A slave of sin changes to become a slave of God and Christ and righteousness (Romans 6:18). Sometimes the change is described as being born again (John 1:12, 13; 3:3-5). But in our text we have read, "one died for all, and therefore all died" (2 Corinthians 5:14). Thus the figure here is like that in Romans 6:1-4. There we see that becoming a Christian is dying to sin, being buried in baptism, and rising to a new life. This new life of being reconciled to God brings certain changes with it.

### A. NEW OUTLOOK (v. 16)

16. So from now on we regard no one from a worldly point of view. Though we once regarded Christ in this way, we do so no longer.

A whole person is "spirit, soul and body" (1 Thessalonians 5:23). To know someone *from a worldly point of view* is to know that person superficially from appearance and what he or she is seen to do. Paul's opponents make a mistake when they glory "in what is seen rather than in what is in the heart" (2 Corinthians 5:12).

Paul's own mistake had been to think of *Christ* as an enemy of God and of God's people. But Paul resolved to make that mistake no more. Really knowing anyone involves acquaintance with that person's thoughts and feelings, values and ambitions, as well as desires and motives.

### B. NEW STATUS (v. 17)

17. Therefore, if anyone is in Christ, he is a new creation; the old has gone, the new has come!

Whether we think of a Christian as born again or as dead to sin and risen to new life, the point is that he or she is *a new creation*—a different person, a saint instead of a sinner. Love of sin and bondage to sin have *gone*; the person's whole

---

*WHAT DO YOU THINK?*

How many believers feel the constraint that Paul describes? What can be done to lead disciples to know that same compulsion to live and testify for Christ?

---

*DAILY BIBLE READINGS*

Monday, Nov. 15—Christ's Ministers Act Boldly (2 Corinthians 3:12-18)

Tuesday, Nov. 16—Paul Serves for God's Glory (2 Corinthians 4:1-15)

Wednesday, Nov. 17—We Must Live by Faith (2 Corinthians 4:16—5:5)

Thursday, Nov. 18—Serve God with Confidence (2 Corinthians 5:6-10)

Friday, Nov. 19—Paul Serves God Faithfully (2 Corinthians 5:11-15)

Saturday, Nov. 20—Paul's Ministry of Reconciliation (2 Corinthians 5:16-21)

Sunday, Nov. 21—Now Is the Day of Salvation (2 Corinthians 6:1-10)

nature and way of life have become *new*. Compare also Romans 8:1, 10; Galatians 6:15; and Revelation 21:5.

## C. NEWNESS FROM GOD (v. 18)

**18. All this is from God, who reconciled us to himself through Christ and gave us the ministry of reconciliation:**

The *all this* that is *from God* refers to our new outlook and new status according to verses 16 and 17, above. The verse now before us speaks of the change as being reconciled to God, and God is the one *who reconciled us to himself through Christ*. By our sinning we made ourselves to be God's enemies (Colossians 1:21). We could not end our enmity, but God could. He sent Jesus, who died to pay sin's penalty. As a result, God could forgive us.

So our redemption and reconciliation are God's work, not ours. But don't miss the next two verses! They reveal that we do have a part in changing people from being sinners to being saints. That revelation is begun in the last clause of the verse before us: to Paul and other Christians, God has given *the ministry of reconciliation*, the work of presenting to God's enemies the opportunity to be reconciled to God.

## D. MESSAGE OF NEWNESS (v. 19)

**19. . . . that God was reconciling the world to himself in Christ, not counting men's sins against them. And he has committed to us the message of reconciliation.**

This is the *message* that was and still is delivered to the sinners of the world: because Jesus took to himself the punishment that was due sinners, God can forgive the sinners, no longer holding them accountable for the wrongs they have done. Thus he reconciles to himself the sinners who have been his enemies (Romans 3:24, 25; Colossians 1:19, 20). God *committed* that message to Paul and other preachers to be delivered to sinners, and Christians are delivering it yet today.

## E. MESSENGERS OF NEWNESS (v. 20)

**20. We are therefore Christ's ambassadors, as though God were making his appeal through us. We implore you on Christ's behalf: Be reconciled to God.**

Because God committed to Paul and other preachers the message of reconciliation and newness, those preachers have become his *ambassadors*, his representatives, his spokesmen to all the sinners of the world (also Ephesians 6:20). Speaking for Christ, they said and still are saying to sinners, *be reconciled to God*.

This makes it very plain that each sinner decides whether he or she will be reconciled to God or not. God is eager to forgive, and thereby to justify and reconcile; but a sinner can choose to remain unforgiven.

### AN UNLIKELY ROLE

Sergio Gutierrez is a Roman Catholic priest in Mexico, but he is better known for his unlikely role as a professional wrestler. Gutierrez-the-priest is also "Fray Tormenta," who has a passionate following among wrestling fans in his country. His two roles in life are incongruous, and many people come to his matches just to see if he will actually fight.

Others come to give him money for use in another role that Gutierrez has: running an orphanage near Mexico City. The eighty-plus orphans who live there rely almost totally on his wrestling earnings for their physical needs. Many were rescued from among the thousands of parentless children roaming the streets of Mexico City. "Fray Tormenta" is more than an entertainer or sports figure; he sees himself

### WHAT DO YOU THINK?

What is "new" for you as a Christian? What change in your life are you most grateful for?

### WHAT DO YOU THINK?

To what extent do you share the "message of reconciliation"? Why?

*If any man be in Christ, he is a new creature: old things are passed away; behold, all things are become new.*

2 Corinthians 5:17

*Use this visual to ask your learners how their "newness" in Christ is real right now.*

PRAYER

*We do love you, Father, and we love our brothers and sisters in your family. We treasure the companionship, the joy, the learning, the help, and the encouragement that we find in our association with the church.*

*Help us to make our witness for the church reflect the benefits we receive—even the benefit of eternal life. May we guard the worthy reputation that Christ has given us. In his name, amen.*

THOUGHT TO REMEMBER

*"Live down" your past by "living up" to God's Word.*

as an ambassador who shows Christ's love and reconciliation to children who might otherwise never experience it. (Even after a wrestling victory, "Fray Tormenta" goes to his knees to ask forgiveness for any "overenthusiastic" holds that he may have used in the match!)

In the person of Jesus, God came to earth in an unlikely role—one diametrically opposed to who he really was. The sinless Son of God became sin personified so that we who have been "orphaned" by sin could be reconciled to God and experience his love and care. Some who knew Jesus in the flesh were scandalized by the idea that a man could also be God (or vice versa). But scandal or not, the dual roles Jesus played have become the means of salvation for us all.     —C. R. B.

## F. METHOD OF NEWNESS (v. 21)

**21. God made him who had no sin to be sin for us, so that in him we might become the righteousness of God.**

All are sinners (Romans 3:23). God wants to make us into new creatures (2 Corinthians 5:17). How does he go about it? First, he sent his Son to be one of us, but without *sin* (Hebrews 4:15; 1 Peter 2:22). Second, God laid the penalty for our sins on that guiltless one (Isaiah 53:6; Galatians 3:13). Since the penalty for our guilt is gone, we can have God's *righteousness* as our own, if we want it (1 Corinthians 1:30; Philippians 3:9).

Of course we are not interested in that offer unless we believe it to be genuine, unless we believe that Jesus really did die for our sins, and that we really can be (and need to be) forgiven. Even if we believe in Jesus the Savior, God will not make us new if we prefer to go on sinning—we must repent. When we repent and are baptized (Acts 2:38), then we are new creatures. We have died to sin and have risen to walk in newness of life (Romans 6:3, 4).

Then it must be our intent to be free from sin throughout our lives. But sometimes we fail to live up to our intention. Every Christian can sin. The apostle Paul did (Romans 7:19-25), and not many of us are better than he! But we can praise God for his continuing forgiveness (1 John 1:9).

## CONCLUSION

From my long-ago youth I remember my first date with Louise. Her mother was a charming and vivacious lady. With almost no help from me, she kept up a sparkling conversation while Louise went upstairs for her coat. As we were leaving, her mother gave her daughter a quick hug and said, "Now don't forget who you are."

That instruction intrigued me. As we drove away I asked Louise, "Who are you?"

"I'm a Hampton," she said with a smile. "I guess you might call Mom a snob. She thinks everybody named Hampton is super-good."

"And your mom was afraid I might get you into something dishonorable?"

"No, not you. Somebody else at the party, maybe. When I asked her about dating you, she said, 'Sure, Honey. I know his mother and father.' So I guess I'm not the only one with a proud family name to live up to."

It's important to have an honorable family name, isn't it? And it's good to add honor to that name by what we do. This is especially true for those of us in "the family of God" (cf. Mark 3:35).

Christians are privileged to have both eternal life and the chance to offer that privilege to others. But the example we set is important to the credibility of our message. The way we "live down" a sinful past is to "live up" to the high standards of being a new creature in Christ. Are you making progress in this regard?

# Discovery Learning

*This page contains an alternative lesson plan emphasizing learning activities. Classes desiring such student involvement will find these suggestions helpful. The next page is a reproducible activity page to further enhance discovery learning.*

## LEARNING GOALS

After this lesson each student will be able to:

1. Summarize the message of the "ministry of reconciliation" that Paul describes in the text.

2. Note specific evidence for the need of this ministry in his or her own community.

3. Suggest one specific way he or she can participate in this ministry of reconciliation in the coming week.

## INTO THE LESSON

*Option #1:* Write the words "New Beginnings" on the board. Say, "We often experience new beginnings in life, such as in a new job. What other 'new beginnings' do people experience?" Examples include new homes, remarriages, new locations, new cars. After compiling the list, tell the class, "The greatest new beginning one can enjoy is revealed in today's Scripture. However, with this new beginning comes a new responsibility."

*Option #2:* Distribute copies of the reproducible activity "A New Creation" from page 112. Allow about five minutes for students to complete the activity.

*Option #3:* Write the word "Ambassador" on the board. Ask, "What does an ambassador to other countries do?" Then ask, "To which country would you enjoy being an ambassador? Why?" Ask members to share answers with two others. Make the transition to Bible study by saying, "Christians have been called to be ambassadors. Today we'll discover why, where, and what we are to do as ambassadors."

## INTO THE WORD

Begin the Bible study with a brief lecture based on the Lesson Background notes on Corinth. Prepare a visual with the following words to be used as an outline.

*Corinth—korinthiazesthai*

*Aphrodite*

*1st Letter to Church at Corinth*

*2nd Letter to Church at Corinth*

Prepare a handout titled "Reconciled and Reconciling!" and include the following questions. Give the handout to teams of no more than five people.

1. Underline 2 Corinthians 5:17. Discuss what Paul means when he says old things are passed away and all things are become new.

2. Clarify Paul's statement when he uses the phrases *out of our mind* and *in our right mind* (v. 13).

3. Discuss and explain "the righteousness of God" in verse 21. What is it? Why are we to become the righteousness of God?

4. Paul assumes that our reconciliation with God leads to reconciliation with one another. Review today's text and find clues as to why he affirms this should happen.

5. How would you define a ministry of reconciliation? What is its purpose? What should we be doing?

6. How do the teachings of verse 16 help us keep our focus in this ministry?

Encourage teams to work quickly. After they are finished, ask team leaders to review their conclusions. If you have large numbers of teams, form clusters of three teams to share their conclusions with each other.

## INTO LIFE

*Use as many of the following activities as time allows.*

*Activity #1:* Note that Paul calls us "ambassadors" (v. 20). Ask the class to brainstorm the characteristics and mission of a Christian ambassador. They should list these under a column headed "Christian Ambassadors."

*Activity #2:* Remind the class that Paul also calls believers to a ministry of reconciliation. Ask the class how this ministry and the concept of a Christian ambassador are related. Why does Paul include both? Make a second column on the board. Ask the class to brainstorm a list of the needs for a ministry of reconciliation in your community and ways to help in this ministry.

*Activity #3:* Distribute copies of the reproducible activity "A New Righteousness" from page 112. This activity will help learners make personal application of the text.

*Activity #4:* Before class, prepare a Thanksgiving card to God for each class member. Use a standard letter-size sheet of paper, folded once. On the front cover print the words "My Thanksgiving Card to God." You may include a simple piece of thanksgiving artwork.

On the left inside page, print the words, "Lord, in my community I am especially thankful for. . . ." Ask class members to list things in their community for which they are grateful. This may include such matters as values, opportunities, places, and relationships.

On the second inside page, print the words, "Lord, in order to be an ambassador of reconciliation I will. . . ." Ask class members to respond by writing at least one thing they intend to do to complete this commitment. Also include a signature line at the bottom of this page.

# A New Creation

Today's text reminds us that we are a new creation. Newness implies change. In the left column, list a few illustrations of life activities that may have been included in the old, sinful life. In the right column, list illustrations of the believer's new life. The words you select are to include one of the letters of the word *creation*.

| THE OLD CREATURE | A NEW CREATION |
|:---:|:---:|
| C | C |
| R | R |
| E | E |
| A | Ambassador for Christ |
| T | T |
| I | I |
| PORNOGRAPHY | O |
| N | N |

# A New Righteousness

Second Corinthians 5:21, the last verse of our text, tells us that "God made him who had no sin to be sin for us, so that in him we might become the righteousness of God." To appreciate this wonderful blessing, complete the following:

1. What does Isaiah 64:6 teach you about earning "righteousness"?

2. Read Romans 3:21-24. What does this passage teach you about how to obtain righteousness?

3. Now, reread the last verse of our text, 2 Corinthians 5:21. In light of the passages you have just studied, how do you apply this text? What new understanding and appreciation do you have about the phrase *righteousness of God*?

# A NEW RELATIONSHIP

**LESSON 13**

## WHY TEACH THIS LESSON?

In late 1989 the world began to witness an amazing spectacle as the infamous Berlin Wall was opened and eventually torn down. Since 1961 that wall had artificially divided a people who were in reality one in language and in culture. Those of us who watched on TV from thousands of miles away couldn't help but share the joy of those who were actually there. In reality a figurative wall had collapsed along with the physical wall as a divided people became one again.

Sometimes relationships cannot begin (or cannot be renewed) until a wall first comes down. As God has torn down the wall of sin between him and us, so he expects that there will be no walls to separate his people one from another. Yet even two thousand years after Christ started the church we still seem to have much to learn in this regard! Let today's lesson fill us with a renewed resolve that there be "No Walls!"

## INTRODUCTION

### A. VANISHING WALLS

The church in a certain hot-weather town was generous in giving its new preacher a vacation. "You may as well take the whole month of August," he was told. "The town practically closes down then. Half the people go to the mountains and the other half go to the beach. Those who are left just have Communion and Sunday school."

So when August came the preacher and his wife gratefully went back home to visit parents and old friends. When they again drove up to the parsonage at sunset on the last day of August, they saw that the long-vacant house across the street was now occupied. A younger man was mowing the lawn; a woman of comparable age was operating an edger along the walk. Instead of entering the parsonage, the preacher and his wife went across the street to get acquainted.

Quickly they learned that the newcomers were Jim and Jane Meyers, that Jim was the new custodian at the nearby school. He had been working overtime to get the place ready for classes, and he hoped never to see a hotter place to work!

To that wordy introduction the preacher responded, "I'm the minister of that church over there." He pointed with a wave of his hand toward the spire. "We hope to see you there on Sunday."

"I don't know about that." Jim's voice was morose, but there was a gleam of fun in his eye. "It can't be much of a church. We watched last Sunday. They didn't have even a handful of people."

"That won't be the case next Sunday," the preacher promised. "Come and see. Come to Sunday school at nine-thirty."

Jane spoke up then, with an edge to her voice. "Those people don't want us here. We've been here nearly a week, and not one of them has come near us."

"They don't know you're here," the preacher countered. "They don't live across the street. We do, and we came over as soon as we saw you. We want you in church. There's not one person in the congregation who doesn't want you here. Come and see."

DEVOTIONAL READING:
EPHESIANS 2:4-10
BACKGROUND SCRIPTURE:
EPHESIANS 2:11-21
PRINTED TEXT:
EPHESIANS 2:11-21

### LEARNING AIMS

After participating in this lesson, each student will be able to:

1. Describe the new relationship between Jews and Gentiles that made their differences unimportant in Ephesus.

2. Mention groups in today's church that are drawn together by a similar relationship.

3. Use his or her influence for unity and peace in the church.

### KEY VERSE

You are no longer foreigners and aliens, but fellow citizens with God's people and members of God's household. —Ephesians 2:19

Nov
28

The preacher and his wife soon went home, but they made some telephone calls before they unpacked their suitcases. Before darkness fell, two couples stopped to greet Jim and Jane, chat a little, and invite them to church.

Each evening that week, two or three more couples came over. Women stopped by while Jim was at work. They were eager to help Jane get settled in her new home. When Jim and Jane came to Sunday school at nine-thirty, they were greeted happily by friends. Never again did Jane suspect they were not wanted. The walls had come down.

### B. LESSON BACKGROUND

Jews of the first century often presented a strange contrast, almost a self-contradiction. Many became merchants as they scattered from their homeland in Palestine to all the countries around the Mediterranean Sea. Swiftly they learned the languages and business customs of the countries where they settled. As they made friends they also embraced some of the foreign cultural practices.

At the same time, the Jews fiercely maintained their Jewish identity. Many of them traveled long distances to attend the religious festivals at Jerusalem. They built synagogues so that they could worship separately in most of the cities where they lived.

These practices of the Jews occasionally caught the attention of others around them. In those days some pagans were losing faith in the imaginary gods of their ancestors. When they went to synagogue meetings they were welcomed, and many were attracted by the teaching about the one true God. Some were converted to the Jewish faith, becoming circumcised and taking the law of Moses as their own.

This was the situation when Paul (a Jew who became a Christian) arrived in Ephesus in about A.D. 53 to teach in the synagogue (Acts 19:8). Both Jews and Gentiles heard his message. When the hostility of some Jews drove him from the synagogue, he probably had even more Gentile listeners as he taught in another place (Acts 19:9, 10). Consequently both Jews and Gentiles became Christians. And when they became Christians, the wall between Jew and Gentile vanished.

Paul wrote a letter to the Ephesian church about five years later. In that letter he reaffirmed that Christians are new creatures (Ephesians 2:1-10). This is just as true of the Gentile Christians as it is of the Jewish Christians. The truth still stands: there is no longer a wall between them.

### I. FOREIGNERS (EPHESIANS 2:11-13)

In verses 8-10, just before our lesson text, Paul reminds the readers that they did not make themselves into new creatures. Rather, they are God's workmanship, "created in Christ Jesus to do good works." Paul has more to say about Christians as new creatures as our text begins.

### A. THAT WAS THEN (vv. 11, 12)

**11. Therefore, remember that formerly you who are Gentiles by birth and called "uncircumcised" by those who call themselves "the circumcision" (that done in the body by the hands of men)—**

Although the Ephesian church is a mixture of Jews and *Gentiles*, Paul specifically addresses the latter here. Two important thoughts loom before us. First, the verse refers to time past, meaning the time before the Ephesian Gentiles became Christians. Second, in that past time the Jews had been immensely proud to call themselves *the circumcision* and immensely scornful in calling the Gentiles *uncircumcised.*

But circumcision is only *in the body,* a physical thing administered *by* human *hands.* It does not in and of itself make any difference in the spirit (cf. 1 Corinthians 7:19; Galatians 5:6; 6:15; Colossians 2:11). What really counts with God is a circumcision of the heart (Romans 2:29). This has always been the case (Deuteronomy 10:16; 30:6; Jeremiah 4:4).

**12. . . . *remember that at that time you were separate from Christ, excluded from citizenship in Israel and foreigners to the covenants of the promise, without hope and without God in the world.***

*At that time,* meaning the time before they became Christians, the Gentiles now in the Ephesian church truly were alienated from God. Those Gentiles who previously attended the synagogue had had, at most, a tenuous connection with the commonwealth of *Israel* and the *covenants of the promise.* Even so, all the Gentiles in Ephesus had been *separate from Christ,* by whose blood some were later made near (v. 13, below).

What a hopeless existence that previous condition was! These Gentile Christians had worshiped many gods. Undoubtedly these included Artemis (also known as Diana; see Acts 19:28). Perhaps they also worshiped the gods Sarapis, Isis, Aphrodite, Zeus, and a dozen others. But even though they had worshiped all these gods, in truth they had been *without God in the world.*

## B. THIS IS NOW (v. 13)

**13. *But now in Christ Jesus you who once were far away have been brought near through the blood of Christ.***

But now things have changed! The Gentiles whom Paul addresses are *in Christ* —they are Christians. It is *the blood of Christ* that has bridged the gap. Paul has already stressed this in this letter (Ephesians 1:7) as he does in other letters (e.g., Colossians 1:20).

Only through Christ can people be *brought near* to God. In fact the Gentile Christians at Ephesus are now much nearer to him than are the devout non-Christian Jews who still rely solely on the covenants of promise that were made before Christ appeared. The Christian Gentiles now have the assurance of being God's people along with those Christian Jews who also acknowledge the blood of Christ as payment for their sins.

### CHRIST AND CULTURE: THE NECESSARY CHOICE

Before the 1917 Bolshevik Revolution brought atheistic Communism to Russia, the Orthodox Church was the state church and the keeper of Russian culture. With the coming of Communism, however, religion was suppressed and thousands of churches closed. The Orthodox Church was able to stay feebly alive by accommodating itself to the limitations that the Soviet state placed upon it. As a result, the church lost its power to influence the culture.

When Communism fell in 1989, Russian Orthodoxy again found freedom. With that freedom came a renewed closeness to Russian culture. But a new problem has since developed: the Orthodox Church now has gained so much power in its closeness with the current culture that other denominations and sects fear a revival of the repressive treatment of non-Orthodox Christians as in Czarist Russia of old.

How aghast Paul would be were he to see this situation! Notice how he speaks of Gentile Christians who had once been part of pagan culture, but now have turned from paganism to a close relationship with the living God. In so doing, they left behind the closeness they once had had with a pagan culture that was steeped in idolatry.

Paul commends this principle to us: the church is always faced with the task of distinguishing between what God wants and what our culture expects. Sometimes

*WHAT DO YOU THINK?*

*What groups are excluded from our church—not by command but in practice? How can we demonstrate the reconciliation that Christ offers?*

Ye are no more strangers and foreigners, but fellow citizens with the saints, and of the household of God. Ephesians 2:19

Visual for lesson 13. *Use this photograph to allow your learners to reflect on the ways that they were once "foreigners" and "aliens" to God.*

cultural expectations are radically opposed to God, and sometimes they are not. But the distinction between the two always must be made. If we fail to make this distinction, then how will we know how or when to make godly choices?—C. R. B.

## II. PEACEMAKER (EPHESIANS 2:14-18)

For centuries the Jews, proud of being God's people, had scorned the Gentiles, who did not share that privilege. For centuries the Gentiles had responded with enmity of their own, scorning the scorners. Now in the city of Ephesus some of the Jews are God's people in a different way: they have been born again.

They are new creatures. They are children of God in a way they had never been before. Some Gentiles also are born again—born anew in the same way. They, too, are new creatures. They, too, are children of God. All God's children are brothers and sisters. There is no room for scorn, no room for enmity.

### A. DESTRUCTION (vv. 14, 15a)

*14. For he himself is our peace, who has made the two one and has destroyed the barrier, the dividing wall of hostility,*

Sometimes peace comes about only when something is first *destroyed*. Christ is the one who is *our peace* (Micah 5:5) because he came to destroy the devil and his work (Hebrews 2:14; 1 John 3:8).

In bringing us peace with God in this way, Jesus performed another act of destruction at the same time when he broke down *the dividing wall of hostility* that had existed between Jew and Gentile for centuries (cf. 1 Corinthians 12:13). Jews are still Jews and Gentiles are still Gentiles in a biological sense, but now all Christians stand as equal before God (Galatians 3:28).

*15a. . . . by abolishing in his flesh the law with its commandments and regulations.*

As we saw in lesson 10, Jesus, in his Sermon on the Mount, said that his purpose was not to destroy the law, but to fulfill it (Matthew 5:17). Additional light is cast on that statement by Paul's comment that, "The law was put in charge to lead us to Christ that we might be justified by faith. Now that faith has come, we are no longer under the supervision of the law" (Galatians 3:24, 25). The law was thus to guide the Jews until they came to Christ.

But Jewish Christians are now no longer under the law (Romans 3:19-21). What Jesus did in his flesh served to destroy the enmity between God and sinner that had come about because people had broken that law. Thus Paul can speak of Christ's work as "having canceled the written code, with its regulations, that was against us and stood opposed to us" (Colossians 2:14).

### B. CONSTRUCTION (vv. 15b, 16)

*15b, 16. His purpose was to create in himself one new man out of the two, thus making peace, and in this one body to reconcile both of them to God through the cross, by which he put to death their hostility.*

Both Jews and Gentiles are sinners. Their sins make them enemies of God (Colossians 1:21). But because of the cross, reconciliation between God and all those created in his image is now possible.

All reconciled people form one body, one group. They are the family of God, for all of them were born again as his children. This is an important New Testament theme (Mark 3:35; 1 Corinthians 12:12-27; Ephesians 3:6; 4:4).

### C. INSTRUCTION (vv. 17, 18)

*17. He came and preached peace to you who were far away and peace to those who were near.*

## WHAT DO YOU THINK?

*If Christ has broken down the "dividing wall of hostility," why do so many people not want to be a part of the church? How do we reach people who do not care to be reconciled to God?*

## WHAT DO YOU THINK?

*Some people want to claim Jesus as Savior, but they want nothing to do with the church— his "body." How would you try to convince such a person that the church is important?*

Those *who were far away* are the Gentiles, while *those who were near* are the Jews. The message of Jesus to both groups (in other words, to everyone) is that peace with God is now possible. See also Isaiah 57:19.

**18. For through him we both have access to the Father by one Spirit.**

Jesus said, "I am the way and the truth and the life. No one comes to the Father except through me" (John 14:6). It is through him and him alone that all Jews and Gentiles in the world can *have access to the Father.* If we choose this path, God's Holy *Spirit* leads us every step of the way. We must allow ourselves to be led by the Spirit in all things (Romans 8:14; Galatians 5:18).

## III. TEMPLE (EPHESIANS 2:19-21)

If the body of each Christian may be called a temple where the Spirit dwells (1 Corinthians 6:19), how much more may the church—the whole assembly of Spirit-filled Christians—be described as a temple where the Spirit dwells! All the "little temples" like you and me are brought together in one holy and magnificent edifice. That is the grand thought that climaxes and completes our text today.

### A. ONE HOUSEHOLD (v. 19)

**19. Consequently, you are no longer foreigners and aliens, but fellow citizens with God's people and members of God's household,**

In times past the Gentiles had been *foreigners and aliens,* left out of all the gracious providence of God for his special *people.* That was the thought that began our text (vv. 11, 12), but the status of pagan Gentiles changed when they became Christians.

Taking the one true God as their King, they have been naturalized into his kingdom and have become *fellow citizens* with the saints. They are born again and are *members of God's household,* his family. They are brothers and sisters of the Jewish believers who have been reborn in the same way. Elsewhere Paul describes Gentile believers as branches of a wild olive tree that have been grafted in among the branches of a cultivated tree (Romans 11:17).

### B. ONE FOUNDATION (v. 20)

**20. . . . built on the foundation of the apostles and prophets, with Christ Jesus himself as the chief cornerstone.**

Modern builders have learned to leave a hole in a wall so a cornerstone can be inserted during a ceremony when the building is completed. But in ancient times the building began with the cornerstone. That stone was squared precisely and laid in exactly the right place. Then the other foundation stones were lined up with it, and the stones of the walls were placed on the foundation.

In the church *Christ* is *the chief cornerstone* (Isaiah 28:16; 1 Corinthians 3:11; 1 Peter 2:6). He is exactly right in every respect. Inspired by the Holy Spirit, the apostles and prophets took positions that lined up precisely with Christ (Matthew 16:18; Revelation 21:14). Church leaders of every age must resist the temptation to follow their own fancies. They must build securely *on the* one true foundation. The consequences of doing otherwise are dire indeed (cf. Matthew 7:24-27).

### CORNERSTONES AND TIME CAPSULES

Cornerstones have fallen on hard times. As our lesson writer tells us today, at one time the cornerstone was the most important stone in the building, since it was the basis for all that was built upon and around it. In recent times their primary uses have been ceremonial, informative, and, on occasion, as receptacles for time capsules.

**WHAT DO YOU THINK?**

If the church's message is one of peace, then what happens to the church's witness and credibility when church members fight and quarrel with one another? How can we prevent internal differences of opinion from destroying our church's witness?

**HOW TO SAY IT**

Aphrodite. Af-ruh-DITE-ee.
Artemis. AR-teh-miss.
Bolshevik. BOL-shuh-vik.
Colossians. Kuh-LOSH-unz.
Corinthians. Ko-RIN-thee-unz
　(th *as in* thin).
Czarist. TSAR-ist.
Deuteronomy. Due-ter-AHN-uh-
　me.
Ephesians. Ee-FEE-zhunz.
Ephesus. EF-uh-sus.
Galatians. Guh-LAY-shunz.
Gentiles. JEN-tiles.
Hebrews. HEE-brews.
Isaiah. Eye-ZAY-uh.
Isis. EYE-sis.
Jeremiah. Jair-uh-MY-uh.
Micah. MY-kuh.
Sarapis. Suh-RAP-is.
synagogue. SIN-uh-gog.
Zeus. Zoose.

## PRAYER

*Our Father, thank you for your church that unites your people in happy fellowship and earnest work and cordial love. May we nobly do our part to increase and improve it. In Jesus' name, amen.*

Yet even the latter use has declined. As a result many time capsules have been lost. Back in the 1970s, a time capsule was buried in Fillmore, California, to preserve the memory of the culture of that decade. Now no one can remember exactly where or even when it was buried.

In 1986 an attempt was made in Los Angeles to retrieve seventeen time capsules from the 1930s. Concrete was dug up all around the Civic Center, but not a single one was found. The International Time Capsule Society reports that most of the world's ten thousand or so time capsules have been lost, and with them much valuable information.

Christ is the cornerstone of the church, and the New Testament is the "time capsule" that helps us to remember him. If we ignore the reminder of his role that the New Testament provides for us, or if we attempt to build the church without regard for the fundamental place Christ and his teachings should have in it, then we will have lost an essential tie with the past. In that case the church will neither be square with the truth nor stand tall against falsehood and heresy.    —C. R. B.

### C. ONE BUILDING (v. 21)

**21. In him the whole building is joined together and rises to become a holy temple in the Lord.**

Let every church leader take note of what the two words *joined together* imply. Those who would build the church in a spiritual sense must take care not only to build securely on the right foundation, but also to build well with "materials" that will stand the test of time (1 Corinthians 3:10-15).

Consequently, let no one be enrolled in the church until he or she is a real Christian, truly born again, a genuine brother or sister of other Christians. However, let us not expect newborn Christians to be mature Christians. Everyone knows that newborn babies need special care. If you have any newborn Christians in your congregation, don't let them die of neglect (Ephesians 4:15, 16).

## WHAT DO YOU THINK?

*What is your role in building God's "holy temple"? How did you decide this role was what God wanted you to do?*

### CONCLUSION

In the twenty-first century, not many churches have both Jews and Gentiles in their membership. But every church has different kinds of people. Churches need to plan their evangelism to reach all peoples, not just "targeted demographics." Every church needs to plan carefully so that no one is left out or left behind.

For example, every growing church has old-timers and newcomers. This was considered briefly in the Introduction of this lesson. Blessed is the church where the newcomers are neither too hasty nor too slow about finding their places of service! And blessed is the church where the old-timers are neither too hasty nor too slow in helping them find those places!

We may also pause to consider the relationship between the young(er) and old(er) members of the church. The work of the church is very impressive in providing Christian education that is nicely adapted to learners of all ages. Allied with the Sunday school in many churches are graded youth programs. The Sunday school is for teaching, some educators say, and the youth groups are for learning by experience. With wise adult counselors to guide, young people meet with those their own age to discuss and debate questions of Christian doctrine or Christian living. Still with wise adult counselors, they carry out Christian service projects. From the "oldest" youth group, young adults move easily and capably into the adult life of the church.

## THOUGHT TO REMEMBER

*Cherish the unity of the church*

*—and work to maintain it.*

Today many churches have more than one service on Sunday morning to appeal to differing worship styles and preferences. It is good to serve and be served as well as possible, but in so doing let care be taken to preserve the unity of the church as a holy temple in the Lord.

# Discovery Learning

*This page contains an alternative lesson plan emphasizing learning activities. Classes desiring such student involvement will find these suggestions helpful. The next page is a reproducible activity page to further enhance discovery learning.*

## LEARNING GOALS

After this lesson, each student will be able to:

1. Describe the new relationship between Jews and Gentiles that made their differences unimportant in Ephesus.

2. Mention groups in today's church that are drawn together by a similar relationship.

3. Use his or her influence for unity and peace in the church.

## INTO THE LESSON

Set up the classroom with physical barriers between chairs. Cluster small groups of chairs facing you with barriers made of cardboard, tables on their sides, and blankets over sawhorses. After the class is seated in these clusters, say, "The church often has barriers between its people. These barriers keep us from knowing each other well and keep us from working together. They may breed hostility, jealousy, or anger."

Ask the class to name barriers between people that churches experience. Examples include disabilities, race, economic status, age, traditions. As the students name these, affirm their answers as you remove the barriers you had built. Example: "Yes, newcomers often have a hard time adjusting to a new church setting. The church must work to understand and respond to their needs."

Make the transition to Bible study by saying, "The problem of barriers that separate Christians is not a new one. It was a problem in the first days of the church. Fortunately, God gives us some powerful teaching about how to overcome this problem."

## INTO THE WORD

Display a picture or diagram of Herod's temple. If neither is available, simply describe the temple and its four walled courts, each more exclusive than the one outside it. The outer court, Court of the Gentiles, was as far as non-Jews were allowed, even if they believed in God. Inner courts included the Court of Women, as far as female Jews were allowed. Then there was the Court of Israel, available to Jewish men only, and the Court of Priests. Point out the divisive nature of these courts. In Jewish history and in the New Testament church, a very real racial barrier caused division and needed healing.

Hand out copies of today's printed text. Explain the lesson background, and then read the text. Ask students to review verses 11-13 and underline every divisive word or phrase they find. Let a "scribe" write the findings on a poster with a heading, "Division and Tension." Use the commentary to explain the following terms as students cite them: "foreigners to the covenants" (v. 12) and "far away have been brought near" (v. 13).

After this list is complete, remind the class that the early church had a problem accepting Gentile Christians. God used powerful lessons to teach that, in spite of backgrounds, nationality, and gender, we are all united in Christ's body.

Then ask the class to review verses 14-21 and circle terms that indicate the unity that believers are to enjoy. After a few minutes, ask class members to share their findings. While they do, have a "scribe" write the responses on another poster board with a heading, "The Church United." As in the previous exercise, you may need to explain a few terms or phrases such as "create in himself one new man out of the two" (v. 15) and "reconcile" (v. 16).

## INTO LIFE

*Activity #1:* Remind the class of the opening discussion about barriers that divide the church. Recall these and list them on a marker board.

*Activity #2: Small Groups:* Give the following instructions, poster board, and marking pens to groups of four to six people.

Group 1: Discuss and list why practicing unity with fellow believers and breaking down barriers to that unity is important to the church today.

Group 2: Name things or values that bind a church together in spite of barriers or differences that stand between us. List these on the poster board provided.

Group 3: Select one or two barriers to Christian unity in your congregation and offer ways to break them down so the church can stand united. List your suggestions on your poster board.

*Option, Group 3:* Work together to complete the activities on the reproducible page that follows.

Encourage groups to work quickly. Allow each group to report their findings.

*Activity #3:* Give each class member an index card. State: "Identify a believer that has a different background (racial, economic, a church newcomer, etc.) and make a commitment to get acquainted with that person. Write that person's name on the index card and two ways your goal can be achieved."

# Building Unity in Christ's Church

Today's text challenges believers to resolve differences for the sake of Christian unity. Described below are a few situations that may mirror a challenge in your own church. Offer a few suggestions on how to build unity in each of the situations described.

## NEWCOMERS LEAVING

A church of about 200 has visitors nearly every Sunday. However, a large percentage of these newcomers are not staying at the church. They seem to visit a few weeks, then leave and join other churches. What steps could this congregation take to help each newcomer become a valuable part of this congregation?

## A RACIAL BARRIER OR A RACIAL OPPORTUNITY

This rural church of about 125 is primarily composed of white and middle-class farming families. A new family moved to town, opening a pharmacy. They have begun to attend church regularly. The husband is from Taiwan and the wife comes from mainland China. She is a Christian, and he is still studying the Bible and exploring Christianity. What are some ways you might suggest to help break down cultural and racial barriers that may prevent this new couple from feeling at home in this new church?

## A CHURCH DIVIDED ABOUT DIVIDING

A congregation of about 1,500 has decided to send about one-third of its membership to start another suburban congregation. Some church members are very upset about this decision. What are some ways to help these members accept this decision and contribute in meaningful ways to make this plan successful?

## UNDERSTANDING UNITY—SCRIPTURALLY

Many Scriptures highlight the importance of the church standing united. Use a Bible concordance to identify a few of these. Words to look up may include *church*, *unity*, *united*, *outsiders*, *peace*, and *peacemakers*. Jot the emphases of some of these verses below.

## CELEBRATING UNITY—MUSICALLY

Write lines of hymns or choruses that teach church unity or celebrate our oneness in Christ. Let these tunes flow through your mind as you enjoy this exercise.

# Winter Quarter, 2004–2005

## *Called to Be God's People*

### Special Features

### Lessons

#### Unit 1: God Calls a People

#### Unit 2: Jesus Calls His Followers

#### Unit 3: Whosoever Will—Come!

## About These Lessons

When the telephone rings at dinnertime, we often assume it's just a telemarketer calling. But we dare not jump to such an indifferent conclusion when God calls to us from the pages of his Word! God will be calling you to greater service in his kingdom through the lessons of this quarter. As you study, will you "pick up" or merely "let the machine get it"?

Dec 5

Dec 12

Dec 19

Dec 26

Jan 2

Jan 9

Jan 16

Jan 23

Jan 30

Feb 6

Feb 13

Feb 20

Feb 27

# The Caller

*by Thomas D. Thurman*

When I was a high school boy, I got a job one summer working for the Louisville and Nashville Railroad. My duties were few and simple. I worked the graveyard shift, and when a particular train was to leave on a run, I had to locate the engineer and the fireman and inform them of the schedule.

The railroad yards were just across the street from a couple of cheap hotels where many of the railroad men slept while waiting to be called. On the corner near the hotels was a little all-night restaurant, and there, in that restaurant, I spent my working hours. When men were to be called, I was notified by phone, left the restaurant for a few minutes, located and informed them of the situation, and returned to the restaurant. It was really a plush job for a high school boy.

I wore the glamorous title of "calling boy." Well, maybe it wasn't so glamorous, but it was certainly accurate. It described the exact nature of my work—I called people.

So does God. I suppose we could give him the title, "The Calling God," but I prefer just "The Caller."

From the beginning of time, God has been calling people. He began to do so in the Garden of Eden. After Eve had eaten of the forbidden fruit and given it to Adam, they "heard the sound of the Lord God as he was walking in the garden in the cool of the day." He "called to the man, 'Where are you?'" (Genesis 3:8, 9).

Thus began God's role as The Caller, a role seen in both the Old and New Testaments. A classic example is the case of Elijah the prophet. "What are you doing here, Elijah?" God asked his despondent prophet, who had taken up residence in a cave in Mount Horeb (1 Kings 19:9).

Elijah had been waiting for just such an opening, and he lost not a minute in pouring out his complaints to God. "I have been very zealous for the Lord God Almighty. The Israelites have rejected your covenant, broken down your altars, and put your prophets to death with the sword. I am the only one left, and now they are trying to kill me too" (1 Kings 19:10).

In effect, Elijah was saying, "I've had it, Lord. I'm tired and weary, despondent and discouraged. I'm ready to quit."

Having listened patiently to Elijah's gripes, God spoke up and said, "Go out and stand on the mountain in the presence of the Lord" (1 Kings 19:11). When the prophet obeyed, "a great and powerful wind tore the mountains apart and shattered the rocks before the Lord, but the Lord was not in the wind. After the wind there was an earthquake, but the Lord was not in the earthquake. After the earthquake came a fire, but the Lord was not in the fire. And after the fire came a gentle whisper" (1 Kings 19:11, 12). God was in that gentle whisper.

Perhaps you will hear God's voice through the pages of Scripture this quarter as we learn the meaning of being "Called to Be God's People." This theme will tie our thirteen lessons together. It is a theme that must be kept before the class throughout the quarter if your learners are to keep the "big picture" about what it is that we're trying to accomplish. During this time we will examine several situations where The Caller spoke to his people.

## GOD CALLS A PEOPLE

Our unit of lessons for December offers us four examples of how God called people to help him bring about his magnificent and long-range plan of redemption. **Lesson 1** concerns God's call to Abram: "Leave your country, your people and your father's household and go to the land I will show you" (Genesis 12:1). That seventy-five-year-old man obeyed! His faithful response to a call must resonate with us today.

In **Lesson 2** we will journey with the prophet Samuel to Bethlehem. There we will hear The Caller say concerning Jesse's youngest son, David, "rise and anoint him; he is the one" (1 Samuel 16:12). In this anointing of a future king, Samuel learns that God considers inner qualities to be more important than outward appearance. This is a lesson that those of us who live in a mass-media-driven culture need to learn and relearn.

For **Lesson 3** we'll examine again the thrilling account of God's call to the earthly stepfather of Jesus: "Joseph son of David, do not be afraid to take Mary home as your life, because what is conceived in her is from the Holy Spirit" (Matthew 1:20). This lesson will challenge us to consider how unexpected circumstances often present a possibility for responding to God in trust.

**Lesson 4** will be about an old man named Simeon. God had communicated "that he would not die before he had seen the Lord's Christ" (Luke 2:26). We also will meet an elderly woman named Anna, who "spoke about the child to all who were looking forward to the redemption of Jerusalem" (Luke 2:38). We will celebrate with these two the hope that Christ's birth brought to the world.

## JESUS CALLS HIS FOLLOWERS

JANUARY

The five lessons for January are from the Gospel of Mark. In **Lesson 5** we'll hear Jesus' call to Simon and Andrew (and a similar call to James and John), "'Come, follow me,' Jesus said, 'and I will make you fishers of men'" (Mark 1:17). As the early disciples were challenged to spread the good news, so shall we be.

**Lesson 6** introduces us to the tax collector Levi (Matthew) and Jesus' call to him to "Follow me" (Mark 2:14). This lesson will challenge us to identify ways that we can reach out to people whom others may think are "unacceptable" in some way.

**Lesson 7** allows us to witness the call of Jesus to twelve of his disciples to "be with him," and to be available so "that he might send them out to preach" (Mark 3:14). Their call is, in a sense, our call as well. As we consider our call, we shall also identify our own ministry roles in the church and how Jesus equips us to serve.

The final two studies for January are **Lessons 8 and 9.** These will allow us to examine some important considerations in our response to Jesus' call. In Lesson 8 we'll hear Jesus say, "If anyone would come after me, he must deny himself and take up his cross and follow me" (Mark 8:34). This is a call to total commitment. In Lesson 9 we'll learn of the necessity to be ministers and servants in imitation of his example. In so doing we will learn to avoid reaching for "greatness" as culture defines that idea.

## WHOSOEVER WILL—COME!

FEBRUARY

The four lessons for February will acquaint us with individuals who had to overcome personal obstacles in order to answer God's call. We look first to the ancient story of Ruth in **Lesson 10.** In the midst of personal loss and tragedy, Ruth reached out to support her mother-in-law, whose own loss was greater still. God still calls his people to have the faith and commitment of Ruth.

**Lesson 11** comes from 2 Kings 5. There we will see a prideful man known as Naaman seeking a cure for a skin disease. To find healing for his disease, this non-Jew had to overcome his pride in following the command of God's prophet. Our exploration of this man's situation will remind us of the dangers of pride. Our walk with God is in jeopardy if we let pride dominate our thoughts and dictate our actions.

Nicodemus, Jesus' nighttime visitor, will be the subject of **Lesson 12.** Our study will focus upon this man's need to reevaluate his thinking regarding the requirements for admission to the kingdom of God. Once again we'll hear Jesus' famous words, "No one can see the kingdom of God unless he is born again" (John 3:3). What joy for those who indeed have been born again!

**Lesson 13** concludes both the unit and the quarter. This will be a study of Jesus' encounter with the woman of Samaria to whom he testified, "God is spirit, and his worshipers must worship in spirit and in truth" (John 4:24). Jesus had to overcome more than one barrier to reach this person. His example calls us to identify barriers that bias and prejudice create today and to consider ways to break down those barriers.

## THE CALLER, THE CALLED, AND THE CALLING

*ANSWER THE CALL!*

Remember, The Caller is still active today as he invites men and women to come out of the world and into his kingdom. To answer that call is vital! Eternal destinies depend on it.

But while we anticipate eternity with the Master, we must remember that God calls us to serve in the here and now. Like Timothy, Christ calls us to a holy life (2 Timothy 1:9). Like those at Corinth, we are "called . . . to live in peace" (1 Corinthians 7:15). Like those in Galatia, we are "called to be free" (Galatians 5:13). As we meet these challenges, may we "live a life worthy of the calling [we] have received" (Ephesians 4:1). Expect God's rich blessings as you and your learners embrace your calling through this quarter's studies!

# Jesus Calls Us

To Follow in Faith . . . like Abraham

To Lead with Integrity . . . like David

To Respond with Grace . . . like Joseph

To Hope in Christ . . . like Simeon

To Fish for Men . . . like the Disciples

To Repent from Sin . . . like Matthew

To Tell Good News . . . like the Twelve

To Give 100% . . . like Jesus

To Become as a Child . . . like the Disciples

To Overcome Grief . . . like Ruth

To Overcome Pride . . . like Naaman

To Overcome Doubt . . . like Nicodemus

To Overcome Prejudice . . . like the Samaritan Woman

# CALLED TO FOLLOW IN FAITH

## WHY TEACH THIS LESSON?

As preparations were being made for the war with Iraq in 2003, some friends of mine were to be part of the effort. They were preparing to go forth to war—either to Iraq itself or as support in some other area. Some of them did not know exactly where they would be going or when they would leave. They just knew their government had called them to serve, and they were ready at a moment's notice to go to places unknown for a task not fully understood.

As servants of God we are really soldiers in his army. We are called to be ready at all times to go to any place our Commander in Chief may lead us. We are not told what the full extent of following is at the start. What we are called to do is to follow by faith. In our text today Abram exemplifies such an attitude of faithful following. But not only does Abram serve as an example, he leads his family in this journey of faith as well. And the family willingly follows.

As you study and prepare this lesson today, allow it to challenge your life of faithful following of Christ.

## INTRODUCTION

### A. THE TENSIONS OF TRAVEL

The questions most frequently heard on an extended family trip in an automobile are probably the following: "How much longer?" "Are we there yet?" "Do you know where you are going?" "Are we lost?" "How long till we reach a rest area?" "When can we eat?" Such questions demonstrate the personality traits of impatience, a lack of trust in the driver's navigational abilities, and a compulsion to meet physical needs or wants.

When my daughter arranged a vacation trip for her family, she planned so that such tensions would be minimized. This involved researching and securing the best prices for airlines, car rentals, and motels. Upon their return it was announced that everything had gone just as it had been planned, without tensions or adjustments. In one sense this demonstrates what Jesus said about planning and counting the cost before undertaking a project (Luke 14:28).

The lesson for today tells of a different type of journey, a trip to an unknown destination. In a sense it demonstrates a tension with the well-planned trip described above. At times it is essential to organize carefully. But advance planning can go only so far. Certain tasks, however, involve the unexpected and the unknown by their very nature. Trust in God is required to secure the outcomes God has intended.

### B. LESSON BACKGROUND

The early chapters of the Book of Genesis move quickly from creation to an emphasis on events that involve *all humanity*: the making of the first man and

DEVOTIONAL READING:
*JEREMIAH 1:4-10*
BACKGROUND SCRIPTURE:
*GENESIS 11:27–12:9*
PRINTED TEXT:
*GENESIS 11:27–12:9*

### LESSON AIMS

After participating in this lesson, each student will be able to:

1. Describe the historical situations of Abram as he and his family obeyed the call of God to leave Ur and then Haran.

2. Evaluate the faith of Abram through his positive responses to God's call to venture into the unknown.

3. Make changes personally in order to conform to the call of God as given in his Word.

### KEY VERSE

The LORD had said to Abram, "Leave your country, your people and your father's household and go to the land I will show you."
—Genesis 12:1

woman, the consequences of sin that culminate in the flood, an explanation for the many languages, and how all this led to the formation of nations.

The lesson text for today is transitional in Genesis, for it marks the beginning of God's working with selected *individuals*. God's ultimate purpose is the redemption of every tribe, tongue, and nation, but this is made possible through a selective process that begins with Abram.

Abram (later called Abraham) is one of the heroes of the faith. His name is mentioned about three hundred times in the Bible, in twenty-seven of the sixty-six books. There are more verses about him in the New Testament's "faith chapter" than any other person listed there (Hebrews 11:8-19, or twelve verses). The apostle Paul says that Abraham is the father of all who have a genuine faith (Romans 4:16). He is the first person in Scripture of whom it is said that he "believed the Lord" (Genesis 15:6).

The lesson for today gives the beginnings of Abram's journey of faith. Biblical data reveal that it was about 2091 B.C. when he entered the land of Canaan.

## I. PEOPLE OF ABRAM (GENESIS 11:27-32)

The verse previous to the beginning of our text concludes a genealogical listing that begins with Shem, Noah's son, in Genesis 11:10. This grouping ends by noting Terah, Abram's father.

### A. DESIGNATING THE MEN (vv. 27, 28)

**27. This is the account of Terah.**
**Terah became the father of Abram, Nahor and Haran. And Haran became the father of Lot.**

Terah, in addition to being *the father of Abram,* is usually remembered for a statement that Joshua made about him as being one of Israel's ancestors who worshiped other gods on the other side of the Euphrates River (Joshua 24:2). Some attempt to soften this statement by citing Genesis 31:53, which states that the God of Abram and *Nahor* was also "the God of their father" Terah. It is then suggested that Terah's departure from the land of Ur was his break with idolatry.

#### GENEALOGY

In his book *Midnight in the Garden of Good and Evil,* author John Berendt contrasts three Georgia cities. He says that a newcomer to Atlanta is always asked about his business. A newcomer to Macon is asked where he goes to church. A newcomer to Augusta is asked, "What was your grandmother's maiden name?" This reveals a concern for ancestry.

Why are we told the name of Lot's father and the name of his grandfather? Why are we told where Abram (Abraham) was born? It is to convey to us that these are real persons. They are not just names from a book or characters in a story.

We can relate to Abram because we share many of his experiences. Like Abram, many of us have moved to a strange place or have dealt with the sorrow of being childless. Like Abram, we have had domestic difficulties, faced danger, and been tempted to lie.

If Abram was like us in so many ways, then we can be like him in return. We can have the same unquestioning obedience. We can have the same stubborn faith. Three times in Hebrews 11 the writer begins a reference to this man with the words "by faith." Truly he is "the father of the faithful"! Being his spiritual descendants means that we walk by faith, not by sight. —R. C. S.

Visual for lesson 1. *This map will help your students visualize where the events of today's lesson—and several lessons this quarter—took place.*

**28. While his father Terah was still alive, Haran died in Ur of the Chaldeans, in the land of his birth.**

It is not the natural order of things for a child to predecease a parent. This marks the first such recorded incident after the great flood. The narrative that follows suggests that Abram began to serve as the father figure for Lot after *Haran died* (see Genesis 12:4).

*Ur of the Chaldeans* is usually associated with a city that is about one hundred and twenty miles southeast of Babylon (cf. Genesis 15:7; Nehemiah 9:7). Ur is a progressive city with well-arranged streets and a sewer system. It is a trading center, so it is considered a desirable place to live. It is also a city of much idolatry.

## B. DESCRIBING THE WOMEN (vv. 29, 30)

**29. Abram and Nahor both married. The name of Abram's wife was Sarai, and the name of Nahor's wife was Milcah; she was the daughter of Haran, the father of both Milcah and Iscah.**

The *wives* of the two surviving brothers are mentioned. *Abram's wife* is *Sarai*, who later becomes "Sarah" (or "princess") in Genesis 17:15. Genesis 20:12 states that Sarai is also Abram's half-sister, having had a different mother. Over six hundred years later, God's instructions for the nation of Israel will prohibit marrying someone who is closely related (see Leviticus 18:6; 20:17). But at this time there is no such restriction.

*Nahor*, for his part, marries *Milcah*. She is one of the two daughters of *Haran*, the brother who had died. Milcah is mentioned in Genesis 22:20-24 as having eight sons. Bethuel, her youngest son, becomes the father of Rebekah, who will later marry Isaac, Abram's only son through Sarai.

**30. Now Sarai was barren; she had no children.**

The fact that *Sarai is barren* becomes a major factor in the developing faith of Abram. The factor of temporary barrenness also plays an important part later in the lives of Rebekah (Isaac's wife), Rachel (wife of Jacob, Isaac's son), and, in the time of Jesus, Elizabeth (Zechariah's wife).

## C. DEPARTING FROM UR (v. 31a)

**31a. Terah took his son Abram, his grandson Lot son of Haran, and his daughter-in-law Sarai, the wife of his son Abram, and together they set out from Ur of the Chaldeans to go to Canaan.**

The fact that it is *Terah* who is in charge of this move indicates that he is still the head of the family. *Abram* and the others, therefore, have had many years of being in submission to Terah. Respect for parental authority is often entwined with a spiritual faith that respects God's authority.

The real factor behind Terah's decision is that God called Abram while the family was still in the land of Mesopotamia, an area between the Tigris and Euphrates Rivers (Acts 7:2). Genesis 12:1; Acts 7:3; and Hebrews 11:8 reveal that at this time Abram does not know that the ultimate destination is *Canaan*.

Abram's experiences thus far are the early steps in a life that will be counted among the great examples of faith. There are some events in his life over which he has no control, but he does not permit them to move him from the path of righteousness. Abram's life to this point includes the death of a brother, the reality of having a barren wife, and leaving behind everything that is familiar.

## D. DELAYING IN HARAN (vv. 31b, 32)

**31b. But when they came to Haran, they settled there.**

For some unknown reason the family stops at *Haran*. The name of this town is the same in English as the name of the deceased brother, but the first letter is different in Hebrew.

DAILY BIBLE READINGS

*Monday, Nov. 29—God Calls Isaiah (Isaiah 6:1-8)*

*Tuesday, Nov. 30—God Calls Jeremiah (Jeremiah 1:4-10)*

*Wednesday, Dec. 1—Jesus Calls the First Disciples (Luke 5: 4-11)*

*Thursday, Dec. 2—God Calls Saul (Acts 9:1-9)*

*Friday, Dec. 3—Abram and Sarai Live in Haran (Genesis 11: 27-32)*

*Saturday, Dec. 4—God Calls Abram (Genesis 12:1-9)*

*Sunday, Dec. 5—God Makes a Covenant with Abram (Genesis 15:1-6)*

## WHAT DO YOU THINK?

*What are some things we may need to "leave behind" in order to answer God's call or to follow his leading?*

*[Consider using 2 Corinthians 6:14-16 and 1 Peter 2:9-12 as starting points for discussion.]*

## WHAT DO YOU THINK?

*How might God use similar situations in our lives to prepare us to serve him in the future?*

Some have pointed out that both Ur and Haran are centers of worship for the same moon god and goddess. It is speculation, however, to assert that this is the reason for the pause in the journey.

**32. Terah lived 205 years, and he died in Haran.**

If the text provides any reason for the family's stopping *in Haran*, it may have been the final illness and death of *Terah*. Stephen's comments about this event say that Abram left Haran after his father had died (Acts 7:4). Genesis 12:4 states that Abram was seventy-five when he left Haran.

## II. PROMISES TO ABRAM (GENESIS 12:1-3)

The Lord plans to separate Abram from the other members of his family. We can only guess as to why this is done. It would seem that Abram's faith is stronger than theirs, and the challenges ahead of Abram do not need any negative influences.

### A. REMINDER TO CONTINUE (v. 1)

**1. The LORD had said to Abram, "Leave your country, your people and your father's household and go to the land I will show you.**

Scholars debate whether this call refers back to the first call at Ur, or if this is a restatement of that original call. One thing is certain: the call indicates that a drastic change is about to take place. Each phrase becomes more demanding as Abram is told to depart from his *country*, his relatives, and the familiar surroundings of his father's dwelling.

The call of Abram causes other thoughts. To our knowledge, this is the first definite message from God since the flood in the time of Noah. Several hundred years have passed since that event. What are people thinking during those days? Is there a restlessness without a sure word from God? We know that there is faith in the earth, for Melchizedek is a good example of such (Genesis 14:18-20). The larger question may be this: why do so many people today live as if they are unaware that God has spoken through his Son (Hebrews 1:1, 2)?

### B. REHEARSAL OF THE PROMISES (vv. 2, 3)

**2. "I will make you into a great nation**
**        and I will bless you;**
**    I will make your name great,**
**        and you will be a blessing.**

This verse begins a series of seven special promises. God has called a man having no children, a man who is just the unknown son of Terah, and a man who seems not to have any land of his own. Now God makes promises that involve both present and future blessings that will change his situation dramatically.

The first promise is that Abram will now become the progenitor of *a great nation*. Abram will realize instantly that this demands many descendants and much time. God, however, provides comfort by emphasizing his own part in the fulfillments: the expression *I will* occurs or is implied over and over throughout these verses.

These thoughts lead naturally into the following promise that God will *bless* Abram. If God is the one who calls, then it is his task to provide the blessings as he determines. Some form of the word *bless* occurs five times within verses 2 and 3.

Abram will also have a *name* that is *great*. As noted earlier, his name is one of the most frequently mentioned in God's Word. His faith and obedience have been the subjects of many sermons and books throughout the centuries.

*HOW TO SAY IT*

Abraham. AY-bruh-ham.

Abram. AY-brum.

Ai. AY-eye.

Bethel. BETH-ul.

Bethuel. Be-THU-ul.

Canaan. KAY-nun.

Canaanites. KAY-nun-ites.

Chaldeans. Kal-DEE-unz.

Esau. EE-saw.

Euphrates. You-FRAY-teez.

Haran. HAIR-un.

Isaac. EYE-zuk.

Iscah. IS-ka.

Ishmael. ISH-may-el.

Keturah. Keh-TOO-ruh.

Melchizedek. Mel-KIZ-eh-dek.

Mesopotamia. MES-uh-puh-TAY-me-uh.

Milcah. MIL-kuh.

Moreh. MOE-reh.

Nahor. NAY-hor.

Rebekah. Reh-BEK-uh.

Sarai. SEH-rye.

Shechem. SHEE-kem or SHEK-em.

Terah. TAIR-uh.

Tigris. TIE-griss.

Ur. Er.

Zechariah. ZEK-uh-RYE-uh.

Abram is also assured that he *will be a blessing*. In Abram's case, this has spiritual implications, but it also lends itself to another thought: everyone should want to live so that his or her life is a blessing to others. This includes being a spiritual example and benefit to family, friends, employers, neighbors, etc.

3. *"I will bless those who bless you,*
    *and whoever curses you I will curse;*
 *and all peoples on earth*
    *will be blessed through you."*

Individuals who are "sold out" to God draw different responses from those whom they encounter. Some feel prompted to want to *bless* such dedication. Others, perhaps because they are forced to admit their own spiritual lacks, are inclined to *curse* the one who compels them to do a spiritual self-assessment.

The seventh promise by God finds its ultimate fulfillment in the Messiah. It is interesting that the first verse of the New Testament states that Jesus Christ is a son of David and a son of Abraham.

God gave the same or similar promises to each of the three great patriarchs: in six different chapters to Abram (Genesis 12:1-3, 7; 13:14-18; 15:4, 5, 13-18; 17:1-8; 18:17-19; 22:15-18), twice to Isaac (26:4, 23, 24), and twice to Jacob (28:14, 15; 35:9-12).

## III. PILGRIMAGE OF ABRAM (GENESIS 12:4-9)

Earlier it was Terah who had moved the family. This time it is Abram leading in this regard.

### A. RESUMING THE JOURNEY, PART 1 (vv. 4-6)

4. *So Abram left, as the LORD had told him; and Lot went with him. Abram was seventy-five years old when he set out from Haran.*

This is no longer just the travels of a family. It has become a spiritual pilgrimage, and Abram acts decisively. Abram is a man who is looking "forward to the city with foundations, whose architect and builder is God" (Hebrews 11:10).

The presence of *Lot* with Abram indicates a personal decision for him to accompany his uncle. We can only speculate whether this is a religious conviction or a concern for a favorite uncle who had attained such an age.

5. *He took his wife Sarai, his nephew Lot, all the possessions they had accumulated and the people they had acquired in Haran, and they set out for the land of Canaan, and they arrived there.*

The separation from other family members must be an emotional moment, but that is concealed for us only to imagine. Abram now has the responsibility of leading, encouraging, and meeting the needs of the entire group.

The childless state of Abram and *Sarai* can produce either a greater closeness or a falling apart. The choice is theirs. These two may have moments of frustration as well as curiosity as to how God will make a great nation through them.

The one who penned these words originally was Moses, and he also experienced a call from God. One wonders if he reflected on the parallels and differences between himself and Abram as each of them start from opposite directions to lead a group to *Canaan*.

6. *Abram traveled through the land as far as the site of the great tree of Moreh at Shechem. At that time the Canaanites were in the land.*

The journey from Haran to *Shechem* is almost four hundred miles. There are no conveniences of travel that we take for granted. Shechem and its environs will later become special places for Abram's descendants. (See Genesis 33:18-20; Joshua 24:32; etc.)

*VISUALS FOR THESE LESSONS*

The visual pictured in each lesson (e.g., page 128) is a small reproduction of a large, full-color poster included in the Adult Visuals *packet for the Winter Quarter. The packet is available from your supplier. Order No. 292.*

*WHAT DO YOU THINK?*

*Abram demonstrated his faith in God by his prompt obedience to God's call to leave everything behind to go to a new land and a new life. What can we learn from the first four verses of Genesis 12 that will help us respond to God today with the same trusting obedience?*

PRAYER

Thank you, Lord, for the example of Abram, who waited, struggled, and slowly matured in his faith. Like him, we sometimes fail, but we give thanks that you never do. In Jesus' name, amen.

## B. RECEIVING THE PROMISE OF LAND (v. 7a)

**7a. The LORD appeared to Abram and said, "To your offspring I will give this land."**

The word *offspring* reaffirms that *Abram* will have children, and it is added that his descendants will possess the *land*. Restrictions on the promise will be given in the future, for the land-promise in view here does not extend to the descendants of Ishmael, Abram's son through his wife's handmaid. Neither does it include Abram's sons by Keturah (his wife after Sarai dies; cf. Genesis 25:1, 2) nor the descendants of grandson Esau (the twin brother of Jacob).

## C. REVERENCE DEMONSTRATED (vv. 7b, 8)

**7b. So he built an altar there to the LORD, who had appeared to him.**

Abram makes a bold statement by building *an altar* to *the Lord*, for pagan altars are already in existence in this place. Abram is not called to compromise the one true faith, but to express it.

**8. From there he went on toward the hills east of Bethel and pitched his tent, with Bethel on the west and Ai on the east. There he built an altar to the LORD and called on the name of the LORD.**

Abram continues his journey to the south by traveling another twenty miles to a site between *Bethel* and *Ai*. Having *pitched his tent*, he again erects *an altar* for worship. His worship involves invoking *the name of the Lord*. In this way he sets an example for anyone who moves from location to location but ignores or defers the spiritual aspects of life.

WHAT DO YOU THINK?

What can we learn from the fact that Abram built an altar to God each place he moved? In what ways (figuratively) can we do the same thing today?

### LANDMARKS

A visitor to Zimbabwe was shown an aeronautical map of that African country. He noticed that the most frequent landmarks on the map were mission stations. In a land where most villages look alike and where there are few modern roads or structures, the mission stations became the landmarks by which pilots could navigate.

Notice that when Abraham pitched his tent, he built altars. In effect Abraham marked his journey by those altars. Centuries later they still serve as mental reference points by which we can retrace his journey of faith.

This leads us to consider the marks of faith that we will leave on the landscape of life. Fame is fleeting. Wealth vanishes. Human accomplishments are soon surpassed. But the footprints of faith remain. That is the greatest legacy we can leave. Abraham didn't just travel through life pitching his tent here and there, and neither should we.                                                    —R. C. S.

## D. RESUMING THE JOURNEY, PART 2 (v. 9)

**9. Then Abram set out and continued toward the Negev.**

The *Negev* is a particular desert region. It is also the Hebrew word for "south." Although we might like to know more about Abram's continued journey on to this area, the most important thing is that he follows in faith when God calls.

WHAT DO YOU THINK?

How can we maintain our faith in God as we face detours and obstacles on the journey of life?

## CONCLUSION

When people view a drama, there is a tendency to identify with the leading characters rather than the members of the supporting cast. Without the latter, however, the fame that is achieved by the heroes would never become a reality.

Most of those studying this lesson today will never see their "names in lights" like Abram. What is important is that they faithfully fulfill whatever God has called them to do by the precepts and principles of his Word. In the end, having your name in the Lamb's book of life means much more than having it "in lights."

THOUGHT TO REMEMBER

Expect stages and crises in your growth of faith.

# Discovery Learning

*This page contains an alternative lesson plan emphasizing learning activities. Classes
desiring such student involvement will find these suggestions helpful. The next page
is a reproducible activity page to further enhance discovery learning.*

## LEARNING GOALS

After participating in this lesson, each student will be able to:

1. Describe the historical situations of Abram as he and his family obeyed the call of God to leave Ur and then Haran.

2. Evaluate the faith of Abram through his positive responses to God's call to venture into the unknown.

3. Make changes personally in order to conform to the call of God as given in his Word.

## INTO THE LESSON

Ask students to think about people they trust, then ask whether they trust you. When several students have nodded their heads in agreement, ask for a volunteer to come up to the front of the room. Tell the class that this student is going to demonstrate his or her trust in you.

Have the student stand behind you, placing a hand on one of your shoulders. Then have the student close his or her eyes, and follow you wherever you go. Emphasize no peeking! Lead the student on a simple course throughout the room. Make sure you take the student around several obstacles. (If your classroom has a small platform with stairs, so much the better!) Sometimes you'll want to warn the person that an obstacle is coming. Other times, simply walk around it and have the person follow you.

End the activity after about two minutes. Send the student back to his or her seat with a round of applause for being such a good sport. Then ask a few general questions for the whole class. "Would you be willing to go through a day this way?" "What would make it hard to do?" "What would make it less difficult?"

Close the activity by summarizing the activity and the discussion. It's hard to trust someone completely, but it's less difficult when the person is completely trustworthy. Then say, "Today we'll learn about Abram's trust in God. God told him to leave his home, and he obeyed—even though he had no idea where God would lead him."

## INTO THE WORD

Using the lesson commentary, relate the story of Abram's journey from Ur to Canaan. Have your learners trace Abram's movements on either a classroom map or a map in the back of their Bibles. Note each place along the way: Ur, Haran, Shechem, and Bethel. Have them jot down the main events that happened at each place. (Be sure to emphasize the provisions of God's covenant, which was given while Abram was in Haran. Your learners can use space in the student book to jot down the seven promises God made to Abram in this covenant.)

After leading students through today's text, ask your learners to share what they've noted for each place. Here are some possible answers:

*Ur:* Starting point. Haran died there.

*Haran:* Terah dies. God calls Abram. God makes a covenant with Abram. (Review the provisions of the covenant.)

*Shechem:* God appears to Abram again. God renews the promise of the land. Abram builds an altar to the Lord.

*Bethel:* Abram builds an altar to the Lord.

*Toward the Negev:* No information about Abram's activities there.

Conclude this review by asking, "Why is Abram called a man of faith?" Ask students to share responses. Be supportive of any reasonable answer, but make sure that you emphasize that Abram followed God to a place where he (Abram) had never been. Also mention the fact that Abram built altars to God. He was showing his dependence upon God and identifying himself with God's purposes.

## INTO LIFE

Ask: "Have any of you had an experience of trusting God's direction, even though you didn't know what would happen?" This could be a decision relating to career, relocation, finances, family matters, or a number of other issues. Give opportunity for several students to share briefly their experiences.

Divide the class into groups of three or four. Ask students to share a major decision they're facing now, if they feel free to do so. Then have students pray for one another in their groups. Ask them to pray for insight into what God wants them to do and courage to follow his leading.

(Note: Your learners can use their student books to write down their commitment to follow God's leading. If your students have the book, have them do this now.)

Close the class with prayer, asking God to help your students develop the faith of Abraham—to obey God and trust him for the results.

# Family Tree

From today's text, sketch Abram's family tree. Be sure to include all these people, showing how each is related to the others:

TERAH

ABRAM

NAHOR

HARAN

LOT

SARAI

MILCAH

ISCAH

# Contract Terms

From Genesis 12:2, 3 list the seven promises that God made to Abram in the covenant.

1.

2.

3.

4.

5.

6.

7.

# My Commitment

Is God directing you to do something specific? Do you find yourself wavering and hesitating? Today, affirm your determination to follow God and trust Him in this area of your life. Then sign and date it.

Lord, I know you want me to _____.
Today I promise to step out in faith, like Abram, and follow You.

Signed: _____ Date: _____

# CALLED TO LEAD WITH INTEGRITY

**LESSON 2**

## WHY TEACH THIS LESSON?

When the space shuttle Challenger exploded in 1986, NASA began an immediate investigation to determine the cause. Attention soon focused on the "o" rings that served as a type of gasket. Eventually, a NASA spokesman declared that the explosion was the result of a loss of the integrity of this "o" ring.

The loss of seven lives because of this problem with integrity was tragic. Unfortunate things also happen when people are placed in positions of leadership and authority but fail miserably in the area of integrity. Our lesson today helps us focus on how God evaluates potential leaders. A key ingredient for a leader of God's people—an ingredient that should be found in any leader, from government to business to athletics—is the need for integrity.

## INTRODUCTION

### A. LEAD WITH INTEGRITY

The politician was "working the crowd" at the state fair. Just as he entered a livestock area, one of the show horses was startled and reacted by trying to get loose. The trainer grabbed the politician and asked him to take the halter for the other horse while he tried to calm the horse that was in fright. The politician said, "Sir, I am a member of your state legislature, and . . ."—but the trainer quickly said, "Just take the halter; I'll trust you anyway."

Is it true that the words *business* and *ethics* no longer can be used in the same context, unless it is being stated that good ethics have all but disappeared? The scandals of recent years have served notice that the breakdown of morals has affected homes, schools, the courts, and governments. It often seems that those elected to public office are the ones who have the least amount of mud still clinging to them on election day.

But certain questions must be considered. Which is more important, political survival or integrity? How long can a godless society survive? How did the business world reach the place that balance-sheet falsification is common?

Just as important is to ask what it will take to reverse the process. What responses are appropriate for a Christian, especially one in leadership? Does morality have to be sacrificed in order to get ahead? Is it really worth it if "a man . . . gains the whole world" in exchange for his soul? (See Matthew 16:26.)

The title of today's lesson stands in stark contrast to the leadership portrayed by many business and world leaders of today. God, however, has always desired integrity for every leader, from the home to the highest levels of government.

### B. LESSON BACKGROUND

One millennium plus another sixty years—that is the period of time between the call of Abram in about 2091 B.C. in last week's lesson to the lesson for today.

DEVOTIONAL READING:
2 SAMUEL 7:18-29

BACKGROUND SCRIPTURE:
1 SAMUEL 16:1-13; 2 SAMUEL 7:8-16

PRINTED TEXT:
1 SAMUEL 16:1-13

### LESSON AIMS

After participating in this lesson, each student will be able to:

1. Share with others the purpose and results of Samuel's journey to Bethlehem.

2. Understand that integrity in the hearts of leaders at all levels of society is pleasing to God.

3. Resolve to honor God, whether leading or following.

### KEY VERSE

The LORD does not look at the things man looks at. Man looks at the outward appearance, but the LORD looks at the heart.
—1 Samuel 16:7

LESSON 2 NOTES

During that time God worked with two types of leaders to accomplish his purposes: family leaders and national leaders. *Family leaders* in the book of Genesis include the three great patriarchs Abram, his son Isaac, and grandson Jacob. Moses became the first *national leader* of Israel as it grew into a mighty nation in Egypt. After forty years Moses turned the leadership over to Joshua. His task was to conquer the land that God had promised to Abram over six hundred years previously.

When Joshua died, the only national leaders were the high priests. Each tribe had its leaders during the sojourn to Canaan, and that system remained in place after the conquest of the land. The Lord had promised abundant blessings if the people would obey his law. But the people did not resist the temptations of idolatry that are often combined with immorality. God punished Israel with periods of oppression. Then he raised up judges as deliverers.

Samuel is considered to be the last such judge in Israel. His sons were not worthy successors, so the people asked for a king. God then had Samuel anoint Saul as the first king of Israel. Saul began well, but his faith faltered in two critical situations (see 1 Samuel 13 and 15).

Samuel may have felt that much of his life had been a failure: his sons were dishonest judges (1 Samuel 8:3), and Saul's disobedience caused him to be rejected by the Lord.

## I. CONVERSATION WITH GOD (1 SAMUEL 16:1-3)

The Lord can see the big picture, involving both the past and the future. It has been over eight hundred years since Jacob gave the prophecy that the scepter of royalty would belong to the tribe of Judah, Jacob's fourth son (Genesis 49:10). The fulfillment is ready to begin, and it will extend into the future so as to include the everlasting reign of the Messiah, the Son of David (Revelation 5:5).

### A. COMMAND TO SAMUEL (v. 1)

*1. The LORD said to Samuel, "How long will you mourn for Saul, since I have rejected him as king over Israel? Fill your horn with oil and be on your way; I am sending you to Jesse of Bethlehem. I have chosen one of his sons to be king."*

Through a reprimand and a command, *the Lord* prompts *Samuel* to action. The reprimand involves Samuel's mourning *for Saul*. God understands that a period of mourning is normal and necessary in many situations, but there is a time for the grief to end. Spiritual maturity demands that Samuel accept the fact that the Lord has *rejected* Saul.

The command is for Samuel to take a *horn with oil* in order to anoint a new *king* from among the sons of *Jesse*. But the people present at the anointing will not necessarily know that the anointing is to a kingship. Jesse is in the lineage of Judah (Matthew 1:2-5).

### B. CONCERN BY SAMUEL (v. 2)

*2. But Samuel said, "How can I go? Saul will hear about it and kill me."*

*The LORD said, "Take a heifer with you and say, 'I have come to sacrifice to the LORD.'*

Samuel has valid reasons to be concerned. He has already informed *Saul* that the Lord is seeking "a man after his own heart" (1 Samuel 13:14). If Saul discovers the purpose of Samuel's trip, it could be construed as treason. That would give Saul a valid reason to *kill* Samuel.

The Lord resolves Samuel's concern by telling him that he should also engage in one of his normal functions by taking *a heifer* as a *sacrifice to the Lord*. Samuel's

*WHAT DO YOU THINK?*

*What factors should we consider in determining when it is time to go on to other responsibilities?*

response to any queries will be truthful, but he will not tell everything he plans to do. This is in accord with the advice given in Proverbs 12:23: "A prudent man keeps his knowledge to himself, but the heart of fools blurts out folly."

The use of a heifer indicates that this will be a peace or fellowship offering as prescribed in Leviticus 3. This will be an enjoyable occasion of feasting.

### THE ONLY SAFE PLACE

A man was serving a small-town church in a peaceful community when there came a call to go to Africa and teach in an emerging Bible college. That particular African country was going through a very unsettled time, and tensions were high. Someone asked him, "Is it really safe for you to go?" He replied, "The only safe place is where God wants you to be."

To do our duty in the face of danger is always honorable. It is especially praiseworthy when it is God who calls us. While we cannot expect to have a call as explicit as had Moses, Samuel, or Paul, we can have a sense that God wants us in a certain place for a certain purpose. When we have that conviction, we must respond.

Of course, faith does not demand foolishness. We are not condemned for being prudent and careful. God does not expect us to take unnecessary risks. We can be faithful without being foolhardy. We can trust without trying to parade our faith. God was not angry when Samuel expressed reservations. Instead, God provided a solution that calmed Samuel and still sent him on his way to do God's work.

To be daring in order to prove or flaunt our faith is a mistake. But to trust God means that we do what we are convinced he wants us to do. It's reflected in so many of our hymns: "Trusting Jesus," "Trust and Obey," etc. God understands our insecurity and our fears, but he does expect our unqualified obedience.   —R. C. S.

### C. COMMISSION FOR SAMUEL (v. 3)

3. "Invite Jesse to the sacrifice, and I will show you what to do. You are to anoint for me the one I indicate."

Samuel's commission also includes calling Jesse to the sacrifice. Jesse seems to be a man for whom no further identification is needed. It is customary in the Bible to designate a person with a reference to his father or other ancestors, but this is not done in Jesse's case.

God does not reveal to Samuel which of Jesse's sons (16:1) is to be anointed as the next king. Some people want to know all the answers "up front," but God is deliberately planning to provide a lesson in leadership for Samuel and for us.

The examples of Scripture are that three groups of people receive special anointing: prophets (1 Kings 19:16b), priests (Exodus 30:30), and kings (as here). It has been suggested that those who witness David being anointed may assume that Samuel is anointing him to become a prophet. David also receives a gift of the Holy Spirit (1 Samuel 16:13). This special inspiration enables him to write many of the psalms. Peter will later say that David was a prophet (Acts 2:30).

### II. CONVOCATION AT BETHLEHEM (1 SAMUEL 16:4, 5)

Samuel is probably in his hometown of Ramah as he prepares for his journey (see 1 Samuel 16:13). Ramah is a few miles north of Jerusalem, and the usual way for Samuel to travel to Bethlehem would take him through Gibeah, Saul's hometown and capital (10:26; 15:34). It is interesting to speculate whether Samuel took another route or left early enough not to be noticed.

### A. CONCERN BY THE ELDERS (v. 4)

4. Samuel did what the LORD said. When he arrived at Bethlehem, the elders of the town trembled when they met him. They asked, "Do you come in peace?"

HOW TO SAY IT

Abinadab. Uh-BIN-uh-dab.
Absalom. AB-suh-lum.
Bethlehem. BETH-lih-hem.
Eliab. Ee-LYE-ab.
Gibeah. GIB-ee-uh (G as in get).
Herod. HAIR-ud.
Jesse. JESS-ee.
Naomi. Nay-OH-me.
Ramah. RAY-muh.

Samuel provides an example of obedience to the Lord's call. His valid question to God has been answered, and he acts promptly.

In this month of December, it is fitting to mention other people in the Bible who make Bethlehem journeys. They include Ruth (an ancestress of David) and Naomi (Ruth 1:19), plus soldiers of David (2 Samuel 23:15, 16). Of course, most of us know about Joseph and Mary, the shepherds who heard the angelic announcement (Luke 2:10-12), the wise men, and soldiers of Herod.

*The elders of the town* tremble as they inquire about the purpose of this visit. To have God's prophet suddenly appear on the scene is a matter of great concern!

### B. CONSECRATION FOR ALL (v. 5)

**5. Samuel replied, "Yes, in peace; I have come to sacrifice to the LORD. Consecrate yourselves and come to the sacrifice with me." Then he consecrated Jesse and his sons and invited them to the sacrifice.**

Samuel's answer is positive. His arrival is peaceful in intent, and even includes having a sacrificial meal for everyone to enjoy. The nature of the occasion also demands a spiritual emphasis that includes ceremonial cleansing to be sanctified. This requires a washing of clothing and the body (Exodus 19:10; Numbers 8:21).

Special mention is made of Samuel's participation in the consecration of *Jesse and his sons*. Samuel's commission makes it imperative that they be present. This also provides him an opportunity to become better acquainted with them, to discern the attitudes within the family, and to begin to determine which one would be chosen by the Lord.

### III. CONSIDERING JESSE'S SONS (1 SAMUEL 16:6-13)

At this point the elders of Bethlehem drop from the narrative. The emphasis shifts to the sons of Jesse.

### A. CONTRASTING STANDARDS (vv. 6, 7)

**6, 7. When they arrived, Samuel saw Eliab and thought, "Surely the LORD's anointed stands here before the LORD." But the LORD said to Samuel, "Do not consider his appearance or his height, for I have rejected him. The LORD does not look at the things man looks at. Man looks at the outward appearance, but the LORD looks at the heart."**

Samuel initially judges *Eliab* by two things: *his height* and his looks. Samuel is confident that the Lord's anointed is before him; the Lord, however, has an entirely different assessment!

The two qualities cited above can be a positive advantage to someone who is chosen to be one of God's leaders, but the Lord is much more concerned with a person's *heart*. The standards of acceptance for the Lord's leaders demand that extra dimension of the inner self.

It is especially true in ancient times that height is a desirable attribute for a king (cf. 1 Samuel 9:2). First, there is the assumption that a person who is tall is more competent. Second, in hand-to-hand combat the person with long arms has a distinct advantage. Third, a king who is tall can be seen more easily by his soldiers whenever battles are fought; they will know to continue fighting if they see that their king is still present with them.

It also seems that these genetic features of height and handsomeness are frequent in David's family. David's son Absalom later leads a rebellion against his father, and his handsomeness is noted in 2 Samuel 14:25, 26. An extra dimension is added for him—that of his abundant hair. (In recent years some election results have led to the conclusion that men with the greater amount of hair are

Man looks at the outward appearance, but the LORD looks at the heart.

1 Samuel 6:7, NIV®

Visual for lesson 2. *Use today's visual to spark a discussion of how much concern for "outward appearance" is appropriate in view of today's text.*

more likely to win! This may explain why some candidates go to stylists who fluff the hair to a pleasing fullness.)

Contemporary publications on leadership may feature the "Top Ten Traits of Trailblazers and Trendsetters." But remember that God stresses the most important factor of all: a person with a pure heart.

### TELEGENIC

The word *telegenic* entered our vocabulary in 1939. It refers to someone who looks good on television. Nowadays, successful political candidates need to be telegenic. Many who were elected to high office in the past would not even be considered as candidates today because of their appearance. Abraham Lincoln comes to mind!

Samuel was warned against making a person's looks a criterion for leadership, and we need the same warning now. In an age of superficiality, when so many never see beyond the outward appearance, it is important for believers to judge by a different standard. Some of our greatest preachers did not really look the part. The apostle Paul was not impressive in his physical appearance (2 Corinthians 10:10).

We all have had the experience of meeting someone who seemed unattractive until we got to know him or her. Then we thought that person to be very appealing. We all have known someone who gave the appearance of holiness, only to discover that it was outward and not inward.

While we cannot look at the heart in the way that God does, there are windows into every person that give us a glimpse of what is "really in there." We need to value what we see through these windows. Our challenge is to value character over appearance, and spiritual stature as more significant than physical stature. —R. C. S.

## B. CONTINUING THE REVIEW (vv. 8-10)

**8. Then Jesse called Abinadab and had him pass in front of Samuel. But Samuel said, "The LORD has not chosen this one either."**

Many people tend to hurry by this verse in order to reach the discussion about the chosen son. But we may pause to wonder about the reactions of the first two sons who did not "pass inspection." Are they disheartened or dismayed at being rejected, or do they experience a sense of relief that they will not have to make the changes that Samuel may require?

How a person handles not being accepted for leadership in the church is very revealing. Some have reacted in anger or even abandoned the fellowship of believers. This speaks volumes about whether such people are really qualified spiritually to lead others. Mature individuals may be disappointed, but their faith and faithfulness will not be diminished. Such reversals can become very important in a person's spiritual and emotional development.

**9, 10. Jesse then had Shammah pass by, but Samuel said, "Nor has the LORD chosen this one." Jesse had seven of his sons pass before Samuel, but Samuel said to him, "The LORD has not chosen these."**

The third son of Jesse is the final named son in these verses until David is mentioned. Samuel, however, has learned his lesson well. He no longer judges by outward appearances. He simply makes his pronouncements, and the people in attendance can only wonder why the (apparently) finest young men in Bethlehem are not *chosen* by the Lord.

A minor concern is with the phrase that says *seven* of Jesse's *sons pass before Samuel* before David makes his appearance. The alert student may be aware that the genealogy of this family in 1 Chronicles 2:13-15 says that David is the seventh. The usual reconciliation is to assume that one son died early in life, and he

### WHAT DO YOU THINK?

*How can we train ourselves to see people as God sees them, focusing on the heart instead of outward appearance?*

### WHAT DO YOU THINK?

*We are not told in the text how the older sons of Jesse handled the fact that they were not chosen, but it does prompt us to ask ourselves the question: "How should we respond to such a rejection?"*

PRAYER

*Lord, bless with wisdom, courage, and endurance the leaders of this nation, the church, and especially those who have the fearful tasks of preaching and teaching. In Jesus' name, amen.*

WHAT DO YOU THINK?

*What can we learn from David's example about waiting on God's timing for our opportunity to lead?*

THOUGHT TO REMEMBER

*Lead and follow with integrity.*

WHAT DO YOU THINK?

*If we are to have leaders in the church who are filled with integrity, we must pray for them with passion and consistency. What are some of the things about which we should pray? Are any of these things more important than any of the others? Why, or why not?*

is not listed in the official records. The rate of infant mortality is very high in the ancient world.

## C. CALLING FOR DAVID (vv. 11, 12)

**11. So he asked Jesse, "Are these all the sons you have?"**

**"There is still the youngest," Jesse answered, "but he is tending the sheep."**

**Samuel said, "Send for him; we will not sit down until he arrives."**

The absence of David is often explained by saying that the role of caring for *the sheep* falls to *the youngest* son. Others conclude that David is about ten years old, making him too young to be considered. It is a hasty action to dismiss young people as unimportant, for one never knows which ones will become great leaders for God and humanity.

To mention the fact that David is a shepherd is a reminder that he is also the author of Psalm 23, a favorite of many. David's most famous descendant, Jesus Christ, said of himself, "I am the good shepherd" (John 10:11).

**12. So he sent and had him brought in. He was ruddy, with a fine appearance and handsome features.**

**Then the LORD said, "Rise and anoint him; he is the one."**

*Ruddy* is usually interpreted to mean that there is a reddish cast to David's hair or skin. David may have been young, but the blending of all his features demonstrates that he already has some of the qualities that are desired in leaders.

The selection process has come to an end as the Lord commands Samuel to *anoint* young David. This anointing of Israel's second king occurs approximately twenty years before David actually takes on his special, kingly role in God's plan in about 1010 B.C. During many of those years, he will be a fugitive from Saul. But David behaves with honor as he waits patiently for the time when he will become the king of Israel.

## D. CONFIRMING GOD'S CHOSEN (v. 13)

**13. So Samuel took the horn of oil and anointed him in the presence of his brothers, and from that day on the Spirit of the LORD came upon David in power. Samuel then went to Ramah.**

Samuel's task is finished. Josephus, a Jewish historian of the first century A.D., reflects a tradition of his time by writing that Samuel whispers into David's ear that he will become a king. It is not known what the onlookers think. As indicated above, they may wonder if David is being *anointed* to become a prophet. It is doubtful that they make any assumptions about his becoming a king, for simply being present for such an event could put all their lives in jeopardy.

The shepherd boy, with the help of *the Spirit of the Lord*, grows to become ancient Israel's most famous king. His accomplishments will be many, and his name will be used by later prophets to foretell the coming kingdom that God will establish with the Son of David as King of kings and Lord of lords.

## CONCLUSION

One of the famous remarks of Samuel is that it would be a sin if he did not pray for Israel (1 Samuel 12:23). The apostle Paul encouraged people to pray for him (1 Thessalonians 5:25). Prayer is therefore a mutual obligation for those who lead and those who follow.

The leaders in spiritual projects especially need prayer, for souls are involved. The spiritual implications are sobering. In the church there are the extra meetings, people with problems, plus the added stresses on the families of the leaders. Pray for your leaders at all levels—and for their spouses and families!

# Discovery Learning

*This page contains an alternative lesson plan emphasizing learning activities. Classes
desiring such student involvement will find these suggestions helpful. The next page
is a reproducible activity page to further enhance discovery learning.*

## LEARNING GOALS

After participating in this lesson, each student will be able to:

1. Share with others the purpose and results of Samuel's journey to Bethlehem.

2. Understand that integrity in the hearts of leaders at all levels of society is pleasing to God.

3. Resolve to honor God, whether leading or following.

## INTO THE LESSON

Make three columns on the board. The first column is headed "Category." Underneath the heading list the categories of movie actor/actress, musician, television personality, business leader, politician, and athlete. The second column is headed "Name." The third column is headed "Why?" Ask: "Who do you think is 'number one' in each of these categories? Why?" As you read each category in turn, ask two or three students to give their answers to that category. Be sure each one gives a reason for the choice.

When you've gone through all the categories, ask students to look over all the answers they wrote in the "Why?" column. Ask: "What does it take to be 'number one' today?" Many of the answers will relate to characteristics we value in our celebrities: good looks, attractiveness, achievement, talent, power, wealth, and so on.

Now ask: "How important is integrity in rating someone 'number one'?" Tell them that today's lesson will present God's criteria for leadership.

## INTO THE WORD

*Lecture.* Following the commentary notes, talk about the events in 1 Samuel 16:1-5. This will provide background for the next verses, which form the core of today's lesson.

Before reading 1 Samuel 16:6-13, tell students that in these verses God will inform Samuel which of Jesse's sons is to be anointed king. Have them pay attention first to Samuel's expectations, and then to God's choice.

After reading verses 6-13, ask: "What kind of man did Samuel expect God to choose?" Note that Samuel looked at physical size and appearance. Perhaps he was expecting another Saul (see 1 Samuel 9:2).

"How was God's perspective different from Samuel's?" God looked on the heart. Spiritual qualifications are more important than physical ones.

Ask: "What clues do these few verses provide about David's qualifications for leadership?" Since God was looking at the heart (v. 7) we can assume that David passed that examination by God. In addition students may mention the fact that he was a shepherd and that working in that capacity may indicate that he would be a servant leader.

Ask: "What effect do you think this event had on David, especially since it would be twenty years before he became king over all Israel?" The text tells us he was filled with the Holy Spirit. This affected his thinking and his actions, preventing him from taking revenge on Saul, for one thing.

## INTO LIFE

Ask students to think about the areas of their lives in which they are called to lead. They might mention a position of responsibility at work, a ministry in the church, a position of leadership in the community, membership in an organization, and so on.

Now ask them to think about their own qualifications for leadership in these areas. Why were they selected for that position? How is their leadership evaluated? How will they know if they're successful in that position?

Write on the board the following quotation from General Norman Schwarzkopf: "Leadership is a combination of strategy and character. If you must be without one, be without the strategy." If your class is large, you can break them into small groups for a few minutes to allow your learners to discuss this statement among themselves.

Next, ask one or more of the following questions: "Why do you think the general would say something like this? Why is integrity important in military campaigns? What could be some consequences of acting without integrity? What would tempt a person to violate his or her personal integrity?"

After a time of discussion, close the class in a period of prayer. Ask students to pray for each other, that they will be men and women of integrity in the leadership roles to which God has called them. Also ask them to pray for their leaders—in civil government and in the church—that those people would perform their responsibilities with integrity. Pray also for God's help in realizing that integrity in leadership begins with integrity of "followership."

# Chosen by God!

Look at the following Bible passages. After you've read each passage, write down whom God chose and why.

Acts 6:3, 4

Acts 13:1-3

Acts 16:1-3

How did God call each of the following people to lead? What qualified them for their leadership roles?

Moses (Exodus 3:1-14)

Samuel (1 Samuel 1:1-21)

Isaiah (Isaiah 6:1-8)

Jeremiah (Jeremiah 1:4-10, 17-19)

Ezekiel (Ezekiel 2:1–3:15)

Look over your conclusions. In one or two sentences, summarize how God chooses the leaders of his people.

# CALLED TO RESPOND WITH GRACE

LESSON 3

## WHY TEACH THIS LESSON?

The Christmas season is characterized as a season of joy. There is the joy of being with family, the exchanging of gifts, and, for Christians, the remembrance of the birth of Christ. But statistics bear out that it is also a season of despair and depression. The season is one of loneliness for those who have lost a loved one in the past year or who feel estranged from family and friends. It is a season of great swings in emotion.

The first Christmas was a time of emotional swings as well. Joseph was experiencing the joy of his upcoming marriage. But the joy came crashing down as he was confronted with the pregnancy of Mary and his feelings of being betrayed by her. There was the fear in the confrontation by the angel. Then there was acceptance of his position in life.

From this story of Joseph we have a tremendous example of responding with grace. From it we learn some principles of dealing with the curves life throws at us through the acceptance of the message of Christ.

## INTRODUCTION

### A. DREAMS AND DREAMERS

People have dreams all the time, don't they? You may have had one just last night. Perhaps it was so "wild and woolly" that you couldn't wait to tell someone about it after you awoke. When you did, everyone had a good laugh. Then you just forgot about it and went on with your day.

In the ancient world, however, dreams were enormously important. They were seen as providing divine guidance and knowledge. In the Bible such dreamers are rare. There are only eighteen people who receive dreams from God in Scripture. Five are in the New Testament: Joseph, the wise men (assuming there were three), and Pilate's wife. Joseph is therefore in select company! He is important enough for God to use a direct and dramatic mode of communication.

### B. LESSON BACKGROUND

Joseph, the man in our text this week, is the "father" of Jesus. We know at least six important things about Joseph. First, Matthew 1:19 calls him "a righteous man." In the ancient context, this means he was an upstanding, respected citizen who feared God and kept God's commandments. We see this in his obedience to the expressed will of God twice in Matthew (1:24; 2:21).

Second, Matthew 13:55 tells us that Joseph was a carpenter, a skilled tradesman in his community. Third, Matthew indicates that Joseph became the father of a large family. Four brothers are listed for Jesus, and Matthew 13:55, 56 indicates at least three sisters. Fourth, we know from both Matthew 1:20 and Luke 1:27 that Joseph was a descendant of King David and thus from the tribe of Judah.

DEVOTIONAL READING:
LUKE 1:26-32.
BACKGROUND SCRIPTURE:
MATTHEW 1
PRINTED TEXT:
MATTHEW 1:17-25

LEARNING AIMS

After participating in this lesson, each student will be able to:

1. Recount the events that led to Joseph's gracious response to Mary's pregnancy.

2. Explain how Joseph's obedience to God's command revealed his character.

3. Make a commitment to respond with obedience to God's leading in a specific life situation.

WHAT DO YOU THINK?

What are some ways God may guide us or give us reassurance when we are thrust into unexpected circumstances?

KEY VERSE

When Joseph woke up, he did what the angel of the Lord had commanded him and took Mary home as his wife.
—Matthew 1:24

LESSON 3 NOTES

Fifth, Joseph was a resident of Nazareth, a small town in Galilee approximately sixty-five miles north of Jerusalem (see Luke 2:4, 39). Sixth, we learn that Joseph was a dreamer. He was not a dreamer in a negative sense—one who lives in a dreamland and refuses to face the realities of life. Rather, he was one who received messages from God in his dreams.

Matthew presents the birth circumstances of Jesus in a surprising way. Jesus has all the right credentials to be the Messiah, as Matthew shows in the genealogy (Matthew 1:1-17). Jesus is the descendant of Abraham and the descendant of David. A major agenda in Matthew, then, is to show how Jesus fulfills the prophesied expectations for the Messiah. Why must he do this?

The reason is that many other details about Jesus' birth are not what the ancient Jews would have expected. His parents come from Nazareth, a tiny village in Galilee. Shouldn't the anointed king's parents be from the grand and ancient city of Jerusalem? Shouldn't they be rich, famous, well educated, and influential? No, they are simple, rural people.

To make matters worse, there is some messiness involved in their marriage. Mary is pregnant before the marriage is consummated! Wedding customs of that day required that a marriage be arranged months or years before the couple actually lived together as husband and wife. Normally, the husband would pay a "bride price" to the father of the bride at the time of this arrangement.

After this, the woman was promised to this man, and any activity with other men was considered adulterous (see Deuteronomy 22:23, 24). Mary's pregnancy signaled to all the gossips of little Nazareth a violation of her commitment to Joseph. What was Joseph to do? Our lesson today is the story of his response, a response of grace and righteousness.

## I. BACKGROUND TO BIRTH (MATTHEW 1:17)

*17. Thus there were fourteen generations in all from Abraham to David, fourteen from David to the exile to Babylon, and fourteen from the exile to the Christ.*

Matthew explains the purpose and structure of the genealogy given in 1:1-16. The list is broken down into three sections of *fourteen generations*. This employs two significant numbers for the Jewish readers (who loved numbers!). Fourteen is double seven, the number of creation and perfection (Genesis 2:3). Three is a number of reverence and holiness (Isaiah 6:3). Further, the letters of David's Hebrew name add up to fourteen. This isn't some kind of secret "Bible code," but is a simple memory device.

Matthew also highlights the most important people in the genealogy: *Abraham* and *David*. Two thousand years earlier, God had promised that Abraham would bless the earth, presumably through a descendant (Genesis 12:3). Matthew 21:15 presents Jesus as the "Son of David," an obvious messianic title. Jesus is the fulfillment of the promise to David of an eternal kingdom (2 Samuel 7:13).

One might ask why the genealogy of Joseph is given if Jesus is not really the son of Joseph. Matthew does make it clear in the following story that Joseph is not the biological father of Jesus. However, in the ancient world an adopted son is a rightful heir and, in effect, inherits the genealogy of his father.

## II. PROBLEM TO SOLUTION (MATTHEW 1:18-21)

### A. STICKY SITUATION (vv. 18, 19)

*18. This is how the birth of Jesus Christ came about: his mother Mary was pledged to be married to Joseph, but before they came together, she was found to be with child through the Holy Spirit.*

### HOW TO SAY IT

*Abraham.* AY-bruh-ham.
*Alcmene.* Alk-MEE-nee.
*Athena.* Uh-THEE-nuh.
*Athens.* ATH-unz.
*Babylon.* BAB-uh-lun.
*Deuteronomy.* Due-ter-AHN-uh-me.
*Galilee.* GAL-uh-lee.
*Hercules.* HER-kew-leez.
*Hoshea.* Ho-SHAY-uh.
*Isaac.* EYE-zuk.
*Jerusalem.* Juh-ROO-suh-lem.
*Joshua.* JOSH-yew-uh.
*Messiah.* Meh-SIGH-uh.
*Nazareth.* NAZ-uh-reth.
*Nun.* None.
*Parthenon.* PAR-thuh-non.
*parthenos (Greek).* par-THEN-ahss.
*Pilate.* PIE-lut.
*Zeus.* Zoose.

*Mary* already has been committed to the first stage of marriage *to Joseph* by the time he receives the disappointing news that his future wife is pregnant. Unlike many today, they are not living together nor have they had any sexual relationship. Matthew explains that Mary's child is of *the Holy Spirit*.

There are several Old Testament accounts of births that took place as a result of divine intervention, including Isaac (Genesis 18:11-14) and Samuel (1 Samuel 1:4-20). There is nothing like this in the Old Testament, however, where the child is conceived without a human father.

This text is perhaps even more remarkable for what it doesn't contain. There is no hint of a deity having sexual intercourse with a human woman, a story oft repeated in the ancient world (e.g., Zeus impregnating Alcmene, the mother of Hercules). This conception is not the work of a naughty god; rather, it is a miracle of the true God.

*19. Because Joseph her husband was a righteous man and did not want to expose her to public disgrace, he had in mind to divorce her quietly.*

We are comforted by the fact that despite the devastating news of apparent infidelity, *Joseph* is *a righteous man*. The meaning of this description, however, is often unclear to many readers. If he is such a righteous man, then why doesn't he follow the letter of the Old Testament law and have Mary punished as an adulteress?

Matthew explains the character of Joseph's righteousness by noting that he is not willing to make her a public example. Instead, he decides to break the marriage agreement in private. He does not let his disappointment turn into anger. To say that Joseph is a righteous man is to say that Joseph is a good man.

The Greek word translated *to divorce* is the same word used of dissolution of marriage elsewhere (see Matthew 5:31; 19:3). This is more than breaking an engagement. Joseph is legally obligated to wed Mary, and she is legally promised to him. Joseph is considering making arrangements for Mary to stay in her father's household, have the baby, and, perhaps, never marry.

But this arrangement can never do for God's chosen Messiah. To lose Joseph as legal father would mean throwing the Davidic lineage into doubt. It would mean that the sinless one would grow up and be perceived as having been conceived in sin. It would mean that Mary, God's chosen vessel, would live all her life as a disgraced adulteress. It would mean that God's plan to bless the earth through a son of Abraham and to establish an eternal King through a son of David had been tragically derailed. A different resolution is needed, and God is the one who can provide it!

## B. REMARKABLE RESOLUTION (vv. 20, 21)

*20. But after he had considered this, an angel of the Lord appeared to him in a dream and said, "Joseph son of David, do not be afraid to take Mary home as your wife, because what is conceived in her is from the Holy Spirit.*

Joseph now gets his first divinely-inspired *dream*, his first experience of God's miraculous intervention in his life. The child is not the product of adultery. His beloved Mary is not a tramp or a rape victim. God gives him a little push to do what his heart wants to do: *take Mary* as his full-fledged *wife*.

Surely Joseph does not understand all of this. He cannot possibly know that two thousand years later there will be two billion followers of Mary's child. But he takes to heart the command of the angel in the dream: *do not be afraid!* When he obeys, "Joseph the righteous" and "Joseph the gracious" become "Joseph the fearless"! He goes ahead with the marriage. He claims his divinely-ordered destiny.

WHAT DO YOU THINK?

What characteristics in Joseph's life should we strive to develop as parents today?

[Ephesians 5:22-33 can be a starting point for discussion.]

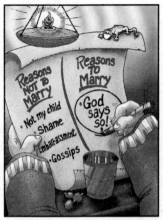

Visual for lesson 3. *This visual points out that obedience can require hard choices. Discuss how that is true today.*

## THE DREAMTIME

The aborigines of Australia have many stories from the past that have been passed down for generations. These stories embody their myths and legends about the time of the creation of the world and the beginning of their people. They call this period the Dreamtime.

We use the word *dream* rather differently! While one should be cautious about interpreting dreams, psychologists may ask their patients about their dreams because the subconscious mind is allegedly important in understanding the conscious mind. When we can remember a dream when we wake up, we usually realize that its content was ludicrous, logically impossible, or downright laughable.

But God has a right, of course, to use dreams for his own purposes. We are glad that Joseph took seriously God's message to him in this dream, and the later one that led the family to escape to Egypt. Today we have the full revelation of God for the New Testament era in Scripture. We do not need to sift through any "dream-time" to figure out the past or to know what God wants us to do next.

The apostle Paul says that the revelation we have in Scripture is just what we need (2 Timothy 3:16, 17). And the apostle Peter put the word of the prophets above personal experience (2 Peter 1:19-21). Surely it is a dangerous vanity to expect God to speak with individuals in unique and personal ways when he has already revealed his will to everyone!                                    —R. C. S.

**21. *"She will give birth to a son, and you are to give him the name Jesus, because he will save his people from their sins."***

This is the climactic verse in this section, and one of the most important verses in Matthew. Long before ultrasound was invented, the gender of the unborn child is revealed by the angel. It is to be a boy, *a son!*

The angel also gives Joseph the correct name for the boy: *Jesus.* This name is actually the Greek version of the famous Hebrew name *Joshua.* This was the name of several men in the history of Israel, but the most recognized was Joshua, the son of Nun, the protégé of Moses. Numbers 13:16 tells us that Moses changes the name of Hoshea to Joshua. This is a very slight spelling change in Hebrew—the addition of a single, small letter at the beginning of the name. It is an enormous change in meaning, however. Hoshea simply means "salvation," but Joshua means "Yahweh is salvation."

Jesus, then, is clearly identified as the promised Savior of his people. His mission of salvation is given from the beginning. But he is not the type of Savior that the Jews expect. He is not a military messiah, a secular savior who will deliver them from the hated Roman overlords. His mission is far more important than that.

Jesus is to be a spiritual Savior—one who will deliver his people from their sins. Only in this way can he be the son of Abraham, to bless the whole of humanity. Only as a spiritual Savior can he reign eternally on the everlasting throne of David. Part of Matthew's job from here on is to explain to the Jews what kind of Messiah God has sent.

## III. FULFILLMENT TO OBEDIENCE (MATTHEW 1:22-25)

### A. PREDICTIONS (vv. 22, 23)

**22, 23. *All this took place to fulfill what the Lord had said through the prophet: "The virgin will be with child and will give birth to a son, and they will call him Immanuel"—which means, "God with us."***

For the first time, Matthew shows us one of his major agendas and its associated method. The agenda is to demonstrate that Jesus is truly God's intended

Messiah, the Savior promised to the Jews. The method is to use the Jewish Scriptures (our Old Testament) in a selective way to explain God's prophesied intentions. A dozen times Matthew uses some form of the formula *this took place to fulfill what the Lord had said through the prophet*. This is how Matthew relates the Old Testament prophecy to Jesus.

In this case the prophesied event is the creation of a child in the uterus of a *virgin* woman. The prophecy is found in Isaiah 7:14. Matthew uses the Greek word for virgin here, *parthenos*. This is the root word for the famous Greek temple in Athens, the Parthenon. This was a shrine to Athena, the virgin goddess of mythology.

Matthew does not intend a pagan reference here, but uses a word that everyone in the ancient world knows to represent an unmarried young woman who has not engaged in sexual intercourse. To describe Mary at this point seems to be stating a self-contradiction: a pregnant virgin. It is the paradoxical double truth of being a virgin and being pregnant at the same time. It is important to notice why Matthew emphasizes Mary's virginity. He tells us that Jesus' conception in the womb of a virgin is a miraculous sign, a fulfillment of prophecy. It marks Jesus as unique.

This phenomenon is further explained by Isaiah's prophesied name for the child: *Immanuel*. Jesus is not given this title as a personal name. His given, personal name is Jesus, not Immanuel. Matthew's point is in the meaning of the title. Immanuel means *God is with us*.

Isaiah's prophecy takes a marvelous turn at this point. A mighty miracle is here, and God is showing that he is the Creator, the Master of the biological universe. A baby is created where there should be no baby. We cannot help but conclude: surely, God is here with us! The further truth is that God will continue to be with us.

## B. ACTIONS (vv. 24, 25)

**24, 25. When Joseph woke up, he did what the angel of the Lord had commanded him and took Mary home as his wife. But he had no union with her until she gave birth to a son. And he gave him the name Jesus.**

Now we see the character of Joseph displayed in a powerful way. He is both fearless and obedient. He completes the marriage, brushing aside any potential criticism that his wife is "damaged goods."

The phrase *had no union with her* means that Joseph honors the sacred child that Mary is carrying by having no sexual relationship with his new wife until after the birth. He completed his obedience by faithfully giving his new son *the name* given by the angel: he is *Jesus!*

### THE GREATEST EVENT

Many years ago, twenty-eight historians and journalists were asked to name the most significant events in human history. Columbus's discovery of America came in first. The invention of the printing press was second. There was a tie for third through thirteenth places among eleven events. After those came the writing of the U.S. Constitution, the discovery of anesthesia, the discovery of the X-ray, and the invention of the airplane. The birth of Jesus came after all these!

In fact nothing since creation even approaches the significance of the birth of Jesus Christ. It is more than mere convenience that divides history into B.C. and A.D. There are stiff-necked unbelievers who have changed B.C. (before Christ) to B.C.E. (before the Common Era); they have changed A.D. (anno Domini—in the year of the Lord) to C.E. (Common Era). Though they refuse to acknowledge the

### WHAT DO YOU THINK?

*To some people the names and titles of Jesus and the doctrine of the virgin birth may seem like dry theological facts. In what ways should these things actually play a meaningful role in our life and obedience?*

### WHAT DO YOU THINK?

*Joseph probably invited scorn from the people in his community by following through with his marriage to the pregnant Mary. How can we respond to God's calls in our lives without being intimidated by peer pressure and public perception?*

### WHAT DO YOU THINK?

*Joseph's role in the unfolding plan of God's redemption was quiet and unassuming, but vitally important. In what ways can God use our "small" acts of obedience in the larger plan of the kingdom of God?*

PRAYER

*Mighty God, who formed Jesus in the body of Mary, who revealed the circumstances to Isaiah seven hundred years earlier, who chose the faithful Joseph to rear your own Son, to you we offer our amazement, our wonder, and our praise. May we be more like Joseph, acting with courage and grace to do your will. In the name of Jesus we pray, amen.*

name of the Lord Jesus Christ, they cannot escape the fact that history is dated from his birth, even with their new designations.

Civil rights activist and 1950 Nobel Peace Prize-winner Ralph J. Bunche (1904–1971) said, "If you want to get across an idea, wrap it up in a person." God knew the truth of this idea long before Bunche did! God expressed his love for the world in the person of Jesus Christ. His entry into the world forever changed the world. He interrupted history and forever set it on a new path.

More specifically, in bringing the love and grace of God, Jesus brought eternal life. Thus his arrival, life, death, and resurrection were the greatest events of history. How does this fact affect the way you live your life each day?     —R. C. S.

## CONCLUSION

We may think that Joseph's situation is unlike ours. We may be tempted to admire him at first, and then dismiss him as a remote hero of olden days. But Joseph was very much like us. He was a simple man living an honest life. He had plans to marry a girl from his village, raise a family, and enjoy life.

It didn't turn out that way for Joseph. God called him to a ministry under cloudy circumstances. The plan of God stepped on Joseph's plans. He was not to have a traditional wedding nor the joy of a long-anticipated wedding night. He was called to make a difficult decision. He was called to a difficult obedience.

We must remember that Joseph's obedience was no sure thing. He could have rejected Mary and her child to follow a safe course. He easily could have found another wife, another family, another life. He didn't. He obeyed God. He gave family stability and a Davidic heritage to Jesus.

Before ending this lesson time, examine your own heart and ask yourself questions that Joseph had to answer. First, has God given me a "dream" about what he wants me to do? We're not talking about the appearance of an angel in a dream. Remember: even in the Bible there are few people who received this type of dream. But God is alive and active in our lives; he cares about you.

Maybe the dream was planted by a speaker at a camp or retreat many years ago. Maybe the dream is the desire to serve in some type of missions capacity. There are many short-term missions opportunities for people of all ages today. Your dream may be fulfilled by serving as a forwarding agent for a missionary and visiting him or her every year. It may be volunteer assistance in fund-raising for a ministry of compassion and benevolence. Rekindle your dream, or ask God to give you a new one!

Second, am I willing to obey God's call in spite of public disapproval? When the demand of God was clarified for Joseph, he obeyed. Those who obey God's leading are often criticized, even inside the church. If you are a senior willing to take a short-term missions trip, your children, your doctor, and your friends might all say that you are crazy. Imagine this, though: how would you like to write a letter asking for funds for your trip and send it to your grandchildren!? That would be a turn of the tables, and you may be surprised at how willing they are to help and how proud they will be of you.

Third, how long will I wait? Today's Scripture seems to tell us that Joseph began to act as soon as he woke up. He did not spend days in doubt. His obedient heart pushed him to act faithfully and boldly, no matter the consequences.

The older we get, the more we realize that life is short and many opportunities slip by us. We are often in no position to know the importance of our acts of obedience in the larger picture of the kingdom of God. Joseph probably saw himself doing the right thing in a small-town drama, a family matter. Yet his obedience was a key part of God's plan for the Messiah. God honors obedience to all ministries, great and small. May we honor them, too!

THOUGHT TO REMEMBER

*Obedience to God is never a mistake.*

# Discovery Learning

*This page contains an alternative lesson plan emphasizing learning activities. Classes desiring such student involvement will find these suggestions helpful. The next page is a reproducible activity page to further enhance discovery learning.*

## LEARNING GOALS

After participating in this lesson, each student will be able to:

1. Recount the events that led to Joseph's gracious response to Mary's pregnancy.

2. Explain how Joseph's obedience to God's command revealed his character.

3. Make a commitment to respond with obedience to God's leading in a specific life situation.

## INTO THE LESSON

Before class begins, write on the board in large letters, "News We Don't Want to Get." Just below it write in smaller letters, "What is the worst news you can imagine?" Your learners should naturally begin thinking and talking about this question as they arrive.

After class begins, encourage responses from those who are interested in sharing their answers. Typical answers will include news of a death in the family, a diagnosis of cancer, etc.

Then tell your learners that in today's lesson Joseph gets the message he dreads most about his fiancée, Mary. Challenge your learners to put themselves in Joseph's place as you begin the study of today's text.

## INTO THE WORD

*Joseph's reactions.* Inform the class that you want them to think about three questions before you read the text: (1) "What did Joseph think when he found out Mary was pregnant?" (2) "What did he plan to do?" and (3) "What did his plan say about his character and integrity?" (Write these questions on the board. You may instead distribute individual pieces of paper with the questions preprinted on them.)

Next, read today's text aloud, pausing after verse 19. Then ask your learners to respond to the three questions. Take time to discuss issues that may come up. (The lesson commentary will prepare you for this discussion.)

Then read through verses 20-25. Ask for responses to the same questions. (Options: allow time to write answers down, or discuss them in small groups if your class is large.) Some possible answers to the questions include "Joseph thought Mary had been unfaithful to him," "He planned to divorce her quietly," "He loved her too much to disgrace her; he cared more for her welfare than for his own reputation."

*Angel message.* Conclude the discussion by noting that the angel said that the baby Mary was carrying was conceived by the Holy Spirit in fulfillment of Isaiah's prophecy. The baby would one day save his people from their sins.

Since this type of birth hadn't happened before, Joseph probably had no idea what the angel's message meant. He took Mary as his wife, as the angel had told him to do. Stress that Joseph was a man of faith. He obeyed the word of the Lord, even though he didn't necessarily understand it.

## INTO LIFE

Remind your class of the words of William Cowper: "God moves in a mysterious way his wonders to perform." This was certainly the case in the conception of Jesus, and Joseph no doubt struggled to understand this "mysterious way" of getting a child. God is still a God of surprises today.

Divide your class into small discussion groups of three or four, if your seating arrangement allows for this. Pose this question to the groups: "When did God surprise you in a life-changing way?" Allow time for several learners to offer answers. Some may say that it was in their choice of spouse, school, or occupation. Others may mention discovering a spiritual gift that was unexpected. Perhaps it was the birth of a child. Perhaps it was a difficult situation, such as a serious illness or the death of a loved one.

Ask: "How might God surprise you in the next five years?" In a sense this is a rhetorical question, since no one can predict the future. However, the answers to the previous question may suggest some possibilities.

Next, encourage your learners to think about how they would respond if God were to surprise them in one of the ways that they previously mentioned. Would they be resentful because their previous plans had been upended? Would they obey, but only grudgingly? How would they know that it was really God who was leading them into such and such a path, and not mere human desire or the natural course of life?

Close the class with an exhortation to respond to God's surprises the way Joseph did—in faith and obedience. Move to a time of prayer, asking God to prepare your learners for the future surprises that he will bring into their lives.

# A Significant Genealogy

As background for today's lesson, look at Joseph's genealogy in Matthew 1:1-11. It is printed for you here.

A record of the genealogy of Jesus Christ the son of David, the son of Abraham:

Abraham was the father of Isaac, Isaac the father of Jacob, Jacob the father of Judah and his brothers, Judah the father of Perez and Zerah, whose mother was Tamar, Perez the father of Hezron, Hezron the father of Ram, Ram the father of Amminadab, Amminadab the father of Nahshon, Nahshon the father of Salmon, Salmon the father of Boaz, whose mother was Rahab, Boaz the father of Obed, whose mother was Ruth, Obed the father of Jesse, and Jesse the father of King David.

David was the father of Solomon, whose mother had been Uriah's wife, Solomon the father of Rehoboam, Rehoboam the father of Abijah, Abijah the father of Asa, Asa the father of Jehoshaphat, Jehoshaphat the father of Jehoram, Jehoram the father of Uzziah, Uzziah the father of Jotham, Jotham the father of Ahaz, Ahaz the father of Hezekiah, Hezekiah the father of Manasseh, Manasseh the father of Amon, Amon the father of Josiah, and Josiah the father of Jeconiah and his brothers at the time of the exile to Babylon.

Look at the names that are listed below. Read or skim the verses beside the names. Then jot down one fact that you think is significant about that person.

Abraham—Romans 4:18-22
Isaac—Genesis 21:1-7
Jacob—Genesis 27
Judah—Genesis 44:16-34
Tamar—Genesis 38
Boaz—Ruth 4:1-17
Rahab—Joshua 2
Jesse—1 Samuel 16:1-13
King David—1 Samuel 24
Solomon—1 Kings 3
Uriah's wife—2 Samuel 11
Rehoboam—1 Kings 12:1-17
Abijah—1 Kings 15:1-4
Asa—1 Kings 15:9-14
Jehoshaphat—1 Kings 22:41-46
Jehoram—2 Kings 8:16-19
Uzziah—2 Chronicles 26
Jotham—2 Kings 15:32-35
Ahaz—2 Chronicles 28
Hezekiah—2 Kings 18–20
Manasseh—2 Kings 21:1-16
Amon—2 Kings 21:19-24
Josiah—2 Kings 22:1–23:30

Now glance over the facts you've written. What does this list tell you about the people God uses to accomplish His purposes?

# CALLED TO HOPE IN CHRIST

## LESSON 4

## WHY TEACH THIS LESSON?

Another year is upon us. For some, 2004 has been a hard year and you've anticipated the changing of the calendar at midnight this coming Friday night. This change of the calendar, you hope, will bring a change of fortune and direction for your life. But as we sing "Auld Lang Syne" one more time, we know that old acquaintances will not be forgotten and that events of the "old long ago" will still be with us.

We know that a simple change of the calendar cannot change the basic issues of life. Even becoming a Christian does not always change the hard times we face. But one thing we can have at the change not only of the calendar but also from minute to minute, second to second, is the hope that comes in knowing Jesus Christ.

It was when Simeon and Anna came face to face with Jesus that they were able to speak words of peace and hope for the future. As we study this lesson, we learn from them where the true source of hope for the future lies.

## INTRODUCTION

### A. BRIEF ENCOUNTERS, IMPORTANT ENCOUNTERS

Can you think of a person whom you met only briefly but who had an impact on your life? I remember a few years ago when I was staying in a hotel while attending a convention. I had no car, so I went down at suppertime to see if I could share a cab to a restaurant. I did find a couple of willing people who shared my situation and we ended up at an Outback Steakhouse.

I realized in the taxi ride that these men were not Christians. They were a fascinating pair, however, both scientists for the National Oceanographic and Atmospheric Administration (NOAA). We spent the evening discussing the problems facing the world's oceans, and I learned a lot. I learned that the average depth of the ocean is five miles. This gave me new understanding of the promise in Habakkuk 2:14: "For the earth will be filled with the knowledge of the glory of the Lord, as the waters cover the sea." What I managed to learn and appreciate from such a brief encounter!

Today's lesson tells the story of the encounter of Jesus and his parents with two special people. We meet these two only briefly in the pages of Scripture, but their witness has the power to have a lasting impact on our lives. They are Simeon and Anna, and they have waited their entire lifetimes to see the promised Messiah. Their personal experience, however, served to do more than allow them to glimpse God's promised Messiah with their own eyes. Both Simeon and Anna have a prophetic ministry to fulfill.

### B. LESSON BACKGROUND

From one perspective the birth of Jesus was a spectacular event. It was heralded by a sky full of angels. A supernatural star marked the occasion. The infant was sought out by wealthy magi from foreign lands. An evil king feared for his throne.

DEVOTIONAL READING:
PSALM 71:1-8
BACKGROUND SCRIPTURE:
LUKE 2:22-38
PRINTED TEXT:
LUKE 2:22-38

Dec
26

LESSON AIMS

*After participating in this lesson, each student will be able to:*

*1. Summarize the encounter between Joseph and Mary and the two prophetic persons in the temple.*

*2. Explain how Jesus' birth gives hope to the world today.*

*3. Identify a practical way to follow the example of Simeon and Anna in proclaiming the hope found in Jesus.*

KEY VERSES

*My eyes have seen your salvation, which you have prepared in the sight of all people.*
—Luke 2:30, 31

From another perspective, Jesus' birth was remarkably mundane. This is seen in today's lesson as Jesus' parents follow the traditional rituals required of the Jews in regard to a firstborn son. The incident reveals both the faithfulness and the poverty of Joseph and Mary. While this trip to the temple may have been exciting for this rural couple, it was a common exercise among their people.

Yet in the midst of the routine, God had a few more surprises for them. They met Simeon and Anna, people with divine insight beyond the visible circumstances. These two had an understanding of God's master plan for redemption and the central role of Jesus in that plan.

Sometimes we have been taught that the office of prophet ceased with the completion of the Old Testament and that Malachi was the last of the line. Reading the New Testament, however, reveals a lively interest in prophets and prophecy at the time of Jesus. Prophets were not necessarily those who foretold the future, although that may be an aspect of their ministry. Prophets were inspired by the Holy Spirit to preach God's message: a call for justice and repentance among the people and a proclamation of Israel's hope for a Messiah. Several people serve a prophetic role in the Gospel of Luke, including Elizabeth (1:41-45), Zechariah (1:67), John the Baptist (7:26; 20:6), and even Jesus himself (7:16).

In this lesson, Simeon and Anna are prophetic people. Anna is specifically called a prophetess (Luke 2:36), while Simeon speaks prophetically under the influence of the Holy Spirit (2:25-35).

## I. OBEDIENCE TO THE LAW (LUKE 2:22-24)

### A. PARENTS' ACTIONS (v. 22)

**22. When the time of their purification according to the Law of Moses had been completed, Joseph and Mary took him to Jerusalem to present him to the Lord**

The Jews of Jesus' day have strict rituals associated with the birth of a son. In keeping with *the law of Moses* (which Jesus kept all his life), Jesus was circumcised and named on the eighth day (Leviticus 12:3; Luke 2:21).

The *purification* being referred to in this verse is that of the mother. After the birth of a son, the mother is ceremonially unclean for seven days until the circumcision. Although considered "clean" at this point, the mother is required to remain at home another thirty-three days (see Leviticus 12:1-4). At the end of this forty-day period, she goes to the temple in Jerusalem (if she can) and offers a sacrifice.

### B. LAW'S REQUIREMENTS (vv. 23, 24)

**23. ... (as it is written in the Law of the Lord, "Every firstborn male is to be consecrated to the Lord"),**

Associated with the purification rites of the mother are the dedication rites for the son. God's instruction to the Jews was that all *firstborn males* belong to him (see Exodus 13:2, 12). Therefore, this son must be "bought back" or redeemed from the Lord. A formula for redeeming firstborn sons is given in Numbers 18:15, 16.

**24. ... and to offer a sacrifice in keeping with what is said in the Law of the Lord: "a pair of doves or two young pigeons."**

Luke includes a detail here that reveals the financial status of Joseph and Mary. The law requires an offering of a yearling lamb and a small pigeon or dove. However, the law allows poor women to bring two birds and no lamb (Leviticus 12:6-8). One of these birds would be burned as a sacrifice while the other was killed and retained as an offering for the temple. "Dove" is a somewhat generic term for small birds used as sacrificial animals (cf. Numbers 6:10).

WHAT DO YOU THINK?

*What inspiration can we gain from the fact that Joseph and Mary faithfully fulfilled their obligations under the Old Testament law, despite having been shown special, miraculous attention by God?*

## II. ENCOUNTER WITH SIMEON (LUKE 2:25-35)

### A. SIMEON'S BACKGROUND (vv. 25, 26)

**25. Now there was a man in Jerusalem called Simeon, who was righteous and devout. He was waiting for the consolation of Israel, and the Holy Spirit was upon him.**

Simeon is the name borne by a man who encounters Jesus' family in the temple. This is a famous name, the name of the second son of Jacob by Leah, and therefore the name of one of the twelve tribes of Israel.

Beyond his name we are told three things about Simeon. First, Luke gives a description of his character: he is *righteous and devout*. Being righteous means that he is a good man. Being devout means that he is a man of worship and faith. These two attributes probably make Simeon a regular fixture in the temple.

Second, Luke tells us that Simeon is waiting for the consolation of Israel. This means he is waiting for God's Messiah, but the expression gives us insight into what type of Messiah that Simeon expects. The rabbis of Jesus' day sometimes refer to the Messiah as the "consoler" or the "comforter." This is based on Scriptures such as Isaiah 40:1, 2, where Israel looks forward to God's comfort, meaning his forgiveness and national restoration. Jews like Simeon believe that the Roman occupation of Israel and Jerusalem is a punishment from God that can be lifted only by God's forgiveness and miraculous intervention. As we will see, however, the vision of Simeon is much bigger that mere military victory.

Third, Luke relates that Simeon is a man filled with *the Holy Spirit*. This shows that he is a deeply spiritual man, in tune with God in an extraordinary way.

**26. It had been revealed to him by the Holy Spirit that he would not die before he had seen the Lord's Christ.**

While Simeon is never called a prophet, Luke describes him in prophet-like terms. Simeon has received a direct message from God, a revelation. This is a prophecy of a personal nature. Simeon has been told that his life will extend past the birth of the Messiah and that he will lay eyes on this promised *Christ* (which means "anointed one"). We do not know how old Simeon is, but Luke portrays him as one who has waited quite a long time, so he is probably a very old man.

### B. SIMEON'S SONG (vv. 27-32)

**27. Moved by the Spirit, he went into the temple courts. When the parents brought in the child Jesus to do for him what the custom of the Law required,**

This is a "divine appointment," a meeting arranged by the Holy Spirit. Such meetings are rarely understood through foresight, but rather through hindsight. For the author Luke and for the participants, this is not a chance meeting. Many Christians experience the work of God in their lives in such a way. God arranges circumstances according to his will, but rarely reveals this to us ahead of time.

**28. Simeon took him in his arms and praised God, saying:**

There must be something both commanding and reassuring in the presence of *Simeon* for the young mother to allow a stranger to hold her baby! Notice that Simeon does not presume to bless the child, for that is not his role. He sees and knows that this is the Messiah and gives a blessing of praise to God for his faithfulness.

**29-32. "Sovereign Lord, as you have promised,**
    **you now dismiss your servant in peace.**
**For my eyes have seen your salvation,**
    **which you have prepared in the sight of all people,**
**a light for revelation to the Gentiles**
    **and for glory to your people Israel."**

*HOW TO SAY IT*

Asher. ASH-er.
Benedictus. BEN-eh-DIK-tus.
Bethlehem. BETH-lih-hem.
Gentiles. JEN-tiles.
Habakkuk. Huh-BACK-kuk.
Hannah. HAN-uh.
Jerusalem. Juh-ROO-suh-lem.
Leviticus. Leh-VIT-ih-kus.
Magnificat. Mag-NIF-ih-cot.
Malachi. MAL-uh-kye.
Messiah. Meh-SIGH-uh.
Nunc Dimittis (Latin). Nunk
   Dih-MIT-us.
Phanuel. Fuh-NYOO-el.
Simeon. SIM-ee-un.
Zechariah. ZEK-uh-RYE-uh.

**Whose EYES need to see the Lord's salvation today?**

See Luke 2:30, 31

Visual for lesson 4. This visual reminds us that the eyes of all people need to see the Lord's salvation. Who will show them?

Luke now records his third great canticle, the Song of Simeon. This canticle is known as the "Nunc Dimittis," its Latin title, and it has often been set to music in the history of the church. (The other two are the Song of Zechariah, also called the "Benedictus," and the Song of Mary, also called the "Magnificat.")

There is a simple lesson in this song that still applies today. When we have seen Jesus (believed in him), we may face death with *peace*. This assurance is not for Simeon alone, but should guide every believer as he or she prepares for death. This is a promise that we should all claim!

There are also some important doctrinal teachings in this song. First, Simeon understands God's Messiah to be more than a military leader. He is *salvation*, a Savior. This is in keeping with Matthew's own understanding of Jesus' mission from last week's lesson (Matthew 1:21).

Second, while the Messiah is certainly the fulfillment of Israel's hopes (*for glory to your people Israel*), he has a ministry to all people, Jews and *Gentiles*. Simeon has been given an understanding of Jesus' mission to be a Savior for all humanity. This is certainly crucial for those of us who have no Jewish blood in our veins.

Third, we gain insight into God's plan for redemption. He did not choose the best candidate among available men or women (like he did with King Saul). Rather, he prepared someone from birth for this unique and essential role. Thus Simeon can look at a helpless baby and know what the future holds.

### LET THERE BE LIGHT

Many travelers who suffer from jet lag have tried using the supplement melatonin. This supplement is said to help regulate the body's "clock" so that one adjusts more quickly to a different time zone. Recently, researchers claimed that melatonin, which the body produces naturally, is a defense against cancer. The report said that melatonin builds in the darkness. Too much light works against the production of melatonin. The report concluded that we are not getting enough darkness!

That may be true physically, but we certainly have enough darkness spiritually. Many live in spiritual darkness for years. Some live all their lives in this kind of darkness, never seeing the true light of life! And that is exactly what Simeon was talking about—spiritual light.

One of the first acts of creation was, "Let there be light," and it is interesting that the Bible should use the term *light* to describe the knowledge of God. Eventually, Jesus came as the light of the world (John 1:4-9). What Simeon foresaw the apostle John experienced. And so have we. There is no life spiritually without Jesus, the light of the world.    —R. C. S.

### C. SIMEON'S PROPHECY (vv. 33-35)

**33. The child's father and mother marveled at what was said about him.**

Who could blame them! These simple, faithful people are being bombarded by the supernatural elements surrounding the birth of their son. Yet this "marveling" does not lead to disbelief. While Joseph and Mary may not understand everything, they act with faith.

**34. Then Simeon blessed them and said to Mary, his mother: "This child is destined to cause the falling and rising of many in Israel, and to be a sign that will be spoken against,**

Simeon has a private message for Mary. This may indicate his prophetic foresight of Joseph's death before Jesus' adult ministry. Simeon's reference to the *falling and rising* of many brings to mind the image of Jesus as both a cornerstone and a stumbling stone. Some build upon him, others are offended by him (see

---

## WHAT DO YOU THINK?

*Simeon received a special personal blessing, but focused even more on the blessing Jesus would be to others. How can we each develop that kind of missionary mind-set?*

## DAILY BIBLE READINGS

*Monday, Dec. 20—You, O Lord, Are My Hope (Psalm 71: 1-8)*

*Tuesday, Dec. 21—New Things I Now Declare (Isaiah 42:1-9)*

*Wednesday, Dec. 22—Jesus Is Born (Luke 2:1-7)*

*Thursday, Dec. 23—Angels Appear to the Shepherds (Luke 2:8-14)*

*Friday, Dec. 24—The Shepherds See Jesus (Luke 2:15-20)*

*Saturday, Dec. 25—Jesus Is Taken to the Temple (Luke 2: 22-26)*

*Sunday, Dec. 26—Simeon and Anna Praise God (Luke 2: 27-38)*

Romans 9:33; 1 Peter 2:4-8). The word for rising is the word for "resurrecting." This may indicate that Simeon foresees Jesus' later victory over death and his role as the firstfruits of the resurrection of all believers (1 Corinthians 15:20).

Simeon also prophesies that Jesus will be *a sign . . . spoken against.* The word *sign* is used here in the sense of "miracle" (cf. Luke 11:16; 23:8). Jesus will do more than perform miraculous signs. He is a miracle! His life is a sign of God's presence and activity (see Luke 11:20). This wondrous life will not be well received by all, however. Some will see Jesus as a threat and oppose him, even to his death.

**35. "... *so that the thoughts of many hearts will be revealed. And a sword will pierce your own soul too."***

Jesus' ministry will bring hidden thoughts and motives to the surface. Many who give an outward appearance of holiness and righteousness will be revealed as impostors as they oppose Jesus. Simeon gives Mary a hard promise that these attacks on her good and righteous Son will tear her *soul* apart as well.

## III. ENCOUNTER WITH ANNA (LUKE 2:36-38)

### A. ANNA'S BACKGROUND (vv. 36, 37)

**36, 37. *There was also a prophetess, Anna, the daughter of Phanuel, of the tribe of Asher. She was very old; she had lived with her husband seven years after her marriage, and then was a widow until she was eighty-four. She never left the temple but worshiped night and day, fasting and praying.***

One of the most intriguing women in the Bible is *a prophetess* by the name of *Anna* (the Hebrew equivalent is Hannah). Luke seems to know quite a lot about her. Her father's name is *Phanuel,* which means "face of God." She is from *the tribe of Asher,* one of the northern ten tribes deported by the Assyrians in the eighth century B.C.

Anna's age may be understood two ways. Luke may be giving us her actual age (i.e., *eighty-four* years old), or he may be stating how long she has been a *widow.* If the second option is correct, then Anna could be over one hundred years old.

At any rate Anna is of a great age. Any age we can compute means that she has been alive long enough to remember when the Romans conquered the Jewish homeland in 63 B.C.

Most interesting, though, are her spiritual qualifications. She is a prophetess, one blessed with divine insight and messages. Being a prophet is a vocal occupation. We can imagine that Anna speaks words of encouragement and exhortation to the temple pilgrims she encounters. This prophetic vocation consumes her to the point that she lives at the *temple* and participates constantly in the ongoing prayers and religious fasts that take place there.

### SERVING GOD WITH PRAYER

A minister had been called to serve as the interim preacher in a small church. He was standing at the front door one Sunday morning when an elderly lady came in. She asked for two bulletins. That seemed puzzling.

Then she explained that every week she sent a church bulletin to the man who had been their minister years before. He was now in a nursing home, but every week he received in the mail a bulletin from the church he had served faithfully for many years.

But why not just send him the one she herself used in the worship service? Then he realized that she needed two because she kept the other to pray that week for everyone on the prayer list. He thought, "There is no one I'd rather have praying for me than this aging, thoughtful Christian sister."

**WHAT DO YOU THINK?**

*In what ways can Simeon's predictions about Jesus also come true in our lives?*

**WHAT DO YOU THINK?**

*It is obvious that both Simeon and Anna enjoyed an extraordinary relationship with God. What can we learn from that to strengthen our own walk with the Lord?*

## PRAYER

*Dear God, may we be people of hope. May we live as if we know our future is secure. May our lives sing of our hope to a world living desperately without hope. We pray in the name of the one who brings hope to all, Jesus the Christ, amen.*

Anna, in our text, was like that. At her advanced age her strength and energy must have been limited. There were many things she could not do, but she saw prayer as something she could do. Luke saw it as a way of serving God! Perhaps we think of prayer and service as two very different things, but Luke saw them as the same thing.

Work and worship are not opposites. Sometimes the hardest work we do is worship. And sometimes the most productive work we do is worship. So we should never take it lightly when someone says, "I am praying for you." And we should never take it lightly when someone says, "Pray for me." That could well be the most important service you can offer. —R. C. S.

### B. ANNA'S REMARKS (v. 38)

**38. Coming up to them at that very moment, she gave thanks to God and spoke about the child to all who were looking forward to the redemption of Jerusalem.**

Luke indicates that God has arranged another divine appointment. Anna's reaction differs from Simeon's, however. Rather than speak to Jesus' parents, Anna does her usual thing: she talks with anyone who will listen. The time for *redemption* has come!

## CONCLUSION

### A. HOPE IN THE HEART

What a difference hope makes! I am reminded of the little boy who had been promised a fishing trip with his father for the next day. As he went to bed he joyfully hugged his father and said, "Thanks, Daddy, for tomorrow." That's hope! Israel had hoped for a Redeemer for centuries before Jesus came. Jesus is hope realized. Paul dedicated himself to preaching this "hope of Israel" (Acts 28:20).

Hope makes life livable. How can we possibly endure tragedy if we have no hope? How can we face death without the hope of the resurrection? Hope is faith's view of the future. We believe that no matter how bad things may get, God loves us and will never desert us. As John promises, "perfect love drives out fear" (1 John 4:18).

Dread of the future is the opposite of hope. Fear of the future leads to worry, anxiety, even depression. Hope for the future gives us the strength to face what life throws at us. For decades Simeon and Anna hoped, and God did not disappoint them. He will do no less for us.

### B. SINGING OUR HOPE TO THE WORLD

How can we share hope with our fearful, terrified world? Here are some practical suggestions. First, let your joy out. Don't hoard your joy, share it! Share it with both your believing and nonbelieving friends. A remarkable thing will happen. You won't run out of joy, because God will replenish your supply endlessly.

Second, anticipate good things for the future. Anna endured decades of loneliness as a widow for the moment of pure joy she experienced when she saw Jesus. Not everything in the future will be pleasant. But God loves you and will bless you immeasurably if you trust him. Ultimately God will receive you into his presence and say, "Well done, good and faithful servant."

Third, focus your hope on Jesus, not yourself. If all you have to show a terrified world is your own life, you will not bring hope. We probably all have known people who have been betrayed so many times that they trust no one. They depend only on themselves. What miserable, futile lives they lead! How much better to trust Jesus, the Son of God, the conqueror of death. How much better to live and serve in a community of believers that has the common hope of abundant life because of Jesus Christ! When your life sings hope, it must sing Jesus.

## WHAT DO YOU THINK?

*How can we allow true hope to develop and grow in our hearts? Why is it easier to live with hope when we share it with others?*

## THOUGHT TO REMEMBER

*Live without fear of the future because of the hope Jesus brings.*

# Discovery Learning

*This page contains an alternative lesson plan emphasizing learning activities. Classes desiring such student involvement will find these suggestions helpful. The next page is a reproducible activity page to further enhance discovery learning.*

## LEARNING GOALS

After participating in this lesson, each student will be able to:

1. Summarize the encounter between Joseph and Mary and the two prophetic persons in the temple.

2. Explain how Jesus' birth gives hope to the world today.

3. Identify a practical way to follow the example of Simeon and Anna in proclaiming the hope found in Jesus.

## INTO THE LESSON

Before class begins, write on the board, "I'd be happy if only . . . " As your learners arrive, they should naturally begin thinking and talking about how to complete the statement.

As class begins, ask your learners to think not only of their own answers, but answers they have heard from other sources. Allow time for several to give both their own answers and answers that they have heard elsewhere. If you hear the answer "more money," challenge your class to be specific regarding exactly how it is that more money would make them happy.

Then say, "Today's lesson is about two people who also had a driving desire. Once that desire was met, they were happy and content."

## INTO THE WORD

To set the background for Simeon's hymn, summarize Luke 2:22-28 using the lesson commentary. Then discuss Simeon's hymn itself (vv. 29-32), phrase by phrase. Ask students the significance of each line. Below is the hymn, with some possible answers interspersed.

"Sovereign Lord . . . now dismiss your servant in peace" *[his life is fulfilled; nothing else is needed, so he can die without regret]*, "as you have promised" *[God apparently had promised Simeon that he would see the Messiah before he died]*, "For my eyes have seen your salvation" *[Jesus' name means 'the Lord saves']*, "which you have prepared in the sight of all people" *[God's Messiah was publicly displayed, for all to see]*, "a light for revelation to the Gentiles" *[non-Jews share in the salvation that this Jewish baby brings; see God's promise to Abram in Genesis 12:3]*, "and for glory to your people Israel" *[the Messiah is the hope of the Jewish nation, the fulfillment of prophecy]*.

Comment on the remaining verses, which cover Simeon's prophecy to Mary, and Anna's encounter with the baby Jesus.

## INTO LIFE

State that Simeon and Anna are great examples for us. Their lives were focused on one great hope, and that hope kept them going—even through old age and possible poverty. When that goal was reached, they considered their lives to be complete.

Ask: "What gives you hope during the hard times? What keeps you going when life is tough? What do you consider to be the ultimate purpose of your life?"

These are difficult and sometimes disturbing questions. Stress to the class that you are not expecting audible responses. In fact it might be best to have students simply think about the questions rather than give glib answers that sound spiritual. If time is up, you can close the class at this point with your learners still in a reflective mood.

As an optional activity, write on the board, "My Testimony of Trust." Then ask someone to give a dramatic reading of Habakkuk 3:17, 18. Point out to your learners that they may not be facing the exact situations described in verse 17, which was written for people in an agricultural situation. To make this verse more personal, allow your learners time to substitute mentally certain words that apply to their own situation. (For example they could say, "Even if my company goes bankrupt and I get laid off . . . " or "Even if I do not recover from my arthritis . . . ")

After students have had a few minutes to create their own versions of verse 17, ask for volunteers to share their work. You may have several learners who normally are very quiet and never speak up. They may be the ones who have the most thoughtful answers! Seek out some responses from them.

After several have read their "personal verses," ask the whole class to read verse 18 in unison.

Close in prayer, thanking God for the hope that he provides—hope that can sustain us in every situation that we may face. Ask that your learners be given the satisfaction of knowing, when they reach the end of their lives, that they have accomplished what God gave them to do. Pray that each would hear from God, "Well done!"

# Senior Hall of Fame

Simeon and Anna weren't the only people who had an impact in their old age. Identify the "senior saints" in these passages, what they did, and why those achievements were remarkable.

Genesis 7:6

Genesis 12:4

Joshua 14:10, 11

Acts 7:23, 30-34

Philemon 9

# A Promise Regarding the Elderly

"The righteous shall flourish like a palm tree: they will grow like a cedar of Lebanon; planted in the house of the Lord, they will flourish in the courts of our God. They will still bear fruit in old age, they will stay fresh and green, proclaiming, 'The Lord is upright; he is my Rock, and there is no wickedness in him.'"—Psalm 92:12-14

*For class discussion:* Is there an elderly person you know of who remains "fresh and green" in the Lord? In the space below, write down how you will thank this person today and how you will you pray for him or her.

*For the privacy of your own thoughts:* Is there an elderly person you know of who has grown stale and wilted in the service of the Lord? If so, how will you encourage this person? How will you pray for him or her?

# JESUS BEGINS HIS MINISTRY

**LESSON 5**

## WHY TEACH THIS LESSON?

Throughout history there have been cultic leaders able to rally people around them. From the past one hundred years, we think about Hitler and Hussein in the political arena or Jim Jones or David Koresh in religious movements. Often these cultic leaders were much more interested in themselves—their comforts, glory, and prestige—than they were in the interests and needs of their followers.

As a leader Jesus was just the opposite. He used his position and authority for the good of others. When he called people to follow him, it was not for what they could do for him but what he could and would do for them.

The message of this lesson is that when the voice of authority of Jesus spoke, people followed and demons departed. We learn from this lesson that Jesus is worthy to be followed. It is a lesson that should challenge us to "forsake our nets" and follow him.

## INTRODUCTION

### A. THE COST OF DISCIPLESHIP

A teenage friend of mine recently volunteered for a mission to the children in an inner-city area. She and her teammates spent several days teaching Vacation Bible School lessons to children who otherwise might not have had the opportunity to learn about Jesus.

A few weeks after returning home, she began to suffer with itch, and her mother took her to their family doctor. He examined her, asked her about recent activities, and correctly diagnosed that she was suffering from scabies.

Scabies, in case you've forgotten, is a disease that's supposed to affect the unclean poor of the world, not an American girl from an immaculately clean family. That's how mother and daughter felt, but it didn't alter the diagnosis. Both, but especially the daughter, felt humiliated, embarrassed, and, for no reason, ashamed. As any teenage girl might do, that young lady burst into tears right there in the doctor's office.

The Christian doctor, who correctly diagnosed the ailment, also correctly evaluated the situation. Calling the girl by name, he said, "Don't let this keep you from going on future mission trips. Remember that Jesus himself had to take risks when he came to earth."

He surely did; and, on a lesser scale, so did Peter, Andrew, James, John, and the other apostles. So have many of his other disciples down through the ages.

When Jesus calls, take up whatever cross comes your way and follow him. There may be some rough times, some uncomfortable situations, but in the end you'll be glad you answered his call.

### B. LESSON BACKGROUND

Our previous lesson ended in Jerusalem, the city to which Mary and Joseph had taken the baby Jesus "to present him to the Lord . . . and to offer a sacrifice" (Luke 2:22, 24). Our present lesson begins more than thirty years later, and we switch from Luke's Gospel to Mark's.

DEVOTIONAL READING:
MATTHEW 4:18-25
BACKGROUND SCRIPTURE:
MARK 1:14-28
PRINTED TEXT:
MARK 1:14-28

Jan
2

### LESSON AIMS

After participating in this lesson, each student will be able to:

1. Describe the activities of Jesus' early ministry and the effect he had on people.

2. Explain how Jesus demonstrated his authority.

3. State one specific way that he or she will submit to Jesus' authority.

### KEY VERSE

"Come, follow me," Jesus said, "and I will make you fishers of men."          —Mark 1:17

LESSON 5 NOTES

With the exception of one brief glimpse of Jesus as a twelve-year-old (Luke 2:41-52), we know nothing of his life from his birth until he was about thirty years old (Luke 3:23). That was when he went to the Jordan to be baptized of John (Luke 3:21, 22).

After his baptism Jesus was led into the wilderness where he fasted and was tempted for forty days. He then returned to the scene of John's baptizing, enlisted his first disciples, and journeyed to Cana in Galilee where he performed his first miracle. At this time he relocated his base of operations from his hometown of Nazareth to Capernaum, which is spoken thereafter as "his own town" (Matthew 9:1).

Having changed his residence to Capernaum, Jesus set out on a journey to Jerusalem to attend the first of the four Passovers of his ministry (John 2:23). During this visit to the Holy City, he cleansed the temple (the first of two times) and had his famous nighttime conversation with Nicodemus (John 2:12–3:21). On his return trip to Galilee, he passed through Samaria, where he had his conversation with the woman at the well. At this time John the Baptist was arrested (Luke 3:19, 20), which sets the scene for our present lesson.

## I. MESSAGE JESUS PREACHES (MARK 1:14, 15)

### A. KINGDOM OF GOD (v. 14)

**14. After John was put in prison, Jesus went into Galilee, proclaiming the good news of God.**

Matthew and Luke begin their Gospels with the birth of Jesus. John begins his Gospel by discussing the pre-existence of the Christ. Mark, however, begins his Gospel with the ministry of John the Baptist (Mark 1:2-8). John the Baptist is remembered as a fearless preacher who never hesitated to condemn sin wherever he found it. At one point he singled out Herod Antipas, the tetrarch of Galilee, and condemned him for living adulterously with his brother Philip's wife. Herod responded by imprisoning John (Mark 6:17-29).

As well as can be determined, *John was put in prison* about a year after Jesus launched his own ministry. We are in the second year of Jesus' three-year ministry; it is the so-called "year of popularity." The people in the region of Galilee are about to hear preaching and teaching concerning the long-awaited kingdom of God.

### B. REPENTANCE AND FAITH (v. 15)

**15. "The time has come," he said. "The kingdom of God is near. Repent and believe the good news!"**

The message that Jesus preaches is that *the kingdom of God is near.* That is *the good news* that the ancient Jews have been anticipating for hundreds of years. This is the culmination of the dreams that the Old Testament prophets had instilled in the hearts of God's people.

It will be some time before those who first hear this good news fully comprehend the true nature of this kingdom. It is not to be, as they think, a political or military force that will exalt a newly formed Jewish nation above all the other nations of the earth. Instead, it is to be a spiritual kingdom. It will include all individuals who respond with repentance and belief in the gospel. Jesus' message is similar to that which John has been preaching (see Matthew 3:1, 2).

In preaching to nonbelievers today, the logical and biblical procedure calls for submission to the entire plan of salvation. This includes, among other things, placing faith and belief in Christ, to be followed by repentance of sins. In Jesus' message to the Jews, however, the order is reversed. The Jews, who are already

*WHAT DO YOU THINK?*

*What can Jesus' announcement of the nearness of the kingdom teach us about determining the right timing for something?*

believers in the one true God, are first commanded to repent of their wicked resistance to God's will. That seems to be a prerequisite to believing the gospel message that the kingdom of God is near.

## II. CHALLENGE JESUS ISSUES (MARK 1:16-20)

### A. CALL OF SIMON AND ANDREW (vv. 16-18)

16-18. *As Jesus walked beside the Sea of Galilee, he saw Simon and his brother Andrew casting a net into the lake, for they were fishermen. "Come, follow me," Jesus said, "and I will make you fishers of men." At once they left their nets and followed him.*

If we had only Mark's Gospel, we would assume that Jesus' call to these four disciples is extended and accepted at their first meeting. This, of course, is not the case, as the first chapter of John makes clear. From that text we learn that *Simon* (Peter) and *Andrew* already are acquainted with Jesus and have some level of attachment to him. Perhaps this can be thought of as a loose, informal relationship between Jesus and these men. Now, an official call is extended and accepted.

We do well to remember that when we first expose our friends to Jesus, it can be premature to expect them to "leave *their nets*" and follow him immediately. Jesus allows time for his words to sink in and be accepted, and so should we.

### FISHING FOR PEOPLE

We always should be careful not to press an illustration that Jesus uses in ways that he would not intend. For instance, there are many things about fishing that do not fit evangelism. A fisherman will often use artificial lures, and that is certainly not an example for evangelism. We are not to win people by deceiving them, nor by promising them something that we cannot deliver.

Perhaps we may use "bait" in the sense that we address "felt needs" in order to get a chance to show people their deepest need, which is Jesus. There is no harm in churches offering recreational, social, or entertainment programs to unbelievers as long as they don't win people "to" what they're winning them "with." Ultimately, we must offer them Christ and eternal life.

In the days of our text, fishing was done with a cast net. Perhaps that idea fits evangelism best of all. As fishermen threw the net around the fish, so we throw arms of love and care around people. Our nets of compassion may include programs for people in prison, for the needy, for the aged, for the sick and dying, for unwed mothers, and for parents with troubled children. When we cast a net of love about them, we will certainly win some of them.

Of course, we will never win all of them. Jesus himself didn't. But we must be like the persistent fisherman, determined to keep on trying and never give up. Someday conditions will be right, people will respond, and our patience and persistence will pay off. Remaining faithful is the key. God will grant the victory.—R. C. S.

### B. CALL OF JAMES AND JOHN (vv. 19, 20)

19, 20. *When he had gone a little farther, he saw James son of Zebedee and his brother John in a boat, preparing their nets. Without delay he called them, and they left their father Zebedee in the boat with the hired men and followed him.*

After his call to Simon Peter and Andrew, Jesus goes *a little farther* along the shore to where the sons *of Zebedee, James* and *John, are preparing their nets.* Jesus calls them into a close discipleship as well.

Luke gives us some information that Mark omits. He says that James and John were "Simon's partners" (Luke 5:10). Mark adds his own tidbit when he relates that Zebedee has *hired men.* This seems to indicate that he is a man of some means.

---

**WHAT DO YOU THINK?**

In what sense does Jesus call people today to be "fishers of men"?

**WHAT DO YOU THINK?**

How does Jesus' call to the fishermen help us understand the difference between being a committed disciple and simply being a follower?

**HOW TO SAY IT**

Babylonian. Bab-ih-LOW-nee-un.
Capernaum. Kuh-PER-nay-um.
Galilee. GAL-uh-lee.
Herod Antipas. HAIR-ud AN-tih-pus.
Jerusalem. Juh-ROO-suh-lem.
Messiah. Meh-SIGH-uh.
Nazareth. NAZ-uh-reth.
Nicodemus. NICK-uh-DEE-mus.
Pharisees. FAIR-ih-seez.
Satan. SAY-tun.
synagogue. SIN-uh-gog.
tetrarch. TEH-trark or TEE-trark.
Zebedee. ZEB-eh-dee.

## III. AUTHORITY JESUS DEMONSTRATES (MARK 1:21, 22)

### A. LOCATION OF HIS TEACHING (v. 21)

**21. They went to Capernaum, and when the Sabbath came, Jesus went into the synagogue and began to teach.**

Capernaum is commonly thought of as Jesus' "headquarters" during his Galilean ministry (Matthew 4:13; Mark 2:1). It is situated on the northwest shore of the Sea of Galilee and must be a town of considerable size in Jesus' day.

Although this town is repeatedly mentioned in the Gospels (and only there in the New Testament), it is never mentioned in the Old Testament. This has led some students to conclude that it wasn't founded until after the Babylonian captivity. The apostle Paul will later use the same "freedom of the *synagogue*" that we see here in his own preaching and teaching (see Acts 13:15).

Bible students know that Capernaum becomes the scene of some of Jesus' miracles as well as some of his teaching. Because its citizens refuse to repent, however, Jesus predicts a horrible future for them (see Matthew 11:23, 24). Today, the exact location of Capernaum is subject to debate, perhaps testifying to the completeness of its destruction.

### B. EFFECT OF HIS TEACHING (v. 22)

**22. The people were amazed at his teaching, because he taught them as one who had authority, not as the teachers of the law.**

The *teachers of the law* are referred to as "scribes" in older translations. These are men employed to handle correspondence and to keep records. In the New Testament, they are learned men who study, interpret, and expound the law. Thus the translation "teachers of the law" thus accurately describes their function. Many references to them can be found in the Gospels, where they are usually associated in a bad light with the Pharisees.

Their teaching is here contrasted with that of Jesus' *teaching*. His teaching is fresh, open, straightforward, and spontaneous. The teaching of these learned men, on the other hand, is little more than a repetition of the sentiments and traditions of the great rabbis of the past. Such teaching lacks both freshness and practicality, often consisting of debates and disputes. When Jesus teaches *as one having authority*, it is little wonder that he thrills his audiences and creates in them a thirst for more of such teaching.

## IV. DEMON JESUS TERRIFIES (MARK 1:23-26)

### A. DEMON DESCRIBED (v. 23)

**23. Just then a man in their synagogue who was possessed by an evil spirit cried out,**

Some in the Greco-Roman world of Jesus' day believe that *an evil spirit* or demon is the ghost of a dead person that has taken possession of the living and is controlling them. Greeks also believe that some demons are beneficial, doing good for people.

The Bible, however, doesn't share these views. The evil spirits of the New Testament are always described as unclean—that is, wicked agents of the devil, laboring to carry out his unholy will. Although the precise expression "demon possession" is not a biblical term, it is a convenient phrase to use to describe people who have an evil spirit or demon.

Today many believe that demon possession is restricted to the period surrounding the life of Jesus on earth and is the result of the devil's bold attempt to meet and defeat Jesus in battle. Others, especially missionaries to third-world countries, feel that people are still demonized in the remote areas of the world

Visual for lessons 5, 13.
*This visual provides a summary of the lessons for this quarter. Leave it on display for the next several weeks.*

that have not been penetrated successfully by the light of the gospel. The Bible isn't clear as to which viewpoint is correct.

## B. DEMON REBUKED (vv. 24, 25)

**24, 25.** *"What do you want with us, Jesus of Nazareth? Have you come to destroy us? I know who you are—the Holy One of God!"*

*"Be quiet!" said Jesus sternly. "Come out of him!"*

The demon's message is expressed through the voice of the man. The demon not only recognizes that *Jesus* is from *Nazareth*, he also knows him to be *the Holy One of God*. This is a phrase used to describe the Messiah (Psalm 16:10; Acts 2:27). The demon is also aware that Jesus possesses the power to *destroy* him and other demons (note the use of the plural *us*).

Skeptics today may claim that what the ancient people thought of as "demon possession" actually was an illness such as schizophrenia or epilepsy. But the ancient people certainly knew the difference; Matthew 4:24 shows this distinction very well. Since children could have evil spirits, the cause of demon possession is not always moral (see Mark 9:14-29).

Jesus' two commands to *Be quiet!* and *Come out of him!* are quite forceful. Note that this encounter occurs in what seems to be an unlikely place—a synagogue. All sorts of people come to church!

## C. DEMON EXPELLED (v. 26)

**26.** *The evil spirit shook the man violently and came out of him with a shriek.*

The expulsion of this *evil spirit* is not without pain as *the man* is shaken violently by the departing spirit. Later in his Gospel, Mark relates the account of the expelling of a dumb spirit from a child (9:17-27). In that instance, as here, pain is involved.

The New Testament makes it clear that Satan does not want to lose control or influence over a person. Nor does Satan wish to surrender one of his earthly children to the Lord today. Quitting sin is a difficult business that seldom happens without some pain being involved.

## V. FAME JESUS EARNS (MARK 1:27, 28)

### A. PEOPLE'S AMAZEMENT GROWS (v. 27)

**27.** *The people were all so amazed that they asked each other, "What is this? A new teaching—and with authority! He even gives orders to evil spirits and they obey him."*

From the end of the Old Testament until the time of Jesus—more than four hundred years—the world has been without miracles. Not even John the Baptist is empowered to perform them (John 10:41). This lengthy period, void of the miraculous, contributes to the effect produced by Jesus as he performs "miracles, wonders and signs" (Acts 2:22). That he has the ability to command *evil spirits* naturally causes amazement.

### B. JESUS' FAME SPREADS (v. 28)

**28.** *News about him spread quickly over the whole region of Galilee.*

Jesus permits a limited testimony of this evil spirit that Jesus is the Holy One of God or Messiah (v. 24, above). But it is not Jesus' desire that demons should testify on his behalf. Such testimony may well have an adverse effect on Jesus' ministry (cf. Acts 16:16-18). On this occasion, however, the testimony of the demon and his expulsion contribute toward the growth of Jesus' fame *over the whole region of Galilee.*

*WHAT DO YOU THINK?*

Jesus rescued many who were harassed and hindered by unclean spirits. How can we limit the devil's influence in our own lives?

[Acts 2:38; Galatians 5:16-26; and 1 John 4:4 can start your thinking.]

*WHAT DO YOU THINK?*

In what ways can we (and can we not) teach with authority as Jesus did?

## FAME

The fame of Jesus has continued to spread. Today there is no name better known on the face of the earth. Jesus is better known than Buddha, better known than Mohammed, and better known than any figure of history or fiction. But that does not mean that everybody knows him.

There are more than six billion people on planet Earth. A large percentage call themselves Christians. But there are at least one billion people who live in lands where there is no access even to knowledge about Jesus Christ. At the same time that we are comforted in the knowledge that so many have heard of him, we also are disturbed by the fact that so many have not!

Think about how many one billion is: it is nearly four times the population of the United States! That many people have never had a chance to accept Jesus Christ. We have a lot of work to do to fulfill the Great Commission.

Although the task of world evangelism is far from finished, today we have better tools than ever to accomplish it. With television, the Internet, the ease of printing, and the ease of world travel, we have the best opportunity that Christians have ever had to really finish what Jesus commanded. Imagine yourself among the one billion who have never heard of him. Wouldn't you want someone to come and tell you?　　　　—R. C. S.

## CONCLUSION

Peter, Andrew, James, and John were called by Jesus to become his disciples. In the case of the first two, the nature of their future work is told them—they were to be fishers of men. Probably a similar explanation is given to James and John, but it is not recorded in any of the Gospel accounts of the event.

More than fifty years ago, I received a similar call from the Lord to become a preacher. Note that I said "similar," not "same." It is similar in that it came from the Lord and was a definite call.

But it was not the same. No, Jesus didn't appear to me in bodily form. He did not come to me in a dream, point his finger at me like Uncle Sam in a famous World War II poster, and say, "I want you." I would have been happy had it been that way, especially had he told me the specific kind of ministry he had in mind for me. That would have made my life much simpler!

Since "my call" didn't include a specific assignment, I have had to use my intelligence to determine where I could best serve. I'm not sure that my judgments have always been the best, but at the time of making each choice I felt it was the thing the Lord wanted me to do. I have served as a preacher, a missionary, a professor, and an editor. I have pursued all of these ministries because I felt led by God to do so.

I know there are those who contend that their calls were of a supernatural nature. I also know that many who have made such claims have been miserable failures, their efforts resulting in much harm to the kingdom of God.

My call came to me from the Lord, but it came through the Bible. As a young man I read Jesus' command, "Go into all the world and preach the good news to all creation" (Mark 16:15). I assumed that Jesus was speaking to me and to every other Christian. I had the two essentials that I think constitute a call: a desire to preach and the talent to do so. I put the two together along with the command of Christ, so I went! It was as simple as that.

Jesus is calling you to his service. It may be to become a preacher, a teacher, an elder, or a deacon. Add your desire to serve to your talent and spiritual giftedness to do so. To these also add the need that exists, and you have a call "similar" to that given to Peter, Andrew, James, and John. When you answer that call, you submit to Jesus' authority.

# Discovery Learning

*This page contains an alternative lesson plan emphasizing learning activities. Classes desiring such student involvement will find these suggestions helpful. The next page is a reproducible activity page to further enhance discovery learning.*

## LEARNING GOALS

After participating in this lesson, each student will be able to:

1. Describe the activities of Jesus' early ministry and the effect he had on people.

2. Explain how Jesus demonstrated his authority.

3. State one specific way that he or she will submit to Jesus' authority.

## INTO THE LESSON

Before class write "Symbols of Authority" on the board. Ask the students to think of things in our society that symbolize some kind of authority. As an example you might cite the label on the gasoline pumps indicating that a government official has inspected the pumps and certified their accuracy. The consumer can trust the authority of the county government that he or she is getting gasoline that is accurately measured. (Or distribute copies of the reproducible activity "Symbols of Authority" from the next page.)

Allow a few minutes for the class to think about this, perhaps discussing it informally among themselves. If your class enjoys coffee and pastries during a "fellowship time" before the class starts, ask the students to put this time to good use by talking about these symbols of authority as they visit with one another.

Call the class to order and ask for suggestions. Some of the following may be voiced: a badge (worn by police or fire department personnel or even by convention officials or state-fair judges), the state or county seal (found on government buildings, vehicles, and letterhead), the black robe and gavel of a judge, and a crown.

When the class seems to have exhausted its list of ideas, ask, "Do you know any person who seems to be a symbol of authority—someone whose actions or speech convey authority without any tangible symbol like a badge?" Allow time for responses. Then say, "Jesus was such a person. Again and again, the people who heard him marveled at his authority. Today's lesson includes one such event."

## INTO THE WORD

Ask a volunteer to read Mark 1:14-28 aloud. Then divide the class into five groups and ask each one to take part of the text and to list evidence of Jesus' authority as found in the assigned verses. Assign the text according to the five major subdivisions of the outline on page 154. Provide posters, markers, and other helps for the groups to work and compile their results. Allow six to eight minutes for the groups to work; then call for reports. Some possible answers are:

I. Mark 1:14, 15—preaching implies a certain authority, especially the call to repent.

II. Mark 1:16-20—in calling disciples, Jesus requires a submission to his authority. The four fishermen acknowledge that he is worthy of it by following.

III. Mark 1:21, 22—Jesus' teaching is unique. The people can sense his authority.

IV. Mark 1:23-26—in commanding that the demon leave the man, Jesus demonstrates an authority that goes beyond the physical and earthly. He has spiritual authority of a kind that does not expire; this is divine authority.

V. Mark 1:27, 28—the discussion by the people is still focused on the authority that Jesus has over the demon. As his fame spreads, it surely includes this awe-inspiring authority.

## INTO LIFE

Say, "To acknowledge that Jesus demonstrated authority two thousand years ago is well and good, but it's not enough. Jesus still has authority today." Ask someone to read Matthew 28:18. Note that Jesus' claim to have "all power" has not been rescinded.

Then ask, "How, then, do we demonstrate our submission to his authority?" Have learners return to their five groups. Each group is to come up with an idea for demonstrating submission to Jesus' authority based on the example they found earlier. Call for reports after a few minutes.

Groups 1 and 2 should come up with something on the order of following as Jesus' disciples today. Group 3 should acknowledge that Jesus' teaching, as well as that of his inspired representatives (apostles and other writers of the New Testament), is authoritative and worthy of our complete acceptance. Groups 4 and 5 should focus on the spiritual and eternal nature of Jesus' authority.

Next, ask your learners to consider one specific way each of them will acknowledge Jesus' authority. Say, "Consider your week ahead. What's on your agenda? How will Jesus' authority make a difference in the decisions that you make and the activities in which you participate?" Close with a prayer of submission to his authority.

# Symbols of Authority

Use the letters of the word authority to suggest nine words or phrases that symbolize authority in our culture today. The key letters may begin, end, or merely appear in the words and phrases you suggest. One example has been done for you to "prime the pump" of your imagination.

BAdge
U
T
H
O
R
I
T
Y

# Submission to Authority

Choose one of the symbols of authority from the acrostic above and answer the following questions.

1. What is the symbol of authority? _____

2. Who wields the authority represented by that symbol? _____

3. Who or what empowers that person with authority? _____

4. How does one express submission to this authority? _____

5. What consequences follow if one does not submit to this authority? _____

6. What parallels do you see in submission to this authority and submission to the authority of Christ? Write your reflections in the space below. Include a statement of commitment to submit to the Lord's authority.

# JESUS CALLS LEVI (MATTHEW)

**LESSON 6**

## WHY TEACH THIS LESSON?

What do Saul of Tarsus and Matthew the tax collector have in common? Both were men who by their lives and actions could have been considered unreachable with the message of Christ, yet who became followers of Christ nonetheless. In a Sunday school class I was attending in the Spring of 2003, the students were asked to name some people they felt would never become Christians. Answers included Osama bin Laden, Saddam Hussein, Ted Turner, and Bill Gates, along with the names of many Hollywood stars and political figures.

All of us have those people we feel will never become Christians. And no one of us may ever be able to do anything directly to reach some of the higher profile people we feel this way about. But there are those who are close to us: a family member, a coworker, a neighbor. We may feel that they are unreachable for Christ. But that is not the case, any more than it was the case with Matthew.

Our lesson today reminds us that even those we think are hardest to win to Christ can be converted. It also should convict us to quit finding excuses for not reaching our "unreachable" acquaintances and to begin to share the message of Christ with them.

## INTRODUCTION

### A. JESUS AND SINNERS

Luke tells of an occasion when a Pharisee named Simon invited Jesus to dine with him. While Jesus was reclining at the table in the style of eating in that day, a sinful woman of the city somehow managed to gain access to the house. As she began to weep profusely, her tears fell on Jesus' feet. She used her hair to wipe his feet and then she poured on them the perfume that she had brought for the purpose.

Well! It was all just too much for Simon to endure. Luke 7:39 records that he said to himself, "If this man were a prophet, he would know who is touching him and what kind of woman she is—that she is a sinner."

Simon was only partially correct in what he thought. A prophet of God would not necessarily know the moral state of a person. Having such discernment is not a requirement of the office of prophet. But applied to Jesus, the statement is true. As the omniscient Son of God, he should have known everything about the woman. And he did.

That's the beauty of the story. The perfect, sinless Son of God happily accepted the ministrations of sinful people when they came to him in genuine faith and repentance. "Her many sins have been forgiven," he said, "for she loved [me] much" (Luke 7:47).

Today's lesson offers us a similar case—that of Levi. To the Pharisees, Levi, a tax collector, was as repulsive as the woman who anointed Jesus' body, perhaps

DEVOTIONAL READING:
EPHESIANS 4:25-32
BACKGROUND SCRIPTURE:
MARK 2:13-17
PRINTED TEXT:
MARK 2:13-17

Jan
9

### LESSON AIMS

After participating in this lesson, each student will be able to:

1. Tell how the call of Levi (Matthew) illustrates Jesus' purpose in coming to seek and to save the lost.

2. Identify individuals or groups in the local community who need to hear Jesus' call.

3. Suggest some method by which to bring the lost to Christ.

### KEY VERSE

Jesus said to them, "It is not the healthy who need a doctor, but the sick. I have not come to call the righteous, but sinners."
—Mark 2:17

even more so. Yet Jesus was willing to accept an invitation to eat with him and others of his profession.

What the Pharisees failed to recognize is that people can change. Anyone can become a child of the King!

## B. LESSON BACKGROUND

The call of Levi occurred during Jesus' great Galilean campaign. It was perhaps a year or fifteen months after his baptism that Jesus began this preaching and teaching tour. In the Gospel of Mark, this campaign of ministry extends from 1:14 to 9:50.

Not all of this time was spent in Galilee, however. There was an excursion to Jerusalem to attend a Passover feast (John 5:1-47), another to Phoenicia (Matthew 15:21-28; Mark 7:24-30), and four recorded visits to the eastern side of the Sea of Galilee. After each such visit, Jesus returned to Galilee to carry on his ministry there. Levi was called in the early part of this campaign, perhaps sometime in late A.D. 27 or early A.D. 28.

## I. SEEKERS AND SOUGHT (MARK 2:13, 14)

### A. TAXING CROWD (v. 13)

**13a. Once again Jesus went out beside the lake.**

Much of Jesus' ministry occurs in Galilee, the northernmost province of Palestine. Jesus seems to spend a lot of his time near the sea that carries the area's name. The Sea of Galilee is fed by the Jordan River, which passes through it from north to south. The sea (better thought of as a lake because of its size) is thirteen miles in length and eight miles in width at its widest spot. Its greatest depth is about one hundred and fifty feet.

In last week's lesson we learned that it was by this lake that Jesus called four disciples, all of whom were later to become apostles. In today's lesson Jesus goes *out beside the lake,* where he attracts the usual crowd of people.

John 21:1 refers to this body of water as "the Sea of Tiberias," so designated because of the city of that name on its western shore. John evidently chooses to use this Roman name since his Gospel is to circulate in the Roman world. Elsewhere in the Bible it is called "the Lake of Gennesaret" (Luke 5:1), and "the Sea of Kinnereth" (Numbers 34:11).

In Jesus' day the area around the lake teems with people. Several cities of fifteen thousand or more ring its shores. Today, only two of them remain, and these are small and insignificant.

**13b. A large crowd came to him,**

Everywhere Jesus goes there seems to be *a large crowd.* Most of the inquisitive people come to him with good motives. But there are exceptions, as some people show up to see what they can manipulate Jesus into doing for them (Luke 12:13; John 6:26). Crowds certainly can be fickle! The crowd that proclaims "Hosanna!" one day (Matthew 21:9) can shout "Crucify him!" a short time later (Matthew 27:22).

**13c. . . . and he began to teach them.**

Jesus is both teacher and preacher (see Matthew 4:23), and he uses whichever method best suits the occasion. Notice from Matthew 5:2 that the so-called "Sermon on the Mount" is not a preached sermon, but a lesson he taught. Concerning the occasion at hand, teaching seems to predominate.

If digital video recorders had been in existence in Jesus' day, and if one had been in the hand of a disciple who faithfully captured every lesson Jesus taught and every sermon he delivered, how would we feel about those lessons and mes-

## HOW TO SAY IT

Augustine. AW-gus-TEEN or Aw-GUS-tin.

Alphaeus. AL-fee-us.

Barnabas. BAR-nuh-bus.

Bartholomew. Bar-THAHL-uh-mew.

Galilean. Gal-uh-LEE-un.

Galilee. GAL-uh-lee.

Gennesaret. Geh-NESS-uh-ret.

Jerusalem. Juh-ROO-suh-lem.

Jordan. JOR-dun.

Josephus. Jo-SEE-fus.

Kinnereth. KIN-e-reth.

Levi. LEE-vye.

Maccabees. MACK-uh-bees.

Macedonia. Mass-eh-DOE-nee-uh.

Nathanael. Nuh-THAN-yull.

Pharisees. FAIR-ih-seez.

Phoenicia. Fuh-NISH-uh.

Silas. SIGH-luss.

Silvanus. Sil-VAY-nus.

Tiberias. Tie-BEER-ee-us.

sages? Would we find his illustrations too simple? His pronouncements too dog-matic? His requirements too demanding? His concepts too "prudish"?

Jesus is, of course, the greatest teacher of all time. His every word is the Word of God. Even so, we must not assume that people in any particular era all will be pleased with what he says or how he says it.

We're probably correct in assuming that DVDs of his lessons and sermons would be kept on shelves just like his printed words are now. After all, wouldn't it be more enjoyable to watch a science fiction presentation, a romantic movie, or a gangster thriller than to listen to a controversial rabbi who lived two thousand years ago? Human motives do not change, despite advances in technology. In short, the crowds of today are just as "taxing" in their motives and expectations as those of the first century!

## B. TAX COLLECTOR (v. 14)

**14a. As he walked along, he saw Levi son of Alphaeus sitting at the tax collector's booth.**

When Matthew tells of his call in the Gospel that he writes, he refers to him-self by that name rather than *Levi*. That he has two names isn't unusual in his day. We know of Silas/Silvanus, John/Mark, Joseph/Barnabas, Saul/Paul, and Nathanael/Bartholomew. Perhaps Jesus renames Levi to be Matthew, as in the case of Simon Peter (Cephas in John 1:42); or Levi may have changed his own name. The name Matthew means "gift of Yahweh" and is still a popular name among Christians.

The name *Alphaeus* is also noted in connection with a disciple named James in Matthew 10:3; Mark 3:18; Luke 6:15; and Acts 1:13. Consequently, some be-lieve that Matthew is a brother to that particular James. Against this view is the fact that they are never called as such in the New Testament, nor are their names ever grouped together in the way that is true of other brothers.

The phrase *sitting at the tax collector's booth* tells us that Matthew is a tax col-lector. To his fellow Jews, this occupation brands Matthew as being a collaborator with the hated Romans. Matthew thus would seem to be an unlikely choice for a disciple and eventual apostle! But Jesus obviously sees in him qualities of great-ness that only need to be developed. As a tax collector, Matthew has skills such as writing and record-keeping that will serve him well when it comes time for him to write his own Gospel about Jesus.

Matthew is mentioned here and in the lists of the Twelve in Matthew 10, Mark 3, Luke 6, and Acts 1 but nowhere else in the New Testament. Tradition has it that he stayed for fifteen years in his homeland, after which he went to several foreign nations and preached. He may have died a natural death in either Mace-donia or Ethiopia, but some legends have it that he died as a martyr.

**14b. "Follow me," Jesus told him,**

It seems unreasonable that Matthew should respond instantly to such a sim-ple call as Jesus extends to him here if they are total strangers. Probably, as with the fishermen whom we saw called in last week's lesson, Matthew is already ac-quainted with Jesus—his mission, message, and methods—prior to receiving this call.

Various levels of relationship to Jesus are evident in the New Testament. Many (such as those mentioned in John 1) are attracted to him, intrigued no doubt by his teaching. From this larger group, a few are more dedicated (such as the ones who constitute the hundred and twenty of Acts 1:15). The twelve chosen to be apostles are men whom he desires to be with him constantly during his ministry (Mark 3:14-19).

Visual for lesson 6. *The Lord came to call even the notorious sinners. Discuss, "Are we ready to receive them?"*

## WHAT DO YOU THINK?

How can the church become more of an inclusive community where all unbelievers find hope?

Before we move on, notice that Jesus doesn't issue some kind of general appeal to the crowd in Mark 2:13 to call forth volunteers to be his very closest disciples. Jesus doesn't say to the crowd, "I'm looking for twelve apostles. If anyone is interested, please step forward for an interview." Instead, he zeroes in on the one he wants and invites him personally. This may say something about the best way to choose church leaders today.

**14c. . . . and Levi got up and followed him.**

Matthew answers the call to enter into a deeper relationship with Jesus. In Mark 3:13-19, Matthew and eleven others are called into a relationship with the Lord that is deeper and more meaningful still. In that passage Jesus "appointed" them "that they might be with him and that he might send them out to preach and to have authority to drive out demons."

Luke 5:28 tells us that Matthew "left everything and followed him." Perhaps Matthew's humility keeps him from making the "left everything" claim for himself in Matthew 9:9.

## II. DINNER AND SINNERS (MARK 2:15-17)

### A. FOLLOWERS (v. 15)

**15. While Jesus was having dinner at Levi's house, many tax collectors and "sinners" were eating with him and his disciples, for there were many who followed him.**

This feast appears to be something of a farewell party given by Matthew as he makes ready to travel with Jesus. It serves as a threshold in Matthew's life, an event that he can later look back upon as a major fork in his earthly journey.

To this feast Matthew has invited *many* of his friends and former associates. No doubt he presents Jesus to them, hoping that he will change their lives as he has changed Matthew's own.

There are many ways to open the doors of people's hearts so that they will be receptive to the gospel. One oft-used method is "evangelism of the table." Most people will accept an invitation to your home if the invitation includes a meal. Sitting around a table at a meal provides a relaxed atmosphere for guests to converse about your faith.

### "FOLLOW ME"

Road repairs often involve closing a lane of traffic for a certain distance. When this happens on a two-lane road, the repair crew has to figure out a way to keep a flow of traffic alternating in each direction on the single usable lane.

Sometimes the road repair crew will use a little pickup truck with a big sign on the back that says, "FOLLOW ME." That truck leads traffic to the point where the single lane again becomes two. The various drivers in the cars being "led" do not know the name of the person driving the truck, nor have they ever met. Yet they follow him or her with every confidence that the driver of that little truck will safely lead everyone. The pickup truck driver has credibility!

When Jesus said to those first disciples "Follow me," they had no doubt that Jesus would lead them the right way. They knew he would not lead them into sin. They knew he would not lead them to a useless and purposeless life. They did not know exactly where he would lead them—to what cities or towns they would go. But faith grounded in Christ's credibility made them follow.

For us, too, faith demands that we follow him. We do not always know the exact direction he will lead us. But we know he will not lead us astray. We know he will lead us to the places where life can really count for something. If we follow him, we will have no regrets. The important thing to remember, however, is that it is we who are following Jesus, and not the reverse.

**WHAT DO YOU THINK?**

How much contact should we as Christians maintain with unbelievers today? At what point do we make ourselves too vulnerable to dangerous influences (see James 4:4)?

**WHAT DO YOU THINK?**

Why is hospitality such an effective method of reaching out to other people in the name of Jesus?

Humility, faith, and commitment will ensure that we follow our Guide. Even those who would be leaders in the home, the church, or the community must first of all be followers. Jesus still says to people, as he did so long ago, "Follow me."          —R. C. S.

## B. PHARISEES (V. 16)

**16a. When the teachers of the law who were Pharisees saw him eating with the "sinners" and tax collectors, they asked his disciples:**

The *Pharisees,* meaning "separated ones," compose the most prominent religious party of the Jews in Jesus' day.

The first-century Jewish historian Josephus indicates that there were only about six thousand Pharisees at the height of their power. Considering this against a population of perhaps a quarter of a million or more, the Pharisees exercise influence that is out of proportion with their numbers. Their origin is somewhat uncertain, but they apparently date to the time of the Maccabees, about one hundred and sixty years before Christ.

The Pharisees are noted for their strictness (Acts 26:5) and for adherence to such doctrines as special divine providence, immortality of the soul, and future reward for the righteous and punishment for the wicked. They strongly believe in the coming of the Messiah, but most refuse to accept Jesus as being "the One." Pharisees are repeatedly mentioned in the Gospels, where, like a pack of wild dogs, they constantly snarl and snap at Jesus. But Jesus can snap back at times, as we see in Matthew 23:13-36.

**16b. "Why does he eat with tax collectors and 'sinners'?"**

To the Jews in general and to the Pharisees in particular, no group of men is more detestable than the *tax collectors.* The animosity stems in part from the fact that tax collectors are servants of Rome, the pagan power that occupies the land.

Another factor is that the Jews know the character of the tax collectors all too well—most are unjust, noted for their extortion and oppression. The accusation that Jesus eats and drinks with such people is true! See Luke 7:34. Jesus' motive in doing so, of course, is to change them.

## C. PHYSICIAN (v. 17)

**17. On hearing this, Jesus said to them, "It is not the healthy who need a doctor, but the sick. I have not come to call the righteous, but sinners."**

Notice that the Pharisees do not register their objection directly with Jesus, but with his disciples (v. 16a). Perhaps they are reluctant to lock horns with him at this time and in this place. Although the criticism is made to the disciples, it is Jesus who responds.

The application of Jesus' statement is apparent, and the logic underlying it is such that none can question it. We shouldn't conclude from Jesus' statement that he is affirming that the Pharisees are indeed *healthy* or *righteous*—only that they considered themselves to be so. In reality, they are quite ill spiritually.

Whether speaking of the physically, mentally, or spiritually ill, the first step toward recovery is always the admission that a problem exists. Examples abound of sick people whose condition continues to deteriorate because of their refusal to go to *a doctor.* At one time or another, most of us have heard a friend or acquaintance who was obviously sick or injured say, "Who needs a doctor? I can take care of myself." We have watched the person's health worsen until it took its toll, and have then found ourselves expressing sympathy to the next of kin at a visitation. "If only she had admitted her problem," we've said to ourselves.

And what about friends and neighbors whose problem isn't physical but spiritual? Think of people who have a pregnant, unmarried daughter, whose children

## WHAT DO YOU THINK?

How can we as Jesus' disciples avoid the tendency of the Pharisees to focus only on "people as they are now"? What steps would help us show mercy toward others without condoning sinful actions or lifestyles?

## WHAT DO YOU THINK?

What do we learn about how God views people from the way that Jesus reacted to the people in this lesson? Realizing that we don't have the miraculous ability that he had, how can we apply this knowledge?

## PRAYER

*Father, our world is filled with people like Matthew who are spending their time in worldly pursuits, unaware of the happiness that could be theirs as your servants. Help us to befriend them, discover things we have in common with them, and invite them to our homes.*

*May we do what it takes to bring them to your Son, the great physician, that they may have eternal life. We can do no less for the one who died for us. In Jesus' name, amen.*

## THOUGHT TO REMEMBER

*All Christians, like physicians, should be concerned with the sick.*

are on drugs, who think that getting drunk each weekend is what life is all about, whose loud arguments keep the entire neighborhood upset. I'm talking about people, who, when approached about the healing of the great physician, respond, "Hey, we're all right. There's not a thing wrong with us. Just leave us alone, okay?" Those who do not admit to having a problem are not motivated to get it fixed.

Jesus' mission to the world is seen in his name, "Yahweh is salvation." It was explained to Joseph by "the angel of the Lord," who told him concerning Mary, "She will give birth to a son, and you are to give him the name Jesus, because he will save his people from their sins" (Matthew 1:20, 21).

Nowhere is Jesus' mission made clearer than in Luke 19:10 where he said of himself, "For the Son of man came to seek and to save what was lost." Our text expresses the same truth: *I have not come to call the righteous, but sinners.*

### A CALL TO REPENTANCE

Few people have influenced the course of Christianity more than Augustine of Hippo (A.D. 354–430). But before his conversion he was, by his own account, a great sinner.

When Augustine came to repentance, he reportedly described it like this: "I carried inside me a cut and bleeding soul. How to get rid of it I just didn't know. . . . My soul floundered in the void and came back upon me. Where could my heart flee from my heart? Where could I escape from myself?" That is repentance—genuine, deep repentance!

Properly understood, repentance involves the mind, the emotions, and the will. It means that we turn around and walk a different path. But emotionally, it means we have a sense of sin that sears the soul. If we take our sins lightly, we will take our forgiveness lightly. But if we are truly moved by the awfulness of our sins, then we will truly rejoice at the magnitude of our forgiveness.

John Newton (1725–1807) had himself been a great sinner. One of his greatest sins had been to be involved in the slave trade of his day. Yet this one who had tasted the dregs of sinful disobedience could also greatly revel in the joy of forgiveness. He expressed both the realization of his sin and the joy of God's forgiveness when he wrote what is perhaps the most famous of all hymns, "Amazing Grace."

Like King David, the apostle Paul, Augustine, and Newton, we must repent at the deepest level of our being, and then rejoice in our salvation. Only then will we truly know God.

—R. C. S.

## CONCLUSION

Matthew was excited. His life was being changed for the better and he wanted his old friends to know why. So he prepared a feast and invited them to attend so that he might introduce them to Jesus.

Such an exact situation is rare. The reason? Just after Matthew became a disciple of Jesus, Matthew's circle of friends included his old buddies who were not disciples. But as time moves on Matthew naturally would have less and less contact with his old friends who reject Christ (and reject Matthew as well). Thus Matthew eventually will not be able to witness in the same way that we see in today's lesson.

So it is with present-day disciples. Soon after conversion, a Christian may number many lost individuals as friends and associates. But the longer he or she remains a Christian, the smaller that old circle becomes. This is why it is imperative that the freshly won, while still remembering what it's like to be "sick," testify to those still suffering from the disease of sin. Such testimony, accompanied by a godly lifestyle, can have a tremendous impact on the lives of the lost.

# Discovery Learning

*This page contains an alternative lesson plan emphasizing learning activities. Classes desiring such student involvement will find these suggestions helpful. The next page is a reproducible activity page to further enhance discovery learning.*

## LEARNING GOALS

After participating in this lesson, each student will be able to:

1. Tell how the call of Levi (Matthew) illustrates Jesus' purpose in coming to seek and to save the lost.

2. Identify individuals or groups in the local community who need to hear Jesus' call.

3. Suggest some method by which to bring the lost to Christ.

## INTO THE LESSON

As students arrive, give each a copy of the following list: an inexpensive watch, a pair of eyeglasses, a twenty-dollar bill, a car title, a picture drawn by a preschooler, a button that fell off a shirt or blouse, last year's tax return, and a shopping list. Ask each to tell how long he or she would look for each item if it were lost.

After a few minutes, ask for volunteers to tell what items they would search longest for. What items would they not look for much at all? Why?

Obviously, we search longest and hardest for those things we value most. Sometimes what we value is not valued by others. Such is the case in today's lesson. Jesus said he came to seek that which was lost. When he came seeking Levi (Matthew), there were some who thought he was wasting his time. But Jesus saw the value of every human. Today's lesson is intended to help us see that value as well.

## INTO THE WORD

Distribute copies of the reproducible activity "Responding to Jesus" from the next page. Ask a volunteer to read Mark 2:13-17 aloud. Tell the students to use their handouts to note how the different individuals or groups (the crowd; Levi; tax collectors and "sinners"; teachers of the Law and Pharisees) responded to Jesus. Have them mark these as the text is read. *Suggested answers include the following: (1) The crowd was enamored of Jesus (v. 13); they were more curious than committed. (2) Levi became a disciple, leaving his tax collector's booth to follow Jesus (v. 14). (3) The tax collectors and sinners, apparently at Levi's invitation, also received Jesus' message and became followers (v. 15). (4) The Pharisees were critical.*

Discuss how the same attitudes are present today. Some people are enamored with Jesus as a celebrity.

They like to talk about his teachings or his "revolutionary" behavior, but they are not disciples. Others, of course, are true disciples. They want to follow Jesus. Some of these come from what we may consider to be unlikely sources, but the gospel is for all. And there are some who are openly hostile to the Lord. Sum up with the commentary's description of the various levels of relationship to Jesus under the discussion of verse 14c.

Call attention back to the individuals or groups on the students' charts. Ask, "Why were these people coming to Jesus?" Contrast these purposes with Jesus' purpose. Discuss how Jesus' purpose to call sinners to repentance is seen in his interaction with each.

## INTO LIFE

Ask, "What is our purpose today?" Easily your learners might repeat Jesus' own purpose: to call sinners to repentance. Challenge them to defend that statement with evidence. Do our behavior and church programming support the claim? Are we deliberate about calling sinners to repentance?

Divide the class into four groups. Each group will have two assignments. First, group members will suggest potential church programs to reach people in the assigned category. Second, they are to suggest some things individuals can do to reach them.

The four categories, one for each group, correspond with the categories on the chart used earlier. Ask group one to suggest some ways to reach those who are merely curious about Jesus, like the crowd. Group two will suggest ways to minister to new believers, like Levi. Ask group three to suggest ways to reach those who are seeking, like the tax collectors and "sinners." Finally, ask group four to suggest methods to reach those who are hostile to the gospel, like the Pharisees.

Allow time for discussion; then call for brief reports. Have the class choose one of the group-effort suggestions and decide how to implement it. Ask each learner to adopt one of the personal methods suggested and implement it to reach out to someone he or she knows who needs the Lord.

At the close of class, allow any to pray audibly who so desires. Ask that the prayers would focus on requesting God's help in strengthening everyone in the class to adopt Jesus' purpose to reach out to those who need him.

# Responding to Jesus

Read Mark 2:13-17 and note how different individuals or groups responded to Jesus. Note these on the chart below.

| THE CROWD | LEVI | TAX COLLECTORS AND SINNERS | TEACHERS OF THE LAW AND PHARISEES |
|---|---|---|---|
| | | | |

# Reaching Out for Jesus

Just as Jesus found differing responses to his message in ministry, today's church gets a different reaction from different people when it reaches out in Jesus' name. Think of the different kinds of people in your community. What can you or your church do to minister to these people to draw them closer to Jesus? Consider the following kinds of people and suggest one program or activity to appeal to each.

People who are merely curious about Jesus

New believers

Those who are seeking Jesus

Those who are hostile to the gospel

# JESUS SENDS OUT THE TWELVE

**LESSON 7**

## WHY TEACH THIS LESSON?

Have you ever heard of the "Dependent Order of Really Meek and Timid Souls"? When you make an acrostic of its first letters, you have "Doormats." The Doormats have an official insignia—a yellow caution light. Their official motto is: "The meek shall inherit the earth, if that's OK with everybody!"

As humorous as that stereotype is, it is misleading when applied to Christians. When Jesus commissioned the Twelve, he did not commission a dozen doormats. Rather, he commissioned a dozen men to open the door to salvation to a world that was not fully ready to receive them or their message. Our text tells us that they went out and did just as the Lord has commanded them to do.

Today's lesson reminds us that we are not doormats either, cowering in the face of a hostile world. Instead, we are commissioned to open the door of salvation to a world that may not be fully ready to hear, but needs to fully hear.

## INTRODUCTION

### A. SIMULTANEOUS REVIVALS

When revivals were in vogue some years ago, it was not uncommon for churches in a given area to participate in simultaneous meetings. Usually it was the preachers who led out in the endeavor, choosing an acceptable time and, perhaps, even suggesting a theme. The meetings stirred a lot of interest and often resulted in the conversion of many of the lost.

I remember most pleasantly working in a simultaneous campaign held in the entire country of Australia. Reggie Thomas, an international evangelist, along with his team of workers had contacted many churches in Australia and secured their cooperation. My assignment was to go to a participating church and preach and evangelize for a week. My wife and I have never forgotten the experience, nor have the other preachers who shared in the simultaneous campaign.

Of course, the best part of the entire venture was that lost souls were won to the Lord. It would be too much to claim that the entire country was stirred, but I'm certain that numerous areas were. Many Australians will never be the same again because of those meetings.

Simultaneous undertakings didn't originate with contemporary preachers. Jesus sent out the Twelve on such a campaign, as we see in today's lesson. The impact of their labors must have been tremendous throughout Galilee. As was true of my experience in Australia, I'm sure the apostles never forgot those happy days when two by two they went about preaching that people should repent.

### B. LESSON BACKGROUND

According to the Gospel of Luke, the calling of the twelve apostles was followed (apparently on the same day) by the teaching of the lesson we've come to

DEVOTIONAL READING:
LUKE 9:1-6.

BACKGROUND SCRIPTURE:
MARK 3:13-19; 6:6b-13.

PRINTED TEXT:
MARK 3:13-19; 6:6b-13.

## LESSON AIMS

After participating in this lesson, each student will be able to:

Jan 16

1. Tell how Jesus called and commissioned the twelve apostles.

2. Compare and contrast the ministry of the Twelve with the ministry of today's church.

3. Identify his or her own ministry role in the church.

## KEY VERSE

[Jesus] appointed twelve—designating them apostles—that they might be with him and that he might send them out to preach.　　—Mark 3:14

*LESSON 7 NOTES*

call the Sermon on the Mount. This has led one writer to refer to it as "The Ordination Address to the Twelve." These events were of tremendous importance to the ministry of Jesus. As part of his preparation before choosing the Twelve, he "went out to a mountainside to pray, and spent the night praying to God" (Luke 6:12).

It was probably sometime in A.D. 28 when Jesus "appointed" the twelve apostles. Several months would pass before the Master would send forth those Twelve on their mission.

## I. THE TWELVE—THEIR CALL (MARK 3:13-19)

### A. PLACE OF THE CALL (v. 13)

*13. Jesus went up on a mountainside and called to him those he wanted, and they came to him.*

As stated in the Lesson Background, the calling of the Twelve is followed by the teaching of the Sermon on the Mount. Since both events occur *on a mountainside,* the logical assumption is that the two locations are actually one and the same.

But exactly which mountain this is has been a matter of some controversy. The Sea of Galilee has numerous ridges that rise up from its shores, several of which would be suitable for the two events. From the days of the Crusades, Karn Hattin (the Horns of Hattin) has been suggested by many; this location is four or five miles southwest of Tiberias, on the road to Nazareth. Perhaps the best solution is to understand *up on a mountainside* as a general reference to "hill country."

No explanation is given as to how Jesus called *to him those he wanted.* Apparently some signal is given, or a runner sent, to inform certain of his disciples that he wishes them to join him. Pleased no doubt by the invitation, they are more than happy to obey.

Jesus continues to call people to himself today. Although the call is not the same as that heard by these early disciples, it is an equally thrilling call to which the spiritually alert gladly respond.

### WHAT DO YOU THINK?

*How much training and teaching are necessary before a person can serve in Christ's church effectively?*

#### UNQUESTIONING RESPONSE

There was a mission recruiter who received a request from a young woman wanting to be considered for a mission assignment. The recruiter wrote back, "Your interview is scheduled for 4:00 A.M. in the station boiler room."

She was troubled, but at 4:00 A.M. on the appointed day she appeared. The recruiter was late. When he came in, he sat across from her and said, "State your name." She did, but he didn't even write it down. Instead he promptly got up and left, saying merely, "We'll be in touch."

Surely this had to be a joke. But two days later the young woman was called to meet with the board. When the recruiter was asked if he would recommend her, he replied, "Absolutely. Her credentials are good, but most importantly, she followed directions, as unusual as they were. She did not question or rant at the bizarre request. I believe she will be a great servant."

Often the disciples must have had the natural inclination to wonder "why?" when they received their calls. In service to God there always is a "why?" but we should not expect an immediate answer. Even so, that should not hinder the call to duty. What God commands, first and foremost, is to be followed. —J. D. R.

### B. PURPOSE OF THE CALL (vv. 14, 15)

*14, 15. He appointed twelve—designating them apostles—that they might be with him and that he might send them out to preach and to have authority to drive out demons.*

Mark expresses a double purpose for the ordination of these *twelve*. First, they are to *be with him*. This may reveal to us a "change of allegiance" in their hearts (see Mark 10:28).

But to *be with him* doesn't mean that these twelve will just "hang out" with Jesus. He calls them so that they will be available to be sent *out* as his official emissaries *to preach and to have authority to drive out demons*.

In formally setting these men apart, Jesus has yet a third purpose in mind for them, one not mentioned by Mark: they are to become the foundation stones upon which Jesus' church is to be built (see Ephesians 2:20). This concept is far more extensive than the other two and certainly has an importance beyond what any of the Twelve can comprehend at the time.

## C. PEOPLE OF THE CALL (vv. 16-19)

**16, 17. *These are the twelve he appointed: Simon (to whom he gave the name Peter); James son of Zebedee and his brother John (to them he gave the name Boanerges, which means Sons of Thunder);***

Luke 6:13, a parallel account of this event, says that Jesus called *the twelve* men "apostles." That word refers to what we would think of as ambassadors or envoys. It does not refer to an ordinary messenger, but to a fully authorized and commissioned representative of the sender.

Jesus renames *Simon* to be *Peter* (Greek meaning "rock"), or, as John 1:42 has it, "Cephas" (Aramaic word for "rock"). Peter is the most prominent of the Twelve and one of the great leaders of the early church. He will go on to author the two epistles in the New Testament that bear his name.

*James, John,* and Peter make up Jesus' inner circle of disciples (cf. Mark 5:37; 9:2). Like Peter, James and John are fishermen. There are four or five different men bearing the name of James in the New Testament, so we should take care not to get them confused. This particular James will be martyred by Herod Agrippa I in about A.D. 44 (see Acts 12:2).

John, who authors five books of the New Testament, will live to a ripe old age. Tradition says that he spent much of his "golden years" in the city of Ephesus.

We are not told why Jesus gives to James and John the nickname *Boanerges*, meaning *Sons of Thunder*. The most popular view is that it results from Jesus' recognition of their aggressive personalities as we see in Mark 10:35-37 and Luke 9:54. At no other time in the New Testament is this name used of these two.

**18, 19. . . . *Andrew, Philip, Bartholomew, Matthew, Thomas, James son of Alphaeus, Thaddaeus, Simon the Zealot and Judas Iscariot, who betrayed him.***

*Andrew*, whose name means "manly," is Peter's brother (John 1:40; 6:8). The only reference to Andrew outside the Gospels (as is true of other apostles) is in Acts 1:13. Tradition holds that he was martyred in Achaia (part of Greece) on an X-shaped cross, now called an Andrew's cross.

Andrew is associated on two occasions in the Gospels with *Philip*, a fellow townsman. These two occasions are the feeding of the five thousand (John 6:5-9) and the Greeks' request to see Jesus (John 12:22).

Philip's name means "lover of horses." From the few references to him, he is believed to be a timid man, but not so timid that he won't witness concerning his convictions (see John 1:45). He is last mentioned in Acts 1:13. Tradition says he evangelized in Asia Minor. As a result, the historian Eusebius refers to him as "a great light of Asia."

The man called *Bartholomew* by Matthew, Mark, and Luke is frequently identified with the Nathanael of John 1:45. In favor of this view is the possibility that the word "Bartholomew" could be spelled "Bar-Tholami," meaning "son of

## HOW TO SAY IT

*Achaia.* Uh-kay-uh.
*Alphaeus.* Al-fee-us.
*Barnabas.* Bar-nuh-bus.
*Bar-Tholami.* Bar THAL-uh-me.
*Bartholomew.* Bar-THAHL-uh-mew.
*Cephas.* SEE-fus.
*Didymus.* DID-uh-mus.
*Ephesus.* EF-uh-sus.
*Eusebius.* You-SEE-be-us.
*Galilee.* GAL-uh-lee.
*Gentiles.* JEN-tiles.
*Herod Agrippa.* HAIR-ud Uh-GRIP-puh.
*Judas Iscariot.* JOO-dus Iss-CARE-e-ut.
*Kerioth.* KEE-rih-oath.
*Levi.* LEE-vye.
*Nathanael.* Nuh-THAN-yull (TH as in THIN).
*Nazareth.* NAZ-uh-reth.
*Pisidian* ANTIOCH. Puh-SID-ee-un AN-tee-ock.
*synagogue.* SIN-uh-gog.
*Thaddaeus.* Tha-DEE-us.
*Tiberias.* Tie-BEER-ee-us.

Tholami"; this means that "Bar-Tholami" would actually be a surname. Thus the man's full name would be "Nathanael Bar-Tholami." Nothing is known about his life after his being mentioned in Acts 1:13. Even traditions concerning him are subject to question.

We discussed *Matthew* (Levi) in last week's lesson, so we need not repeat that information here.

John informs us that *Thomas* is also called "Didymus," a word meaning "twin" (John 11:16; 20:24; 21:2). If this means that he is a twin as we use that term, we know nothing about his sibling. In the Gospel of John, Thomas is shown to play an important role in Jesus' ministry (see John 11:16; 14:1-6; 20:24-29; 21:1-8).

Unfortunately, Thomas is best remembered for his expression of doubt about Jesus' resurrection. The incident in question has earned him and his kind the title, "Doubting Thomas." But why not call him, "Thomas, Man of Conviction"? After seeing the resurrected Jesus, Thomas certainly became that. Thomas also showed great conviction when he challenged the rest of the disciples to accompany Jesus to death (again, John 11:16). A tradition holds that Thomas labored as far east as India.

Almost nothing is known of *James the son of Alphaeus, and Thaddaeus, and Simon the Zealot.* The first of these three may also be "James the less" of Mark 15:40. The man whom Mark calls "Thaddaeus" (see also Matthew 10:3) must be the "Judas" who is a relative of James in Luke 6:16 and Acts 1:13. Luke 6:15 and Acts 1:13 also identify Simon's surname as *the Zealot.* It is a common practice for a man to have more than a single designation in this era.

The man whose name occupies the last position in the list is the traitor, *Judas Iscariot.* He is the son of a certain man named Simon (see John 6:71; 13:2, 26). The word "Iscariot" suggests that the men were from Kerioth, a town in Judah (Joshua 15:25). Judas seems to be highly regarded by the other apostles to the point of being made the treasurer of the group (John 12:6). None of the other apostles will suspect him of his forthcoming treachery.

Before moving on, we can pause to note that there are four listings of the apostles in the New Testament (see Matthew 10:2-4; Mark 3:16-19; Luke 6:13-16; Acts 1:13). In those lists Peter always appears first, Philip is always fifth, and James the son of Alphaeus is always ninth. Furthermore, the first four names of the Twelve always remain the first four (although the order of the names changes). The same is true of the second and third groups of four. It's possible that Peter, Philip, and James the son of Alphaeus are something like "captains," each in charge of the three others in his group, thus helping expedite various tasks.

## II. THE TWELVE—THEIR MISSION (MARK 6:6B-11)

### A. EXAMPLE SET (v. 6b)

6b. Then Jesus went around teaching from village to village.

Time has now moved forward several months. Jesus has been in his old hometown, Nazareth, where he taught in the synagogue on a Sabbath day. Although many of the people had been astonished at his teaching, they nevertheless "took offense at him" (Mark 6:3). No reason for the offense is stated, but it probably has to do with the people's disbelief that a hometown boy could amount to much.

When Jesus left Nazareth, he *went around teaching from village to village.* He thus sets an example for his apostles, who are soon to be sent on a mission of their own.

## B. APOSTLES SENT (v. 7)

**7. Calling the Twelve to him, he sent them out two by two and gave them authority over evil spirits.**

Since the time that Jesus ordained *the twelve* apostles, he has taught them by word and example of the kind of ministry they are to perform. Now he sends them out to be extensions of his own work. As stated in verses 4, 5 above, when he calls them he specifies three things they are to do. One of these is to have *authority over evil spirits*. The fuller account in Matthew 10:8 adds two other things: they are to cleanse lepers and raise the dead.

There are definite advantages to going *out two by two*. These include a pooling of wisdom, fellowship, and encouragement. It also results in a more-powerful testimony. Modern-day church calling programs also follow this procedure, with significant results.

## C. EQUIPMENT LIMITED (vv. 8, 9)

**8, 9. These were his instructions: "Take nothing for the journey except a staff—no bread, no bag, no money in your belts. Wear sandals but not an extra tunic.**

Only essential items are to be taken on the *journey*. No reason is given for the limitations, but perhaps Jesus doesn't want his emissaries to appear affluent. Such an appearance can give the wrong impression of discipleship. No one, then or now, should be induced to become a follower of Jesus for the material things that he or she can get out of following him.

Interestingly, Jesus specifies in this passage that they are to take *a staff* while Matthew 10:10 and Luke 9:3 prohibit them from taking such an item. D. A. Carson suggests that, "It may be that Mark's account clarifies what the disciples are permitted to bring, whereas Matthew's assumes that the disciples already have certain things . . . and forbids them from 'procuring' anything more."

Jesus also places restrictions on taking *a bag* (a kind of knapsack; see 1 Samuel 17:40), *bread*, and *money in* their *belts*. Their needs apparently are to be met by those among whom they labor (cf. 1 Corinthians 9:14; 1 Timothy 5:17, 18).

Further, they are to wear *sandals* (often made of hard leather, better for rough wear than shoes), but not *an extra tunic*. The picture is that of taking the barest of necessities and traveling light. These limitations, however, are temporary (see Luke 22:35, 36).

## D. STRATEGY OUTLINED (vv. 10, 11)

**10. "Whenever you enter a house, stay there until you leave that town.**

This verse makes clear that the disciples are not to be *"house* jumpers," always moving about in the hope of getting better accommodations (see also Matthew 10:11 and Luke 9:4). Such action could turn the townspeople against them and make void their testimony.

**11. "And if any place will not welcome you or listen to you, shake the dust off your feet when you leave, as a testimony against them."**

The Jews believe that even *the dust* of Gentiles is impure and is to be shaken *off* when leaving Gentile territory. By Jesus' instruction, those who reject his messengers are to be treated like profane, pagan Gentiles. Paul and Barnabas apply this teaching toward the people of Pisidian Antioch in Acts 13:51.

### MAKING IT WORK

Jesus' allowance for his disciples' turning their backs on others were those cases where people don't "receive you" or "hear you." That can be determined only by first trying, instead of (as Jonah) just believing that "this won't do any good."

Visual for lesson 7. *Use today's visual to launch a discussion of how the Lord calls people to his service today.*

### WHAT DO YOU THINK?

*How can we make sure to remember that we are working for God and others, and not for personal gain?*

### PRAYER

*Dear God and Father, we know there are still many sick and sinful people in this world. Help us to bind up the wounds of the physically ill and preach to the lost a message of repentance unto salvation. In Jesus' name, amen.*

## THOUGHT TO REMEMBER

*Jesus still calls people to be with him and to go forth.*

Frankly, we may wish that the Lord would give a bit more latitude here, because there are some people in our lives with whom cooperation seems next to impossible. We all have our MIPs—our "Most Irritating Personalities." For you it might be the perfectionist or the inflexible person with whom you work. (One lady said, "When I wanted to marry 'Mr. Right,' I didn't know his first name would be 'Always'!") Maybe for others it is the phony, or the obnoxious braggart, or the gushy-touchy-feely-huggy person. But we seldom see ourselves as irritants to others, do we?

If we are going to be effective "point people" for Christ, we must overcome our tendency to avoid the MIPs. This will mean moving beyond mere tolerance. The second greatest commandment, "Love your neighbor as yourself" (Mark 12:31), requires much more than superficial, outward civility.    —J. D. R.

## III. THE TWELVE—THEIR TRIUMPHS (MARK 6:12, 13)

### A. THEIR MESSAGE (v. 12)

**12. They went out and preached that people should repent.**

John the Baptist's message had been one of repentance (Mark 1:4). When Jesus began preaching, he echoed the same theme (Mark 1:15). It is logical, then, that the apostles should preach a message of repentance.

This is a message that never becomes irrelevant. Certainly our times call for it. We need to repent of our practice of abortion, our immoral movies and TV programs, our drunkenness and drug use, our immodest dress that we flaunt before people and God, our indifference to suffering, our disregard of law, and our greed that grows more excessive with each passing year.

Our preachers today, like the apostles of old, need to preach *that people should repent.* When was the last time that you heard such a message from your church's pulpit?

## WHAT DO YOU THINK?

*Why is the message of repentance that was preached by the apostles so important? How does an extreme view of "tolerance" cause us to neglect the idea of repentance today?*

*[Mark 1:15; Luke 13:1-5; Acts 2:38; and 3:19 are important to consider in your answers.]*

### B. THEIR SUCCESS (v. 13)

**13. They drove out many demons and anointed many sick people with oil and healed them.**

The results of the apostles' efforts are outstanding! *Many demons* are exorcised, and many *sick* are made well. Nothing is said concerning how many repent, but undoubtedly we are correct in assuming that many hearts are softened while many others are hardened. The message of Jesus tends to have those two effects on people! Those who refuse to repent face a dismal future (Revelation 16:8-11).

The anointing *with oil* may have been for medicinal reasons, added to the miraculous healings performed by the apostles. God desires that we use the natural means at our disposal in addition to relying on God's ability to heal as the result of prayer (cf. James 5:14).

## CONCLUSION

An old poem says, "Christ has no hands but our hands to do his work today; he has no feet but our feet to lead men in his way." The poem is true. There is no other way for the work of Christ to be done except through people who respond when they hear his call to service. That is God's plan on how he chooses to accomplish the work of his kingdom.

Undoubtedly, our service will be different in significant ways from that of the Twelve. Most of us will not face martyrdom. Most of us will not become traveling evangelists. The "tools" we have—cars, airplanes, computers, video, etc.—for spreading the gospel are far different from anything the original Twelve had. But whatever the case or situation, God still expects us to respond.

## WHAT DO YOU THINK?

*What factors were involved in Jesus' process of preparing some of his disciples to become the "apostles" who later established his church? Why is this important today?*

*[Hint: think in terms of "seeking," "exposure," "challenge," and "learning by doing."]*

# Discovery Learning

*This page contains an alternative lesson plan emphasizing learning activities. Classes desiring such student involvement will find these suggestions helpful. The next page is a reproducible activity page to further enhance discovery learning.*

## LEARNING GOALS

After this lesson, each student will be able to:

1. Tell how Jesus called and commissioned the twelve apostles.

2. Compare and contrast the ministry of the Twelve with the ministry of today's church.

3. Identify his or her own ministry role in the church.

## INTO THE LESSON

Prepare a handout with the heading "Help Wanted." Have students work individually or in small groups to make a list of personal qualities they would look for if they were putting together a team to evangelize your community or a mission field where your church supports a missionary. After few minutes, ask for reports of ideas.

List the ideas as they are presented. Some ideas may include a history of evangelistic zeal and efforts, compatible personalities, a certain level of education, and a personal reputation for being patient and compassionate.

After a bit of discussion ask, "From what you know of the twelve apostles—before the resurrection—how many of them do you think you would want on your team?" You probably will note that these characteristics are not typical of the apostles. Jesus took an unlikely group of men and molded them into a dynamic force that "turned the world upside down."

## INTO THE WORD

Have a volunteer read aloud Mark 3:13-19. Provide some research resources such as Bible encyclopedias, Bible dictionaries, etc., that provide information about the apostles. Divide the class into three or four groups and ask each group to research three or four apostles. You may wish to use the groupings suggested in the lesson commentary.

Have each group give as much detail about their assigned disciples as possible: occupation before joining Jesus' ministry, family connections, etc. Ask them also to suggest what may have made it difficult for each to follow Jesus: What did they have to leave? How hard was it to partner with some of the other disciples? etc. Allow a few minutes for research; then give a reporter from each group two or three minutes to summarize the group's findings.

Now ask another good reader to read Mark 6:6b-13 aloud. Have your learners return to their groups and consider the same disciples they researched earlier. Have them answer the following questions:

1. If you were pairing the disciples, whom would you have selected for each of the disciples you researched earlier? Why?

2. Whom do you think each disciple would least want paired with him? Why?

3. What do you think the disciples you researched thought about the restrictions Jesus put on them for the journey? Why? What could they have learned from the experience?

Once again, allow a few minutes for research and also for each group to report. Add to the reports the information from the verse-by-verse commentary regarding what Jesus intended in giving these instructions. Ask how each disciple may have responded.

## INTO LIFE

Note that Jesus called the Twelve "that they might be with him and that he might send them out" to spread the good news and to minister to physical needs. Ask, "What is the relationship between being with Jesus and going forth to serve?" Discuss how to keep the two roles in balance in your church and in individual lives. Many believers today want to be with Jesus—in worship, in Bible studies, in fellowship with other believers, etc.—but they do not share the gospel or minister to other needs. How can we help such believers move to full obedience?

Ask, "What if you had been one of the Twelve? Which apostle would you have wanted to pair up with for this mission? Why? Which would you have least wanted to pair with? Why?" Use the students' answers to launch a discussion about what we today need to learn about working together to serve the Lord. How would a mission tour like that of the disciples be received today? What principles—if not the actual practice—of what Jesus told the disciples are most important for evangelism today? Why? Of these, in which does our church excel? Where do we need some improvement?

Then ask each learner to think of his or her own role in this ministry. What does each add to the church's effort to win the lost? In the closing time of prayer, ask God to expand their outreach.

*Option:* Use the reproducible activity page that follows to lead the students in applying the message of today's lesson in their lives.

# Imitating the Apostles

The Scripture tells us that Jesus "appointed twelve—designating them apostles—that they might *be with him* and that he might *send them out* to preach and to have authority to drive out demons" (Mark 3:14, 15). We today do not serve as "apostles," but we still serve the Lord. We want to "be with him," knowing his presence and growing in our relationship with him. And we want him to "send us out" into ministry in some form: sharing our faith, teaching, helping the sick or elderly, and others. Use the chart below to examine yourself on these two points and to challenge yourself to do better.

*TO BE WITH HIM*

What am I doing to spend time with Jesus?

How often or consistently do I practice this (these things)?

How can I improve on my time spent with Jesus (either by spending more time or by making the time spent more productive)?

*TO SEND THEM OUT*

What am I doing to serve others in behalf of Jesus?

How often or consistently do I serve in this way (these ways)?

How can I improve in my ministry?

What step(s) will I take *this week* to begin to make an improvement in one or both of these areas?

# JESUS CALLS FOR TOTAL COMMITMENT

**LESSON 8**

## WHY TEACH THIS LESSON?

The pig and the chicken were in the barnyard together and overheard the farmer and his wife discussing meal plans for the weekend as they had several guests coming in. The wife said breakfast would not be a problem, as they would have ham and eggs. At this the pig began to cry uncontrollably. The chicken asked what was the matter. The pig responded, "Didn't you hear what she said? They're going to have ham and eggs." The chicken stood there perplexed still not discerning what the problem was. So the pig continued speaking to the chicken saying, "For you, ham and eggs is not problem. All you have to do is make a contribution. For me, ham and eggs requires a total commitment."

When Jesus calls us into his service, it is not for us to make some small contribution of time or money or ability. Instead, he calls for a total commitment, a total sacrifice. Our lesson today reminds us of this call to a life of complete surrender that the Lord has placed upon all who have accepted his call.

## INTRODUCTION

### A. COMMITMENT?

Imagine crossing paths with an old friend whom you haven't seen for a half-dozen years. After the usual greetings that include a handshake and a pat on the back, you hold your friend at arm's length and evaluate her. She doesn't appear to have aged much, and you tell her so. She looks to be in great shape and you compliment that. Similar remarks are returned about you and your appearance.

Then you notice that she has about her neck a gold chain to which something that looks like a miniature chair is attached. She sees that you notice, so she volunteers an explanation.

"It's not just an ordinary chair," she says, "but a replica of an electric chair—you know, one used to electrocute people."

While you stand there startled and speechless, she continues. "It's a miniature of the electric chair in which [and she cites the name of a notorious revolutionary] was put to death."

Your astonishment is magnified, but somehow you manage to stammer, "You must really be committed to that man and his philosophies."

Your friend laughs dismissively. "Not really," she says. "I don't even know a whole lot about what he stood for. I just wear the chair because I think it's pretty. Don't you like it?"

After you've said your good-byes, you shake your head in disbelief and mutter under your breath, "She's weird; she's still weird."

The application is pretty obvious. There are many people who wear a cross, the emblem of another revolutionary—a peace-loving, sinless one who proved himself to be the Son of God. Unfortunately, many of these folks know little

DEVOTIONAL READING:
MATTHEW 16:24-28
BACKGROUND SCRIPTURE:
MARK 8:27-38
PRINTED TEXT:
MARK 8:27-38

### LESSON AIMS

After participating in this lesson, each student will be able to:

1. Tell what Peter did and did not understand about who Jesus was and what he had come to do.

2. Express the level of commitment that Jesus expects from his followers.

3. Evaluate his or her own level of commitment in following Jesus, and state one specific means of deepening that commitment.

Jan 23

### KEY VERSE

[Jesus] said: "If anyone would come after me, he must deny himself and take up his cross and follow me.          —Mark 8:34

about the one the cross represents. And some of those who do know show little commitment to him. Let it be understood that Jesus never asked anyone to *wear* a cross, but he did insist that those who truly follow him must *bear* one. That's what today's lesson is about.

## B. LESSON BACKGROUND

Our previous lesson concluded with the successful ministry campaign of the apostles. That endeavor apparently began as the third year of Jesus' ministry—his "year of opposition"—got under way.

Between last week's lesson and today's, one of Jesus' miracles was to feed the five thousand (Mark 6:30-44). The people "intended to come and make [Jesus] king by force" (John 6:15) as a result. When Jesus refused to accept such an earthly crown, his Galilean campaign began to collapse (John 6:66).

Jesus was on the move over the next several months. He went westward to Phoenicia (Mark 7:24-30), and then to the southeast through Galilee to the eastern side of the Sea of Galilee and into the Decapolis. Jesus healed many people in that place (Matthew 15:30), including a deaf man with a speech impediment (Mark 7:31-37). Next, Jesus miraculously fed a multitude of four thousand men, in addition to women and children (Mark 8:1-8).

Then Jesus and his disciples crossed the lake to Dalmanutha, where they were challenged by some Pharisees (Mark 8:10-12). Following this encounter, Jesus returned to the other side of the lake (Mark 8:13).

Jesus restored sight to a blind man upon arrival at Bethsaida Julias (Mark 8:22-26). From that place Jesus and his apostles traveled approximately twenty-five miles northward into the vicinity of Caesarea Philippi. This is where today's lesson commences.

## I. TRUE IDENTITY (MARK 8:27-30)

### A. JESUS' QUESTION (v. 27)

27. *Jesus and his disciples went on to the villages around Caesarea Philippi. On the way he asked them, "Who do people say I am?"*

The city of *Caesarea Philippi* (now called Banias) is located about thirty miles east of the seaport of Tyre and some fifty miles southwest of Damascus. While in this region, *Jesus and his disciples* are at the far northern end of what is considered Israelite territory.

The city of Caesarea Philippi must not be confused with the Caesarea that is on the seacoast (e.g., Acts 10). It is while Jesus and his disciples are near (not in) Caesarea Philippi that Jesus inquires as to what people *say* concerning his identity.

Jesus' question is worded in a slightly different form in each of the three records. Luke 9:18 has it, "Who do the crowds say I am?" Matthew 16:13 gives the fullest form, "Who do people say the Son of Man is?" The existence of these three forms may indicate that Jesus intentionally words his question in more than one way, a device often used by teachers to seek clarity. Each Gospel writer chooses the best way to present the question to a specific audience.

### B. VARIOUS OPINIONS (v. 28)

28. *They replied, "Some say John the Baptist; others say Elijah; and still others, one of the prophets."*

Some people, influenced no doubt by Herod Antipas (Herod the Tetrarch), confuse Jesus with *John the Baptist*, whom they think has been raised from the dead (Matthew 14:1, 2). The great Gospels professor R. C. Foster suggested that

Bethsaida Julias. Beth-SAY-uh-duh JOO-lee-ahs.

Caesarea Philippi. Sess-uh-REE-uh Fih-LIP-pie or FIL-ih-pie.

Dalmanutha. Dal-muh-NEW-thuh.

Damascus. Duh-MASS-kus.

Decapolis. Dee-CAP-uh-lis.

Elijah. Ee-LYE-juh.

Galilean. Gal-uh-LEE-un.

Galilee. GAL-uh-lee.

Herod Antipas. HAIR-ud AN-tih-pus.

Isaiah. Eye-ZAY-uh.

Jeremiah. Jair-uh-MY-uh.

Leviticus. Leh-VIT-ih-kus.

Messiah. Meh-SIGH-uh.

Phoenicia. Fuh-NISH-uh.

Tetrarch. TEH-trark or TEE-trark.

Tyre. Tire.

Herod made this false identification because he suffered from a guilty conscience for having beheaded John.

Others identify Jesus with the prophet *Elijah*, whose coming had been predicted in Malachi 4:5, 6. We, of course, know that it was John the Baptist, not Jesus, who fulfilled Malachi's prediction (see Matthew 17:10-13.)

After mentioning John the Baptist and Elijah, Matthew adds the name of Jeremiah before concluding with the generalization *one of the prophets*, as Mark does. People are letting their speculations run wild!

The disciples mention no rumor that Jesus could be the promised Messiah. Even so, there seems to be some thinking in that direction, according to Matthew 9:27; 15:22; and John 4:29. We should note that Jesus doesn't first inquire of his disciples what they think of him. Perhaps his motive is to have a backdrop of rumors and then paint upon it the truth. Against such a background, truth always shines more gloriously.

## C. CORRECT UNDERSTANDING (v. 29)

29. *"But what about you?" he asked. "Who do you say I am?"*

    *Peter answered, "You are the Christ."*

After the apostles cite various rumors that are circulating about Jesus' identity—answers that Jesus requests for their sake, not his—the Master then inquires about their own understanding. Bold *Peter*, recognized leader of the Twelve, responds with *You are the Christ*.

The word *Christ* comes from a Greek word that means "anointed one." The word *Messiah*, from a Hebrew word, means the same thing. Three classes of people received sacred anointing in the Old Testament: prophets (e.g., 1 Kings 19:16), priests (e.g., Leviticus 8:12, 30), and kings (e.g., 1 Samuel 10:1). Jesus' anointing came from the Holy Spirit at the time of Jesus' baptism (Mark 1:9-11).

## D. JESUS' PROHIBITION (v. 30)

30. *Jesus warned them not to tell anyone about him.*

Jesus' prohibition to the apostles is in keeping with similar restrictions given to those blessed by his healing power in Mark 1:43, 44; 5:43; and 7:36. The prohibition may have to do with the Twelve's understanding (or misunderstanding) of the nature of Jesus' messiahship. The Jews of the first century are expecting a political Messiah (cf. Acts 1:6). Great harm thus can follow from the apostles' public pronouncement that Jesus is the Christ.

Jesus' entire mission leads to the cross. No action or proclamation from the Twelve can be allowed to derail this plan. This problem has come up among the people at least once already, and Jesus had to fight it off (John 6:14, 15). But even though he commanded the people not to tell anyone, "the more he did so, the more they kept talking about it" (Mark 7:36).

The apostles probably struggle to keep from saying to people, "Come, see the Christ!" How easy it would be for them to brag on their Teacher. Later they will gain the true concept of his messiahship. When that happens and the prohibition is lifted, they will proclaim joyfully, "Therefore let all Israel be assured of this: God has made this Jesus, whom you crucified, both Lord and Christ" (Acts 2:36).

## II. COMING DEATH (MARK 8:31-33)

### A. REVELATION BY JESUS (v. 31)

31. *He then began to teach them that the Son of Man must suffer many things and be rejected by the elders, chief priests and teachers of the law, and that he must be killed and after three days rise again.*

*WHAT DO YOU THINK?*

*Why is confessing Jesus as the Christ so important for the church, for the individual, and for society? How is this difficult in a postmodern, pluralistic culture?*

*[Hint: John 14:6; Acts 4:12; and Romans 10:8-10 are important to consider.]*

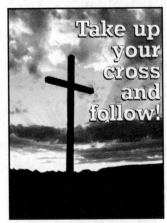

Visual for lesson 8. *On the cross Jesus gave his life—100%. Discuss how modern disciples give 100%. Or do they?*

*WHAT DO YOU THINK?*

*In what ways might we be guilty of attempting to correct or rebuke God as Peter did?*

Jesus already has hinted of his death in Mark 2:20. Now the prediction is much clearer. Other predictions that follow are found in Mark 9:9, 30-32; and 10:32-34.

It is not by accident that Jesus makes this prediction at the time of Peter's great confession. As stated above, Jesus is very likely concerned that the apostles may give the wrong impression of what is involved in his messiahship. So he warns them to keep this fact a secret. By explaining that he is going to *suffer many things and . . . be killed*, he is making an effort to help them understand that he is the one to suffer as predicted in Isaiah 53. At his first coming, Jesus is not some political or military leader who will oust the Romans and establish a world power.

After Jesus is raised from the dead, the apostles will remember this prediction. They will understand that Jesus had been aware of his approaching death. They will then comprehend his words, "I lay down my life—only to take it up" (John 10:17, 18).

### B. REBUKE BY PETER (v. 32)

**32. He spoke plainly about this, and Peter took him aside and began to rebuke him.**

Jesus' open prediction is very forthright. He uses neither parable nor other figure of speech. Although Jesus is completely candid about his coming death and resurrection, the apostles struggle with both concepts right up to the point when Jesus' resurrection becomes an established fact. See Luke 18:31-34.

*Peter* certainly seems to grasp the first part of Jesus' statement concerning Jesus' death. But the promise of his resurrection—the most wonderful of all promises—Peter seems to miss totally. Unhappy that Jesus could even talk about dying, Peter speaks in order *to rebuke him*.

Matthew 16:22 states the content of Peter's rebuke: "Never, Lord! . . . This shall never happen to you!" As D. A. Carson sums it up, "Peter's strong will and warm heart linked to his ignorance produce a shocking bit of arrogance. He confesses that Jesus is the Messiah and then speaks in a way implying that he knows more of God's will than the Messiah himself."

### C. RESPONSE BY JESUS (v. 33)

**33. But when Jesus turned and looked at his disciples, he rebuked Peter. "Get behind me, Satan!" he said. "You do not have in mind the things of God, but the things of men."**

Peter's shallow proposal recalls the devil's temptation of Jesus in the wilderness. There *Satan* proposed that Jesus should become a spectacular Messiah rather than a suffering servant (Matthew 4:1-11). At that time Jesus had commanded Satan to depart. Now, addressing Peter with that same name—so that Peter would know whose agent he is—Jesus commands Peter, *Get behind me.*

Satan had offered Jesus a shortcut to kingship, and Peter is following the same path. Although Peter is not "literally" Satan, Peter's idea certainly is in line with that demonic source. In Matthew 16:23, Jesus further says to Peter that he is an offense, that is, a stumbling block. This is because Peter's idea will only serve to pull Jesus away from his true mission to accomplish the Father's will. After the resurrection the tables will be turned as Jesus and his crucifixion become a stumbling block to others (1 Corinthians 1:23).

### III. TRUE DISCIPLESHIP (MARK 8:34-38)

#### A. ITS REQUIREMENTS (vv. 34, 35)

**34, 35. Then he called the crowd to him along with his disciples and said: "If anyone would come after me, he must deny himself and take up his cross and follow**

me. For whoever wants to save his life will lose it, but whoever loses his life for me and for the gospel will save it.

The crossbearing of which Jesus speaks is not merely the same as having a few bad breaks or enduring the normal hardships of life. Rather, it is the enduring by a Christian of whatever afflictions come upon him or her in laboring for the Master.

The crossbearing of which Jesus speaks involves a denial of self (Romans 14:7-9; 15:2, 3). A Christian certainly should not seek after trouble or delight in opposition. But when these things come, he or she must accept them in the spirit of him who bore his *cross* for all.

Notice that this statement isn't made just to the Twelve, who through their future afflictions will come to understand the high cost of discipleship. It is also made to *the crowd*, some of whom may be considering becoming Jesus' disciples. Better for would-be disciples—both then and now—to be shown the whole picture. They must be made aware of what is entailed in following Jesus before they make a commitment to follow him. (See Luke 14:25-33.)

*WHAT DO YOU THINK?*

*Why is self-denial such a difficult thing for most people?*

*WHAT DO YOU THINK?*

*What are some questions we could ask ourselves to help us determine the amount of risk we should take in serving Christ?*

*WHAT DO YOU THINK?*

*Why is it good to explain the cost of Christian discipleship as clearly as possible to a potential disciple?*

*WHAT DO YOU THINK?*

*How can we prepare ourselves to stand up boldly for Jesus so that we will not disgrace him through our fear and shame?*

### ACCEPTING THE PAIN

There are many stories and legends that surround Patrick, the great missionary to Ireland who lived about A.D. 389–461. One of the stories that comes from his ministry concerns a time when he was baptizing converts in a river.

Patrick, it seems, had waded out into waist-deep water and had called for the new believers to come to him, one by one, to be baptized. He was holding a staff, called a crosier, in his hands as the people made their way into the water. One who came forth to be baptized was a certain mountain chieftain. While lowering the chief down under the water, Patrick also pressed his staff down into the river bottom.

People on the riverbank noticed that the chief was limping as he came out of the water. Someone explained to Patrick that he must have bruised the foot of the chief in pressing the wooden staff into the riverbed. Patrick went to the chief at once and asked, "Why didn't you cry out when I struck your foot?" Surprised, the chief answered, "I remembered you telling us about the nails on the cross and I thought my pain was part of my baptism."

How do you handle the pain that Christianity brings?

—J. D. R.

## B. ITS WISDOM (vv. 36, 37)

36, 37. *"What good is it for a man to gain the whole world, yet forfeit his soul? Or what can a man give in exchange for his soul?*

Here Jesus employs an illustration from the world of commerce. Profit and loss are the concern of all people who engage in buying, selling, and investing. In the business world, it doesn't make sense to gain a thousand dollars today if that gain will result in a million-dollar loss tomorrow. How much more foolish it is to trade anything, even *the whole world*, for one's own *soul!*

Jesus believed in Hell and unashamedly taught about it. Jesus said that Hell is a place of "eternal fire" (Matthew 18:8), a place of "darkness" where there is "weeping and gnashing of teeth" (Matthew 8:12), and a place of "eternal punishment" (Matthew 25:46). "God's wrath" will abide upon those who lose their souls in Hell (John 3:36).

Unfortunately, this fact does not square with modern ideas of "enlightenment" and "tolerance," where various viewpoints and "alternate lifestyles" are not to be judged. This is obviously at odds with the clear teaching of Scripture that a judgment day is coming. On that day some will be given eternal life, while others will be sent away into everlasting punishment (again, Matthew 25:46).

## PRAYER

Dear Father, because we know that Jesus is the Messiah, may we heed the call to follow him. May we lose our lives that we may find the everlasting life that only he offers. In his name we pray, amen.

## THOUGHT TO REMEMBER

The way of a cross leads home.

## C. ITS ALTERNATIVE (v. 38)

38. *"If anyone is ashamed of me and my words in this adulterous and sinful generation, the Son of Man will be ashamed of him when he comes in his Father's glory with the holy angels."*

The alternative to true cross-bearing discipleship is an attitude of shame toward *the Son of Man*. It is also an attitude of shame toward his *words*. Those who possess such an outlook while they live in this world will endure extreme humiliation when the Son of Man—Jesus himself—returns to claim his own. On that day those disobedient, miserable souls will hear Jesus say, "I never knew you. Away from me, you evildoers!" (Matthew 7:23).

### THE WIMP FACTOR

Pepper Rodgers was the football coach of the UCLA Bruins from 1971 to 1973. Alumni and fans made his life miserable during a season when his Bruins got off to a horrible start. No one would hang out with him. "My dog was my only true friend," Rodgers said. "I told my wife that every man needs at least two good friends. She bought me another dog."

Pepper Rodgers could be rigid in the face of adversity, however. When his players were having difficulty adapting to the wishbone offense he had installed—and the school's alumni demanded that he adopt another system—Rodgers didn't budge. The wishbone, he reasoned, "is like Christianity. If you believe in it only until something goes wrong, you didn't believe in it in the first place" (*Washington City Paper*, October 26, 2001). During his final year at UCLA, Rodgers's team had a record of nine wins and two losses, putting it ninth in the nationwide United Press International rankings.

A disturbing trend that we witness in Christianity is what we may label (although very un-theologically) as "the wimp factor." Modern Christians have too little staying power. Their convictions and dedication last only as long as their circumstances remain ideal (see Matthew 13:5, 20, 21).

Satan must marvel at how often some Christians crumble when just a little heat is applied. Can our faith take some attacks, even "friendly fire," and still hold? Or is there too much "wimp" in our walk?          —J. D. R.

## CONCLUSION

Various people from my past come to mind when I think of the word *commitment*. Having been a missionary, I naturally focus on those who served on foreign fields. I think of Mac Coffey, Eleanor Brown, Art Morris, Max Randall, and Cyril Simkins—all great soldiers of the cross. They served in Europe, Africa, and Asia. They struggled with new languages, strange customs, debilitating diseases. They were deprived of the advantages of America, not only for themselves, but for their children as well. One of them, Eleanor Brown, was martyred during an African uprising.

As I recall these friends and acquaintances of my youth—all of them now dead—I ask myself what sort of people they were. And I answer, "ordinary folks." They were all just ordinary people who had an extraordinary commitment to Jesus Christ. That's how it was with them; that's how it was with the apostles; and that's how it always seems to be. It's amazing what God can do with ordinary folks who are willing to lose their lives for him.

The question that follows next is obvious: are you one of those who is willing to lose your life for him? If that question seems too difficult to deal with, try this one instead: are you willing to lose *anything at all* for him? Whatever you're willing to lose for him reveals your level of commitment. As you ponder this, keep in mind what he was willing to lose for you!

# Discovery Learning

*This page contains an alternative lesson plan emphasizing learning activities. Classes desiring such student involvement will find these suggestions helpful. The next page is a reproducible activity page to further enhance discovery learning.*

## LEARNING GOALS

After participating in this lesson, each student will be able to:

1. Tell what Peter did and did not understand about who Jesus was and what he had come to do.

2. Express the level of commitment that Jesus expects from his followers.

3. Evaluate his or her own level of commitment in following Jesus, and state one specific means of deepening that commitment.

## INTO THE LESSON

Before the class arrives, write "R H I P" on the board. Below that list the following positions: CEO of a company; head of a prestigious hospital; president (or prime minister) of your country; head of a respected brokerage firm; principal of the local high school; and head of the bank branch office located in a suburban grocery store.

As students arrive, say: "Imagine that you have been selected to fill one of the positions listed. Sure, there will be a lot of responsibility and hard work; but think of the perks that go with each position. If you were selected for one of these positions, what kind of recognition and fame would you expect to receive?" (Remind them that RHIP stands for "rank has its privileges.")

Allow time for discussion, perhaps while your learners are getting coffee and doughnuts. Then ask volunteers to tell which position they would most like to have—at least, if only the benefits had to be considered—and why.

Then point out that today's lesson is about the one who held the highest position imaginable. Yet, instead of seeking the fame and accolades one might have expected, he ordered those closest to him to keep his high rank private. We have much to learn from this One!

## INTO THE WORD

Invite a man who is not a member of your class to come and portray the apostle Peter. Provide him with information from today's commentary and the student handout described below. Encourage him to "get into the part," putting drama and passion into his presentation.

Tell the class, "We have a real treat today. We have present with us someone who was there when the Person of rank we mentioned told his followers to keep things quiet. You can imagine his surprise! I'd like him to tell you about it, and about his Leader, in his own way. Then you'll have a chance to ask questions. Our guest is Simon Peter!"

Bring "Peter" into the room and ask him to tell his story. He should begin by paraphrasing Mark 8:27-33, told from Peter's perspective. Allow a little embellishment, particularly to add remarks about Peter's thinking and emotions along the way.

When "Peter" finishes, invite questions. Refer your learners to Mark 8:27-33 as a source for questions. Also, note that you have prepared a few sample questions to get them started. Distribute a handout, which includes these questions:

1. Where were the wrong ideas of Jesus' identity coming from? Who was saying those things?

2. How quickly did you respond when Jesus asked who you believed him to be? Did you blurt it out, or was there a silent pause?

3. What did you think when Jesus charged you not to tell anyone? Did that seem strange to you?

4. You were surprised when Jesus spoke of his death. What was the reaction of the others?

5. How could you have been so bold as to rebuke Jesus?

6. How long did it take for you to really understand what Jesus meant when he said that you "do not have in mind the things of God"?

Ask "Peter" to go on with the story as he paraphrases Mark 8:34-38. Have him tell a little of his personal struggle as he came to grips with the concepts of self-denial and servant leadership. He should close with a challenge for modern disciples to take up their crosses and follow.

## INTO LIFE

Ask your learners to think about Peter's level of commitment to Jesus on different occasions, ranking them 1 (low) to 5 (high). Where would they rate him at Caesarea Philippi? Where would they rate him at Gethsemane? How about in Acts 4? (*The reproducible page that follows will be a helpful resource for this activity.*)

Next, challenge the learners to think privately of their own level of commitment. (No discussion is needed.) Are they like Peter at Caesarea Philippi—confessing Jesus with their lips but also contradicting him? Are they sleeping when they should be praying and fighting when they should be passive as in Gethsemane? Or are they bold to speak even when it may be costly?

# Peter's Level of Commitment

Look at Peter's behavior, including things he did and things he said, at various episodes in his life. How do these reflect his level of faith in, and commitment to, Jesus at those particular times? Rate his level of commitment, ranking it 1 (low) to 5 (high) for each of the following events.

When Jesus called him to follow ...................................... 1 ...... 2 ...... 3 ...... 4 ...... 5
*(Matthew 4:18-22; Mark1:16-21; Luke 5:1-11)*

When the tempest was raging—and Jesus was sleeping! ............... 1 ...... 2 ...... 3 ...... 4 ...... 5
*(Matthew 8:23-27; Mark 4:35-41; Luke 8:22-25)*

When the crowds were disillusioned and leaving ...................... 1 ...... 2 ...... 3 ...... 4 ...... 5
*(John 6:60-68)*

When he made his "Good Confession" at Caesarea Philippi ........... 1 ...... 2 ...... 3 ...... 4 ...... 5
*(Matthew 16:13-20; Mark 8:27-30; Luke 9:18-21)*

When he reacted to Jesus' prediction of death ......................... 1 ...... 2 ...... 3 ...... 4 ...... 5
*(Matthew 16:21-25; Mark 8:31-35)*

In Gethsemane, when Jesus left him with James and John to pray ...... 1 ...... 2 ...... 3 ...... 4 ...... 5
*(Matthew 26:36-46; Mark 14:32-42; Luke 22:39-46)*

In Gethsemane, when Jesus was arrested ............................. 1 ...... 2 ...... 3 ...... 4 ...... 5
*(Matthew 26:47-56; Mark 14:43-50; Luke 22:47-51; John 18:10, 11)*

When Jesus was on trial ............................................. 1 ...... 2 ...... 3 ...... 4 ...... 5
*(Matthew 26:58, 69-75; Mark 14:54, 66-72; Luke 22:54-62; John 18:15-18, 25-27)*

When he met the risen Jesus on the shore of Galilee ................. 1 ...... 2 ...... 3 ...... 4 ...... 5
*(John 21)*

When he was arrested for preaching about Jesus ..................... 1 ...... 2 ...... 3 ...... 4 ...... 5
*(Acts 4:5-31)*

# My Level of Commitment

Think back to the events of the past month. How have your actions and words demonstrated your own level of commitment? Consider the following.

1. What event or set of circumstances provided an occasion to demonstrate a low level of commitment?


2. When was my commitment level the highest? Why?


3. What can I do this week to keep my commitment level high?

# JESUS DEFINES GREATNESS

**LESSON 9**

## WHY TEACH THIS LESSON?

The world is impressed with the concept *up*. We speak of those who are "up and coming," "the upwardly mobile," as well as "the upper class." When a team is winning, they are said to be "up." In his book *Descending Into Greatness*, Bill Hybels says that "from the world's perspective, [up] is the only direction to go. Just as a compass needle points north, the human needle points up" (p. 16).

The Bible view of success is different! Jesus' teaching in our text today should challenge us to reconsider our lives and our goals. Perhaps our lesson will cause a little "shifting in our seats" as we see how much the culture has influenced our thinking about what constitutes true greatness.

## INTRODUCTION

### A. GREATNESS?

Alfred (A.D. 848–899) was the fifth and youngest son of Ethelwulf, King of the West Saxons. At the death of Alfred's brother Ethelred in 871, Alfred ascended to the throne. It was not an ideal time to be crowned king—a Danish invasion of England was under way. Eventually, Alfred managed to assemble an army and defeat the Danes. By 886 he had captured London and soon afterward was recognized as king of all England.

Alfred is the only king the English have ever designated "the Great." And what did he do to merit the title? Among other things he laid the foundation for the unification of England, was a patron of learning, and established trial by jury.

From an earthly point of view, Alfred surely deserves to be labeled "the Great." But the standards by which people judge greatness are not, and never have been, God's standards. Today we'll examine the words of Jesus on this topic. We will see that exercising lordship and authority over people does not fit into his definition of greatness. We will also see that for Jesus and his followers the key words are *ministry* and *service*.

### B. LESSON BACKGROUND

Our present lesson takes us into early A.D. 30, several months after Peter's great confession (studied in last week's lesson). It's now probably less than a month before Jesus' crucifixion.

During the months between the events of last week's lesson and today's, Jesus continued his ministry of healing and teaching. His labors covered more than two hundred miles, from Caesarea Philippi in the north to Jerusalem in the south.

Along the way Jesus had passed quietly through Samaria where he rebuked James and John for wanting to call down fire from Heaven upon a Samaritan village (Luke 9:51-56). For a period of time he labored on the eastern side of the Jordan River in Perea.

We also know that Jesus was in Jerusalem to attend the Feast of Tabernacles (John 7:11-52) and back there later to share in the Feast of Dedication (John 10:22-39). Much of the material for this period of Jesus' life is found in either Luke or John, but not in Matthew or Mark.

DEVOTIONAL READING:
MATTHEW 20:20-28

BACKGROUND SCRIPTURE:
MARK 10:13-45

PRINTED TEXT:
MARK 10:32-45

### LESSON AIMS

After participating in this lesson, each student will be able to:

1. Summarize Jesus' prediction of his death and the account of James and John's quest for chief seats in the kingdom.

2. Contrast Jesus' plan with that of James and John.

3. Explain how he or she plans to help someone who is in need.

Jan
30

### KEY VERSES

Whoever wants to become great among you must be your servant, and whoever wants to be first must be slave of all.
—Mark 10:43, 44

Just prior to the events of today's lesson, Jesus had his famous encounter with the rich young ruler (Mark 10:17-22) and had spoken to his disciples concerning the peril of riches (Mark 10:23-31). Having just heard Jesus' lecture on the dangers of wealth, it is strange that James and John should request places of leadership in Jesus' kingdom, as we will see them doing today. It's true that they specifically asked for high honor rather money, but it's also true that those two concepts have a way of "finding each other."

## I. CONDITION OF THE TWELVE (MARK 10:32a-c)

### A. THEIR AMAZEMENT (vv. 32a, b)

*32a, b. They were on their way up to Jerusalem, with Jesus leading the way, and the disciples were astonished,*

Jesus and his entourage are moving toward Jerusalem when the event described here occurs. On this journey they will pass through Jericho where Jesus restores sight to blind Bartimaeus (Mark 10:46-52) and has his encounter with Zacchaeus (Luke 19:1-10). Jesus will arrive in Bethany shortly (John 12:1). Following that, he will enter Jerusalem in triumph (Mark 11:1-10).

Jesus recently has been in the Jerusalem area, at Bethany, to raise his friend Lazarus from the dead. That event has stirred more opposition, and a council meeting is called to deal with Jesus. John 11:53 says, "So from that day on they plotted to take his life." Now Jesus is on his way back to Jerusalem, and his apostles are *astonished* that he should so soon return there after having encountered such harsh opposition. They undoubtedly must possess a vague sense of foreboding that some awful event is about to unfold. This feeling probably has been with them for a while now (cf. John 11:8).

### B. THEIR FEAR (v. 32c)

*32c. . . . while those who followed were afraid.*

The apostles' amazement is for their leader; their fear is for themselves. It is easy for us to imagine that the apostles are such spiritual giants that they never experience the emotions common to the rest of us, but the Gospel records do not so portray them. Even after seeing so many miracles, they have their doubts as well as their fears, their pride as well as their arrogance. At times they are quarrelsome, at other times vengeful (see below).

Jesus already has taught the apostles concerning fear. When he sent them forth on their evangelistic campaign (two lessons ago), he told them, "Do not be *afraid* of those who kill the body but cannot kill the soul. Rather, be afraid of the one who can destroy both soul and body in hell" (Matthew 10:28). But even though they had been taught not to fear, still they yield to their natural inclination under the circumstances.

There is a measure of comfort here for all of us. Though we know and love the Master and desire above all else to obey his words, sometimes, like the Twelve, we fail to do so. The spirit is often willing but the flesh proves to be weak.

## II. PREDICTION OF JESUS (MARK 10:32d-34)

### A. TO BE DELIVERED TO ENEMIES (vv. 32d, 33)

*32d, 33. Again he took the Twelve aside and told them what was going to happen to him. "We are going up to Jerusalem," he said, "and the Son of Man will be betrayed to the chief priests and teachers of the law. They will condemn him to death and will hand him over to the Gentiles,*

Jesus predicts his death several times in the Gospels (see Matthew 26:2; Mark 8:31; 9:9, 30-32). When the Twelve learn that he is to be delivered into the

WHAT DO YOU THINK?

*Fear sometimes can keep us from serving God. What are some ways God can teach us and use us despite our fears?*

WHAT DO YOU THINK?

*What can we learn from the fact that Jesus predicted his own death so many times?*

hands of *the Gentiles*, we might think that this will increase their bitterness and multiply their resolve to oppose such an atrocity. But just how much of what Jesus says at this time do they really comprehend? Luke 18:34 states that, "The disciples did not understand any of this" and gives as an explanation that the reality of Jesus' pending death was "hidden from them."

This fact raises a question: Who is bringing about the hiding? Does God in some miraculous way do it? Isn't it possible that the mind-set of the apostles won't allow themselves to believe it, and in this sense it is hidden from them?

We've all had experiences with things too horrible to believe, things rejected on that basis. For many people—citizens of the United States and their friends, especially—the 9/11 experience fits into this category.

### B. TO BE ABUSED AND KILLED (v. 34a)

*34a. " . . . who will mock him and spit on him, flog him and kill him.*

In none of his other predictions of death is Jesus so graphic in describing his suffering as here. Not only is he to be killed, but prior to his death he is to be tortured and abused in various ways.

Mark 14:65 later describes the accuracy of Jesus' predictions. At the conclusion of his trial before Caiaphas, "some began to spit at him; they blindfolded him, struck him with their fists, and said, 'Prophesy!' And the guards took him and beat him."

Still later, after Pilate has abdicated his responsibility and turned Jesus over to his soldiers, "They put a purple robe on him, then twisted together a crown of thorns and set it on him. And they began to call out to him, 'Hail, king of the Jews!' Again and again they struck him on the head with a staff and spit on him. Falling on their knees, they paid homage to him" (Mark 15:17-19). Such abuse of the Messiah had been predicted long before. See Isaiah 53.

### C. TO BE RAISED (v. 34b)

*34b. "Three days later he will rise."*

As the apostles don't grasp that Jesus is to die, neither do they understand that *he will rise*. Like the sad news of his death, the glorious revelation of his resurrection is hidden from them. And it stays hidden until after that event.

Immediately after the resurrection, two angels will remind the women at the tomb of Jesus' prediction, and "they remembered his words" (Luke 24:8). His apostles and other disciples similarly became convinced.

### III. REQUEST OF ZEBEDEE'S SONS (MARK 10:35-41)

#### A. REQUEST MADE (vv. 35-37)

*35-37. Then James and John, the sons of Zebedee, came to him. "Teacher," they said, "we want you to do for us whatever we ask."*

*"What do you want me to do for you?" he asked.*

*They replied, "Let one of us sit at your right and the other at your left in your glory."*

Matthew 20:20 notes that the mother of *James and John* comes "to Jesus with her sons." Obviously, all three are heavily involved in making this misguided request. If we combine Matthew 27:56 with Mark 15:40, we discover that the mother's name is Salome. She is neither the first nor last mother to have ambitions for her children. See Genesis 27:5-10.

Shortly before the time of this request, Jesus spoke of the twelve thrones upon which the apostles are to "sit . . . judging the twelve tribes of Israel" Matthew 19:28). It may be this promise that inspires James and John to make

WHAT DO YOU THINK?

How can we sometimes show spiritual immaturity like James, John, and the other disciples did in today's lesson?

their request for the most important of the twelve seats. To sit on the *right* hand and *left* hand of a sovereign indicates special favor and hence additional authority.

Since these two men, along with Peter, comprise an "inner circle" among the apostles, it's understandable that they will assume that they will continue to be singled out for special honor. As for the reason for making this request at this time, we are indebted to Luke. Shortly after this incident, that Gospel writer explains that the apostles "thought that the kingdom of God was going to appear at once" (Luke 19:11).

### ME FIRST

Eric Ritz tells of a certain executive who was traveling. While waiting at an airport, he learned his flight had been canceled. This forced him to go to another airline to rebook his journey. His patience was gone, so he shoved his way to the front of the ticket line and angrily demanded a first-class ticket on the next available flight. The agent explained that he'd be happy to help, but the man would just have to wait in line like everyone else.

That was too much for the man's ego. He leaned over the counter and said, "Young man, do you have any idea who I am?" Whereupon the ticket agent picked up the microphone and said, "Attention, please. There is a gentleman at the ticket counter who doesn't know who he is. If anyone can identify him, please come to the counter."

That man was really "asking for it"! An inflated view of self indicates a shallow spirit. But when there is genuine communion with God, there is humility; there is the absence of seeing oneself as greater than others. See Romans 12:3.    —J. D. R.

### B. DIALOGUE INTENSIFIES (vv. 38, 39)

38, 39. *"You don't know what you are asking," Jesus said. "Can you drink the cup I drink or be baptized with the baptism I am baptized with?"*

*"We can," they answered.*

*Jesus said to them, "You will drink the cup I drink and be baptized with the baptism I am baptized with,*

*Jesus* responds to the two in particular and the Twelve in general that they don't understand the full import of the request (cf. Romans 8:17; 2 Timothy 2:12; Revelation 3:21). He illustrates with two figures to teach that the leaders in his kingdom can expect suffering and death rather than greatness and power in their earthly lives. The use of *cup* represents sorrow, judgment, or retribution (see Psalm 75:8; Isaiah 51:17, 18; Jeremiah 25:15-26; 49:12). Jesus previously used the figure of *baptism* in Luke 12:50 to represent immersion in sorrow.

James will experience his cup and baptism of suffering in becoming the first apostle to be martyred (Acts 12:2). John will live a long life, but will be cast into exile (Revelation 1:9).

### WALKING THE WALK

Several years ago, *USA Today* reported from an extensive survey that 48 percent of American workers admitted to taking unethical or illegal actions on the job in the year past. Insurance companies state that 20 percent of car write-offs represent deliberate acts by the owners.

Worker's compensation cases are inflated by bogus claims. Female absenteeism for claimed sickness and injury peaks four times a year, just prior to school holidays. Retail stores are paying high prices for more sophisticated electronic equipment in an attempt to capture shoplifters—a multi-billion-dollar annual loss. Such equipment detects one out of every fifty-two customers carrying away at least one

HOW TO SAY IT

Bartimaeus. BAR-tih-ME-us.

Caesarea Philippi. Sess-uh-REE-uh Fih-LIP-pie or FIL-ih-pie.

Caiaphas. KAY-uh-fus or KYE-uh-fus.

Corinthians. Kor-IN-thee-unz (TH as in THIN).

Gentiles. JEN-tiles.

Jericho. JAIR-ih-co.

Jerusalem. Juh-ROO-suh-lem.

Lazarus. LAZ-uh-rus.

Perea. Peh-REE-uh.

Salome. Suh-LO-me.

Samaria. Suh-MARE-ee-uh.

Samaritan. Suh-MARE-uh-tun.

Zacchaeus. Zack-KEY-us.

Zebedee. ZEB-eh-dee.

item that is not paid for. Throw in cheating on exams, spouses, and tax returns and you have a cloudy picture of modern-day honesty and integrity.

It's easy to get swept up in so much dishonesty, isn't it? After all, "everyone else is doing it." Yet part of the cup that Christ had to drink involved going against the grain of cultural expectations that were opposed to God's will. His disciples are to do so as well. When we do, will we be surprised by the fiery baptism and bitter-tasting cup that can result?             —J. D. R.

## C. EXPLANATION OFFERED (v. 40)

40. " . . . but to sit at my right or left is not for me to grant. These places belong to those for whom they have been prepared."

Notice that Jesus does not deny that there will be chief places in the kingdom, only that they *belong to those for whom they have been prepared.* Matthew 20:23 further explains that it is the Father who has assigned the positions for which James and John ask.

Matthew 25:31-40 and John 5:22-30 show that Jesus will indeed have a key role in dispensing reward and punishment. But the authority of Jesus is derived from the Father (Matthew 11:27; 28:18; John 14:28), and the Father evidently reserves some functions for himself.

## D. DISPLEASURE EXPRESSED (v. 41)

41. When the ten heard about this, they became indignant with James and John.

Nothing is stated to show that *the ten* are equally anxious to have the chief places in the kingdom. But from Jesus' reprimand of all twelve, we may fairly surmise that the ten are of a similar mind as the other two. *James and John* have shown themselves to be spiritually immature by attempting to grab the chief spots. The other ten now show their own spiritual immaturity as they express displeasure out of jealousy. This is not the first time that these twelve have squabbled among themselves (see Mark 9:33-37).

## IV. NATURE OF DISCIPLESHIP (MARK 10:42-45)

### A. UNLIKE THAT OF THE GENTILES (v. 42)

42. Jesus called them together and said, "You know that those who are regarded as rulers of the Gentiles lord it over them, and their high officials exercise authority over them.

Jesus defuses this potentially explosive situation by suggesting that the apostles' conduct is similar to what would be found among *Gentiles.* The authority and power of the Roman Empire undoubtedly comes to everyone's mind. In effect, Jesus says that the actions of the apostles are not only unworthy of them, but they are not even Jewish-like. Such a statement should certainly grab the apostles' attention!

### B. LIKE THE PATTERN SET BY JESUS (vv. 43-45)

43-45. "Not so with you. Instead, whoever wants to become great among you must be your servant, and whoever wants to be first must be slave of all. For even the Son of Man did not come to be served, but to serve, and to give his life as a ransom for many."

In verse 40 Jesus indicated that there will be places of honor in his kingdom; he now indicates that these positions will not be based upon earthly standards such as Gentiles employ (v. 42, above). He explains the basis of true leadership in the kingdom. In so doing he switches from discussing the kingdom of God in an "end times" sense (v. 40) to speak of it in a "here and now" sense—that is, the

Visual for lesson 9. *Workers with International Disaster and Emergency Services display true servants' hearts in India and Brazil.*

church age. True greatness, Jesus explains, comes from ministering and serving, not from craving and grasping.

The Greek word translated *servant* is the word for the office of deacon in 1 Timothy 3:12, but it does not have that sense here. This word is used of any sort of servant, especially of one who serves at the table. All Christians—whether they hold an official church office or not—are to be ministering servants.

The word *slave* is used in a similar way in 1 Corinthians 9:19 and 2 Corinthians 4:5. What a concept: a "slave" and a "servant" who will be *great* and *first!* The apostles are not to follow the pattern seen in worldly Gentile kingdoms. Rather, they are to imitate the example that Jesus is living out before them.

The concept of Jesus' giving *his life as a ransom for many* is a rare explanation in the Gospels regarding the reason for Jesus' death. (The apostle Paul will offer a much more extensive explanation of this idea in the book of Romans.) What a life of humility and service!

### JUST LIKE JESUS

In his book *Reach Out for New Life*, Robert Schuller tells about Dr. Henry Poppen, who served for many years as a missionary to China. Poppen related going to a remote village where, presumably, missionaries had never been. He told the people about Jesus, stressing his kind and gentle manner and his great servanthood. He also stated that Jesus was able to forgive and love those who were unlovable.

When Dr. Poppen finished telling them about Christ, a few of the men came up to him and said, "We know Jesus! He has been here." "No," Dr. Poppen corrected. "He lived and died in a country far from here years ago." "No, no," they insisted. "He died here. Come, we will show you his grave."

They led him outside the village to a cemetery. On one tombstone was the name of a Christian medical doctor, who, on his own, had felt called by Christ to go, live, and die in China. The people had so admired him that they thought he was Jesus, the one Poppen had revealed.

Would anyone confuse your life with that of the Lord? Servanthood is the key to godly greatness.        —J. D. R.

## CONCLUSION

The little church had a real problem. One of its elders—perhaps the most capable man in the congregation—had passed away. His death had left a real void. Because the church was so small, there was no one with the necessary qualifications to take the place of the deceased elder. At least that's how many in the church saw it.

But not everyone agreed. One man in particular had other ideas. He was sure he was ideally qualified to be an elder. So he began a campaign to get "elected."

The trouble is that the man was an alcoholic, and a foul-mouthed one at that. In spite of his character faults, he somehow managed to get his name on the ballot for "election day." But that's as far as he got. The Christian people of the little church, knowing him for what he was, denied him the office that he so diligently sought.

The man reminds us of Simon the sorcerer from Acts 8. Both the would-be elder and the sorcerer thought too highly of themselves; both craved power in the church for the wrong reason; both were kept from sharing in the ministry of the kingdom because of their wrong attitudes.

In effect Jesus said, "You twelve know all too well what the Gentiles are like. My definition of greatness is not the same as theirs. Beware!" Which model of greatness will we choose to follow today?

# Discovery Learning

*This page contains an alternative lesson plan emphasizing learning activities. Classes desiring such student involvement will find these suggestions helpful. The next page is a reproducible activity page to further enhance discovery learning.*

## LEARNING GOALS

After this lesson each student will be able to:

1. Summarize Jesus' prediction of his death and the account of James and John's quest for chief seats.

2. Contrast Jesus' plan with that of James and John.

3. Explain how he or she plans to help someone who is in need.

## INTO THE LESSON

Provide a handout with the heading, "Opposites." In a column on the left side of the page list several words that have obvious opposites. Provide the opposite for the first as an example, like "light" and "dark." Some suggested words include high, sweet, positive, age, off, truth, strength, arrogance, righteousness, and selfishness.

As students arrive, distribute the handouts. Ask the learners to complete the handouts as they visit with other class members, get coffee, etc., before class begins.

After the class comes to order, quickly review the list of opposites. Note that the presence of an opposite tends to emphasize the power of an item. For example, the sour taste of grapefruit is more pronounced if it follows something sweet.

Point out that today's lesson puts some opposites into an interesting juxtaposition. Jesus, the epitome of humility and self-denial, is seen in stark contrast to some of his followers, who hope to thrust themselves into positions of leadership ahead of others. What makes the contrast even more striking is that their request comes on the heels of Jesus' predictions of his death.

## INTO THE WORD

*When more than one Gospel includes details of the same event, it is can be helpful to note the information provided by the parallel texts. The reproducible activity page that follows will help your students do that. Use it in addition to the activities described on this page.*

Ask a volunteer to read Mark 10:32-45 aloud. Divide the class into three groups for the following assignments.

*Group 1.* Review the text and compile a report on the emotions expressed by different persons or groups of people. Explain the reason for each emotion expressed and comment on whether the emotion was warranted or if some other emotion would have been more appropriate. In the latter case, explain how the person(s) could have been expected to display a different emotion.

*Group 2.* Review the text and compile a report on the dangers or potential dangers cited. Comment on the response to each danger (whether or not those involved responded properly).

*Group 3.* Review the text and compile a report on the contrasts seen in this passage. Point out the strengths and weaknesses of each side of the contrasts.

Allow about ten minutes for the groups to work; then ask for reports. Expect the following details to emerge from the reports; use the comments in the verse-by-verse exposition to note the significance of these details.

*Group 1.* The disciples displayed both amazement and fear (v. 32). James and John displayed an attitude of pride or selfishness (vv. 35-37). The ten were displeased with James and John (v. 41).

*Group 2.* Moving back to Judea put Jesus and the disciples in danger from the Jewish leaders (v. 32). Jesus elaborated on the danger to himself and how it would turn from potential to actual (vv. 32-34). Jesus told James and John—and also the other ten—of danger they would face in his name (vv. 38, 39).

*Group 3.* The disciples displayed a contrast in their emotions—amazement and fear (v. 32). The stark contrast here is between Jesus' attitude of self-sacrifice (vv. 33, 34) and James and John's attitude of self-promotion (vv. 35-37). Jesus then pointed out the contrast between the worldly attitude of leadership (v. 42) with the attitude he expects (vv. 43-45). Even within Jesus' remarks is contrast in that "whoever wants to become great among you must be your servant, and whoever wants to be first must be slave of all."

## INTO LIFE

Distribute a handout for students to note their own response to Jesus' call. The handout should include the following questions:

1. Is your attitude about service more like that of the world or that of Jesus? How is it demonstrated?

2. Who is someone in need of some service or ministry that you can provide? (This may be a person either inside or outside the church.) How can service on behalf of this person demonstrate Christlike leadership?

3. What will you do this week to follow Jesus' pattern of servant leadership?

Close the session with a prayer for each student to behave more like Jesus and less like James and John.

# Gospel Harmony

Today's lesson text, Mark 10:32-45, has parallels in Matthew 20:17-28 and Luke 18:31-34. Use the chart below to list all the details contained in any of the accounts. Note the proper verse notation(s) for each incident in the corresponding column. (See the examples below.)

| DETAILS | MATTHEW 20:17-28 | MARK 10:32-45 | LUKE 18:31-34 |
|---|---|---|---|
| On the way to Jerusalem | v. 17 | v. 32 | v. 31 |
| Disciples were astonished | | v. 32 | |
| Other followers were afraid | | v. 32 | |
| Jesus spoke privately to the 12 disciples | v. 17 | v. 32 | v. 31 |

# OVERCOMING GRIEF

**LESSON 10**

## WHY TEACH THIS LESSON?

A friend shared with me about the death of a husband. The young widow was left all alone to care for the house and two small children. Several days after the funeral a neighbor, who had never made an effort to make contact before, decided it was time to say something. He saw this bereaved neighbor out mowing her overgrown yard and went over to introduce himself to her. In the course of the conversation he also invited her and her children to church, then said, "If I can ever be of help to you, please let me know." Then he walked off, leaving her with the yard to finish on her own.

Too often it is in the time of grief that we reach out to people, but that can be too late. And when we do reach out, we give pious platitudes and weak offers to assist, while failing to take the initiative to assist in ways that are blatantly obvious.

In our text today, we see the pain of grief, but we also see the desire to care for the grieving. This lesson should challenge us to be more proactive in our efforts in ministering to people in their times of grief.

## INTRODUCTION

### A. SURROUNDED BY FRIENDS

A reporter from the *Cincinnati Enquirer* went to New York City following the terrorist attacks of September 11, 2001. Her assignment was to observe the rescue operations and to report on the efforts of police and firefighters to find survivors amidst the staggering devastation. One of the firemen at "the hole," which was another name for "Ground Zero," told the reporter that whenever one of the workers found a firefighter they could identify, they immediately sent for that man's company to come down. They would carry him out so that he could be surrounded by his friends.

Later that same day the reporter watched, tears filling her eyes, as a fire truck with sirens blaring raced through an intersection and stopped in front of the firehouse. Out came all the firefighters in full attire. Upon boarding the truck, the group headed toward "the hole," apparently to pick up the body of another friend.

In some funeral services, pallbearers surround the deceased and carry the body in a casket to the place of burial. Others, however, are needed who will surround the bereaved, offering to support and "carry" them when the burden of their loss seems too great to bear. Ultimately, God is the great carrier in this regard, as described by the prophet Isaiah: "Even to your old age and gray hairs I am he, I am he who will sustain you. I have made you and I will carry you; I will sustain you and I will rescue you" (Isaiah 46:4).

Today's lesson draws our attention to Ruth and Naomi, each of whom had experienced the death of a husband. For Naomi the loss was especially severe, since Ruth's husband was one of Naomi's sons. Through their experiences, we learn that our God is indeed "the God of all comfort, who comforts us in all our troubles" (2 Corinthians 1:3, 4).

DEVOTIONAL READING:
PSALM 31:9-16
BACKGROUND SCRIPTURE:
RUTH 1
PRINTED TEXT:
RUTH 1:3-9, 14-18

LESSON AIMS

*After participating in this lesson, each student will be able to:*

*1. Relate the series of events that led to Ruth's expression of devotion and loyalty to Naomi.*

*2. Explain how faith in God makes a difference in dealing with grief.*

*3. Think of a situation where he or she may be able to help someone in overcoming grief, and pray for wisdom in carrying out such a ministry.*

Feb
6

KEY VERSE

*Ruth replied, "Don't urge me to leave you or to turn back from you. Where you go I will go, and where you stay I will stay. Your people will be my people and your God my God."* —Ruth 1:16

LESSON 10 NOTES

WHAT DO YOU THINK?

*Christians are sometimes guilty of condemning those who are not like them in all matters of church life. From the story of Ruth, what do we learn about those who are outside of "our" group and how we are to relate to them?*

## B. LESSON BACKGROUND

The book of Ruth has been compared to a beautiful, delicate flower that emerges from the ground and survives amidst an abundance of worthless, unsightly weeds. Or one could think of it as a breath of fresh air, providing some relief from a smog-filled, polluted atmosphere. The first verse of the book gives us the setting: "in the days when the judges ruled." These days were not part of Israel's "golden age"; rather, they were the time characterized by the far from flattering assessment that appears at the conclusion of the book of Judges: "In those days Israel had no king; everyone did as he saw fit" (Judges 21:25).

In contrast, the book of Ruth highlights the exemplary faith and devotion of a Moabite woman—an individual outside the "chosen nation" of Israel. Yet she demonstrated the kind of loyalty to the Lord that was sadly missing from God's own people at this time in their history. What Jesus said of a certain centurion could also be spoken of Ruth: "I have not found anyone in Israel with such great faith" (Matthew 8:10).

## I. FAMILY'S DISASTERS (RUTH 1:3-5)

While the book of Ruth provides a welcome exception to the generally depressing tone of the book of Judges, it does not begin that way. The opening verse mentions a famine that had struck the land, a famine that became so severe as to necessitate a family move from Bethlehem of Judah to Moab, a mountainous region east of the Dead Sea. This would have been a journey of fifty or sixty miles.

### A. DEATH OF NAOMI'S HUSBAND (v. 3)

**3. Now Elimelech, Naomi's husband, died, and she was left with her two sons.**

Sometime after the move (the exact time is not given in the text), a tragedy far worse than famine occurs: *Elimelech, Naomi's husband,* dies. The text gives no details as to the cause. All we are given is the consequence of his passing: Naomi is *left with her two sons.* One can only imagine how devastated these three individuals feel. Perhaps they question the wisdom of their move and wish they had remained in Judah.

### B. DEATH OF NAOMI'S SONS (vv. 4, 5)

**4. They married Moabite women, one named Orpah and the other Ruth. After they had lived there about ten years,**

Whether the family discusses returning to Judah after Elimelech's death is not known. Mahlon and Kilion, the two sons (v. 2), take wives from the women of Moab. Kilion marries a woman named *Orpah,* while Mahlon marries a woman named *Ruth* (Ruth 4:10).

That these two Israelite men marry *Moabite women* may seem questionable in light of earlier restrictions given in the law of Moses regarding the marriage of foreigners (see Deuteronomy 7:1-4). But marriage with Moabites is not specifically forbidden in the law. The only restriction involving Moabites is found in Deuteronomy 23:3: "No Ammonite or Moabite or any of his descendants may enter the assembly of the Lord, even down to the tenth generation." Certainly there is a kind of stigma attached to the Moabites, part of it perhaps stemming from the rather sordid account of their origin (Genesis 19:30-38). Apparently there is not yet any relief from the famine in Judah, so Mahlon, Kilion, and their wives, along with Naomi, dwell in Moab *about ten years.*

**5. . . . both Mahlon and Kilion also died, and Naomi was left without her two sons and her husband.**

After the ten-year period mentioned in verse 4 passes, *Mahlon and Kilion* die. While Ruth and Orpah no doubt grieve over their respective losses, the deaths of these two men constitute an especially crushing blow to Naomi. Again, she is *left* (as in v. 3)—only now she is *left without her two sons and her husband*.

Naomi is thus both widowed and childless, a doubly disastrous condition in the ancient world. The first situation leaves her vulnerable to being taken advantage of—a problem that had not improved by Jesus' day (Luke 20:46, 47) and is still evident at times in today's society. The second situation leaves Naomi in a position that carries with it a sense of dishonor or disgrace: she has no sons and thus no means of continuing the family line of her husband Elimelech. In a sense, Naomi has lost her identity.

### THE SHADOW OF DEATH

*Leadership* magazine relates a story about Donald Grey Barnhouse, a great preacher of the past, who lost his wife. In his great grief, he was faced with the daunting task of rearing children alone. On the way to the funeral, the well-dressed youngsters sat quietly in the car. Barnhouse knew their pain was as intense as his. He also knew that their fear was coupled with an uncertainty even greater than his own.

The car stopped at a railroad crossing. Everyone stared ahead as the freight train passed swiftly by, casting an eerie sequence of shadow, sunlight, shadow, sunlight across the car. It was then that the father turned to his oldest child, who was seated in the front.

"Son," he asked, "would you rather be hit by that train or its shadow?" The puzzled boy asked his father to repeat the question. So again the father asked, "Would you rather be hit by that freight train or by its shadow?" Softly came the answer, "The shadow—it can't hurt."

"Kids," the father continued, "because your mom loved Jesus and let him be her Lord, he made sure death was just a shadow, it couldn't hurt her, only take her from our sight for a while. We'll see her again, in Jesus. That's what's going to help us through."

Historical hindsight reveals God's guiding hand on the lives of Ruth and Naomi as they worked through their grief, although it may not have seemed like it in the pain of the moment. Now that we have the firm and clear hope of the resurrection, how much more are we able to know of God's hand as it guides us through our own pain of loss!                                                                —J. D. R.

## I. NAOMI'S DECISION (RUTH 1:6-9)

Once more one can only surmise the barrage of questions and doubts that flood Naomi's mind following the deaths of her sons. Why did her family leave Judah to begin with? Is all of this a punishment from God for leaving the promised land and residing with foreigners? Is it only a matter of time until Naomi herself dies?

### A. CONCERNING HER DWELLING (vv. 6, 7)

**6. When she heard in Moab that the LORD had come to the aid of his people by providing food for them, Naomi and her daughters-in-law prepared to return home from there.**

Eventually news arrives from back home—good news, for a change. For the first time in the book of Ruth, *the Lord* is mentioned, perhaps an indication that Naomi's plight will begin to improve (though slowly at first). Specifically, the Lord has *come to the aid of his people by providing food for them*. The famine is over.

### DAILY BIBLE READINGS

**Monday, Jan. 31**—*I Am Weary with Weeping* (Psalm 6:1-7)

**Tuesday, Feb. 1**—*My Life Is Spent with Sorrow* (Psalm 31:9-15)

**Wednesday, Feb. 2**—*My Soul Refuses to Be Comforted* (Psalm 77:1-10)

**Thursday, Feb. 3**—*Naomi Loses Her Husband and Sons* (Ruth 1:1-5)

**Friday, Feb. 4**—*Go Back to Your Home* (Ruth 1:6-11)

**Saturday, Feb. 5**—*Orpah Goes, Ruth Stays* (Ruth 1:12-17)

**Sunday, Feb. 6**—*Naomi and Ruth Travel to Bethlehem* (Ruth 1:18-22)

**7. With her two daughters-in-law she left the place where she had been living and set out on the road that would take them back to the land of Judah.**

The picture set forth in this verse is a touching one. Here are three women united by the common bond of tragedy. All three have lost their husbands. Perhaps they determine, at first, that they will try to survive together in Naomi's homeland of Judah. Certainly there is something to be said for such companionship; people who have gone through a similar tragedy or crisis can often lend encouragement to one another by forming a kind of "support group."

### B. CONCERNING HER DAUGHTERS-IN-LAW (vv. 8, 9)

**8. Then Naomi said to her two daughters-in-law, "Go back, each of you, to your mother's home. May the LORD show kindness to you, as you have shown to your dead and to me.**

At some point Naomi seems to realize that it is really not in the best interest of her *daughters-in-law* for them to travel to Judah with her. They will be much more apt to find husbands (and therefore security) in their homeland of Moab.

So Naomi urges them to return each to her *mother's home*. In some instances in the ancient Near East, the mother's house seems to serve as a kind of bridal chamber. Genesis 24:67 tells how Isaac brought Rebekah to the tent of his mother, Sarah.

Naomi concludes her plea to her daughters-in-law with a blessing: *the Lord show kindness to you, as you have shown to your dead and to me*. Naomi thus commits these two women, though they are Moabites, to the Lord's care. Her words reflect her desire that the Lord would reward them for being so kind to her during the tragedies that have befallen them all. She knows that they already have made a genuine sacrifice by being willing to come with her this far.

**9. "May the LORD grant that each of you will find rest in the home of another husband."**

**Then she kissed them and they wept aloud.**

Again, Naomi expresses her wish that *the Lord* provide each of her daughters-in-law with *rest* by allowing each to settle down in Moab with a *husband*. The concept of rest includes the sense of security and well-being that will be missing from their lives if they remain widows.

From a practical standpoint, Naomi's advice is sound. Actually carrying it out is another matter entirely. The bonds that have been forged from the tears of grief and sorrow are not easy to break. Now come new tears as the three women prepare to part company.

### III. RUTH'S DECISION (RUTH 1:14-18)

In verses 10-13, not included in our printed text, both Ruth and Orpah voice their loyalty to Naomi and state their desire to accompany her to Judah. Naomi then tries to persuade the two of them to look at their situation realistically. She herself has nothing to offer Ruth and Orpah in the way of providing the "rest" mentioned in verse 9. Naomi's advanced age makes childbearing an impossibility for her. Even if through some means she is able to become pregnant and bear sons, it does not make sense for Ruth and Orpah to wait until these sons became old enough to marry. It is far better for both of the younger women to resettle in Moab.

Naomi concludes her appeal by declaring, "The Lord's hand has gone out against me!" (v. 13). From her viewpoint, her current situation appears hopeless. She has resigned herself to the fact that the Lord has determined to bring disaster upon her.

---

### HOW TO SAY IT

Ammonite. AM-un-ite.
Bethlehem. BETH-lih-hem.
centurion. sen-TURE-ee-un.
Chemosh. KEE-mosh.
Corinthians. Kor-IN-thee-unz
 (TH as in THIN).
Elimelech. Ee-LIM-eh-leck.
elohim (Hebrew). el-o-HEEM.
Isaac. EYE-zuk.
Judah. JOO-duh.
Kilion. KIL-ee-on.
Mahlon. MAH-lon.
Moab. MO-ab.
Moabites. MO-ub-ites.
Naomi. Nay-OH-me.
Orpah. OR-pah.
Rebekah. Reh-BEK-uh.

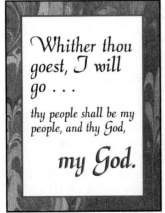

*Whither thou goest, I will go . . . thy people shall be my people, and thy God, my God.*

Visual for lesson 10. *Discuss how Ruth's kind of devotion to God and to one's family can be demonstrated today.*

Yet it is out of such seemingly hopeless scenarios that the Lord often does his greatest work. In his time his hand will provide abundant blessings to Naomi. However, that thought probably gives little comfort to her at this particular moment.

## A. NAOMI'S PLEA (vv. 14, 15)

**14. At this they wept again. Then Orpah kissed her mother-in-law good-by, but Ruth clung to her.**

Naomi's counsel to the daughters-in-law makes perfect sense, but that does not make it any easier to obey. More weeping follows. Finally, *Orpah* decides to bid farewell and kisses *her mother-in-law* one last time. *Ruth*, however, refuses to do so. She clings to Naomi.

**15. "Look," said Naomi, "your sister-in-law is going back to her people and her gods. Go back with her."**

At this point, Naomi is able to add another reason why Ruth should return to Moab: *your sister-in-law is going back*. By mentioning that Orpah is returning to both *her people and her gods*, Naomi highlights two crucial marks of a person's identity in the ancient world. Is Ruth really willing to sever ties with these?

The Hebrew word translated *gods* is *elohim*. Though it is actually a plural form in Hebrew, it is also one of the primary names for the one true God in the Old Testament. While the Moabites worship many gods, they recognize a chief god, who is known as Chemosh. In 1 Kings 11:7 this god is called "the detestable god of Moab." Second Kings 3:26, 27 tells how the king of Moab sacrificed his first-born son (apparently to Chemosh) in an effort to turn the tide of a battle with the Israelites in his favor.

Perhaps Naomi's plea reflects her earlier lament in verse 13: "The Lord's hand has gone out against me." Is she expressing her own frustration with the Lord by encouraging Ruth to go back to the chief god of her homeland?

## B. RUTH'S PLEDGE (vv. 16-18)

**16. But Ruth replied, "Don't urge me to leave you or to turn back from you. Where you go I will go, and where you stay I will stay. Your people will be my people and your God my God.**

If Naomi is determined that her daughters-in-law return to Moab, *Ruth* is even more determined to travel on to Judah with Naomi. Naomi may as well "save her breath," because Ruth has her mind made up. For her, there is no turning back.

Ruth's statement of devotion in this verse may be considered a kind of "Good Confession" from the Old Testament point of view. She is expressing a firm decision to break ties with the two primary sources of her identity: her *people* and her god. No longer will she see herself as a Moabite; she will be an Israelite. No longer will she honor Chemosh, whose worship includes the sacrifice of children; she will worship the *God* of Israel through the "sacrifice" of her heart and mind. Note that in spite of Naomi's claim that the hand of her God has gone out against her (v. 13), Ruth is still willing to acknowledge him as her God!

**17. "Where you die I will die, and there I will be buried. May the LORD deal with me, be it ever so severely, if anything but death separates you and me."**

The words *Where you die, I will die, and there I will be buried* reflect the uncompromising commitment that Ruth is making. One's place of burial testifies to one's sense of identity and belonging. Thus Joseph, just before he died in Egypt, requested that his bones be carried from Egypt to Canaan when the Lord delivered his people from bondage there (Genesis 50:24, 25).

WHAT DO YOU THINK?

Why is it important to "be there" for those going through times of grief? How can we do a better job at this?

[Genesis 2:18 and Romans 12:15 can help start your thinking on this issue.]

WHAT DO YOU THINK?

Family loyalty is a lost concept in many cases today. How can we demonstrate loyalty to family? Or is this really that important?

[Make sure to use Exodus 20:12 in your discussion.]

## WHAT DO YOU THINK?

We often struggle with the right thing to do in certain circumstances. What do we learn about the right thing from Ruth and Orpah?

## WHAT DO YOU THINK?

Sometimes we can be fickle! We are hot and cold, up and down. In spiritual matters this is a dangerous way to live. How can we steadfastly focus on the way of God? How have you been able to do this?

[Joshua 24:15; 1 Corinthians 15:58; and Philippians 3:13 can help frame your thinking.]

## PRAYER

Father in Heaven, thank you that in your Son Jesus we can be "more than conquerors." Whenever circumstances such as death tear us away from those we love, may we remember that nothing can separate us from your love. Grant us remembrance as well that there will be a day when tears are no more. In Jesus' name, amen.

## THOUGHT TO REMEMBER

His oath, his covenant, his blood,
Support me in the whelming flood;
When all around my soul gives way,
He then is all my hope and stay.
    —Edward Mote (1797–1874)

Although Ruth has been unquestionably clear in her statement of loyalty, she concludes her words with an oath, using the name of Naomi's God: *the Lord deal with me, be it ever so severely, if anything but death separates you and me.* Her pledge can be considered the equivalent of the phrase "till death do us part" in modern marriage vows.

Ruth is making herself accountable to the Lord himself. If she should in any way break the promise of loyalty she is voicing to Naomi, she is willing to pay whatever consequences the Lord will determine.

**18. When Naomi realized that Ruth was determined to go with her, she stopped urging her.**

What can Naomi say in rebuttal to such a thorough declaration of devotion? Similar to Jesus, who "resolutely set out for Jerusalem" (Luke 9:51), Ruth is *determined to go with* Naomi. Naomi knows that there is nothing she can do to dissuade Ruth from her intentions, so *she stopped urging her.*

### STAND BY ME

In his work *A Grief Observed*, the great C. S. Lewis discussed the personal and aching loss of his wife. He stated that there was "an invisible blanket between the world and me. I find it hard to take in what anyone says. It is so uninteresting."

But he continued, "Yet, I want others to be about me. For I dread the moments when the house is empty. I want them, only if they can be there to talk to one another and not to me. I want them there."

In times of grief, we need each other! This is how God designed us. One of the most powerful ministries (and evangelistic opportunities) that the church can have involves grief recovery. And this isn't just "the preacher's job." It's a job for us all.
    —J. D. R.

## CONCLUSION

In considering the topic of grief, it is also instructive to consider the example of Mary and Martha in their grieving over the death of their brother Lazarus. John 11:20 records the initial reactions of both women when Jesus came to Bethany, the town where the sisters lived. The contrast is striking: "When Martha heard that Jesus was coming, she went out to meet him, but Mary stayed at home."

Two points are of special note. The first is that this description echoes what we are told of the sisters in other passages in the Gospels, particularly Luke 10:38-42. There Martha is the aggressive initiative-taker, concerned that everything be "just right" for her guests (Jesus and his disciples). Mary, on the other hand, is the quiet, meditative individual, satisfied to sit at Jesus' feet and take in whatever he has to say. Observe that in John 11:20, it is Martha who immediately goes out to meet Jesus when he arrives. Mary, the more reflective of the two, prefers to remain in the house.

The two sisters' different responses illustrate the important truth that people express grief in different ways. Some are very open and verbal about how they feel; others are more withdrawn and introspective. Some need the company of other people; others prefer to be alone. For some, tears come easily and frequently; others carry the look of those who are grief-stricken, but there are no tears.

To both sisters Jesus offers his presence and, even more significantly, his power. He raised Lazarus from the dead with only a command. Death submitted to the Master just as quickly as the winds and waves of a raging storm had done earlier. Jesus remains, by virtue of his own resurrection, the great overcomer. He empowers us to be overcomers as well (Romans 8:37-39).

# Discovery Learning

*This page contains an alternative lesson plan emphasizing learning activities. Classes desiring such student involvement will find these suggestions helpful. The next page is a reproducible activity page to further enhance discovery learning.*

## LEARNING GOALS

After this lesson each student will be able to:

1. Relate the series of events that led to Ruth's expression of devotion and loyalty to Naomi.

2. Explain how faith in God makes a difference in dealing with grief.

3. Think of a situation where he or she may be able to help someone in overcoming grief, and pray for wisdom in carrying out such a ministry.

## INTO THE LESSON

*Option 1:* Before class make copies of the word search puzzle below. Give each student a copy when he or she arrives. Your learners should naturally start working on the puzzle during the informal time of visiting before class starts. If needed, allow a few minutes to complete the puzzle after class begins.

```
H N B U O E T E O C A N N P B
I U O U H O U S E H M D T C E
C T S R R E N O N I J O O M H
F L M B P I E T U L D T A A O
V E A A A A E L E I R E Y B L
O E V V H N H D H O N L A O D
I E I S E L D T D N T C Y T I
C L S H M O O E T S H R D M H
E I I V B T S N A A T R D M B
R M T C A S R F D N O Y H D R
U E E U I P D U U L N B E O E
T L D K E A J O K I N D L Y A
H E E F E D C M N I N A E W D
W C H T N A O M I I H R E S T
E H S O D E A D M P E O P L E
```

Inform your learners that there are sixteen words from today's lesson text in the puzzle grid. See how many they can find before you reveal the following list of the hidden words: buried, Kilion, dead, death, Elimelech, husband, Judah, kissed, Lord, Mahlon, Moab, Naomi, Orpah, people, rest, Ruth.

*Option 2:* Use the reproducible activity "Coping with Grief" from the next page to introduce the lesson. (You can distribute copies or simply introduce the subject and discuss it.) Note that companionship is a great help in times of grief. Our lesson today tells of Ruth, who was a wonderful companion to one who had suffered much grief in her life.

## INTO THE WORD

Ask a volunteer to read Ruth 1:3-9, 14-18 aloud. Briefly review the story, pointing out locations on a map. Then ask your learners to imagine what Naomi might have written to a friend or relative in Judah while she was in Moab. Ask students either to write these imaginary "letters" or to discuss in small groups what she could have included. Challenge your learners to consider the following occasions for writing: the death of Elimelech (v. 3), the marriages of Kilion and Mahlon (v. 4), the deaths of Kilion and Mahlon (v. 5), the decision to return to Judah (vv. 6, 7), the anticipation of arriving in Judah with Ruth (vv. 8, 9, 14-18).

Encourage the learners to write their letters with feeling consistent with the facts being related. The earlier letters should be filled with the grief of bereavement in a foreign land. That grief should be apparent even in the second letter, which concerns the sons' marriages as Naomi comes to terms with the idea of her Hebrew sons marrying Moabite women. (See Deuteronomy 23:3-6.)

The final letter should indicate Naomi's grief as it is tempered by the compassionate love of Ruth, who is accompanying Naomi to Judah. Your best letter writers may even include a note of anticipation for the future.

## INTO LIFE

Ask the learners to suggest situations that produce grief today. Write these on the board. (*Ideas include death of a loved one, rejection by a prodigal son or daughter, loss of a job, relocation to a new city, an incident that divides a family or church, and divorce.*) Ask, "How does one's faith in God help make these events easier to bear?"

Try to get learners to avoid "glittering generalities" in their responses. Challenge them to be specific about some of the ways that their faith encourages them in times of grief. Two situations should become clear in this discussion. First, one's personal faith helps him or her to bear up under trial better than one without faith. Second, the presence of others who share that faith is comforting to the believer. Ruth provided this benefit to Naomi.

Ask your students to consider the people they know in their "circles of influence." Are some of these suffering through grief? Encourage your learners to look for ways to minister to those who grieve. Provide copies of the list of "Comforting Scriptures" from the next page. Close with prayer, asking for God's guidance.

# Coping with Grief

Most adults have lost someone close to them and know others who have experienced the same. Think about some of the losses you have experienced and losses that people you know have experienced. What was most helpful in getting through the acute pain of the grief?

What kinds of "help" from well-meaning friends was not helpful? Why?

# Comforting Scriptures

If you or someone you know is experiencing a time of grief, the following Scriptures may be found helpful. If you are sharing these with another, be careful not to offer them flippantly. Discuss in class how Scripture may be offered in a way that gives hope instead of sounding like "pious platitudes."

| | |
|---|---|
| Psalm 9:9, 10 | Psalm 142:1-5 |
| Psalm 23 | Psalm 145:13b, 14 |
| Psalm 27:1, 4-6 | Isaiah 25:6-9 |
| Psalm 30:1-5 | Isaiah 40:1-5 |
| Psalm 31:7, 9, 10, 24 | Isaiah 41:10, 13 |
| Psalm 33:20-22 | Isaiah 43:1-3a |
| Psalm 34:1-8, 17-20 | Isaiah 49:13 |
| Psalm 40:1-6 | Isaiah 61:1-3 |
| Psalm 42 | Jeremiah 31:13b |
| Psalm 43:5 | Lamentations 3:22-26 |
| Psalm 46:1-3, 10, 11 | Nahum 1:7 |
| Psalm 55:1, 2, 16, 17, 22 | Matthew 10:29-31 |
| Psalm 56:3, 4, 8-11 | Matthew 11:28-31 |
| Psalm 61:1-3 | John 14:1-4, 27 |
| Psalm 62:1, 2, 5-8 | Romans 8:28-39 |
| Psalm 69:28 | 2 Corinthians 1:3-5 |
| Psalm 71:19-21 | 2 Corinthians 4:16-18 |
| Psalm 73:25, 26 | Philippians 1:19, 21 |
| Psalm 86:1-4 | Philippians 4:4-7 |
| Psalm 91:1, 2 | 1 Thessalonians 4:13-18 |
| Psalm 94:17-19 | 2 Thessalonians 2:16, 17 |
| Psalm 102:1, 2 | James 5:8-11 |
| Psalm 103:8, 13, 14 | 1 Peter 4:12-19 |
| Psalm 121:1, 2 | 1 Peter 5:7 |
| Psalm 130:1, 2, 5, 6 | Revelation 7:15-17 |
| Psalm 141:1, 2 | Revelation 21:3, 4 |

# OVERCOMING PRIDE

**LESSON 11**

## WHY TEACH THIS LESSON?

In the summer of 1986, two ships collided in the Black Sea off the coast of Russia. Hundreds of passengers died as they were hurled into the icy waters below. News of the disaster was further darkened when an investigation revealed the cause of the accident. It wasn't a technology problem like radar malfunction—or even thick fog. The cause was human stubbornness. Each captain was aware of the other ship's presence nearby. Both could have steered clear, but according to news reports, neither captain wanted to give way to the other. Each was too proud to yield first. By the time they came to their senses, it was too late (*Closer Walk*, December 1991).

In our text today we meet a man who just about allowed his pride to keep him from realizing the healing and blessing God wanted to give to him. This lesson should bring to our mind areas where we are so filled with pride that God is unable to bless us. In turn, this lesson should cause us to repent from the sin of pride and lead us into a life of submission.

## INTRODUCTION

### A. IT'S ALL ABOUT ME

During a National Football League game in October 2002, a player caught a pass and scored a touchdown for his team. Following his dash into the end zone, the player reached down to his shoes, pulled out a felt-tip marker, autographed the football, and handed it as a souvenir to a friend sitting conveniently in the front row.

While some harshly criticized the player for his actions, others saw the incident as just another example of the self-promotion that characterizes so much of the sports world today. As one columnist noted, the motto in sports these days seems to be, "Wake up and smell the *me*."

People often have referred to the 1960s as the "Me Generation." But that label could be attached to every generation of humanity, for pride knows no limits or restrictions of time or geographical boundaries. In our lesson today, we will see pride manifest itself in the thinking of Naaman, an Aramean military commander afflicted with leprosy. His pride almost resulted in his rejection of the only remedy for his condition.

Some of Naaman's servants, however, had the courage to speak up and call attention to the folly of his behavior. To Naaman's credit, he was willing to swallow his pride and obey the Lord's word as conveyed through his prophet.

If only God's own people had demonstrated such humility, how different their history would have been!

### B. LESSON BACKGROUND

The story of Naaman occurred during the ministry of the prophet Elisha. At this point in the history of God's people, the twelve tribes had been divided into two separate nations for a little less than a hundred years. Elisha's ministry was primarily to the northern kingdom (usually referred to as Israel), where Baal

DEVOTIONAL READING:

MARK 7:1-5, 14-23

BACKGROUND SCRIPTURE:

2 KINGS 5

PRINTED TEXT:

2 KINGS 5:1-15a

LESSON AIMS

After participating in this lesson, each student will be able to:

1. Relate how Naaman overcame his pride in order to receive the divine cure from his leprosy.

2. Explain how pride keeps people today from enjoying divine favor.

3. Identify an area in his or her own life where pride needs to be defeated and express a commitment to release that pride.

KEY VERSES

Naaman's servants went to him and said, "My father, if the prophet had told you to do some great thing, would you not have done it? How much more, then, when he tells you, 'Wash and be cleansed'!" So he went down and dipped himself in the Jordan seven times, . . . and his flesh was restored and became clean.

—2 Kings 5:13, 14

Feb
13

worship had made serious inroads because of the influence of King Ahab and his pagan wife Jezebel.

The text for today from 2 Kings refers to the king of Israel and the king of Aram, though it does not mention either by name. Most likely the king of Israel was Joram or Jehoram (but usually spelled as Joram in most English Bibles to distinguish him from the Jehoram who was king of Judah at about the same time). The king of Aram (sometimes called Syria) was probably Ben-Hadad II.

## I. SYRIAN'S PLIGHT (2 KINGS 5:1-4)

### A. NAAMAN'S SITUATION (v. 1)

**1. Now Naaman was commander of the army of the king of Aram. He was a great man in the sight of his master and highly regarded, because through him the LORD had given victory to Aram. He was a valiant soldier, but he had leprosy.**

*Naaman* is introduced to us as *commander of the army of the king of Aram*. This means that he is a high-ranking officer in the army of that country. (He is called Naaman the Syrian by Jesus in Luke 4:27.) He has distinguished himself in this capacity, as indicated by the descriptions that he is *a great man*, *highly regarded*, and *a valiant soldier.*

But while Naaman is unquestionably a capable leader, he is in truth an instrument in the greater, more honorable, and mightier hands of the Lord. It is through Naaman that *the Lord had given victory to Aram*.

When we study Old Testament history, we usually think of God's activity in delivering his people from their oppressors (as in the exodus or in the days of the judges). But God is the Lord of all nations (Isaiah 14:26, 27). He is as capable of aiding them as he is of aiding the Israelites. In this case his deliverance of Aram may refer to a victory that that nation achieved over the Assyrians around the middle of the ninth century B.C., the time in which the events in today's lesson take place.

One might think that the fact that Naaman has *leprosy* would prevent him from carrying out any kind of military activity. However, the Hebrew word often translated *leprosy* in our Bible does not always indicate the severe, debilitating affliction ("Hansen's Disease") that we often associate with that term. It can also describe less serious skin conditions, such as psoriasis or eczema.

Naaman's condition, whatever it may be, is most likely in its earliest stages. Note Naaman's reference to "the spot" in verse 11, as if there is a specific place on his skin that is particularly troublesome.

### B. POSSIBLE SOLUTION (vv. 2-4)

**2, 3. Now bands from Aram had gone out and had taken captive a young girl from Israel, and she served Naaman's wife. She said to her mistress, "If only my master would see the prophet who is in Samaria! He would cure him of his leprosy."**

The strategy of the Arameans against Israel at this particular time involves dispatching a series of smaller *bands* of troops that engage the Israelites in brief skirmishes at certain key locations. Often both captives and goods are seized in the process.

During one such excursion, the Arameans *had taken captive a young girl*. Many of the captives exhibit bitterness or hatred toward their captors. This Israelite girl, however, apparently develops a great respect for Naaman, whose *wife* she serves. (This may say something about how Naaman and his wife treat this girl.)

One day the girl voices her concern for her *master* (Naaman) to *Naaman's wife*. The girl is convinced that if only Naaman could consult *the prophet* (Elisha) *who is in Samaria*, then *he would cure him of his leprosy*.

**WHAT DO YOU THINK?**

*People face many needs in life. The ultimate answer to life's most pressing needs are found in God. How can you be used to point people to the God who gives help?*

*4. Naaman went to his master and told him what the girl from Israel had said.*

Naaman tells *his master* (here the word *master* refers to the king of Aram) about the Israelite girl's suggestion. This explains why the king of Aram responds in the next verse of our text.

## II. KING'S PANIC (2 KINGS 5:5-7)

### A. LETTER SENT (v. 5)

*5. "By all means, go," the king of Aram replied. "I will send a letter to the king of Israel." So Naaman left, taking with him ten talents of silver, six thousand shekels of gold and ten sets of clothing.*

The words used by the king convey a sense of urgency. In speaking them, *the king of Aram* indicates his concern for Naaman's health. The king, too, respects this "valiant soldier" (v. 1) and values his skill on the battlefield.

The fact that the king of Aram could send a letter to *the king of Israel* may reflect more cordial relations than could be indicated by the skirmishes mentioned earlier. However, a treaty was agreed to by the Israelites and the Arameans during the reign of King Ahab (1 Kings 20:34). The existence of this treaty seems to be recognized during King Joram's reign as well, in spite of the occasional Aramean raids into Israel.

In the ancient Near East, it is common to provide some kind of payment whenever certain services are requested of a prophet. This is characteristic of pagan prophets more than it is of the Lord's prophets, as illustrated by Elisha's later refusal to accept any such offer from Naaman (2 Kings 5:15, 16). But Naaman, coming from a pagan background, believes that such a payment is part of the "protocol" when dealing with a prophet.

The Syrian's gift is impressive indeed: *ten talents of silver, six thousand shekels of gold, and ten sets of clothing*. A shekel weighs just a bit over four-tenths of an ounce. At three hundred dollars per ounce today, this amount of gold equates to over seven hundred thousand U.S. dollars!

To get an idea of the value of ten talents of silver, consider that King Omri of Israel bought the hill on which he built the city of Samaria for just two talents of silver (1 Kings 16:24). *Ten sets of clothes* would be quite an addition to anyone's wardrobe, even today.

### B. LETTER READ (vv. 6, 7)

*6. The letter that he took to the king of Israel read: "With this letter I am sending my servant Naaman to you so that you may cure him of his leprosy."*

The contents of this *letter* may provide another illustration of the pagan mind-set of the Arameans. Apparently the king of Aram assumes that the prophet in Samaria is under the control of the king (as prophets usually are in pagan countries). So the Aramean king directs his request for Naaman's healing directly to Joram, *the king of Israel*. Another possibility is that the king of Aram assumes that Joram knows of Elisha and will convey the message of the letter to him.

*7. As soon as the king of Israel read the letter, he tore his robes and said, "Am I God? Can I kill and bring back to life? Why does this fellow send someone to me to be cured of his leprosy? See how he is trying to pick a quarrel with me!"*

The king of Aram probably is not aware of the tension that exists between the prophet Elisha and the spiritually weak King Joram (see 2 Kings 6:30-32, where Joram is most likely the king described in the text). When Joram reads *the letter*, he does not think of Elisha at all. He views the letter as nothing more than a political ploy devised by the king of Aram to start a conflict with *Israel*.

### HOW TO SAY IT

Abana. AB-uh-nuh or Uh-BAN-uh.
Ahab. AY-hab.
Aram. AIR-um.
Aramean. AR-uh-ME-un (strong accent on me).
Assyrians. Uh-SEAR-e-unz.
Baal. BAY-ul.
Ben-Hadad. Ben-HAY-dad.
Damascus. Duh-MASS-kus.
eczema. EK-zuh-muh.
Elisha. E-LYE-shuh.
Jehoram. Jeh-HO-rum.
Jezebel. JEZ-uh-bel.
Joram. JO-ram.
Naaman. NAY-uh-mun.
Omri. AHM-rye.
Pharpar. FAR-par.
psoriasis. suh-RYE-uh-sis.
Samaria. Suh-MARE-ee-uh.
Syria. SEAR-ee-uh.

## III. PROPHET'S PROPOSAL (2 KINGS 5:8-15a)

### A. ELISHA'S COMMAND (vv. 8-10)

**8. When Elisha the man of God heard that the king of Israel had torn his robes, he sent him this message: "Why have you torn your robes? Have the man come to me and he will know that there is a prophet in Israel."**

When the prophet *Elisha* hears of the king's alarmed reaction, he chides *the king* for such a faithless response. This issue is nothing to tear one's clothes over. *"Have the man come to me and he will know that there is a prophet in Israel"* (even if King Joram doesn't).

Joram has asked the question, "Am I God?" (v. 7). Certainly, he is not, nor is Elisha; but Elisha is a *man of God* who will address the concerns expressed by the king of Syria. The real King in *Israel* is still the Lord.

**9. So Naaman went with his horses and chariots and stopped at the door of Elisha's house.**

Elisha's message is passed on to Naaman, who proceeds to the prophet's *house*. The text mentions Naaman's *horses and chariots,* perhaps to highlight the fact that Naaman has brought his typical military entourage.

Naaman probably hopes to impress *Elisha* with just how worthy he is of the prophet's attention. So he stands *at the door of Elisha's house,* waiting (perhaps somewhat impatiently) for the prophet to come out.

**10. Elisha sent a messenger to say to him, "Go, wash yourself seven times in the Jordan, and your flesh will be restored and you will be cleansed."**

In most pagan environments, a prophet shows great respect for the king and for other important leaders (such as someone of Naaman's reputation). Perhaps Naaman expects *Elisha* to emerge from his house and express his admiration that such a renowned individual would come all the way from Aram for his assistance. If so, how surprised and offended Naaman must be that Elisha himself does not even bother to appear!

Instead, the prophet merely sends a *messenger,* whose word is simple: Naaman must *wash* in the *Jordan* River *seven times;* then his leprosy will be cured. To Naaman, however, things are not as simple as they may seem to Elisha!

### B. NAAMAN'S PRIDE (vv. 11, 12)

**11. But Naaman went away angry and said, "I thought that he would surely come out to me and stand and call on the name of the LORD his God, wave his hand over the spot and cure me of my leprosy.**

Naaman is *angry,* both at the prophet's refusal to *come out* to see him and even more by such a seemingly ridiculous "prescription" for his leprosy. Again, perhaps Naaman's more pagan-oriented thinking contributes to his reaction. He expects a much more elaborate, flamboyant display of power—something appropriate for a man of his standing. To be told he must go to the Jordan River, probably about twenty miles away, is an insult.

**12. "Are not Abana and Pharpar, the rivers of Damascus, better than any of the waters of Israel? Couldn't I wash in them and be cleansed?" So he turned and went off in a rage.**

From the standpoint of sheer logic, Naaman's response to the prophet's suggested cure seems to make sense. If a river is part of the remedy for his leprosy, why does it have to be the Jordan, which is often sluggish and muddy? There are rivers in Aram and its capital *Damascus* that are just as good, if not better.

Clearly, Naaman's ego has taken a beating. He has come to Elisha with a certain set of expectations, and none of them has been met. So he turns and leaves in a rage.

WHAT DO YOU THINK?

*The directives of God, though straightforward, sometimes seem strange to us. Why does God choose to work in this way?*

WHAT DO YOU THINK?

*How does pride keep us from following God's will today?*

### PRIDE BEFORE A FALL

Sometimes pride encourages people to get into deep trouble. Pride manifests itself in various ways, one of which is known as "résumé padding." Perhaps one of the saddest such cases came to an ominous close on May 16, 1996, when Admiral Jeremy M. "Mike" Boorda, U.S. Navy Chief of Naval Operations, committed suicide.

U.S. President Bill Clinton had appointed Admiral Boorda to his prestigious post in early 1994. Subsequently, word got out that one or more of the combat decorations that the admiral claimed as his own may not have been officially awarded. Rather than "face the music," Admiral Boorda ended his life with a gunshot through the chest.

After expressing deep regret over the incident, one Navy officer said, "No officer should ever be in a position where he or she fears the truth. But integrity is like virginity—once you've lost it, it's gone for good." That analogy may be a bit overstated, but the danger of pride is still shockingly clear. After leading us into wrong paths, pride can yield horrible consequences if we don't take steps to reverse it.

—J. D. R.

### C. SERVANTS' COUNSEL (v. 13)

*13. Naaman's servants went to him and said, "My father, if the prophet had told you to do some great thing, would you not have done it? How much more, then, when he tells you, 'Wash and be cleansed'!"*

Naaman is blessed to have some very discerning (not to mention courageous!) servants, who take it upon themselves to approach the frustrated Aramean. They bring their own brand of logic to the situation. They begin by addressing Naaman as *father,* another indication of the high respect in which Naaman is held by all who know him.

They then point out that if Elisha had told Naaman to perform some feat of strength or endurance (*some great thing*) to prove his worth, Naaman would have accepted the challenge. He ought therefore to accept the very simple request of the prophet, even though it seems absurd. The issue comes down to this: how badly does Naaman want to rid himself of his leprosy?

### "I REALLY MEAN IT!"

Picture this: you hire a reputable company to paint the exterior of your house. You are going on vacation, so you anticipate that the job will be finished when you return. You choose the colors and negotiate the price. You want it basic white with green trim. The contract is signed and you depart.

When you come back, your contractor has painted your house yellow with blue trim. He says to you, "I know what you asked for, but I think this will be a more appealing combination and will really stand out in this community. So I took the liberty of changing your color scheme."

Perhaps your painter will think that your complaints sound unreasonable and restrictive. But you don't think so, and neither will a judge!

Why is it, then, that when the Almighty gives a specific command, his subjects have the audacity to declare that something else—something less or more—is what they'll do? How can we expect him to be pleased and accept us with this kind of an attitude?

God was clear in Old Testament times that his commands were not negotiable or optional. In the New Testament era, we may be tempted to pay less attention to God's commands and laws because we live under grace. But it is vital to remember Jesus' words from John 14:15: "If you love me, you will obey what I command." First John 5:3 also declares our task: "this is the love of God: to obey his commands."

—J. D. R.

**DAILY BIBLE READINGS**

**Monday, Feb. 7**—*These Evil Things Defile a Person* (Mark 7:17-23)

**Tuesday, Feb. 8**—*Trap My Enemies in Their Pride* (Psalm 59:10-17)

**Wednesday, Feb. 9**—*God Will End Arrogant People's Pride* (Isaiah 13:9-13)

**Thursday, Feb. 10**—*Naaman Hopes for a Cure* (2 Kings 5:1-5a)

**Friday, Feb. 11**—*Elisha Tells Naaman What to Do* (2 Kings 5:5b-10)

**Saturday, Feb. 12**—*Naaman Is Cured* (2 Kings 5:11-14)

**Sunday, Feb. 13**—*Naaman Accepts the God of Israel* (2 Kings 5:15-19)

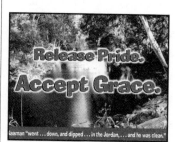

Visual for lesson 11. *The Jordan river, where Naaman exchanged his pride for God's grace. Discuss how people today need to release pride to find grace.*

## D. NAAMAN'S COMPLIANCE (v. 14)

14. *So he went down and dipped himself in the Jordan seven times, as the man of God had told him, and his flesh was restored and became clean like that of a young boy.*

It is never easy to confront and try to reason with an angry person. Naaman's servants are to be commended for their willingness to do so. Their gentle but persuasive and firm logic convinces Naaman that his immediate reaction was wrong.

So he proceeds to go to the *Jordan* River and dip himself *seven times*. And as *the man of God* had promised, Naaman's *flesh* becomes *like that of a young boy*. It should be noted that Naaman's heart has become as that of a little child as well, for he has humbled himself before the Lord and his messenger Elisha.

## E. NAAMAN'S CONFESSION (v. 15a)

15a. *Then Naaman and all his attendants went back to the man of God. He stood before him and said, "Now I know that there is no God in all the world except in Israel.*

Naaman's attitude is radically different from what it had been previously. He is a different man—both on the outside and on the inside. Given what he's just been through, should it be otherwise?

Naaman could now just go on his way home, but he doesn't. Like the one leper that was cured (out of ten!) in Luke 17:11-19, Naaman returns to acknowledge the source of his healing. Interestingly, neither Naaman nor the leper of Luke 17:16 are Israelites. But they both go out of their way to express gratitude for their healing.

The inward change in Naaman is reflected in his words to *the man of God*, Elisha: *Now I know that there is no God in all the earth except in Israel.* We noted in last week's lesson that Ruth made a kind of "Good Confession" in her declaration of commitment to Naomi's God (Ruth 1:16). Naaman now makes a similar statement.

Notice that Naaman is not merely adding the God of Israel to the list of gods that he already worships. Rather, he is acknowledging that *there is no God in all the earth except in Israel.* Earlier, Naaman had referred to the Lord as Elisha's God (v. 11). Now he is affirming, like Ruth, that "your God is my God."

## CONCLUSION

For a number of years, Richard Halverson served as chaplain of the United States Senate. One of his duties in this position was to offer a prayer at the beginning of each session of the Senate. On May 2, 1984, Halverson gave the following prayer. As you read it, consider its relevance to our lesson and our lives.

"Almighty God, we have come a long way since our birth as a republic, but we have wandered somehow. Our Founding Fathers held freedom of religion as fundamental. We have translated their deep conviction into freedom from religion.

"We have become technological giants, and spiritual and moral dwarfs. We are sophisticated in scientific progress and primitive in spiritual development.

"We are knowledgeable in the ways of the world and ignorant in the ways of God. We live as though man is the center of the universe and God a peripheral invention of pious enthusiasts.

"We are abundantly rich in material resources and abysmally poor in spiritual and moral capital.

"Dear God, help us get our act together before it is too late. In the name of him who is the Way, the Truth, and the Life. Amen."

---

WHAT DO YOU THINK?

Simply doing things God's way is the best way. What foundational areas of obedience concerning God's will are you lacking in?

[Matthew 10:42 and James 1:27 can start your thinking.]

---

PRAYER

Father, we confess how often pride has kept us from a closer walk with you. Break down our self-made walls this day in Jesus' name, amen.

---

WHAT DO YOU THINK?

It was after he was cleansed that Naaman finally confessed his belief in the one true God. Considering John 20:29, how are we even more blessed in our acknowledgment of God?

---

THOUGHT TO REMEMBER

"A proud man is always looking down on things and people: and, of course, as long as you are looking down, you cannot see something that is above you."
—C. S. Lewis (1898–1963)

# Discovery Learning

*This page contains an alternative lesson plan emphasizing learning activities. Classes desiring such student involvement will find these suggestions helpful. The next page is a reproducible activity page to further enhance discovery learning.*

## LEARNING GOALS

After this lesson each student will be able to:

1. Relate how Naaman overcame his pride in order to receive the divine cure from his leprosy.

2. Explain how pride keeps people today from enjoying divine favor.

3. Identify an area in his or her own life where pride needs to be defeated and express a commitment to release that pride.

## INTO THE LESSON

Begin the session by telling the students you'd like their help in proposing to the major TV networks a new reality show. The program will bring famous people onto the set to determine who is the most arrogant! You need their help in coming up with a list of athletes, performers, politicians, and others who have a chance at the title, "World's Most Arrogant Human." (No local people allowed! All suggestions must be famous people not personally acquainted with anyone in the class.)

Let the students enjoy this exercise without allowing it to get out of hand. Poking a little good-natured fun at athletes who dance or gyrate after they score or at politicians who promise the sun, moon, and stars to get elected should be harmless. But don't let the talk turn political or into personal attacks at certain celebrities based on your learners' opinions or positions.

After a few minutes, ask, "Who would want this title? Anyone?" After the class acknowledges that this would not be a coveted position, ask, "Why is arrogance (or pride) looked on so negatively?" Discuss the irony of pride's being universally recognized as bad, but just about as universally practiced. Observe that today's lesson looks at an example of one who could have earned the title, "World's Most Arrogant." But when he released his pride, he became one of the world's most blessed.

*Option:* Introduce the lesson by using the reproducible activity "Key Concept" from the next page.

## INTO THE WORD

Today's lesson comes from a text that is a favorite source of Bible drama for children. If possible, recruit some children from grades 5 and 6 who enjoy acting to act out the events of 2 Kings 5:1-15. (You'll need to recruit and work with the children in advance.) Otherwise, have a good reader read the text aloud.

Provide a handout to guide students through the Bible study. Students may work individually or in small groups to complete the table described below. At the top of the handout should be the title, "The Problem of Pride." Below that should be a table or grid with the following headings: *Potential Reasons for Pride; Evidence or Demonstrations of Pride; Reasons Pride Was Inappropriate.* Down the left side should be the following: Naaman, Servant girl, King of Israel, Elisha.

When you call for reports, fill in a copy of the chart with your learners' answers, supplementing as necessary. Naaman may have been proud because of his high position and success. His pride is evidenced by his hurt feelings and his initial refusal to submit. He had no reason for pride because he himself was powerless to do anything about his condition; he was dependent on God. Had he continued in pride, he would have forfeited his opportunity for healing.

The servant girl could have been proud because she knew the God who could heal Naaman. She showed no evidence of pride, however. She was God's servant first.

The king of Israel was likely proud of his position. He shows pride in that he thought the request for Naaman's healing was "all about him"; he failed to recognize the opportunity to point Naaman to God. He should have been humbled, knowing God to be the true king.

Elisha could have shown pride because he was specially blessed by God to do miracles and foretell future events. But he shows none of that. He recognized his power was from God, not himself.

Option: Use the reproducible "Just the Facts" from the next page to explore today's Bible text.

## INTO LIFE

Point out the potential result of Naaman's pride: forfeiture of healing. Ask, "How does pride keep people today from enjoying divine favor?" Potential answers include the failure to find salvation, as those who take pride in their own efforts are unable to appreciate salvation by grace. Be sure to explore potential results of pride among Christians—what blessings do we who are saved also miss out on because of pride? Also, think of fractured relationships that are not mended because of pride.

Wrap up the class with a challenge for each student to examine his or her life for signs of pride. Close with prayer for greater humility.

# Key Concept

Complete the following verses by supplying the missing word in each. Then unscramble the highlighted letters to find a key word for today's lesson.

[The Lord] mocks __ □ __ __ __ mockers but gives grace to the humble (Proverbs 3:34).

The fear of the Lord teaches . . . __ □ __ __ __ __ , and humility comes before honor (Proverbs 15:33).

The Lord detests all the proud of heart.
Be sure of this: they will not go __ __ □ __ __ __ __ __ __ __ (Proverbs 16:5).

Before his downfall a man's __ □ __ __ __ is proud, but humility comes before honor (Proverbs 18:12).

Haughty eyes and a proud heart, the lamp of the __ __ __ __ __ □ , are sin! (Proverbs 21:4).

Fill in the key word in the following sentence: Release __ __ __ __ __ ; accept grace!

# Just the Facts

Read 2 Kings 5:1-15 and answer the following questions.

1. Who was Naaman, and what was his problem?

2. Who suggested a solution for his problem, and what did she suggest?

3. With permission of his master, Naaman went to Israel. To whom did he go, and what did he take with him to purchase a cure?

4. What did this person think when he found out what Naaman wanted?

5. What did Elisha do when he heard that the king of Israel had torn his robes?

6. When Naaman stopped at Elisha's house, who communicated the prophet's message to Naaman? What was that message?

7. How did Naaman initially respond? What changed his mind?

8. Having been cleansed, Naaman said, "Now I know. . . ." What did he know?

9. What saved Naaman from his leprosy? Could he in any way say he had "earned" his cure? Why or why not?

10. Could he have been cured without obedience? Why or why not?

# OVERCOMING UNCERTAINTY

**LESSON 12**

## WHY TEACH THIS LESSON?

Millions sat glued to their televisions on July 20, 1969, when Neil Armstrong took those first steps on the moon. Some were skeptical, thinking it all a great ruse being foisted on the public. When Columbus declared his belief that the world was round and could be circumnavigated, he was ridiculed. The reports of the resurrection of Jesus were doubted by even his closest followers. We are quick to question and even deny things that are not part of our experience or previous teaching, aren't we? We consider it the "conservative" thing to do.

Jesus came teaching principles and lessons that did not always make sense to the accepted way of thinking. A message of new birth, a message of eternal life, a message of hope for all peoples everywhere are difficult things to comprehend. If there are doubts in your mind about God's will for saving the world today, about God's desire to save you, then acceptance of Jesus' teaching in this lesson should dispel those doubts and provide you with the hope and peace only he can give. And if you are already in Christ, it should be your desire to proclaim the possibility of being "born again" to those around you who need this message.

## INTRODUCTION

### A. HOW TO FIND GOD

The topic "how to find God" is not new. People have been attempting to make a connection with God (or "the gods," as the case may be) throughout history. The early twenty-first century is no exception.

There seems to be no consensus, however, on how God may be found. For example, a 2001 Barna Research survey reported that 51 percent of American adults believe that it is possible to earn a place in Heaven by being "generally good" or by "doing good things." A 1994 Barna survey revealed that only 39 percent of Americans believe that a failure to accept Jesus as Savior will result in being "condemned to Hell." A 2002 Barna survey showed that 37 percent of U.S. adults consider themselves to be "Christians," while they also declare that they have not been born again.

The existence of so many religious beliefs with contradictory ideas certainly presents us with a mess! Yet in the midst of such confusion, Jesus says without hesitation that people will not see the kingdom of God unless they are born again.

### B. LESSON BACKGROUND

John writes his Gospel to convince his readers that Jesus is "the Christ, the Son of God" (John 20:31). John does this by recording important miracles and teachings.

One of the earliest recorded teachings of Jesus focuses on a private conversation with a certain Nicodemus, a very religious Jew who was a teacher himself. When Nicodemus sought out Jesus to learn more about him, Jesus confronted that learned man with the most important challenge of his life. This challenge made him step beyond his beliefs to examine his relationship with God in a new and powerful way.

DEVOTIONAL READING:
JOHN 3:18-21
BACKGROUND SCRIPTURE:
JOHN 3:1-21
PRINTED TEXT:
JOHN 3:1-17

LESSON AIMS

After participating in this lesson, each student will be able to:

1. Recount what Jesus told Nicodemus about the new birth.

2. Compare and contrast the lifestyles of those who have been born again with the lifestyles of unbelievers.

3. Give thanks to God for sending Jesus and giving us new birth.

KEY VERSES

Jesus answered, "I tell you the truth, no one can enter the kingdom of God unless he is born of water and the Spirit. Flesh gives birth to flesh, but the Spirit gives birth to spirit." —John 3:5, 6.

Feb 20

# I. NEED FOR A NEW BIRTH (JOHN 3:1-3)

Jesus' days are busy. So on occasion he looks forward to quiet time (e.g., Luke 4:42). But this particular evening is interrupted by a visitor.

## A. INQUIRY (vv. 1, 2)

**1. Now there was a man of the Pharisees named Nicodemus, a member of the Jewish ruling council.**

The Pharisees consider themselves to be the guardians of God's laws. They have counted more than six hundred commands in the Old Testament, which they then interpreted and supplemented. Ultimately, they ended up making their interpretations into a protective hedge around God's laws. Most Pharisees reject Jesus because they believe he broke the law (e.g., Matthew 12:1-14).

Not only is Nicodemus a Pharisee, but he is also *a member of the Jewish ruling council.* This means that he is part of the Jewish Supreme Court known as the Sanhedrin, which also opposes Jesus.

### ON TARGET?

Tony Evans tells about a man who visited a farm and noticed that on the barn were several bull's-eye targets. On closer inspection he discovered that in the middle of each of those targets was a single shot, dead center.

The man complimented the farmer upon learning that he was the one who had handled the rifle. "You must be an expert marksman—smack in the middle every time." The farmer replied, "Well, to be truthful, I just fired away and painted all those bull's-eyes after I shot."

Evans concludes: "I've run across a lot of thoughtless and aimless people. Are you clear and purposeful, aiming at a legitimate target, or are you just trying to learn how to paint well?"

Right here was where the Pharisees had a problem. The Scripture interpretations they came up with were justified by painting bull's-eyes around them. But unlike the farmer in the story above, the Pharisees were unwilling to recognize the illegitimacy of what they were doing. What about us?                    —J. D. R.

**2. He came to Jesus at night and said, "Rabbi, we know you are a teacher who has come from God. For no one could perform the miraculous signs you are doing if God were not with him."**

Many Pharisees believe that Jesus performs miracles by satanic power (e.g., Matthew 12:24). Nicodemus proves that he is not one of them when he addresses Jesus as *Rabbi* (teacher). Nicodemus risks much by holding this opinion in opposition to his fellow Pharisees.

Even so, many today criticize Nicodemus for coming *at night.* Is Nicodemus using the cover of darkness out of fear of his fellow Pharisees? (See John 9:22.) Perhaps Nicodemus purposely hides his beliefs because he thinks that this is the only way to retain his seat on the council.

We should not overlook the fact that John uses the word *night* in his Gospel figuratively to include moral and spiritual darkness (see John 9:4; 11:10; and 13:30). This may be John's subtle way of telling us that Nicodemus's spiritual darkness is worse than he realizes, despite his confession "Rabbi." We see this darkness lift as Nicodemus later speaks in Jesus' defense (John 7:50-53) and helps Joseph of Arimathea prepare Jesus' body for burial (John 19:38, 39).

## B. CONFRONTATION (v. 3)

**3. In reply Jesus declared, "I tell you the truth, no one can see the kingdom of God unless he is born again."**

### WHAT DO YOU THINK?

Nicodemus serves as an example of a (somewhat) humble person coming to a spiritual awakening. In what ways were you like Nicodemus in coming to Christ in the beginning? How can you follow the example of Nicodemus as you draw closer to the Savior?

Jesus often begins discussions by saying something so bold that he immediately grabs people's attention. Nicodemus wants to learn more from Jesus, but does not expect him to teach a radical transformation. The implication is that the scholarly and distinguished Nicodemus still lacks this transformation.

When Jesus begins with *I tell you the truth,* he is stating something of utmost importance: only those who undergo a new birth will see God's *kingdom.* The Greek word translated *again* can also mean "from above," and Jesus may be using both meanings at once. Thus this new birth is not only a rebirth but it is also "from above" as it is accomplished by the power of God.

No one is exempt, not even Nicodemus. Certainly he is very religious. As a Pharisee he keeps himself from everything that breaks God's law. He does not dream of lying, stealing, or killing. But Jesus makes it clear that even Nicodemus must be *born again.* No matter how "religious" he is, he will not *see* God's *kingdom* without a new birth.

Jesus' kingdom is not of this world (John 18:36). Most of the Jews in Jesus' day expect God's kingdom to be a political realm where Jews will be militarily, politically, and materially greater than all Gentile nations. But God's kingdom is within, where God rules in the heart (Luke 17:21).

God so loved the world that he gave his only begotten Son.
John 3:16

Visual for lesson 12.
*Today's visual illustrates the climax of Jesus' conversation with Nicodemus.*

## II. RECEIVING THE NEW BIRTH (JOHN 3:4-11)

Jesus certainly has the attention of Nicodemus. Nicodemus is full of questions and Jesus now answers them—and more!

### A. WATER AND SPIRIT (vv. 4-7)

4. *"How can a man be born when he is old?" Nicodemus asked. "Surely he cannot enter a second time into his mother's womb to be born!"*

*Nicodemus* is incredulous, even scornful, in his reply. He wants an explanation. "A *man* cannot reenter *his mother's womb* and be reborn, can he? Exactly what do you mean, Jesus, by saying that a man must be 'born again'?"

5. *Jesus answered, "I tell you the truth, no one can enter the kingdom of God unless he is born of water and the Spirit.*

Jesus' response is very similar to what he has just declared in verse 3. The main difference is that he substitutes *born of water and the Spirit* for "born again."

Very few Christians doubt that the Holy Spirit plays a vital part in being born again (see Romans 2:29; 2 Corinthians 3:6). After we are born again, we "are led by the Spirit of God" (Romans 8:14) and we walk in his ways (Romans 8:4; Galatians 5:16, 25).

On the other hand, there is a great deal of disagreement over the meaning of *water* in this context, and there are numerous ideas. One idea is that the reference is to the amniotic fluid that surrounds a baby in the womb before physical birth occurs. Another idea is that Jesus is talking about John's baptism as practiced, for example, in Matthew 3:6. Still another idea is that Jesus is thinking about Christian baptism such as we see Peter proclaim in Acts 2:38. A fourth idea is that Jesus is drawing upon Old Testament images of water and Spirit. These four theories do not exhaust the list of proposals!

Since Jesus seems to want "born again" in verse 3 to mean the same thing as *born of water and of the Spirit,* then the reference cannot be to amniotic fluid. What Jesus has in mind is one spiritual rebirth, not a physical birth plus a spiritual rebirth. The idea that *water* refers to John's baptism is not strong, because that baptism is designed to be temporary (Acts 19:1-5).

The idea that *water* may refer to Christian baptism has a great appeal when we consider the importance that this concept receives in the New Testament (e.g.,

### HOW TO SAY IT

*Arimathea.* AIR-uh-muh-THEE-uh.

*carpe diem (Latin).* kar-pay DEE-um.

*Ezekiel.* Ee-ZEEK-ee-ul or Ee-ZEEK-yul.

*Gentile.* JEN-tile.

*Isaiah.* Eye-ZAY-uh.

*Nicodemus.* NICK-uh-DEE-mus.

*Pharisees.* FAIR-ih-seez.

*Rabbi.* RAB-eye.

*Sanhedrin.* SAN-huh-drun or San-HEED-run.

Colossians 2:12). However, the problem with this idea is that Christian baptism does not come into being until the Day of Pentecost (Acts 2:38). If Jesus is referring to Christian baptism here, then it means that he is scolding Nicodemus in verse 10 (below) for failing to understand something that has not yet even come into practice.

A good case can be made for a reference to the Old Testament ideas of water and Spirit. See especially Ezekiel 36:25-27. There, *water* stands for cleansing from impurity while *Spirit* points to transformed hearts. Nicodemus, the Old Testament scholar, should understand these things. In passing we may note that as the Old Testament Passover celebration foreshadows the Lord's Supper of the New Testament era, so also do certain Old Testament images of water point toward the New Testament practice of baptism (1 Peter 3:18-22).

6. *"Flesh gives birth to flesh, but the Spirit gives birth to spirit.*

God's *Spirit* produces the new *birth*. "Not because of righteous things we had done, but because of his mercy. He saved us through the washing of rebirth and renewal by the Holy Spirit" (Titus 3:5). This rebirth, then, is a renewal. It is accomplished as the Spirit of God brings new life to our dead spirits.

We come into this world by *flesh*. But our rebirth is by *the Spirit!* This rebirth produces spiritual fruit—"love, joy, peace, patience, kindness, goodness, faithfulness, gentleness and self-control" (Galatians 5:22, 23). Those who are born of the Spirit mind the things of the Spirit, while those born only from the flesh mind the things of the flesh (Romans 8:5).

7. *"You should not be surprised at my saying, 'You must be born again.'*

Jesus has said that people *must be born again*. Now he changes to the pronoun *you* (which is plural in the Greek) to make the idea even stronger. The word *must* tells us that being born again is not optional. All of this apparently causes Nicodemus to *be surprised*, but it shouldn't! An Old Testament scholar such as he should realize the importance of the need for a new nature.

### B. WIND AND SPIRIT (v. 8)

8. *"The wind blows wherever it pleases. You hear its sound, but you cannot tell where it comes from or where it is going. So it is with everyone born of the Spirit."*

Jesus refers to *the wind* to illustrate the unseen work of *the Spirit*. When the wind *blows*, it blows where it wishes, so to speak. We hear *the sound*, but we do not know where that gust of wind has come from or where it will go after it passes. The wind itself is unseen, but the effect that it has on us is quite noticeable. We see the branches of the trees bending. We feel a cool breeze.

Similarly, no one can see the movements of the Holy Spirit himself. No one can see the gift of the Spirit or the Spirit's indwelling (Acts 2:38). Physically, the renewed person looks the same, but the fruit of the Spirit will show the Spirit's effects (see v. 6, above).

In Ezekiel 37, God's breath or Spirit brings life from death in the valley of dry bones. So it is with all genuine Christians. (The ancient word for *wind* is the same as the word for *Spirit*, making the comparison even more interesting.)

### C. QUESTION AND ANSWER (vv. 9-11)

9, 10. *"How can this be?" Nicodemus asked.*

*"You are Israel's teacher,"* said Jesus, *"and do you not understand these things?*

Nicodemus is still struggling to understand, so Jesus reminds him that a *teacher* of Israel should not be mystified at these concepts. The original language has the word *the* before *teacher*, which has caused some to speculate that Nicodemus is a teacher with an official position.

---

*WHAT DO YOU THINK?*

Birth is followed by life. This is a straightforward thought, but one that often is neglected spiritually. How do we demonstrate our life in the Spirit?

[Make sure to consider Romans 12; 1 Corinthians 12; and Ephesians 4.]

---

*DAILY BIBLE READINGS*

Monday, Feb. 14—You Have Been Born Anew (1 Peter 1:18-23)

Tuesday, Feb. 15—Born of God, Children of God (1 John 2:29–3:5)

Wednesday, Feb. 16—Born of God, Conquer the World (1 John 5:1-5)

Thursday, Feb. 17—How Can I Be Born Again? (John 3:1-5)

Friday, Feb. 18—How Can These Things Be? (John 3:6-10)

Saturday, Feb. 19—God So Loved the World (John 3:11-16)

Sunday, Feb. 20—Jesus Came to Save the World (John 3:17-21)

Nicodemus, who is very familiar with what we call the Old Testament, should know about God's power to renew. He should also know of his own need for renewal. Further, Nicodemus should know that people are not justified by their own righteousness (Isaiah 64:6) and that people need God's mercy to be cleansed from sin (Psalm 51:1, 2).

It is God's Spirit who can breathe new life into the heart of someone who is dead in sins. And it is only the Spirit who can do so. The Pharisees are blind to these facts, however (Luke 18:9-14).

**11. "I tell you the truth, we speak of what we know, and we testify to what we have seen, but still you people do not accept our testimony.**

This is the third time Jesus uses *I tell you the truth*. As before, these words create an air of authority and seriousness regarding the discussion at hand. By using the plural *we*, Jesus may be mocking the "we know" that Nicodemus uses in verse 2, above. The phrase *you people* sounds disdainful. These are the people who have rejected John the Baptist's testimony, and now they are rejecting Jesus as well (Luke 7:29, 30).

## III. UNDERSTANDING THE NEW BIRTH (JOHN 3:12-17)

People must be born again. Yet no one would have that opportunity were it not for the fact that God chooses to love lost humanity. "This is love: not that we loved God, but that he loved us and sent his Son as an atoning sacrifice for our sins" (1 John 4:10).

### A. LIFE, NOT DEATH (vv. 12-15)

**12. "I have spoken to you of earthly things and you do not believe; how then will you believe if I speak of heavenly things?**

Jesus informs this teacher of Israel that the things thus far spoken of are relatively easy compared with other topics. Although the new birth is from above, it is *earthly* in the sense that it takes place here on earth. If Nicodemus cannot understand this, then how can he possibly comprehend the grandeur of *heavenly things*?

**13. "No one has ever gone into heaven except the one who came from heaven—the Son of Man.**

No one has ever gone *into heaven* to learn about that place (Proverbs 30:4). But Jesus knows about Heaven because he *came from* there. Thus Jesus has the authority to speak about things that only he has seen. Jesus is no average person!

**14, 15. "Just as Moses lifted up the snake in the desert, so the Son of Man must be lifted up, that everyone who believes in him may have eternal life.**

The Israelites sinned, so God sent poisonous snakes. But to save those who wanted to be spared, God commanded Moses to construct a brass serpent on a pole. People were invited to look up at the serpent. If they looked in faith, God saved them from the snakes' venom (Numbers 21:4-9).

It can be said that humanity has been "bitten" by the old serpent, Satan (Genesis 3; Revelation 12:9). In a way somewhat similar to the brass snake, Jesus is lifted up on a cross (John 8:28; 12:32, 34). People who look to him in faith will be saved. A worse fate awaits those who are lost—the lake that burns with fire and brimstone (Revelation 21:8). But those who look in faith to Jesus will not perish but will have eternal life. See the next verse.

### DOING RIGHT, WRONG, AND NOTHING

A certain life insurance agent had a unique way of encouraging potential clients to make timely decisions. The agent would make his presentation and lead right to

*WHAT DO YOU THINK?*

*Like Nicodemus, we sometimes fail to know or understand foundational things. Why do we fail in this regard?*

*WHAT DO YOU THINK?*

*What principles for living do we learn from Jesus' descent into this world? How do we emulate him in this regard?*

*[See especially Luke 14:11; 18:14; and Philippians 2:1-11.]*

PRAYER

*Father, thank you for your great love that sent Jesus to die for our sins. Thank you that we can experience a new birth so that no matter how bad our sins have been we can find forgiveness and new life through the power of your Holy Spirit. But Father, our thankfulness is not enough. Help us to take the message of transformed hearts to others! In Jesus name, amen.*

WHAT DO YOU THINK?

*Jesus came into the world for the sake of saving this world, not condemning it. How should this guide us as we live out our lives of Christlikeness?*

THOUGHT TO REMEMBER

*"Everyone who believes that Jesus is the Christ is born of God" (1 John 5:1).*

the moment of closing the sale. If the potential client said, "That's such a big decision, I'd really like to think on it," the agent had a ready response.

"Of course, I can see that," the agent would say. "Tell you what: you sleep on it. And *if* you wake up in the morning, we'll talk some more." What a powerful point!

The Latin phrase *carpe diem* is also powerful. This phrase, popularized in the 1989 movie *Dead Poet's Society*, means "seize the day." Jesus said something similar when, in talking about his own ministry, he stressed that "night is coming, when no one can work" (John 9:4). Time is running out!

Theodore Roosevelt (1858–1919) once said, "In any moment of decision the best thing you can do is the right thing, the next best thing is the wrong thing, and the worst thing you can do is nothing." There is a lot of truth in this observation. However, when it comes to accepting Christ as Savior, "doing the wrong thing" and "doing nothing" really amount to the same thing.

Each of us is just a heartbeat away from eternity. Can we risk deciding *anything* but the right thing as we seize this day?      —J. D. R.

### B. SALVATION, NOT CONDEMNATION (vv. 16, 17)

**16. "For God so loved the world that he gave his one and only Son, that whoever believes in him shall not perish but have eternal life.**

This single verse contains the gospel in a nutshell. God's love is self-sacrificing and embraces the entire *world* (not just Israel). People are lost in sin and will *perish* if something is not done. Jesus is God's *Son*, a gift to the world. Eternal rewards and punishment await. People either perish or they have *eternal life*, depending upon how they respond to Jesus.

**17. "For God did not send his Son into the world to condemn the world, but to save the world through him."**

Jewish teachers believed that Messiah came *to condemn* Gentile nations, setting Israel over the nations. But Jesus here says that he came to save *the world*. Jesus has indeed come to judge the world (John 9:39), but that is not the same as condemning the world. Eventually he will return to both judge and condemn those who reject the gospel. But when he first comes to earth, his purpose is to be their Savior.

### CONCLUSION

Jesus has made it clear: everyone must be born again. This new birth results in a complete transformation. It is made possible by the power of God's Holy Spirit.

However, many today want to hold back part of their lives for themselves. They want to straddle the fence. They don't want to truly change, because that would mean giving up some favorite vices. But Jesus demands complete transformation. "Therefore, if anyone is in Christ, he is a new creation; the old has gone, the new has come!" (2 Corinthians 5:17).

When writing later, the apostle John will list tests by which people can judge whether or not they have been born again. Consider the following, all from the letter we call 1 John:

"You know that everyone who does what is right has been born of him" (2:29).

"No one who is born of God will continue to sin" (3:9).

"Everyone who loves has been born of God" (4:7).

"Everyone who believes that Jesus is the Christ is born of God" (5:1).

"Everyone born of God overcomes the world" (5:4).

So the new birth that Jesus demands is not merely some theological term to be studied by Bible scholars. It is a radical change of heart and lifestyle. Do you meet these tests?

# Discovery Learning

*This page contains an alternative lesson plan emphasizing learning activities. Classes desiring such student involvement will find these suggestions helpful. The next page is a reproducible activity page to further enhance discovery learning.*

## LEARNING GOALS

After this lesson each student will be able to:

1. Recount what Jesus told Nicodemus about the new birth.

2. Compare and contrast the lifestyles of those who have been born again with the lifestyles of unbelievers.

3. Give thanks to God for sending Jesus and giving us new birth.

## INTO THE LESSON

Begin the session by asking learners to take the following quiz. (Answers in parentheses are the results of a 1999 Gallup poll in the U.S., which may be somewhat different from the Barna Research surveys noted in the Introduction.)

1. In the U.S., what percentage of people believe in God? *(86%)*

2. What percentage believe that good people go to Heaven, whether or not they believe in God? *(44%)*

3. What percentage believe that religions other than their own offer true paths to God? *(75%)*

4. What percentage believe that they earn a place in Heaven by being good and doing good things? *(60%)*

Briefly discuss how the students' expectations compare with the Gallup survey. Which statistic surprises them most? Why? Observe that there is obviously much confusion about the issue of salvation. This confusion is not new. A similar confusion was evident from the earliest days of Jesus' ministry—even from a learned teacher who ought to have known better. His name was Nicodemus, and what Jesus told him is as important for us today as it was for him.

## INTO THE WORD

Prepare in advance to have three good readers to read John 3:1-17 from the reproducible activity "A Conversation with Jesus" from the next page. One should read the words of Nicodemus, another the words of Jesus. The third will narrate, reading all the words that are not quotes from Jesus or Nicodemus. Have the one who reads the words of Nicodemus also prepare a brief report about the Pharisees.

After the text has been read, ask "Nicodemus" to tell about the Pharisees. What was their purpose? *(They wanted to maintain the observance of God's law in society.)* What was wrong with them? *(They became legalistic,*

*keeping a rigid form of the law but not its spirit.)* Why did they oppose Jesus? *(He did not cater to their interpretations or their expectations of who they thought the Messiah ought to be.)* Note that all this made Nicodemus's interview with Jesus quite remarkable.

Point out that the Pharisees had the wrong idea about salvation—as many today do as well. Jesus attempted to set him straight. His words will help set people today straight as well.

Ask, "How does this text answer some of the misconceptions about salvation that we discussed earlier?" Give a few minutes for the class to make some comparisons, working individually or in small groups. Then ask for reports. The following points should be noted:

1. Only 86 percent of the people surveyed even believe in God. Salvation depends on believing in God in order to believe in his Son (vv. 14-17).

2. Forty-four percent believe that good people go to Heaven, whether or not they believe in God. However, see Romans 3:10-18; Hebrews 11:6.

3. Three-fourths believe religions other than their own offer true paths to God. Jesus said that only He, the One "who came from heaven," is capable of granting salvation (John 3:13).

4. Sixty percent believe that they earn a place in Heaven by being good and doing good things. However, see John 3:3-8; Ephesians 2:8, 9.

Say, "Our actions reflect our beliefs. How does one who believes in God's Son differ in behavior from one who does not?" Take a few minutes to field answers. This is a "what?" question, but push deeper by asking, "why?"

## INTO LIFE

Ask class members, "Do you ever find yourself slipping into the same behaviors as those we have noted that characterize unbelievers? What do you do to reaffirm your faith and redirect your behavior?" Discuss this issue briefly, encouraging your learners to take seriously the matter of acting on faith.

Point out that God's gracious plan of salvation is a wonderful gift. The fact that salvation is not a matter of works should give each of us great joy. Salvation could only have come about as it did—by Jesus' paying the price for our sins himself. Ask each student to write a brief prayer, poem, or song of thanks to God for sending Jesus and giving us new birth.

# A Conversation with Jesus

Use the following to facilitate a dramatic reading or a skit of the visit of Nicodemus to Jesus.

**Narrator:** Now there was a man of the Pharisees named Nicodemus, a member of the Jewish ruling council. He came to Jesus at night and said,

**Nicodemus:** "Rabbi, we know you are a teacher who has come from God. For no one could perform the miraculous signs you are doing if God were not with him."

**Narrator:** In reply Jesus declared,

**Jesus:** "I tell you the truth, no one can see the kingdom of God unless he is born again."

**Nicodemus:** "How can a man be born when he is old? Surely he cannot enter a second time into his mother's womb to be born!"

**Jesus:** "I tell you the truth, no one can enter the kingdom of God unless he is born of water and the Spirit.
"Flesh gives birth to flesh, but the Spirit gives birth to spirit.
"You should not be surprised at my saying, 'You must be born again.'
"The wind blows wherever it pleases. You hear its sound, but you cannot tell where it comes from or where it is going. So it is with everyone born of the Spirit."

**Nicodemus:** "How can this be?"

**Jesus:** "You are Israel's teacher, and do you not understand these things? I tell you the truth, we speak of what we know, and we testify to what we have seen, but still you people do not accept our testimony. I have spoken to you of earthly things and you do not believe; how then will you believe if I speak of heavenly things?
"No one has ever gone into heaven except the one who came from heaven—the Son of Man. Just as Moses lifted up the snake in the desert, so the Son of Man must be lifted up, that everyone who believes in him may have eternal life.
"For God so loved the world that he gave his one and only Son, that whoever believes in him shall not perish but have eternal life. For God did not send his Son into the world to condemn the world, but to save the world through him."

(from John 3:1-17, NIV)

# Give Thanks to God

Use the space below to write a brief prayer, poem, or song of thanks to God for sending Jesus and giving us new birth.

# OVERCOMING PREJUDICE

## LESSON 13

## WHY TEACH THIS LESSON?

Prejudice is an ugly sin that won't seem to go away. Take the case of Benjamin O. Davis, Jr. (1912–2002), who graduated in 1936 from West Point. During his time there he had to room alone because no one would room with him. He had to eat alone in the mess hall. Davis graduated thirty-fifth in a class of 276, so he was not shunned for being a slackard. He was shunned for being black.

Yet Davis did not sit back and feel sorry for himself. Instead, he went on to lead with distinction a squadron of fighter pilots during World War II. Rubel Shelly observed, "Resentment, malice, and trying to get even are self-destructive. Resolve and steadiness at a noble task can overcome prejudice. Ben Davis proved it." (Adapted from *Faith Matters*, July 29, 2002.)

It has often been said that Sunday morning is the most segregated hour in American society. Some like to cite cultural differences as being the reason for this. But deep down inside of the hearts of many, it is simply a matter of racial, cultural, and economic prejudice. Our lesson today should remind us that in the worship of God, there is no place for prejudice.

## INTRODUCTION

### A. CENTURIES OF PREJUDICE

Gene Brown tells of two apples that were looking down upon the world. One said, "Look at all those people fighting, robbing, rioting—no one seems willing to get along with his fellow human being. Someday we apples will be the only ones left. Then we'll rule the world." The second apple replied, "Which of us—the reds or the greens?"

Today's lesson will help us to understand that even though the power of prejudice wrecks society and brings misery to everyone in some way, Jesus Christ has the power to transform our lives and break down barriers of prejudice. *The American Heritage Dictionary* defines prejudice as an "irrational suspicion or hatred of a particular group, race, or religion." People have been long divided by these very things. India's caste system divides one billion people by profession, wealth, religion, and family heritage. Many religious groups fight over power, territory, and sacred sites.

Prejudice is learned. Children of many races may be playing happily together until one parent says, "Stay away from those people." Such preconceived notions fail to treat people individually, are not based on all the facts, and forget God's love for the entire world.

Prejudice is sin and has its roots in selfishness, pride, anger, and hatred. It ignores compassion, mercy, love, and forgiveness. The power to overcome prejudice comes from God. In today's lesson Jesus will brush aside the prejudices of his day and help a social outcast find new hope.

### B. LESSON BACKGROUND

While in Judea, Jesus decided to travel north to preach in Galilee (John 4:3). To get there he had to go through Samaria (4:4) if he wanted to take the shortest

---

*DEVOTIONAL READING:*
JOHN 4:35-42
*BACKGROUND SCRIPTURE:*
JOHN 4:1-42
*PRINTED TEXT:*
JOHN 4:7-10, 19-26

### LESSON AIMS

After participating in this lesson, each student will be able to:

1. Tell how Jesus' love defeated prejudice in the case of the woman from Samaria.

2. Explain how acceptance of people from different backgrounds can present opportunities to lead others to Christ.

3. Identify a personal prejudice and suggest a specific action that he or she can take to replace it with Christ's love.

### KEY VERSE

There is neither Jew nor Greek, slave nor free, male nor female, for you are all one in Christ Jesus.
—Galatians 3:28

Feb
27

LESSON 13 NOTES

### DAILY BIBLE READINGS

**Monday, Feb. 21**—*Christ Is All and in All (Colossians 3: 11-17)*

**Tuesday, Feb. 22**—*Jesus Travels to a Samaritan City (John 4:1-6)*

**Wednesday, Feb. 23**—*Jesus Speaks About Living Water (John 4:7-12)*

**Thursday, Feb. 24**—*The Samaritan Woman Wants Living Water (John 4:13-18)*

**Friday, Feb. 25**—*I Am the Messiah (John 4:19-26)*

**Saturday, Feb. 26**—*Come and See the Man (John 4:27-34)*

**Sunday, Feb. 27**—*Many Samaritans Believed Jesus' Word (John 4:35-42)*

### WHAT DO YOU THINK?

*Discrimination toward women is still a reality in modern culture. How can the church demonstrate God's expectations in this area while still maintaining God-ordained role distinctions (1 Timothy 2:12)?*

route. At midday Jesus and his disciples arrived at a well about a half-mile from the village of Sychar (4:5). Jesus was weary, so he sent his disciples for food (4:8) while he stayed at the well (4:6).

History was all around him as he sat there. Tradition holds that Jacob himself had dug that well nearly two thousand years earlier. This is "near the plot of ground Jacob had given to his son Joseph" (John 4:5; see also Genesis 48:22). A short distance away were Mounts Gerizim and Ebal, where people had recited God's blessing and curses at the command of Moses (Deuteronomy 27:4-26). Some fourteen centuries earlier, Joshua stood on Mount Ebal and encouraged all Israel to keep God's law (Joshua 8:30-35). Also nearby was Joseph's tomb.

But Jesus did not have time to dwell on history. A woman had appeared, carrying a water jar. The woman who approached the well had no idea that she was about to come face to face with the long-awaited Messiah. She had no idea that she was about to have a conversation that would change her life.

A story is told about U.S. President Thomas Jefferson and a group trying to cross a raging river. The bridge was washed away, so each rider crossed the river on horseback, fighting the deadly current. A stranger who had no horse asked the President to take him across the river. He agreed.

So the man climbed on, and the two of them made it safely to the other side. As the stranger came down from the horse, someone asked him why he had asked the President for help. The man was shocked because he had no idea that he had been talking with the President! The woman in today's lesson who has come to draw water was about to talk with someone greater than any president or earthly king.

## I. UNEXPECTED CONVERSATION (JOHN 4:7-9)

### A. STARTLING REQUEST (vv. 7, 8)

**7, 8. When a Samaritan woman came to draw water, Jesus said to her, "Will you give me a drink?" (His disciples had gone into the town to buy food.)**

Jesus is thirsty, but he cannot just turn on the tap. A water vessel will need to be lowered on ropes into the well and hauled back up again. If Jesus' disciples had been there, they would have brought him *water*. But they are in nearby Sychar finding food (John 4:5). Having no container for drawing water, Jesus asks this *Samaritan woman* for help.

Jewish men of this period usually do not address women in public. The first-century Jewish historian Josephus says that women are inferior to men in all things. A certain Jewish prayer for men includes thanks for not being made a woman! In about 180 B.C., a Jewish writer penned the following: "Better is the wickedness of a man than a woman who does good; it is a woman who brings shame and disgrace" (Sirach 42:14). When Jesus' disciples return, even they will be amazed that he is talking with a woman (John 4:27).

Jesus does not condone this demeaning attitude. Several women follow him and supply material help to his ministry (Luke 8:1-3). Also, Paul mentions many women who were his fellow laborers in the gospel. He publicly praises them for their hard work and valuable contribution for Christ's church (Romans 16:1-16).

We should not overlook the fact that the woman in today's lesson is a person of loose morals (see John 4:17, not in our text for today). Married five times, she now lives with a man who is not her husband. This may explain why she is alone at the well at noon. Women usually come to the well when it is cooler (morning or evening) and chat with their friends. Perhaps they shun this woman for her lack of morals, forcing her *to draw water* in the heat of the day, alone.

## B. ANCIENT ANIMOSITY (v. 9)

**9. The Samaritan woman said to him, "You are a Jew and I am a Samaritan woman. How can you ask me for a drink?" (For Jews do not associate with Samaritans.)**

The name Samaria comes from 1 Kings 16:24. The reason that *Jews do not associate with Samaritans* is an interesting and sad story.

When King Solomon died in about 930 B.C., the nation of Israel split into two parts. Some tribes appointed their own king, and that king established idolatrous worship sites involving two golden calves (1 Kings 12:28-30). God's prophets warned them, but their continued idolatry brought judgment.

As a result, many people in these tribes were scattered into various countries by their Assyrian captors in 722 B.C. Other captive peoples were brought into Israel, where they intermarried with those Israelites who were left in the land (2 Kings 17).

The descendants of those intermarriages became the Samaritans of Jesus' day. The "pure-blood" Jews had come to view them, to put it crudely, as "half-breeds." This taint resulted in antagonism between the Jews who returned from the Babylonian exile after 539 B.C. and the Samaritans. When the Samaritans offered to help rebuild the temple, the Jews refused (Ezra 4:1-5). This angered the Samaritans, and we see some of this anger come out when Nehemiah begins to rebuild the city walls (Nehemiah 4:1, 2).

In Jesus' day the Jews still look with suspicion upon this group of people. Jews are afraid of being corrupted by people who are not pure Israelites. So by the time that Jesus is born, Jews have few dealings with Samaritans (although the disciples apparently think it is okay to buy food from them; see John 4:8).

Jesus' enemies will try to discredit him by calling him a Samaritan (John 8:48). Perhaps we can compare the Samaritans' experience with that of African-Americans, who once were not allowed to use the same drinking fountains or dining facilities as whites.

Thus it is no wonder that the woman is amazed that this Jew not only talks with her, but also actually asks for a drink from her vessel! The woman probably recognizes Jesus as *a Jew* either by his clothing or by his accent (cf. Matthew 26:73). Certainly after she experiences his attitude of openness she will be more ready to hear what he has to say.

Christians are challenged to overcome prejudice yet today. How do people perceive our attitudes toward those of a different race, social background, religion, or culture? Even when it comes to religion, Christians can love and show respect to others without compromising foundational Christian truth. Jesus broke social and religious taboos, and so must we.

### WHAT DO YOU THINK?

*Just as with discrimination toward women, we also like to think that we do not have any racial prejudice and that we do not practice racial discrimination. How can we go beyond talk and really demonstrate this?*

## CATEGORIES

Years ago, the magazine *Psychology Today* reported on a survey taken of eleven major symphony orchestras to learn what players in one section of instruments thought of the musicians in other sections. The survey revealed that those playing stringed instruments were thought of as effeminate wimps and prima donnas. Brass players were seen to be loud, beer-drinking jocks. Percussionists were categorized as insensitive, unintelligent, and hard-of-hearing, yet humorous and fun at parties. Those who played woodwinds were held in the highest esteem—described as quiet, meticulous, and intelligent, though quite egotistical.

Can you believe that professional musicians could hold such critical and stereotypical views of each other? Before we gasp too much, however, perhaps we should stop and take a look at our own biases.

## HOW TO SAY IT

Assyrian. Uh-SEAR-e-un.

Bethel. BETH-ul.

Deuteronomy. Due-ter-AHN-uh-me.

Ebal. EE-bull.

Ezra. EZ-ruh.

Galilee. GAL-uh-lee.

Gerizim. GAIR-ih-zeem or Guh-RYE-zim.

Jacob. JAY-kub.

Jeremiah. Jair-uh-MY-uh.

Jerusalem. Juh-ROO-suh-lem.

Josephus. Jo-SEE-fus.

Judea. Joo-DEE-uh.

Nehemiah. NEE-huh-MY-uh.

Samaria. Suh-MARE-ee-uh.

Samaritans. Suh-MARE-uh-tunz.

Sirach. SIGH-rak.

Solomon. SOL-o-mun.

Sychar. SIGH-kar.

Zechariah. ZEK-uh-RYE-uh

We often are guilty of generalizations, aren't we? We practice "lumping" when we note someone from another part of the country, or from another school or community, and have some experience with them. We destroy those biases when we remember that "there is neither Jew nor Greek, slave nor free, male nor female, for you are all one in Christ Jesus" (Galatians 3:28).                     —J. D. R.

## II. UNEXPECTED SOLUTION (JOHN 4:10, 19-26)

### A. DEEPEST THIRSTS (v. 10)

*10. Jesus answered her, "If you knew the gift of God and who it is that asks you for a drink, you would have asked him and he would have given you living water."*

A stranger is asking the woman for a *drink* and yet claiming to have a supply of *water* that is somehow greater than the water in Jacob's well. This woman has no idea what a privilege it is to be there at that moment in history! God has a *gift* for all of humanity—Jews, Samaritans, and Gentiles alike. This gift, freely given, is greater than any earthly thing that the woman can possibly imagine.

Hundreds of years earlier, the Israelites had forsaken God, "the spring of living water" (Jeremiah 2:13). Even so, God had predicted through a prophet that a day would come when "living water will flow out from Jerusalem" (Zechariah 14:8). Jesus is the one who has that *living water!*

### B. PROFOUND TRUTH (vv. 19-22)

*19. "Sir," the woman said, "I can see that you are a prophet.*

The dialogue of verses 11-18 (not in today's text) leads up to this point. The woman considers Jesus to be *a prophet* because he has told her things about herself (in vv. 16-18) that a stranger could not know without having divine knowledge. He knows about her five previous marriages and how she is now living with a man who is not her husband.

*20. "Our fathers worshiped on this mountain, but you Jews claim that the place where we must worship is in Jerusalem."*

With this statement the woman zeroes in on the major point of theological dispute between Jews and Samaritans. Jacob had built an altar near this very spot (Genesis 33:20). Later, Moses warned the people that they were to worship at one altar only, the one chosen by God (Deuteronomy 12:1-14). The tabernacle served as the one sacred site until it was replaced by the temple (1 Kings 6).

When King Solomon died, the northern tribes established sacred sites in Bethel and Dan (1 Kings 12:25-33). The Jews rebuilt the temple in *Jerusalem* after the exile (Ezra 6:13-15), while the Samaritans worshiped on Mount Gerizim, a bit to the southwest of Mount Ebal. These rival places of worship perpetuate the differences between these two peoples. But the woman assumes that *a prophet* from God can settle the matter.

*21. Jesus declared, "Believe me, woman, a time is coming when you will worship the Father neither on this mountain nor in Jerusalem.*

This is "part one" of a three-part response by Jesus. With the coming of the Christian age, sacred sites lose their meaning except for historical purposes. As beautiful as the Jewish temple is, it is only made out of gold, stones, and cedar; it is subject to destruction (Matthew 24:1, 2).

The church, however, is made of living stones. It is not limited by geographical boundaries. Believers everywhere are the living stones that comprise it (Ephesians 2:19-22; 1 Peter 2:5, 6). This temple is not made with human hands and cannot be destroyed. Christians must not argue over sacred sites as people of other religions do. Instead, Christians must encourage others to become stones in Christ's living temple.

## WHAT DO YOU THINK?

God cannot be contained in a building, yet often we try to do so. What are some dangers of equating worship with a particular place?

**22. "You Samaritans worship what you do not know; we worship what we do know, for salvation is from the Jews.**

Although Jesus treats the woman with respect and compassion, he does not support her false ideas. Some people think that to be free from prejudice means to accept all points of view as valid. Christians can treat Jews and Muslims with respect and demonstrate Christ's love without compromising Christian truth that Jesus alone is the way, the truth, and the life.

Jesus tells the woman that the *Samaritans* are wrong about their *worship*, and that God offers *salvation* through *the Jews* (cf. Romans 1:16). Jesus, after all, is a Jew from the line of David as the Scriptures promise for the Messiah (Jeremiah 33:15). Salvation is to be offered first to the Jews. After that, the gospel is to be taken to Samaria and then to the Gentiles (Acts 1:8).

Visual for lessons 5, 13. *Display the same visual as was used for lesson 5. Use it to review the lessons of the past quarter.*

### INTOLERANCE AT ITS WORST AND BEST

As I write this, it is April 29, 2003, a date designated as "Holocaust Remembrance Day." The beginning of the Holocaust can be dated to 1933, the year that Adolf Hitler became Reichs Chancellor (or Prime Minister) of Germany. His reign of terror came to an end in 1945 with the fall of his Third Reich.

In the intervening years, Hitler and his cronies conducted a campaign that resulted in the state-sponsored murder of six million Jews. The Nazis had deemed this group of innocent people to be "life unworthy of life." This was intolerance at its worst!

The mind-set that resulted in this tragedy is still with us today. Television images from around the world remind us of this nightly. In order to stem this tide of hatred, we see a greater emphasis on teaching "tolerance" at all levels of society. People are encouraged to accept and respect differences of race, culture, and religion.

Somewhere along the way, however, we seem to have lost the distinction between "tolerance for all people" and "tolerance for all ideas." As Christians we must embrace the former while we reject the latter.

Our model for this distinction is Jesus as he speaks to the Samaritan woman at the well. Jesus sets an example for us as he crosses social and religious barriers to reach out in respect to someone who needs salvation. But at the same time his compassion and love require him to confront her about her false religious viewpoint. This is intolerance at its best!

—R. L. N.

### C. TRUE WORSHIPERS (vv. 23, 24)

**23, 24. "Yet a time is coming and has now come when the true worshipers will worship the Father in spirit and truth, for they are the kind of worshipers the Father seeks. God is spirit, and his worshipers must worship in spirit and in truth."**

At the most foundational level, *worship* means to ascribe worth to God. We can do this properly only when our worship is *in spirit* (is centered on nothing but God) *and in truth* (is faithful to God's Word).

God is interested in what happens in our hearts. The first and greatest commandment is to love God with the entire heart, soul, and mind (Matthew 22:37, 38). We must worship with the feelings of the heart, the fervency of the soul, and the power of the will. We must worship with sorrow over sins and joy over God's mercy and grace. We must worship with gratitude for God's blessings of creation and redemption through Jesus. Only this kind of worship changes the heart and life of the worshiper.

Worship that is concerned only with outward form and ritual lacks the key elements of love, gratitude, and repentance. When those things are missing, God is not truly worshiped. He rejects all such attempts.

WHAT DO YOU THINK?

*Sometimes our worship becomes merely a performance of certain traditions. How can we transform our worship services beyond mere ritual?*

## PRAYER

*Father, thank you for Jesus who offers salvation to all. Help us to show others by our words and actions that Jesus can solve our deepest needs, even the need for eternal life. In Jesus' name, amen.*

## WHAT DO YOU THINK?

*Two of the more prevalent types of prejudice discussed involve race and gender. What are some other types of prejudice that the church needs to be aware of and confront?*

## THOUGHT TO REMEMBER

*"Consequently, you are no longer foreigners and aliens, but fellow citizens with God's people and members of God's household" (Ephesians 2:19).*

Passages such as Amos 5:21-23; 6:5, 6; Malachi 1:6-8; and James 2:1-4 show us that God is well aware of improper motives in worship. When we think of worshiping in spirit and in truth, let us remember that Jesus himself is truth (John 14:6), and it is he who gives the Spirit without limit (John 3:34).

### D. DIVINE SAVIOR (vv. 25, 26)

**25, 26. The woman said, "I know that Messiah" (called Christ) "is coming. When he comes, he will explain everything to us."**

**Then Jesus declared, "I who speak to you am he."**

The word *Messiah* refers to someone anointed or selected by God for a special mission. The woman knows something of this promised one. She may be thinking of Moses' promise of a prophet "like" him (Deuteronomy 18:15) as he instructed the people to listen to this prophet.

So the woman knows that the Messiah will have the answers. Jesus tells her plainly that he is that promised Messiah.

## CONCLUSION

As the Messiah, Jesus brings salvation to the lost—Jew, Samaritan, and Gentile alike. He came to bring all together as part of one family in his church. In fact that is what happened. The gospel was first offered to Jews in Jerusalem (Acts 2:17-41). These Jewish Christians then took the gospel to Samaritans (Acts 8:4-8, 14-17). Then Jewish Christians took the gospel to Gentiles (Acts 13 and following).

As a result, old barriers of hostility and prejudice were broken down (Ephesians 2:11-22). Jews, Samaritans, and Gentiles can forget old divisions; they can enjoy oneness in the church (Galatians 3:28; Ephesians 4:4-6).

General Robert E. Lee (1807–1870) is said to have been a devout follower of Jesus Christ. Soon after the end of the American Civil War, he visited a church. During the Communion service, so the story goes, he knelt beside a black man. An onlooker said, "How could you do that?" Lee is said to have replied, "My friend, all ground is level beneath the cross." When Christians have that attitude, prejudice will end.

But smashing such barriers is not really the ultimate goal. Instead, the ultimate goal is eternal life. The woman in today's lesson responded by bringing others to Jesus. She left her water jar and returned to town saying, "Come, see a man who told me everything I ever did. Could this be the Christ?" (John 4:29).

Many Samaritans of Sychar believed on him because of the testimony of the woman. They even begged him to stay with them (4:40), and they believed Jesus' teachings (4:39-41). This shows that the woman was able to make an impact on her community, in spite of her past, because of the power of Jesus' words.

Today we see religious groups continue to squabble over sacred sites around the world, especially in Jerusalem. Yet while all this fussing goes on and on, Jesus still offers a message that goes beyond geographical and ethnic barriers. Jesus can still break down racial barriers so that all peoples can belong to the greatest family in the world.

As we think about our part in proclaiming this message, we as Christians can and must do several things. First, ask God to forgive our past prejudices. Second, ask God to substitute love, compassion, and mercy for hatred, suspicion, and pride in our hearts. Third, follow Jesus' example in how he treated the woman in today's lesson. Fourth, offer Jesus as the Savior to all members of the human race. What a privilege it is to spread that message by our actions, attitudes, and words!

# Discovery Learning

*This page contains an alternative lesson plan emphasizing learning activities. Classes desiring such student involvement will find these suggestions helpful. The next page is a reproducible activity page to further enhance discovery learning.*

## LEARNING GOALS

After participating in this lesson, each student will be able to:

1. Tell how Jesus' love defeated prejudice in the case of the woman from Samaria.

2. Explain how acceptance of people from different backgrounds can present opportunities to lead others to Christ.

3. Identify a personal prejudice and suggest a specific action that he or she can take to replace it with Christ's love.

## INTO THE LESSON

Before class make arrangements with two students to perform a very brief skit. For their "costumes" find some large pieces of cardboard, such as the shipping carton for a range or refrigerator. Cut out two apple shapes large enough for the students to hold in front of themselves and expose only their heads (and perhaps their feet). Paint one cutout red and one green.

Have the students memorize the dialogue between the apples in the Introduction to today's lesson (page 218). Introduce the skit by saying, "Two apples looked down upon the world." Let the two actors perform. Then say, "Why is it so easy for us to focus on negatives and differences instead of positives and similarities?" In the discussion note how this attitude is the basis for racism and other forms of prejudice. Ask, "What is the solution to this kind of prejudice?" Observe that the love of Jesus breaks down barriers instead of putting them up. Indicate that today's lesson gives us a concrete example of that fact.

## INTO THE WORD

Read John 4:7-10, 19-26 aloud. Ask students to make a list of differences between Jesus and the woman, things that might be cause for separation. Provide paper and pencils as needed. Your learners should note the following differences: man/woman; Jew/Samaritan; worship in Jerusalem/worship in "this mountain"; highest morals/loose morals; knowledgeable worship/ignorant worship.

Ask learners for the differences they noted, writing each in a single column on the board or overhead transparency. Also ask, "How did Jesus overcome these distinctives? What did this communicate?" A list like the following should develop: he ignored the social distinc-

tive (gender) by talking with the woman. This communicated a sense of value; he did not consider the woman inferior or worthless.

Jesus also overcame the religious distinctives with his willingness to address a religious issue in a kind but firm way. This communicated not only truth but personal respect. The woman, with her misguided religious viewpoint, needed to hear both.

Point out that Jesus acted from love. No matter what potential barriers stood between Jesus and this woman, love was the key to breaking them down. It was in the woman's best interest to receive the living water Jesus had to offer. That is love: acting in the best interest of another.

## INTO LIFE

Point to your list of distinctives between Jesus and the woman. Ask, "How are these same differences and prejudices seen in society today?" Discuss the problems of social, racial, and religious prejudice. Observe that some prejudices are based in purely externals (gender, race, etc.). Other matters are more internal, based on decisions we make (social issues, morality issues, etc.).

Ask, "How can we take a proper stand on such issues without disrespecting people themselves?" As the class talks about this, note Jesus' method. He told the truth, even pointing out faults in the woman's religion, but he did not accuse. He did not withdraw. He did not treat her unkindly. Try to get the learners to suggest tangible ways of doing that today.

For example, if racial prejudice is a particularly troublesome issue in your community, what can your church do to demonstrate that this issue is not a barrier—or that you do not want it to be? If your church is 99 percent one race, how do you demonstrate that people of other races are welcome? What are you doing to reach out to people of other races? Are you targeting ministry events for people of various races and economic statuses? Are you taking a public stand for issues of justice that will benefit people of other races more than yourself?

Encourage your learners to be as specific as possible. Then close with a prayer that God will help you and your class to practice the love of Christ in ways that will tear down the walls that divide your community.

*Option:* Use the "Case Studies" activity on the reproducible page that follows as the basis for making personal application of today's text.

# Case Studies

Choose one or both of the following case studies and determine how you would address the issue if it were one you were facing.

## THE CASE OF THE MONOCHROMATIC CONGREGATION

First Church is a suburban church that has between 250 and 300 in worship each Sunday. The church has two worship services, one quite traditional in format and the other more contemporary. By many standards, the church is quite healthy, but some of the leadership is growing increasingly troubled by the fact that the congregation is monochromatic (one color). The neighborhood where it is located is split fairly evenly between African-Americans (42%) and those of European descent (45%). There is also a growing number of Hispanic residents (11%).

A meeting has been called to discuss the issue. What recommendations would you bring to the meeting if you were a member of First Church? Consider the following areas:

What programs, traditions, or practices are you unwilling to change for racial integration? Why?

What programs, traditions, or practices are you willing to drop for racial integration? How would that help?

What new programs, traditions, or practices are you willing to adopt for racial integration? How would that help?

## THE CASE OF THE THIRSTY CULT MEMBER

Fred is a Christian. Tom, one of Fred's co-workers, is a member of a cult. He has been reprimanded twice for "proselytizing" on the job. By now most people avoid him like the plague. They make jokes about him in the break room, and many look for ways to get him dismissed. But he is very good at what he does, so even the two reprimands have not seriously jeopardized his job.

Having read John 4, Fred believes he has not acted properly toward Tom. He has never offered him the "living water" Jesus told the Samaritan woman about. So he has asked for your advice. What will you tell him?

# Spring Quarter, 2005

## God's Project:
## Effective Christians

Mar 6

Mar 13

Mar 20

Mar 27

Apr 3

Apr 10

Apr 17

Apr 24

May 1

May 8

May 15

May 22

May 29

## Special Features

## Lessons

### Unit 1: Saved by God

### Unit 2: The Christian Life

### Unit 3: Set Free

## About These Lessons

This quarter's lessons are taken from Paul's letters to the Romans and the Galatians. While all of Paul's writings in the New Testament are important for Christians to study, Romans and Galatians could be considered his "dynamic duo." Their emphasis on such crucial themes as justification by faith, the role of the law of Moses, and the proper use of Christian freedom will contribute significantly to helping you achieve this quarter's goal: producing effective Christians.

# Participants in God's Project

*by Marshall Hayden*

"The gospel according to Paul." That's what many students of the Bible have called the book of Romans, and that is the section of the Word of God that draws our attention for the first eight lessons of this quarter. The shorter, possibly earlier, letter to the Galatians will be the focus of our study for the remaining Sundays. The lessons from Galatians will be a splendid supplement to the faithful doctrine/faithful life studies from Romans. Like Romans, Galatians discusses what it means to be justified by faith in Jesus Christ, not by the works of the law of Moses (or of any works-oriented system). Both books also discuss the proper and godly use of our freedom in Christ and our need to appreciate the freedom that other Christians have. We should be stronger, surer, and more clearly characterized by joy after we have finished this study together.

Have you ever heard someone open a series of remarks with the words, "I have bad news and good news"? In Romans the apostle Paul first presents the bad news that sets the stage for the good news. In Romans 3:23 (a verse many have memorized) he writes, "For all have sinned and fall short of the glory of God." That's the bad news. We have missed the mark; we have failed to honor the image of God in which he created us (Genesis 1:26, 27). The prodigal son in Jesus' well-known parable speaks for every human being when he declares, "I have sinned against heaven and against you. I am no longer worthy to be called your son" (Luke 15:21). The first three chapters of Romans make that truth very clear. Jews have sinned. Gentiles have sinned. No one is exempt from this disheartening news: we *all* have sinned.

But then comes the good news! God himself has made a way to cure our terminal condition of sin-sickness.

## UNIT 1: SAVED BY GOD

**Lesson 1: All Have Sinned.** As we read the first three chapters of Romans, some may recall a statement that became associated with a former President of the United States: "Let me make one thing perfectly clear." That's what Paul is doing. And what he says is clearly distressing! By the time we have completed reading our Scripture text for the first lesson, his point cannot be missed: *we have sinned.* Yet even as Paul admits that grim truth, he cannot restrain himself from mentioning the good news. Part of the text for this lesson removes our self-made excuses, but the other part presents a God-made answer: the gospel of Christ that remains "the power of God for the salvation of everyone who believes" (Romans 1:16).

**Lesson 2: God's Judgment Is Just.** This lesson leaves us ready to approach the judgment seat of God and confess, "Guilty, your honor. I have no excuse." We know it's true. Paul helps us see that. He encourages us to avoid all pretense of superiority. He reminds us that judging is God's business, that he is very good at it, and that he does not need our help! Like the first lesson, this one is not silent about the good news. We will learn about repentance and about Christ, the Way.

**Lesson 3: Justified by Faith.** Here the good news becomes especially clear. We will be reminded of what faith means, what it does, how it begins, and what it produces. The theme of this lesson makes it abundantly clear that only in Christ does justification occur.

**Lesson 4: Victory in Christ.** This is the Easter Sunday lesson—always a time to celebrate what sets Christian faith apart from anything the world has to offer. The key word for this study is *life*. The thrilling message that we will study from the Gospel of John (in addition to our continued study from Romans) calls to mind the story of a little boy who was standing outside the window of a small-town hardware store where he had been permitted to paint an Easter scene. A man came by and asked him about the hillside, the crosses, and the people he had painted. "That's Jesus," he said, pointing to the center cross. "Them's the soldiers. They killed him." Then he was silent. But as the man began to walk away the boy shouted, "Hey, Mister, there's more—he rose again!"

Thank God there's more.

APRIL

## UNIT 2: THE CHRISTIAN LIFE

**Lesson 5: Live by the Spirit.** This lesson introduces Unit Two in our study of Romans. In Unit One we lay a foundation of biblical doctrine, which is essential for living the Christian life. Here we will see how Paul discusses some of the practical applications of doctrinal truth. Romans 8:12 is a key verse in this lesson: "Therefore, brothers, we have an obligation—but it is not to the sinful nature, to live according to it." The fleshly part of each person exerts a powerful pull, but a Christian's spiritual part, empowered by God's Holy Spirit, makes him or her a champion in the "tug of war."

**Lesson 6: Find Salvation in Christ.** In this lesson we will talk about lives that call on the name of the Lord. Confessing the Lord Jesus" is something that we do before other people—not just once, as part of accepting Christ as Savior—but regularly before others whose reaction may be less than encouraging. In response to this study, we should also think about appealing to others to call on the name of Jesus. We should consider our responsibility as Christians to support other Christians willing to travel to both faraway and nearby places—individuals who have feet ready to go and tongues ready to speak the "good news."

**Lesson 7: Display the Marks of a Christian.** Romans 12 is a clear and helpful description of several of the characteristics that should mark our lives as we live out our Christian walk. With this study we shall see how the book of Romans demonstrates a pattern often seen in Paul's letters—moving from foundational doctrine to practical personal conduct. This will be a good week for making a list, checking it twice, and examining what God thinks about our daily living and what alterations we need to make.

**Lesson 8: Accept One Another.** In the previous lesson, Paul led us to examine whether we handle our personal lives faithfully. This week we study a passage that challenges us to handle our Christian fellowship faithfully. There are reminders about personal value to God, freedom, and responsibility. And there is a call to unity in Christ, something not always easy to achieve. But it is immeasurably important for us to practice it—for ourselves, for seekers who may be watching, and for the Lord.

MAY

## UNIT 3: SET FREE

**Lesson 9: Believe No Other Gospel.** Our studies in Galatians will remind us not to drift into any concept of a "works" salvation. God is the author of grace, Jesus Christ is the deliverer of grace, and we are the recipients of grace. We shall see that first-century Christians were tempted to look for a counterfeit "salvation" that was more complicated than Christ and less dependent on Christ. It is a temptation from which twenty-first-century Christians are not exempt, and one we must be prepared to resist.

**Lesson 10: Know Salvation by Faith.** Some of the Galatians, it seems, had come to think that the gospel of grace was just too good to be true. Surely we need some "additional" revelation, they thought. Surely there must be other good works that we need to do. Not so! This study will offer some significant insights into what it means for Christ to live in us (Galatians 2:20).

**Lesson 11: Understand the Purpose of the Law.** This week's lesson begins to make the transition in Galatians that we saw in Romans—moving from essential doctrinal truth to essential practical application. The Old Testament law prepared people to meet Jesus. It defined sin; now Jesus has been offered to remove sin. He removes old burdens, and he removes old barriers.

**Lesson 12: Live in Christian Freedom.** Jesus Christ sets us free—free from sin and death, and free from continuing in sin. We will be reminded this week that we are not free to do whatever we want, but we are gloriously free to do what Christ wants. We are also free to serve others.

**Lesson 13: Participate in the Community of Faith.** This is a great concluding lesson for the quarter—practical and terrifically important! Paul describes what life is like when the Holy Spirit of God is in charge. The class will be challenged to take a long, hard look at the implications and applications of the fruit of the Spirit in the Christian's life and within the community of Christians. We will see the importance of personal accountability (carrying our own loads), and with that the importance of helping and being helped with loads when they are just too much for one person to handle.

Thirteen lessons about being effective Christians! What better topic could we study?

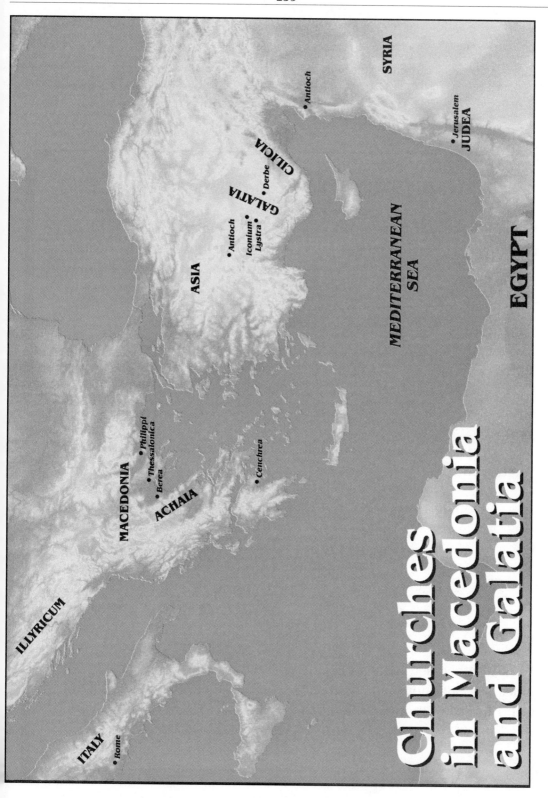

# Churches in Macedonia and Galatia

# The Gospel of Grace

Romans and Galatians share themes. Written at about the same time, these two letters contain some of Paul's most explicit explanations of the difference between the gospel of grace and the law of works. We will explore some of those themes in the coming quarter. Note some of the similarities on the chart below.

| Romans | Galatians |
|---|---|
| "The gospel . . . is the power of God unto salvation" (Romans 1:16) **Lesson 1** | "The gospel . . . is not after man. . . . but by the revelation of Jesus Christ" (Galatians 1:11, 12) **Lesson 9** |
| "Justified by faith" (Romans 5:1) **Lesson 3** | "Not justified by the works of the law, but by . . . faith" (Galatians 2:16) **Lesson 10** |
| The law was weak and ineffectual (Romans 8:3) **Lesson 5** | The law was temporary, until faith came (Galatians 3:23-25) **Lesson 11** |
| Serve one another (Romans 12) **Lesson 7** | Use the fruit of the Spirit, not provoking or envying one another (Galatians 5:22-26) **Lesson 13** |
| Work together, not judging one another, but glorifying God "with one mind and one mouth" (Romans 14; 15:5, 6) **Lesson 8** | Exercise Christian liberty to "serve one another" (Galatians 5:13) **Lesson 12** |

# ALL HAVE SINNED

**LESSON 1**

## WHY TEACH THIS LESSON?

"Our dear departed friend John was such a good man. He was an upstanding citizen and a genuinely nice person. We remember him fondly."

If this is all there is to John's eulogy, our friend John is a soul lost for eternity. It makes no difference that he was kind to strangers, never cheated on his taxes, and didn't litter. If he was not living under God's grace, he is condemned.

"You couldn't say that if you had known John," a friend might suggest. We know one thing: God does not forgive those who die while mired in the sin of unbelief. We may know something of John's outward actions, but God has perfect knowledge of every thought, deed, and motive.

Your learners probably know many "good" people. But God teaches a tough class where only those who score 100 percent pass. Fortunately, we can opt to let God's star pupil, Jesus, "take the final exam" for us. He did just that when he died in our place. But before we can acknowledge God's solution, we have to recognize our problem and our need. Today's lesson helps us in just this way.

## INTRODUCTION

### A. NO SINGULAR SAINTS

The headings on the Gospels and epistles that we find in our modern Bibles were not in the original text. Someone added the word *saint* to names such as Matthew and John (for example), resulting in "The Gospel According to Saint Matthew" or "Saint John." Interestingly, the word for *saint* (meaning "holy one," or someone "set apart," thus describing any Christian) never occurs in the singular form in the New Testament. It is always plural. Songs in Heaven are not going to be solos. They are going to be sung by "a great multitude that no one could count" (Revelation 7:9). The Christian life was never intended to be a solo. It is designed to be lived with and for *others*.

It is true also that all of us together are plagued by the curse of sin. Each of us has fallen short of the glory of God, just as the first human beings, Adam and Eve, did. The seductive summons from our fleshly side has pressured all of us, has been most enticing, and cannot be successfully resisted in our own strength.

"Misery loves company," an old saying tells us. We have abundant company in the misery caused by sin, but in Christ we have company in the victory that he provides (company that we can really love!). Throughout this quarter, we are going to talk a good deal about both kinds of "company."

### B. LESSON BACKGROUND

Paul, formerly Saul the persecutor of Christians, is the author of the letter to the Romans. He is sending it to the congregation of believers in Rome, with the hope that he would follow the letter personally before very long (Romans 1:10, 11). Some of the men and women whom he had loved and taught and led to Christ seem to have traveled to Rome ahead of him for one reason or another (persecution, employment, or other factors). That is clear from the list of personal greetings that Paul includes at the end of the letter in chapter 16.

DEVOTIONAL READING:
PSALM 59:1-5

BACKGROUND SCRIPTURE:
ROMANS 1:16-20; 3:9-20

PRINTED TEXT:
ROMANS 1:16-20; 3:9-20

LESSON AIMS

After this lesson, a student should be able to:

1. Summarize what Paul says about people's need for a solution to their sin problem and the helplessness of the law to provide it.

2. Compare the problems Paul cites with the problems we see in our own culture.

3. Memorize Romans 1:16, 17.

WHAT DO YOU THINK?

How has your own life been influenced by the community of saints or the community of sinners? In what ways have others influenced you to some specific act, either good or evil?

KEY VERSE

As it is written: "There is no one righteous, not even one."
—Romans 3:10

A church was growing in Rome—made up of individuals who were likely present in Jerusalem on Pentecost (Acts 2:10) and of newly converted believers. It seemed most important to Paul that they grow in the right direction. They needed a strong doctrinal base, and they needed some practical spiritual direction. In this letter they received both.

Paul wrote Romans about the year A.D. 56 or 57, which would have been approximately twenty years after his own conversion. Apparently the letter was written from Corinth during Paul's third missionary journey. He refers to the hospitality of a man named Gaius in Romans 16:23; Gaius was a convert of Paul's in Corinth (1 Corinthians 1:14).

The contents of Romans reflect Paul's experience in presenting a gospel that is both thorough and orderly, as well as one that deals with some of the normal daily issues and relational matters faced by growing Christians. He is in the prime years of his ministry, and he is able to present the fruit of his personal familiarity with bringing people to Christ and providing an atmosphere for their growth. He is prepared to send a letter that covers many important issues, counters some spiritual errors, and emphasizes core truths of the Christian faith.

The maturity of the church in Rome was already well known. "Your faith is spoken of throughout the whole world," Paul writes in Romans 1:8. He wanted to meet the Christians there and share in their growth. His desire was to help them, while also benefiting from their gifts (Romans 1:12).

## I. ANSWER TO SIN (ROMANS 1:16, 17)

### A. GOSPEL OF CHRIST (v. 16a)

*16a. I am not ashamed of the gospel,*

In this verse we read one of the most familiar statements in all of the letters written by Paul—a statement that is important for us to affirm to ourselves, to our family in Christ, and to our neighbors who are in need of good news. Paul indicates in the previous verses (13-15) that he is eager to preach Christ to the faithful in Rome and to work with them in reaching others for Christ in that great city.

### B. POWER OF GOD (v. 16b)

*16b. . . . because it is the power of God for the salvation of everyone who believes: first for the Jew, then for the Gentile.*

It is difficult to determine whether the church in Rome consisted of mostly Jews or Gentiles. Clearly there were some of both present. As noted earlier, some of the Jewish believers in the church in Rome were likely present in Jerusalem to observe Pentecost. They heard the gospel from Peter, who presented Jesus as the Messiah and Savior. Those Jews were among the *first* to hear the good news; but back in Rome were Greeks, who also needed to know this *power of God for the salvation of everyone.*

The Greek word translated *power* is the source of such English words as *dynamite, dynamo,* and *dynamic.* Not only did the gospel possess the power to save *everyone,* it also had the power to break down the walls separating Jews and Gentiles—a point discussed further by Paul in Ephesians 2:11-22.

### C. RIGHTEOUSNESS BY FAITH (v. 17)

*17. For in the gospel a righteousness from God is revealed, a righteousness that is by faith from first to last, just as it is written: "The righteous will live by faith."*

Why is the gospel such a crucial message? Because *in the gospel a righteousness from God is revealed.* The gospel tells sinful people how to become right with God. That is something that we can never earn or achieve through our own efforts; Isaiah 64:6 says that "all our righteous acts are like filthy rags" before God. Our only hope is to accept by faith the gift of God's righteousness provided by him through the death of Jesus. As Paul wrote to the Corinthians, "God made him who had no sin to be sin for us, so that in him we might become the righteousness of God" (2 Corinthians 5:21).

What does the phrase *by faith from first to last* mean? Perhaps Paul is indicating that faith must govern our approach to God throughout our walk with him. We never outgrow our need for faith. And God never changes that requirement.

## II. RESPONSIBILITY FOR SIN (ROMANS 1:18-20)

### A. UNGODLINESS REVEALED (v. 18)

18. *The wrath of God is being revealed from heaven against all the godlessness and wickedness of men who suppress the truth by their wickedness,*

Sin can never be taken lightly. *The wrath of God* is the reaction of a holy, righteous God to something that blatantly violates that holiness and righteousness. That wrath, says Paul, is *revealed from heaven against all the godlessness and wickedness of men*. Paul's use of the present tense is noteworthy. God's wrath is not associated with only the final Judgment Day. His wrath is manifested in this life. Paul describes how this takes place in verses 21-32 of this chapter.

Paul also describes how sinful humans *suppress the truth by their wickedness*. He is concerned with how those in rebellion against the Creator suppress his truth and hinder its progress by their sinfulness. Human beings have always been experts at drowning divine truth in an ocean of excuses and evil behavior. It goes without saying that the present day is no exception.

### B. UNGODLINESS INEXCUSABLE (vv. 19, 20)

19, 20. *. . . since what may be known about God is plain to them, because God has made it plain to them. For since the creation of the world God's invisible qualities—his eternal power and divine nature—have been clearly seen, being understood from what has been made, so that men are without excuse.*

God's creative *power* shouts through all he has made, and it echoes throughout the universe. David observed, "The heavens declare the glory of God; the skies proclaim the work of his hands" (Psalm 19:1). This marvelous world, our amazing bodies, the atmosphere, the cycle of life involving plants and animals—all of this communicates one clear message: "Creator." *From what has been made* we can see the Maker. God's *divine nature* includes those attributes that make God who he alone is.

We can also understand that along with God's designs in nature are his designs for those made in his image. And it is not difficult to understand that we have violated them. We are indeed *without excuse*.

In Romans 1:21–2:29, Paul continues to provide support for the "bad news"—every human being is a sinner. This includes Gentiles, who do not have the benefit of what may be termed the "special revelation" of God's law, and Jews, who do. In the remainder of our printed text, Paul reaches the conclusion of his argument and paves the way for his discussion of the grace of God.

### INVISIBLE BUT ABUNDANTLY EVIDENT

On May 24, 1844, Samuel Morse opened the telegraph age when he sent a message by his special "code" from the United States Capitol to his partner in Baltimore, Maryland. The message he sent was brief but stirring: "What hath God wrought?" The telegraph enabled people to communicate with each other over great distances by means of wire and a pair of telegraph keys (and, of course, a

---

*WHAT DO YOU THINK?*

*What is the difference in these two statements: "the righteous will live by faith," and "living by faith will make a person righteous"? What is the significance of God's choosing the first statement rather than the second one?*

*WHAT DO YOU THINK?*

*What are some of the "invisible qualities" (attributes of God) that you have "clearly seen" in creation? How does seeing God's character and power in creation remove the excuses that we and others might make for our sin?*

knowledge of Morse code). Technology changed again on March 10, 1876, when Alexander Graham Bell demonstrated his new invention, the telephone.

However, on January 18, 1903, a totally new era dawned in the field of communications when Guglielmo Marconi (Goog-lee-*el*-mo Mar-*coe*-nee) stood on Cape Cod and sent through the airwaves a fifty-four-word greeting from President Theodore Roosevelt across the Atlantic Ocean to King Edward VII of England. King Edward responded with a message to President Roosevelt. Today, we take for granted the fact that even our telephones are wireless and are beginning to rival computers in their many functions.

Before electricity was discovered and before the telegraph, telephone, radio, and television were invented, the average person had no sense of the unseen forces that would allow modern communications. On the other hand, the evidence of God's invisible power has *always* been all around us. According to Paul, there's no excuse for missing it.                                                                    —C. R. B.

## III. EXPERIENCE OF SIN (ROMANS 3:9-12)

### A. SAME FAILURE IN EVERYONE (v. 9)

**9. What shall we conclude then? Are we any better? Not at all! We have already made the charge that Jews and Gentiles alike are all under sin.**

In Romans 3:1, 2, Paul cites the spiritual benefits associated with being one of the *Jews.* Do those benefits automatically make them *better* than the *Gentiles? Not at all!* Both groups have "missed the mark" in God's eyes, and such failure is called *sin.*

### B. SAME FAILURE TO SEEK GOD (vv. 10, 11)

**10, 11. As it is written:**
> **"There is no one righteous, not even one;**
> **there is no one who understands,**
> **no one who seeks God.**

At this point, Paul begins to marshal an impressive array of evidence from the Old Testament to strengthen his argument for the sinfulness of humanity. The quotations begin with the authoritative phrase *as it is written:* "*There is no one righteous, not even one*" as drawn from Ecclesiastes 7:20. The remainder of the verse is found in Psalms 14:2, 3 and 53:2, 3. These bold, uncompromising statements (note the repetition of *no one*) strike hard at the proud, self-confident, God-defying attitude of many in our society.

### C. SAME FAILURE TO DO GOOD (v. 12)

**12. "All have turned away,**
> **they have together become worthless;**
> **there is no one who does good,**
> **not even one."**

These statements continue Paul's use of Psalms 14:3 and 53:3 as cited under the previous verse. Note once again Paul's all-inclusive language, letting no one off the hook. *All* are guilty; *there is no one who does good, not even one.*

That people *have turned away* means that we have departed from God's way and "each of us has turned to his own way" (Isaiah 53:6). One might also consider how so many go "out of their way" to *become worthless.* Some of the profitless living that people pursue requires a great deal of creativity, energy, and deception, when a profitable, godly life would give greater immediate return as well as the glorious long-term return on their investment.

"They have together become worthless" has a very familiar ring to it. It's quite a contemporary perversion, and it's also quite foolish.

"There is none righteous, no, not one."
—Romans 3:10

Visual for lesson 1. *This visual of people from around the world helps emphasize the fact that no nation or people-group is unaffected by sin.*

## IV. CHARACTER OF SIN (ROMANS 3:13-18)

### A. AFFECTS OUR TONGUES (vv. 13, 14)

13. *"Their throats are open graves;*
*their tongues practice deceit."*
*"The poison of vipers is on their lips."*

Here Paul uses the words of Psalms 5:9 and 140:3 to continue his indictment of humanity. The word pictures that Paul employs are instructive. Both *open graves* and *the poison of vipers* convey the image of death. *Deceit* is often necessary to cover one's tracks after unkind or bitter words have been uttered. Colossians 4:6 offers a more positive word picture: "Let your conversation be always full of grace, seasoned with salt."

14. *"Their mouths are full of cursing and bitterness."*

*Cursing* is often thought of in terms of blasphemy against God. But cursing can also be aimed at human beings. That is what the context of Psalm 10:7, cited by Paul in this verse, is describing.

**WHAT DO YOU THINK?**

In his description of the effect of sin, Paul seems to focus particularly on our speech. In what ways does sin affect our speech?

### THE POWER OF SPEECH

An old joke tells of a "space saucer" that landed at 3:00 A.M. in the driveway of a deserted gas station. The space aliens got out of their ship, examined the pumps, looked around a bit, then reboarded their ship and flew off into space. The pilot radioed back home and said, "The Earthlings look very much like us, but they refused to talk to us. All they do is stand around with their tails in their ears." Watching people today walk around with their heads tilted sideways and with one arm holding a tiny cell phone to an ear may cause one to think the old joke has come true. Everyone seems to be talking on the phone most of the time—in restaurants, theaters, church services, and even funerals!

The number of minutes per year that Americans spent talking on cell phones skyrocketed from 20 billion in 1993 to 580 billion in 2002—an increase of almost 30 times! The number of cell phone users has increased at a similar rate. The number of automobile accidents caused by distractions from cell phone usage has also climbed so much that many cities and states have outlawed the use of such phones while driving.

It cannot be denied that "talk" has changed the way we live and act—and that is exactly the point Paul makes in Romans 3 as he describes humanity's sinfulness. Evil speech can produce evil actions. If we wish to live righteously, we must pay attention to the way we talk.                                                —C. R. B.

### B. AFFECTS OUR FEET (vv. 15-17)

15. *"Their feet are swift to shed blood;*

The way we talk affects the way we walk. Bitter action follows bitter words. The shedding of *blood* is the fruit of unchecked anger.

Verses 15-17 include a reference to the words of Isaiah 59:7, 8, as Paul's unflattering picture of humanity without God continues.

16, 17. *" . . . ruin and misery mark their ways,*
*and the way of peace they do not know."*

Picture a tornado that leaves a path of *ruin and misery* in its wake. Such are the consequences of sinful ways—both in the sinner's life and in those affected by his or her wayward words and deeds.

In the twenty-first-century Western world, one finds numerous living illustrations of the apostle's insights into human sinfulness drawn from the Old Testament. "We can get along just fine without God," say the secular humanists. But even just a cursory survey of the past forty years demonstrates the emptiness of their claim. Our knowledge has increased significantly in many fields during that

**VISUALS FOR THESE LESSONS**

The small visual pictured in each lesson (e. g., page 240) is a reproduction of a large, full-color poster included in the Adult Visuals packet for the Spring Quarter. The packet is available from your supplier. Order No. 392.

PRAYER

*Help us, dear Father, to see our sin and the consequence of it. How thankful we are that we can rest in Jesus, your Son, our Savior. How thankful that we do not rest there alone, but in fellowship with others who name the name. Thank you for providing the good news, for no one else could have provided an answer for our sin. Through Christ, our perfect redeemer, we pray. Amen.*

WHAT DO YOU THINK?

*If we are saved by grace, what role does God's law play in our lives?*

WHAT DO YOU THINK?

*What do you think of the statement, "I can worship God just as well on my own as I can in a church"?*

*[Consider Romans 12:1-8 and 1 Corinthians 12:12-27 in your response.]*

THOUGHT TO REMEMBER

*Instead of trying to cover up our sin on our own, let us allow Jesus' blood to cover it.*

time, but *the way of peace* is known less and less as people depart further and further from the Prince of peace.

### C. AFFECTS OUR EYES (v. 18)

**18. "There is no fear of God before their eyes."**

Here we see the root of all the trouble described in the previous eight verses. *There is no fear of God before their eyes* (Psalm 36:1). God is not treated with reverence. He is not the reference point for the discussion of issues involving human conduct. He is viewed by many as a hindrance to their desire to be their own god. It is the same lie whispered by the serpent in the Garden of Eden (Genesis 3:4, 5).

## V. DEFINER OF SIN—THE LAW (ROMANS 3:19, 20)

### A. CONFIRMS OUR GUILT (v. 19)

**19. Now we know that whatever the law says, it says to those who are under the law, so that every mouth may be silenced and the whole world held accountable to God.**

The *law* in this verse may refer to more than just the law of Moses. Since Paul has just finished a series of quotations from different portions of the Old Testament, he may be using *law* as a designation for the entire Old Testament. Those quotations have not described Jews only; they have been clear in their emphasis that "there is no one righteous, not even one" (v. 10). The effect is to reinforce what Paul stated in verse 9: that "Jews and Gentiles alike are all under sin." Or, as he states in the verse before us, *the whole world* is *held accountable to God. Every mouth* must be *silenced* before the Creator.

With the precision of a skilled prosecutor, Paul has presented an airtight case for humanity's guilt. The evidence is irrefutable; we have no choice but to agree with it. We are indeed guilty as charged.

### B. FAILS TO ADDRESS GUILT (v. 20)

**20. Therefore no one will be declared righteous in his sight by observing the law; rather, through the law we become conscious of sin.**

The *law* plays a pivotal role in the plan of God. The law points out our need, our spiritual nakedness as it were. That's its job—to highlight the bad news: *no one will be declared righteous in his sight by observing the law*. If that were the end of the story, what a dismal picture! But it isn't; now we are ready to receive the good news, to which Paul turns in the next portion of Romans.

## CONCLUSION

### A. NO SUPERIORITY IN SINNERS

As we noted at the beginning of our study, there are no singular saints. None of us should try to go solo in faith's pilgrimage or toward faith's destination.

In addition, there are no singular sinners. We have all fallen short of God's glory. And there is no superiority in sinners—big ones and little ones, favored ones and disdained ones. Both Jews and Gentiles are guilty. Both need a Savior. And both have a Savior.

### B. EVERY GLORY IN SALVATION

Consider the words of the Bible's Golden Text: "For God so loved the world that he gave his one and only Son, that whoever believes in him shall not perish but have eternal life" (John 3:16). To Paul's words, "There is no one who does good, not even one" (Romans 3:12), we can answer, "There is 'not even one' for whom Jesus did not die." *Whoever!*

# Discovery Learning

*This page contains an alternative lesson plan emphasizing learning activities. Classes desiring such student involvement will find these suggestions helpful. The next page is a reproducible activity page to further enhance discovery learning.*

## LEARNING GOALS

After this lesson, a student should be able to:

1. Summarize what Paul says about people's need for a solution to their sin problem and the helplessness of the law to provide it.

2. Compare the problems Paul cites with the problems we see in our own culture.

3. Memorize Romans 1:16, 17.

## INTO THE LESSON

Take three cards measuring at least six by eight inches. Write the letters L-A-W on one side and the letters S-I-N on the other side, one letter per side of card. Tape the cards as lift flaps to the wall or chalkboard, with the letters L-A-W showing. As class begins, say, "Under each of these letters is the letter of a related word. What letters would you expect to find?" As soon as someone guesses an S, an I, or an N and you show the underside of the flap, someone will probably identify the hidden word. Once a learner does, ask, "How are these two words related?" Expect such responses as, "The law reveals sin" and "The law is the target; sin is the miss."

Next, distribute to the class a copy of two lists from an exhaustive concordance of the Bible. One list will contain occurrences of the word *law* and the other list occurrences of the word *sin* in the Epistle to the Romans. Note that the two words *sin* and *law* are very common in this letter: *law* occurs more than sixty times; *sin* occurs more than forty times. Have someone quickly read the reference list for law, asking all others to follow the sin reference list with the direction to yell "Stop!" whenever the lists coincide. Have those verses read to show the relationships between the two concepts as Paul describes them.

## INTO THE WORD

Give learners a copy of Romans 3:20 in this format: "Therefore, no one will be declared righteous _____ _____; rather, _____ we become conscious _____." In addition, give them this list of prepositional phrases deleted from the verse and printed here alphabetically: "by observing the law," "in his sight," "of sin," "through the law." Tell them this is the "Prepositional Proposition" that is the key truth of today's study. Give them time to put the prepositional

phrases into the appropriate spaces. Emphasize the key truth: the law makes sin clear, but it does not justify anyone of his or her sins.

Recruit two of your best oral readers to read Hebrews 8:6–9:15, alternating verses. Though this will take three to four minutes, it will provide an excellent explanation of the relationship between the law and the gospel. The Holy Spirit, through the writer of that text (and surrounding contexts), develops the full contrast between the righteousness that comes by the law and the righteousness that comes by faith in Christ.

Direct attention to verses 12-18 of Romans 3, in which Paul notes the sins common in his culture. Say, "Paul highlights some of the sins common in his first-century Roman world. Those of you whose age is an even number, make a list of those sins. Those of you whose age is an odd number, make a list of the common sins of our twenty-first-century world." Give three or four minutes, then ask for the "Roman" list of sins. After each is mentioned, ask those with the "our time" list if they have included the same or a corresponding sin. Deceit, cursing, shedding blood, no fear of God—all are as common today as in Paul's lifetime. Conclude with a clause from today's text (Romans 1:20): "The Romans of Paul's time—they are 'without excuse.' Those of our time—they are 'without excuse.'"

## INTO LIFE

Remind the group: "Romans 1:16 must be the motto for the Christian's daily experience. Find that verse and put your finger on it." Ask for volunteers to stand and affirm that truth, personalizing it in whatever way each one finds appropriate. For example (and you as the teacher may need to be the first to do so): "I, *[insert your name]*, am not ashamed of the gospel; for it is the power of God for the salvation of everyone who believes, including me!" After several have volunteered, ask the class to read this verse in unison. Make sure everyone has the same version of the passage. (This activity is included in the student book.)

Point out that having no shame in the gospel implies that one will stand up for and promote its truths at every opportunity. Suggest that class members keep a mental "log" this coming week of occasions when they show no shame in the gospel and occasions when they are more hesitant to stand up for it.

# Sin Is . . .

Look in the following word find puzzle for words that will accurately complete the sentence "Sin is . . ."

```
S  I  N  S  I  N  S  I  N  S  I  N  L
E  V  I  T  C  U  R  T  S  E  D  A  A
S  I  I  N  S  T  D  I  N  S  S  I  W
N  O  S  I  N  S  E  D  I  R  P  S  L
E  L  B  A  S  U  C  X  E  N  I  I  E
N  E  S  I  N  L  E  V  I  L  S  I  S
U  N  G  O  D  L  I  N  E  S  S  N  S
S  T  V  I  N  N  T  S  I  N  S  I  N
N  S  I  I  U  N  F  S  I  N  S  I  E
N  S  I  N  C  L  U  F  E  M  A  H  S
C  H  O  I  C  E  L  S  I  N  S  I  S
```

[Words to be found: *choice, deceitful, destructive, evil, inexcusable, lawlessness, lust, pride, shameful, ungodliness, universal, vice, violent.*]

# What About Me?

Look at Romans 1:16 carefully.

"I am not ashamed of the gospel, because it is the power of God for the salvation of everyone who believes: first for the Jew, then for the Gentile."

Begin by answering the following questions *yes* or *no*.

*Do I ever act as if I am ashamed of the gospel?*

*Are there any groups or individuals for whom I act as if they can't be saved?*

*Have I "written off" the Jews from the gospel?*

Now confront yourself honestly: is there any shame in any of the answers you have given? What will you do to remove that shame?

# GOD'S JUDGMENT IS JUST

**LESSON 2**

## WHY TEACH THIS LESSON?

At an Alcoholics Anonymous meeting, a member introduces himself: "Hi. I'm Jeff. I'm an alcoholic." Other members applaud—not because Jeff has a problem, but because he's come to an emancipating recognition of that problem.

In the church, we must lay bare our guilt. And, to function as a healthy community of believers, we have to support other sinners in their efforts to avoid sin. Like a support group, we hold each other accountable.

Wouldn't it be ridiculous for one alcoholic to condemn another because the other abused mixed drinks instead of wine or beer? Our lesson will show that it's just as inconsistent for us to judge others while ignoring our own shortcomings. We all must stand on our simple profession: "I'm a sinner. But with God's help, I'll try not to sin today."

## INTRODUCTION

### A. JUDGE WITHOUT LIMITS

Several times in the Scriptures we read strong cautions about our all-too-human tendency to make ourselves seem better by depicting others as somehow worse. As we study the Scripture for today, we will talk more about that. One aspect of this matter should never be ignored. There is one who has every right to judge and whose judgment is administered with true justice. His nature requires it. The patriarch Abraham asked this poignant question found in Genesis 18:25: "Will not the Judge of all the earth do right?" The implied answer is yes, he will. God is the Judge without biases or limits of any kind. His judgment is flawless.

Within today's generation are those who insist that no authoritative standard of right and wrong exists. Each person has the power to decide what is right for himself or herself. Everything is relative. As much as some may think that this is a new position, it is, of course, not new at all. (See Judges 21:25 for an example of how Old Testament Israel embraced this same philosophy.)

God has established his laws, and they are to be obeyed. He is the ultimate Supreme Court before whom all are accountable (Romans 14:10).

### B. JUDGES WITH LIMITS

How different is the subject of judging when human beings are doing it! Our Scripture today, along with others, carries strong warnings against judging. It is addressed to Christians, who are not immune to imperfect attitudes or behavior in this area. We are not to exhibit superiority over others, or suggest that we are without flaws, or claim that we "would never be caught dead" doing what has ensnared another (especially if we have engaged in the same behavior).

Beside the many prohibitions against improper judging are other Scriptures that encourage judging of the proper kind. That is not the focus of today's lesson, but it is a teaching that we must keep in mind. Jesus told those skeptical of him to "make a right judgment" (John 7:24). Paul reminded the Corinthian church that "the saints will judge the world" (1 Corinthians 6:2). And they are to use God's clear teaching (such as that cited in 1 Corinthians 5 and 6 involving sexual

DEVOTIONAL READING:
PSALM 50:1-15

BACKGROUND SCRIPTURE:
ROMANS 2:1-16

PRINTED TEXT:
ROMANS 2:1-16

LESSON AIMS

After this lesson, a student should be able to:

1. Contrast the perfect judgment of God with the faulty judgment of people.

2. Explain why something better than "justice" is needed.

3. Commit to live with a non-judgmental attitude toward others, keeping in mind the coming judgment of God.

WHAT DO YOU THINK?

What would the world look like if there were no such concept as judgment? Would it be better or worse? Why?

[Judges 21:25 could be an interesting passage to include in your discussion.]

KEY VERSE

God will judge men's secrets through Jesus Christ, as my gospel declares. —Romans 2:16

## WHAT DO YOU THINK?

How should the knowledge of God's ultimate judgment influence our judgment of others? Does this mean that we should never exercise judgment of others' morality, wisdom, or interpretation of Scripture?

immorality) to call each other to purity and to separate themselves from the impure who claim to be Christians.

Christians must not try to judge unbelievers for their wrongdoing; that is the job of civil authorities (Romans 13:1-5). But they must apply Christian standards to those who profess faith in Christ, and they must address failure with an eye toward repentance and recovery. And they are to settle disputes among themselves by themselves, rather than bringing other Christians before a pagan court.

There are no limits to God's judgment. There are limits to ours. That's why the Scripture for today is so important!

### C. LESSON BACKGROUND

In today's text from Romans 2, Paul is taking an approach with the Christians in Rome that is similar to the disarming, yet effective, approach taken by Amos, the prophet to Israel (the northern kingdom), in the middle of the eighth century B.C. Plagued by ungodly leadership and spiritual apathy, Israel was falling apart. The people needed to understand that God's judgment was imminent. But how would this sheep farmer and fig picker from the south (Judah) get their attention?

First, Amos brought up the topic of judgment in such a way as to gain the attention and the approval (maybe even cheers) of his listeners. He told them how God was going to rain down judgment on other peoples with whom the northern kingdom was often at odds. "Yes!" they shouted. "They deserve to be destroyed!" He even capped his introduction with a word of judgment against Judah, Israel's spiritual sibling and archrival. Then, before the residents of the north could stop cheering, Amos unloaded God's word of judgment against *them*. So they got the message through a very clever, "back door" method.

Paul takes a very similar approach in the book of Romans. The Jews knew (as Paul confirms) that the Gentiles were vile and sinful. And they were without excuse for being so. As Paul states in Romans 1:18-32, they could see the evidence for God all around—an orderly, powerful Creator, who had not hidden himself at all. And within them was created the capacity for responding to him in faith. They simply chose to ignore the evidence and thus the source of the evidence.

With the beginning of Romans 2, Paul will begin to make the case that the Jews have sinned as well. Thus they have the very same need for salvation that the Gentiles possess.

## I. UNQUALIFIED JUDGE (ROMANS 2:1-4)

### A. CONDEMNS WHAT HE DOES (v. 1)

1. *You, therefore, have no excuse, you who pass judgment on someone else, for at whatever point you judge the other, you are condemning yourself, because you who pass judgment do the same things.*

We know this pattern within ourselves all too well. We tend to raise our voices loudest against those sins in others that are no temptation at all for us (so we can feel quite superior), or against those that have been the greatest problem for us (so we can divert attention away from our own flaws). Any Christian who commits a sin against which he or she has spoken passionately has ruined his or her witness—possibly beyond repair.

This is what upsets Paul the most—the double standard. "Don't do as I do—do as I say." One set of rules for you and another for me!

### B. EXPECTS AN EXEMPTION (vv. 2, 3)

2. *Now we know that God's judgment against those who do such things is based on truth.*

**We are not to judge— God will judge.**

Visual for lesson 2. The visual for today's lesson can be used to highlight the truth that God is our ultimate judge.

Most certainly *God's judgment* will be carried out *against* anyone who dares to commit the sins that he himself would condemn in another. Do we really believe that God will let us get by with that?

We can also be certain that God's judgment *is based on truth*. His judgment is not tarnished by any of the biases, prejudices, or limited insight that affect our perspective. His judgment is truly just.

3. *So when you, a mere man, pass judgment on them and yet do the same things, do you think you will escape God's judgment?*

We are familiar with how modern society has attempted to "repackage" certain sins so as to mask their true identity and lessen their offensiveness. Homosexuality is an "alternative lifestyle"; abortion is just another means of "birth control." Christians are not immune from this same practice. Stealing is never acceptable, but my inaccurate accounting to the Internal Revenue Service is justified because of how the government wastes money. Other people gossip; I "pass along helpful information." Get serious! We know better! And we had better live according to what we know.

Keep in mind that the phrase *a mere man* is not directed just to male human beings. It is a generic term and speaks to both men and women.

## C. DECLINES REPENTANCE (v. 4)

4. *Or do you show contempt for the riches of his kindness, tolerance and patience, not realizing that God's kindness leads you toward repentance?*

If we are so arrogant as to judge others while ignoring our own sin, we may be too blind to see the need for our *repentance* and to avail ourselves of the *riches* of *God's kindness*. That condition will never change unless we are honest with ourselves and with God and repent. Surely we can see how patient God has been—with people such as Old Testament Israel, the first disciples of Jesus, and us. We should not deceive ourselves by thinking that such patience reflects God's indifference to our sinfulness. It does not!

### FIREFIGHTERS OR FIREBUGS?

In 1991, within a span of just a few weeks, three firefighters were arrested in Southern California. One was a fire captain, who was also a highly respected arson investigator. He was charged with setting three fires and implicated in several others. A second firefighter was charged with setting nine fires, and a third with starting twenty-two fires.

Among the nineteen thousand arsonists arrested each year in the United States, only a small percentage are firefighters. One study indicates that only four percent of firefighters are also arsonists, but some experts think the problem is much more extensive.

Why would someone who makes a living fighting fires *start* them? The evidence indicates some common factors in this phenomenon. The guilty person is usually a volunteer or someone who gets paid for each fire he fights. Often he is new at the job and wants to be accepted into the firefighting fraternity. What better way to gain acceptance than to fight a fire—even if you have to start it yourself? Often the firefighter/arsonist will be the first to arrive at the scene of the fire— "a hero on the front lines," so to speak.

In a sense, all of us have the potential to wear the "hat" of either firefighter or "firebug." Perhaps we try to put out "moral fires" by calling attention to the sins of others, in hopes of gaining acceptance from the morally upright. Paul says we have no excuse for such judging, if at the same time we are guilty of starting similar moral conflagrations ourselves. There is no room in the kingdom for such a double standard.      —C. R. B.

### WHAT DO YOU THINK?

*What is the difference between our judgments and God's judgments?*

### DAILY BIBLE READINGS

*Monday, Mar. 7—God Is a Righteous Judge (Psalm 7:6-17)*

*Tuesday, Mar. 8—God Himself Is Judge (Psalm 50:1-15)*

*Wednesday, Mar. 9—Do Not Judge Others (Romans 2:1-5)*

*Thursday, Mar. 10—God Will Judge All (Romans 2:6-11)*

*Friday, Mar. 11—Doers of the Law Are Justified (Romans 2:12-16)*

*Saturday, Mar. 12—Do Jews Follow the Law? (Romans 2:17-24)*

*Sunday, Mar. 13—Real Jews Obey the Law (Romans 2:25-29)*

## II. QUALIFIED JUDGE (ROMANS 2:5-16)

### A. RENDERS RIGHTEOUS VERDICTS (vv. 5-8)

**5. But because of your stubbornness and your unrepentant heart, you are storing up wrath against yourself for the day of God's wrath, when his righteous judgment will be revealed.**

Notice that in verses 5-11, Paul's focus is on two groups (and only two!). Just as there are only two ways (Matthew 7:13, 14), there will be only two groups assembled at the final judgment—as Jesus noted in describing the judgment (Matthew 25:31, 32). Some individuals will come with hard hearts and will reap condemnation. Some will approach the Judge with repentant hearts and righteous lives; they will reap glory. And that will be true for both Jews and Gentiles.

The phrase *stubbornness* and *unrepentant heart* brings to mind the Pharaoh of Egypt, who initially hardened his heart against God and whose heart God eventually hardened. God's action with the Pharaoh seems similar to the process described in Romans 1, where God "gave [sinners] over" to the consequences of the actions they chose to do (vv. 24, 26, 28). Each resistance moves one's heart further from repentance. It is worth noting that the Greek word translated *storing up* is the same word used by Jesus in Matthew 6:19, 20 to describe laying up treasures in Heaven. What are we "storing up"—wealth or wrath?

**6. God "will give to each person according to what he has done."**

One day God's judgment will be administered, in the form of both punishment and reward. This final rendering will not be determined arbitrarily. *Each person* will face the consequence of his or her choices and of the actions based on those choices. God has made this clear repeatedly in Scripture.

**7. To those who by persistence in doing good seek glory, honor and immortality, he will give eternal life.**

Back and forth Paul goes, from one side of the truth to the other. His point is very, very hard to miss. Our deeds matter. Our deeds show on whose side we are. They demonstrate whose message we have accepted and under whose authority we live. We can be our own conductor and follow our own "road map" (which is ultimately Satan's). That means that we will experience God's wrath. Or we can accept God as our conductor, follow his directions, and find *glory, honor and immortality,* and *eternal life.*

In this verse are some good words for Christians: *persistence, doing good,* and *seek.* Don't give up!

**8. But for those who are self-seeking and who reject the truth and follow evil, there will be wrath and anger.**

Here once more is the other side, the other choice. Some will be *self-seeking* and resist God's authority. Like stubborn children they will *reject the truth.* They see no need for God (perhaps they see faith in him as a "crutch" for the weak); they will *follow evil* (bad judgment blended with a bad attitude) instead.

If that is the path I choose to follow, I can count on God's *wrath and anger.* The two choices are pretty clear, aren't they?

### CHOICES

Mary Hutto was a very frugal woman, but few knew her motivation for it. This 1927 graduate of Western Kentucky University in Bowling Green, Kentucky, married and became an English teacher. She and her husband had no children. After he died in an auto accident in 1953, she never remarried.

When Mary's father died in 1957, she began operating the family-owned boarding house near the university campus. Her great appreciation for her alma mater moved her to do all she could for the students of the school. To make as much

---

### WHAT DO YOU THINK?

*If we are under God's grace, why does Paul emphasize that God "will give to each person according to what he has done"? Is Paul advocating a works salvation? Explain.*

space as possible available for university students, she lived in a makeshift cubicle, separated from the rest of the hallway by a sheet she hung there.

Mary Hutto saved her money and invested it carefully, in part because she was afraid she might not have enough for her old age. It turned out that she did. When she died in 2001 at the age of 95, she left her estate to her alma mater in the form of an endowment for scholarships. The gift totaled three and a half million dollars! Mary Hutto chose to live carefully, thus enabling her to bless the lives of others.

Paul tells us that God's judgment will evaluate each of us according to the choices we make in our lives. Wise choices will bring rich rewards; foolish choices will be appropriately punished. Which kind of choices are we making? Are others being blessed by them?
—C. R. B.

### B. Exhibits No Favoritism (vv. 9-11)

9. There will be trouble and distress for every human being who does evil: first for the Jew, then for the Gentile;

The warning continues. The *trouble and distress* of final judgment will be the lot of all those who are outside Christ—those who have made *evil* their trademark and who have refused to surrender their valued self-rule. But it is also true that a great deal of spiritual tribulation and anguish is the plight of unbelievers and evildoers in this life, as Romans 1:18-32 indicates.

Here Paul highlights another truth that he is passionate about conveying: an evildoing, Christ-rejecting *Jew* will be treated the same as an evildoing, Christ-rejecting *Gentile*. There is no difference!

10, 11. . . . but glory, honor and peace for everyone who does good: first for the Jew, then for the Gentile. For God does not show favoritism.

The phrase *first for the Jew, then for the Gentile* is reminiscent of what Paul stated in Romans 1:16 about the recipients of the gospel's powerful salvation message. Since the Jews were the first to hear such a message, they are to be judged first. However, the standard of judgment is to be the same for both Jews and Gentiles. *Glory, honor and peace* will be the precious possession of everyone *who does good*. Keep in mind, though, that generous levels of glory, honor, and peace are already the possession of Christians who live each day exercising the kind of goodness that only one in Christ is equipped to practice.

*God does not show favoritism* means that God does not operate arbitrarily or selectively. All outside of Christ will receive the judgment that a sinner deserves.

### C. Upholds the Law (vv. 12-15)

12. All who sin apart from the law will also perish apart from the law, and all who sin under the law will be judged by the law.

This verse summarizes Paul's comments in chapter 1 that disarm any Gentiles who may plead ignorance regarding the reality and the will of God. They are "without excuse," because the visible world provides adequate instruction on these matters (Romans 1:18-20). They have not lived up to the knowledge of God that they were given. Therefore, without a Savior they will *perish*.

Moreover, those who have had *the law* (Jews) are reminded that they have not kept it. They have not lived up to the knowledge of God they possessed (an even brighter light than the Gentiles had). They *will be judged by the* (written) *law*, and without a Savior they too will be lost.

13. For it is not those who hear the law who are righteous in God's sight, but it is those who obey the law who will be declared righteous.

Here is an additional truth to consider: just to *hear* God's *law* (from teachers or parents) will not save anyone either. Were either Jews or Gentiles to have kept faithfully the law of which they were aware, that law would have been

How to Say It

Amos. AY-mus.
Corinthians. Ko-RIN-thee-unz
    (th as in thin).
Pharaoh. FAIR-o.

**What Do You Think?**

What should we conclude about those who have never heard the gospel? Can they be saved? What about those who live by the Old Testament law but do not believe in Christ?

## PRAYER

*Our Father, most of us studying today have gratefully confessed Christ and accepted your good news. Now we present for your use our lives, willing to confess Jesus before those who do not know him. To you be the glory forever for all you have done. In Jesus' name. Amen.*

their salvation. Keep in mind that Paul is speaking hypothetically in this verse; neither he, nor any other Jew, nor any Gentile, had been able to do that.

*14. (Indeed, when Gentiles, who do not have the law, do by nature things required by the law, they are a law for themselves, even though they do not have the law,*

What could be termed a "godly instinct" was available to the *Gentiles*, even though they did not have the opportunity to study or know the law that was revealed to the Jews. When the Gentiles obeyed God's law, even though they possessed it through instinct rather than revelation, they were acknowledging that there is a law, that it comes from God, and that they are accountable to it.

This needs to be kept in mind in understanding the phrase *a law for themselves.* This language does not mean that the Gentiles are free to make up their own standard of conduct and to do as they please. Within themselves, they have been given a moral awareness of God's standards of right and wrong. They demonstrate that awareness in the manner described in the following verse.

*15. . . . since they show that the requirements of the law are written on their hearts, their consciences also bearing witness, and their thoughts now accusing, now even defending them.)*

Gentiles have the capacity for distinguishing between right and wrong. Conscience, which compares our deeds with a certain standard of judgment and convicts us of wrongdoing when we violate that standard, is part of that capacity. The Gentiles are capable of knowing in *their hearts* what God's requirements are. They can understand their obligation to and their accountability to their Creator. When they do right, they are excused from any feeling of wrongdoing. When they do wrong, they are accused and feel a sense of guilt.

### D. JUDGES THROUGH JESUS (v. 16)

*16. This will take place on the day when God will judge men's secrets through Jesus Christ, as my gospel declares.*

Verses 13-15 are treated as a parenthesis, providing added commentary on the theme of judgment raised in verse 12. With the verse before us, Paul concludes his comments on judgment by calling attention to *the day* when *men's secrets* will be judged. Yes, the doers of the law will be justified rather than the hearers (v. 13), but God's judgment will also examine the inner thoughts and motives. Such a universal failure and a universal need serve to introduce the universal solution.

That solution is highlighted by the reference to *Jesus Christ* as the one by whom God will carry out his judgment. How can this be part of the *gospel*, or good news? The good news is that our judge is also our advocate (1 John 2:1)—the one who, as one illustrative image has described it, removed his royal robes, came down from the judicial bench, and offered to take the punishment that we, though guilty, should have received. Those who refuse to accept that solution of grace will face condemnation.

## THOUGHT TO REMEMBER

*Don't take God's grace for granted.*

## CONCLUSION

Our own failures put us in no position to judge someone else's failures. Whatever our heritage or our history, we are all in the same boat (and the boat is sinking!). We need help. We need to be rescued. And in order for that to happen, there must be a confession on our part. We must acknowledge that we are to blame for our condition. Even though we may be inclined to confess our neighbor's sin or compare ourselves with someone far worse in our eyes, we must end such self-deceit. We must confess our personal sin and our personal need for Jesus as our Savior. That will change our perspective on our neighbor, too, as we realize that judging is not our job—it's God's.

## WHAT DO YOU THINK?

*How can our judgment of our neighbors affect our evangelism of them? Isn't witnessing itself a form of judgment?*

# Discovery Learning

*This page contains an alternative lesson plan emphasizing learning activities. Classes desiring such student involvement will find these suggestions helpful. The next page is a reproducible activity page to further enhance discovery learning.*

## LEARNING GOALS

After completing this lesson, a student should be able to:

1. Contrast the perfect judgment of God with the faulty judgment of people.

2. Explain why something better than "justice" is needed.

3. Commit to live with a non-judgmental attitude toward others, keeping in mind the coming judgment of God.

## INTO THE LESSON

Recruit a class member to introduce you as follows: "All rise! Court is now in session; the honorable [your name] presiding." Walk in (or simply stand). If possible, wear a black robe and carry a gavel. As an alternate introduction, ask if anyone in the class has ever served as a spokesperson for a jury. If so, have the person describe what the experience was like. If not, ask class members, "How would you feel if you were asked to serve in such a capacity?"

## INTO THE WORD

Say, "Paul's strategy as he writes to the Roman Christians (and to us) is to ask questions and then give the Spirit's answer to the question. I have a series of questions for which the answers are found in the verses of today's text from Romans 2:1-16." Assign a verse of today's text to each learner. (If you have more than sixteen learners, assign some verses to pairs of learners; if you have fewer, give more than one verse to several.)

Ask the following questions—best done in random order—and ask learners to cite their verses as answers. Give them an opportunity to explain their connections as well. (It is possible that a learner will be able to justify a match other than that suggested as follows.) Each question's answer can be found in the verse with the same number as the question.

Questions: (1) Can a judge preside over a case dealing with a crime (sin) of which he or she is guilty? (2) How will God judge those who accuse others of a sin of which the accuser is guilty? (3) Will an accuser get away with judging others for sins of which he or she is guilty? (4) What should a guilty accuser/judge remember about the character of God? (5) What characteristic in a person will result in having to face God's wrath and righteous judgment? (6) On what basis will God judge every person? (7) What attitude is necessary in one who seeks eternal life? (8) In the matter of obedience, what is our choice? (9) What will be the ultimate end of the one who does evil, whether Jew or Gentile? (10) What will be the ultimate reward for everyone who (through faith) does good? (11) As a judge, what is God's most outstanding attribute? (12) Is this statement true: "Ignorance of the law will be no excuse"? (13) Is awareness of the law's teaching sufficient to provide justification? (14) Is it possible for a person who does not possess the written law of God to know how God wants him or her to live? (15) What role does one's conscience play in holding him or her accountable to the law of God? (16) Through whom will God carry out his final judgment? Allow discussion and comments with each issue introduced.

## INTO LIFE

Tell your class, "A critical, condemning attitude is learned behavior. To unlearn it, one must replace critical, condemning statements with praising, edifying statements." Divide the group into two sides. Ask one side to suggest common negative statements that may be said (or at least thought) in each of the following situations. Ask the other side to suggest an alternative positive remark.

*Situation 1:* a person comes to a church service wearing what many would consider to be inappropriate clothing. *Situation 2:* a family habitually positions itself to be first in line at a church fellowship dinner. *Situation 3:* a preacher occasionally makes grammatical errors in his oral presentations. *Situation 4:* an older lady with diminished hearing talks out loud in a worship service. *Situation 5:* a youth minister allows elementary children to run noisily before the adult worship is concluded. *Situation 6:* a driver regularly parks in a drop-off area at church and leaves his car there for a period of time. If time allows, suggest other situations at church or from everyday life.

As learners leave today, hand each of them a toothpick with a small "flag" attached that has the Scripture reference *Matthew 7:1-3* printed on it. Tell the learners that the toothpick and the reference are to encourage them to think about the "toothpick/two-by-four" principle of Christian living.

# Qualifications

Look up the following Bible texts and briefly explain how each qualifies God to be Judge.

Exodus 32:34—

Deuteronomy 4:31—

Psalm 94:9-11—

Psalm 139:1-6—

Isaiah 40:10, 28—

Jeremiah 32:27—

Matthew 10:29, 30—

Revelation 22:12—

# Judging and Discerning

Matthew 7:1-6 teaches important principles relative to judging and discerning. Read the verses carefully, and then write three principles you will use in dealing with people in the days to come. One example is given to get you started.

Example: I must be very careful in speaking against a fault in others that is very obviously present in my own behavior.

1.

2.

3.

# God's Project: Effective Christians

Unit 1: Saved by God

(Lessons 1-4)

# JUSTIFIED BY FAITH

## WHY TEACH THIS LESSON?

Christianity differs from other world religions in a striking way: Christianity is the only religion that is not works-based. Buddhism, Hinduism, and Islam all have rungs on a ladder that one must climb to approach reward. This week's lesson shows that our ladder had no rungs. Jesus alone is the source of our reconciliation with God. (Even our faith is not a "work," but rather our acknowledgment of Jesus' completed work on our behalf.)

Because Jesus' atoning work buys us access to the living God, Christianity is more a "relationship" than a "religion."

The final take-home lesson is peace and assurance. Because we are not striving, working out our salvation on our own, we can rest in our hope and rejoice because we know we are not worthy, yet are accepted. We can even have peace and joy when things are rough, because our future is secure.

## INTRODUCTION

### A. ONE WAY TO PEACE

Peace! What a wonderful word! Think for a moment about the Christmas cards that you received just a few months ago. Wasn't that word the focus of many of them? If you had asked individuals during that season what gift they wanted, wouldn't many have mentioned peace?

Today, Palm Sunday, begins what many refer to as "Passion Week" in the life of Christ. The events of this week reveal the climax of God's plan to bring his kind of peace—real peace—to the world. While that plan involved the agony and brutality of the cross, the week itself started with a celebration. As Jesus rode into Jerusalem on a donkey, the people rejoiced and expressed their welcome by placing palm branches and garments in his path.

As the week progressed, the opposition to Jesus from his enemies intensified. The climax was the crucifixion, when God's peace was achieved through man's terror. Isaiah described this vividly: "The punishment that brought us peace was upon him, and by his wounds we are healed" (Isaiah 53:5). Three days later came resurrection morning. And today he lives!

This is the way to real peace. God planned it. Jesus provided it. And we can accept it. Peace talks are often held in today's world to suggest ways to reach the ever-elusive goal of peace. Consider today's lesson on this "Triumphal Entry" Sunday a genuine "peace talk."

### B. LESSON BACKGROUND

The first two lessons of this quarter came from the opening chapters of Romans, drawing a clear picture of the need of sinners, both Jewish and Gentile. "For all have sinned and fall short of the glory of God" (Romans 3:23). Having spelled out this need, Paul then begins to explain the remedy. In chapter 4 he introduces an example, Abraham, who through faith was justified by God. This was not by Abraham's works! God's grace was required—even for this Old Testament saint. Abraham was a good man, but he could not have done enough to

DEVOTIONAL READING:
2 CORINTHIANS 3:4-11
BACKGROUND SCRIPTURE:
ROMANS 5:1-21
PRINTED TEXT:
ROMANS 5:1-11, 18-21

Mar
20

### LESSON AIMS

After this lesson, a student should be able to:

1. Tell about our need for peace with God, the source of that peace, and the attending result of that peace.

2. Compare what Christ did for us as "sinners" with the "much more" that he does for those who have been reconciled.

3. Resolve to face with joy, patience, and hope a situation that currently causes tribulation.

### WHAT DO YOU THINK?

Why did some people find Jesus' entry into Jerusalem objectionable? Why do people today find Jesus objectionable?

### KEY VERSE

Therefore, since we have been justified through faith, we have peace with God through our Lord Jesus Christ.      —Romans 5:1

WHAT DO YOU THINK?

Is there a conflict between faith and works? What is their relationship to each other? How does the example of Abraham illustrate this relationship?

[James 2:14-26 should provide some guidance for this discussion.]

"Therefore being justified by faith, we have peace with God through our Lord Jesus Christ."
—Romans 5:1

Visual for lesson 3. *The dove is considered a symbol of peace. Use this visual as you study Romans 5:1.*

WHAT DO YOU THINK?

*How do we determine whether we really "hope" for something or only "wish" for it? Do we merely "wish" for Heaven? What is the difference?*

earn God's favor. He trusted God, and that trust was the reason for his being considered "righteous" in God's sight.

Like Abraham, we are called to travel the same route—the way of faith.

## I. FAITH'S PROVISIONS (ROMANS 5:1, 2)

### A. BRINGS PEACE (v. 1)

**1. Therefore, since we have been justified through faith, we have peace with God through our Lord Jesus Christ,**

Any occurrence of the word *therefore* should encourage the Bible student to ask what it is "there for." In this case, it points back to Paul's use of Abraham as an illustration of grace and *faith* in the previous chapter. That example may have been cited by Paul in an effort to appeal to the Jews to accept the concept of salvation by grace and faith. If the man considered the "father of the Jewish people" was a recipient of grace and was counted righteous by faith, then his descendants should not try to create some other means of coming to God.

Also worth noting is what Paul has already said about the desperate human condition. All have sinned—Jews and Gentiles; no one is excluded. The finger of God has been pointed at every human being, and our sins have been painted in the dark colors they deserve.

Then the sun breaks through (or perhaps we should say, "Son"). *Jesus* "was delivered over to death for our sins" and was "raised to life for our justification" (Romans 4:25). We are *justified* by God's actions, not ours. He simply asks for our trust—our faith—which is exactly what he asked from Abraham.

One definition of justification is a play on the English word: being justified means being treated "just as if I'd" never sinned. God himself has provided the means for bridging the rift between us, for making *peace.* That means is Jesus.

### B. ACCESSES GRACE (v. 2a)

**2a. . . . through whom we have gained access by faith into this grace in which we now stand.**

By using the word *grace,* the apostle reinforces his central point. There are no "works" that gain our justification. Salvation has been provided by God. It is a gift that we must receive. *Faith* in Jesus gives us *access* to grace.

Think of it this way. To gain an audience with a world leader, the chief executive of a large organization, or someone with a very full calendar, we must not only make an appointment, we also need to be ushered in by someone close to the important person. Jesus (through our trust in him) ushers us into the presence of the God of grace. And Jesus continues to give us access to God and his grace (Hebrews 7:25).

### C. PRESENTS HOPE (v. 2b)

**2b. And we rejoice in the hope of the glory of God.**

*Hope* is a frequently misunderstood word. Often people use it to talk about something they would love to have or see happen, but they don't know whether they will get it and see it or not. "One can only hope," they reply rather passively as to whether what they desire will really occur.

But the Bible uses the word *hope* quite differently. In Christ we *rejoice* in *hope.* What he has promised, he will do. For one in Christ there is no doubt. The quality of hope hinges on the character of the one in whom hope is placed. What more needs to be said? We acquire true hope when we abandon the futile practice of trusting in ourselves to shape the future and put our future in the hands of God. When we are in Christ we have peace, grace, and hope. And there is more!

## II. FAITH'S PROGRESS (ROMANS 5:3-5)

### A. FROM TRIBULATION TO PATIENCE (v. 3)

**3. Not only so, but we also rejoice in our sufferings, because we know that suffering produces perseverance;**

In Christ we have resources for handling the circumstances that come our way, such as suffering. When faith is our guiding principle, what appear to be very bad situations can yield good results. (Read Paul's later affirmation in Romans 8:28.) Those results are not always immediately seen. (Think of what happened to Joseph in the Old Testament and his declaration concerning God's purpose in Genesis 45:4-8.) Thus there is often a need for *perseverance*. This is not a passive resignation, but rather an active patience. Trouble teaches us to wait, and it teaches us to cope by use of the resources that God provides.

### B. FROM PATIENCE TO EXPERIENCE (v. 4a)

**4a. . . . perseverance, character;**

Lessons in *perseverance* come from several directions and at various stages of life. When tribulation comes in different forms and at different times, perseverance is necessary. Yet through the patient handling of circumstances, the discovery of solutions, and the discipline of waiting, *character* is developed. And the person of character can often provide encouragement to someone who needs advice from an individual who's "been there" (2 Corinthians 1:3, 4).

### C. FROM EXPERIENCE TO HOPE (vv. 4b, 5)

**4b. . . . and character, hope.**

At this point, Paul may appear to be going in circles. As Christians we possess a faith-based *hope*. In living out that hope, we will encounter suffering. The suffering will teach us perseverance. The perseverance will help develop character. And that character, in turn, will cause us to hope in God. However, let us not think of this as a circle as much as an advancing spiral. With each round of faith-guided living (which blends trouble and joy and lessons learned), we gain strength and we become more valuable to the Master.

**5. And hope does not disappoint us, because God has poured out his love into our hearts by the Holy Spirit, whom he has given us.**

When we place our *hope* in God, we will not be disappointed. All of the attributes Paul describes in this passage come from God, who guides the entire process by which they are acquired. He even provides the means for maintaining what he has *given*, namely, *the Holy Spirit*, who gives us *love* and helps us grow in love. When love is clearly visible in the church, it is a sure sign of the Holy Spirit's presence.

### TRIUMPHING OVER TROUBLES

The headline read, "'Runner' Wins the Inspiration Prize, Hands Down." The "runner" was Bob Wieland, a Vietnam veteran who lost both legs in that war. The "inspiration prize" was simply finishing the 26.2 miles of the 2003 Los Angeles Marathon, using his hands to swing his torso along the course. Wieland has been doing marathons and triathlons for twenty years. He has even done a "walk" across America! He wears padded trousers that allow him to rock backward and forward as he uses his hands like legs. His "hand shoes"—as he calls them—are gelpads with handles. The 57-year-old Wieland crossed the finish line of the Los Angeles Marathon in a total time of 173 hours and 45 minutes—more than seven days!

Some of us who are able-bodied and younger than Wieland may well question our own physical, emotional, and spiritual stamina when compared with his. He gives God the credit for his feat and says, "It was done only by the grace of God."

**HOW TO SAY IT**

Abraham. AY-bruh-ham.
Isaiah. Eye-ZAY-uh.

**WHAT DO YOU THINK?**

What has your experience taught you about hope? How has God's work in your life given you hope for his work in the future?

Wieland's efforts illustrate what Paul says in our text today about "tribulations." Overwhelming difficulties can produce patience, experience, and hope—if we place our trust in God. At first, this hope may simply be that we will find a "normal" life again, but ultimately it becomes the hope—the assurance—that God will someday make all things right. —C. R. B.

## III. CHRIST'S ATONEMENT (ROMANS 5:6-11)

### A. DEATH FOR SINNERS (vv. 6-8)

**6. You see, at just the right time, when we were still powerless, Christ died for the ungodly.**

The right time is God's time! (See Galatians 4:4.) It is remarkable to study the prophecies fulfilled by Jesus, especially those surrounding his death. But the most remarkable aspect of the death of *Christ* is that he *died for the ungodly*—the undeserving, those *powerless* to save themselves. That includes all of us.

**7. Very rarely will anyone die for a righteous man, though for a good man someone might possibly dare to die.**

What is the difference between a *righteous man* and a *good man*? Some would say that the righteous man describes an especially pious individual who possesses a "holier-than-thou" attitude. He may be highly respected, but he is not the kind of person for whom someone else would be willing *to die*. The good man would be someone whose good deeds make him a much more likable individual, and thus someone for whom others would be more apt to die.

Others believe that there is basically no difference between the righteous man and the good man and that Paul is making the same claim in two different ways. The first part of the verse states Paul's claim in a negative way; the second states it in a more positive manner. Either way, the gist of Paul's thought is this: people are not likely to give their lives on behalf of even the best of human beings.

**8. But God demonstrates his own love for us in this: While we were still sinners, Christ died for us.**

Here is the dramatic difference between us an *God*. He has shown *his own love for us*, in the form of his crucified Son. And he has done this for *sinners*—not righteous men, not good men, but those who were anything but righteous and good! This is real love—the kind of love that can come only from God.

Not only does God demonstrate such love, but he also commands that Christians demonstrate that love to others (John 13:34, 35; 1 John 4:11), even to our enemies (Matthew 5:44).

### B. BLESSINGS FOR THE RECONCILED (vv. 9-11)

**9. Since we have now been justified by his blood, how much more shall we be saved from God's wrath through him!**

Justification is the present possession of the Christian. We can be at peace with God. The work of Christ has been done. We are new creatures (2 Corinthians 5:17), we wear a new name, and we have a new destiny that will not be realized until this time in our present world is finished and our time in Heaven has begun. We will be *saved from God's wrath*, from Hell, from the place prepared for those who have trusted in their way rather than God's way. Thus our past, present, and future are all in God's hands.

**10. For if, when we were God's enemies, we were reconciled to him through the death of his Son, how much more, having been reconciled, shall we be saved through his life!**

Here is a reminder of the change in our status, thanks to Jesus. The ungodly, the sinners, are *God's enemies*. Sin severed the relationship between sinner and

### WHAT DO YOU THINK?

*If Jesus died for sinners, why do so many churches exist primarily for the benefit of the saints? How can our churches do a better job of sharing the love Christ has for the ungodly?*

Creator. God provided the way by which those who are separated from him can come back and be *reconciled* to the one who bore no responsibility for the breach. Only he could take care of this, and he has.

Next comes the consequence of that reconciliation through Jesus' *death*. Now that Jesus is alive and reigning as Lord, how *much more* will he help those who have accepted his gift of salvation! We can have no doubt that Jesus will return someday and complete God's plan of redemption.

**11. Not only is this so, but we also rejoice in God through our Lord Jesus Christ, through whom we have now received reconciliation.**

From our study of verse 3, we can see that Paul's phrase *not only is this so* is simply an expression that he uses to say, "There is more." We have been reconciled (reunited) to *God*. We have been saved from sin and death by means of his grace. As a result, we can have joy. Like hope, joy is more than just a fleeting emotion; it is a constant sense of gratitude and praise for all that God has done and will do.

Paul notes that all of what he has just described comes *through our Lord Jesus Christ*. This includes the atonement, which is often defined as being made "at one" with God. The Greek word used here is a form of the same word that is translated "reconciled" in verse 10.

## IV. CHRIST'S ACHIEVEMENTS (ROMANS 5:18-21)

### A. RIGHTEOUSNESS (v. 18)

**18. Consequently, just as the result of one trespass was condemnation for all men, so also the result of one act of righteousness was justification that brings life for all men.**

In the verses of chapter 5 not included in our printed text (vv. 12-17), Paul raises the issue of Adam's sin and its impact versus Christ's death and its impact. The primary emphasis of Paul's teaching is that Jesus' death has reversed the effects of Adam's sin. Life, not death, reigns for the followers of Jesus.

In the verse before us, Paul states that Adam's *trespass*, or sin, cost him, and it has cost *all* of humanity. In a sense, Adam acted as a representative for the entire human race (some use the term "federal head"), just as Jesus represented all humanity when he died for all on the cross (2 Corinthians 5:14). Specifically what God's *condemnation for all men* as a result of Adam's sin involved is not defined by Paul. What is important to understand is that the impact of Christ's death *(justification)* countered the impact of Adam's sin *(condemnation)*. The phrase *the one act of righteousness* most likely describes one act (Jesus' death) rather than one man (Jesus). Jesus' perfect life of righteousness qualified him to be the perfect sacrifice who died in the place of sinners so that the free gift of *life* could be made available to them (2 Corinthians 5:21).

### B. OBEDIENCE (v. 19)

**19. For just as through the disobedience of the one man the many were made sinners, so also through the obedience of the one man the many will be made righteous.**

This reinforces the teaching of the last verse. Adam disobeyed God, and he has been our model. Because of his *disobedience*, sin intruded and scarred the atmosphere of peace and harmony that God created, and it has been doing so ever since. And we have been good students of our "model." We have disobeyed God as well; "death came to all men, because all sinned" (Romans 5:12).

Jesus provided a different kind of "model." We can be *made righteous* by his redeeming act, his *obedience* to God through his death on the cross (Philippians

---

**WHAT DO YOU THINK?**

*Why does Paul emphasize that we were God's "enemies"? How can such language help to clarify our spiritual focus?*

---

**DAILY BIBLE READINGS**

**Monday, Mar. 14**—We Are Justified and Become Heirs (Titus 3:1-7)

**Tuesday, Mar. 15**—Ministry of Justification Abounds in Glory (2 Corinthians 3:4-11)

**Wednesday, Mar. 16**—Like Abraham, We Have Faith (Romans 4:13-25)

**Thursday, Mar. 17**—We Are Justified by Faith (Romans 5:1-5)

**Friday, Mar. 18**—Christ Died for Us Sinners (Romans 5:6-11)

**Saturday, Mar. 19**—Christ Brings a Free Gift (Romans 5:12-17)

**Sunday, Mar. 20**—Grace Abounds All the More (Romans 5:18-21)

2:8). (*The obedience of the one* highlights one act, Jesus' death, as did "one act of righteousness" in the previous verse.)

## C. GRACE (vv. 20, 21)

**20. The law was added so that the trespass might increase. But where sin increased, grace increased all the more,**

As we noted in the previous lesson, *the law* has spelled out right and wrong very well. Its revelation of God's standards makes it painfully clear that that we have violated them. But there is more power in *grace* than there is in *sin*.

**21. . . . so that, just as sin reigned in death, so also grace might reign through righteousness to bring eternal life through Jesus Christ our Lord.**

Sin's rule has an expiration date, and that will be whenever Christ returns (Matthew 13:40-42). However, the reign of sin in an individual's life can be overthrown when he or she accepts *Jesus Christ* as Lord. At that point, the *reign* of *grace* replaces the reign of *sin*. In addition, *eternal life* becomes one's possession through a knowledge of Christ (John 17:3).

But don't misunderstand or become too complacent: sin will keep picking at the Christian. Sin will be relentless in attempting to trap him or her. It may even win some skirmishes. In Christ, however, the war has been won; sin's reign is at best shaky. And when the Christian dies and goes to be with Christ (Philippians 1:23), sin's influence in that person's life is finished. The reign of grace and the overthrow of sin will be complete.

### STILL REIGNING

Sin is everywhere. We have grown used to (and in some cases even inoculated against) the reality of auto theft, embezzlement, drunk driving, and even murder and war—except, of course, when we ourselves or those we love are victims. But doesn't it seem as if people are constantly finding new ways to sin? For example, the Internet has created many opportunities for such twisted "creativity."

An example of this is the too-good-to-be-true opportunities to cash in on someone else's apparent difficulties that often come in the form of Internet scams. Sexual predators in America search "chat rooms" for unsuspecting young people.

One troublesome example of this new-way-to-sin phenomenon occurred recently when a twenty-one-year-old committed suicide in front of his computer videocam. While he was online "chatting" with a large number of strangers, he was overdosing on drugs. Many of those with whom he was chatting were indifferent to what they saw happening on their computer monitors. Some were even arguing about who would get his drug paraphernalia after he died!

As Paul tells us, sin "increased" and "reigned in death" (Romans 5:20, 21). We're seeing more of this as time goes on. The only answer for this world and all its hurting people is the abundant grace of God through Jesus.

How good a job of communicating that grace is our church doing?     —C. R. B.

## CONCLUSION

You may have heard the advice often given to a prospective husband and wife who are Christians. If each of them will maintain a strong relationship with Jesus, they will strengthen their union with one another. The same principle is true for friendships in general. If two people are close friends with Jesus, that common bond with him will make them close friends with each other.

That's the primary reason that peace is lacking around our world. There is no common bond with Jesus. Why should we expect peace in these places? The presence of such situations reinforces the missionary mandate of Matthew 28:19, doesn't it? There is only one way to peace—the Prince of peace!

# Discovery Learning

*This page contains an alternative lesson plan emphasizing learning activities. Classes
desiring such student involvement will find these suggestions helpful. The next page
is a reproducible activity page to further enhance discovery learning.*

## LEARNING GOALS

After this lesson, a student should be able to:

1. Tell about our need for peace with God, the source of that peace, and the attending result of that peace.

2. Compare what Christ did for us as "sinners" with the "much more" that he does for those who have been reconciled.

3. Resolve to face with joy, patience, and hope a situation that currently causes tribulation.

## INTO THE LESSON

Display the word *suffering* twice on the board with letters top to bottom to form two acrostics. Divide the class into two halves for responding to the following exercise. Ask one half to suggest negative words that are synonymous with or related to suffering. Ask the other half to suggest only positive words, essentially the opposite of what people would normally associate with suffering.

Here are two possibilities; first, for the negative side: S—sorrow, U—unfairness, F—failure, F—frustration, E—enmity, R—ridicule, I—insults, N—need, G—grief. For the positive side, here are some suggestions: S—salvation, U—understanding, F—freedom, F—favor, E—eternal life, R—rejoicing, I—inspiration, N—nurturing, G—gratitude.

If the groups have difficulty getting started, write in a sample word or two for each. Alternate between the two sides until most letters are accounted for. Say, "Though this first column represents what we most often associate with suffering and tribulation, the right column represents what suffering and tribulation can be to the Christian. The positive side of suffering is what Paul stresses in today's study."

## INTO THE WORD

Establish groups small enough for discussion, and give each group one of the following case studies. Tell the groups, "Decide what you would say or write to these Christians upon hearing of their difficulties, based on Romans 5:1-11."

*Situation 1:* The Dooley family has just been told that Mrs. Dooley, age 47, has stage two breast cancer. The family was already struggling with the marital difficulties of one of their children and the college academic problems of another. What do you say to them?

*Situation 2:* Cliff Davis, age 60, has just lost his job of thirty-five years to "downsizing." His wife does not work. The Davises had recently made a commitment to support a young couple planning to go as missionaries to the Czech Republic and had also made a down payment on a small retirement property at a nearby lake. Without "giving advice," what do you say to them?

*Situation 3:* Effin Hubersch has recently become a Christian in a predominantly Muslim nation. Animosities abound from his family, at his job, and in his community. He faces social shunning, job loss, harassment, vandalism of his property, and possible violence. Without "giving advice," what do you say to him?

*Situation 4:* Kathy Rogers has recently canceled her marriage engagement. She has friends who blame her for what happened. Some friends of the prospective groom have cut off all contacts with her and will not return telephone calls. She has gifts to return. Her own family lives about a thousand miles away and can offer little support. Without "giving advice," what do you say to her?

After a short time of discussion, let each group report its decision. Though you should allow each group the freedom of thought, you can anticipate remarks about the peace (v. 1), hope (vv. 2, 4, 5), love (vv. 5, 8), salvation (vv. 9, 10), and joy (v. 11) that Paul emphasizes.

At this point, ask learners to look at verses 18-21 of the text. Ask, "What is there in these verses that speaks of the calamities and anxieties that beset us in this life?" Also ask, "What other words of comfort and grace do these truths suggest for occasions of tribulation and suffering?" Once again, allow for the freedom of insights, but expect comments on the awful consequences of sin in the world and the fact that by God's grace there is a life coming that will be free of such struggles.

## INTO LIFE

Ask the class to suggest godly commitment statements based on the pattern "Even when . . . I will . . . " based upon truths in today's text. For example, "Even when death stares me in the face, I will anticipate eternal life in Christ"; and "Even when another person's self-centeredness has harmed my relationships, I will forgive that person as God forgave me in Christ." (A similar activity is included in the student book.) Close the class with a prayer along these lines.

# What Do You Have?

Romans 5:1-11, 18-21 recites a glorious list of the blessings that are ours in Christ. Read that text and fill in the following list of what we have.

We have peace with _____ .

We have access by _____ .

We have rejoicing in _____ .

We have the Holy Spirit in our _____ .

We have salvation from _____ .

We have reconciliation to _____ .

We have righteousness by _____ .

We have eternal life by _____ .

We have strength in Christ's _____ .

We have justification by his _____ .

# What Can You Give?

Because of what we have been given freely in Christ, we have much to give others, especially to those who have suffered. Complete each of the following statements as an expression of your intention.

I will give knowledge of Christ's salvation to one who . . .

I will give forgiveness to one who . . .

I will give the hope of eternal life to one who . . .

I will give grace to one who . . .

I will give love to one who . . .

# Is Your Heart Full?

The Spirit says, "God has poured out his love into our hearts by the Holy Spirit, whom he has given us" (Romans 5:5). In the heart image to the right, write in some of what God has poured into your heart. If there are "empty places," fill in some of the gifts of God you want to receive.

# VICTORY IN CHRIST

**LESSON 4**

## WHY TEACH THIS LESSON?

Pivotal moments. You see them in every book and movie. The main character is challenged and outnumbered. The odds against him or her seem insurmountable. All looks bleak. Then comes the unexpected. The twist. The turn of events that no one could have imagined and that changes everything.

Peter and John witnessed the pivotal moment in all of history. They had believed that Jesus would change the world. One short week before, he was being honored in Jerusalem. Then came his arrest, mock trial, and brutal murder. Their thoughts of freedom and kingdom were shattered. They were stunned, confused, lost. Then, the unfathomable plot twist: Christ arose from the dead, changing the fate of mankind forever. Our mortal enemies—sin and death—are crushed.

Today's lesson not only dramatizes this pivotal moment in human history, but also shows how each individual's baptism mirrors Christ's victory over death. Today's lesson will show us how baptism can be a pivotal moment in our lives.

## INTRODUCTION

### A. TAKE HEART—JESUS LIVES!

As Christians around the world celebrate Easter Sunday today, many will read from 1 Corinthians 15—the "resurrection chapter" of the Bible. In verses 19 and 20 of this chapter, Paul offers a striking contrast between life without and with the hope of resurrection: "If only for this life we have hope in Christ, we are to be pitied more than all men. But Christ has indeed been raised from the dead, the firstfruits of those who have fallen asleep." He concludes the chapter on this triumphant and encouraging note: "Therefore, my dear brothers, stand firm. Let nothing move you. Always give yourselves fully to the work of the Lord, because you know that your labor in the Lord is not in vain."

The apostle's words ring just as true in the twenty-first century as they did in the first. To those who at times may envy the prosperity and self-assurance of the godless or who become discouraged at the lack of fruit in their labors for Christ, take heart! Today provides a wonderful opportunity to remind ourselves of what distinguishes Christian faith from other "faiths." The difference is like night and day—or, to use today's emphasis, death and life.

### B. LESSON BACKGROUND

Following the crucifixion and burial of Jesus, those who felt the deepest disappointment were most likely the eleven faithful disciples of Jesus. These men had left their families and jobs; they had spent most every day since then listening to his teaching and assisting him as he carried out his ministry.

There were also several godly women who had invested their time, care, and resources in the ministry of Jesus. They had traveled with Jesus and his disciples and had been "helping to support them out of their own means" (Luke 8:3). Perhaps they, along with the disciples, held expectations that Jesus would establish his kingdom (political in nature) and overthrow the Romans. Now he was disgraced and dead.

---

DEVOTIONAL READING:
ROMANS 6:15-23
BACKGROUND SCRIPTURE:
JOHN 20:1-10; ROMANS 6:
1-14
PRINTED TEXT:
JOHN 20:1-10; ROMANS 6:
1-14

Mar
27

LESSON AIMS

After completing this lesson, a student should be able to:

1. Recount the events of resurrection morning, and tell how that event is "replayed" every time a believer is baptized.

2. Contrast the life of sin with the "resurrected" life of the believer raised to "walk in newness of life."

3. Use poetry, art, or music to celebrate the victory over death that we have because of Jesus.

KEY VERSE

For we know that since Christ was raised from the dead, he cannot die again; death no longer has mastery over him.
—Romans 6:9

Some of Jesus' followers realized that the least they could do was to be sure that Jesus was buried with proper dignity. So Joseph of Arimathea and Nicodemus prepared his body (John 19:38-42). Some of the women watched as he was placed in Joseph's new tomb (Matthew 27:61). Then early on the first day of the week, the women went back to the site, eager to add their skillful and sensitive touch to the burial preparation. They were concerned about how the stone could be rolled back from the tomb in order to give them access to Jesus' body.

Today's printed text includes John's account of resurrection morning. Although he focuses especially on Mary Magdalene, it is clear from the other three accounts that other women came to the tomb early that day (Matthew 28:1; Mark 16:1; Luke 23:55–24:1). Mary serves as a model of devotion to Jesus—present at the cross, the burial site, and the empty tomb.

The other part of the lesson text continues our study of Romans by including a section of chapter 6. There we will consider the kind of resurrection that we are to experience in response to Christ's resurrection.

## I. JESUS' RESURRECTION (JOHN 20:1-10)

### A. MARY'S DISTRESS (vv. 1, 2)

1. *Early on the first day of the week, while it was still dark, Mary Magdalene went to the tomb and saw that the stone had been removed from the entrance.*

It is *early* (perhaps as early at 4:00 A.M.) on *the first day of the week* when *Mary Magdalene* approaches the *tomb*. She is eager to carry out her act of devotion to Jesus. Like the other women, she wonders about the *stone* being rolled back so that his body can be respectfully attended to; but she is dismayed to find the tomb is open. Has someone stolen or mistreated the body?

2. *So she came running to Simon Peter and the other disciple, the one Jesus loved, and said, "They have taken the Lord out of the tomb, and we don't know where they have put him!"*

Mary leaves the scene in a panic. She hurries to report to *Peter and the other disciple*. Apparently this *other disciple* is John, who keeps himself in the background through use of this phrase (see similar references to *the one Jesus loved* in John 19:26; 21:7, 20).

Notice that Mary's words to Peter and John reflect her belief at this point that the body of Jesus has been *taken* away. For now, she is not thinking in terms of a resurrection. She also uses the term *we*, referring to the other women who had accompanied her to the tomb.

### B. PETER AND JOHN'S DISCOVERY (vv. 3-10)

3-5. *So Peter and the other disciple started for the tomb. Both were running, but the other disciple outran Peter and reached the tomb first. He bent over and looked in at the strips of linen lying there but did not go in.*

*Both* disciples hurry to *the tomb*. Most commentators propose that John was somewhat younger than *Peter* and therefore more athletic. Perhaps Peter is stouter and stronger, but not as fast afoot as John. John arrives at the tomb *first*, but he is not as inquisitive as Peter. He sees *the strips of linen* used for burial lying inside the tomb, but he does *not go in*.

6, 7. *Then Simon Peter, who was behind him, arrived and went into the tomb. He saw the strips of linen lying there, as well as the burial cloth that had been around Jesus' head. The cloth was folded up by itself, separate from the linen.*

Bible students are accustomed to Peter's bold, daring words and actions (although sometimes ill-advised!) as recorded in the Gospels. Here he goes *into the tomb* and notes *the strips of linen* and the *burial cloth* that had been wrapped *around Jesus' head*. This cloth is now *folded up by itself*. Such neatness does not support the view, touted by some skeptics, that thieves had stolen Jesus' body (Mary's first thought). Robbers are not concerned with good manners!

Notice the hurrying and running that has already taken place in response to the empty tomb. The good news of the resurrected Christ should put some urgency in our steps—not only on Easter Sunday but every day.

**8. Finally the other disciple, who had reached the tomb first, also went inside. He saw and believed.**

Drawing on Peter's courage, John also enters the tomb. He sees the items noted in the previous verse. Remember that John is the one writing this report, especially when it is noted that he not only sees, but also believes at this time. Exactly what John believes is not stated, but he must believe that Jesus is indeed alive. That John's belief in Jesus is not fully informed is clear from the next verse.

**9. (They still did not understand from Scripture that Jesus had to rise from the dead.)**

*Still* none of the disciples understand the messianic expectation of the *Scripture* (in this case the Old Testament) correctly. Like many, they expect a triumphant, earthly ruler, who will restore Israel's greatness by overthrowing the hated Romans—not a man who will be executed as a common criminal and then *rise from the dead*.

**10. Then the disciples went back to their homes.**

Uncertain about what else to do or think, these *disciples* take the only course of action available at this point: they go *back to their homes*. Later in this chapter, John records Jesus' appearances to Mary Magdalene (vv. 11-18), the disciples minus Thomas (vv. 19-23), and the disciples with Thomas (vv. 24-29). Another appearance to seven of the disciples, recorded in John 21, concludes with a focus on the future service of Peter and John (vv. 15-23).

### Fact and Artifact

The "most studied artifact" in history is said to be the Shroud of Turin. Many believe it to be the actual burial cloth of Jesus referred to in today's text from John's Gospel. It is a linen cloth, fourteen and a half feet long and three and a half feet wide, bearing the image of a man who was beaten and crucified. Reliable records of the shroud go back to about A.D. 1350 when it was owned by Geoffrey de Charny, a French knight.

Since 1578, the shroud has been kept in a special repository in a cathedral built in Turin, Italy, specifically for housing the relic (thus the name, "Shroud of Turin"). It has been inspected and investigated innumerable times and is the subject of considerable speculation. In 1988, the shroud was subjected to radiocarbon dating by three different laboratories. The researchers concluded that it dates to approximately A.D. 1325, plus or minus about sixty years.

All of this may be interesting to contemplate; but when all is said and done, the matter of the shroud is irrelevant to our faith. The basis of the Christian faith lies in the risen Lord, who appeared over a forty-day period to numerous individuals and to more than five hundred at one time (Acts 1:3; 1 Corinthians 15:6). We believe, not because of a "most studied artifact," but because of an indisputable fact of history: Christ is risen!

—C. R. B.

## I. THE CHRISTIAN'S RESURRECTION (ROMANS 6:1-14)

### A. DEAD TO SIN (vv. 1-3)

**. What shall we say, then? Shall we go on sinning so that grace may increase?**

Last week's lesson was taken from Romans 5. There we noted Paul's concluding contrast between the reign of sin (leading to death) and the reign of *grace*

---

**What Do You Think?**

Why does the resurrection matter? Some believe that the only important thing about Christianity is the positive example of Jesus' life—are they correct? Why, or why not?

**What Do You Think?**

Why was it so hard for Jesus' disciples to understand and believe in the resurrection? Do you think it is easier or harder to believe today?

**What Do You Think?**

What convinced you of the reality of Jesus' resurrection? What is the best way to convince someone else of that reality?

(leading to eternal life) that is meant to overthrow sin's power. At the beginning of chapter 6, Paul anticipates a question that some may raise concerning grace. If it is indeed true that "where sin increased, grace increased all the more" (Romans 5:20), isn't the next "logical" step to say, "Let's sin all we want, then we'll really give God's grace a chance to work"? (Perhaps some in the church in Rome were actually proposing such a concept, so it was an idea that needed to be addressed quickly and decisively.)

True, God is a God of grace. He is able and willing to forgive the most terrible sins. But God wants us to grow toward righteousness, as Paul will emphasize in this chapter. As someone has put it, "God loves us as we are, but he loves us too much to let us stay that way."

*2. By no means! We died to sin; how can we live in it any longer?*

Paul's answer to the question raised in verse 1 is unmistakably clear: *By no means!* ("Of course not!"). A vital part of the acceptance of Jesus Christ as Savior and Lord is becoming dead to sin through repentance. The Christian is "under new management," so to speak. How curious and sadly inconsistent it is for the Christian to go back "under the old management" from time to time!

*3. Or don't you know that all of us who were baptized into Christ Jesus were baptized into his death?*

Baptism is designed to be a defining moment in our relationship with God. Just as *Jesus* was buried in a tomb, the one who accepts Jesus is buried in the "watery grave" of Christian baptism. We are *baptized into his death*; that is, baptism represents our acceptance of Jesus' death as our own. It is a burial of the old self. The penalty for our sin is removed in accepting Jesus' death as the substitute for ours. And sin, as the controlling force in our lives, is dead. Its mastery over us has been broken.

## B. RAISED WITH CHRIST (vv. 4, 5)

*4. We were therefore buried with him through baptism into death in order that, just as Christ was raised from the dead through the glory of the Father, we too may live a new life.*

Paul continues his explanation of the dynamic image of Christian *baptism*. A candidate is *buried* in water and raised from that water in an act that identifies him or her with the Son of God, who was buried and *raised* for us. God's power and love raised Jesus, and in baptism his power is also at work in those who have chosen to follow Jesus. Paul notes this in Colossians 2:12: "buried with him [Christ] in baptism and raised with him through your faith in the power of God, who raised him from the dead."

Paul also calls attention to what is to take place following the act of baptism. This is clear from the phrase *live a new life*. Baptism is a spiritual turning point in one's life; a baptized individual must never live the same as he or she did prior to baptism.

Clearly baptism is much more than just a ritual or ceremony. It marks a transformation from death to life; it is, spiritually, a matter of life and death.

*5. If we have been united with him like this in his death, we will certainly also be united with him in his resurrection.*

Jesus was buried and raised for us. And when we have surrendered to Jesus' lordship, after our *death* and burial in baptism, we will *be united with him in his resurrection*. Christian baptism is a demonstration or reenactment of the central facts of the gospel message as defined by Paul in 1 Corinthians 15:1-4 (the death, burial, and *resurrection* of Jesus). Baptism provides a wonderful opportunity to be like Jesus!

## WHAT DO YOU THINK?

If we are "dead to sin," why do so many of us struggle with temptation?

## HOW TO SAY IT

Arimathea. AIR-uh-muh-**THEE**-uh (TH as in THIN).

Elijah. Ee-**LYE**-juh.

Lazarus. **LAZ**-uh-rus.

Magdalene. **MAG**-duh-leen or Mag-duh-**LEE**-nee.

Nicodemus. NICK-uh-**DEE**-mus.

## C. FREED FROM SIN (vv. 6-11)

*6, 7. For we know that our old self was crucified with him so that the body of sin might be done away with, that we should no longer be slaves to sin—because anyone who has died has been freed from sin.*

In the remainder of this chapter and in chapters 7 and 8, Paul will continue to describe the ongoing battle in which Christians are engaged—a battle of which we are all keenly aware. As long as we live in this world, the fleshly part of us (the body) will be calling for attention; and that will be the part of us through which Satan will work the hardest to capture our allegiance and erode our faith.

Here the apostle insists that we do not take orders from *sin* anymore or from its headquarters. He uses the term *our old self* to describe the individual under sin's rule. But now that we are new creatures in Christ Jesus (2 Corinthians 5:17), we live under a new master, or by the "new self" (Ephesians 4:24). We are not *slaves to sin*. We serve a new master—Christ. We are not freed from temptation, but we are *freed from sin* as the controlling factor in our lives. God has also given us his Holy Spirit to equip us for the battle, and the Spirit is stronger than Satan (1 John 4:4). Sin will continue to entice, but now it has "met its match." The will to resist temptation operates only in the person in whom the Holy Spirit is at work.

*8. Now if we died with Christ, we believe that we will also live with him.*

Our symbolic death and burial in baptism illustrates our death to the old way of life—the time when we were living under the power of sin. Now we are dead to that; now we truly *live*, with *Christ* at the helm. That eternal life begins with our relationship with Christ (John 17:3), and it extends into eternity.

*9. For we know that since Christ was raised from the dead, he cannot die again; death no longer has mastery over him.*

Prior to Jesus, other individuals had been raised from the dead, such as the widow's son in the time of Elijah (1 Kings 17:17-24) and Lazarus (John 11:38-44). But these all eventually died again. *Christ was raised from the dead* to die no more. The Christian faces death knowing that it is a beaten enemy because of Jesus' resurrection. Thus what is true of Jesus is true of the Christian: *death no longer has mastery over him.*

*10. The death he died, he died to sin once for all; but the life he lives, he lives to God.*

When Jesus *died*, it appeared that *sin* had won. The enemies of truth rejoiced. But their celebration was short-lived. Christ's victory over the power of sin was decisive. Jesus' death does not need to be repeated; it happened *once for all* (Hebrews 9:24-28). Jesus now lives *to God*, dwelling with the Father as he did before laying aside his glory to come to earth.

*11. In the same way, count yourselves dead to sin but alive to God in Christ Jesus.*

As Christians we are *dead to sin*. Paul has already made that clear. But that is more than just a point of doctrine; we are to live like that—*alive to God*, alive in the presence of God, alive for God and his eternal purposes.

### "FREE" BUT STILL A PRISONER

J. C. Fuller declined his girlfriend's request that he go to church with her one Sunday morning in 1952. Instead, he went out drinking. Later that day his girlfriend saw him talking to another girl. They argued, and in his drunken state Fuller fired the shotgun he was carrying. He was arrested and convicted of attempted murder.

While in the middle of his four-year prison sentence, Fuller was on a work crew building a bridge. He saw poisonous cottonmouth snakes swimming in the stream where the crew was required to work. He was deathly afraid of snakes, so he complained to the guard, who shrugged and said with no sympathy, "There's the

Visual for lesson 4. *This visual can help reinforce the message of victory over death through Jesus' resurrection.*

*WHAT DO YOU THINK?*

*Whom do you know who exemplifies the phrase, "alive to God"? What can you learn from him or her about living for God?*

## PRAYER

*To the truths that we celebrate on this glorious day, our Father, we commit our lives. That you would permit your only begotten Son to be crucified for us is beyond our comprehension, but it is the reason for our profound gratitude. That you brought him back to life is the cause for our celebration. And that we shall live as children of life rather than as slaves of death is our commitment. In Jesus' name. Amen.*

## WHAT DO YOU THINK?

*What does it mean to have victory in Christ? What difference does this victory make in our lives—both now and in the future?*

road." The next morning Fuller took to the road and disappeared for forty-seven years. Early in 2000, a prison fugitive squad was reviewing old cases and tracked Fuller down. Because by then he was seventy-six years old, he was allowed to serve out the rest of his sentence with no penalty for his escape.

J. C. Fuller was never actually free from his wrongdoing, although he lived all those years without being confined in any prison. Nearly five decades were spent in a captivity of the spirit, knowing that the debt for his crime had never been paid. How different it is with us who know Christ! We are dead to sin—no longer under its control. We are alive to God, living under his dominion by the miracle of the grace he showed to us at the cross of Christ!     —C. R. B.

### D. CALLED TO RIGHTEOUSNESS (vv. 12-14)

**12. Therefore do not let sin reign in your mortal body so that you obey its evil desires.**

"Live according to who (and whose) you are," the apostle writes. You have been set free, so live as a free individual. You have become a child of God. You have an alternative to the path of *sin*. Sin no longer has to *reign* over you; through Christ you can reign over it.

**13. Do not offer the parts of your body to sin, as instruments of wickedness, but rather offer yourselves to God, as those who have been brought from death to life; and offer the parts of your body to him as instruments of righteousness.**

Christians live in the era between the moment that *God* dealt *sin* a deathblow through Jesus' death and resurrection and the final victory that will occur at Jesus' return. During this interval, we are to live under God's authority, reflecting the *righteousness* that he requires of his people (Ephesians 4:24).

Here Paul tells us that the *parts* of our *body* are not Satan's possession now; they are God's *instruments*. We are to use our eyes, our hands, our feet, our minds, and our mouths in a way that shows we are people *who have been brought from death to life*. That does not simply mean avoiding wicked uses of those features; it also means putting them to work to serve, to bless, and to draw others to the righteous God.

**14. For sin shall not be your master, because you are not under law, but under grace.**

This may be considered a summary of Paul's answer to the question raised in verse 1. We must not keep sinning, because *sin* is our former *master*. Although Paul has not mentioned the *law* yet in this section, the law is part of the reason for sin's mastery; it points out our sin. The problem is that the law cannot provide an answer to that mastery. It cannot free us from the guilt it produces. Only God's *grace* can supply what we need and solve our dilemma. By grace, death has been destroyed, sin's hold has been broken, and the law has been fulfilled through the perfect obedience of Jesus.

### CONCLUSION

One of God's commandments to Old Testament Israel was to remember the Sabbath and keep it holy—the seventh day, the day he rested from creation. It was to be a day for worship and for rest. God knew that both were essential for an effective, obedient life. The Sabbath principle is still vital to observe. Our bodies, minds, and spirits still need worship and rest.

So why do we Christians worship on Sunday instead of Saturday? Because it is the resurrection day! Through Jesus' death and resurrection, a New Covenant with God has been established. He was raised for us, and we shall be raised with him. The empty tomb has opened up the fullness of Heaven. The church is a place of *life*, and that life is in Christ.

## THOUGHT TO REMEMBER

*"Because I live, you also will live"* (John 14:19).

# Discovery Learning

*This page contains an alternative lesson plan emphasizing learning activities. Classes desiring such student involvement will find these suggestions helpful. The next page is a reproducible activity page to further enhance discovery learning.*

## LEARNING GOALS

After this lesson a student should be able to:

1. Recount the events of resurrection morning, and tell how that event is "replayed" every time a believer is baptized.

2. Contrast the life of sin with the "resurrected" life of the believer raised to "walk in newness of life."

3. Use poetry, art, or music to celebrate the victory over death that we have because of Jesus.

## INTO THE LESSON

Display this caption: "Nothing There—Good or Bad?" Bring several empty containers, such as an opaque two-liter bottle, a cereal box, a shoebox, and a paper bag. Say, "Empty objects like these seem to promise something, but do not deliver. Ask the group to make two lists: one, of items whose emptiness is associated with something bad, and the second, of items whose emptiness suggests something good. For the former list, such items as a car's fuel tank, a depleted bank account, a burglarized home, or a computer's hard drive may be suggested. The latter list may be a bit more difficult to compile, but such items as a completed regimen of oral medication, garbage cans at the end of pick-up day, and a dry basement after heavy rains may be suggested. (Consider prompting class members for this second list by asking, "When are the times that you are happy to find nothing when something bad could be there?") As the discussion ensues, someone may suggest Christ's empty tomb. That is the item you should add to the list, if no one does.

## INTO THE WORD

As learners look at John 20:1-10, designate three sections of the class to be the Mary group, the Peter group, and the John group. As you read the following "clues," ask the appropriate group to stand after each. (1) "I stood at the empty tomb . . . and ran away." (2) "I stood at the empty tomb . . . and looked in but did not enter right away." (3) "I stood at the empty tomb . . . and rushed right in." (4) "I stood at the empty tomb . . . first of all the followers of Jesus to do so." (5) "I stood at the empty tomb . . . and thought the body of Jesus had been stolen." (6) "I stood at the empty tomb . . . ahead of a slower disciple." (7) "I stood at the empty tomb . . . and saw Jesus' empty burial clothes."

(8) "I stood at the empty tomb . . . and was the second to go in." (9) "I stood at the empty tomb . . . and immediately understood the Scripture that Jesus had to rise from the dead." Groups that should stand are as follows: 1—Mary; 2—John; 3—Peter; 4—Mary; 5—Mary; 6—John; 7—John, Peter; 8—John; 9—no one stands; see verse 9. (A similar activity is included in the student book.)

Say, "Most of us have seen the old frontier 'Wanted' posters that read 'Dead or Alive.' Paul's words in Romans 6:1-14 are directed to Christians and may be summarized: 'Wanted: Dead *and* Alive!'" Ask your learners to scan that text quickly and make a count of the number of times *dead* (and derivatives) and *live* (and derivatives) appear. (They should find more than ten for *dead* and about eight for *live*.) Once several indicate their count, ask, "How is it that we as Christians are both dead and alive?"

After a discussion that includes references to the text, have two class members pantomime a baptismal scene of one lowering the other into and out of the water. Afterward, ask, "How is the early church's practice of baptism (immersion) a perfect picture of the Christian's dying to sin and being resurrected to new life?" Such elements as submission and humility, stopping one's breathing, being washed/cleansed, beginning one's breathing again, and others may be suggested.

## INTO LIFE

The reproducible page that follows has an activity entitled "Dead in the Water." It calls for the learner to write an epitaph for himself or herself based on Romans 6:1-14.

Direct attention once again to the text from Romans 6, and assign the learners to compose an appropriate epitaph for their tombstones. Give an example or two, such as, "Raised up from the dead; By Jesus I'm led" and "Buried with Christ ____(date)____; Made Alive with Him ____(date)____."

Choose a familiar hymn or gospel song dealing with our new life in Christ, and have a musical class member lead in singing it. Such songs as "Because He Lives" by the Gaithers, "Christ the Lord Is Risen Today" (especially the stanza beginning, "Soar we now, where Christ has led"), "Buried With Christ" by Ryder and Kirkpatrick, or another your class enjoys may be used.

# Dead in the Water

As Paul reflects, "All of us who were baptized into Christ Jesus were baptized into his death" (Romans 6:3). Examine Romans 6:1-14, write in your name on the "tombstone" below, and write an epitaph for yourself in some way related to those verses.

# Resurrection Realities

The verse preceding today's text reads, "As sin reigned in death, so also grace might reign through righteousness to bring eternal life through Jesus Christ our Lord" (Romans 5:21). Paul's development of ideas in today's text in Romans 6:1-14 is in support of that truth: sin ends in death; grace allows eternal life. Under each of the headings below, write some of the sad realities of living a life in sin and the resurrection realities of new life in Christ.

SIN RESULTS IN DEATH                    GRACE RESULTS IN LIFE

---

# LIVE BY THE SPIRIT

## WHY TEACH THIS LESSON?

Empowerment is a trendy buzzword in healthcare, business, and the social sciences. Simply stated, to be empowered is to be equipped with the tools, resources, knowledge, energy, and/or authority to get one's goals accomplished.

This lesson declares the Christian is enabled, wired, and empowered for victory over sin. The Holy Spirit empowers us with everything we need.

Many experience significant inner struggle after accepting Christ. While this might seem upsetting, it is proof that there are now two natures warring within. This lesson should help us be sensitive to this spiritual battle, while providing comfort that we are no longer slaves to the flesh. It should help us to acknowledge the Spirit's work in us, always showing us God's way. Finally, it should encourage us to grow more sensitive to his leading.

## INTRODUCTION

### A. IT'S NO CARTOON

Those of us who read the comic pages in the newspaper every morning have developed our favorites over the years. One of the great favorites from yesteryear for this writer was "Priscilla's Pop." The lingering image that comes to mind is young Priscilla (who is eight to ten years old) listening to a little angel on one shoulder debate with a little devil on the other shoulder. Most of us can readily relate to such an image. For Christians, it should bring to mind Paul's words about the tug-of-war that we experience between the flesh and the Spirit. In this case, it's no cartoon and nothing to laugh about.

How can we learn to listen to the right message and stand on the right side? That's what today's lesson will help us understand.

### B. LESSON BACKGROUND

Last week we read a portion of John's record of resurrection morning. The dawning of a new day brought the dawning of a new era of life and hope by virtue of Jesus' resurrection. Such news should put a spring in our step, as it did for Mary Magdalene, Peter, and John, all of whom started running when confronted with the astonishing (but true!) news of an empty tomb. Then we read Paul's words in Romans 6, challenging all Christians to live as resurrected people. We don't live under sin's control anymore. Being alive unto God and to righteous living is now the order of the day. Christian baptism is the landmark event that dramatizes the change from death to life by the picture of being buried in and then emerging from water.

As we proceed in our study of Romans, we see Paul continuing to contrast the old life under sin and the law with the new life in Christ. In particular, he focuses on the ongoing tension between those two paths experienced by himself (and all of us). This leads to the frank and challenging comments in our text from Romans 8.

A brief word is in order concerning Paul's teaching in Romans 7, especially verses 7-25. Is Paul relating his experience before or after becoming a Christian?

DEVOTIONAL READING:
*ROMANS 7:1-6*
BACKGROUND SCRIPTURE:
*ROMANS 8:1-17*
PRINTED TEXT:
*ROMANS 8:1-17*

Apr
3

### LESSON AIMS

After participating in this lesson, a student should be able to:

1. Tell how Paul contrasts the life lived in the flesh with one lived in the Spirit.

2. Cite contemporary evidence of living in the flesh and living in the Spirit.

3. Identify a compulsive or addictive behavior that interferes with his or her life in the Spirit, and commit to greater submission to the Spirit in that area of life.

### KEY VERSE

Those who are led by the Spirit of God are sons of God.
—Romans 8:14

LESSON 5 NOTES

It is probably best to see these verses as a description of Paul's (and the Christian's) continual struggle with the sin factor following conversion. That struggle—the issue of whether sin or righteousness should "reign" in our lives—is introduced in Romans 6:12. At the end of chapter 7, Paul expresses the intensity of the struggle in these words: "What a wretched man I am! Who will rescue me from this body of death? Thanks be to God—through Jesus Christ our Lord! So then, I myself in my mind am a slave to God's law, but in the sinful nature a slave to the law of sin" (Romans 7:24, 25). In Romans 8 Paul elaborates on the deliverance offered to us in Christ.

## I. WAY TO FREEDOM AND LIFE (ROMANS 8:1-8)

### A. IN CHRIST JESUS (vv. 1, 2)

**1. Therefore, there is now no condemnation for those who are in Christ Jesus,**

God has solved what we cannot solve. God has paid a price that we cannot and could never pay. His Son took the *condemnation* that we deserved because of our sin. Even though our past is shot through with inconsistencies and failures, even though our present practice is imperfect, and even though we can count on facing Satan's "fiery darts" in the future, *there is now no condemnation*—because we *are in Christ Jesus*.

To be in Christ, however, involves more than just a position or standing. To accept Christ as Savior marks the beginning of a process of growth.

**2. . . . because through Christ Jesus the law of the Spirit of life set me free from the law of sin and death.**

A new *law* is at work in the Christian. This law is not loaded with restrictions, prescriptions, accusations, or condemnations. It offers *life*, not death—including possibilities, opportunities, freedom from *sin and death,* and help through God's Spirit.

### B. NOT IN LAW AND FLESH (vv. 3-8)

**3. For what the law was powerless to do in that it was weakened by the sinful nature, God did by sending his own Son in the likeness of sinful man to be a sin offering. And so he condemned sin in sinful man,**

The law called people to obedience. It pointed out failures, but it provided no forgiveness for those failures and no power to do better. The law itself was good; in fact, Paul calls it "holy" in Romans 7:12. But it was *weak through the flesh*. Humanity has not been able to keep the standards set forth in the law. And the flesh always pulls us in the opposite direction from that established by God's law.

God addressed the law's failure by *sending his own Son in the likeness of sinful flesh*. "The Word was made flesh" (John 1:14) but came only in the *likeness* of sinful flesh. Jesus had a human body, but Jesus controlled that body and did not allow the flesh to become the starting point for sin (as we have done). His perfection qualified him to become the sacrifice at the cross for those who had sinned (all humanity). Thus God *condemned* our *sin in the flesh* of Jesus. Then God brought Jesus back to life. Sin, death, and the flesh were defeated.

**4. . . . in order that the righteous requirements of the law might be fully met in us, who do not live according to the sinful nature but according to the Spirit.**

On our own, we could never fulfill *the righteous requirements of the law*. Jesus did so—first, by keeping the law perfectly, and, second, by suffering the punishment of death that the law required of lawbreakers (again, describing all human beings). Those who accept Christ as Savior accept his death on their behalf and are thereby viewed as righteous by God. "God made him who had no sin to be sin for us, so that in him we might become the righteousness of God" (2 Co-

WHAT DO YOU THINK?

How does a law of life differ from a law of death? What difference does the awareness of this make in your own life?

WHAT DO YOU THINK?

Since the law came from God, why was it not sufficient to save us? Why did Jesus have to die? What does that death mean for us?

rinthians 5:21). But as noted earlier, to be in Christ is more than a position. Here Paul encourages those in Christ not to *live according to the sinful nature but according to the Spirit*. Thus the law is *fully met in us* who live under the control of the Holy Spirit.

*5. Those who live according to the sinful nature have their minds set on what that nature desires; but those who live in accordance with the Spirit have their minds set on what the Spirit desires.*

So many people in our world today invest their lives in the immediate. They live for the moment. They take orders from their impulses and their appetites. Consequences mean little or nothing to them. To *have their minds set on what* their *nature desires* is to follow the standard of conduct described so clearly by the apostle John: "For everything in the world—the cravings of sinful man, the lust of his eyes and he boasting of what he has and does—comes not from the Father but from the world" (1 John 2:16). The flesh conveys a signal, and if we are committed only to this world and to the moment, we rush to obey that signal. But when the *Spirit* of God is actively working in us, we are receiving input from another "signal." And we must listen to that which is higher and permanent, not that which is lower and temporary.

*6. The mind of sinful man is death, but the mind controlled by the Spirit is life and peace;*

It is important that we know the consequences of having a sinful *mind*. If we take orders from our sinful nature, *death* will be the unavoidable result. Death is primarily separation from God; therefore it includes not only physical death but also spiritual death in sin. But if we take orders from God's *Spirit*, we will share the quality and quantity of *life* in the Spirit. Which will it be—death or life, torment or *peace?* Whose orders will we follow? Which signal will we heed?

*7. . . . the sinful mind is hostile to God. It does not submit to God's law, nor can it do so.*

All we have to do is read again the Ten Commandments that God gave his people through Moses to see the contrast between *the sinful mind* and *God's law*. When one submits to the sinful nature, he or she is not subject to God but is God's enemy.

The warning against being driven by the flesh does not mean that all of our physical requirements or interests are evil. God created us. And he made life to be enjoyed. But it is clear that some appetites are in opposition to the will of God and that even the good appetites or desires can be abused by someone who does not honor God and his law.

*8. Those controlled by the sinful nature cannot please God.*

Later in this letter, Paul writes the following: "Therefore, I urge you, brothers, in view of God's mercy, to offer your bodies as living sacrifices, holy and pleasing to God—this is your spiritual act of worship" (Romans 12:1). We *please God* when we present our bodies for his use, not when we let fleshly desires control how we use our bodies.

### THE PRICE OF LIVING IN THE FLESH

A complaint Muslims have directed at those of us in the Western world in recent years is that we are exporting a fleshly, materialistic message through the television programs that all too many love to watch. (It seems there are two extremes involved here: one culture has few restrictions on what it allows people to do to express themselves; the other is highly repressive of any kind of individual expression.) Nevertheless, it's no secret that Westerners live in a worldly, sensuous culture.

*WHAT DO YOU THINK?*

*What are some "things of the sinful nature"? What are some "things of the Spirit"? How can we tell the difference?*

*[Hint: see Galatians 5:19-23.]*

*WHAT DO YOU THINK?*

*What is a good life? Can you live a truly good life without God's Spirit?*

*WHAT DO YOU THINK?*

*Why is it impossible to please God "in the flesh"? What about those who believe they are "good enough" or that God will not punish people who live a moral life?*

## HOW TO SAY IT

*Abba.* AB-buh.

*Aramaic.* AIR-uh-MAY-ik.

Advocates of personal freedom sometimes miss the point that freedom calls for responsibility. For example, Erika Harold—Miss America 2003—was roundly criticized for advocating sexual abstinence for young people. The pageant was caught in the bind of hypocrisy: in previous years one winner had been forced to resign because she had posed for revealing photos in a popular men's magazine; another resigned under pressure after a former boyfriend claimed to have seminude photos of her. This prompted one observer to ask about the 2003 pageant, "Who would have thought a virtuous winner would be censured for her virtue?"

Western culture seems to be schizophrenic on moral matters. While wanting freedom to do as they please, most people don't want to pay the price that living for the sinful nature always exacts. The ultimate price is death, because the flesh sets itself against God, who is the only source of life.    —C. R. B.

## II. WALK OF FREEDOM AND LIFE (ROMANS 8:9-14)

### A. IN DEBT TO THE SPIRIT (vv. 9-11)

**9. You, however, are controlled not by the sinful nature but by the Spirit, if the Spirit of God lives in you. And if anyone does not have the Spirit of Christ, he does not belong to Christ.**

Again, Paul highlights the contrast between being *controlled* by a *sinful nature* and *by the Spirit*. Christians, by virtue of their alignment with *Christ* and the "new life" that they have been given (Romans 6:4), are not flesh-guided people. "You have the *Spirit of God* in you," says Paul. So we must take our cues from the Spirit, not from the flesh. If we are controlled our sinful nature, we are not of Christ. If we are guided by the Spirit, we show that we are His; and we witness to others of the difference our faith makes.

"Are you for me or against me?" God would ask. We can't sit on the fence, and we can't have it both ways. Flesh or Spirit?

Let us also notice the word *you.* This word is a second person plural in the Greek text. The business of the Christian walk, of living with Christ in us, is carried out in a fellowship of believers. In fact, in the first Corinthian letter Paul writes, "Don't you know that you yourselves are God's temple and that God's Spirit lives in you?" (1 Corinthians 3:16). The Spirit of God energizes the individual believer, and the Spirit of God energizes the church.

Have you noticed in this passage how Paul refers to the Holy Spirit as the Spirit of life, the Spirit of God, the Spirit of Christ, and later as the Spirit of sonship (v. 15)? Don't be stymied by these different names. With each one Paul refers to the holy presence whom God gives to each Christian. The same divine person is described each time.

**10. But if Christ is in you, your body is dead because of sin, yet your spirit is alive because of righteousness.**

Here the apostle makes the same point in a slightly different way. The Christian's *body* will die *because of sin.* But because of God's grace and because the *righteousness* of Christ has covered our sins, the result is that the Christian's *spirit is alive.* It should be noted that some have suggested that the word *spirit* does not refer to the human spirit but to the Holy Spirit. The *King James Version* gives another possible way to interpret Paul's words in this regard. (The Greek word translated *spirit* is not capitalized, even when it refers to the Holy Spirit.)

**11. And if the Spirit of him who raised Jesus from the dead is living in you, he who raised Christ from the dead will also give life to your mortal bodies through his Spirit, who lives in you.**

The death of the body, mentioned in the previous verse, is not the last word on the subject. The same Holy *Spirit* who lives in us and empowers us spiritually will also *give life* to our *bodies*. The Spirit's presence in us now is considered a "deposit" of greater blessings to come (2 Corinthians 1:21, 22; Ephesians 1:13, 14).

## B. NO DEBT TO THE FLESH (vv. 12-14)

**12. Therefore, brothers, we have an obligation—but it is not to the sinful nature, to live according to it.**

We don't owe our *sinful nature* anything. When our fleshly appetites scream for our attention, they don't have to be fed. They must be evaluated in light of our higher, spiritual citizenship. Satisfying them may be acceptable, or it may be improper to do so. The Holy Spirit provides the Christian the power to say no to those cries of the body that it would be sinful for us to satisfy. We *have an obligation* to God who has provided us with such power.

**13, 14. For if you live according to the sinful nature, you will die; but if by the Spirit you put to death the misdeeds of the body, you will live, because those who are led by the Spirit of God are sons of God.**

To *live according to the sinful nature* is a path to certain death—spiritually, physically, and eternally. What we must do is *put to death*, or kill, *the misdeeds of the body*, meaning those deeds that reflect the influence of the flesh. Accepting the Spirit's guidance indicates our status as *sons of God*.

It should be clear that at some point all of us must face the harsh reality of death. The key question is when we shall do this. Through Jesus we can address it now, by dying to sin and putting to death the deeds of the flesh, so that we can receive abundant and eternal life. If we fail to address it now, we will remain spiritually dead in our sins and we will face physical death without the hope available in Christ.

## III. PROMISE OF FREEDOM AND LIFE (ROMANS 8:15-17)

### A. ADOPTION AS SONS (vv. 15, 16)

**15. For you did not receive a spirit that makes you a slave again to fear, but you received the Spirit of sonship. And by him we cry, "Abba, Father."**

The Aramaic word *Abba* is rather close to our very familiar and warm "Daddy." Jesus addressed his *Father* in this manner (Mark 14:36). Through Jesus we are made heirs to a magnificent inheritance, for we have been adopted into the Father's family. In a sense we are slaves, or servants, as Paul says in Romans 6:16-22. But that servanthood is offered willingly on our part as Christians, in gratitude to the Lord for all he has done for us in Christ. The motivation is love, not *fear*.

#### WANTED! (IN THE BEST SENSE OF THE WORD)

Key in the word *adoption* in an Internet search engine and about a tenth of a second later you are likely to get nearly eight million Web sites! There are sites for "adopting" such creatures as fairies, centaurs, mermaids, pegacorns—a combination of the mythical unicorn and the winged-horse Pegasus—and other imaginary creatures. Many other sites give information about subjects of more worthwhile adoptions such as abandoned animals.

One of the ironies of contemporary culture is the vocal group of people who show more concern for mythical creatures and abandoned animals than they do for unwanted children! During the "abortion wars" of the last few decades, those involved in the debate have sometimes acted as if the only issue were whether a baby (or "product of conception," depending on one's position on the subject) is killed or carried to full term. Even though many thoughtful people have advocated adoption as an alternative to abortion, the heated rhetoric on both sides has occasionally obscured the quiet voice of reason.

WHAT DO YOU THINK?

*How does one "put to death" the flesh? Is the practice of certain individuals in church history who beat themselves to remove impure thoughts an appropriate example for us?*

Visual for lessons 5, 11. *Use today's visual when focusing on the freedom Jesus gives us from sin and death.*

## PRAYER

*Forgive us, Father, when we boast of anything except the cross of our Lord Jesus Christ. Accept our joyful gratitude that comes from knowing that he has paid the debt we owed. Help us understand what it means to live as debtors to the Spirit, not the flesh. May we do away with any "interference" that keeps the Spirit's signal from being heard. In Jesus' name. Amen.*

The fact is, a multitude of potential parents would love to adopt someone else's unwanted child. Such people are demonstrating God's kind of love: we may be lost, fearful of the future, unwanted, or unloved by family or friends who should care for us, but God will graciously adopt us into the wonderful warmth of his spiritual family.

—C. R. B.

### 16. The Spirit himself testifies with our spirit that we are God's children.

When we cry "Abba, Father," we testify that we recognize God as our Father and ourselves as *God's children*. God's *Spirit* confirms this by testifying *with our spirit*. Two possible interpretations of this verse have been suggested. Some believe we are to allow the Holy Spirit to be in clear and constant communication with our spirits, as we eagerly submit to his shaping of our attitudes, our words, and our walk. Others see the Spirit's witness as directed toward the Father, similar to the intercession that he makes for us before God, according to Romans 8:26, 27.

### B. JOINT-HEIRS WITH CHRIST (v. 17)

### 17. Now if we are children, then we are heirs—heirs of God and co-heirs with Christ, if indeed we share in his sufferings in order that we may also share in his glory.

Here Paul raises the possibility that we may suffer for Christ's sake. Certainly that was true for some of the Christians in Rome. It was true for Paul. It is true for many Christians today—in the Western world as well as in other countries. Paul encourages us to keep the "big picture" in mind: we are *heirs of God and co-heirs with Christ*. The path of suffering ends with sharing with Christ *in his glory* and with all who have traveled the same path.

In his commentary on the book of Romans in the *Standard Bible Studies* series, Bruce Shields has a keen insight into this promise that as heirs we shall be glorified:

"*Glory* refers to the image of God in which Adam was created, the glory Adam lost as a result of the fall, the glory of God, which each sinner lacks (Romans 3:23), the glory of the life that Jesus led, and the glory for which we may hope (Romans 5:2). Thus Paul, with this promise of glorification, reaches back to original creation, deals with the reality of new creation, and looks forward to the restoration of God's purpose in creation—a restoration that awaits the final judgment" (Bruce Shields, *Romans*, Standard Publishing, 1988, p. 99).

## CONCLUSION

Our role in this business of life is not to take the "lead" part. That is the role the devil wants us to think we are taking, when in reality he is calling the shots. The devil is stronger than we are. He seeks to set up headquarters in our flesh. He desires to take our God-given appetites and twist them to accomplish his evil ends. He's like the little demon on the shoulder of the cartoon character Priscilla (mentioned in the Introduction), using persuasive words and attractive images to turn her head his way.

God, however, is far stronger than the devil. And he has put in place a plan for our redemption. He has done all of the grace-founded work to make it possible. The devil still harasses us, but the "angel" on the shoulder of the Christian is the Holy Spirit. This means that as a Christian, I am the weakest party in this situation, yet the exercise of my will determines the outcome. God is already the winner, by virtue of the death and resurrection of Jesus. But he has so limited himself, through a free will that he has given me, that I must decide to let the winner win. It may sound strange, but the pathway to victory lies in surrender.

## THOUGHT TO REMEMBER

*Jesus gave up his glory and put on flesh so that we could conquer the flesh and share in his glory.*

# Discovery Learning

*This page contains an alternative lesson plan emphasizing learning activities. Classes desiring such student involvement will find these suggestions helpful. The next page is a reproducible activity page to further enhance discovery learning.*

## LEARNING GOALS

After completing this lesson, a student should be able to:

1. Tell how Paul contrasts the life lived in the flesh with one lived in the Spirit.

2. Cite contemporary evidence of living in the flesh and living in the Spirit.

3. Identify a compulsive or addictive behavior that interferes with his or her life in the Spirit, and commit to greater submission to the Spirit in that area of life.

## INTO THE LESSON

Buy and bring enough of the following stickers to class to allow you to give one of each to each learner: one, a sticker of an angel; two, a sticker of a small imp or devil. Have an angel sticker stuck to one of your own shoulders; have a devil sticker stuck to the other. Direct everyone to follow your example with the stickers they have received. Recruit a good reader to read aloud the following short poem: "Got the devil on your shoulder?/ Hear him whisper in your ear?/ Can you tell he is a-lying?/ Do you know it's right to fear?/ He says, 's'Better, child, it's better,/ Than the burden God will lay/ On your shoulder: heavy, hurting;/ Better, better, child, I s-s-s-say!'/ Got the devil on your shoulder?/ Hear him shouting in your ear?/ Can you tell he is a-lying?/ Do you know it's right to fear?"

Use the lesson commentator's introductory paragraph, "It's No Cartoon," to lead to the study of today's text from Romans 8.

## INTO THE WORD

Recruit a person to don Roman-style clothing and a prisoner's shackles to play the role of Paul for a monologue, using Romans 7:14-25. This text, preceding today's printed text, is Paul's very personal statement of the deep spiritual tension that all Christians experience. If your actor can memorize the passage and deliver it passionately, so much the better.

Once that text has been presented, introduce the following activity that you will entitle, "Split Personality." Divide a letter-size sheet of paper into two vertical halves and six left and six right sections. Write the following words randomly into the twelve resulting rectangles, one word per area: *alive, sinful, child, condemned, obligation, enemy, freed, friend, heir, slave, spirit, weak.* Make a copy of this sheet for each learner and distribute the copies. Then give this direction: "Fold and tear apart the sections of this sheet. In the hand on the side where you have the devil/imp sticker stuck to your shoulder, hold the six terms the devil is 'whispering in your ear.' In the other hand, hold the ones your 'angel' is encouraging you to be." (If you are not using the stickers, simply specify left and right.)

Once the learners have had the opportunity to tear their paper and decide where to place the pieces, tell them you are going to read today's text and that as you do they should pull out appropriate words from their stacks. For example, after reading verses one and two, the appropriate words to be drawn are *condemned* and *freed.* Say something to this effect: "The devil's side keeps reminding us that we are sinners through and through and that we don't stand a chance. But the Spirit's side affirms that we are free!" Using the labels will help the class members focus as you deal with the basic principles of the text, employing notes from the commentary.

## INTO LIFE

Many adults include walking in their daily exercise regimen. Give learners a copy of this list of seven "daily walking mottoes" to quote to themselves—one per day for the next week. (These can be used by learners even if they do not engage in any kind of walking activity.) (1) Though I have sin in my life, today I walk without the condemnation of sin; (2) Though I have aches and pains, today I walk free from the law of sin and death; (3) Though my mind keeps drifting to the needs of my physical body, I walk thinking of the things of the Spirit; (4) Though death is sure and true, I walk alive in the Spirit of righteousness; (5) Though fears and fearful things surround me, I walk as a child of God, not a slave of fear; (6) Though I may share in the sufferings of my Lord, I walk also in his glory; (7) Though others I pass may walk with the burden of sin, I walk free in Christ Jesus.

When each learner has a copy, read the list antiphonally; that is, you read the "Though" clause of each, and ask the class to read the "I walk" clause in unison. Suggest that the learners modify the wording to make a rhythm as they walk, possibly creating a simple tune for each grand truth.

# Me *vs.* Me

Today's text in Romans 8 is about the internal conflict we all face because the lure of sin in the world is strong, even for those who have the indwelling Spirit. Fill in some of the personal conflicts that challenge your spiritual wholeness. Use the stimulus statement given to fill in the "two sides" of your person.

I WANT TO . . . ,                    BUT I FIND MYSELF. . . .

# Either/Or

Certain truths are mutually exclusive; that means that either one thing is true or the other, but not both. From today's text in Romans 8:1-17, decide what the "either/or" is in each of the following. Do not simply complete the statements with the words "not" or "does not"—put some real substance in your answers!

Either I am still condemned by God, or because of Jesus I am. . . .

Either a person has his or her mind set on the things the fleshly nature desires, or. . . .

One is either controlled by the nature of the flesh, or. . . .

Either one has the Spirit of Christ, or. . . .

One has either an obligation to live according to the "sinful nature," or. . . .

Either we have received a spirit that makes us a slave to fear, or. . . .

Either we are children of God, or. . . .

# FIND SALVATION IN CHRIST

### LESSON 6

## WHY TEACH THIS LESSON?

I admit it. Even as a child I was a bit disappointed at the ending to *The Wizard of Oz*. Oh, yes, it's a great film. But I felt somewhat cheated. After the harrowing journey through peril after mortal peril, with each character facing their greatest fears and challenges, Dorothy only had to click her heels to get back home. She never even had to leave Munchkinland!

Today's lesson leads us to the same dilemma with simplicity. We don't have to follow thousands of rules, laws, and codes flawlessly. We don't have to scale mountains or make pilgrimages. Jesus did the saving work on the cross. The key to eternal life has always been as close as our decision to accept him.

The next compelling message of the lesson is this: we must tell others we see along the way that their wizards are fake and that the road home is an easy one. When you're looking forward to Heaven, "There's no place like home."

## INTRODUCTION

### A. THE RIGHT QUESTION

The jailer in the city of Philippi surely had heard what was being said over the "grapevine" about Paul and Silas and about the impact of their preaching. Then he found himself personally involved with these two men after they had cast the fortune-telling demon from the slave girl, were accused of causing social chaos by the owners of the girl, and were stripped and beaten. After the jailer had done his duty, placing Paul and Silas in an inner cell and fastening their feet in the stocks, he probably figured he was finished with them.

Then came the earthquake at midnight. When the jailer saw that the prison doors all were opened, he thought the prisoners had fled, putting his own life in great jeopardy. Then when he realized that no one had escaped, he seems to have been overwhelmed with a sense that what he was witnessing was not a natural occurrence. There was something or someone divine at work. Perhaps the jailer realized that he needed to know more about the message Paul and Silas had been preaching. "Sirs, what must I do to be saved?" he asked (Acts 16:30). He could not have asked a more important question!

In our text for today from Romans 10, Paul says that the "righteousness that is by faith" does not ask questions such as "Who will ascend into heaven?" to bring Christ down, or "Who will descend into the deep?" to bring Christ from the dead (vv. 6, 7). It is not by any mighty deeds of ours that we become right with God. It is only by the "mighty deeds" of Christ's death and resurrection that we are saved. It is not our place to suggest what we should do to be saved; it is our place to follow the plan established by God. The jailer's question revealed a searching mind. Paul and Silas were happy to provide the answer, and later the jailer and his household were baptized (Acts 16:31-34).

### B. LESSON BACKGROUND

In last week's study from Romans 8, we considered the ongoing battle that Christians face between the flesh and the Holy Spirit, who enables us to over-

DEVOTIONAL READING:
HEBREWS 5:5-10
BACKGROUND SCRIPTURE:
ROMANS 10:5-21
PRINTED TEXT:
ROMANS 10:5-17

## LESSON AIMS

After this lesson a student should be able to:

Apr
10

1. Tell what Paul means when he concludes, "Faith comes from hearing the message, and the message is heard through the word of Christ."

2. Explain the importance of confessing faith as it relates to one's own salvation and to the salvation of others.

3. Prepare a personal testimony about what it means to be saved.

## KEY VERSE

If you confess with your mouth, "Jesus is Lord," and believe in your heart that God raised him from the dead, you will be saved.    —Romans 10:9

*LESSON 6 NOTES*

come the flesh. Paul reminded us that the law plays a prominent part in our sin problem, in that the law points out our sins and makes them abundantly clear. The law, however, offers no solution to the guilt it creates. That solution is found only in Christ.

In the rest of chapter 8 (not covered last week), Paul continues to focus on the blessings provided through our relationship with Christ. He especially highlights the assurance of final victory over the fallen sinful world, proclaiming that we are "more than conquerors through him who loved us" (Romans 8:37).

In chapter 9 Paul introduces a new theme in his letter—the place of the Jews in God's redemptive plan. His discussion springs from his personal passion for his people (he calls the Jews his "brothers" and "those of [his] own race" in verse 3) and his desire that they know the Christ who has done so much for him (Romans 9:1-5). That concern continues in chapter 10, which begins with Paul writing, "Brothers, my heart's desire and prayer to God for the Israelites is that they may be saved" (v. 1). The apostle describes them as zealous, yet lacking knowledge. Their desire to follow the law of Moses and thus pursue righteousness that is "their own" (v. 3) is ill-founded, now that "Christ is the end of the law so that there may be righteousness for everyone who believes" (v. 4). A new way, the way of salvation by grace through faith, is now open for all to accept, but, sadly, many of Paul's kinsmen have rejected it.

Paul proceeds to contrast the righteousness based on keeping the law with the righteousness available through faith. He shows that the way of faith in Christ is the way by which both Jew and Gentile must come to God. He also challenges Christians to accept the responsibility for making that message known so that others may call on the name of the Lord and be saved.

## I. KEEPING THE LAW (ROMANS 10:5-7)

### A. MOSES' WORDS ON LAW (v. 5)

5. *Moses describes in this way the righteousness that is by the law: "The man who does these things will live by them."*

There are only two potential ways to obtain *righteousness*, or a right standing with God: law-keeping and grace through faith. *Moses* is recognized as Israel's lawgiver. So it is fitting to cite him as an authority on law-keeping.

The passage Paul uses is from Leviticus 18:5: "the man who obeys them will live by them." In other words, with the principle of righteousness by law-keeping the responsibility is squarely ours. If one should obey every aspect of the law, then he or she would be right with God. But that *if* is huge! In fact, Paul has shown earlier that no one can be justified through keeping the law (Romans 3:20).

### B. MOSES' WORDS ON FAITH (vv. 6, 7)

6, 7. *But the righteousness that is by faith says: "Do not say in your heart, 'Who will ascend into heaven?'" (that is, to bring Christ down) "or 'Who will descend into the deep?'" (that is, to bring Christ up from the dead).*

Now Paul describes *the righteousness that is by faith*. In so doing he quotes from Deuteronomy 30:12-14 (which is included in verses 6-8 of our text). He pictures someone trying to *ascend into heaven* in order to *bring Christ down* from above or making an attempt to *descend into the deep* in order to *bring Christ up*. It should be noted that Paul's citation varies somewhat from the words in Deuteronomy, which speak of going "beyond the sea" rather than *into the deep* to bring someone back from the dead. Paul should be seen as giving an inspired interpretation of Moses' words and applying them to a New Covenant setting. His desire is to show that the righteousness obtained by faith is not based on our deeds. Even if we could perform heroic deeds such as those described in these verses, that would not be enough to gain right standing with God.

Some Bible commentators have noted the significance of Paul's use of the book of Deuteronomy to make his case for righteousness by faith. Moses spoke the words of Deuteronomy when the Israelites were on the brink of entering the promised land. He wanted to impress upon the people the covenant that God had made with them. Here in Romans, Paul desires to impress upon his Jewish readers the New Covenant that God has established. Just as God brought his word to Israel through Moses (see Deuteronomy 30:11-14), God now has brought his living Word through Jesus Christ, whom Paul has already declared to be "the end of the law" (Romans 10:4).

Thus it is not by human good works or devoted efforts that righteousness with God is obtained. Salvation is not the result of our perfection or hard work. Salvation is the result of Christ's perfection and God's work through him on our behalf. Indeed, we do not have to bring *Christ down*; he has already come. Nor do we have to bring him *up* from the grave; God has done that (Romans 8:11).

## II. LIVING BY FAITH (ROMANS 10:8-13)

### A. AN AFFIRMING FAITH (vv. 8-10)

**8. But what does it say? "The word is near you; it is in your mouth and in your heart," that is, the word of faith we are proclaiming:**

Here is the difference between the way of law keeping (works) and the way of *faith*. We do not have to travel to a distant realm and accomplish daring feats in order to impress God. *The word is near you; it is in your mouth and in your heart.* The message is close to us and ready to be accepted—if we respond in faith. Salvation is not a matter of trying through our own efforts to reach God; it is accepting God's love that is offered to us. Righteousness is received, not achieved.

**9. That if you confess with your mouth, "Jesus is Lord," and believe in your heart that God raised him from the dead, you will be saved.**

This verse calls to mind what Jesus said about the importance of confessing him before others (Matthew 10:32, 33). On the basis of this emphasis, many churches ask those who desire to accept Christ to express a "confession" of *Jesus as Lord*. In some cases, a person is asked to repeat a statement of faith in Jesus; in others, people are asked to express their faith in their own words. It should be noted that the declaration "Jesus is Lord" was a pivotal part of Christian confession and belief early in the history of the church.

Notice the requirement of both an external response (confessing the Lord Jesus) and an internal one (believing in one's *heart*). These should not be considered works to earn righteousness, but expressions of faith that accept the righteousness God is eager to give.

Consider also that Paul is addressing Christians who are living in a pagan context. It isn't always easy to confess Christ in such a setting, is it? Today we are living in an increasingly pagan environment. The number of opportunities to "confess" our faith in Christ are many; are we using them as we should?

**10. For it is with your heart that you believe and are justified, and it is with your mouth that you confess and are saved.**

A verse such as this one should not be considered to be the entirety of God's plan of salvation to receive his righteousness. The lesson from two weeks ago examined Paul's teaching about baptism in Romans 6. And just because this verse says nothing about repentance does not mean that Paul considers it insignificant or unnecessary. In the context of Romans 10, Paul has been focusing in particular on the *heart* and the *mouth* (mentioned in verses 6-8 in the reference from

### WHAT DO YOU THINK?

If salvation is primarily an issue of a penitent heart, then why even bother with a physical act such as an audible confession? Why not just confess within our hearts "Jesus is Lord" and let it go at that?

Deuteronomy). He wants to show that becoming right with God does not require the kind of efforts described in verses 6 and 7; it requires simple obedient faith.

Both believing and confessing are meant to be more than one-time actions associated with becoming a Christian. Faith in Jesus and confession of him as Lord must become the hallmarks of a Christ-centered life. While living a godly life is crucial, we must also be able to put our faith into words—at the right time and in the right way.

### TWO KINDS OF CONFESSION

During the aftermath of the corporate financial scandals of the late 1990s, many corporate executives were convicted of their crimes; but few of the guilty actually confessed to having done any wrong. One of the companies that had illegally "cooked" their books was Peregrine Systems, a San Diego software company. Months after the investigations began, the Chief Financial Officer (CFO) of the company finally admitted in court that he had conspired with others in the firm to deceive investors into thinking the company was strong and growing when it actually was doing much worse.

The CFO confessed to having signed nine quarterly reports and two annual reports that he knew to contain "materially false statements and omissions." He also implicated the company's outside accounting firm, saying it had encouraged unethical accounting practices. So while the CFO was selling his stock for four million dollars, the company was collapsing, costing shareholders more than *two billion dollars!* By admitting his guilt, the man was able to decrease significantly his time served in prison.

How different our confession of Christ is! Of course, there must be an admission of guilt for our sins. We can't get around that! But our confession is also meant to be part of a daily lifestyle demonstrating to the world the fact that Christ has rescued us from sin and its eternal consequences.                    —C. R. B.

### B. AN AVAILABLE FAITH (vv. 11-13)

**11. As the Scripture says, "Anyone who trusts in him will never be put to shame."**

Paul cites another Old Testament passage—Isaiah 28:16 in this instance. It reinforces the point he made earlier in Romans 10:4, that "Christ is the end of the law so that there may be righteousness for everyone who believes."

**12. For there is no difference between Jew and Gentile—the same Lord is Lord of all and richly blesses all who call on him,**

Jews and Gentiles enter into God's promise on the same basis—through faith in Christ. That is the only way! *There is no difference!* Paul's language is reminiscent of what he stated earlier about the sin problem that Jews and Gentiles have in common. "There is no difference, for all have sinned and fall short of the glory of God" (Romans 3:22, 23). What a refreshing change from bad news to good news! *The same Lord* whose righteous standard we have failed to meet offers his riches to *all who call on him.*

**13. . . . for, "Everyone who calls on the name of the Lord will be saved."**

*Everyone!* It's the same promise found in the Bible's "Golden Text"—John 3:16. But note the condition: each must call *on the name of the Lord*—on the name of Jesus. This is another example of Paul's use of the Old Testament; he cites Joel 2:32, as Peter did on the Day of Pentecost when preaching the first gospel sermon (Acts 2:21).

Again, we should mention the importance of taking all that the Scriptures say about what is necessary to be *saved*. Calling on the Lord is in line with Paul's emphasis in this passage that "it is with [the] mouth that [we] confess and are saved"(vv. 9, 10).

We should also add that when Jesus returns, everyone will pay homage to him and call on his name (Philippians 2:10, 11); but those who wait until that time will have waited too long. If we do not call on his name voluntarily now, we will be forced to do so at his return.

## III. SPREADING THE FAITH (ROMANS 10:14-17)

### A. HELPING PEOPLE CALL (v. 14)

**14. How, then, can they call on the one they have not believed in? And how can they believe in the one of whom they have not heard? And how can they hear without someone preaching to them?**

Paul follows his statement of the responsibility of all people to call on the Lord with a challenge to those who have called on him and are saved to do all they can so that others will know of that responsibility. *How* will people be made aware of whom they need to *call on* to be saved? How will they know how to accept God's gracious gift of salvation?

Calling on the name of the Lord and receiving God's salvation only happens when one believes. And one can't *believe* until he or she has *heard*. And one can't hear unless there is someone—a preacher—who is willing to tell the story.

God has chosen to use humans to convey his message of salvation. Paul himself, although addressed by Jesus on the road to Damascus, did not hear the gospel from Jesus. Instead, Jesus told him to "go into the city, and you will be told what you must do" (Acts 9:6). Paul was instructed by another human being. And so it is today; we are God's instruments to make known his grace to others.

The Greek word translated *someone preaching* describes a herald or an announcer who runs ahead of a king and proclaims what the king wishes others to know. Certainly the task of preaching can be done by any Christian who tells the good news to someone else. At the same time, there must be those who will give their lives to preaching and teaching in the setting of the local church. The church always has needed those willing to answer such a calling. And those who are ready to do so need to be supported and sent, as the next verse indicates.

### B. HELPING MESSENGERS GO (v. 15)

**15. And how can they preach unless they are sent? As it is written, "How beautiful are the feet of those who bring good news!"**

Ultimately, Jesus sends us to go and carry his message to the world; we call his words the "Great Commission." But the church also plays a vital part in sending, as illustrated by Barnabas and Saul, who were "sent" by the church in Antioch on their first missionary journey (Acts 13:1-3). Once again, Paul cites an Old Testament reference (Isaiah 52:7) to make his point. In their original context, Isaiah's words described the *good news* of the deliverance of God's people from captivity in Babylon. Paul uses these words to refer to the good news of deliverance from sin through the gospel.

Those who bear such good news are pictured as having *beautiful . . . feet*. Usually the heralds who traveled many miles to convey a message arrived at their destination with dusty, dirty feet. The appearance of their feet was anything but beautiful; the beauty was to be found in the contents of the message delivered. Later Paul will describe the Christian's armor as including "fitted with the readiness that comes from the gospel of peace" (Ephesians 6:15).

### CLEAR COMMUNICATION

Autism is a developmental disorder that is found in every country and region of the world. It affects about one or two people in every thousand. A typical autistic

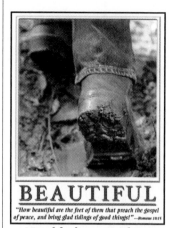

**BEAUTIFUL**

*"How beautiful are the feet of them that preach the gospel of peace, and bring glad tidings of good things!"—Romans 10:15*

Visual for lesson 6. This visual helps highlight the reference to "beautiful feet" in Romans 10:15.

PRAYER

*Father, use our feet to carry the gospel around the corner or around the world—wherever you would have us go. Use our hands to enable other feet to go. Use our tongues to confess that Jesus Christ is Lord. Help us to speak and live in his name. We pray in his name. Amen.*

WHAT DO YOU THINK?

*Why are people so resistant to the gospel? And why are we as Christians so often afraid to share the gospel?*

THOUGHT TO REMEMBER

*"How beautiful are the feet of those who bring good news!" (Romans 10:15).*

WHAT DO YOU THINK?

*Is there a distinction between religion and Christianity? If so, what is it? Do we want to be "religious" people? Why, or why not?*

trait is the inability to communicate or interact normally with others. Sometimes the person is a "savant"—a person possessing extraordinary abilities with mathematical calculations, for example. More often autism is characterized by repetitive motions such as rocking the body or flailing the limbs, as if the brain were not in control.

A breakthrough in the study of autism occurred just a few years ago when doctors were introduced to Tito, a fourteen-year-old autistic boy from India. He had trouble speaking, but could express himself eloquently in written form. He has said that his constant random movements are a way for his brain to "prove that he exists," by developing an awareness of his connection with his body. Doctors are excited about having Tito's first-person information on autism. For the first time, they can better understand the condition by communicating with an autistic child who can explain his disorder.

With the spiritual "disorder" of sin, our problem is not that the doctor (God) cannot understand us. Rather, it is that we seem unable or unwilling to hear him! However, the world's sinfulness can be transformed into spiritual wholeness and "order" if we who possess the gospel will send those who can speak, so that those who need Christ can hear and believe.                                                                  —C. R. B.

### C. HELPING SINNERS LISTEN (vv. 16, 17)

**16. But not all the Israelites accepted the good news. For Isaiah says, "Lord, who has believed our message?"**

Here is a harsh reality that can dampen the enthusiasm of confessing, preaching, and sending. Not *all* to whom we tell *the good news* will receive it gladly. In the context, Paul is lamenting the fact that so many Jews, "those of [his] own race," have neither *believed* nor *accepted* the gospel. Again, the words of *Isaiah* are cited. This verse, from Isaiah 53:1, comes in the context of one of the most powerful messianic prophecies in the Old Testament.

**17. Consequently, faith comes from hearing the message, and the message is heard through the word of Christ.**

It is up to the church, the body of Christ, to see that everyone hears about Jesus. That means missionaries, sent and supported. That means teachers, trained and developed within the body. That means preachers, called, prepared, and supported both prayerfully and financially. There are many "parachurch" organizations that can accomplish these important tasks, but the local church remains God's primary appointed vehicle for making it possible for men and women to hear *the word of God*.

### CONCLUSION

Religion is not a bad word. James speaks of "religion that God our Father accepts as pure and faultless" (James 1:27). But when the issue is how to be right with God, the word *religion* may communicate the wrong message—a message that our works can somehow save us. It is not through our efforts that we are saved. You may know someone who is waiting until he or she is living a "better life" before accepting Christ. That may seem like a noble desire. But we do not need to be "better" to be right with God; we need a Savior *now*. To wait until we are more "presentable" to God misses the point of the gospel. God wants us as we are. As an old gospel song puts it, "Why do you wait, dear brother?"

God offers life, salvation, and peace. He has reached out to us. "The word is near"—not in a distant realm. We can do everything outlined by Paul in today's text. We can believe. We can confess. We can call on the name of the Lord. God has not made the way difficult. Sometimes people make the way hard because of their own attitudes, and sometimes, sadly, God's own people make it difficult for others because of their inconsistent witness.

# Discovery Learning

*This page contains an alternative lesson plan emphasizing learning activities. Classes
desiring such student involvement will find these suggestions helpful. The next page
is a reproducible activity page to further enhance discovery learning.*

## LEARNING GOALS

After this lesson a student should be able to:

1. Tell what Paul means when he concludes, "Faith comes from hearing the message, and the message is heard through the word of Christ."

2. Explain the importance of confessing faith as it relates to one's own salvation and to the salvation of others.

3. Prepare a personal testimony about what it means to be saved.

## INTO THE LESSON

Have a class member ready to repeat (annoyingly) everything you say as you begin. Announce your intention to read a key definition for today's study, and then read aloud the following definition of the word *confess*: "to admit a weakness or mistake; to affirm a view or opinion; to declare a personal faith in; to acknowledge guilt." Hesitate after each phrase to allow your "echo" to chime in. At the end, note that the Greek word for *confess* is *homologeo* (hom-uh-luh-*geh*-o), essentially meaning, "to say the same thing." Thank your learner for his or her help.

Ask the class, "What are some things that absolutely cannot be done unless the doer has certain vital information?" Though learners may identify others, answers may include opening a combination lock without the combination or accessing a person's e-mail without his password. When these items have been noted, say, "Without certain information about God's character and will, no one can be saved. In today's text from Romans 10, Paul declares some of those truths foundational for salvation."

## INTO THE WORD

Give students a copy of the following statements. Ask them to write in the verse number most closely related to each idea, using the numbers 5 through 17 from today's text in Romans 10. Each number is to be used once. (1) Believing is not quite enough. (2) Certain truths never bring shame. (3) Each good deed I do is another rung up the ladder to Heaven. (4) Even the best news is not always well received. (5) Faith is intrinsically tied to facts. (6) Foot models are relatively anonymous, but they show something most people value. (7) My physical heritage means nothing to God. (8) If I could just never do anything wrong, life would be good. (9) It's right on the tip of my tongue! (10) Knowing where a person goes after death would help me trust God. (11) Rhetorical questions do not make good test questions. (12) Some names have even more value than their etymology implies. (13) When it's in my heart, I will talk about it.

Though learners may be able to justify other choices, here are the choices intended here: 1—v. 9; 2—v. 11; 3—v. 6; 4—v. 16; 5—v. 17; 6—v. 15; 7—v. 12; 8—v. 5; 9—v. 8; 10—v. 7; 11—v. 14; 12—v. 13; 13—v. 10. (This activity is included in the student book.) After learners have time to examine the text and respond, read the text a verse at a time and ask learners to identify what they have chosen for the "matching" idea. When differences occur, ask for an explanation.

Note that in Romans 10:14, 15, Paul uses a series of rhetorical questions ("How can . . . ?") to show the need for the presentation of the gospel. Put these letters on display: A C E H N T T Y. Ask the group to identify two words that answer Paul's rhetorical questions. (The words are *They can't*.) Say, "Certain truths are obvious, and this is one: 'Unless we act to see that the gospel is preached and taught, no one can be saved!'"

## INTO LIFE

Prepare two sets of peel-and-stick lapel labels with the following statements printed on them: *Set one:* "I Confess!"; *Set two:* "I Have Pretty Feet!" Let each learner choose the one he or she wants. Suggest that learners wear their label one day during the coming week as a possible stimulus toward sharing a basic gospel truth with someone who inquires as to the tag's significance. Those who choose to do so will need a short, non-threatening response. As a group, develop such a statement for each label. For example, for the former, "I confess that Jesus is Lord over all, and he is rich to all who call upon him." For the latter, "Peacemakers always come on beautiful feet. I want mine to carry a word about peace with God in Christ."

To conclude, have a world map displayed where all can see it. Ask learners to identify some of the Christian peacemakers who are taking the gospel to various locations around the world. Write each name on a self-stick note and apply in the approximate location. Then ask for class members to volunteer to pray and thank God for these "beautiful feet" people. (Or use the reproducible activity "Sending" from the next page.)

# A Preacher

Who was the first "preacher" who told you the good news? Is there any way you can express your appreciation to that person? Will you?

Who is the preacher that most often brings the good news to you and your congregation? List some specific ways to express your appreciation for that preacher's ministry to you in the Word.

# Heart and Tongue

In Romans 10:10, Paul declares that both heart and tongue are involved in salvation. On the heart image, write what it is that Paul says must be in the heart. On the tongue image, what Paul says must be on the tongue or from our mouth.

# Sending

Below, write the names of the Christians that you and your congregation are supporting to take the gospel to places around the world. Use arrows to identify their locations. As you write in each name, stop to pray for God's blessing on their efforts.

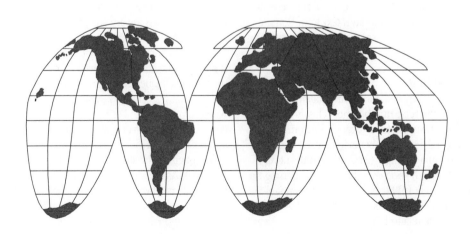

# DISPLAY THE MARKS OF A CHRISTIAN

**LESSON 7**

## WHY TEACH THIS LESSON?

Radical Christianity. Has there ever been a more redundant phrase? To be Christian means to follow Christ . . . to be like him. Therefore, all we need to do to worship him is . . . light a candle? No. Whisper a few prayers? No. Today's lesson text says our worship includes the following:

Living out of step with our culture.

Developing deep emotional bonds with brothers and sisters in Christ.

Blessing those who persecute us.

Serving others; doing what's best for them, no matter what it costs us.

Being disgusted by sin.

Does this sound like extreme Christianity? Today's lesson shows us that this is *simply* Christianity. It's our appropriate lifestyle response to a radical Savior!

## INTRODUCTION

### A. POSITIVE CHRISTIANS IN A NEGATIVE WORLD

There are two ways of looking at the sin-tainted world around us. The first sees people's hatred and disregard toward others and despairs. "It's no use. Why try to make any difference? Just look out for yourself and don't bother anyone else." The second sees the same needs and the same failures, but thinks of the possibilities for improvement and the divine resources behind them. "Yes, sin abounds; but grace abounds more. Yes, sin may win some occasional battles, but God's righteousness will win the war."

Too many Christians have bought into the idea that serious faith fosters an outlook of worry, gloom, and doom. One is reminded of the story of two men who met along the street. "Say," said one to the other, "aren't you a minister?" "No," said the other man, "I've just been sick a lot recently."

As Christians we should live out the hope we have found in Christ and do so with a joy that will cause others to crave what they see in us.

### B. LESSON BACKGROUND

Last week's study came from Romans 10, where Paul contrasts a "works" approach to being right with God with a "faith" approach. This teaching is found within a larger portion of Romans (chapters 9-11), where Paul considers the place of the Jews in God's plan of redemption. Paul concludes chapter 11 with a doxology praising God for the "depth of the riches of the wisdom and knowledge of God!" (v. 33).

Today's lesson is taken from Romans 12. This chapter begins a new direction in Paul's train of thought. Chapters 1-11 have been primarily doctrinal in their focus. With chapter 12 the apostle begins to examine some of the practical issues that relate to living for Christ in both the church and the world—

DEVOTIONAL READING:
ROMANS 12:3-8
BACKGROUND SCRIPTURE:
ROMANS 12:1-21
PRINTED TEXT:
ROMANS 12:1, 2, 9-21

## LESSON AIMS

After this lesson a student should be able to:

Apr
17

1. List several actions that characterize those who are "living sacrifices."

2. Suggest some ways these behaviors can have a positive impact on the community in which he or she lives.

3. Identify one of these behaviors that is particularly challenging, and express a resolve to make it more typical in his or her life.

## KEY VERSES

Love must be sincere. Hate what is evil; cling to what is good. Be devoted to one another in brotherly love. Honor one another above yourselves.

—Romans 12:9, 10

among Christians and non-Christians. However, this "new" section is very clearly linked with what has preceded through Paul's use of the word *therefore* in verse 1. Paul's purpose in doing this should be clear: doctrine is practical as well as theological. What we believe must affect how we live. If it doesn't, then the world has every right to question the value of what we believe. For if our faith in Christ is making no real difference in our lives, why should others embrace it?

## I. REASON FOR GOODNESS (ROMANS 12:1, 2)

### A. God's Mercy (v. 1)

1. *Therefore, I urge you, brothers, in view of God's mercy, to offer your bodies as living sacrifices, holy and pleasing to God—this is your spiritual act of worship.*

Apparently some of those in the church in Rome had not fully grasped the necessity of combining Christian faith with godly living. Perhaps their pagan background made it especially challenging to sever ties with the past and die to sin (Romans 6:2). Here Paul encourages Christians to understand that it is our *spiritual act of worship* to live in this manner. The thought of this idea would be to emphasize that worship is not something that is meant to occur on Sundays only but on a daily basis through the holy lives we lead.

Why is this lifestyle *spiritual*? Paul says *in view of*, or because of, *God's mercy*. The word *therefore* links this phrase to what Paul has written previously—not only in the immediately preceding verses, but also in the entire epistle to this point. Everything that Paul has discussed in the letter thus far, particularly concerning God's grace as demonstrated in Jesus Christ, could be summarized by *God's mercy*. God in mercy gave his only begotten Son to die as a sacrifice to cover our sins. Therefore, it is perfectly reasonable for us to live *holy* lives in service to one who provided such a sacrifice. The concept of *living sacrifices* contrasts the Christian's sacrifice with the slain sacrifices of the Old Testament system.

To be *holy* means to be "set apart." We are not to do this physically, which would make it impossible for us to have any impact on others, but spiritually. If we set apart our lives to God in this way, our sacrifices will be acceptable and enthusiastically received.

### "Glory" at What Price?

Steve Fossett was dropping toward the inky South Pacific at thirty-five hundred feet per minute. A violent, nighttime storm had ripped open his balloon's skin, and most of the burners that heated air to keep the ship aloft had blown out. Fossett was certain he would die in his fourth unsuccessful attempt to fly around the world alone; this time he was *really* going to fail!

At one point, something knocked Fossett unconscious. When he came to, the balloon's capsule was upside down in the ocean, more than five hundred miles from land. Fossett managed to get his life raft free and swim with it to the surface where, twenty-one hours later, he was rescued by a sailboat.

Fossett made one more unsuccessful attempt to be the first person to attain his goal, and the five tries cost him six million dollars! But instead of accepting numerous failures, his thinking was renewed by the noble goal ahead of him. Finally, on July 2, 2002, Steve Fossett entered the record books as his *sixth* solo attempt to circumnavigate the globe in a hot-air balloon succeeded!

As Christians, we seek a different kind of glory from what Steve Fossett sought; and we make a different kind of sacrifice to attain it. He almost sacrificed his life to find fame; we are called upon to turn our bodies into *living* sacrifices to find eternal life in the glory of the perfect will of God. Ours is the better way, by far. —C. R. B.

## B. RENEWED MIND (v. 2)

*2. Do not conform any longer to the pattern of this world, but be transformed by the renewing of your mind. Then you will be able to test and approve what God's will is—his good, pleasing and perfect will.*

Some are familiar with how the first part of this verse reads in J. B. Phillips' translation: "Don't let the world around you squeeze you into its own mold." Most parents have had to confront a child about some wrongdoing, only to hear the reply, "But everyone is doing it!" (That is usually a better reason *not* to do something!) Yet even adults can wrestle with "peer pressure."

Conformed or *transformed*? That is the question Paul challenges us to ask. To be transformed must start from the inside out, or as Paul says, *by the renewing of your mind.* Wicked thoughts precede wicked deeds (Matthew 15:18-20); godly thoughts produce godly deeds. When our minds are renewed, we are ready to practice those *good, pleasing, and perfect* qualities that Paul will mention later in this chapter.

The renewing Paul describes is part of the "newness of life" that we receive in Christ (Romans 6:4; Colossians 3:10). It cannot occur through our own efforts. "Self-help" is out of the question in this area!

**WHAT DO YOU THINK?**

*Should we be governed by "majority rule" in matters of faith and practice? Why is conforming to the majority opinion in such matters displeasing to God?*

## II. SHOWING GOODNESS TO GOD'S PEOPLE (ROMANS 12:9-13)

### A. LOVING (v. 9)

*9. Love must be sincere. Hate what is evil; cling to what is good.*

In the remainder of Romans 12, Paul elaborates on what being a living sacrifice entails. In the portion of the chapter not included in our printed text (verses 3-8), Paul highlights the importance of using our various gifts in the Lord's service. Verse 9 begins a section of short, specific commands concerning the attitudes and actions that should characterize every Christian.

*Love* is the starting point. This is in keeping with what Paul writes elsewhere in his epistles, most notably in 1 Corinthians 13. Jesus pointed out that love is the essence of the Old Testament law (Mark 12:28-34). Love is also the central feature of the New Covenant era (John 13:31-35). This kind love can be defined as "wanting the best for another"; and, although feelings are a part of it, it is primarily a matter of the will. Note that when Paul describes the fruit of the Spirit in a Christian's life, he starts with love (Galatians 5:22).

Paul states that love must be *sincere*. This means that love must be genuine, without hypocrisy. In addition, Paul tells us to *hate what is evil* and to *cling to what is good*. There is room for hatred in the Christian life, but it is not a hatred of people. This describes a loathing of sin and a sense of disgust at the destruction that it causes both in individual lives and in the fabric of society.

**WHAT DO YOU THINK?**

*How can we show God's love to others? What is the difference between the love God wants us to share and the love we often see demonstrated in worldly relationships?*

### B. HONORING (v. 10)

*10. Be devoted to one another in brotherly love. Honor one another above yourselves.*

These words describe a code of conduct that is far removed from the "me first" mentality of the modern world. They include the words *to one another* and *one another*—words found in other New Testament passages that remind us that we do not live the Christian life in a vacuum.

### C. SERVING (v. 11)

*11. Never be lacking in zeal, but keep your spiritual fervor, serving the Lord.*

The Greek word translated *fervor* describes the *zeal* one should have for *serving the Lord*. Our fire can burn even through difficult times, because it is fed by the presence of the Holy Spirit.

### D. REJOICING (v. 12)

**12. Be joyful in hope, patient in affliction, faithful in prayer.**

We noted in Lesson 3 that biblical *hope* does not have any "maybe" in it. It is confident assurance. It rests in God's promises through Christ. Those who possess it have every reason to rejoice, because they know that in the end, Christ and Christ's people will triumph. So we can be *patient in affliction*, calm in the face of any storm.

The last phrase in this verse describes a key ingredient to developing the attitudes and actions found in this verse and in this passage: think of an open line to the Father! A life that is *faithful in prayer*, or that prays without ceasing (1 Thessalonians 5:17)! A mind-set that is ready for prayer at any time!

### E. SHARING (v. 13)

**13. Share with God's people who are in need. Practice hospitality.**

Just as God makes the sun to shine and the rain to fall on the just and the unjust (Matthew 5:45), his children are called to assist those who have needs. But Scripture emphasizes our singular responsibility for our brothers and sisters in Christ (see Galatians 6:10).

*Hospitality* is one of the characteristics of those who serve as elders (also called overseers, 1 Timothy 3:2). But it should also be a trademark of all Christians. Those in God's family should be able to count on one another for food, shelter, security, and friendship in times of need.

#### YOU MEAN IT'S NOT ABOUT ME?

A California woman was surfing the Internet when she "met" a man in North Carolina. She decided to meet him in person—in hopes of marrying him, she later admitted—so she traveled to North Carolina to do so. Perhaps that would have been nobody else's business, except that she left behind, uncared for and alone, her two children, ages four and seven. She left frozen food in the refrigerator and told them to hide if anyone came to the apartment. After she had been gone for three weeks, a neighbor heard the children crying and notified the police. When the mother returned home, she told authorities that the relationship with her newfound fiancé had foundered. They informed her that she was facing criminal charges of child abandonment.

This woman's story is an illustration of a serious ailment in modern culture: the selfish tendency to think, "It's all about me." We can forgive this in small children, since they haven't developed the mental or emotional maturity to know differently. But as our children grow, a part of the socializing (or we could say civilizing) process that we engage in is to help them mature into adults who care for someone other than themselves. And, as Paul says, true *Christian* maturity is demonstrated when we think of the needs of others ahead of our own. Christians learn from the example of Christ and his selfless spirit that life is about others, and not "all about me."

—C. R. B.

### III. SHOWING GOODNESS TO THE WORLD (ROMANS 12:14-19)

#### A. ACTING, NOT REACTING (v. 14)

**14. Bless those who persecute you; bless and do not curse.**

Now we come to the more challenging part of Paul's exhortations—the ones requiring a higher measure of Christian maturity. It's one thing to help the "saints" (v. 13); it's quite another to show kindness to those who are "unsaintly" in some way. Yet, as Jesus pointed out in the Sermon on the Mount, if we love only those who love us, how are we any different from the pagans (Matthew 5:46, 47)?

**WHAT DO YOU THINK?**

How does being "joyful in hope" relate to being "patient in affliction"? How does being "faithful in prayer" make these other two possible?

Visual for lesson 7. This visual calls attention to the dos and don'ts that constitute the "marks of a Christian" as found in Romans 12.

In this area, as in others, the master teacher guides us not only by his words, but also by his example. The prophet Isaiah spoke of his behavior during his so-called "trial": "He was oppressed and afflicted, yet he did not open his mouth; he was led like a lamb to the slaughter, and as a sheep before her shearers is silent, so he did not open his mouth" (Isaiah 53:7). Instead of cursing his accusers and tormentors, he prayed for them: "Father, forgive them, for they do not know what they are doing" (Luke 23:34).

## B. EMPATHIZING (v. 15)

**15. Rejoice with those who rejoice; mourn with those who mourn.**

Notice the word *empathizing* in the heading of this section of the lesson. "Empathy" goes much deeper than sympathy. While sympathy describes a compassion or "suffering with" another, empathy is the ability to experience the feelings and emotions of another.

Generally speaking, it is easier to *mourn with* those who *mourn* than it is to *rejoice with* those who *rejoice*. Most of us can offer examples of weeping with those who have gone through situations such as a critical illness, a death in the family, a job loss, or some other crisis. (Or we can recall times when others have mourned with us.) Sometimes sitting and weeping with another Christian, without words, speaks volumes of love.

On the other hand, when someone else receives a promotion that we thought we had earned or is able to purchase a special possession that we had hoped for, it can be a bit harder to rejoice at that person's success. In truth, however, both the hardships and the blessings that others experience can be a gauge of whether we have learned to be Christlike in our attitudes.

## C. SHOWING NO FAVORITISM (v. 16)

**16. Live in harmony with one another. Do not be proud, but be willing to associate with people of low position. Do not be conceited.**

James challenges our tendency, even in the church, to treat the well-to-do with more respect than we treat the "have-nots" who enter our facilities. He pictures saying, "Here's a good seat for you" to a rich man, and, "Sit on the floor by my feet" to a poor man in shabby clothing (James 2:3). That is hardly an example of living *in harmony with one another*.

To treat others in the body of Christ as equals—despite clothes, checkbooks, education, or heritage—is to treat them the way the head of the church would. One of the most compelling descriptions of Jesus' ministry is this: "the large crowd listened to him with delight" (Mark 12:37). Jesus was not be ashamed to be seen with those *of low position*, and neither should we be. Nor should we worry about what others will think of us. Jesus' opinion is the only one that matters.

## D. PROMOTING PEACE (vv. 17-19)

**17. Do not repay anyone evil for evil. Be careful to do what is right in the eyes of everybody.**

This reinforces some of Paul's earlier teaching. Revenge and dishonesty are never acceptable for the Christian. Paul's emphasis on no man and all men show that his words apply to our conduct in the world as well as in the church.

**18. If it is possible, as far as it depends on you, live at peace with everyone.**

Here, too, is a challenge concerning *everyone*—not just fellow Christians. It is important that we wage peace, not war, even among those who are not peaceful themselves. At the same time, Paul realizes that peace does not lie completely

### WHAT DO YOU THINK?

*Why should we "rejoice with those who rejoice; mourn with those who mourn"? What are some practical ways we can do this?*

### DAILY BIBLE READINGS

*Monday, Apr. 11*—Instructions for Living (*Colossians 4: 2-6*)

*Tuesday, Apr. 12*—Live a Life Pleasing to God (*1 Thessalonians 4:1-12*)

*Wednesday, Apr. 13*—Hold Fast to What Is Good (*1 Thessalonians 5:12-22*)

*Thursday, Apr. 14*—Do What Is Right (*2 Thessalonians 3:6-13*)

*Friday, Apr. 15*—Members One of Another (*Romans 12:1-5*)

*Saturday, Apr. 16*—Marks of the True Christian (*Romans 12: 6-13*)

*Sunday, Apr. 17*—Overcome Evil with Good (*Romans 12: 14-21*)

with us and that some will resist our well-intentioned efforts. "Do all that you can," he says.

**19. Do not take revenge, my friends, but leave room for God's wrath, for it is written: "It is mine to avenge; I will repay," says the Lord.**

Concerning those individuals who remain stubbornly hostile to our initiatives on behalf of peace, or who oppose us in any way, Paul tells us not to *take revenge* on others. *Leave room for God's wrath* literally reads in the Greek text, "Give place to the wrath." The remainder of the verse makes it clear that we should give proper place to the wrath of God, allowing him to render judgment in his own way and in his own time. Paul is saying, "Don't let your anger lead you to take upon yourself something that is God's prerogative. You are not God. He will take care of administering vengeance." The Old Testament reference cited is from Deuteronomy 32:35.

## IV. SHOWING GOODNESS TO AN ENEMY (ROMANS 12:20, 21)

### A. PERSON (v. 20)

**20. On the contrary:**
  **"If your enemy is hungry, feed him;**
    **if he is thirsty, give him something to drink.**
  **In doing this, you will heap burning coals on his head."**

It is one thing to offer food and *drink* to brothers and sisters in Christ. Here Paul describes the "second mile" attitude that should characterize those who walk with Jesus. We should be prepared to help even an *enemy*.

The meaning of heaping *burning coals* on someone's *head* has been subject to much discussion. The reference itself is found in Proverbs 25:21, 22. One suggestion is that it pictures the sense of shame or remorse that "burns" within a person when treated with kindness by someone whom the person deliberately tried to hurt in some way. Possibly such a gesture of kindness will serve as a witness to the person of the difference that our faith in Christ has made in our lives.

### B. PRINCIPLE (v. 21)

**21. Do not be overcome by evil, but overcome evil with good.**

Simply put, the world should not be influencing the Christian; the Christian should be influencing the world. As noted in the introductory material to today's lesson, Christians should seek to be a positive force in a negative world. They should take the initiative on behalf of what is *good*. When they do, they will "act, not react."

## CONCLUSION

Even the most challenging among Paul's exhortations in today's text (such as the positive treatment of people outside the circle of the church, and even of enemies) are not unreasonable. But we cannot carry them out without looking to Jesus. In many instances, we can read examples in the Gospels of Jesus doing just what Paul tells Christians to do. We must also remember that we experienced Jesus' patience with us when we were acting as his enemies. We continue to experience his patience whenever remnants of our old life disturb our relationship with him and we need forgiveness.

As Paul tells us in Romans 12:1, to offer our bodies as a living sacrifice, holy and acceptable to God, is our reasonable service. What could be more reasonable than a practical Christianity that touches my hands, my heart, my tongue, my feet, my attitude, and my acts of generosity—even toward enemies?

# Discovery Learning

*This page contains an alternative lesson plan emphasizing learning activities. Classes desiring such student involvement will find these suggestions helpful. The next page is a reproducible activity page to further enhance discovery learning.*

## LEARNING GOALS

After this lesson a student should be able to:

1. List several actions that characterize those who are "living sacrifices."

2. Suggest some ways these behaviors can have a positive impact on the community in which he or she lives.

3. Identify one of these behaviors that is particularly challenging, and express a resolve to make it more typical in his or her life.

## INTO THE LESSON

Near the entrance to your classroom, display a large sheet of paper with a drawing of a large tin can. Beside the can, draw the outline of a human figure at least four feet in height. To the left of the "can," have the word *Ingredients;* under the figure to the right, have the label *A Living Sacrifice.* As members arrive, draw their attention to the figure, provide a marker, and ask each person to add something to the "list of ingredients" that make up a "living sacrifice." If you need to help them get started, put one or two "ingredients" on the list, such as *faithfulness* and *humility.* You will use this drawing and list later during "Into the Word."

## INTO THE WORD

Recruit one of your better oral readers to stand beside you as you read today's text from Romans 12 verse by verse. After each verse, have that reader read the corresponding verse from a paraphrase such as J. B. Phillips' *The New Testament in Modern English* or *The Promise* (Contemporary English Version).

Read Romans 12:1, 2 again, with emphasis, then assign each learner one of the verses from Romans 12:9-21. (As an assigning method, cut thirteen strips an inch wide and four inches long, write the number of a verse on each, 9 through 21, and insert the strips into your Bible, with the number placed at the center and one or two inches of the paper sticking out. As learners write on the "can" after entering the room, have each pull out a slip from the Bible.) Later you can say, "Look at the verse assigned to you from Romans 12 by the numbered slip. The Bible lists the ingredients of a living sacrifice, and we want to draw our 'recipe' from there."

Then say, "The challenge is clear: we are to be living sacrifices. Examine the verse assigned to you to find the 'ingredients' of a living sacrifice. Compare what you find with our 'can' we have labeled. If you find in your verse an ingredient we have listed, say, 'It's in there!' and come to the sketch and check the ingredient off. If you find an ingredient we have not included, come to the 'can,' write the new ingredient in, and then say, 'It's in there!'" After each ingredient is confirmed or added, ask the learner to identify and read his or her assigned verse. Though you will allow the learners latitude in the "ingredients" they write in, such elements as the following will be appropriate: love (v. 9), honor (v. 10), zeal (v. 11), joy (v. 12), generosity (v. 13), graciousness (v. 14), sympathy (v. 15), humility (v. 16), honesty (v. 17), peace (v. 18), and submission to God (v. 19).

As a way of reviewing these ideas through the coming week, suggest to your learners that they each set a clean, empty can on a work space near them. The can will spur their thinking concerning our daily need to "stir in" the ingredients of holiness and righteousness.

## INTO LIFE

Say, "I want you to take the following 'Report Card' home with you this week to evaluate how 'living' you are as a Christian sacrifice." Make copies of the following and distribute one to each learner with directions to "grade yourself, using a *D* for 'barely breathing' to an *A* for 'fully alive.' When you're done, take the report to your heavenly Father for his commendation and challenge." (A similar activity is in the student book.)

REPORT CARD for _____ (name) _____.

This learner shows the following progress in *Basic Christian Living*:

____ sincere love

____ association with good

____ devotion to the brothers and sisters

____ deferring to the well-being of others

____ zeal and spiritual fervor

____ joy and hope

____ patience in difficulty

____ faithfulness in prayer

____ generosity with the needy

____ hospitality

____ kindness to persecutors

____ rejoicing with achievements of others

____ empathizing with those who hurt

____ harmonious, peaceful living

____ humility

# Alive in Christ

In the picture frame to the right, either sketch an image of yourself or attach a small photograph.

Display this in a place where you will see it each morning as you are preparing for the day. Let it remind you of the continual need to be a living sacrifice.

WANTED: Alive in Christ Jesus!

# Overcome or Overcomer

At the conclusion to today's text, we are admonished: "Do not be overcome by evil, but overcome evil with good" (Romans 12:21). Clip the letters G-O-O-D and E-V-I-L below, or write the letters out on three-by-five cards. This week as you find yourself overcoming evil with good, tape or glue one of the letters from G-O-O-D over one of those in E-V-I-L. Finding joy in another's success (v. 15), expressing honesty when deceit or cheating is possible (v. 17), or doing good for an enemy (v. 20) will be appropriate occasions to overlay evil with good!

# G O O D

# E V I L

# ACCEPT ONE ANOTHER

**LESSON 8**

## WHY TEACH THIS LESSON?

"Dad! He's taking my folder!" "Mom, she's still on the phone!" And—my personal favorite—"Dad, he's breathing my air." Few things are more annoying to a parent than children bickering over the tiniest issues. Don't you think that Christians fussing with each other over matters of opinion grieves our heavenly Father?

The take-home message from today's lesson is relational. Dozens of verses address how we in the body should treat each other. Jesus words in John 13:35 make it clear: brotherly love is not a suggestion—it's our trademark. This love requires us to put our fellow Christian's best interest in front of our own.

God values unity. The Father, Son, and Spirit live in perfect unity. We are created to live in harmony with each other. Unity is not about *uniformity*—agreeing on every minute point. It's about holding one another in the highest respect and helping each other grow in God's grace. Today's lesson will convict us of that.

## INTRODUCTION

### A. TO JUDGE OR NOT TO JUDGE

When it comes to judging, criticism, rebuke, or discipline, a Christian must carefully consider what he or she says and does in the light of three key principles. The first principle is found in Romans 2: one must not judge using a "double standard." It is wrong for me to censure a brother or sister in Christ for a particular action if I am engaging in the same kind of behavior myself (Romans 2:1). The second principle is that anything that is spoken to a wayward brother or sister must be done in the interest of restoring that person to fruitful service (Galatians 6:1). And the third principle is that our opposition to a particular action must be grounded in the teaching of Scripture (2 Timothy 3:16, 17).

Parents face similar issues with their children all the time. If we who are parents desired to correct every childish mistake, we would have to be full-time shadows. We would end up robbing a child of the opportunity to learn through experience. And we would risk bringing up a child who becomes a duplicate of us, not his or her own person, and not necessarily what God created him or her to be. Generally speaking, with children we have to "choose our battles." We must stand firm on the issues that are truly important—those that relate primarily to what God has clearly defined as right and wrong.

When it comes to confrontation within the body of Christ, we must also, in a sense, "choose our battles." Or, to be more accurate, we must let God choose them. Sin cannot be glossed over and ignored. It hurts the sinner and the body of Christ as a whole too much to let that happen. In 1 Corinthians 5 Paul describes a situation that the church in Corinth had to address. A man was treating his father's wife as though she were *his* wife, which clearly broke God's law. In such a case discipline had to be applied.

On the other hand, matters of opinion are not in the same category as the precepts that God has set; matters of opinion are issues of individual conscience. We must not allow such as these to become causes of division in the body of Christ. Each of us must be sparing with judgments and unsparing with love.

DEVOTIONAL READING:

JAMES 4:7-12

BACKGROUND SCRIPTURE:

ROMANS 14:1-13; 15:5, 6

PRINTED TEXT:

ROMANS 14:1-13; 15:5, 6

### LESSON AIMS

After participating in this lesson, a student should be able to:

1. Summarize Paul's teaching about the need for Christians not to judge each other.

2. Discuss the importance of Christians being united by their relationship with Jesus Christ, even when they hold differing opinions on some issues.

3. Suggest a specific issue that divides believers in his or her church, and suggest a means of coming to unity.

Apr
24

### KEY VERSES

May the God who gives endurance and encouragement give you a spirit of unity among yourselves as you follow Christ Jesus, so that with one heart and mouth you may glorify the God and Father of our Lord Jesus Christ.

—Romans 15:5, 6

## B. LESSON BACKGROUND

In this quarter's second lesson, taken from Romans 2, we discussed God's judgment and some issues concerning our judging of others. Today's lesson continues our study of the concluding portion of Romans where Paul examines the practical side of our walk with Christ. It is a continuation of what it means to "present your bodies as living sacrifices" (Romans 12:1). We spent last week examining some of what Paul says in Romans 12 about those attitudes and actions that strengthen the fellowship in the church and the church's witness in the world.

In Romans 13 Paul considers the topic of a Christian's duty to civil authorities. He refers to the "governing authorities" as "established by God" (v. 1) and to the person in civil authority as a "God's servant" (vv. 4, 6). Living by the principles of Christian conduct outlined in chapter 12 constitutes a witness to a person in authority: "Do what is right and he will commend you" (Romans 13:3). The chapter concludes with exhortations such as "put aside the deeds of darkness" (v. 12), "put on the armor of light" (v. 12), "behave decently" (v. 13), and "clothe yourselves with the Lord Jesus Christ" (v. 14). In today's lesson, which is primarily from Romans 14, we consider another aspect of life in the church. The topic is disagreements among Christians over what may be termed "nonessentials."

## I. EATING DIFFERENT FOODS (ROMANS 14:1-4)

### A. RESPECT THE WEAK (vv. 1-3)

1. *Accept him whose faith is weak, without passing judgment on disputable matters.*

The meaning of *whose faith is weak* must be determined by the context of this passage and by the specific issues Paul raises. Judging from the following verses, Paul is not dealing with faith in relationship to salvation (as in a phrase such as "justified by faith"). He is concerned mainly with the practical side of Christian faith. Those whose faith is weak are those Christians who do not seem to understand fully what their faith in Christ allows and does not allow them to do. Perhaps they had not yet been able to break away from former scruples they had strongly held.

Although Paul does not specifically mention the "strong" Christians until Romans 15:1, he suggests in the verse before us how the strong are to treat the weak. The strong must *accept* the weak, welcoming them *without passing judgment on disputable matters.* In other words, the issues that have the potential to create such disputations should not be raised so as to make the weak Christian uncomfortable or put him or her on the defensive. These are matters of opinion (which will become clear in the following verses) and should not be allowed to cause tensions or rifts in the body of Christ.

2. *One man's faith allows him to eat everything, but another man, whose faith is weak, eats only vegetables.*

In Rome and in other first-century churches where there were both Jews and Gentiles, some of the "disputable matters" mentioned in verse 1 included questions related to which foods were acceptable to *eat*. For many Gentile Christians, the Old Testament laws regarding food were of no concern. They accepted what Paul would later tell Timothy: "For everything God created is good, and nothing is to be rejected if it is received with thanksgiving" (1 Timothy 4:4). But many Jewish Christians were not able to go that far. When the meat served to them did not come from an acceptable animal (according to what they had been taught from the law of Moses), they would simply eat *vegetables.*

In other settings, the Gentile Christians would have been considered *weak.* During their pre-Christian days, the meat they ate was often used in presenting sacrifices to pagan idols. For some who had become Christians, it was difficult for

WHAT DO YOU THINK?

What are "disputable matters"? How can we determine what items are essential (where there is no room for compromise) and what items are not essential (where there is room for compromise)?

them to eat such meat when they were aware of its pagan connections. To the "strong," however, their freedom in Christ eliminated all of these old scruples. They could eat such meat, recognizing that since an idol was nothing, there was no way that good meat could be "contaminated" by a superstitious ceremony. Paul deals with these issues more specifically in 1 Corinthians 8, but they also would have been prominent in Rome as well.

**3. The man who eats everything must not look down on him who does not, and the man who does not eat everything must not condemn the man who does, for God has accepted him.**

Here's the guideline. The key issue is not what is eaten; it is the attitude of the eaters. The "anything goes" eater must not *look down on,* or be critical of, the one who eats only vegetables. And the one who cannot bring himself to eat the meat in question is not to put down the one who enjoys it. If each one has surrendered to the lordship of Jesus Christ, then *God* has *accepted him.* And if God has accepted him, he is my brother. If she belongs to the Lord, she is my sister. Who am I to exclude someone whom God has adopted into his family?

## B. DO NOT JUDGE (v. 4)

**4. Who are you to judge someone else's servant? To his own master he stands or falls. And he will stand, for the Lord is able to make him stand.**

We are all servants of one *master*—the Lord. No individual is the master of another. The master makes the rules, and we help each other keep the master's rules. But we don't make the rules for each other, particularly where matters of opinion are concerned. *The Lord* alone determines whether someone stands or falls—that is, whether someone's conduct is acceptable or not.

We must constantly bear in mind that God's grace is the only hope that any of us has to *stand* before him. I must recognize that, in spite of my numerous flaws and my imperfect service, God is ready and willing to help me stand. Shouldn't I treat others with the same measure of grace with which I want God to treat me?

## II. OBSERVING DIFFERENT DAYS (ROMANS 14:5, 6)

### A. ONE'S CHOICE (v. 5)

**5. One man considers one day more sacred than another; another man considers every day alike. Each one should be fully convinced in his own mind.**

Here is another subject where Christians will hold differing opinions: the observance of special days. Most likely the issue for Paul's readers involved the observance of various Jewish holy days by those who came to Christ from a Jewish background. We know that Paul himself continued such observances after he became a Christian (Acts 20:16). But he did not try to force his opinion on others, nor did he condemn those who chose not to observe the days that he honored. This perspective is reflected in his advice to the Roman Christians: *Each one should be full convinced in his own mind.*

This issue probably gives us a more contemporary illustration than the discussion over food. Some thoroughly enjoy the celebration of various holidays such as Christmas and Easter. Others do not believe in observing those days at all because they are troubled by possible links to paganism. Those who try to include a Christian emphasis in their observance of these days reason that the world's attention is already drawn somewhat to Jesus' birthday and to his resurrection. Why not take advantage of that attention to get a word in for the truth?

Whatever our convictions on this matter, Paul would tell us to be loyal to them, to put energy into whatever God-honoring activity we believe in, and to realize the right of another to see such a matter as this differently from us.

*WHAT DO YOU THINK?*

How can we tell if we are the "strong" Christian or the "weak" one? How do our responsibilities toward each other differ depending on which type of Christian we are?

*WHAT DO YOU THINK?*

Should Christians celebrate Christmas and Easter? In what manner should Christians observe national holidays (such as a country's Independence Day)?

## B. ONE'S CREATOR (v. 6)

**6. He who regards one day as special, does so to the Lord. He who eats meat, eats to the Lord, for he gives thanks to God; and he who abstains, does so to the Lord and gives thanks to God.**

This is a review of the principle Paul has stated, as applied to both the observance of certain days and the eating of certain foods. If I celebrate special days, I should celebrate them to the glory of *the Lord*. If I treat every *day* the same, I must make sure that today, and the next day, and the next honor God. If I feel free to eat anything, I should enjoy it, giving *thanks* to the Provider of everything. If I choose to eat with more discretion, I should do that to honor God as well. In other words, the lordship of Christ should affect all I do.

### WHAT WERE THEY THINKING?

Ted VanCleave is an inventor. One of his "bright ideas" was the creation of an inflatable greeting card, but he couldn't get a patent for it. However, in the process he discovered patents for several other interesting inventions. Here are examples:

• a helium-filled bed that floats to the ceiling during the day to provide more room in small apartments.

• three-legged panty hose (so when one leg is ruined, you don't have to throw them away).

• an alarm that beeps and flashes a light when the baby wets his diapers.

• a fork for dieters (when you take a bite a red light comes on, encouraging you to wait for another bite until the light turns green).

• a watch that counts "dog time" (it multiplies seconds, minutes, and hours by seven so you can see how "Fido" keeps time).

Your reaction may be much like mine: What were they thinking? We may have the same question about the religious scruples of other people, similar to those that surfaced in Paul's day about eating (or not eating) certain foods, or keeping certain days as holy days. Today it could be some other matter of opinion related to Christian conduct. Here is Paul's instruction: each person should be fully persuaded about the issue in his or her own mind, and no one should judge others regarding matters where God has not given specific directions.          —C. R. B.

## III. RECOGNIZING A COMMON BOND (ROMANS 14:7-9)

### A. WE NEED OTHERS (v. 7)

**7. For none of us lives to himself alone and none of us dies to himself alone.**

Each Christian is a child of God; thus, we are all brothers and sisters in Christ. We are far more interdependent than we are independent. Our primary dependence is upon the Lord, as Paul points out in the next verse.

### B. WE ARE THE LORD'S (vv. 8, 9)

**8. If we live, we live to the Lord; and if we die, we die to the Lord. So, whether we live or die, we belong to the Lord.**

In this context, Paul is emphasizing that every Christian is responsible to the Lord, even in matters of opinion such as observing special days and eating certain foods. The lordship of Christ should influence every aspect of life, not just what may be considered "major" decisions.

To *die to the Lord* should provide a most comforting thought. Whatever the circumstances of one's death may be, whether quiet, peaceful, violent, or catastrophic, whether at home or in a hospital bed, the Lord will never abandon one of his own.

**9. For this very reason, Christ died and returned to life so that he might be the Lord of both the dead and the living.**

Here Paul reinforces his teaching on "disputable matters" by reminding us of that concerning which there can be no doubt whatsoever: the central facts of the gospel (cf. 1 Corinthians 15:1-4). Let us never lose sight of what really matters in all of this! Christ's death spells death for death. And his resurrection spells life for those who belong to him. The Calvary/burial/resurrection events seal Jesus' lordship. Any matters of opinion must pale in comparison with this glorious message.

## IV. RECOGNIZING A COMMON DUTY (ROMANS 14:10-13; 15:5, 6)

### A. WITHHOLDING PRESENT JUDGMENT (v. 10)

*10. You, then, why do you judge your brother? Or why do you look down on your brother? For we will all stand before God's judgment seat.*

It is *God* who has the ultimate right to *judge a brother.* We must remember that Paul has not been writing about immoral behavior or heresies that are practiced or endorsed by individuals or groups within the church. He has been talking about matters of opinion. To judge our brothers and sisters on such issues and to *look down on* them because their perspective is different from ours is out of line. We are all accountable to God, and we must allow him to be the pattern for all our attitudes and actions toward others. *God's judgment seat* is most likely the same as "the judgment seat of Christ" in 2 Corinthians 5:10.

### B. AWAITING FUTURE JUDGMENT (vv. 11, 12)

*11. It is written:*

> *"'As surely as I live,' says the Lord,*
> *'every knee will bow before me;*
> *    every tongue will confess to God.'"*

In our study of Romans, we have witnessed Paul's frequent use of the Old Testament Scriptures to support his teaching on various topics. Here he quotes from Isaiah 45:23 to reinforce what he has stated previously concerning final judgment. Someday *every knee will bow* and *every tongue will confess to God.* The question is whether we will do that gladly and willingly (because we chose to do it during our earthly lives) or fearfully (because we refused to make spiritual matters a priority).

*12. So then, each of us will give an account of himself to God.*

We owe an accounting, but not to another person. We owe it *to God.* Together *each one of us* will stand before God's judgment seat. No one will be exempt!

### C. MAINTAINING BROTHERHOOD (v. 13)

*13. Therefore let us stop passing judgment on one another. Instead, make up your mind not to put any stumbling block or obstacle in your brother's way.*

Here Paul provides a positive alternative to the kind of negative judging that has been his primary concern thus far. Whenever we find ourselves dwelling on our differences with others and becoming frustrated and impatient with them, it may be a good time to stop and consider how we can be a help to them—to enable them to obey Christ and serve him more fully.

Instead of dwelling on the occasions when an individual has stumbled, let us determine what we can do to keep that person from stumbling again. Staying in touch, becoming a prayer partner, providing words of encouragement, and offering good options to potentially harmful choices can help someone stand rather than *fall.* And possibly someday that brother or sister whom we help may be the person who helps us stand strong and avoid a fall of our own.

**WHAT DO YOU THINK?**

*How does our modern sense of independence and self-centeredness compare to the Bible's sense of interdependence and self-sacrifice? How would you evaluate contemporary culture after reading Romans 14: 7-9?*

**WHAT DO YOU THINK?**

*When we judge others, what role are we usurping? What do we have in common with those whom we judge?*

**WHAT DO YOU THINK?**

*When Paul (quoting Isaiah) says "every knee will bow . . . every tongue will confess," is he teaching a universal salvation? Defend your answer.*

"As I live, saith the Lord, every knee shall bow to me, and every tongue shall confess to God." —Romans 14:11

Visual for lesson 8. *Today's visual encourages us to bow the knee before God now—while we have the opportunity.*

HOW TO SAY IT

Corinthians. Ko-RIN-thee-unz.
Isaiah. Eye-ZAY-uh.

## LOOKING OUT FOR OTHERS

SAD—Seasonal Affective Disorder—seems to affect especially those people who live in the far north, where winter brings on what may be described as a "darkness of the spirit." Alcoholism is a frequent side effect of SAD, as people try to anesthetize themselves against the gloom of shortened days and long winter nights. Of course, since alcohol is itself a depressant, the problem is compounded.

Alaska rates at or near the top in America in incidents of drunken driving, vehicle fatalities, and other deaths related to alcohol. Alaska also has high rates of suicide and abusive home situations. To combat this problem, more than a hundred native Alaskan villages control the use and/or sale of alcohol.

A few years ago, two Alaskan villages experimented by relaxing their laws on alcohol use. After six months of winter had passed, they decided to reinstate the restrictions. Families were starving, teenagers were becoming drunk in public, sexual assaults increased, and public officials were drinking on the job. In essence, the two villages decided that they needed to look out for the "weaker brothers" by removing a "stumblingblock" from their paths.

Whatever we think secular society's role should be in such matters, Christians who seek to practice biblical principles are obligated to ensure that their behavior does not lead other believers into sin. It's not only a case of following the "golden rule"; it's a matter of helping one another "with one heart" to glorify Christ.

—C. R. B.

### D. BEING LIKEMINDED (15:5, 6)

**5. May the God who gives endurance and encouragement give you a spirit of unity among yourselves as you follow Christ Jesus,**

God has shown extraordinary *endurance* and patience with us. Should we not try to exhibit patience with one another—for example, concerning the kind of issues Paul has addressed in this section of Romans? We would do well to reread Jesus' parable of the unforgiving servant—a man who all too quickly forgot the grace with which his master had treated him (Matthew 18:21-35).

Having *a spirit of unity* does not mean that we agree on every issue that surfaces. Paul has already stated in Romans 14 that there will be disagreements among Christians on certain subjects. To be likeminded means that we all determine to have the same attitude toward one another—an attitude that develops as we *follow Christ Jesus.*

**6. . . . so that with one heart and mouth you may glorify the God and Father of our Lord Jesus Christ.**

Here is a picture of what Heaven will be like—speaking with united attitudes and singing with united voices as we praise the *Father* and the *Christ.* Shouldn't we be "rehearsing" now? We will not always sing the same notes, but we will be in harmony because our minds are focused on the same goal: seeking to *glorify* God.

### CONCLUSION

Don't you like the way Paul points us in the direction of positive judging? "Make up your mind not to put any stumbling block or obstacle in your brother's way" (Romans 14:13). Do I apply myself to figuring out how I can help my brother or sister to stand, and not fall?

The writer of Hebrews encourages Christians to get together and to exhort each other, to help each other hold fast to the profession of their faith. "Let us consider how we may spur one another on toward love and good deeds" (Hebrews 10:24). That's the kind of positive judging that will make Almighty God smile, will draw his family closer together, and will give the world a taste of what they're missing when they remain outside of God's family.

# Discovery Learning

*This page contains an alternative lesson plan emphasizing learning activities. Classes
desiring such student involvement will find these suggestions helpful. The next page
is a reproducible activity page to further enhance discovery learning.*

## LEARNING GOALS

After this lesson a student should be able to:

1. Summarize Paul's teaching about the need for Christians not to judge each other.

2. Discuss the importance of Christians being united by their relationship with Jesus Christ, even when they hold differing opinions on some issues.

3. Suggest a specific issue that divides believers in his or her church, and suggest a means of coming to unity.

## INTO THE LESSON

Prepare the following handout. (This activity is included in the student book.) Put the word *WEAK* at the top of a piece of paper and *STRONG* at the bottom. Leave enough space in between for eight lines of writing. Tell the class, "It takes some real work to go from being WEAK to being STRONG, especially when applied to Christian growth. Listen to the following clues and fill in this 'ladder' by changing or adding one letter at each 'rung' in order to go from WEAK to STRONG." (Note that at the clues with a plus sign, a letter will be added.)

### WEAK

–top of a mountain      _ _ _ _   (PEAK)
–a type of moss      _ _ _ _   (PEAT)
–holding one's anger, with "up"

     _ _ _ _   (PENT)
–a small liquid measure   _ _ _ _   (PINT)
–to put words into visible form (+)

     _ _ _ _ _   (PRINT)
–a quick, short race (+)

     _ _ _ _ _ _   (SPRINT)
–a season of the year

     _ _ _ _ _ _   (SPRING)
–what impels and restricts a yo-yo

     _ _ _ _ _ _   (STRING)

### STRONG

*Option:* Ask two or three class members to sit before the group for a "Likes and Dislikes" survey. Allow each to respond to the following (or similar) statements: (1) My favorite food is . . . ; (2) One thing I will not eat is . . . ; (3) My favorite sports team is . . . ; (4) My favorite singer is . . . ; (5) My ideal vacation site is . . . ; (6) My attitude toward going to the movies is . . . ; (7) My favorite color is . . . ; (8) The TV newscast I am most likely to listen to and watch is . . . .

After the variety of responses, say, "It is clear that we do not agree on many matters. Some differences may have consequences as to our relationships with others. Most do not." (Be sure to limit the discussion of each statement.)

## INTO THE WORD

Give learners paper and pen to use in responding with AGREE or DISAGREE to the following statements related to points made in today's lesson. You can either copy the statements onto the papers or simply read them aloud for learner response. (1) We must not allow matters of opinion or matters of individual conscience to become tests of fellowship. (2) For "strong" Christians, freedom in Christ eliminates all of the old scruples of behavior from their concern. (3) The "weak"—with more sensitive consciences—are the ones with stronger principles and stronger feelings. (4) I must not exclude or look down on someone who is part of the family of God, even if his or her eating habits are questionable. (5) We help each other keep the Master's rules, but we don't make the rules for each other. (6) Each of us is related to God, so we cannot help being related to each other. (7) Christ's death spells death for death. (8) When we are tempted to evaluate another person's conduct, we should remember that our time is better spent evaluating how we can encourage that person. (9) We can still be of one mind, even though we disagree concerning certain issues. As you listen to the responses, ask learners to identify verse numbers from the printed text that support their comments.

## INTO LIFE

Have class members divide into small discussion groups, and give the following directions to each group: "What are some matters with which you find yourself disagreeing with fellow church members, or even church leaders? List them. Establish a 'Consequence Sequence'; that is, number your entries from most serious to least serious. Decide which of the principles from today's study apply to dealing with each matter. Decide what these principles tell you about how to relate to your 'disagreeable' brothers and sisters." Give the groups enough time to work on this assignment, then call them together for reports from each. (A similar activity is included in the student book.)

# UNITY and DIVERSITY

Write down your impressions: How does this paper doll chain accurately represent how we are all alike in Christ? In what ways does the "sameness" in this chain fail to represent our actual relationships with Christ and with each other?

# HOLY DAYS, HOLIDAYS,
## and PLAIN OLD DAYS

Today's text notes the differing values that Christians might hold regarding debatable matters of Christian lifestyle, such as attitudes toward certain days and certain foods. What are some specific issues of Christian lifestyle about which today's Christians hold differing values? Write some of those below.

Now think of the verse from today's text that best states the principle for each Christian to follow when relating to other Christians who hold different values. Write it here: _____.

Next, use the space below to "personalize" the application of this passage for your own use in relating to other Christians who may not always see things the same way you do. (As you personalize this passage, make sure you do not violate Paul's intent.)

Finally, sign your commitment to follow both Paul's instructions and your personalized application. (You may find it helpful to enlist an "accountability partner" who will help keep you on track in following this Scripture.)

"With the strength of the Holy Spirit, I commit to relating to other Christians in ways that God desires."

_____
Signed

# BELIEVE NO OTHER GOSPEL

### LESSON 9

## WHY TEACH THIS LESSON?

Choices. We are accustomed to them. Dozens of flavors of soda line store shelves. Ads boast custom-designed investment options "to fit your individual needs." Entertainment providers offer hundreds of channels of programming. We even prefer multiple-choice tests.

It's no wonder we want to believe people have an assortment of faith options. Many Christians hate to think of people going to Hell because they chose the wrong belief system. We hear, "Why do you Christians always have to be so narrow-minded?"

We *must* see this from God's view. He provided a solution to our sin problem at great personal expense. If it were your son who died to bring an undeserving people back into a harmony with you, would you mind if they de-valued his death, then asked to have your favor anyway?

God word says, "Salvation is found in no one else, for there is no other name under heaven given to men by which we must be saved," (Acts 4:12). Not a long list of choices . . . not a short list . . . just one. Bottom line: for variety, go to the supermarket. For salvation, go to Jesus—that's why you need today's lesson.

## INTRODUCTION
### A. Is It Really Good News?

In our Scripture text today, Paul expresses his concern over a school of thought that referred to itself as *gospel* but wasn't. It called on people to depend on their own righteousness, particularly as expressed in Old Testament law-keeping, to get into Heaven. This message that Christians must fulfill all the Jewish laws was being specifically imposed upon the Gentile converts to Christianity. Paul could not call this good news, because it went back to a system that could not save people in the first place.

Let's say you and a companion are stranded on a desert island. Your companion says, "Guess what, there is a ship willing to pick us up. It is only one hundred miles away. The problem is we have to swim to meet it." That would not be good news. But if the ship has promised to come and pick you up, *that* would be good news. Certain teachers had been telling the Christians in Galatia that they had to, in effect, "swim" for their salvation. That can hardly be good news.

Paul was the ideal person to address this issue for at least three reasons. First, he himself had tried the system of salvation through keeping the law of Moses. If there was anyone who knew the fruitlessness of trying to get to Heaven by rigorous law-keeping, it was Paul. He described himself as "faultless" concerning "righteousness . . . that comes from the law." Yet he came to realize that only "the righteousness that comes from God and is by faith" is worth possessing (Philippians 3:6, 9).

Second, Paul was the right person to convey this message to Gentile Christians since, although he was an exemplary Jew, he had grown up in the Gentile world. In fact, when Jesus appeared to Paul (then called Saul) on the road to Damascus, he told him that he was being sent to the Gentiles (Acts 26:17).

DEVOTIONAL READING:
ACTS 13:26-33
BACKGROUND SCRIPTURE:
GALATIANS 1
PRINTED TEXT:
GALATIANS 1:1-12

### LESSON AIMS

After this lesson a student should be able to:

1. Give reasons why there is only one gospel revealed by God.

2. Identify ancient and modern false gospels.

3. Make a commitment to remain faithful to the gospel of Jesus Christ.

May
1

### KEY VERSE

I want you to know, brothers, that the gospel I preached is not something that man made up.
—Galatians 1:11

LESSON 9 NOTES

DAILY BIBLE READINGS

Monday, Apr. 25—Do Not Be Led Astray (2 Corinthians 11:1-15)

Tuesday, Apr. 26—In Christ All Things Hold Together (Colossians 1:15-23)

Wednesday, Apr. 27—We Bring You the Good News (Acts 13:26-33)

Thursday, Apr. 28—Everyone Who Believes Is Set Free (Acts 13:34-41)

Friday, Apr. 29—Bring Salvation to All (Acts 13:44-49)

Saturday, Apr. 30—Do Not Turn to Another Gospel (Galatians 1:1-7)

Sunday, May 1—Only One Gospel Directly from God (Galatians 1:8-12)

WHAT DO YOU THINK?

What are some occasions when we may need to remind someone of our authority or position? Have you ever had your position or authority challenged? What was the result?

Third, Paul was equipped to deal with this matter because he was acquainted with the Galatians by reason of his first missionary journey. During that time, he had introduced them to the gospel of grace. They were more likely to listen to Paul because his earlier conduct among them had testified to his concern for their spiritual welfare.

B. LESSON BACKGROUND

As we begin this series of lessons from Galatians, it is important to look at some general information about the history of both the territory and the church.

While Romans is considered Paul's greatest work, many would rank Galatians a close second. Some have called this book Paul's "Magna Carta." Others have called it the "Christian Declaration of Independence." The sixteenth-century reformer Martin Luther, whose wife's name was Katherine, referred to Galatians as his "Katherine" because of the high esteem in which he held it.

Unlike the majority of Paul's letters, Galatians was not written to a specific church in a city. For example, Romans was sent to Rome, and Philippians was sent to the city of Philippi. But Galatians was written to a group of churches in a province called Galatia. This province received its name from the Gauls who settled there in 279 B.C. The Gauls were originally a warlike Celtic people living in what is today northern France. A colony of them settled in what is now northern Turkey, but they were defeated by the Romans in 189 B.C. Later, in 25 B.C., the Romans captured that area, joined it with another area to the south, and named the province Galatia.

Bible scholars debate whether Paul is writing Galatians to the earlier and more northern area where the Gauls first lived, or whether he has the southern and newer part of the Roman province in mind. Most scholars have settled on the southern area as the most likely option. This would fit very well with events recorded in Acts, and it would date Galatians as one of Paul's first letters, or perhaps the very first. (Suggested dates would range from A.D. 48 to A.D. 52.) The area of southern Galatia would have included the cities of Iconium, Lystra, Derbe, and Pisidian Antioch. These were all churches that Paul founded during his first missionary journey with Barnabas, recorded in Acts 13 and 14.

Two primary issues underlie today's lesson and the entire book of Galatians. The first is that Paul himself is under attack. Some of his opponents claim he is not a real apostle and therefore has no real authority. Paul spends a great deal of time, particularly in the opening chapter of the letter, defending his apostleship; for if his authority is undermined, so is his message. Thus it is not just Paul himself under attack, but also the gospel.

This leads us to the second problem the book addresses. The Galatians had accepted the gospel Paul preached, but were now being seduced into thinking that they had to embrace all the law of Moses to be saved. The uniqueness of the gospel of grace was being compromised.

I. PAUL'S AUTHORITY (GALATIANS 1:1-5)

A. HIS CALLING (vv. 1, 2)

1. Paul, an apostle—sent not from men nor by man, but by Jesus Christ and God the Father, who raised him from the dead—

Paul immediately identifies himself by the title apostle. This claim serves to counter one of the problems noted under the Lesson Background—namely, that there are people doubting the legitimacy of Paul's apostleship.

Admittedly, Paul is not one of the original twelve apostles. He himself points out in this opening chapter that he has no close association with any of the

Twelve (Galatians 1:15-19). Since an apostle was to have witnessed the resurrection (Acts 1:21, 22; 22:12-15), Jesus' appearance to Paul on the road to Damascus enables him to carry the title *apostle* legitimately, though Paul recognizes that he is "one abnormally born" (1 Corinthians 15:8).

The word *apostle* describes an envoy or ambassador. Paul is an apostle with a special assignment to the Gentiles (Acts 9:15; 22:21; 26:17), and Jesus gave him that assignment. No group of *men* or individual *man* is the source of his ministry; he is called *by Jesus Christ* and ultimately *God the Father*.

**2. . . . and all the brothers with me,**

    *To the churches in Galatia:*

At the beginning of his letters, Paul normally identifies by name those who are traveling with him. Here he refers to them by the general term of *brothers*. Paul never considers his ministry a private matter. Others share with him in the preaching of the gospel and are often mentored by him (Timothy is probably the best example).

As stated earlier, the recipients of this letter are a group of *churches* in the region of *Galatia*. The work of the church is carried out primarily through local congregations. Paul intends for all the churches in Galatia to receive this message.

## B. HIS MESSAGE (vv. 3-5)

**3. Grace and peace to you from God our Father and the Lord Jesus Christ,**

Paul continues with his characteristic greeting of *grace and peace*. The words *grace* and *peace* are typical greetings of the day; *grace* is the typical Greek greeting, while *peace* is directed to those from a Jewish background. To any Christian, those two words possess a fuller meaning and significance.

**4. . . . who gave himself for our sins to rescue us from the present evil age, according to the will of our God and Father,**

Paul now describes the ministry of Jesus using three phrases. First, he says that Jesus *gave himself for our sins*. Jesus' death on the cross was not an accident. It was for that reason that he came to earth. To view his death as simply a heroic act or as the death of a martyr is to miss its divinely intended purpose. Paul writes in 1 Corinthians 15:3 that part of the gospel is the fact that "Christ died for our sins."

Second, Jesus is described as the one who came to *rescue us from the present evil age*. Paul is not describing how Jesus will one day take us away from this planet (though he certainly will do that). His primary focus is on Jesus' deliverance of us from the evil system that pervades this planet. The *present evil age* is one under the control of the "evil one," or Satan. A person who becomes a Christian becomes part of a different realm—one that is "not of this world" (John 18:36).

Third, Jesus acted *according to the will of our God and Father*. On one occasion Jesus stated, "My food . . . is to do the will of him who sent me and to finish his work" (John 4:34). As noted earlier, Jesus' death was part of the Father's plan—"God's set purpose and foreknowledge" (Acts 2:23).

**5. . . . to whom be glory for ever and ever. Amen.**

At this point Paul breaks forth into a note of praise. This happens from time to time in his writings, but not in a salutation. Paul may include his praise here because he knows he has to say some difficult things right away to the Galatians.

## II. PAUL'S CONCERN (GALATIANS 1:6-9)

### A. SOME ARE DESERTING THE GOSPEL (v. 6)

**6. I am astonished that you are so quickly deserting the one who called you by the grace of Christ and are turning to a different gospel—**

---

*WHAT DO YOU THINK?*

*How can we identify a "calling"? How can we tell if God has actually called a certain preacher, or if he is speaking on his own authority?*

*WHAT DO YOU THINK?*

*What sets Jesus apart from other spiritual leaders? How can we distinguish Jesus' claims from others in the religious world?*

Usually, following the salutation, Paul continues his letters with a word of encouragement, a prayer, or some personal reminiscences. These items are absent in the letter to the Galatians. The problem threatening the Galatians is too serious to postpone.

Paul is astonished that some among the Galatians are *so quickly deserting the one who called you*. We could say that they were acting like traitors, abandoning the gospel that Paul had so faithfully taught them. In the Greek language, the word Paul uses for *deserting* indicates that this abandonment was ongoing and in the process of occurring even as Paul was writing his letter. It is not something completed or in the past.

Within this verse are two phrases that can be interpreted in more than one way. When Paul marvels at how *quickly* the Galatians have removed themselves, he may be talking about how this occurred so soon after he presented the gospel to them or how quickly they deserted after hearing the "other gospel." The other question concerns the words *the one who called you*. The *one* may refer to God or it may refer to Paul. In the latter case, Paul would be expressing his personal hurt at seeing his message rejected in this way.

What was the other *gospel* that the Galatians were embracing? It was most likely that of a group known as the "Judaizers." These were first-century Jewish Christians who believed in Jesus, but also believed that everyone needed to keep all the Old Testament laws as well. This would particularly include the rite of circumcision. At the gathering in Jerusalem often called the "Jerusalem Conference," the position of the Judaizers was rejected by the leaders of the church in Jerusalem (Acts 15:1-29). They declared that Gentiles could come to Christ alone, without the added requirement of keeping the Old Testament law.

Paul describes this gospel as *a different gospel*. There were two words Paul could have used for *different*. This other gospel is so heinous in Paul's eyes that he sees it as totally different from the genuine gospel.

### B. SOME ARE PERVERTING THE GOSPEL (v. 7)

7. . . . *which is really no gospel at all. Evidently some people are throwing you into confusion and are trying to pervert the gospel of Christ.*

Paul is so opposed to this "different gospel" that he goes on to declare it is not really a *gospel at all*. What makes this situation especially dangerous is that this other gospel resembles the *gospel of Christ* in some ways, but is, in fact, a perversion of it. We could also describe it as a "counterfeit" gospel.

Paul characterizes those promoting this false message as *some people* who *are throwing* them *into confusion*. Those individuals who started the controversy resulting in the Jerusalem Conference are described as those who "disturbed you, troubling your minds by what they said" (Acts 15:24). Jewish traditions were meaningful to people of a Jewish background, but those traditions meant little to Gentiles.

Note how firmly Paul expresses himself in this section of Galatians. We must remember that Paul had started these churches, so he had the authority to speak to them in this manner. To Paul, this is not just an attack on him personally, but an attack on the gospel itself. Someone attacking the gospel has the potential to shake the faith of those Christians who may not be strong enough to withstand such an attack.

### C. A STERN WARNING (vv. 8, 9)

8. *But even if we or an angel from heaven should preach a gospel other than the one we preached to you, let him be eternally condemned!*

---

#### WHAT DO YOU THINK?

*Why do some people abandon the gospel? What makes competing religions and worldviews attractive?*

---

#### HOW TO SAY IT

*anathema.* uh-NATH-uh-muh.

*Antioch.* AN-tee-ock.

*Arabia.* Uh-RAY-bee-uh.

*Barnabas.* BAR-nuh-bus.

*Damascus.* Duh-MASS-kus.

*Derbe.* DER-be.

*Galatians.* Guh-LAY-shunz.

*Gauls.* Gawlz.

*Iconium.* Eye-KO-nee-um.

*Judaizers.* JOO-day-ize-ers.

*Lystra.* LISS-truh.

*Philippi.* Fih-LIP-pie or FIL-ih-pie.

*Pisidian.* Pih-SID-ee-un.

The main point of this verse is simple: the message is more important than the messenger. Paul regarded this other *gospel* that the Galatians had heard as so dangerous that he declared that those who propagate it should be *eternally condemned*. The Greek word translated *condemned* is *anathema*, which describes being under a curse or under the wrath of God. Paul applies the word to himself in Romans 9:3 where he writes of his concern for Jews who are lost: "I could wish that I myself were cursed and cut off from Christ for the sake of my brothers."

Paul reinforces his statement by adding that even if *an angel from heaven should preach* another gospel, he should be sentenced to this same judgment. It does not matter how attractive, appealing, or eloquent a teacher may be; if the content of the message contradicts the true gospel, then both the messenger and the false message come under condemnation.

9. *As we have already said, so now I say again: If anybody is preaching to you a gospel other than what you accepted, let him be eternally condemned!*

Paul states the curse *again*. He reminds the Galatians that they already know the true gospel. It has already been preached to them and they have accepted it. Anyone who preaches any other *gospel* is to *be eternally condemned*.

Visual for lesson 9. *Today's visual includes a map of the region of Galatia. Use it as you introduce students to the book of Galatians.*

### DESERTING AND PERVERTING

You, too, can be a "ghostbuster" (with apologies to the comedy film by that name from several years ago). You can get a college degree from a California-based online institution after taking courses in alchemy, herbology, and both basic and advanced witchcraft. You can buy a book entitled, *Complete Idiot's Guide to Ghosts and Hauntings;* or, for only $150, you can get a home-study course that will declare you a Certified Ghost Hunter™. You will learn such important "facts" (please note the quotation marks!) as these: most ghosts have names; they are harmless; they haunt us because they are trapped outside our world; they miss their loved ones or are trying to avenge some evil done to them in this life; they don't realize they are dead; the really bad ones were never human.

Throughout history, people have been tempted to turn away just a bit (sometimes quite a bit!) from the simple truths found in God's Word. Ghost-hunting and witchcraft are only two examples. In Paul's time, there were Christians who could not believe the simple truth of the gospel: that salvation comes not through our own works or knowledge, but through the grace of God found in Jesus Christ. When we desert the truth, we usually end up perverting it as well!     —C. R. B.

## III. PAUL'S GOSPEL (GALATIANS 1:10-12)

### A. NOT INTENDED TO PLEASE MEN (v. 10)

10. *Am I now trying to win the approval of men, or of God? Or am I trying to please men? If I were still trying to please men, I would not be a servant of Christ.*

Paul raises the questions found in this verse because it is quite likely that his accusers suggested he was preaching grace to *please* his audience. We can see how some could make this erroneous assumption. To some, the message of God's grace looked like it was letting people "off the hook" by relieving them of having to be concerned about their sin. (Paul deals with this issue more directly in Romans 6.)

Is Paul simply currying favor with his listeners by telling them what they want to hear? Paul strenuously denies that he is trying to please people. The reactions of people to what he has to say is not (and never was) a determining factor in Paul's ministry. If he tailors his message to fit what the audience wants to hear, then he will be an unfaithful messenger. Paul's primary concern is to be a *servant of Christ* by speaking the truth.

### WHAT DO YOU THINK?

*Are we ever tempted to soften the gospel message so we do not offend others? Do churches sometimes focus too much on grace and not enough on personal responsibility or moral absolutes? Defend your answers.*

*Gracious Father, we thank you that we do not have to depend on our righteousness to enter into Heaven. If we did, there would be no good news for us. Your gospel is the best news we have ever received. We thank you for Jesus, the author and bearer of this good news, and we pray in his name. Amen.*

## WOULD PAUL "GO FOR RATINGS"?

The quest for audience ratings (and thus advertising income) brings us a variety of television programs, including soap operas, late-night talk and comedy shows, crime-solving dramas, and game shows. In recent years the so-called "reality" shows became some of the most highly rated programs. These shows placed ordinary people in settings that supposedly tested their skills at surviving difficult situations or handling relationships with other people. Most of us haven't figured out how the term *reality* was supposed to fit. Putting strangers in contrived circumstances that bring out their character faults in front of millions of viewers, while TV cameras and crews create the illusion of danger, doesn't seem very "real," does it?

But here's a surprise: the top-rated TV show in New York City on Christmas morning in recent years has been nothing more than a picture of a yule log burning in a fireplace while Christmas carols play in the background! Television station WPIX has found that people are more pleased with tradition than with newness or "pizzazz"—at least on that one day of the year.

If the apostle Paul had been a TV programmer, it's not likely he would have "gone for ratings." He was interested in pleasing God, not men. In a day when most people seem interested only in what is "new," we must also make sure we hold on to what is *true!*                              —C. R. B.

### B. NOT REVEALED BY MEN (vv. 11, 12)

**11. I want you to know, brothers, that the gospel I preached is not something that man made up.**

Paul goes on to state confidently, that not only is his *gospel* not designed to please men, but also its source is not to be found in men. He did not invent it.

**12. I did not receive it from any man, nor was I taught it; rather, I received it by revelation from Jesus Christ.**

Paul affirms that his message came from divine *revelation*. It did not come by way of tradition or by rabbinical instruction, both of which are important sources of truth to the Jews (and to the Judaizers whom Paul seeks to refute). It came *by revelation from Jesus Christ*. This revelation includes not only Jesus' appearance to Paul on the road to Damascus, but also later instruction that may have occurred during the time Paul spent in Arabia (Galatians 1:17).

Like the rest of Scripture, the gospel that Paul teaches is no mere human invention. A way revealed by God was necessary, for left to our own devices and investigations we never would find the way to Heaven.

## CONCLUSION

Every nation or culture has stories of both heroes and traitors. Communities often raise statues to those individuals who are considered heroes. They do no such thing for those regarded as traitors.

Consider an example from one famous traitor story. What do you think of when you hear the name of Benedict Arnold? This man started out as one of George Washington's most trusted generals. Perhaps due to disappointment or jealousy, he offered to join the British side. As a result, neither side respected him. The fact is, you can't be on two sides at once, or as Jesus put it, "No one can serve two masters" (Matthew 6:24).

Paul saw the desertion of the Christians in Galatia in similar strong terms. He could not understand how anyone would embrace a position that endangered one's soul and placed one on the losing side. Paul's message to the Galatians and to us is to stay loyal to the gospel. If we fail to do so, this is the equivalent of being a traitor to the cause. If we do stay true to the gospel, we will be numbered among the heroes of faith.

*"[Jesus] gave himself for our sins to rescue us from the present evil age" (Galatians 1:4).*

# Discovery Learning

*This page contains an alternative lesson plan emphasizing learning activities. Classes desiring such student involvement will find these suggestions helpful. The next page is a reproducible activity page to further enhance discovery learning.*

## LEARNING GOALS

After this lesson a student should be able to:

1. Give reasons why there is only one gospel revealed by God.

2. Identify ancient and modern false gospels.

3. Make a commitment to remain faithful to the gospel of Jesus Christ.

## INTO THE LESSON

Write on the chalkboard: "Why is truth important? What are the consequences of falsehood?" Then write the following circumstances under the above heading:

- From your auto mechanic
- From your doctor
- From your child's schoolteacher
- From your spiritual mentor

As you write each circumstance, allow the class members to share answers about why truth is important in that situation and why falsehood is dangerous.

Make the transition to today's Bible study by pointing out that if we demand nothing but the truth in areas such as these just mentioned, why should we settle for anything less in matters with eternal ramifications? We must be certain that we have the truth when learning about such issues. If we do not, our eternal destiny is at risk. The experience of the Galatian churches will help us keep our eyes on the true gospel.

## INTO THE WORD

*Activity #1.* Begin the Bible study with a brief lecture on the background of the book of Galatians. Use the notes in the Lesson Introduction, the Lesson Background, and the comments on Galatians 1:1, 2 to complete this lecture. Prepare and display the outline below as you speak.

   I. Galatians
     A. Paul's Magna Carta
     B. Christian Declaration of Independence
     C. Esteemed by Martin Luther
   II. Paul's Audience
   III. Paul's Response to Attacks
     A. On Paul Himself
     B. On the Gospel
   IV. Paul, an Apostle

*Activity #2.* The following tasks may be done by small groups or by the entire class, depending upon time available and class preference. If using small groups, give each group a marker and poster board and the following instructions. Also give Group 2 a photocopy of the lesson commentary on Galatians 1:6-9.

*Task #1.* Read Galatians 1:3, 4. These verses summarize what Jesus did on our behalf. Discuss and list the significance of the following phrases about Jesus' work drawn from this text. Be ready to share your notes with the class.

- Gave himself
- For our sins
- Delivered us from this present evil world
- According to the will of God

*Task #2.* Read Galatians 1:6-9 and the lesson commentary on these verses. Your task is to discuss and summarize Paul's concerns for the Galatians and their spiritual welfare.

*Task #3.* Read Galatians 1:10-12. You have two tasks. First, list and comment on the key phrases that give authority to the gospel of which Paul speaks. Second, Paul's opponents were suggesting that he was preaching grace simply to please his audience. How might preaching grace (versus the Old Testament law) be misunderstood as letting people "off the hook"? Why would Paul's critics have viewed this as an easy gospel?

If using groups for the above exercise, allow each group to report its conclusions.

## INTO LIFE

To apply this Scripture to everyday life, ask people to cite ways to be sure we stay connected with the true gospel of Christ. List answers on a piece of poster board. Ideas may include study or know God's Word, maintain a daily Bible study time, attend Sunday school, invite a guest teacher or speaker on apologetics (a defense of basic Christian beliefs), always test teachings against God's Word, pray for wisdom, and other suggestions.

After compiling the list, ask groups of three or four people to discuss and select what they think are the two most important or helpful ideas on the list. Most groups will likely select an answer indicating the need for an intimate knowledge of the Bible.

Conclude the lesson by asking these same groups to pray together. Each person is to pray for himself and for one other person or group in the church, focusing on praying for faithfulness to the true gospel.

# How Do We Know It's True?

The apostle Paul was disappointed that the Galatians would forget the true gospel and be led away by false teachings. As we read the opening verses of this book, we are given a clue about how to discern the true gospel. Fill in the blanks below from Galatians 1:1-12. As you complete each blank, you will find a key word in knowing what is the true gospel.

1. Paul accused some of trying to ___ ___ ___ * ___ ___ ___ ___ the gospel of Christ (v. 7).

2. Paul was astonished that some were ___ ___ * ___ ___ ___ ___ ___ ___ ___ the one who called them to Christ (v. 6).

3. The Lord Jesus Christ ___ ___ ___ * ___ himself for our sins (v. 4).

4. The Lord wants to ___ ___ ___ ___ ___ ___ * us from the present evil age (v. 4).

5. Paul argued that he did not desire man's approval nor did he seek to ___ ___ * ___ ___ ___ ___ men (v. 10).

6. Paul affirms that he did not receive the gospel from any ___ ___ * ___ , but from Jesus (v. 12).

7. Not only did Paul not receive the gospel from any man, he also said he was not ___ ___ ___ ___ ___ ___ it (v. 12).
(asterisk under first blank)

8. This is the one who gave himself for our sins to rescue us from the present evil age. His name is Jesus. His title is ___ ___ ___ * ___ ___ (vv. 3, 4).

9. Anyone preaching a gospel other than the one given them by Paul should be eternally ___ ___ * ___ ___ ___ ___ ___ ___ ___ (v. 9).

10. One way to lure people away from the true gospel is to throw them into ___ ___ ___ ___ ___ ___ ___ ___ ___ * (v. 7).

From the letters with an asterisk (*), you will find the key to discovering the true gospel. It is the gospel given by ___ ___ ___ ___ ___ ___ ___ ___ ___ ___ .

KEY: 1. pervert; 2. deserting; 3. gave; 4. rescue; 5. please; 6. man; 7. taught; 8. Christ; 9. condemned; 10. confusion. Key word: Revelation.

# KNOW SALVATION BY FAITH

## LESSON 10

## WHY TEACH THIS LESSON?

My daughter, who has grown up with personal computers, was fascinated with her grandfather's old IBM typewriter. When he let her type with it, she became even more intrigued with the sheet of royal blue sandwiched between the two white pages. When she realized that the carbon paper created a second copy of what she had typed, she exclaimed, "Wow. With this you don't even need a photocopier!"

Today's lesson shows this type of backward thinking or misunderstood value. Through Christ, the world had received the free gift of salvation. Yet the people were allowing themselves to believe the hopeless idea of earning their righteousness.

Christians today also can misunderstand the role of works. It's important to realize that our Christian service has nothing to do with earning admission to Heaven. Our good works are a fitting response of a grateful heart—a love offering to God. And though we err if we think of our deeds as a negotiating tool to receive God's blessings, when deeds are done in love we are laying up treasures in Heaven.

## INTRODUCTION

### A. SEND ME BACK TO JAIL

Let's suppose you had spent much of your life in prison. At some point the appropriate government official gives you a pardon. You are set free! What would people think if you immediately turned around and walked back into the prison and said, "I don't want to go. I want to stay here." People would think you had lost your mind. And they would probably be right.

A similar kind of decision on the part of the Galatians troubled Paul. These believers had heard Paul's preaching and had learned the glory of God's grace. They had heard the message that liberated Peter and Paul and the rest of the early Christians from a law-oriented means of being right with God. Paul could not understand why anyone would want to go back to a system that was oppressive, frustrating, and did not accomplish what it was intended to do.

Today's lesson shows Paul pleading with the Galatians, both on a logical and an emotional level. It is clear from the apostle's impassioned words that he is greatly concerned that those whom he had worked so hard to bring to Christ remain free in Christ.

### B. LESSON BACKGROUND

Before studying these verses, we must keep in mind that the Jews in Paul's time had a very different understanding of the word *law* than we do. We tend to think of *law* as including civil rules and regulations—prescriptions that govern our conduct with each other. While there was an element of that within Old Testament laws, that system was primarily a way to get right with God. To the Jew in Paul's time, these laws consisted of not only regulations concerning one's relationships with others, but also ceremonial regulations covering such matters as

DEVOTIONAL READING:
GALATIANS 3:6-14
BACKGROUND SCRIPTURE:
GALATIANS 2:15–3:5
PRINTED TEXT:
GALATIANS 2:15–3:5

### LESSON AIMS

After this lesson students should be able to:

1. Define and explain justification by faith.

2. Compare their own awareness of God's grace to that experienced by the early Christians.

3. Prepare a testimony of God's grace to be used in everyday life.

May
8

### KEY VERSE

I have been crucified with Christ and I no longer live, but Christ lives in me. The life I live in the body, I live by faith in the Son of God, who loved me and gave himself for me.
—Galatians 2:20

LESSON 10 NOTES

DAILY BIBLE READINGS

Monday, May 2—Righteousness Through Faith (Romans 3:21-26)

Tuesday, May 3—Grace Given to You in Christ (1 Corinthians 1:3-9)

Wednesday, May 4—Fullness of Life in Christ (Colossians 2:6-14)

Thursday, May 5—Good News for Gentiles and Jews (Galatians 2:5-10)

Friday, May 6—We Are All Saved by Faith (Galatians 2:15-21)

Saturday, May 7—Law or Faith (Galatians 3:1-5)

Sunday, May 8—All Receive the Spirit's Promise (Galatians 3:6-14)

WHAT DO YOU THINK?

Do we ever feel superior to those who do not know Christ? Why is this an easy trap to fall into? What are some ways we can avoid looking down on those who have yet to hear the gospel?

worship and diet. Moral and ethical living was only a part of what the Jews thought of when they used the word *law*.

There is another important factor in the background of this text, and Paul alludes to it in the verses immediately preceding the first part of our text. It concerns Paul's report of a serious disagreement between him and Peter (Galatians 2:11-14). The conflict arose over how Peter treated certain Gentiles at Antioch where Paul and Barnabas were ministering. Antioch was the first church to evangelize large numbers of Gentile converts. Peter had previously spoken eloquently on two occasions about accepting the Gentiles. The first followed the conversion of Cornelius and his household (Acts 11:1-18); the second came at the Jerusalem Conference (Acts 15:6-11).

However, during the incident cited by Paul in Galatians, Peter shunned Gentile believers in order to spend time with Jewish Christians. Paul notes that Peter did this, "because he was afraid of those who belonged to the circumcision group" (Galatians 2:12). Peter seems to have yielded to a measure of "peer pressure" and had demonstrated some of the qualities associated with the "old" Peter (unreliable, quick to falter under pressure). No doubt Peter's actions hurt many of the newer Gentile Christians. Peter's behavior had even affected Barnabas (v. 13), who was known for his generous spirit. Paul confronted Peter and told him that what he was doing was wrong. That surely took some courage!

This confrontation between Paul and Peter, along with the material we are covering in today's lesson, show how controversial the question of Jew/Gentile relations was in the early church. When one reads the book of Acts, he or she cannot help but see that God is nudging and pushing the church to reach out to Gentiles with the gospel message. The gospel first comes to Jews, then to Samaritans, then to an Ethiopian Jewish proselyte, and finally to Cornelius, a Gentile. As noted earlier, it was Peter, not Paul, who welcomed the first Gentile convert. This may be another reason why Paul was so disturbed about Peter's conduct in Antioch.

Following the report of this difficult confrontation, Paul elaborates on the importance of justification by faith. Perhaps this teaching was some of what he shared with Peter.

## I. JUSTIFICATION BY FAITH DEFENDED (GALATIANS 2:15-21)
### A. PROVIDES MAN'S ONLY HOPE (vv. 15, 16)
### 15. "We who are Jews by birth and not 'Gentile sinners'

The word *we* may refer to Peter and Paul, to all the apostles, or to the early Jewish Christians in general. All of these were *Jews by birth*; that is, they were born Jewish. Certainly there were some advantages to being Jewish. The Jews had a long experience with understanding God's law, celebrating God's redemption, and listening to God's prophets tell of a coming Messiah. This was all part of their history as God's chosen people. (See Romans 9:4, 5.)

By referring to the *Gentiles* as *sinners*, Paul is sarcastically using language that was being used against the Gentiles. According to Jewish tradition, it was not that Gentiles were incapable of doing any moral good. They may do some good deeds, but since they do not have the law, they cannot please God. From the law's point of view, they were sinners.

The argument Paul is getting ready to make is essentially the same as his argument in Romans 2:17-29. Physical descent has nothing to do with one's salvation. Christ has come to save all people. As Paul teaches in both Romans and Galatians, the true "sons of Abraham" are those individuals who exercise faith as he did and are thus counted righteous in God's eyes (Romans 4:11, 12, 20-25; Galatians 3:7-9, 29).

16. "... know that a man is not justified by observing the law, but by faith in Jesus Christ. So we, too, have put our faith in Christ Jesus that we may be justified by faith in Christ and not by observing the law, because by observing the law no one will be justified.

When Paul says that a man is not justified by the works of the law, he is not speaking of any person in particular but of all humanity in general. He is confident of this claim, as one who had at one time sought righteousness by means of the law (Philippians 3:6). (Note that he affirms three times in this single verse that the law cannot provide justification.) By using the word we, he maintains that Peter knows this, too. And Peter should have been just as confident of this truth, given his experiences with the household of Cornelius and at the Jerusalem Conference.

There is only one way to be justified, states Paul, and that is by faith in Jesus Christ. The word translated as justified comes from the language of the courtroom. It literally means "to declare innocent." The law of Moses could never produce such an outcome. For one thing, no one can ever keep the law perfectly. Second, it is possible for someone to keep the law outwardly, yet without any inner love, faith, or commitment to God. On one occasion, Jesus noted the Pharisees' failure to observe the "more important matters of the law" while paying close attention to certain external details (Matthew 23:23).

This does not mean that works are unimportant. Good works are meant to be a sign of our love for Christ and evidence of a living faith. Paul tells us in Ephesians 2:10 that Christians are "created in Christ Jesus to do good works, which God prepared in advance for us to do." What Paul is specifically dealing with in Galatians is depending on the Old Testament law as a means of salvation. He asserts that keeping the law can never make anyone good enough to enter Heaven. His teaching on this point is the same as that found in the early chapters of Romans.

### THE FAILURE OF LAW

Some people who live east of the Rocky Mountains refer to the West Coast of America as "the left coast" (for more reasons than just the fact that it appears on the left side of the map of the United States). The San Francisco Bay area, in particular, has long been known for its leftward-leaning politics and more recently for being a bastion of "political correctness."

An example of the kind of thinking that brings derision on some Californians came about in the spring of 2003. In the San Francisco peninsula city of Palo Alto, the city council passed a resolution that forbade city officials from making facial expressions that showed "disagreement or disgust" during council meetings, including rolling the eyes, sticking out the tongue, sneering, and frowning. The council quickly became the butt of jokes by comedians and everyday folks alike, so after a month, they backed down and simply called for "respectful silence and decorum."

These council members finally learned what Paul knew about law. You cannot make a person "good" or "just" simply by passing laws. You can enforce "good" behavior; but unless the heart is in it, there is no moral content to those actions. In urging the Galatians not to revert to the law of Moses, Paul is saying that moral regeneration comes through faith in Christ. That alone can justify us; laws, no matter how well intentioned, cannot.                                        —C. R. B.

*WHAT DO YOU THINK?*

*Have you ever felt that you were not "good enough" for God? How can we address these issues in ourselves and in others?*

### B. DOES NOT PROMOTE SIN (vv. 17-19)

17. "If, while we seek to be justified in Christ, it becomes evident that we ourselves are sinners, does that mean that Christ promotes sin? Absolutely not!

In this verse, Paul attempts to anticipate some objections that might be raised against his position. He seems to be addressing those who think his emphasis on grace will promote sin. Some might argue with Paul that all of his talk of grace

## What Do You Think?

*In what ways do our sins reflect upon the Savior? How do non-Christians tend to react when learning of a Christian's sin?*

and justification by faith will lead to moral laxity. People will think they can do anything they want with impunity, then simply ask to be forgiven. Paul strongly denies that this is the outcome of the gospel of grace. He declares that Christ would never do anything that would make us sin more and thus make Christ to be the minister of sin. The whole idea leads Paul to respond with *absolutely not!*

Once again, we can see a similarity between this teaching and what Paul outlines in his letter to the Romans. In this case the similarity is found in Romans 6, where Paul says, "Shall we go on sinning so that grace may increase? By no means!" (Romans 6:1, 2).

18. *"If I rebuild what I destroyed, I prove that I am a lawbreaker.*

In the previous verse, Paul considered the possible objection of some that the doctrine of justification could actually be promoting sin. In this verse, he maintains that what would constitute sin would be a return to embracing the law as a means of salvation. This is most likely what he means by his reference to *rebuild what I destroyed.* Even though Paul believed that the law is good and has a purpose (Romans 7:7-12), he recognized that he had, in a sense, *destroyed* the system of law by preaching grace, not law, as the way to be right with God.

In its simplest terms, Paul is describing a situation where a person would come to Christ but later try to go back to keeping the law of Moses as a means of salvation. Anyone who does so would be a *lawbreaker.*

Again, it is helpful to compare Paul's teaching here with what he says in Romans: "Christ is the end of the law so that there may be righteousness for everyone who believes" (Romans 10:4). It is also similar to the theme of the book of Hebrews, which seeks to encourage Jewish Christians not to abandon their faith and return to Judaism. The key word in Hebrews is *better,* because the writer wants to show that the New Covenant under Christ is superior to the Old Covenant (Hebrews 8:8-13).

19. *"For through the law I died to the law so that I might live for God.*

*The law* has fulfilled its function when it has led a person to see his or her need for grace. There is no reason to go back to it, once one has experienced grace. The law taught Paul that he was a sinner and that his sins could be dealt with only by dying *to the law.* The law shows us our need for a Savior, thus preparing us for the good news of the gospel. Once one accepts Christ as Savior, there can be no turning back to the law.

Indirectly, Paul is saying that the law demands death for sin and that there has been a death. It is Jesus' death that satisfies the law's demands. To accept his death as the substitute for ours is the only way for us to *live for God.*

## What Do You Think?

*Is Jesus the only way to salvation? If we claim that Jesus is the only way, are we being judgmental and arrogant?*

### C. Honors the Death of Christ (vv. 20, 21)

20. *"I have been crucified with Christ and I no longer live, but Christ lives in me. The life I live in the body, I live by faith in the Son of God, who loved me and gave himself for me.*

This is one of the most well-known verses in Galatians. How are we *crucified with Christ?* He bore our sins on the cross. We are united with him when we accept his death as the substitute for ours. How do we *live?* Once more, it is helpful to consider Paul's teaching on this matter in Romans, particularly in Romans 6. There he says that just as Jesus arose from the dead to live a new life, through baptism we rise from our death to sin to "live a new life" (Romans 6:4). That new life is lived under a new master; as Paul puts it, *Christ lives in me.* He empowers us to keep the law as well as forgiving us of our failures to keep it. Thus our lives are not ours anymore; they belong to Christ. If we accept this, says Paul, why would we want to continue to serve sin? Why should we return to the law?

## What Do You Think?

*How are we "crucified with Christ"? How can we be crucified and yet live? In what ways can we identify with Christ's death?*

*21. "I do not set aside the grace of God, for if righteousness could be gained through the law, Christ died for nothing!"*

Paul has answered his critics and now claims that if they are right, then the death of Christ means nothing. If *the law* were sufficient as a means of making us right with God, Jesus would not have had to die.

## II. JUSTIFICATION BY FAITH TESTED (GALATIANS 3:1-5)

### A. HOW DID YOU RECEIVE THE HOLY SPIRIT? (vv. 1, 2)

*1. You foolish Galatians! Who has bewitched you? Before your very eyes Jesus Christ was clearly portrayed as crucified.*

The Greek word translated *foolish* means literally "to have no mind." It does not mean uninformed or ignorant. The word implies that the *Galatians* know the truth but have not acted on it. They provide an excellent illustration of why Scripture so often warns God's people against being deceived. The Phillips' translation renders *foolish Galatians* as "dear idiots." Perhaps such a phrase captures both Paul's deep love for the Galatians and his disappointment at how quickly they have forsaken the truth of the gospel.

Paul sees the Galatians' rejection of the gospel as so absurd that surely someone must have *bewitched* them. The Greek term carries with it the idea of casting a spell by "the evil eye." This does not mean that Paul actually believes someone can be bewitched. He is simply using a figure of speech to make his point. Today we might say something like, "Who has hypnotized you?" but we would not mean for that to be taken in a literal sense.

Paul goes on to describe Jesus' crucifixion as being *clearly portrayed* before the Galatians' *eyes.* The word translated *clearly portrayed* was normally used to refer to a placard that was set up in a public place. Jesus' crucifixion was clearly, unmistakably set before the Galatians through the preaching of the gospel. How could they reject such a message and act as if they never heard it? Other commentators believe that this verse simply describes how Jesus himself was put on public display when he was *crucified.*

*2. I would like to learn just one thing from you: Did you receive the Spirit by observing the law, or by believing what you heard?*

Paul then asks the Galatians how they received the Holy *Spirit.* Did that happen *by observing the law?* Absolutely not; the Spirit was received *by believing what they heard.* The thought is similar to that found in Romans 10:17: "Faith comes from hearing the message, and the message is heard through the word of Christ."

### B. HOW DID YOU BEGIN TO GROW? (vv. 3, 4)

*3. Are you so foolish? After beginning with the Spirit, are you now trying to attain your goal by human effort?*

Paul asks *Are you so foolish?* using the same word for *foolish* that he used in verse 1. Then, building on his argument in the preceding verse, Paul argues that if the Galatians' Christian lives began by receiving *the Spirit* through faith, how could growth be maintained by striving to live Christ's life *by human effort?* The fact is that this is an impossibility. Moving from life under the control of the Spirit to life under the control of the flesh would be going backward, not forward. The longer a Christian lives, the more he or she should be less tied to the flesh and more attuned to the Holy Spirit. Paul will call further attention to this in Galatians 5:16-26. We will be studying a portion of this passage in Lesson 13.

*4. Have you suffered so much for nothing—if it really was for nothing?*

What have the Galatian Christians *suffered?* We do not know for sure about the *much* to which Paul is referring. He may be describing the kind of physical

"The life which I now live in the flesh I live by the faith of the Son of God, who loved me, and gave himself for me." —Galatians 2:20

Visual for lesson 10. *Use this visual as you discuss what Paul's words, "I am crucified with Christ," mean for Christians today.*

### WHAT DO YOU THINK?

How did you come to faith in Christ? What experiences led you to do so? What is your testimony of your own faith journey?

## HOW TO SAY IT

Antioch. AN-tee-ock.
Barnabas. BAR-nuh-bus.
Cornelius. Cor-NEEL-yus.
Ethiopian. E-thee-O-pee-un.
Galatians. Guh-LAY-shunz.
Gentiles. JEN-tyles.
Judaism. JOO-day-iz-um.
Pharisees. FAIR-ih-seez.
proselyte. PRAHSS-uh-light.
Samaritans. Suh-MARE-uh-
    tunz.

## PRAYER

Dear Father, thank you for setting me free. Having left the prison of sin, help me not to live like a prisoner. Help me to give my life to you, in gratitude for all you have given me. Through Christ, whose death and resurrection made the difference. Amen.

## THOUGHT TO REMEMBER

We are not saved because of how good we are. We are saved because of how good God is.

suffering common to all human beings. He may be citing the persecution experienced by the Galatians.

Another possibility is that Paul is using "suffer" in an older and more general sense to simply describe things that have happened to the Galatians—in other words, their experiences since obeying the gospel. Paul would then be asking, "Does all that you have received since coming to Christ mean nothing to you?"

### C. HOW DID GOD REVEAL HIS POWER? (v. 5)

**5. Does God give you his Spirit and work miracles among you because you observe the law, or because you believe what you heard?**

Paul's final question in this section of Scripture asks the Galatians to think back to when they saw the power of God at work in various *miracles*. When miracles happened, asks Paul, did they come as a consequence of keeping the old law? The answer is no. Paul uses once more the phrase *believe what you heard*. Again, he emphasizes that whatever spiritual blessings the Galatians have experienced have come in response to the message of God's truth rather than through legalistic observances.

### SPIRITUAL PROGERIA

Situations are not always as they appear on the outside. A tragic example of this can be seen in the victims of what is known as Hutchinson-Gilford progeria (pro-jair-ee-uh) syndrome. This syndrome develops because a single DNA molecule (out of three billion DNA units in the human genetic structure) is misplaced. Children born with progeria seem to be normal at birth, but within eighteen months they begin a process of accelerated aging. They become three-foot-tall, thirty-five-pound "old people." Their skin becomes wrinkled and their bones become fragile and subject to fractures—traits we expect in people of advanced years. Most victims of progeria lose their hair by the time they are four years old, and they usually die of heart disease or stroke by the time they are thirteen.

Some among the Galatian Christians apparently thought they could become mature spiritually by going back to the law. However, Paul tells them that situations are not as they seem: legalism is a deadly syndrome that produces only the *appearance* of spiritual health. But legalism quenches the power of the Holy Spirit—God's power to give us life. All too soon it becomes clear that there is no energizing spirit working in those who trust in the works of legalism. They may grow "old," but will never grow to real maturity in Christ.     —C. R. B.

## CONCLUSION

One Sunday morning a small boy entered the sanctuary of a church building for the very first time. He was completely unfamiliar with the Christian faith and with many of the characteristics of a church building that most Christians take for granted. Among the first items he noticed was the large cross attached to the wall at the front of the sanctuary. Turning to the adult who had brought him that morning, he asked, "Say, why is that plus sign on the wall up there?"

That young man spoke far more truth than he realized. The cross is indeed God's "plus sign." It speaks to us of all the blessings God wants to add to our lives. He wants to add all that was subtracted when man sinned in the Garden of Eden.

Some believe that being a Christian is a losing proposition—that one does not get back as much as he or she gives up. That is the very opposite of what Jesus taught: "Whoever loses his life for me will find it" (Matthew 16:25). So the little boy was right. In a world where so much that confronts us is negative, the cross remains God's plus sign.

# Discovery Learning

*This page contains an alternative lesson plan emphasizing learning activities. Classes desiring such student involvement will find these suggestions helpful. The next page is a reproducible activity page to further enhance discovery learning.*

## LEARNING GOALS

After this lesson students should be able to:

1. Define and explain justification by faith.

2. Compare their own awareness of God's grace to that experienced by the early Christians.

3. Prepare a testimony of God's grace to be used in everyday life.

## INTO THE LESSON

Begin this lesson with a brief skit that you should give to three people during the week. Ask them to meet about thirty minutes before class for a brief rehearsal. Encourage them to be creative and to "ham it up." Use simple props to represent a jail cell. A sign on the wall can read "County Jail." Include two chairs with a small table or crate between them. Two prisoners will be playing cards or checkers on the table or crate. Their small talk could include why they are incarcerated, family background, etc. It should be clear that one prisoner has spent most of his adult life in prison. The third character will be the jailer who arrives and announces to the prisoner who has been in jail most of his life that the state governor has given him a pardon. As this prisoner walks out of the cell, he suddenly hesitates and says, "I don't want to go," and goes back into the cell. The jailer asks if he has lost his mind.

Make the transition to Bible study by stating that if something like this actually happened, people would think such a prisoner had lost his mind. Yet this is how many Christians live today. They continue to struggle with a legalism that keeps them from enjoying the freedom of God's grace.

How do we overcome such a mind-set? Paul's letter to the Galatians can help us discover the joy of living in God's grace.

## INTO THE WORD

Use three class members to prepare a series of brief presentations to be used as part of your Bible study time. Select and meet with these people early in the week to explain their tasks. Each person is allowed a maximum of five minutes for his or her presentation. Give each presenter a photocopy of the entire commentary on today's text.

*Presentation #1:* Begin with a brief lecture based on the Lesson Background that is found on pages 309 and 310 of the lesson commentary. The following outline, on a piece of poster board or on the chalkboard, will be useful.

    I. Old Testament Law

    II. The Gentile Controversy: Paul and Peter

    III. Justification by Faith

*Teacher:* Make the transition to the next presentation by emphasizing that we need to understand the difference between justification by faith and justification by the law. Read Galatians 2:15-21 before the transition to the next presentation.

*Presentation #2:* This presentation will focus on Galatians 2:16. Use the lesson commentary and a Bible dictionary to define justification, and explain the difference between justification by faith and justification by the law. Also address the question, "Does this mean that works are unimportant?"

*Presentation #3:* Using Galatians 3:1-5, explain and list on a poster board or on the chalkboard reasons why justification by faith is a better system than justification by the law. After completing this presentation, ask class members if they have other ideas to add to the list.

Make the transition to applying this lesson by reminding the class of the opening skit. It appears that the Galatian Christians, although freed from the law of Moses, wanted to go back to it.

## INTO LIFE

Use all the following activities if time permits.

*Activity #1: Brainstorming.* Ask the class, "What might be symptoms or examples of a Christian who is living with a 'justification by the law' mentality? What kinds of behavior or thoughts might be handicapping this person's sense of freedom?" List these symptoms or examples on the chalkboard.

*Activity #2: Helping a Friend.* Ask the class to imagine a Christian friend who is handicapped by some of the symptoms or examples cited during the previous activity. Ask class members how they would explain the joy of "justification by faith" to such a person.

*Activity #3: Creative Praise.* Celebrate God's grace and justification by faith by compiling a list of songs and lines from songs that highlight faith and grace. Conclude by singing one of those songs (such as "Amazing Grace," "Faith is the Victory," or "I Will Sing of the Mercies of the Lord Forever").

# Strong Words!

Paul isn't playing the "Political Correctness" game in his rebuke of the Galatians. He uses strong and active words to make it clear that he is upset about their doctrinal drift toward "justification by works." He makes it clear Christians are justified by *faith in Jesus Christ!* Just to capture the sense of his strong feelings, write in his strong words in the blanks below.

Twice, Paul calls the Galatians    __F__ __ __ __ __ __ __    (3:1, 3)

About Christ promoting sin, Paul says

__A__ __ __ __ __ __ __ __ __ __ not! (2:17)

What a great "tongue-in cheek" phrase Paul uses in saying the Jews are not

__ __ __ __ __I__ __ __    __ __ __ __ __ __ __ (2:15)

Paul even accuses the Galatians of being

__ __ __ __ __T__ __ __ __ __ (3:1)

Paul asks if they, as believers, have suffered for

__ __ __ __H__ __ __ __ (3:4)

Foolish, Absolutely, Gentile sinners, bewiTched, notHing

# Wonderful Word Pictures

On the more positive side, Paul paints wonderful word pictures of life with Christ. Re-read some of these wonderful word pictures and write a few notes about what these snapshots mean to you.

"Justified . . . by faith in Jesus Christ" (2:16)

"I died to the law" (2:19)

"I have been crucified with Christ" (2:20)

"The life I live in the body, I live by faith in the Son of God" (2:20)

# UNDERSTAND THE PURPOSE OF THE LAW

**LESSON 11**

## WHY TEACH THIS LESSON?

Let's play a game called, "What's wrong with this picture?" A woman gets in her car and tries to drive it down the railroad tracks—what's wrong with this picture? A man on a bicycle tries to ride it across a deep river—what's wrong with this picture? A child picks up a fork and attempts to eat tomato soup with it—what's wrong with this picture?

In each case, there is nothing wrong with the tools themselves; each is designed for a specific function and can perform that function well. The problem in each case lies in trying to use a tool that is not suited for what is desired to be accomplished. The Old Covenant law had a definite purpose. Today's lesson will help us understand what that purpose was as we continue in the grace of God.

## INTRODUCTION

### A. TEMPORARY, BUT NECESSARY

There are many items in life that have a purpose, but are only temporary. Training wheels have a significant part to play in learning to ride a bicycle, but no one would argue that it is superior to riding without them. Braces have a purpose, but no one would argue that wearing braces is superior to unadorned, straight teeth. That something is temporary does not negate its importance or, in some cases, its necessity.

To Paul, the law of Moses was temporary, but necessary. It is fascinating to think that someone like Paul became the one to convey such a message as this. He had, at one time, given his entire life to the law and claimed that he was "faultless" concerning "legalistic righteousness" (Philippians 3:6). Then came the dramatic encounter with Christ on the road to Damascus, after which Paul gave his life to Christ and to the cause he had once tried to eliminate from the face of the earth. This Christ declared on one occasion that he had not come to destroy the law and the prophets, but to fulfill them (Matthew 5:17). Paul accepted this new perspective on the law; however, as we have noted during our studies from Galatians, not all first-century Christians were as willing to do so. Clarifying the purpose of the law was one of the reasons for Paul's letter to the Galatians.

### B. LESSON BACKGROUND

In today's printed text, Paul continues his efforts to instruct the Galatian Christians about the correct relationship between law and grace. Because of Paul's preaching of the gospel of grace, some opponents accused Paul of having no use for the Old Testament law at all. While Paul presented the new message of grace without apology, he also readily acknowledged that there was a purpose for the old law of Moses. He strenuously maintained that the new is superior, but that the old had a purpose in God's plan.

DEVOTIONAL READING:
ROMANS 3:27-31
BACKGROUND SCRIPTURE:
GALATIANS 3:19–4:7
PRINTED TEXT:
GALATIANS 3:19-29; 4:4-7

## LESSON AIMS

After completing this lesson, each student should be able to:

1. Explain the word pictures of law and grace that Paul chose to use in this passage.

2. Identify blessings and responsibilities that come with God's adoption of each of us.

3. Express to God a sense of joy in knowing that they have been adopted by him.

## KEY VERSES

May 15

When the time had fully come, God sent his Son, born of a woman, born under law, to redeem those under law, that we might receive the full rights of sons. Because you are sons, God sent the Spirit of his Son into our hearts, the Spirit who calls out, "Abba, Father."
—Galatians 4:4-6

LESSON 11 NOTES

The verses that precede our printed text from Galatians 3 deal with God's covenant with Abraham. Paul raises this issue in order to show that God dealt with people on the basis of grace before the law of Moses was given. He shows that God's covenant with Abraham was based on grace and that Abraham had to respond to God by faith. He "believed God, and it was credited to him as righteousness" (Galatians 3:6). Paul then notes that in one sense, God "announced the gospel in advance to Abraham: 'All nations will be blessed through you'" (v. 8). We will see in our lesson today how Paul develops this thought and concludes by describing Christians as "Abraham's seed."

## I. THE FAILURES OF THE LAW (GALATIANS 3:19-22)

### A. TEMPORARY (vv. 19, 20)

*19. What, then, was the purpose of the law? It was added because of transgressions until the Seed to whom the promise referred had come. The law was put into effect through angels by a mediator.*

Paul set forth such a strong case for grace and faith that his opponents sometimes accused him of being anti-law. In this verse and the verses to follow, Paul asks and answers the question, *What, then, was the purpose of the law?* He maintains that the law was quite necessary; it had a definite purpose in God's plan.

That purpose is then stated as follows: the law *was added because of transgressions*. One of the purposes of the law of Moses was to expose sin and identify specific sins. This function was only temporary, however. The law was in effect *until the Seed*, or the offspring, *to whom the promise referred had come*. The word *seed* in the Bible often refers to a person's progeny or descendants. In this case it is referring to one individual—Jesus Christ. Paul had made this point earlier in verses 16 and 17 of this chapter. Those verses make it clear that the *promise* mentioned in verse 19 is the promise God gave to Abraham. Verse 19 thus links Jesus to the promise made to Abraham that his seed would bless the entire world.

WHAT DO YOU THINK?

*How should we understand the law of Moses from a Christian perspective? What purpose did (or does) the law serve?*

In illustrating the superiority of the way of grace to the old law, Paul points out that the law was *put into effect through angels by a mediator*. That angels played a part in the giving of the law at Mount Sinai may be drawn from Deuteronomy 33:2. Stephen mentions angels and the giving of the law in his speech before the Sanhedrin (Acts 7:53). Hebrews 2:2 describes "the message spoken by angels" in a context that is referring to the law of Moses. Perhaps this is one reason why Paul mentions the possibility of an "angel from heaven" being the source of another gospel (Galatians 1:8). The *mediator* Paul mentions is Moses.

While all of this is a testimony to the importance of the law, it also helps to highlight how differently the New Covenant was delivered. This will become a bit clearer as we proceed further in our study.

*20. A mediator, however, does not represent just one party; but God is one.*

Paul's argument seems to be as follows: *a mediator* represents both sides of a covenant, but a promise depends on only *one* side. In this way, Paul makes a case for the superiority of the New Covenant. Why is it superior? *God* himself came to us in the person of Jesus Christ. It is true that there are places in Scripture where Jesus is referred to as a mediator (as in 1 Timothy 2:5), but Paul is forming a different kind of argument when he uses the word here. Since Jesus is divine, he can offer the promise of God's grace to us without any outside help.

### B. UNABLE TO SAVE (vv. 21, 22)

*21. Is the law, therefore, opposed to the promises of God? Absolutely not! For if a law had been given that could impart life, then righteousness would certainly have come by the law.*

Here Paul affirms that *the law* must never be considered an enemy to *the promises of God*. Paul does not want his teaching to be misunderstood to say that. Elsewhere Paul maintains that "the law is holy, and the commandment is holy, righteous and good" (Romans 7:12). Both the law and the promises are from God, but each serves a distinct purpose. When we learn that we have broken the law and that the law provides no remedy for our inability to keep it, then it leads us to Christ and to the ability of his grace to provide what the law cannot. In God's plan, law and grace are meant to complement, not contradict, one another. The law diagnoses our illness, and Jesus, the great physician, provides the cure.

**22. But the Scripture declares that the whole world is a prisoner of sin, so that what was promised, being given through faith in Jesus Christ, might be given to those who believe.**

If our hope lies in our ability to keep the law, then we are in serious trouble. Since no one can keep the law perfectly, all we can do is to throw ourselves on the mercy of the court. And there is mercy! We must *believe* in and accept the promise of God given through *Jesus Christ*. Paul's teaching here is quite similar to that found in Romans 3:19-26.

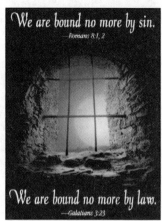

Visual for lessons 5 and 11. *Use this visual when discussing Galatians 3:23 and Paul's description of the law as a prison.*

### ONLY A TEMPORARY THING

More than seventy-five years ago, bubble gum "popped" onto the scene. The popular gooey pink stuff was invented by Walter Diemer, an accountant who was working for a chewing gum company. Diemer wanted to make the gum colorful, and he had no food coloring except pink; so pink it was—and has been since (with some additional colors featured to offer some variety). The first five pounds of the stuff were sold in a Philadelphia grocery store for a penny a piece. It was gone within a few hours.

How about some more statistics to "chew on"? Bubble gum is comprised of sixty to seventy percent sugar. The biggest bubble on record is twenty-two inches in diameter. And, contrary to what your mother may have told you, if you swallow your bubble gum, it won't stay in your stomach for seven years.

Why bring up the subject of bubble gum when today's lesson is about the Old Testament law? (I thought you'd never ask!) Many a mother has responded to the disheartening sight of her child's face covered by a popped bubble by asking, "Won't you *ever* grow up?" By the time most people get through high school—or at least college—they outgrow the need they once felt to have nearly their entire face enclosed in bubble gum. And, at some point in the process of gaining spiritual maturity, most serious seekers after God's will outgrow the illusory and temporary satisfaction that comes from living by law. Eventually the successful quest for spiritual maturity brings one to the joy of living by faith in the grace of God.        —C. R. B.

## II. THE FUNCTION OF THE LAW (GALATIANS 3:23-26)

### A. A PRISON GUARD (v. 23)

**23. Before this faith came, we were held prisoners by the law, locked up until faith should be revealed.**

Here Paul describes us as *prisoners by the law*. We are in such a condition because we are in fact guilty of sin. Every human being has been confined to a place on "death row." But the situation is not hopeless. A pardon has been provided through the death of Jesus. By *faith* in him, we can be released from our prison.

### B. A SCHOOLMASTER (vv. 24-26)

**24. So the law was put in charge to lead us to Christ that we might be justified by faith.**

*WHAT DO YOU THINK?*

*In what ways does law (any kind of law) imprison us? Why are these experiences necessary?*

This verse presents a very meaningful word picture. Behind the idea of the law being *put in charge* stands the idea of a "schoolmaster." The description is that of someone who had a significant role to play in a child's upbringing. Another word for this person might be "guardian" or "tutor." This person was given the responsibility of monitoring and disciplining a child from about six years of age until sixteen. He was not the child's actual teacher; the tutor often supervised the child as he went to and from school each day and monitored the child's behavior after school—checking on the company he kept and the activities in which he participated. He also made sure that the child's homework was done. In addition, the tutor supervised any household chores for which the child was responsible. Usually such a monumental task was given to a trusted slave.

In Paul's day the tutor could sometimes be considered harsh and cruel. After all, he was given full authority to discipline a child. Most any child longed for the day when he would be rid of his tutor, for that day marked his freedom!

It should not be difficult to understand why Paul uses this word picture of a schoolmaster or tutor to describe the function of the law. The law's purpose is *to lead us to Christ that we might be justified by faith*. The law's purpose was never to save anyone; it was to show the need for the one who can save everyone.

**25. Now that faith has come, we are no longer under the supervision of the law.**

Completing his illustration, Paul says that *now that faith has come, we are no longer under the supervision of the law*. The law's supervisory job is only temporary. It is "out of work" once we come to Christ and discover the freedom that he alone can provide. At that point, we have "matured" to where we are part of God's family. The schoolmaster is no longer necessary.

### NEEDED: A GUIDE

Most people in the over-60 generation can remember when Edmund Hillary (now Sir Hillary) and Tenzing Norgay (Ten-sing Nor-gay) became the first men to successfully reach the peak of Mt. Everest and live to tell about it. (Some believe that others may have reached the summit, but lost their lives on the way back down.) The Hillary-Norgay team accomplished their feat in 1953.

Fifty years later, in 2003, a Hillary-Norgay team was on the mountain again. This time it was the sons of those heroes, filming a TV special about the fascination the mountain still has for adventurers. Although people from all over the world have tried to climb the mountain, they always go with an experienced guide, usually a Sherpa—a member of the Tibetan tribe that lives in the vicinity. For the kind of danger the mountain holds, a trustworthy guide is an absolute necessity.

The role of a guide is the role the law of God has played in the spiritual history of the human race. It has taught us about the dangers of the towering cliffs and treacherous crevasses of sin that can bring disaster for the unwary and inexperienced. The law has prepared us for the next guide—Jesus Christ—who can take us to the next spiritual "level." As Paul notes in today's text, eventually we outgrow our need for the law as a "schoolmaster"; but we will always need Jesus to take us the rest of the way to the Father.

—C. R. B.

**26. You are all sons of God through faith in Christ Jesus,**

Previously Paul described us as under the authority of the law—prisoners. How our status has changed! Now we are *sons of God through faith in Christ Jesus*.

### III. THE FULFILLMENT OF THE LAW (GALATIANS 3:27-29; 4:4-7)
### A. BY GRACE WE CLOTHE OURSELVES WITH CHRIST (v. 27)

**27. . . . for all of you who were baptized into Christ have clothed yourselves with Christ.**

Here Paul calls upon the Galatians to reflect upon the time of their conversion. His words are reminiscent of his teaching from Romans 6, noted in Lesson 4, concerning baptism as the time when someone who has died to sin is raised to "live a new life" (Romans 6:1-4).

Paul adds that those who *were baptized into Christ have clothed* themselves *with Christ*. Paul is probably referring to the fact that the righteousness of Christ is now our righteousness. His "robe of righteousness" (Isaiah 61:10) has replaced our "filthy rags" (Isaiah 64:6). As we grow in the Christian life, we should become more and more like Christ and more comfortable wearing his "wardrobe." Note Paul's instructions to the Roman Christians: "Clothe yourselves with the Lord Jesus Christ, and do not think about how to gratify the desires of the sinful nature" (Romans 13:14).

## B. BY GRACE WE ARE UNITED (v. 28)

**28. There is neither Jew nor Greek, slave nor free, male nor female, for you are all one in Christ Jesus.**

Paul goes on to describe the special unity that belongs to Christian believers. When Paul says *there is neither Jew nor Greek, slave nor free, male nor female*, he is not suggesting that all these distinctions are completely eliminated. That would be nonsense. There are still differences of nationality, gender, and status in the Christian community. What Paul is declaring is that these distinctions do not make one better than another in God's eyes. God does not love one race over another. He does not love someone in a higher social class more than someone in a lower social class. He does not love men more than women. Keep in mind that all of these statements would have been considered quite radical and controversial in Paul's day.

It is interesting that Jewish men in New Testament times often prayed a prayer in which they thanked God that they were not born a Gentile, a slave, or a woman. Note that Paul uses this same order of Gentile, slave, and woman when he declares that *all* of these are *one in Christ Jesus*. We will always have our differences in the body of Christ, but our commitment to Christ transcends such barriers.

## C. BY GRACE WE ARE ADOPTED (v. 29, 4:4-7)

**29. If you belong to Christ, then you are Abraham's seed, and heirs according to the promise.**

Jews saw themselves exclusively as children of Abraham and took great pride in such a status (Matthew 3:9; John 8:39). Paul maintains that all Christians are *Abraham's seed*. This concludes Paul's consideration of Abraham, which began in Galatians 3:6. Abraham lived before the law of Moses was given, and his faith was "credited to him as righteousness." Christians who have responded to Christ by faith are thus Abraham's offspring and *heirs* of the *promise* God made to him: "All peoples on earth will be blessed through you" (Genesis 12:3; Galatians 3:8).

**4:4. But when the time had fully come, God sent his Son, born of a woman, born under law,**

God's *law* was the standard *under* which people lived for some time, *but when the time had fully come*, or at just the right time, *God sent his Son*. This suggests that the coming of Christ was planned by God to happen according to his timetable. Scholars have noted that the political, social, economic, and geographical conditions were just right for a Messiah when Jesus entered the world.

By saying that Jesus was *born of a woman*, Paul was simply reminding the Galatians that Jesus was both divine and human. God "gave his one and only

### WHAT DO YOU THINK?

*What does it mean to "be clothed with Christ"? What were we wearing before that? How does "wearing" Christ change us?*

*[Passages such as Isaiah 64:6; Revelation 3:18; and 7:9, 10 can enrich your discussion.]*

### WHAT DO YOU THINK?

*How does God view our racial, ethnic, social, and gender differences? How should we view them?*

### WHAT DO YOU THINK?

*In what ways was Jesus sent "when the time had fully come"? What have we done to prepare for his return?*

## PRAYER

*Father, I thank you for the law, even though I no longer depend on it. I needed to know I was a sinner, so I could come to your Son to save me from my sins. As much as I appreciate your law, I rejoice in the gift of grace. Through Jesus, the grace giver. Amen.*

## WHAT DO YOU THINK?

*What does it mean to be "adopted" by God?*

## THOUGHT TO REMEMBER

*The law diagnoses our illness, and Jesus provides the cure.*

Son" (John 3:16), but he entered our world as all human beings do—through the process of birth. Jesus was not merely sent to humanity; he became humanity (Philippians 2:5-8). Paul describes Jesus in a similar manner in Romans 1:3, 4: "who as to his human nature was a descendant of David, and who through the Spirit of holiness was declared with power to be the Son of God."

When Paul points out that Jesus was *born under law*, he is saying that Jesus was born into the Jewish system, as a citizen of the Jewish nation. It is worth noting that the one who made us free from the law and opened up the way of grace to us was the only one who ever lived that law perfectly. Admittedly, there were times when the Pharisees tried to suggest that Jesus had broken some minor aspect of the ceremonial laws (such as when he healed people on the Sabbath, as in Luke 13:10-17), but this was according to their legalistic interpretation of the law.

**5. . . . to redeem those under law, that we might receive the full rights of sons.**

Jesus lived under the law (as the previous verse tells us), but he came to earth *to redeem those under law*. The term *redeem* means "to buy back." Jesus' ministry was twofold; first, he rescued us from the tyranny of the law. But he did not do that merely to send us out on our own. He has also adopted us into his family as his *sons*. The use of the word *sons* is not meant to exclude women from the family of God, for Paul has previously stated that male and female are one in Christ (3:28). Here he is reinforcing that concept by saying that all can enjoy a "sonlike" status in Christ.

**6. Because you are sons, God sent the Spirit of his Son into our hearts, the Spirit who calls out, "Abba, Father."**

Not only has God sent *his Son* (v. 4), but he has also sent his *Spirit*. With the sensitivity to God that the Spirit gives us, we are moved to cry out to him, *Abba, Father*. We noted in Lesson 5, taken from Romans 8, that *Abba* signifies intimacy, being roughly equivalent to the word *Daddy*. This is the word Jesus used when he prayed in Gethsemane (Mark 14:36).

Paul also notes that we have received the Spirit *into our hearts*. To Paul and other Biblical writers, the heart represents where our will resides as well as our emotions. We know that neither of these originates from the organ that pumps blood, but we still use the word *heart* in similar ways today. When Paul states that the Holy Spirit is in our hearts, it means that we have embraced the Spirit with our entire being.

**7. So you are no longer a slave, but a son; and since you are a son, God has made you also an heir.**

This verse summarizes our transformation. A Christian is *no longer a slave, but a son*. As such, he or she is *an heir* to all the riches that our Father intends for us to have.

## CONCLUSION

Imagine what it would be like to discover that you have a rich, long-lost relative. One day you are going about your business at home and a lawyer knocks on your door. He asks you to identify yourself, and you do. He then tells you that a wealthy, long-lost relative has died and named you an heir to his wealth. You become an instant millionaire. At least that's how the story might unfold. But it seldom happens that way.

Well, something even better *has* happened. As Christians, we have been given full rights as sons of God and are now heirs of the great spiritual blessings that our Father wants to give. We are destined to receive "an inheritance that can never perish, spoil or fade" (1 Peter 1:4). That's even better than the fantasy, don't you think?

# Discovery Learning

*This page contains an alternative lesson plan emphasizing learning activities. Classes desiring such student involvement will find these suggestions helpful. The next page is a reproducible activity page to further enhance discovery learning.*

## LEARNING GOALS

After completing this lesson, each student should be able to:

1. Explain the word pictures of law and grace that Paul chose to use in this passage.

2. Identify blessings and responsibilities that come with God's adoption of each of us.

3. Express to God a sense of joy in knowing that they have been adopted by him.

## INTO THE LESSON

*Option #1:* Invite a parent of an adopted child (or a teen or adult who has been adopted) to give a brief testimony about why adoption is special to both parent and child. If available, both persons may speak to this issue. Try to limit this introduction to around ten minutes.

Make the transition to Bible study by telling the class that these testimonies help us understand the Christian's special relationship with God as he adopts us into his family.

*Option #2:* Write the words *Children of God* on the chalkboard. Tell the class that one of the warmest pictures of our relationship with God is the word *Father*. Our hymns, songs, and choruses often speak of this Father/child relationship. Ask the class to work in groups of three or four (or whatever size is most appropriate for your class size) and make a list of lines from Christian music that speaks of this Father/child relationship with God. Provide each group with two hymnbooks or songbooks. After listing these lines on the chalkboard, use the same transition to Bible study suggested under *Option #1*.

## INTO THE WORD

Summarize the lesson Introduction and Background from the lesson commentary for today's study, found on page 317, 318. Then divide the class into four study teams. Give each team a written copy of its task, a photocopy of the lesson commentary, and a piece of paper for compiling notes.

*Team #1:* Answer the following questions about the Old Testament law. Use them to explain to the rest of the class God's purpose in giving the law to his chosen people.

1. What is the purpose of the law as implied in Galatians 3:19?

2. What limitations of the law are revealed in Galatians 3:21, 22?

3. Galatians 3:21 reveals that the law should not be considered bad or viewed as God's enemy. What do you think are some of the good features of the Old Testament law?

*Team #2:* Paul uses two word pictures of the law in Galatians 3:23-26. Read the text and the lesson commentary. Prepare a brief presentation to the rest of the class, explaining what Paul was trying to teach in each word picture about the role of the law.

Word Picture #1: A Prison Guard (Galatians 3:23)

Word Picture #2: A Schoolmaster (Galatians 3:24-26)

*Team #3:* In Galatians 3:27, Paul offers two snapshots of the purpose of Christian baptism. Read this text and the lesson commentary. Prepare a brief presentation to the rest of the class about what Paul is communicating in these word pictures.

Word Picture #1: Baptized into Christ

Word Picture #2: Putting on Christ

*Team #4:* Read Galatians 3:29–4:7 and the lesson commentary on these verses. Discuss the following questions and share your findings with the rest of the class.

1. Why would Paul emphasize to the Galatians that believers are Abraham's seed?

2. What is the significance of the word *redeem* in Galatians 4:5? Define *redeem*.

3. Why should the phrase *Abba, Father* be special to adopted children of God?

4. What are some of the other blessings that come with being an adopted child of God?

After the groups share their findings, provide a brief summary of the lesson comments on Galatians 3:28.

## INTO LIFE

In closing, focus on the phrase *Abba, Father*. Review the meaning of *Abba*. Tell the class that God wants an intimate relationship with us as his children. Write the words *emotional, social,* and *material* beside each other on the board, creating three columns. Ask the class to share blessings that may come to us as God's children in these areas. Then ask them to share responsibilities that also come to us as God's children in these areas. Ask the teams formed earlier to pray together, expressing the joy that comes from knowing God as Father.

# Slaves or Children of God?

As we read today's printed text, Galatians 3:19–4:7, it becomes apparent there was a purpose for the law, just as there is a purpose to God's adoption of us as children. Take a few moments to list some of the advantages and purposes of being a slave to the law and to being an adopted child of God.

SLAVES TO THE LAW OF GOD                    CHILDREN OF GOD

# A Close Relationship with Our Heavenly Father

The words "Abba Father" invite a wonderful intimacy with God. Commentators often say this is like calling God "Daddy." Use the sentence starters on the letter to God to open your heart to God.

Abba Father (Dear Daddy),

My heart is filled with peace as I struggle with

You have promised me an inheritance. Some things I look forward to in my inheritance include

Father, I really need your help for

I love you, Father!

Signed _____

# LIVE IN CHRISTIAN FREEDOM

**LESSON 12**

## WHY TEACH THIS LESSON?

Over and over in Galatians, Paul points out the crazy, illogical thinking involved in trying to add a doctrine of works to the perfect New Covenant of grace. Today's lesson hits on an area where the Judaizers come the closest to making a rational point. Without all our rules to live by, don't these new Christians have license to live like the devil?

Christian freedom in action isn't unruly or self-centered. Rather, it resembles the church in Acts 2—a group of people known by their selfless giving, unity, and community. Such a community still lives by a code—a better code written on the heart rather than on scrolls of parchment. It's the love code. Today's lesson shows us how and why.

## INTRODUCTION

### A. FREEDOM—NOW WHAT?

Freedom is a word almost universally treasured. We desire freedom, not only for the society where we live, but also for our personal lives. To many, freedom is not a concept readily associated with the church and the Christian life. Often unbelievers see freedom as incompatible with any kind of Christian experience. They view Christian faith as a kind of "ball and chain" that limits one's freedom, or as a "crutch" that one uses only in time of great need.

However, we have seen quite clearly in our studies this quarter that Paul regards the Christian life as a life of wonderful *freedom*—from sin, from law-keeping as a way of salvation, and from death. Paul has spent a major portion of his letter to the Galatians trying to help the Galatians understand their freedom in Christ and avoid returning to the slavery of the law. With today's lesson we come to another series of issues relating to Christian freedom: What does our freedom in Christ allow us to do? How do we best exercise this freedom?

Many countries in our world have desired freedom for a long time. Often they have failed to learn from the examples of other countries that gained freedom, yet didn't quite know what to do with it. These countries were not prepared for what living in freedom is like. They did not anticipate the adjustments in thinking and acting that accompany possessing freedom. The same thing can happen to Christians. Never forget that freedom in Christ carries with it certain responsibilities.

Even though a Christian living in the age of grace does not look to the law for salvation, this does not mean that a person is under no authority at all. He or she has changed masters, is now under the authority of Jesus, and seeks to please him. Love for God and love for others is meant to be the natural (or perhaps more accurately, *supernatural*) outgrowth of being saved and possessing the Holy Spirit. One commentator has observed that in Christ we are not free to sin, but we have become free to not sin.

### B. LESSON BACKGROUND

Today's lesson (and next week's as well) will focus on how the free Christian should live. Our study last week concluded with Paul's statement of our special

DEVOTIONAL READING:
1 PETER 2:11-17
BACKGROUND SCRIPTURE:
GALATIANS 5:1-15
PRINTED TEXT:
GALATIANS 5:1-15

## LESSON AIMS

After participating in this lesson, students should be able to:

1. Explain how God's grace sets us free from bondage to the law.

2. Make the connection between their freedom from the law and their responsibility to love.

3. Identify one way to show love to a Christian brother or sister during the coming week.

## KEY VERSE

You, my brothers, were called to be free. But do not use your freedom to indulge the sinful nature; rather, serve one another in love.

—Galatians 5:13

May
22

status in Christ. We are no longer servants, but sons and heirs (Galatians 4:7). In the remaining verses of chapter 4, Paul addresses some personal issues concerning his relationship with the Galatians. His words deal with how warmly they accepted him when he came and worked among them. Paul also includes some allusions to a physical problem, possibly involving his eyes, with which he apparently struggled (verses 13-15). Paul expresses his fervent love for the Galatians (he calls them "my dear children" in verse 19) and his concern for their spiritual welfare. Later in the chapter, Paul uses an allegory concerning Hagar and Sarah to reinforce his teaching concerning the superiority of the New Covenant.

With chapter 5, Paul moves from the theological to the practical (as he usually does in his letters to churches). This section includes several personal exhortations to the Galatians to remain faithful to Christ.

## I. MAINTAINING FREEDOM (GALATIANS 5:1-6)

### A. STAND FAST (v. 1)
1. *It is for freedom that Christ has set us free. Stand firm, then, and do not let yourselves be burdened again by a yoke of slavery.*

Paul exhorts the Galatians (and us) to *stand firm* so that they do not lose *the freedom* in which *Christ has set* them *free*. We should adamantly refuse to go back to a life characterized by slavery to sin. Paul's words offer a special challenge to avoid the kind of slavery promoted by the Judaizers, who insist that obedience to the law is a condition of salvation.

Notice Paul's reference to a *yoke of slavery*. A yoke is a heavy piece of equipment used on an animal to keep it under control, especially to do farm work. It is a fitting way to illustrate the burdensome demands of the law of Moses. Even Peter used this same word picture when he addressed the Jerusalem Conference concerning the issue of Gentile Christians and the law. He referred to the law as a yoke "that neither we nor our fathers have been able to bear" (Acts 15:10). Jesus also used a yoke as a figure of speech, but in a much different way. He assures us that his yoke is "easy" and his burden is "light" (Matthew 11:28-30).

The Greek word translated *burdened* is a word often used by hunters. It describes a snare that would be placed to trap an animal. Paul earnestly desires that the Galatians and all Christians enjoy their freedom in Christ.

### B. CHOOSE GRACE OVER LAW (vv. 2-4)
2. *Mark my words! I, Paul, tell you that if you let yourselves be circumcised, Christ will be of no value to you at all.*

Paul begins this verse with emphatic words that capture one's attention immediately. He says *mark my words* or "look" (perhaps we could render it "please listen"), and he adds the emphatic *I, Paul, tell you*. He means for his readers to pay close attention to what he is about to say: *if you let yourselves be circumcised, Christ will be of no value to you at all.*

Paul's words appear to condemn circumcision completely. Yet it was not Paul's intent to eliminate the practice of circumcision altogether. He had his "son in the faith," Timothy, circumcised. Timothy's mother was Jewish, but his father was a Gentile. In this case, Paul knew that neither Jew nor Gentile would accept Timothy, for both sides would see him as belonging to the other. To avoid such a controversy and to aid Timothy's ministry among the Jews, Paul circumcised him (Acts 16:1-3). This was a choice made by the parties involved; no outside group was putting pressure on them to do this act or making it a test of salvation.

On the other hand, as Paul relates earlier in Galatians, Titus was *not* circumcised because certain "false brothers" (apparently belonging to the Judaizers)

WHAT DO YOU THINK?

*Why would someone choose to go back into slavery? Do we ever choose slavery over freedom in our own lives?*

were trying to force the matter. As Paul notes, "The freedom we have in Christ Jesus" was at stake (Galatians 2:3-5). This is the view of circumcision that Paul is confronting in the verse before us. To believe that something else besides Jesus is necessary for salvation is the same as saying that Jesus is inadequate. This is why Paul's attitude is so uncompromising. Jesus cannot be a person's Savior unless he is that person's *only* Savior.

3. *Again I declare to every man who lets himself be circumcised that he is obligated to obey the whole law.*

One commentator observes that Paul is not condemning the act of circumcision as much as the theology of circumcision that the Galatians are in danger of embracing. When Paul warns them against letting themselves be *circumcised*, it is because of the reason they are considering circumcision. He explains the devastating consequences of such a decision. If the Galatians accept the Judaizers' position that circumcision is necessary for salvation, they then accept a works-oriented view of salvation. This means that they must also commit themselves to keeping all the other laws and regulations of the Old Covenant. From what Paul states elsewhere in Galatians, this is already happening (Galatians 4:10).

4. *You who are trying to be justified by law have been alienated from Christ; you have fallen away from grace.*

Paul cites two consequences of attempting to be *justified by law*. First, he makes essentially the same point he made in verse 2: they *have been alienated from Christ*. Do the Galatians really want to accept a teaching that leads to such a result as this? Do those who have accepted Jesus' sacrifice on the cross for their sins really want to embrace something that will make that sacrifice of no effect? Surely their goal must be to draw closer to Christ, not to become his enemy.

The second consequence is that those who seek to be justified by the law have *fallen away from grace*. Justification by law and justification by grace are two completely different paths. Those going back to the law are choosing the wrong course, and there will be no grace available to them if they continue that way.

## WHAT DO YOU THINK?

Why did Paul place so much emphasis on the issue of circumcision? What was at stake in this matter?

## WHAT DO YOU THINK?

Few Christians today wrestle with the theology of circumcision, but are there areas in our lives today that may have the moral equivalence of circumcision? Are there aspects of the law that draw us despite our acceptance of God's grace?

### SPIRITUAL RECIDIVISM

The word *recidivism* (re-sid-uh-viz-um) refers to the process of reverting to a previous state of being, and is often used with regard to various addictive behaviors and criminal lifestyles. Sometimes these behaviors work in conjunction with each other. For example, some statistics indicate that more than 30 percent of the people arrested for DUI (driving under the influence of alcohol) are repeat offenders. Most recidivists deny that they either have an addiction to alcohol or are a danger to themselves and others when they drive while drunk. Obviously, the human mind has a tremendous capacity to deceive itself!

When Paul talks about returning to the bondage of the Old Testament law, he is describing a form of addictive behavior. The legalist keeps saying, in effect, "I just know that if I try harder this next time, I can do it right and make myself right with God." But like the alcoholic or drug addict or compulsive gambler, spiritual recidivism is the result.

The real solution to this problem is to admit our failures and trust in Christ's forgiveness and the power of the Spirit of God to bring hope to a hopeless situation. We can never be good enough to deserve God's love. Instead, God offers his love to all who, through faith in Christ, accept his redeeming, renewing power.

—C. R. B.

### C. EXPRESS FAITH THROUGH LOVE (vv. 5, 6)

5. *But by faith we eagerly await through the Spirit the righteousness for which we hope.*

## DAILY BIBLE READINGS

*Monday, May 16*—The Truth Will Make You Free (John 8:31-38)

*Tuesday, May 17*—Live As Free People (1 Peter 2:11-17)

*Wednesday, May 18*—Free in Christ (1 Corinthians 7: 17-24)

*Thursday, May 19*—Freed from Slavery by Christ (Hebrews 2:14-18)

*Friday, May 20*—Christ Has Set Us Free (Galatians 5:1-5)

*Saturday, May 21*—Faith Working Through Love (Galatians 5:6-10)

*Sunday, May 22*—Love Your Neighbor as Yourself (Galatians 5:11-15)

At any point in our growth in Christ, we realize that we still fall short of all he wants us to be. We know that complete righteousness in Christ cannot be ours until we leave this world and go to be with him for eternity. So we *eagerly await through the Spirit the righteousness for which we hope*. Where do we get the stamina to wait? The Holy *Spirit* keeps us strong and focused.

This is a very different perspective from the works-oriented or law-oriented approach to salvation. Rather than seeing the Galatians fall from grace by depending on their own works, Paul would have them live by faith and wait for God's completion of his work in them. Consider Paul's words to the Philippian Christians and his confidence "that he who began a good work in you will carry it on to completion until the day of Christ Jesus" (Philippians 1:6).

**6. For in Christ Jesus neither circumcision nor uncircumcision has any value. The only thing that counts is faith expressing itself through love.**

Paul has already made it quite clear that *circumcision* is worthless as a supposed "supplement" to the gospel of grace. It is hard to miss that message in Galatians. But notice that Paul also says that *uncircumcision* means nothing. He probably does not want the Gentile Christians among the Galatians to view themselves as superior to the Jewish believers for seeing the latter as having participated in a now-obsolete ritual.

Paul is then quick to address the possible suggestion that a Christian living under grace can do anything he chooses to do; since, after all, Paul has just spoken in rather negative terms of law-keeping. His response is that Christian *faith* must express itself through *love*. Faith that saves is a faith that works. This is essentially the same point James makes in his epistle when he affirms that faith without works is dead (James 2:26).

## II. THREAT OF FALSE TEACHERS (GALATIANS 5:7-12)

### A. HINDERING BELIEVERS (vv. 7, 8)

**7. You were running a good race. Who cut in on you and kept you from obeying the truth?**

Paul frequently uses athletic metaphors, referring especially to running and boxing (Acts 20:24; 1 Corinthians 9:24-27; Galatians 2:2; 2 Timothy 4:7). The picture Paul seems to be describing is one in which a runner jumps in and cuts off another runner or in some way impedes the progress of another runner. Notice also that here, as in the previous verse, Paul emphasizes that saving faith must be an active faith.

We must do more than simply believe the truth; we must obey *the truth*. The Galatian Christians had been hampered from doing that.

**8. That kind of persuasion does not come from the one who calls you.**

The word *persuasion* in this verse describes the change of conviction on the part of the Galatians, caused by the influence of the Judaizers. That change did not originate *from the one who calls you*—that is, God. God would not call people to two radically different kinds of approaches to him. He would never call people to law and grace at the same time.

### B. EXERTING GREAT INFLUENCE (v. 9)

**9. "A little yeast works through the whole batch of dough."**

This statement may be a proverb that was in current use in Paul's time. Whether this is the case or not, it certainly reflects the teaching of Jesus, who used the illustration of *yeast* on more than one occasion. In one of his parables, he used yeast in a positive way (Matthew 13:33); other times he used it to describe the influence of false teaching (as in Matthew 16:12).

## HOW TO SAY IT

*Corinthians.* Ko-RIN-thee-unz.
*Galatians.* Guh-LAY-shunz.
*Hagar.* HAY-gar.
*Judaizers.* JOO-day-ize-ers.
*Philippians.* Fih-LIP-ee-unz.
*Timothy.* TIM-o-thee.

In the verse before us, Paul uses yeast to picture the influence of the Judaizers and their false doctrine. Yeast works silently, but is very effective at permeating every part of the bread *dough*. Such is the effect of false teaching in the church, whether in an ancient or modern setting.

### C. CONFUSING THE CHURCH (vv. 10-12)

**10. I am confident in the Lord that you will take no other view. The one who is throwing you into confusion will pay the penalty, whoever he may be.**

Paul is *confident in the Lord* that the Galatians will not be swayed by the Judaizers' teaching and that they will not embrace "another gospel" (Galatians 1:6). Note that Paul speaks of *the one who is throwing* them *into confusion*. Is he speaking of an actual person, or is he using this word in a more general sense? We do not know. Perhaps he is referring to the leading proponent and preacher of the law-based system promoted by the Judaizers. What is quite clear is that there is a *penalty* awaiting such individuals who are obstructing people from the way to Heaven.

**11. Brothers, if I am still preaching circumcision, why am I still being persecuted? In that case the offense of the cross has been abolished.**

This verse indicates that some of Paul's opponents suggest that he still believes in, practices, and preaches *circumcision* in the same manner that they do. But Paul maintains in the verse before us that this is not true at all. His opponents may cite Timothy's situation as proof that Paul still advocates circumcision. Perhaps some use what happened to Titus (Galatians 2:3) to claim that Paul is inconsistent in his teaching.

In his response, Paul raises a valid point: if these critics claim that I agree with them in the matter of circumcision, then *why* do they still persecute me? If this is the reason for him *being persecuted*, the *offense of the cross has been abolished*. This is another way of saying that Paul cannot serve two masters or preach two "gospels." The Judaizers would be glad to accept a gospel that includes the requirement of circumcision. Paul's insistence on the crucified Christ as the heart of his gospel is a stumblingblock to them, as it is to many Jews of the day (1 Corinthians 1:23).

**12. As for those agitators, I wish they would go the whole way and emasculate themselves!**

This is about as strong a statement as Paul can make in his opposition to the Judaizers. He wishes that these false teachers would *emasculate themselves*. It appears that Paul is saying that those who advocate the "cutting off" that occurs at circumcision should continue their action and castrate themselves. If circumcision is really that important, and if it makes someone right before God, then why stop with circumcision itself? Why not go all the way to castration? (Some of the pagan religions of the time practice this act as a sign of devotion to their deities.) The apostle's tone may be sarcastic, but no one can deny his determined opposition to the Judaizers and their message.

### III. DEMONSTRATING FREEDOM (GALATIANS 5:13-15)

### A. SERVING ONE ANOTHER (v. 13)

**13. You, my brothers, were called to be free. But do not use your freedom to indulge the sinful nature; rather, serve one another in love.**

Christian *freedom* must not become license (see Jude 4). The freedom we have in Christ should not be used to satisfy *the sinful nature*. Instead, we should use our freedom as an opportunity to *serve one another*—to care for others rather than satisfy our base desires. The flesh desires to use people; the Holy Spirit

*WHAT DO YOU THINK?*

*What is the difference between suffering and persecution? Is persecution a necessary part of the Christian life?*

Visual for lesson 12. *Use this visual to encourage students to think of creative ways to "serve one another."*

PRAYER

*Dear Father, help me to see my freedom in Christ not as an entitlement but as a gift. In appreciation, help me to use my gift wisely for my sake, for others' sake, but most of all for your sake. Through Christ our Lord. Amen.*

WHAT DO YOU THINK?

*Why is serving one another the antithesis of sinning against one another? How does serving one another relate to loving one another?*

*[Review Paul's definition of love in 1 Corinthians 13.]*

THOUGHT TO REMEMBER

*We are not free to sin, but we have become free to not sin.*

within us desires to serve people. Christian freedom means the freedom to live as our Creator intended us to live.

## THE RIGHT KIND OF SERVICE

Does "Horn & Hardart" mean anything to anyone? How about "Automat"? Those two names were attached to what was once the world's largest restaurant chain. It was also America's first fast-food chain, and its first site opened in Philadelphia in 1902. What set the company apart was a precise business plan that dictated exact uniformity of quality, service, and price. There were no waiters. Food was dispensed from coin-operated machines—similar in principle to what one finds in some hospital waiting rooms these days. You could see the food, make your selection, insert your coins, open a sliding glass window, and take the item from the case. The food is said to have always been of high quality and low cost. The last Automat closed in 1991, but while they lasted, their system was very efficient and automated—and all very impersonal.

When Paul talks about serving one another, efficiency seems not to have been the key factor on his mind. Instead, love is the key. True Christian service is not automatic (or even necessarily efficient). It is not based on a law or an organization handbook that tells us how to do it "the right way." It is not "doing as we please," but "pleasing to do what love calls us to do." It means loving those we serve, not serving only those we love. —C. R. B.

## B. FULFILLING THE LAW (v. 14)

**14. The entire law is summed up in a single command: "Love your neighbor as yourself."**

Why would Paul talk about fulfilling *the entire law,* when he has spoken against a system of law? The reason is that the ultimate fulfillment of the law is something God still desires. Only Jesus and the system of grace can accomplish that ultimate fulfillment. To *love your neighbor as yourself* means demonstrating the attitudes and actions that fulfill the requirements of the law of Moses. Paul elaborates on this in Romans 13:8-10. Verse 10 says, "Love does no harm to its neighbor. Therefore love is the fulfillment of the law."

## C. AVOIDING DESTRUCTIVE BEHAVIOR (v. 15)

**15. If you keep on biting and devouring each other, watch out or you will be destroyed by each other.**

This describes what happens when there is an absence of love and the desire to "serve one another" (v. 13). What a tragedy that alleged Christians should act this way—biting and devouring *each other* through petty squabbles, unkind words, and selfish attitudes! What a sad witness to an unsaved world!

## CONCLUSION

Several times in our studies from Galatians thus far, we have noted that there is something wrong with being set free and then going back into bondage. Today's lesson has emphasized that the new life of freedom in Christ carries responsibility, but it is a joyous responsibility.

Suppose that you risked life and limb to free someone from a deep pit. Would you feel gratified if the person jumped back into the pit? No, you would be outraged! All that effort and sacrifice for nothing! You would want the person you rescued to enjoy his freedom and use it wisely.

God has not freed us to return to a life of bondage or to waste the new life he has provided. Today's Scripture challenges us to "stand firm" in the freedom we have been given. That's the best way to honor the one who set us free.

# Discovery Learning

*This page contains an alternative lesson plan emphasizing learning activities. Classes desiring such student involvement will find these suggestions helpful. The next page is a reproducible activity page to further enhance discovery learning.*

## LEARNING GOALS

After this lesson students should be able to:

1. Explain how God's grace sets us free from bondage to the law.

2. Make the connection between our freedom from the law and our responsibility to love.

3. Identify one way to show love to a Christian brother or sister during the coming week.

## INTO THE LESSON

Write these words at the top of two poster boards, creating one column on each poster: *National Freedoms* and *Christian Freedoms*. Ask the class to work in teams of two and complete the first column. They should list national freedoms guaranteed in the Constitution of the United States (or a similar document, if other nationalities are present) and practical applications or illustrations of each of those freedoms. Cite an example for the class such as the freedom of religion and the freedom to worship as one desires. Ask the teams to share their findings as you list them on the poster board.

After completing the first exercise, ask the entire class to work together to do the same exercise for *Christian Freedoms*. Tell the class that Paul says, "Christ has set us free" (Galatians 5:1). Class members are to give examples of freedom in Christ. Do not provide examples for this column unless the class has a hard time getting started. List answers on the second poster board. Leave these posters taped to the wall. (This exercise is also in the student activity book.)

Make the transition to today's Bible study by telling the class that people treasure freedom. The opposite of freedom is slavery or bondage. Interestingly, however, we find people in the New Testament who found freedom in Christ, but seemed to want to revert back to a system of bondage. Would Christians today ever consider doing such an absurd thing? We may be surprised as we study today's Scripture.

## INTO THE WORD

*Activity #1.* Early in the week, recruit a class member to prepare a brief report on circumcision according to Jewish law. He or she should speak of its role and importance in Jewish life. Even the circumcision ceremony, as practiced by Jews, may be of interest to the class. Give this person a Bible dictionary to assist with preparations.

Begin the Bible study by reading through the printed text from Galatians 5. Then tell the class that circumcision is an important part of Paul's focus in this text. Introduce the class member who is to give a brief introduction of this practice as a background for this study.

*Activity #2:* Begin this activity by giving a brief lecture about the purpose of today's passage. See the Introduction in the commentary for assistance with this part of the presentation. Hand out photocopies of the lesson commentary to the teams used during the "Into the Lesson" segment. Explain that you are going to assign one phrase from this passage to each team. Their task is to read the entire text, read the lesson commentary on the phrase or sentence assigned, and prepare a presentation about how that phrase or sentence fits into today's lesson theme. The phrases to assign are as follows:

*v. 1: Yoke of slavery*

*v. 6: Circumcision nor uncircumcision*

*v. 7: You were running a good race. Who cut in on you?*

*v. 9: A little yeast works through the whole batch of dough.*

*v. 11: The offense of the cross has been abolished.*

*v. 12: I wish they would go the whole way and emasculate themselves!*

*v. 13: Called to be free*

*v. 14: Love your neighbor as yourself*

Allow each team to report its conclusions.

## INTO LIFE

Remind the class that part of Paul's teaching in Galatians 5 is that the privileges of freedom also bring responsibility. Prepare another poster board headed *National Responsibilities*. Ask the class for examples of responsibilities that come with our national freedoms and list them on the poster board. Mount another poster board with the heading *Christian Responsibilities* and ask the class for items to list under this heading.

To conclude, give each student an inexpensive, light-colored pen. Have available several fine-tip markers to write on these pens. Say that Paul makes it clear that our Christian freedom brings with it an obligation to "serve one another" (v. 13). Ask class members to use the list of responsibilities just created to identify one "service project" he or she will do for another person this week. They are to write a one- or two-word reminder of that commitment on the pen. They also should carry and use the pen all week as a reminder of their commitment.

# Words of Freedom and Bondage

Read Paul's words about freedom in Christ and bondage to the law in Galatians 5:1-15. Then complete the chart below by making a checkmark (✔), indicating whether the words and phrases listed are said to be characteristic of freedom in Christ or bondage to the law.

|  | Freedom in Christ | Bondage to the Law |
|---|---|---|
| Yoke (v. 1) | _____ | _____ |
| Circumcised (v. 2) | _____ | _____ |
| Faith (v. 5) | _____ | _____ |
| Love (v. 6) | _____ | _____ |
| Good race (v. 7) | _____ | _____ |
| Confusion (v. 10) | _____ | _____ |
| Indulge (v. 13) | _____ | _____ |
| Sinful nature (v. 13) | _____ | _____ |
| Serve (v. 13) | _____ | _____ |
| Love your neighbor (v. 14) | _____ | _____ |
| Biting and devouring (v. 15) | _____ | _____ |

# Accepting Freedom's Responsibilities

Galatians 5:13, 14 reminds Christians that our freedom brings a responsibility to serve one another. In the left column, jot several ideas that interest you for service to another believer. Then, in the right column, detail a project you have selected as a service to another Christian.

| A Few Service Ideas | My Service Project |
|---|---|
| _____ | _____ |
| _____ | _____ |
| _____ | _____ |
| _____ | _____ |
| _____ | _____ |
| _____ | _____ |

# PARTICIPATE IN THE COMMUNITY OF FAITH

## WHY TEACH THIS LESSON?

Welfare systems in democratic countries have been widely criticized for causing people to feel entitled to something that they have not worked for. As a result, so it is claimed, welfare recipients are made to feel poor and helpless, having no sense that they owe others anything.

Today's lesson offers a different approach for God's people. We are to carry our own loads, yet be quick to help others as well. And we are to do all this without pride or a spirit of competition. Yet this isn't really anything new since it echoes a sentiment God through the Old Testament prophet Micah (and popularized in a song by Stephen Curtis Chapman): "What does the Lord require of you?" In turn, this should cause us to ask, "What does the Lord want from me today?" The answer is, "To act justly and to love mercy and to walk humbly with your God" (Micah 6:8). Today's lesson shows us how and why.

## INTRODUCTION

### A. NO HERMITS HERE

The Christian life cannot be lived in isolation. God has always intended that his people be part of a community. In the New Testament context, that community is the church. All of us at one time or another have found ourselves disappointed in the behavior of others—even of those we believed were Christians. During such experiences, we may wish that we could become a hermit so that we could have no contact with people at all. Yet if we did that, we would soon find such a life boring and unsatisfying. Besides, the community of believers needs us, and we need the community.

Today's lesson focuses on Paul's sensitivity to the church as a community and how the members are to function in relation to each other. Some may think of life in the Spirit as a totally inner experience or as something between "me and God." But life in the Spirit is intended to be lived out among human beings and in the body of Christ, his church. Perhaps we are sometimes like Linus, in the *Peanuts* comic strip, who declared, "I love mankind. It's people I can't stand!" But as followers of Jesus, we have to do more than tolerate each other. We must work together for the good of the greatest cause there is.

### B. LESSON BACKGROUND

This lesson (the final one in this quarter of studies) begins with a look at a passage of Scripture familiar to many: Paul's description of the fruit of the Spirit. In fact, the Holy Spirit is a very prominent part of our lesson text.

Notice that Paul's discussion of the fruit of the Spirit follows a rather dismal section of Scripture. In that section, Paul lists the "acts of the sinful nature." What an evil list it is! His list of vices includes immorality, impurity, debauchery,

DEVOTIONAL READING:
*1 JOHN 3:14-23*
BACKGROUND SCRIPTURE:
*GALATIANS 5:22–6:10*
PRINTED TEXT:
*GALATIANS 5:22–6:10*

## LESSON AIMS

*After this lesson a student should be able to:*

*1. Explain the meaning and application of "the fruit of the Spirit."*

*2. Describe the behaviors Paul associates with the fruit of the Spirit.*

*3. Identify one or more ways he or she will become more Christlike in daily living.*

## KEY VERSE

*Carry each other's burdens, and in this way you will fulfill the law of Christ.*
—Galatians 6:2

May 29

*LESSON 13 NOTES*

idolatry, witchcraft, hatred, discord, jealousy, fits of rage, selfish ambition, dissensions, factions, envy, drunkenness, and orgies (Galatians 5:19-21).

Paul then proceeds to describe the changes that the Holy Spirit brings into our lives. His concern is not just what the Holy Spirit does for us personally, but what he does for us in relationship to the community of faith—the church.

Some note that Paul chose to refer to the *fruit* of the Spirit, not the *works* of the Spirit. Fruit serves as a better analogy, since it is what a tree was created to produce. The fruit is the tree's natural product. We were created by God to live holy lives; such holiness should proceed naturally from our lives.

The metaphor of fruit-bearing is helpful for another reason. Fruit is a positive product. The virtues that make up the fruit of the Spirit are all positive virtues. This is significant, since so many people erroneously define Christianity in terms of negative qualities. In addition, fruit is not just to be seen and admired for its beauty; it is to be used. Fruit may be beautiful to the sight and pleasant to the taste, but most of all it should provide nourishment. That is what a Christian's testimony should offer to those with whom he or she is associated.

Some commentators have called attention to the fact that Paul uses *fruit* (singular) not *fruits* (plural). Is there any significance to this? Perhaps. If the plural form were used, someone might treat these qualities as a kind of checklist ("I'm strong in this area, but weak in this one"). By use of the singular *fruit*, Paul is highlighting the fact that all of these qualities come from one source—the Holy Spirit. Christian growth is not a matter of "self-help" or "self-improvement"; it comes through allowing the Holy Spirit greater control of our lives.

As a final note, many commentators have observed that the qualities listed by Paul in this passage can be studied in groups of three. That is how we will approach the passage in this study. However, it is best not to be too dogmatic about such an order or grouping.

### I. THE SPIRIT AND HIS FRUIT (GALATIANS 5:22, 23)

#### A. GOD-ORIENTED VIRTUES (v. 22a)

*22a. But the fruit of the Spirit is love, joy, peace,*

The first three of the *fruit* appear to be primarily inner virtues. They are virtues that are very much a part of the nature of God himself. It is no surprise that *love* leads the list. Placing love first among the Spirit's fruit is consistent with Paul's teachings elsewhere, particularly in 1 Corinthians 13.

*Joy* and *peace* are similar inner qualities. A close relationship exists between joy and peace. There is an old saying that peace is joy resting and joy is peace dancing. The word translated *joy* does not describe a pleasant feeling brought on by favorable circumstances, but an inner joy that defies circumstances. It is the kind of joy that filled the apostles after they had been beaten for speaking in the name of Jesus (Acts 5:40, 41). Only God can bestow such joy.

*Peace,* as used in the Scriptures, means more than just the absence of conflict. It is a sense of calm assurance at knowing that God is in control. Jesus spoke of such peace to his disciples as crucifixion drew closer (John 14:27; 16:33). Paul could speak of such peace, even when writing from a prison (Philippians 4:6-9).

#### B. OTHERS-ORIENTED VIRTUES (v. 22b)

*22b. . . . patience, kindness, goodness,*

The next three virtues deal more with social situations. *Patience, kindness,* and *goodness* are all best expressed in our relationships with others.

Patience is not just the ability to endure problems, but to triumph over them. The variety of circumstances and people that we encounter in our lives help us

*WHAT DO YOU THINK?*

*Is the "fruit of the Spirit" something given wholly from God, or is there a personal component we contribute? What part of this list comes from our personal efforts, and what part comes from God's grace?*

develop and use this virtue. Someone has remarked that the incidents in life that we refer to as "interruptions" (and usually do not welcome) are really God's appointments that he brings our way for a purpose. Often our spiritual growth is part of that purpose.

The Greek word translated *kindness* became very special to the early Christians. This word actually sounds like the title *Christ*. When Jesus says that his yoke is "easy," this is the word he uses (Matthew 11:30). We should seek to treat others as Jesus has treated us.

The word used for *goodness* is very similar to the word for *kindness*. A form of this word is used later in our printed text to describe how Christians should treat all people (Galatians 6:10). Goodness implies personal moral excellence, but it also means looking beyond oneself to meet the needs of others.

### C. SELF-ORIENTED VIRTUES (vv. 22c, 23)

*22c, 23. . . . faithfulness, gentleness and self-control. Against such things there is no law.*

The last three virtues, *faithfulness*, *gentleness*, and *self-control*, are all linked to one's personal discipline. The word translated *faithfulness* can also be translated as loyalty. It probably carries that meaning in this verse.

*Gentleness,* which could also be translated "meekness," is a quality often viewed in negative terms. Jesus mentioned this quality when he said, "Blessed are the meek" (Matthew 5:5). Perhaps part of our problem is that the word "meek" sounds like "weak." Meekness is not weakness; it is strength under control. Jesus is described as having this trait (Matthew 11:29, 2 Corinthians 10:1).

Finally, there is *self-control*, which has many applications. For an interesting study, see Acts 24:25; 1 Corinthians 7:9; 9:25; Titus 1:8; and 2 Peter 1:6, where this same word occurs in both noun and verb forms.

Paul closes this list by telling his readers that *no law* needs to be enforced to restrain or punish those who possess the fruit of the Spirit. Indeed, their actions fulfill the law.

### A WONDERFUL VARIETY OF FRUIT

Perhaps you've seen the advertisements in the Sunday newspaper "magazine" section offering a plant that grows potatoes underground and tomatoes on the vine above ground. Or possibly you've noticed a nursery catalog selling a fruit tree that will grow several different varieties of fruit. For example, one company offers trees that combine two, three, and even four different varieties on one tree. Or, as one more example of what is horticulturally possible, the branches of a desired variety of fruit can be grafted onto a hardy rootstock for optimum performance in a given climate or environment. Whatever the combination of fruits you are seeking, the desired results can be achieved through the process of grafting.

Our text in Galatians for today suggests that a similar principle is at work in the realm of what we might describe as "spiritual horticulture." God wants us to become like him, and the "root stock" of the flesh does not bear the right kind of fruit. So when we become Christians, God "grafts" his Holy Spirit onto our spirits, and the miracle begins: nine varieties of spiritual fruit growing on one "tree"! And these are far lovelier, far more "tasty" than any we can ever produce by ourselves.

—C. R. B.

### I. THE SPIRIT AND OUR ATTITUDES (GALATIANS 5:24-26)

#### A. CRUCIFYING THE FLESH (v. 24)

*24. Those who belong to Christ Jesus have crucified the sinful nature with its passions and desires.*

*Visual for lesson 13. This visual reminds us of the truth that we reap what we sow—in both the natural world and the spiritual world.*

*HOW TO SAY IT*

Corinthians. Ko-RIN-thee-unz.
Ephesus. EF-uh-sus.
Galatians. Guh-LAY-shunz.
Titus. TY-tus.

## WHAT DO YOU THINK?

*How can we crucify the flesh with its lusts? What role does walking in the Spirit play in this matter?*

This statement is similar in meaning to Paul's declaration in Galatians 2:20: "I have been crucified with Christ." To say that we *belong to Christ Jesus* means to repent utterly and completely of our old way of life, which is patterned after *the sinful nature*. We are to repudiate totally the *passions* associated with that lifestyle. The word *crucified* emphasizes how drastic and decisive we must be about breaking ties with sin and determining to serve Christ.

### B. MAINTAINING A DAILY WALK (v. 25)

**25. Since we live by the Spirit, let us keep in step with the Spirit.**

Since *the Spirit* is the source of our new life in Christ (Romans 8:10), then we need to let the Spirit guide our daily walk. All of our thoughts, words, and deeds should come under his control.

In this verse Paul uses a very specific word for *keep in step*. It is a different word from that used in verse 16, where Paul tells us to "live by the Spirit." The word in the verse before us describes keeping in step as a military unit would do when marching. To place this verse together with the previous one gives us a useful definition of Christian maturity. We must say no to what is evil by crucifying the flesh, and we must say yes to what is good by walking in step with the Spirit.

### HIS FATHER'S WALK

One bright, crisp winter morning in northern Iowa, a young father who stood six feet tall decided to introduce his two-year-old son to the beauty of new-fallen snow. Ten inches had fallen overnight and lay in pristine whiteness on the ground. The toddler only recently had mastered the art of walking, so this was his first real adventure in the snow.

The father started breaking the trail with his son following him, but he forgot how short those little legs were. Soon a plaintive wail came: "Daddy, wait for me!" The boy was trying to put his feet in the footprints of his father, and those footprints were just too far apart for the much smaller legs to match!

Obviously, the moral "steps" that our Heavenly Father can take are much too far apart for us to match in our own power. However, he has given us the Holy Spirit to help us match our steps with His. Through the Spirit's power, we can have our Father's walk.
    —C. R. B.

### C. KEEPING A HUMBLE ATTITUDE (v. 26)

**26. Let us not become conceited, provoking and envying each other.**

While this verse appears at the end of Galatians 5, it also serves to introduce the teaching found in the next chapter about relationships within the body of Christ. Paul warns Christians not to be *conceited;* that is, we should not become so self-centered and self-righteous that we take pleasure in *provoking* one another (to unnecessary and fruitless arguments) and *envying each other*.

Notice that both extremes of our potential responses to people are included in this verse. On the one hand, we may look at our neighbor with pride, thinking that we are better. On the other hand, we may view our neighbor with envy, thinking he or she is better (or more talented, more popular, etc.) than we are. Neither approach is appropriate for someone led by the Spirit.

## III. THE SPIRIT AND OTHERS (GALATIANS 6:1-10)

### A. HELPING THE FALLEN (v. 1)

**1. Brothers, if someone is caught in a sin, you who are spiritual should restore him gently. But watch yourself, or you also may be tempted.**

Here Paul describes a circumstance that provides an excellent test of whether or not we are walking in step with the Spirit. How do we react if someone is *caught in a sin?* The idea of being *caught* conveys the concept of being ensnared in the fault itself rather than being caught by another person. Perhaps it is not an act of blatantly defying God's authority; yet if it is left unchecked, it may lead to more serious actions.

How should we respond? Some would prefer to ignore the situation and assume it is not their responsibility; others would respond by condemning, rejecting, and shunning the guilty party.

Here is Paul's directive: the *spiritual* person will desire to *restore* such an individual. The idea is to make a person whole again. This idea is also found in 1 Peter 5:10, where the same Greek word is used to show God's willingness to restore us.

Notice also that we are to restore the person with gentleness. Restoration likely will never be accomplished if a fallen person is treated with contempt. With this counsel, Paul includes a warning against self-righteousness: *watch yourself, or you also may be tempted.* Elsewhere he issues this warning: "If you think you are standing firm, be careful that you don't fall!" (1 Corinthians 10:12).

## B. BEARING OTHERS' BURDENS (vv. 2-5)

**2. Carry each other's burdens, and in this way you will fulfill the law of Christ.**

The responsibility to *carry each other's burdens* is closely related to Paul's teaching in the previous verse. It may appear that this verse contradicts what Paul says a short time later in verse 5: "Each one should carry his own load." However, the word for *burdens* in verse 2 and the word for *load* in verse 5 are different words in the Greek text.

The word for *burdens* in verse 2 describes a very heavy burden—one that a person cannot possibly carry alone. It is the duty of a fellow Christian to help. The word for *load* in verse 5, on the other hand, refers to a much smaller burden. It is one that need not be shared with anyone else, for it cannot be shared with anyone else; it is each person's accountability before God's judgment seat.

**3. If anyone thinks he is something when he is nothing, he deceives himself.**

Here Paul addresses an attitude that could hinder some from bearing the burdens of others (v. 2). Some may *think* themselves too important or too busy to help another in need. That attitude adds up to *nothing* in God's eyes. We are deceiving ourselves with such thinking; we are certainly not fooling God and probably not too many other people.

**4. Each one should test his own actions. Then he can take pride in himself, without comparing himself to somebody else,**

Rather than trying to judge and critique others, let each person simply *test* himself or herself. We may think ourselves better than someone else until we compare ourselves with God. Taking *pride* in ourselves comes as we grow according to his standard, not our own flawed, self-made standards.

**5. . . . for each one should carry his own load.**

Here is the reason why each person needs to examine himself closely: *each one should carry his own load.* The significance of the word *load* was noted earlier in the comments on verse 2. What Paul is describing here is simply the accountability of each of us to God.

## C. SHOWING GENEROSITY (vv. 6-10)

**6. Anyone who receives instruction in the word must share all good things with his instructor.**

This verse covers a new topic—possibly one that the Galatians needed assistance in addressing. What responsibility does the church have to those who

*WHAT DO YOU THINK?*

When we see a Christian brother or sister involved in the kind of sin described in Galatians 6:1, how should we respond? What does our response say about God, about the behavior, and about ourselves?

*PRAYER*

Dear Father, I pray that my fruit is good fruit. I pray that my conduct is winsome. I pray that my service is sweet. I thank you that through your Spirit you have given me both the graces of Christ and the places to demonstrate them. In the name of our Lord Jesus. Amen.

*WHAT DO YOU THINK?*

*How do we show appreciation to our preachers and teachers? Should a preacher's salary reflect the average salaries in the congregation? Why, or why not?*

teach *the word?* Paul says that those who receive such *instruction* should help in the financial remuneration of those who instruct. In other words, the preacher or teacher of a congregation should expect that those who benefit from his teaching will support him financially. The word *share* implies such generosity.

**7. Do not be deceived: God cannot be mocked. A man reaps what he sows.**

This principle can apply to a variety of areas, including Christian stewardship (2 Corinthians 9:6-8). In this context, Paul's words should be understood in light of what he has stated about living in the flesh and living in the Spirit in chapter 5 (and in the next verse as well).

**8. The one who sows to please his sinful nature, from that nature will reap destruction; the one who sows to please the Spirit, from the Spirit will reap eternal life.**

We should not sow to please the *sinful nature,* because if we do that we will surely *reap destruction.* That destruction includes both the physical and spiritual consequences of choosing to live in sin. Many will recall the old expression, "sowing his wild oats." Someone once remarked that it doesn't make sense to sow your wild oats and then pray for a crop failure. The positive application of the principle is this: the one who sows *to please the Spirit* will *reap eternal life.*

**9. Let us not become weary in doing good, for at the proper time we will reap a harvest if we do not give up.**

This verse adds a word of encouragement that Christians often need. Paul does not want his Galatian readers (or us) to become *weary in doing good. At the proper time,* or when the time is right, we will *reap a harvest.* Paul is picturing the farmer who gets tired in the process of planting, weeding, and watering his crop, while at the same time having to contend with unfavorable weather conditions. But the farmer is encouraged to know that in due time the harvest will make all his labors worthwhile.

This verse reminds us of a very real truth: sometimes the Christian life can be tiring. It can be discouraging trying to help people. But like the farmer, we also wait for a harvest time, when our faithful efforts will be rewarded.

**10. Therefore, as we have opportunity, let us do good to all people, especially to those who belong to the family of believers.**

Paul challenges us to use every *opportunity* we have to *do good.* We should seek to do good to *all* people, but we have as Christians a special responsibility to help those within *the family of believers.* It is a sign of spiritual maturity if Christians are willing to do good to all people and surely a sign of immaturity if they will not do good to those with whom they share the common bond of faith and fellowship in Jesus.

*WHAT DO YOU THINK?*

*Why is there a special emphasis by Paul on fellow believers ("the family of believers") as the recipients of our good works?*

## CONCLUSION

A well-known motion picture illustrates the kind of life that can be created if we are committed to contributing to the well-being of others around us. That movie is *It's a Wonderful Life.* Perhaps you remember that the main character, George Bailey, reaches the depths of despair at one point. He thinks he has been a miserable failure. Then his guardian angel allows him to see what the world would be like if he had never been born. George sees how he had filled his life with simple acts of kindness done for the sake of simple people. When George saw what his community would have been like if those acts had not been done, he realized how significant his life had been. The world was a meaner, crueler world without the influence of George Bailey.

We Christians do not live in isolation. We come in contact with many people every day. Do we allow God to work through us to bless others? If we do, we will find that we have created for others and ourselves a wonderful life.

*THOUGHT TO REMEMBER*

*"Let us not become weary in doing good, for at the proper time we will reap a harvest if we do not give up" (Galatians 6:9).*

# Discovery Learning

*This page contains an alternative lesson plan emphasizing learning activities. Classes desiring such student involvement will find these suggestions helpful. The next page is a reproducible activity page to further enhance discovery learning.*

## LEARNING GOALS

After this lesson a student should be able to:

1. Explain the meaning and application of "the fruit of the Spirit."

2. Describe the behaviors Paul associates with the fruit of the Spirit.

3. Identify one or more ways he or she will become more Christlike in daily living.

## INTO THE LESSON

Prepare a table of sliced fruit for class members to eat as they enter the room. Have two bowls of each kind of fruit prepared. One bowl will be fruit that is old, wrinkled, or spoiling. (Often this can be prepared by just leaving the fruit out and unprotected for a few days.) The other bowl will contain freshly prepared fruit. Suggested fruits include whole bananas, orange slices, melon slices, strawberries, or pineapple. You may wish to have a fruit dip available. Have disposable bowls, silverware, and napkins at the table. As students enter, invite them to have a snack from the table of fruit you have prepared.

After the class is seated, note that people did not make selections from the bowl containing the old and spoiled fruit. Ask the class what the difference is between good and bad fruit. What makes fruit go bad? Make the transition to today's Bible study by telling the class that Paul uses the analogy of good fruit to teach us about the kind of lives followers of Jesus should live.

## INTO THE WORD

Prepare three posters. Each poster should have one of these three headings: "The Spirit and His Fruit" (Galatians 5:22, 23); "The Spirit and Our Attitudes" (Galatians 5:24-26); and "The Spirit and Others" (Galatians 6:1-10). The first poster also should have these statements evenly spaced down the page: "God-oriented Virtues" (that especially reflect God's nature); "Others-oriented Virtues" (expressed in relationships with others); and "Self-oriented Virtues" (that reflect personal disciplines).

*Poster #1 (The Spirit's Fruit).* Read Galatians 5:22, 23. Tell the class that some Bible commentators divide the fruit of the Spirit into three categories of three qualities each. As you cover each quality, write it in the appropriate space on the outline. Offer brief comments on each, using the material in the lesson commentary. After completing the list, ask the class, "Why do you think Paul used the phrase *fruit of the Spirit* instead of *works of the Spirit* or *fruits of the Spirit*? How is the metaphor of fruit helpful?" (See the Lesson Background.)

*Poster #2 (Our Attitudes).* Read Galatians 5:24-26. Write the phrase *Crucify the Sinful Nature* on the poster board while asking, "What does it mean to crucify the flesh?" After this discussion, write "Keep in Step with the Spirit" on the poster board while asking, "What does this phrase mean? What criteria would you use to determine if someone were keeping in step with the Spirit?"

*Poster #3 (Blessing Others).* Ask the class to read Galatians 6:1-10 and then list the ways this text says that we can be a blessing to others. Write these on the poster board. Then ask these discussion questions: "What could make it difficult to restore a person who has been 'caught in a sin'? (Galatians 6:1). How can this be accomplished?" Jot down the class's comments on the poster.

In addition, use the commentary to explain the apparent contradiction when Paul says to "carry each other's burdens" (v. 2) and to "carry [our] own load" (v. 5).

## INTO LIFE

(The following activity is included in the student book activity page.) On another poster board, create a chart with two columns with the heading "Fruit in Real Life." In the left column list the nine qualities of the fruit of the Spirit from Galatians 5:22, 23. Then ask the class to think of persons they know or examples with which they are familiar of people living out one of these qualities. As they share their stories or testimonies, jot down a note in the right column about how that quality was demonstrated. (Be prepared to give an example to start the discussion.)

Tell the class that Paul is encouraging Christians to live out these qualities each day. Ask members to consider the models of application just cited and to identify one of the qualities of the Spirit's fruit that they would like to "bear" in their lives this week. They are to write that target "fruit" on a piece of cardboard you distribute that is about the size of a business card.

Close the class by asking class members to pray for each other in groups of three or four.

# Fruit Basket Upset!

The old childhood game "Upset the Fruit Basket" can be modified for application to Galatians 5:19-24. We are to dump the fruit of evil out of our lives and fill our lives with the fruit of the Spirit. Read this Scripture and write in the fruit we are to avoid and the fruit we need to demonstrate in our lives.

*DUMPING EVIL FRUIT*                    *SHOWING FRUIT OF THE SPIRIT*

# On Being Fruitful

Galatians 6:1-10 tells us that doing good to the family of believers may include tough tasks. Respond to the following concerning the requirement to be fruitful.

1. Verse one challenges believers to hold one another accountable for sinful behavior. What are a few difficulties and dangers of doing what Paul asks?

2. Even though this task is difficult, why is it important?

3. It seems like a paradox! Paul asks us to "carry each other's burdens" (v. 2). Then he says "each one should carry his own load" (v. 5). Reread this passage and try to harmonize these two teachings from Paul.

4. This passage boldly asks Christians to do good, especially to fellow believers. Think about this challenge for a while. Then select one specific action you will do for someone else this week that comes from having God's Spirit within you.

# Summer Quarter, 2005

## Jesus' Life, Teachings, and Ministry

## About These Lessons

This quarter takes us into first Mark, then Matthew, then Luke to focus on the theme of *Christ*. The Old Testament points toward him. The letters of Paul point back to him. The book of Revelation lifts our hearts to consider his return. Could there be anything more important—or could there be any greater privilege—than studying Jesus' life and ministry?

Jun 5

Jun 12

Jun 19

Jun 26

Jul 3

Jul 10

Jul 17

Jul 24

Jul 31

Aug 7

Aug 14

Aug 21

Aug 28

# The Historical Jesus

*by Ronald L. Nickelson*

Many scholars of decades past occupied their time with searches or "quests" for "the historical Jesus." The New Testament, so they thought, presents us merely with "the Christ as preached" by first-century Christians, and the picture of Christ that those early believers painted may or may not square with actual history. Their questions and their "quests" should cause us to ask an important question: Is it plausible that the apostles and other first-century Christians could get so carried away with what they *wanted* to believe that they embellished and stretched the truth?

There are many ways to approach this question, and there are many ways to examine the evidence. In the limited space we have here, we shall consider only one: the martyrdom of the apostles. Historical records and tradition confirm that most of the apostles suffered this fate. This fact raises a powerful question: Would rational people willingly die for a Christ whom they knew wasn't really who they said he was? To think that the apostles would first create a fiction and then be willing to give up their lives for that fiction is an idea with no credibility. Jesus is just who the Bible says he is: the Son of God. This quarter's lessons help us explore that fact from various angles.

In **Lesson 1** we see Jesus' authority declared, by both divine and human voices, at the time of his baptism.

**Lesson 2** looks at miracles as reflections of both Jesus' power and caring. Jesus' miracles establish his power to bring healing.

**Lesson 3** shows how the intense opposition to Jesus eventually led to his trial and crucifixion. Ultimately, however, that rejection fulfilled God's plan.

**Lesson 4** proclaims God's victory in the resurrection. Jesus' empty grave witnesses to God's ultimate power to exceed all human expectations.

In **Lesson 5** we will see Jesus teaching that true happiness is found in the spirit in which one gives and lives. It is also found in how one glorifies God. True happiness is not found in possessions and controls.

**Lesson 6** takes us to the Sermon on the Mount. Truly this is one of the greatest teaching events in all of history!

**Lesson 7** examines Jesus' use of parables as a teaching tool that both clarifies and conceals. Jesus communicated deep truths with this method.

**Lesson 8** focuses on teachings of forgiveness. This can be both our favorite and least favorite topic, depending on which side of the fence we're on!

**Lesson 9**, which deals with teachings on "the last days," explores the relationship between God's future and our present-day living.

**Lesson 10** shows us how focused Jesus was on knowing and completing his mission. He refused to be distracted. And our mission is an extension of his.

**Lesson 11** shows us two instances when Jesus healed others out of compassion. His actions provide us with a window into the relationship between faith and wholeness.

**Lesson 12** challenges us to consider compassion in light of what it means to be and to recognize a neighbor. The Parable of the Good Samaritan is familiar; its lesson is ever new.

**Lesson 13** rounds out our quarter by exploring issues of humility and hospitality. Being a "glory grabber" will interfere with our ability to be compassionate toward others. Being included in God's kingdom is honor enough.

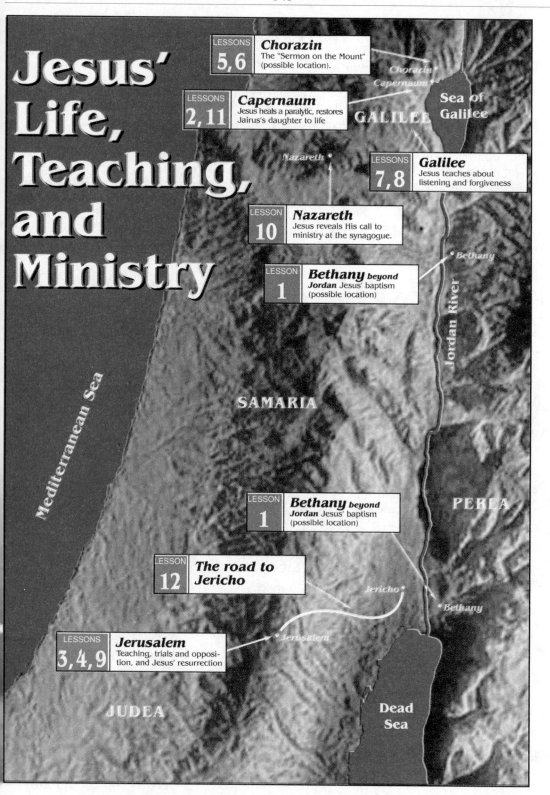

# Jesus' Life, Teaching, and Ministry

**LESSONS 5,6** — **Chorazin** The "Sermon on the Mount" (possible location).

**LESSONS 2,11** — **Capernaum** Jesus heals a paralytic, restores Jairus's daughter to life

**LESSONS 7,8** — **Galilee** Jesus teaches about listening and forgiveness

**LESSON 10** — **Nazareth** Jesus reveals His call to ministry at the synagogue.

**LESSON 1** — **Bethany beyond Jordan** Jesus' baptism (possible location)

**LESSON 1** — **Bethany beyond Jordan** Jesus' baptism (possible location)

**LESSON 12** — **The road to Jericho**

**LESSONS 3,4,9** — **Jerusalem** Teaching, trials and opposition, and Jesus' resurrection

Chorazin
Capernaum
Sea of Galilee
GALILEE
Nazareth
Bethany
Jordan River
Mediterranean Sea
SAMARIA
PEREA
Jericho
Bethany
Jerusalem
JUDEA
Dead Sea

# Jesus Confronts the World
### Chronology of the Summer Lessons

Jesus launched His ministry with His baptism "in the fifteenth year of the reign of Tiberius Caesar" (Luke 3:1). This we know was about a.d. 26 or 27. From there we can with reasonable certainty date the rest of His ministry, although the different arrangement of the material in each of the Gospels does present some chronological challenges.

From the beginning of His ministry Jesus' popularity grew and grew, reaching a climax at the feeding of the 5,000, when many wanted to force Him to become king (John 6:15). His challenging teaching on the next day caused many to abandon Him (John 6:66). The opposition, which had been present almost from the start, began to grow stronger and became more threatening during the last year of Jesus' ministry.

Of course, it all worked together to accomplish the Father's plan. In a final week that began with "Palm Sunday" (the triumphal entry), Jesus challenged the religious leaders, taught His disciples, and laid down His life. Early sunday morning He took it up again and appeared to several of His close followers, starting with Mary Magdalene.

## Launching the Ministry (A.D. 26-27)

| | |
|---|---|
| Lesson 1: Baptism and Temptations | Mark 1:4-13 |
| Lesson 10: Called to a Mission | Luke 4:16-24, 28-30 |

## Growing Popularity (A.D. 27-29)

| | |
|---|---|
| Lesson 2: Miracles | Mark 2:1-12 |
| Lesson 5: Experiencing True Happiness | Matthew 5:1-16 |
| Lesson 6: Practicing Genuine Righteousness | Matthew 6:1-15 |
| Lesson 7: Learning to Listen | Matthew 13:9-17 |
| Lesson 11: Healing the Incurable | Luke 8:40-56 |

## Mounting Opposition (A.D. 29-30)

| | |
|---|---|
| Lesson 8: Receiving and Giving Forgiveness | Matthew 18:21-35 |
| Lesson 12: Being a Good Neighbor | Luke 10:25-37 |
| Lesson 13: Accepting the Invitation | Luke 14:7-11, 15-27 |
| Lesson 9: Meeting Human Needs | Matthew 25:31-46 |

## Climax: Crucifixion & Resurrection (A.D. 30)

| | |
|---|---|
| Lesson 3: Trials and Opposition | Mark 14:53-65; 15:1-3 |
| Lesson 4: Triumph | Mark 16:1-16 |

# BAPTISM AND TEMPTATIONS

### LESSON 1

## WHY TEACH THIS LESSON?

Of all those seeking to be leaders, most are only talkers. They may be powerful talkers, but *leadership* may be nothing more than one of their oft-used words.

Jesus demonstrated true leadership. Yes, his words carried power, but his deeds verified his inner strength and integrity.

Distinguishing true leaders is a skill needed by every adult. At the voting booth, in matters of missions and benevolence endeavors, with employment opportunities, regularly one must decide who is and who is not an effective leader. Seeing the attributes and character Jesus modeled is key to developing discernment in leadership choice. To see the one who can submit to another when it is the right thing to do, to see the one who can resist and reject challenges to his mission, to find the one who has the acclamation of both man and God—then one is beginning that discernment.

As Jesus' leadership qualities are emphasized in today's study, your learners will be closer to making wise leadership choices at every level of their lives.

## INTRODUCTION

### A. GREAT LEADERS

What makes a great leader? What credentials do we look for? Is it dynamism, like that of Alexander the Great? Is it political skill, like that of Abraham Lincoln? Is it integrity, like that of Mohandas Gandhi? Is it determination, like that of General George Patton? Is it a combination?

Christians want to be effective leaders in carrying out their God-given mission. But Christians are concerned with more than the world's standards of leadership. Christians have to ask, "What does God seek in a leader?" Mark's Gospel can help us understand the answer to that question. In certain ways, both Jesus and John the Baptist are models of leadership for us.

### B. LESSON BACKGROUND

The original readers of Mark's Gospel were probably preoccupied with a crucial question: How can a crucified man be the promised Messiah, sent from God? For most observers, suffering crucifixion at the hands of the Roman imperial authorities would signal defeat. How could God's Anointed One be defeated?

One aim of Mark's Gospel is to answer this question. It shows us through the actions of Jesus that he is different from all others. There have been great prophets in the past, but none with the authority of Jesus. But what does Jesus do with his authority? He does not use it to serve himself. Rather, he surrenders himself to the will of God. God's purpose for him is that he is to give his life willingly for the sake of sinners. He dies on the cross at Golgotha, but not because he is defeated. In the cross is his greatest victory as he pays sin's penalty on our behalf.

Mark begins presenting Jesus' credentials as the Messiah from his very first verse, where he declares that Jesus is the "Christ" (synonymous with "Messiah," meaning "Anointed One"). Then he launches immediately into a narrative that

DEVOTIONAL READING:
MATTHEW 12:15-21

BACKGROUND SCRIPTURE:
MARK 1:4-13

PRINTED TEXT:
MARK 1:4-13

LESSON AIMS

After participating in this lesson, each student will be able to:

1. Retell Mark's account of Jesus' baptism and temptations.

2. Explain what Jesus' baptism and temptations tell us about his identity and authority.

3. Name one reason why he or she is willing to follow the leadership of Jesus Christ.

KEY VERSE

And a voice came from heaven: "You are my Son, whom I love; with you I am well pleased." —Mark 1:11

shows both what accredits Jesus as God's Anointed One and what kind of Anointed One he truly is.

## I. FORERUNNER OF THE GREATEST ONE (MARK 1:4-8)

We may be surprised, though, that Mark's Gospel first describes not Jesus but John the Baptist. John is a crucial figure in all the Gospels. He stands at the end of the line of God's prophets. He announces that God is about to fulfill his promises by establishing his rule. But John's testimony about Jesus shows Jesus to be an even greater figure. In fact, John declares that his most important role is to point to the greater one who is to come.

### A. JOHN'S ACTIONS (vv. 4, 5)

*4. And so John came, baptizing in the desert region and preaching a baptism of repentance for the forgiveness of sins.*

John is known in the New Testament as "the Baptist" (Mark 8:28) because he plunges repentant people in water for the cleansing of their sins. The Mosaic law had established situations in which the Jewish people were required to undergo a ceremonial washing (Exodus 19:10; 30:18-21; Leviticus 14:8, 9; etc.). But in those ceremonies, a person washed oneself. John's action is different. As the prophet of God, he plunges the person under the water.

For people accustomed to washing themselves for ceremonial cleansing, this action clearly represents something different. John's *baptism* differs from the washings practiced by the Pharisees and the Essenes of the day. John's baptism calls for *repentance,* and it is for everyone. Only God can wash people so that they are truly cleansed of sins. That is what John's baptism declares.

It is significant that John performs his baptisms in *the desert region.* The Bible uses this phrase to refer to places that are unpopulated, usually wilderness areas. The actual place where John baptizes is the wilderness around the Jordan River; this is not to be confused with the wilderness or desert of Sinai, where the Israelites had wandered (Numbers 14:32, 33; Jeremiah 2:6). Even so, the location serves as a potent reminder of that earlier time. This wilderness was the place of preparation for entering the land of promise.

So John's message is an announcement that God is freeing his people from captivity for entry into a greater promise. This is the very promise that the Old Testament prophets had given: when God brings his magnificent act of salvation, it will be like the exodus, only greater. God begins by using John the Baptist to prepare "the way for the Lord," meaning Jesus—the one who will bring this promise to fruition (see Isaiah 40:3, quoted in Mark 1:3).

We remember that the generation that witnessed the exodus refused to believe in the power of God, and so they died in the wilderness without entering into the promise. John understands that his own generation, like others, is much the same. That is why God's offer of cleansing requires repentance. To receive this cleansing, people must admit their rebellion against God. Baptism can have no significance apart from the faithful trust in the power of God to forgive on the part of the one baptized. John's actions signal that the promise of God to free and forgive his people is about to be fulfilled. John's act of baptism looks forward to the appearance of the one who will bring that salvation.

WHAT DO YOU THINK?

*Some people find times of trial and hardship to be a "wilderness experience." What kinds of "wilderness experiences" have you endured, and what "promise" came after?*

### MAKING A U-TURN

Some comedian once said that the greatest contribution the state of California has made to civilization is the legal U-turn! Of course, the Golden State has made many contributions to civilization, and that is probably the least. But we are happy when we are driving down the street and discover that it both possible and legal to make a U-turn.

We may think of repentance as a "spiritual U-turn." Often the Bible uses the word *turn* for repentance. A cynical world says, "Once a thief, always a thief." But both Old and New Testaments assure us that we can make a U-turn. The message of the prophets was, "Repent" (Ezekiel 14:6; 18:30-32). That was the message of John the Baptist (Matthew 3:2). Later it would become the message of Jesus (Luke 13:3).

All of us know of people who made drastic and lasting U-turns in life. We ourselves, for that matter, are proof that one can turn *from* sin and *to* Christ. Both those prepositions are used in connection with repentance: we turn from something and we turn to something (Acts 20:21). Yet it is not enough to say that a spiritual U-turn is possible. The Bible makes it plain that the U-turn is mandatory. If we do not make that turn, we will certainly perish (again, Luke 13:3).    —R. C. S.

### 5. The whole Judean countryside and all the people of Jerusalem went out to him. Confessing their sins, they were baptized by him in the Jordan River.

John's contemporaries are clearly impressed by his actions. Large numbers gladly submit to this offer of being immersed in water for God's cleansing from sin. Submitting to baptism goes hand in hand with *confessing* one's *sins*. Just as there can be no genuine baptism without faithfully turning toward God and away from rebellion, so there can be no genuine baptism without the heartfelt confession that we have rebelled against God.

### B. JOHN'S APPEARANCE (v. 6)
### 6. John wore clothing made of camel's hair, with a leather belt around his waist, and he ate locusts and wild honey.

John's unusual *clothing* reminds his audience of the great prophet Elijah (2 Kings 1:8). Elijah prophesied over eight hundred years earlier, at a time of crisis for Israel when militant paganism threatened to overwhelm the worshipers of the God of Israel. In that crisis the prophet called on the people to turn away from idols and return to the living God (1 Kings 18). John's appearance puts that message in a similar context.

John's diet fits the setting of his ministry. No conventional crops will grow in the arid wilderness, so John eats what is available from foraging. *Locusts* are what we call grasshoppers. Living in the barren desert, John relies on the food that God provides, like Israel receiving manna (Exodus 16) or Elijah receiving food from ravens (1 Kings 17:6). It is the food of one who waits patiently for God to fulfill his promise of blessing.

### C. JOHN'S ANNOUNCEMENT (vv. 7, 8)
### 7. And this was his message: "After me will come one more powerful than I, the thongs of whose sandals I am not worthy to stoop down and untie.

The entire description of John the Baptist underlines his importance in God's plan. But his message focuses on one of greater importance, one with supreme importance. The coming one will be so superior to John that John regards himself as unworthy even to do the stoop labor, characteristic of slaves, of undoing the *thongs* on that one's *sandals*.

John's statement is very provocative. Who could this be—this mightier person with whom even God's prophet (John) pales in comparison? Not even angels are worthy of such veneration. Humans, all of them, are the pinnacle of God's creation; as such, humans are second only to God himself (Genesis 1:26, 27). Only God is worthy of an honor that places him on a plane far above

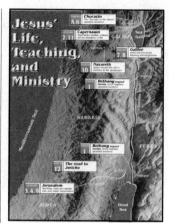

Visual for lesson 1. *Display this map throughout the quarter to provide a geographical perspective of the lessons.*

### VISUALS FOR THESE LESSONS

*The small visual pictured in each lesson (such as the one above) is a reproduction of a large, full-color poster included in the Adult Visuals packet for the Summer Quarter. The packet is available from your supplier. Order No. 492.*

*WHAT DO YOU THINK?*

*John's behavior was not offensive, but it did command attention! John used that attention to point people to Jesus. How can Christians today draw attention to themselves in such a way as to point people to the Lord? What errors need to be avoided in such an effort?*

*WHAT DO YOU THINK?*

*How diligent are we in making sure the world knows we follow Jesus because he is more than a mere man—that he is God himself? What more can we do?*

*HOW TO SAY IT*

*Bezalel.* Bih-ZAL-ih-el.
*Elijah.* Ee-LYE-juh.
*Essenes.* EH-seenz.
*Ezekiel.* Ee-ZEEK-ee-ul or Ee-ZEEK-yul.
*Golgotha.* GAHL-guh-thuh.
*Habakkuk.* Huh-BACK-kuk.
*Isaiah.* Eye-ZAY-uh.
*Jeremiah.* Jair-uh-MY-uh.
*Jerusalem.* Juh-ROO-suh-lem.
*Leviticus.* Leh-VIT-ih-kus.
*Messiah.* Meh-SIGH-uh.
*Pharisees.* FAIR-ih-seez.
*Philistines.* Fuh-LISS-teens or FILL-us-teens.

human beings. So, by speaking of the coming one as fundamentally greater than himself, John opens the door to the central question in Mark's Gospel: Is this one much more than just an ordinary human being? Mark will soon show us that the answer is *yes.*

**8. "I baptize you with water, but he will baptize you with the Holy Spirit."**

Sometimes Christians imagine that *the Holy Spirit* does not appear on the scene until New Testament times, but this is not the case. In the Old Testament, the Holy Spirit was present and active in many ways.

For example, God's Spirit enabled Bezalel to design the tabernacle (Exodus 31:2-5), Samson to overcome the Philistines (Judges 13:25), and especially the prophets to speak the message of God (1 Samuel 10:10). But in the Old Testament the Spirit of God is given to just a few of God's people, not to all.

Even so, the prophets looked forward to the time when God would give his Spirit to all his people. That gift would mean renewed blessing producing real righteousness among his people (Isaiah 32:15; Ezekiel 36:27). It would mean new life (Ezekiel 37:14). It would mean that God's people would speak his message with boldness (Joel 2:28-32).

No one can give God's Spirit but God. John's promise that the coming greater one *will baptize you with the Holy Spirit* says flatly that that one will do what only God can do. Therefore, who can this greater one be but God himself?

John draws a contrast between his own action of baptizing in *water* and the greater one's action in giving the Holy Spirit. Some say that this shows that John's own administration of water baptism is relatively unimportant. But this is not John's implication. John is simply pointing out that as a mere human he does not personally do what only God can do. But as a divinely given aspect of God's plan for humanity, baptism has profound importance.

Is John's practice of baptism the same as Christian baptism in the name of Jesus? The witness of the New Testament shows us that while these are different, they are closely related. Disciples of John who believed in Jesus after his resurrection were rebaptized into the name of Jesus (Acts 19:1-7). John's baptism looked forward to the coming greater one who would fulfill God's promises. Baptism in the name of Jesus looks back to the actual fulfillment of those promises. As such, baptism should have a powerful effect on our thinking and behavior. To discover the meaning of baptism, study passages such as Acts 2:38; Romans 6:1-7; Galatians 3:27; Colossians 2:12; and 1 Peter 3:21.

## II. ARRIVAL OF THE GREATEST ONE (MARK 1:9-11)

In Mark, Jesus' first appearance is at his own baptism. This scene gives us a glimpse of the role that Jesus will play in God's plan.

### A. BAPTISM (v. 9)

**9. At that time Jesus came from Nazareth in Galilee and was baptized by John in the Jordan.**

Jesus comes to *John* to receive the baptism that John offers. Mark's Gospel does not tell us directly why Jesus does this, but we can infer the reason from the context. First, Jesus does not come, as others do, for cleansing from sin. Soon he will begin to cast out demons, showing his mastery over sin and Satan (Mark 3:23-27) and offering forgiveness of sin on his own authority (Mark 2:5).

In Matthew 3:15, Jesus himself provides a direct answer regarding the meaning of his baptism when he notes that it is "to fulfill all righteousness." In this act of submission, Jesus identifies himself with John's message; it is Jesus' ministry that will fulfill that message. Jesus' baptism also identifies him as the greater one of whom John has spoken. The actions that accompany Jesus' baptism will make that clear.

## B. HOLY SPIRIT (v. 10)

**10. As Jesus was coming up out of the water, he saw heaven being torn open and the Spirit descending on him like a dove.**

Following closely on John's promise, the Holy Spirit's appearance identifies Jesus as the one who gives the Holy *Spirit*. Because Mark's Gospel has just related John's promise about the giving of the Spirit, the Spirit's descent from Heaven on Jesus is God's statement that Jesus is the one who will fulfill that promise.

## C. VOICE FROM HEAVEN (v. 11)

**11. And a voice came from heaven: "You are my Son, whom I love; with you I am well pleased."**

By itself, the descent of the Spirit on Jesus may not tell us much. But the *voice* that accompanies that action fills out the picture. Mark does not tell us whose voice this is. But because the voice says something very similar to statements of God in the Old Testament, there is no doubt who is speaking.

The words of the voice are very similar to two important Old Testament passages, namely Psalm 2:7 and Isaiah 42:1. The combination of these texts helps us understand who Jesus is and what he will do.

Psalm 2 is a celebration of God's rule over his people through the King whom he appointed. It begins by commenting on the rage and pretensions of the pagan nations. Where is God, since the wicked seem to rule the world? The psalmist answers that God still rules in Heaven and will establish his rule on earth through his appointed King. It looks forward to the Messiah who will defeat God's enemies and bring about God's will "on earth as it is in heaven."

Isaiah 42 speaks of the servant of the Lord who will make God known to all the nations. His method will not be to conquer with the sword but to serve with gentleness. Thereby he will bring light to the nations.

God's words at Jesus' baptism identify him with these two Old Testament concepts. Jesus is the promised King, the one appointed by God to establish his rule. He will do that, not by conquest, but by mercy. He will defeat God's enemies, but he will do it by what seems to be his own defeat. By submitting to death on the cross, Jesus will make the mercy of God available to all and will reign as God's King.

As Christians look at the world, they can easily sink into frustration and discouragement. It often seems that wickedness has won the day. This outlook is not new (see Judges 6:13; Habakkuk 1:2-4). What God announces here shows us otherwise. God is working out his plan. Yet he does it "not with swords loud clashing, Nor roll of stirring drums," but with the servant-king who rules by giving himself for unworthy people.

## III. TEMPTATION OF THE GREATEST ONE (MARK 1:12, 13)

Mark tells us very little about Jesus' temptation after his baptism. Rather, Mark sets a scene and lets us infer the outcome.

## A. SPIRIT'S ACTION (v. 12)

**12. At once the Spirit sent him out into the desert,**

Having just descended on Jesus, the Holy Spirit sends Jesus *into the desert*. Mark uses a strong verb that implies urgency. What Jesus does in that place is important to his mission and God's purpose.

## DAILY BIBLE READINGS

**Monday, May 30**—*You Are My Son (Psalm 2:7-12)*

**Tuesday, May 31**—*Baptism for Repentance and Forgiveness (Mark 1:4-8)*

**Wednesday, June 1**—*John the Baptist's Message (Matthew 3:7-12)*

**Thursday, June 2**—*Jesus Is Baptized (Matthew 3:13-17)*

**Friday, June 3**—*Jesus Is Baptized and Tested (Mark 1: 9-13)*

**Saturday, June 4**—*Here Is My Servant (Matthew 12:17-21)*

**Sunday, June 5**—*Jesus Is Tempted by the Devil (Matthew 4:1-11)*

## WHAT DO YOU THINK?

In what ways does it seem to you that "wickedness has won the day" in our culture? What do you do to resist the feelings of despair or frustration over that? How can we demonstrate that the victory still belongs to the Lord?

## Prayer

*Heavenly Father, we seek your approval this day on our thoughts and actions as we look in humble gratitude back to the approval you pronounced on your Son. May we live our lives in rejection of the evil that Jesus came to defeat. In Jesus' name, amen.*

## What Do You Think?

*How does our church imitate Jesus' ministry in bringing defeat to Satan and relief to those whom Satan has oppressed? What more can it do? How are you demonstrating these ministry emphases? What more can you do?*

Again, desert or wilderness is an important place for Israel. In the wilderness under Moses, Israel failed its test. How will Jesus stand up to his wilderness challenge?

### B. Elements of Jesus' Temptation (v. 13)

**13. . . . and he was in the desert forty days, being tempted by Satan. He was with the wild animals, and angels attended him.**

Mark's spare details show us the main thrust of Jesus' *desert* experience. As we observed before, the prophets spoke of God's promised salvation as an event like Israel's exodus from Egypt, only greater. Jesus now goes to the desert for *forty days*, like Israel after the exodus for forty years, and confronts temptation. His temptation comes from the chief adversary himself, *Satan*. Though the situation is dangerous, as suggested by the presence of *wild animals*, Jesus receives supernatural care from *angels*.

What, then, is the outcome of this confrontation? Mark will show us in what follows. Jesus' first miracle in Mark is the casting out of a demon (Mark 1:23-26). Jesus continues to prevail whenever he encounters Satan's demonic servants (3:11). In fact, he says that his casting out of demons demonstrates that he has bound the "strong man," Satan himself (3:27). Jesus freely offers forgiveness for the sin that Satan has inspired (2:5).

In all, Jesus' ministry brings defeat to Satan and relief to those whom Satan has oppressed. Clearly, Jesus has prevailed from the beginning.

### Our Enemy

The (in)famous French philosopher Voltaire (1694–1778) was dying. Someone at his bedside asked him to renounce the devil. Voltaire purportedly replied, "I am in no position to make any enemies."

But the devil already was Voltaire's enemy! The apostle Peter referred to the devil as such (1 Peter 5:8). The very word *Satan* means "adversary." Sometimes when a very good man dies, people say, "He never had an enemy." Not true! We all have an enemy. As surely as God wants the best for us, the devil wants the worst for us. As deeply as God loves us, Satan hates us. His promise to Eve didn't come true, and neither will his promises to us. Yet, strangely enough, we keep on believing them. If you trust God, he will never fail you. If you trust the devil, he will always disappoint you.

We may have a hard time visualizing Satan, and we do not need to. (We have an equally hard time visualizing God!) The important thing is that we realize that there is a great spiritual struggle going on. Good and evil, God and Satan, are locked in combat (with the decisive battle already fought at the cross and the empty tomb). We cannot stay out of the struggle that continues. We enlist on one side or the other. Since we already know the final outcome, how foolish we would be to enlist on Satan's side—the losing side. He will always be our enemy until his final defeat (Revelation 20:10).       —R. C. S.

### CONCLUSION

At the end of the story, as Jesus goes to his death, we may think that Satan has prevailed. But the resurrection will show us the real outcome.

Jesus was not defeated in the cross. Rather, in the cross he was victorious over sin and Satan. God had predicted this victory as far back as Genesis 3:15. When it seems that evil cannot be overcome, we can remember the one who has defeated the evil one for all time. We understand this final outcome all the better when we look at how Jesus began his ministry. It began with the Father's approval.

## Thought to Remember

*When in doubt, continue to follow Christ.*

# Discovery Learning

*This page contains an alternative lesson plan emphasizing learning activities. Classes
desiring such student involvement will find these suggestions helpful. The next page
is a reproducible activity page to further enhance discovery learning.*

## LEARNING GOALS

After participating in this lesson, each student will be able to:

1. Retell Mark's account of Jesus' baptism and temptations.

2. Explain what Jesus' baptism and temptations tell us about his identity and authority.

3. Name one reason why he or she is willing to follow the leadership of Jesus Christ.

## INTO THE LESSON

On four or five seats in your classroom place a small gift-wrapped (empty) box. On four or five seats, place a small candy bar. On four or five, tape a quarter (25 cents). Ignore any initial comments regarding the items. As class begins, ask, "Were any of you tempted to open or pocket the item on your seat? Did you find the items tempting?" After a few responses, ask, "How do these items represent temptations common to people?" Curiosity can lead to exploratory behavior; appealing smells and tastes can lead to sampling and overindulgence; money can lead to greed—all are common temptations.

As an alternate introduction, display this letter series: S S E U L B F M C I O S N S T I R O O N L. Ask the class to decipher the word puzzle. (It is the word submission merged with the word self-control—alternating letters.) Once someone suggests the correct intention, note that in today's lesson text Jesus demonstrates how the godly live lives both of self-control and of submission as he yields to John's baptism and as he resists the devil's strongest temptations.

## INTO THE WORD

Display a sketch titled "East Gate Wilderness Mall," showing a basic floor plan for a shopping mall with ten to twelve "business spaces" available. Explain that the ford crossing the Jordan near Jericho, the general location of John's preaching and baptizing, was indeed the "East Gate" for northern travelers coming to Jerusalem. Indicate that you are going to write in the names of "shops" and that you want learners to relate each one to a verse in today's text. Use the following sample "shop" names (or others of your own creation) with verse identification and brief explanation: *4J Travel Agency* (vv. 4, 5)—four Js are Judea, Jerusalem, Jordan, and John; the people all traveled to where John was; *Nothing But San-*

*dals* (v. 7)—the reference to unloosing shoes; *Healthy Diet Shoppe* (v. 6)—a reference to the unusual but kosher diet of John; *Birds from Above* (v. 10)—a reference to the Spirit descending from Heaven in the form of a dove; *Wild Kingdom* (v. 13)—only Mark makes reference to the wild animals in the wilderness; *Dry Goods for Men & Women* (v. 5)—after being immersed in the water the believers needed dry clothing; *Big Amps* (v. 11)—the clear and loud voice from Heaven; *Something Better* (v. 8)—John's act was good, but the better baptism would be later with the Spirit; *UnFriendly Advice Counseling Services* (v. 13)—with the *Un* careted above the line as if a correction; the reference is to Satan's evil suggestions to Jesus in the guise of helping him; *Driven! Taxi Services* (v. 12)—the Spirit drove Jesus to his appointment with the devil.

Rather than suggesting "shop" names yourself, your class may well want to suggest relevant "shop" names, if you explain the sketch and give them an example or two.

## INTO LIFE

Provide a sheet of paper for each learner to make a quick sketch of the "East Gate Wilderness Mall" as you have completed it. Suggest that they save this in their Bibles at Mark 2 for review this coming week. Suggest further that they make a mental connection between today's text and the shops that they walk by or drive by. For example, passing a store specializing in sound equipment should remind them of God's voice from Heaven announcing his pleasure with his Son's submission; passing a health foods store can bring to mind John's careful and healthful diet (and the Bible's general expectations for healthy eating).

Recommend a careful reading of the accounts of Matthew and Luke regarding Jesus' wilderness temptations from Satan. Matthew 4:1-11 and Luke 4:1-13 provide important details regarding the ways Jesus responded to the various temptations. Encourage your learners to look around in the coming week and note those images that speak to the reality of the evil one today. They should also be able to quote a verse that is relevant to the image and context. For example, seeing a demonic tattoo on a passerby could recall, "Worship the Lord your God, and serve him only" (Matthew 4:10). Close with a prayer for discernment to do this.

# Learning from Jesus

Today's text, Mark 1:4-13, describes two events from the beginning of Jesus' public ministry: his baptism by John and his temptations at the villainy of Satan. Look at these "lessons to be learned from Jesus" and decide which are learned in today's text and which are not. For those that are, indicate a relevant verse or verses.

_____ 1. Public assemblies can be the right places to show submission.

_____ 2. True leaders can become followers in the right circumstances.

_____ 3. Receiving God's approval goes hand in hand with humble submission.

_____ 4. Honoring the effective ministry of others is a good choice.

_____ 5. Prayer is the right behavior for major events.

_____ 6. Sometimes one has to go "out of his or her way" to do the right thing.

_____ 7. When one is doing what God wants, there is no reason to fear.

_____ 8. Satan may prefer to come at a time of personal weakness.

_____ 9. God's ministering angels may be present at difficult times.

How would you explain your decisions to another learner?


Select one of the "lessons from Jesus" and describe what you will do that demonstrates you have learned the lesson.


# Submission and Resistance

The person of God must learn two key behaviors: submission to the will of God and resistance to the will of Satan. Make two lists below: one, of the matters of God to which you need to submit; the other, of the lures of the devil that you need to resist.

| *SUBMISSION* | *RESISTANCE* |
|---|---|

# MIRACLES

## LESSON 2

## WHY TEACH THIS LESSON?

Contemporary men and women live with jaded eyes. One might expect to hear, "Ho, hum! I think I've seen it all" in almost any circumstance. Men on the moon, daily intercontinental flights for hundreds of thousands, instantaneous e-mail connections—have we not seen it all?

Mark's report of his generation's reactions to Jesus' power pictures phenomena missing in our generation: amazement at God's power and praise for his marvelous creation. Though we may not be privileged to see the signs and wonders that were New Testament era miracles, marvelous things occur around us all the time—all the results of God's power. Adult learners need to regain that wide-eyed wonder children often express at something new. Glorifying God for all the discoveries of modern science and technology that surround us is as appropriate as the response of Galilean villagers to Jesus' healing word and touch.

Today's lesson enables not only a glimpse at Jesus' power to heal the body but should open the eyes of all to his daily provision of things marvelous, both in the physical world and in the spiritual realm.

## INTRODUCTION

### A. THE CASE OF STEVE

I once was leading a Wednesday night Bible study through 1 Thessalonians. One of the participants was a young man, Steve, afflicted with cerebral palsy. He was nearly helpless from a physical standpoint. He tried diligently to follow our study in his own Bible, but his lack of limb control caused him to rip many pages, leaving a badly tattered Bible. Steve's participation in discussion was ponderous, even painful. He either spelled out words by pointing to a signing board or tried to verbalize his comments using a voice that was difficult to understand. Sometimes the other adults in this group were impatient, for I usually needed Steve to repeat his questions many times before I could understand them.

As we got to 1 Thessalonians 4, we began to talk about the nature of Christ's second coming. Suddenly, Steve motioned that he wanted to ask a question. He was very excited, and this caused the question to be even harder to decipher than usual. He enthusiastically repeated it many times until I finally got it. The question was this, "When Jesus comes, will I get a new body?"

I have always had a relatively healthy body, so it took me a second to appreciate the implications of this question. Steve looked forward to the day when his poor, twisted body would be able to walk and talk just like all the "normal" people he observed around him. What a great day that will be! Steve passed away a few years ago without being healed from cerebral palsy, even though I know he prayed for this healing many times. It thrills my heart to know that he is now praising God with no impediment of his defective earthly body.

Today's lesson is about a "Steve" from the ministry of Jesus. He, too, had a nearly helpless physical condition. Surely he also dreamed of being "normal," of walking without help and talking so that he was easily understood. In today's marvelous story, this man received a new body, a miracle of wholeness from Jesus.

---

DEVOTIONAL READING:
MARK 7:31-37

BACKGROUND SCRIPTURE:
MARK 2:1-12; 3:1-6; 8:1-10

PRINTED TEXT:
MARK 2:1-12

### LESSON AIMS

After participating in this lesson, each student will be able to:

1. Summarize the story of the paralytic who was made whole in body and in spirit.

2. Explain why Jesus' healing ministry was central to his identity as the Son of God.

3. Give praise to God for his power and willingness to make persons whole.

### KEY VERSES

"That you may know that the Son of Man has authority on earth to forgive sins. . . ." He said to the paralytic, "I tell you, get up, take your mat and go home."
—Mark 2:10, 11

LESSON 2 NOTES

## B. LESSON BACKGROUND

The second and third chapters of Mark's Gospel contain several brief stories, sometimes referred to as "conflict narratives." In these accounts Jesus or his disciples do something that causes people to be upset with them.

In Mark 2:1-12 the healing of the paralytic is accompanied by a pronouncement of forgiveness of sins, causing the Jewish leaders to view Jesus as a blasphemer. In 2:13-17 Jesus attends a celebration at the home of his new disciple, Levi (also known as Matthew). The Jewish religious leaders see this party group as "the wrong crowd," and Jesus is again criticized. As with the paralytic, Jesus draws a connection between physical health and spiritual health, saying, "It is not the healthy who need a doctor, but the sick. I have not come to call the righteous, but sinners" (2:17). Mark 2 ends with two more stories in which Jesus and his disciples are criticized over their fasting practices and over a perceived violation of ancient Sabbath-day regulations.

These conflicts reach something of a climax in Mark 3:1-6, the story of the man with the "shriveled hand." Here Jesus is challenged to make a sobering choice: ignore a suffering man or break the Sabbath. By healing the man verbally, Jesus not only avoids obvious Sabbath work, but also takes advantage of the opportunity to expose publicly the hypocrisy of his opponents. This humiliation infuriates Jesus' opponents to the point that they develop a plot to kill him (Mark 3:6). This early foreshadowing of the death of Jesus is then worked out in the remaining chapters of Mark.

The spiritual depravity of Jesus' opponents is illustrated in the last conflict narrative in this part of Mark, a story where Jesus is accused of being demon possessed (3:20-30). The intensity of this clash is shown when Jesus pulls out the heaviest of theological artillery and warns his opponents that they are dangerously near to committing an unforgivable sin (3:29).

Today's lesson, the story of the healing of the paralytic, shows some of the terrible tensions that Jesus encountered in his ministry. On the one hand, he found people in desperate need of the forgiveness and healing that he freely offered. Their faith, their gratitude, and their blessings inspire and encourage us. On the other hand, Jesus was dogged by critics who hoped for his failure, were constantly offended by his claims, and resented his refusal to submit to their authority.

## I. PACKED HOUSE (MARK 2:1, 2)

### A. TRAVELS (v. 1)

**1. A few days later, when Jesus again entered Capernaum, the people heard that he had come home.**

Jesus makes the small fishing village of *Capernaum* his headquarters in the early days of his ministry. This is the town of Simon Peter and Andrew, and Jesus may be staying in Peter's house (Mark 1:21, 29). The word *home* means that he resides there on a semi-permanent basis. This is the place where Jesus had healed the mother-in-law of Peter (Mark 1:30, 31).

Capernaum is a well-known archaeological site in Israel today. It is located on the north end of the Sea of Galilee, about three miles west of the inlet of the Jordan River.

### B. PREACHING (v. 2)

**2. So many gathered that there was no room left, not even outside the door, and he preached the word to them.**

If this takes place at the house of Peter, we may have some remarkable information available to help us understand this setting. Modern archaeologists be-

We've Never Seen Anything Like This!

Jesus' Life
"What manner of man is this, that even the wind and the sea obey him?"
—Mark 4:41

Jesus' Teachings
"When the multitude heard this, they were astonished at his doctrine."
—Matthew 22:33

Jesus' Ministry
"[He] was moved with compassion toward them, and he healed their sick."
—Matthew 14:14

Visual for lessons 2 and 11. *You may wish to keep this visual aid posted to set the tone for each of this quarter's three subunits.*

lieve they have found the actual house of Peter at the ancient site of Capernaum. The foundations of this house were buried under the remnants of various ancient churches that had been built over it. Inscriptions and other evidence indicate that this place was considered holy by Christians from early times, lending credence to the theory that it was originally the house of Peter.

Such homes usually consisted of a rectangular, one-story building surrounded by a large, walled courtyard. Peter's (apparent) house in Capernaum was approximately twenty-eight feet long and would have been fifteen to eighteen feet deep. The interior is now packed with perhaps fifty to sixty people, causing an overflow into the courtyard. The text notes that Jesus preaches *the word* to this spiritually thirsty crowd. This is his message of faith and repentance, announcing the presence of the kingdom of God (Mark 1:14, 15).

## II. DRAMATIC ENTRANCE (MARK 2:3, 4)
### A. "PLAN A" (v. 3)
**3. Some men came, bringing to him a paralytic, carried by four of them.**

What is wrong with this man? His condition is so helpless that he has to be *carried* on a bed or stretcher with one person at each corner. This probably is not a bed rigged up just for the occasion. The man has to be carried anywhere he goes, for he cannot walk. Perhaps he is carried daily to a begging spot in this portable bed (e.g., Acts 3:2).

What, exactly, is his disease? The text only describes his condition, not the underlying cause of the condition. The word that we see translated *paralytic* is the Greek word *paralytikos*. This means the man has use of neither his arms nor his legs. This could be a condition from birth, the result of an accident, or the product of a stroke—we simply don't know. What we do know is that the *four* friends think that if they can bring the man to Jesus then Jesus can help.

### B. "PLAN B" (v. 4)
**4. Since they could not get him to Jesus because of the crowd, they made an opening in the roof above Jesus and, after digging through it, lowered the mat the paralyzed man was lying on.**

The house is so packed with people that the band of stretcher-bearers has no chance of getting their man close to Jesus. The friends of the man who is *paralyzed* are not easily thwarted. "Plan A" didn't work, so now it's on to "Plan B." They carry their disabled friend to *the roof* and proceed to break a hole in it. Then they use the stretcher as a platform to lower their friend to Jesus.

Common houses in Palestine in this time are of one story with a staircase or ladder outside to give access to the roof. The roof area could be used for storage, sometimes having a lightweight shed built on it. The roof itself is made of crossbeams with branches laid across them. This is then covered with mud, hardened by the sun. This is a durable system, hard enough to walk upon.

The drama of this event should not be missed. The *digging* surely showers the packed people below with dirt. The descending bed doubtlessly clears a space near Jesus for the man to rest, perhaps causing some to flee. We marvel at the audacity of these friends to risk the wrath of the homeowner, at their strong faith that Jesus can heal, and at their great love to do such a crazy thing for the paralyzed man. One author has described this as a "silent but dramatic plea for healing."

## III. DRAMATIC PRONOUNCEMENT (MARK 2:5)
**5. When Jesus saw their faith, he said to the paralytic, "Son, your sins are forgiven."**

*How can people see our faith today?*

*[Make sure to consider Matthew 7:20 and James 2:20, 26 in your answer.]*

*WHAT DO YOU THINK?*

*The teachers of the law were moved by jealousy to oppose Jesus. Paul encountered some of the same rival spirit from Christian preachers (Philippians 1:15). How can we be sure we do not yield to a spirit of jealousy when someone else performs a ministry in a way that results in attention and honor that we do not share?*

Jesus maintains control over this chaotic situation. He immediately recognizes an act of *faith* and a need for physical healing. His words, however, are confusing. What is the connection between faith, healing, and the need for forgiveness? Jesus' startling pronouncement, *your sins are forgiven,* elicits three responses from those who hear it.

## IV. THREE RESPONSES (MARK 2:6-12)

### A. OFFENDED HEARTS (vv. 6-9)

**6, 7. Now some teachers of the law were sitting there, thinking to themselves, "Why does this fellow talk like that? He's blaspheming! Who can forgive sins but God alone?"**

Mark first tells of the response of the *teachers* or scribes in the house. Scribes are respected, authoritative interpreters of the Jewish *law.* They instantly detect a possible violation. *Sins* are forgiven by God only, and only through long-practiced methods of sacrifices and priests. See Exodus 34:7 for God proclaiming the power to forgive sins. See also Psalm 103:2, 3 and Isaiah 43:25.

These men already have been portrayed as seeing Jesus as a possible rival teacher, one with extraordinary spiritual authority (Mark 1:27). None of them would presume to be able to pronounce forgiveness. They conclude that Jesus possesses no such rightful authority either, and, therefore, his pronouncement is nothing less than blasphemy. Blasphemy in this context is to infringe upon authority that belongs rightfully to God. Blasphemy is a capital offense under the Jewish law (Leviticus 24:16).

**8, 9. Immediately Jesus knew in his spirit that this was what they were thinking in their hearts, and he said to them, "Why are you thinking these things? Which is easier: to say to the paralytic, 'Your sins are forgiven,' or to say, 'Get up, take your mat and walk'?**

Jesus undoubtedly startles the teachers of the law by reading their thoughts. His comment reflects the ancient way of referring to mental processes. The people of Jesus' time see the heart as more than the center of emotions. For them, the heart is also the intellectual center, and in particular it is the source of the human will. So their reasoning is really a spiritual matter, a lack of faith. To make his purpose completely clear, Jesus challenges the scribes to differentiate between forgiving and healing. Both require authority that they do not possess. Both call for the power of God.

It seems uncomfortable to look at this man as a gross sinner. What is his sin problem? How can a *paralytic* get into sin? To think this way, however is to underestimate the universal, pervasive problem of human sinfulness. Disabled people sin, too! Sin extends beyond our actions. It includes our mental life. The mental life of the paralytic may have been consumed by sexual sin, by bitter rejection of God, or by personal dishonesty. We don't know.

We may not all be physically disabled, but we are all spiritually disabled because of sin. Everyone stands before God as a sinner in need of forgiveness. And just as we have no power to miraculously heal our bodies, we have no power to grant God's forgiveness to ourselves. Both are gracious acts of God that must be received in faith rather than demanded or expected.

### THE PERSONAL TOUCH

There is a gallery in England that displays what many call "holy relics." They say that they have a bone from the skull of John the Baptist. They display a lock of hair said to be from the head of Mary, the mother of Jesus. There is even a column that is supposed to be the one against which Jesus leaned when he was scourged! Of course, it is most unlikely that any of the relics are genuine. They may be a source of inspiration, but little more. Some, though, claim that they have been healed by these things.

You will notice that Jesus healed personally. Most of us think that today healing still comes directly and personally from the Lord, not indirectly and impersonally from some object that may or may not have been associated with Him. When we pray for health or healing today, we should not expect that some object over which someone has prayed will accomplish what we desire. Neither should we expect that there are magic words that, if only said properly, will accomplish healing.

We should expect, rather, that a loving Lord hears our prayers and answers them in accordance with his own wisdom, knowledge, and love. This means that we may have to wait until we are in Heaven to receive the healing for which we pray. It also means that we can pray freely, for if we ask for something we should not have, a wise and loving Father will respond in the way that is best.    —R. C. S.

## B. OBEDIENT HEART (vv. 10-12a)

**10, 11. "But that you may know that the Son of Man has authority on earth to forgive sins . . . ." He said to the paralytic, "I tell you, get up, take your mat and go home."**

Supernatural claims demand supernatural evidence. For example, if I claim the supernatural ability to fly like Superman, no one would believe me unless I demonstrate the fact by soaring into the air unaided. To make the supernatural claim that Jesus is the Son of God requires supernatural evidence.

Jesus deliberately links the healing and the forgiving. Only the power of God can instantly heal a *paralytic*. Only the authority of God can allow for forgiveness of sins. Jesus says, in effect, "I have *authority* in both areas. Because there is no visible sign of forgiveness, I will show my authority in a tangible way by healing this man. I will make him whole spiritually and physically."

Jesus is making a messianic claim by doing this. The Gospel of Mark is very careful in its presentation of Jesus as the Son of God. Mark 1:1 indicates that this is the core of the book's message. At his baptism, Jesus is identified as God's Son (Mark 1:11). Later, at the transfiguration, God not only reinforces this identification, but also commands that Jesus must be heard (Mark 9:7). To truly hear Jesus is to believe him and obey Him. This is what the man is being asked to do. If we are to receive forgiveness, this is what we are asked to do.

**12a. He got up, took his mat and walked out in full view of them all.**

To put it simply, the man believes and obeys. As there can be no certain evidence of the man's forgiveness without the healing, there can be no evidence of his faith without his obedience. By *took his mat*, we envision a portable device that can be rolled up.

## A CHANGED MAN

The advertising slogan for the Louisiana tourist industry is, "Come as you are. Leave different!" That describes the experience of the paralyzed man in today's lesson. It also describes the experience of everyone who receives Jesus as Savior. The man in today's lesson was a changed man in two ways. He was a changed man physically. Four friends carried him in; he walked out carrying his mat. As important as that was to him, there was another change even more important: he was carried in a sinner; he walked out a forgiven man.

Today there are many victims of paralysis, some famous and some unknown. No doubt they pray for the same healing as the man in our text. Some may receive it now and some may have to wait until Heaven. But think for a moment of that other change. When we seek the forgiveness of our sins, we do not go away disap-

*DAILY BIBLE READINGS*

*Monday, June 6—Jesus Heals the Demoniac (Mark 5: 1-13)*

*Tuesday, June 7—He Has Done Everything Well (Mark 7:31-37)*

*Wednesday, June 8—How Many Loaves Do You Have? (Mark 8:1-5)*

*Thursday, June 9—Four Thousand Are Fed (Mark 8:6-10)*

*Friday, June 10—Stretch Out Your Hand (Mark 3:1-6)*

*Saturday, June 11—Son, Your Sins Are Forgiven (Mark 2:1-5)*

*Sunday, June 12—I Say to You, Stand Up (Mark 2:6-12)*

*HOW TO SAY IT*
blasphemer. BLAS-feem-er.
blasphemy. BLAS-fuh-me.
Capernaum. Kuh-PER-nay-um.
Galilee. GAL-uh-lee.
Isaiah. Eye-ZAY-uh.
Levi. LEE-vye.
Leviticus. Leh-VIT-ih-kus.
messianic. Mess-ee-AN-ick.

pointed. We are forgiven, and that change is of far greater magnitude than any physical healing.

Remember that we will have these bodies for only a little while. We will have our souls (and resurrected bodies) for eternity. For the soul to be crippled by sin is the greater tragedy—and to have the inner person forgiven, made whole, is the greater miracle. While we marvel at what this man experienced in his body, we marvel more at what all of Christians have experienced in their souls.       —R. C. S.

### C. "PRAISE GOD" HEART (v. 12b)

**12b. This amazed everyone and they praised God, saying, "We have never seen anything like this!"**

We should not miss the reaction of the crowd to all of this. They are *amazed*. This language is often used in the Gospels and Acts to describe the realization of a crowd that they had just witnessed a miracle (compare Mark 5:42). The Greek term translated *amazed* is the word from which we get our English words *ecstasy* and *ecstatic*. This powerful reaction is followed by an immediate acknowledgement that God is the source of this miracle.

## CONCLUSION

### A. OUR PHYSICAL CONDITION

In the mind of the ancient Jew, illness and disability were thought to be punishment for sin; this is seen clearly in John 9:2. Today, we know this to be true on a limited scale. Behavior defined as sinful by the Bible is often dangerous or even disease-producing. A reckless, pleasure-seeking lifestyle may have consequences for our health. However, we all know of many instances of disease or injury suffered by good and righteous people. Where is the power of God in all of this?

### B. MIRACLES AND US

We use the word *miracle* loosely in today's world. We speak of the latest computer triumph as a "technological miracle." We refer to a new advance in medical treatment as a "miracle drug." We call the rapid growth of a company's stock value "miraculous." But none of these things are really miracles. All can be explained through careful study and analysis.

A true miracle is a supernatural event, something beyond rational or scientific explanation. Such wonders may be spiritual or physical, just as the paralytic is healed spiritually and physically in this story. Spiritual transformation is no less miraculous than unexplainable physical change. May we never forget that God's forgiveness is also a miracle.

### C. OUR REACTION TO THE MIRACULOUS

When God works miraculously, we don't always understand. Here are three suggestions to help us deal with this issue in our lives.

*First, God is in control of his miracles; we aren't.* Why do righteous people suffer diseases, injuries, and personal disasters? Why doesn't God always heal when we ask for healing? The bottom line is that God in his wisdom determines the time, place, and circumstance of his miraculous intervention in our lives.

*Second, since we sometimes don't understand God's miraculous works, our only reaction is to praise him* as the crowd did in today's lesson. God's work is always a cause for worship. To do this is an act of obedience that should be natural for the believer.

*Third, every time we pray we expect the miraculous.* If we petition God with prayers of faith, we are asking him to make "Situation A" into "Situation not-A." Such praying is good and proper; it is an act of both obedience and faith.

---

**WHAT DO YOU THINK?**

The crowd was "amazed" and they "praised God" when the man was healed. What can we do to rekindle that same sense of awe in our worship?

**PRAYER**

Creator God, you formed the universe out of nothing by the power of your Word. You continue to work miracles that are beyond our comprehension. While we are in constant need of your providential power, today we ask that you make us more aware and appreciative of your wonders in our lives so that we may be brought to your throne in praise again and again. We pray in the name of your Son, amen.

**THOUGHT TO REMEMBER**

God's miracles should cause us to give him glory.

# Discovery Learning

*This page contains an alternative lesson plan emphasizing learning activities. Classes desiring such student involvement will find these suggestions helpful. The next page is a reproducible activity page to further enhance discovery learning.*

## LEARNING GOALS

After participating in this lesson, each student will be able to:

1. Summarize the story of the paralytic who was made whole in body and in spirit.

2. Explain why Jesus' healing ministry was central to his identity as the Son of God.

3. Give praise to God for his power and willingness to make persons whole.

## INTO THE LESSON

Display a list of six biblical miracles with the heading "Miracles," and ask the class to number them from "greatest" to "least." Consider these six (or choose your own): Red Sea held back for Israel to cross—Exodus 14:21, 22; Walls of Jericho collapse—Joshua 6:20; Samuel's spirit appears to Saul and his medium—1 Samuel 28:11-19; Elijah is taken to Heaven in a fiery chariot—2 Kings 2:11; Apostles speak in unlearned languages—Acts 2:4; Paul heals the lame man of Lystra—Acts 14:8-10.

Let the class make their decisions, and then ask, "What is it that makes a miracle a miracle?" Expect to receive responses about their extraordinary nature, their value as evidence, and their divine origin. Also ask, "How can we decide if one miracle is greater than another?" After the group responds, make the points that each miracle was God's intervention into his established "natural law," and that each is equally purposeful in the revelation of his will.

Then say, "In today's text in Mark 2, Jesus equates a healing miracle with another act that only God can do. Look carefully for how these two are connected."

## INTO THE WORD

Hand four blank index cards to each learner. Direct everyone to write the following four letters on the cards, one letter per card: F, P, R, S. Have one of your better oral readers stand and read the text, Mark 2:1-12, loudly and clearly.

Next, tell the group to conceal the text from their eyes. Then say to them, "I am going to read several questions regarding the facts of today's text. I want you, after each question, to hold up the card bearing the first letter of the word from the text answering my question." Use the following questions to review the content: (1)

"How many friends carried the man unable to walk?" (Four); (2) "What did Jesus do once the crowd assembled?" (Preached); (3) "What was the condition of the man brought to Jesus?" (Paralyzed); (4) "Of what was it said in this text that there was none?" (Room); (5) "What was it about the men carrying their friend that impressed Jesus?" (Faith); (6) "What was said about the position of the teachers in the house?" (Sitting); (7) "What part of the house was opened to get the lame man to Jesus?" (Roof); (8) "What did Jesus say about the lame man's sins?" (Forgiven); (9) "How did Jesus address the man brought to Him?" (Son); (10) "How did Jesus know the Jewish scholars were accusing Him?" (Spirit); (11) "From what Jesus said, what was the lame man's greater problem?" (Sin); (12) "What was the crowd's reaction to what they witnessed? (Praise).

Let all reveal their cards after each question. Then let one student give the answer orally.

At the end, give this assignment to the learners: "Use the four letters in your hand—in any order you choose—to compose a 'headline' for the events of the text. Feel free to add articles, prepositions, or other words." Give them a few examples:

"Rejoice! Paralyzed Man Saved and Forgiven";
"Scholars Reject Paralytic's Forgiveness";
"Forgiveness Riles Proud Scribes."

Allow enough time and then let several give their "headlines."

## INTO LIFE

The miracle in Mark 2:1-12 begins with faith (read v. 5) and ends with praise (read v. 12). Ask the class to answer this question, "What role do the miracles of the Bible play in your faith?" Ask also, "Compare your own response to Jesus' miracles to that of those present during his ministry. How do you fare in the comparison?" If you think your learners need a few texts to examine, suggest they look at records of miracles in other chapters in Mark's Gospel, perhaps Mark 1:25-28 and 4:35-41.

Ask your class to make a commitment to the following practice by signing the statement you give them (also in the student book accompanying this series): "I will—each time I read of one of the miracles of the Bible—stop to glorify God for his power and grace." Close with a prayer appropriate to this promise.

# In Full View

Jesus' demonstration of divine power did not occur in secret. Mark declares that the man healed in today's lesson "walked out in full view" (2:12). Discover, in the word search puzzle, the answers suggested by the following: (1) Jesus' activity when a crowd gathered; (2) The man's physical condition; (3) The number of men carrying the man; (4) Why the man could not be brought through the door; (5) Where the man gained access to Jesus; (6) How the men got through the roof; (7) What the man was carried on; (8) What Jesus saw in the men; (9) How Jesus addressed the paralyzed man; (10) What Jesus declared of the man's sins; (11) One realm of Jesus' authority; (12) The reaction of the crowd to the events; (13) The accusation the teachers made of Jesus; (14) The way the teachers expressed their views; (15) Who can forgive sin; (16) How Jesus knew the teachers' thoughts; (17) Where Jesus sent the healed man; (18) How the healed man left; (19) The town where the miracles took place. (Answers are at the bottom.)

```
M  I  C  R  A  T  H  I  N  K  I  N  G  H
H  T  R  A  E  C  L  E  M  F  I  O  N  C
T  I  R  I  P  S  R  A  O  C  D  L  I  I
E  M  I  R  R  E  A  O  C  L  E  T  G  H
M  I  R  F  E  A  R  C  L  E  Y  M  G  W
I  R  N  O  A  A  C  N  L  L  E  M  I  R
D  W  O  R  C  M  A  C  A  R  T  L  D  E
E  M  S  G  H  I  A  R  R  U  A  A  C  L
K  E  M  I  I  I  A  Z  H  O  M  E  R  A
L  C  L  V  N  P  E  M  E  F  A  I  T  H
A  I  R  E  G  A  C  L  E  D  M  I  R  A
W  C  G  N  I  M  E  H  P  S  A  L  B  L
```

# In Full Awe

The miraculous acts of God described in the Bible had one consistent effect on the witnesses: total amazement. Read each of the following miracle descriptions and then write a brief reaction in praise to the God of both natural law and miracle. The first gives an example.

Exodus 3:2: God of flame and fire, I stand humbled in your blazing presence.

Numbers 22:21-35

Daniel 6:16-23

Luke 7:11-16

Acts 20:7-12

Answers to word search: (1) preaching, (2) paralytic, (3) four, (4) crowd, (5) roof, (6) digging, (7) mat, (8) faith, (9) son, (10) forgiven, (11) earth, (12) amazed, (13) blaspheming, (14) thinking, (15) God, (16) spirit, (17) home, (18) walked, (19) Capernaum.

# TRIALS AND OPPOSITION

### LESSON 3

DEVOTIONAL READING:
MARK 14:17-21

BACKGROUND SCRIPTURE:
MARK 14:53-65; 15:1-5

PRINTED TEXT:
MARK 14:53-65; 15:1-3

Jun
19

## WHY TEACH THIS LESSON?

Christianity is confrontational. It cannot be otherwise. Truth always meets resistance from both the lie and the liar. Anyone striving to live a life of godliness and peace knows the conflict and confrontation that is likely to come in such a lifestyle. Darkness does not appreciate light's intrusion in the spiritual realm.

The threat of such resistance intimidates some Christians. Why broach the subject of sin and salvation with a friend or associate when it may get a hostile reaction? Why bother with small deeds of kindness when they may simply be resented (or at the least, unappreciated)? Why correct a brother or sister when relationships may be broken?

Jesus' example stands strong. He did not soften the message of personal sin, even when he knew sinners would attack. He did not stop telling the truth, even when others called it a lie. Jesus did not save himself at the cost of the lives of others; rather he gave himself to save others. Every adult who would live successfully and effectively as light in a dark world needs the lessons of today's study.

## INTRODUCTION

### A. BLAMED, BUT INNOCENT

An office helper knocked at the door of my seventh-grade classroom with a note for the teacher. I barely noticed. But terror gripped me when the teacher read the note. It said that I was to report to the vice principal's office immediately. It only took me a few seconds to be escorted down the hall to the vice principal, but my heart pounded and my mind raced. The vice principal was in charge of one thing at that school: student discipline. I was in big trouble! What had I done?

Sitting in the office was a member of the janitorial crew. He simply said, "Yes, that's him," and left. The vice principal closed the door and asked, "Why did you do it? Did you think you would get away with it?" Confused and scared, I pleaded with him to explain. He was so angry that it took him a while to give me an answer. I had been identified as having committed a major act of vandalism in one of the rest rooms. The positive identification by the janitor left no room for doubt in the vice principal's mind.

I tried every way I could to convince the man that I was innocent (which I was), but his mind was made up. He had found a guilty party, and he would not rest until proper punishment had been administered. Now, I must admit that I had been in this vice principal's office before under different circumstances where I was not innocent. I was hardly above suspicion. He was thus resistant to all my pleas of blamelessness.

In today's lesson Jesus is accused of a crime in spite of his innocence. Unlike me, he had no earlier unfavorable marks against him. He had lived a life innocent of any and all sin. Unlike me, too, he did not protest against his accusers. He quietly accepted an unjust sentence of death, and in so doing he changed the world forever.

### LESSON AIMS

After participating in this lesson, each student will be able to:

1. Describe the trial process that led to the death of Jesus.

2. Contrast the innocence of the One accused with the guilt of his accusers.

3. Express gratitude to God for the sacrifice of his innocent Son to save them from their sins.

### KEY VERSE

The chief priests and the whole Sanhedrin were looking for evidence against Jesus so that they could put him to death, but they did not find any.

—Mark 14:55

**LESSON 3 NOTES**

## B. LESSON BACKGROUND

The celebration of Passover in first-century Jerusalem was one of the greatest festivals of the ancient world. Jerusalem was a city of perhaps fifty thousand in population. (Some estimates put the "normal" population as high as one hundred twenty thousand.) Using information from a Jewish historian named Josephus, scholars estimate that this population swelled manyfold during Passover week.

Not all of these visitors were observant Jews. Herod Antipas, ruler of Galilee, came down from his capital city of Tiberias. Pilate, the Roman governor, came up from beautiful Caesarea, bringing plenty of troops with him to keep the peace. It was a time of great pageantry, celebration, and excitement.

The center of attention was the Jewish temple, a marvel of the ancient world. This enormous, magnificent complex of buildings had acres of open space to accommodate all the visitors. Business was brisk as the temple vendors had their biggest days of the year. Profits were high as Jewish pilgrims paid cash for Passover necessities.

The south end of the temple campus housed a colossal "stoa," or covered porch, approximately three hundred yards long and forty-five to fifty yards wide. At the western end of this stoa was an apse that served as the official meeting site of the Sanhedrin, the Jewish High Council. The Sanhedrin was closely connected to the temple. It not only convened there normally, but many of the Sanhedrin councilors probably had commercial interests in the temple businesses. (See a panoramic computer reconstruction of Herod's Temple on the Web site of The Jerusalem Archaeological Park at www.archpark.org.il.)

There is some reason to believe that the author, John Mark, may have been an eyewitness to some of the events he describes in chapters 14, 15, and 16. This is based on the theory that the naked runner of Mark 14:51, 52 was Mark himself. This detail is not used in the other Gospels, so some have seen it as Mark's insertion of a personal detail, almost a "cameo" appearance. If this is true, we should expect to read Mark's account all the more eagerly since we are reading the words of a witness to some of these events.

## I. TAKEN TO TRIAL (MARK 14:53, 54)

### A. JESUS AND HIS ENEMIES (v. 53)

**53. They took Jesus to the high priest, and all the chief priests, elders and teachers of the law came together.**

The high priest is not named here, but the parallel account in Matthew 26:57 indicates it is Caiaphas. John 18:13 notes a trip to the home of Annas, the father-in-law of Caiaphas and former high priest. They may have adjoining homes.

The assembly is called "the whole Sanhedrin" in Mark 14:55 (below). For the Sanhedrin to meet at the house of Caiaphas rather than at its official temple site is highly unusual. This is necessitated by the very early hour and by the nasty nature of the business at hand.

Mark lists three general categories within the assembly. *Chief priests* are the elite of the Jerusalem priests and are members of the Sadducee party. *Elders* are older, respected members of the Jerusalem ruling community. Some of these may be of the Pharisee party. The *teachers of the law* are needed experts in the Jewish legal code; many of these are likely Pharisees. There are seventy-one members in this body during the time of Jesus.

### B. PETER AND THE SERVANTS (v. 54)

**54. Peter followed him at a distance, right into the courtyard of the high priest. There he sat with the guards and warmed himself at the fire.**

*HOW TO SAY IT*

*Annas.* AN-nus.

*Caesarea.* Sess-uh-REE-uh.

*Caiaphas.* KAY-uh-fus or KYE-uh-fus.

*Galilee.* GAL-uh-lee.

*Herod Antipas.* HAIR-ud AN-tih-pus.

*Jerusalem.* Juh-ROO-suh-lem.

*Josephus.* Jo-SEE-fus.

*Leviticus.* Leh-VIT-ih-kus.

*messianic.* mess-ee-AN-ick.

*Pharisees.* FAIR-ih-seez.

*Pontius Pilate.* PON-shus or PON-ti-us PIE-lut.

*Sadducees.* SAD-you-seez.

*Sanhedrin.* SAN-huh-drun or San-HEED-run.

*Tiberias.* Tie-BEER-ee-us.

*Peter* is drawn irresistibly to Jesus, even in this dangerous time. His motives are probably a mixture of loyalty and curiosity, but he is positioned to act out his prophesied denials of Jesus. Many sermons have been preached using this verse to show that following Jesus *at a distance* is a contradiction in terms. True commitment is shown by the desire to be as close to Jesus as possible. Casual Christianity is elsewhere described as "lukewarm" and is rejected by Jesus (Revelation 3:16).

## II. PLOT TO ELIMINATE (MARK 14:55-59)

### A. WITNESSES DISAGREE, PART 1 (vv. 55, 56)

*55, 56. The chief priests and the whole Sanhedrin were looking for evidence against Jesus so that they could put him to death, but they did not find any. Many testified falsely against him, but their statements did not agree.*

There is no intention of giving Jesus a fair trial, for his death is predetermined by God (Mark 8:31; 10:33) and by the council itself (14:1). It is obvious that the witnesses are lying, because their testimony is contradictory. It is sad that in this assembly, which serves as the Supreme Court for the Jews of Jesus' day, there is no one with enough conscience to denounce the entire proceedings. The situation echoes Isaiah 59:4, "No one calls for justice." The people of God forget that God's demand for justice has never gone away.

### THE VERDICT BEFORE THE TRIAL

The following account is true. A minister was conducting a revival meeting in a country church. As was the custom there, every day he was entertained for the noon meal in the home of one of the families of the church. On this particular day the hostess remarked that her daughter-in-law would be absent because of jury duty.

They had barely begun the meal when the daughter-in-law walked in. Of course, everyone asked her what had happened. She replied, "They wouldn't let me sit on the jury. I don't know why. They asked me if I thought the defendant was guilty and I said, 'If he weren't guilty, they wouldn't have arrested him,' and they put me off of the jury."

Something like that happened at the trial of Jesus. Verse 55 makes it plain that the verdict already had been decided before the trial began. The authorities were looking for witnesses who would testify the way they wanted, for they already had decided that Jesus must die.

Since Jesus was guilty of no crime, they had to invent something, twisting his words. In their time as in ours, court testimony is taken very seriously. To testify falsely is both a crime and a sin. To encourage someone to testify falsely also is both a crime and a sin. Many witnesses could have been found to testify in his favor, but none were sought or desired. When people treat us unfairly because we are Christians, will we be surprised?     —R. C. S.

### B. WITNESSES DISAGREE, PART 2 (vv. 57-59)

*57-59. Then some stood up and gave this false testimony against him: "We heard him say, 'I will destroy this man-made temple and in three days will build another, not made by man.'" Yet even then their testimony did not agree.*

In the debate that follows, an issue finally emerges: Jesus apparently poses a threat to the *temple* itself. Threats against sacred sites can draw the death penalty in the Greco-Roman world. This was equally true for the Jews of Old Testament times (see Jeremiah 26:1-11).

Mark does not record Jesus' direct statement concerning destroying and rebuilding this temple as is found in John 2:19. However, Jesus' comments there

### WHAT DO YOU THINK?

Suppose you have been selected by the leadership of the church to join a new ministry effort. Its goal is to identify those church members who follow Jesus "at a distance" to encourage them to a closer walk with the Lord. What ideas would you bring to the first ministry-team meeting?

### WHAT DO YOU THINK?

How does one develop the strength of conscience required to stand up against powerful forces and denounce injustice? How can our church equip people for such acts of character?

**Many bare false witness against Him.**
Is your witness true?

Visual for lesson 3. *Many spoke against Jesus falsely in his day. Use this visual to encourage discussion of how people do this yet today.*

refer to his own body, according to John 2:21. Those who heard Jesus talk of this destruction (including the *false* witnesses here) missed the figurative meaning.

### III. HEART OF THE MATTER (MARK 14:60-65)
#### A. WHO ARE YOU, JESUS? (vv. 60-62)
60. *Then the high priest stood up before them and asked Jesus, "Are you not going to answer? What is this testimony that these men are bringing against you?"*

The plot to kill Jesus is in danger of unraveling because of the lack of integrity in the Sanhedrin's process. Caiaphas sees this and tries a new tactic: he attempts to get Jesus to incriminate himself. A time-tested trial practice is to put the accused on the witness stand and hope for a misstatement.

61. *But Jesus remained silent and gave no answer.*

*Again the high priest asked him, "Are you the Christ, the Son of the Blessed One?"*

Jesus refuses to respond. There is an element of truth in the charge that he claimed to be able to destroy and rebuild the "temple" (see previous discussion), but it is no use explaining his meaning or defending himself (see Isaiah 53:7). *The high priest*, therefore, introduces a new charge: that Jesus claims to be *the Christ*, the Messiah, the long-awaited chosen one. *Son of the Blessed One* is equivalent to "Son of God" (see Matthew 26:63).

62. *"I am," said Jesus. "And you will see the Son of Man sitting at the right hand of the Mighty One and coming on the clouds of heaven."*

Jesus now breaks his silence to respond to Caiaphas's question. To sit *at the right hand* of power is an allusion from Psalm 110:1, a messianic psalm. Jesus thus confirms his identity and claims a Scripture. His answer has the effect of saying, "You won't see my power now, but my time is coming."

#### B. BLASPHEMY! (vv. 63-65)
63, 64. *The high priest tore his clothes. "Why do we need any more witnesses?" he asked. "You have heard the blasphemy. What do you think?"*

*They all condemned him as worthy of death.*

*Blasphemy* is deliberate disrespect for God or divine things. For the ancient Jew, any human claiming to be God is both a deceiver and a blasphemer. The penalty is *death* (Leviticus 24:16). Jewish belief in one God does not allow for any type of divine human being. For Jesus to claim to be the Son of God makes him a usurper of God's authority in the council's eyes. There is only one problem: Jesus' claim is true! Tragically, this possibility is not considered by the Sanhedrin. Both of the charges against Jesus (temple destroyer, messianic pretender) are used as taunts against him as he is on the cross (Mark 15:29, 32).

65. *Then some began to spit at him; they blindfolded him, struck him with their fists, and said, "Prophesy!" And the guards took him and beat him.*

The uncontrolled fury boils over into physical violence. Mark draws a strong contrast between Jesus' power (14:62) and his brutal humiliation. There is no hint that Jesus protests or even protects himself. He fulfills the role of the servant of Isaiah 50:6: "I offered my back to those who beat me, my cheeks to those who pulled out my beard; I did not hide my face from mocking and spitting."

### IV. PILATE THE DUPE (MARK 15:1-3)
#### A. ACCURATE RESPONSE (vv. 1, 2)
1. *Very early in the morning, the chief priests, with the elders, the teachers of the law and the whole Sanhedrin, reached a decision. They bound Jesus, led him away and handed him over to Pilate.*

---

*WHAT DO YOU THINK?*

*Surely Jesus knew the Sanhedrin's plan was in trouble. If he just kept quiet, he might even walk! But then he answered with a declaration that he knew would seal his fate. What kind of courage is required to take such a bold action? What was a time when you deliberately put yourself in jeopardy for the sake of a principle you couldn't compromise?*

*WHAT DO YOU THINK?*

*The scene in the council chamber is almost more than we can bear. Civilized men (religious leaders!) stoop to the level of mob violence. What causes us to "lose control"? How can we safeguard ourselves from acting from sinful motives in our pursuit of doing what we believe is right?*

*[Be sure to consider Romans 10:2.]*

This verse introduces us to Pontius *Pilate*, the Roman governor who will be eternally blamed for his complicity in the death of Jesus Christ. Pilate is the most powerful person in Jerusalem that day, a ruthless man with Roman troops available to impose his will. Yet even the mighty Pilate is not in control of this situation.

We are also presented with the complete Sanhedrin in a *morning* meeting, probably at their appointed place in the southeast corner of the temple. This meeting is designed to get Jesus to Pilate near dawn. Roman officials are known to be early risers, preferring to finish their business by noon and leave the remainder of the day for personal pursuits.

There are a few hours between the initial meeting at the house of Caiaphas and the official meeting of the *whole* council in this instance. These are hours for Jesus to endure the mocking humiliation of his captors.

**2. "Are you the king of the Jews?" asked Pilate.**

**"Yes, it is as you say," Jesus replied.**

The Sanhedrin and the Roman governor are forced into an uneasy alliance in order to maintain order in Judea. While the Jews of the high council surely resent the foreign occupation of their homeland, they know that riots and rebellion will be crushed by the Roman legions, creating risk to their businesses and fortunes.

This tension is shown here. Pilate asks a clever question designed to cover his concerns and to tweak the nose of the Sanhedrin. He interrogates Jesus as a potential political criminal, an illegal king. At the same time he belittles both Jesus and the Jews by asking if a bound, beaten man is *the king of the Jews.*

Jesus' affirmative response gives pause to wonder at the irony of it all. His answer is as much for the mob as it is for Pilate. He is not only the "true temple," the Son of God and the promised Messiah, he is also their King! His rejection by his own people has the effect of saying, "We don't want our own king anymore. We like having a pagan, uncircumcised Roman Caesar as our king" (see John 19:15).

**B. NO RESPONSE (v. 3)**

**3. The chief priests accused him of many things.**

Our lesson ends with a silent Jesus. Silence in the face of charges does not mean guilt. Jesus' silence allows him to rise above the unjust nature of the situation and fulfill the mission for which he has been sent: salvation (Luke 19:10). Earlier, Jesus claimed only to say the things that the Father told him to say (John 12:49). The one who sent him gives him no words here. He speaks the silence of God.

### WHEN SILENCE IS GOLDEN

An old Swiss inscription says, "Silence is golden." Someone else added that sometimes silence is just plain yellow! But it was not cowardice that caused Jesus to be silent before his accusers. Think how much dignity he would have lost if he had shouted back, "Liars! Liars! They are all liars!" Jesus knew the truth of what Solomon said long before: there is "a time to be silent" (Ecclesiastes 3:7). The Roman writer Plutarch (A.D. 46–120) said, "It is a point of wisdom to be silent when occasion requires."

Jesus was intelligent and eloquent enough to defend himself. But he had in mind a plan more important than his own safety. That plan was the salvation of humanity! So when he was brought to trial before Herod, he again said nothing. He would not satisfy the curiosity of Herod nor still Herod's fears that Jesus was really John the Baptist come back from the dead. Nor would he entertain Herod with miracles done for show.

*DAILY BIBLE READINGS*

*Monday, June 13—Jesus Predicts Peter's Denial (Mark 14:26-31)*

*Tuesday, June 14—Jesus Is Betrayed by Judas (Mark 14: 43-50)*

*Wednesday, June 15—False Testimony Is Given About Jesus (Mark 14:53-59)*

*Thursday, June 16—Jesus Is Condemned (Mark 14:60-65)*

*Friday, June 17—Peter Denies Jesus (Mark 14:66-72)*

*Saturday, June 18—Jesus Goes Before Pilate (Mark 15:1-5)*

*Sunday, June 19—Pilate Hands Jesus over to Die (Mark 15:6-15)*

*WHAT DO YOU THINK?*

*Sometimes the best answer is no answer at all. When is it best to ignore the accusations of our opponents, and when is an answer appropriate or even imperative?*

*Father, we come before you to thank you for the willing sacrifice of your Son. How it must have hurt you to see him condemned as a criminal! The death of Jesus at the hands of sinners was the greatest injustice in all of history. Yet, in your providence, this injustice served to justify us, changing us from unrighteous to righteous through Jesus' blood payment of our penalty. For this we thank you, Jesus, and we give the Father all praise and glory. In Jesus' name, amen.*

We must stand in awe and admiration at the self-control of our Lord—and take it as a model for ourselves. Sometimes we must rise above the situation, rather than being caught up in it. May we always see the bigger picture! And with God's help, we shall do so.

—R. C. S.

## CONCLUSION

### A. WHY DID THEY KILL JESUS?

Many have been blamed for the death of Jesus: Judas, Pilate, Caiaphas, Satan, even God. Theologically, we know that Jesus had to die to save us. But what happened historically? Why was the Jewish Sanhedrin so intent on having Jesus killed?

Bible scholars have been debating this question for many years. Some claim that the Jewish leaders sought Jesus' death because he had challenged their authority. Others claim that the Sanhedrin feared Jesus would lead a revolt against the Romans, resulting in the crushing of the Jews in Palestine. Still others see the Jewish authorities as pawns being manipulated by Satan in Satan's attempt to thwart Jesus.

While all of these explanations have merit and Scriptural support, we can find the primary reason on the lips of the Sanhedrin members themselves: "If we let him go on like this, . . . the Romans will come and take away both our place and our nation" (John 11:48). In this passage, *place* can refer to the temple. Many scholars thus theorize that the primary menace posed by Jesus was a threat to the Jerusalem temple. The temple was the engine that drove the economy of Judea. It was still under construction in Jesus' day, so it supplied jobs for construction workers. Thousands worked as priests and attendants. Temple pilgrims needed food and accommodations. Furthermore, the magnificent temple, begun by Herod the Great, was a source of enormous pride for all Jews. It was one of the most beautiful buildings in the ancient world.

Jesus' actions in cleansing the temple and criticizing the gouging business monopolies associated with it were threats that could not be tolerated. If this theory is correct, the misguided Sanhedrin was not trying to protect the religion of Israel. Rather, it was protecting its own economic security. And history has shown repeatedly that money serves well as a motive for murder.

### B. THE INNOCENCE AND SACRIFICE OF JESUS

Skeptics have wanted to say that Jesus is surely responsible for his own death, that he had done something wrong. Yet the authors of the New Testament are consistent in saying that Jesus was not executed for any crime. Even Pilate, the jaded Roman governor, recognized this when he said, "I find no basis for a charge against this man" (Luke 23:4).

While there was no legal reason to execute Jesus, there was a spiritual reason. In 2 Corinthians 5:21 Paul states, "God made him who had no sin to be sin for us, so that in him we might become the righteousness of God." People were separated from God because of sin. We had no way to atone for our sins, because that required a perfect, eternal sacrifice. This was Jesus' purpose.

Jesus' innocence was central to his sacrifice. Without the innocence, his sacrifice was inadequate. Without the sacrifice, his innocence was irrelevant. This is why, at the beginning of Jesus' ministry, John the Baptist cried out, "Look, the Lamb of God, who takes away the sin of the world!" (John 1:29). This is why, many years later, Peter still wrote of "the precious blood of Christ, a lamb without blemish or defect" (1 Peter 1:19). Today, some twenty centuries afterward, will you affirm the same thing?

*The death of the innocent one was history's greatest injustice, yet humanity's greatest hope.*

# Discovery Learning

*This page contains an alternative lesson plan emphasizing learning activities. Classes desiring such student involvement will find these suggestions helpful. The next page is a reproducible activity page to further enhance discovery learning.*

## LEARNING GOALS

After participating in this lesson, each student will be able to:

1. Describe the trial process that led to the death of Jesus.

2. Contrast the innocence of the One accused with the guilt of his accusers.

3. Express gratitude to God for the sacrifice of his innocent Son to save them from their sins.

## INTO THE LESSON

Recruit a person to present the following monologue as Peter on the evening of Jesus' arrest. Have your "Peter" sitting in front of the class, huddled as if warming himself by an open fire. Monologue: "The fire was doing little good. I was cold to the bone. The air was chilly, but the glances of the others around the fire were even more chilling. First one . . . and then another . . . and then another pointed an accusing finger at me, accusing me with the truth. 'You are one of his disciples, a Galilean!' What could I do? There was a threat with every accusation. I had to deny it: 'I am not!' The silent echo of my denial only added to my shuddering. . . . There! [pointing, as he sees Jesus being led by] There my Master is being led away! He sees me! Oh! Mercy for my sin!"

Ask the class how well this portrayed scene represents what the Scriptures say about Peter's traumatic occasion. Suggest they look at the Mark 14:53, 54, 66-72 and the other Gospel accounts (Matthew 26:69-75; Luke 22:54-62; John 18:15-18, 25-27) for an analysis.

## INTO THE WORD

Note to your class that the Hebrew and Greek words transliterated Satan in the Scriptures means *the accuser.* Point out that in the scenes described in today's text "the chief priests accused him [Jesus] of many things" (Mark 15:3). Have a dictionary definition of *accuse* ready to be read aloud. The definition will typically include such elements as blaming, faultfinding, and bringing legal charges. Ask the class to identify the nature of the accusations made against Jesus. Ask them to characterize the accusers.

Give your learners the following two-word sentences to put in the correct chronological order, per the text. This activity is included in the student book.) The sentences are given here in alphabetical order, per first words. Numbers in parentheses indicate the correct chronological order. Jesus affirms (9); Jesus captured (1); Jesus condemned (11); Jesus mistreated (12); Jesus reaffirms (14); Jesus silent (7); Jesus silent (16); Leader dismayed (10); Leaders accuse (15); Leaders assemble (2); Peter follows (3); Pilate questions (13); Priests question (6); Priests question again (8); Witness sought (4); Witnesses lied (5). After a few minutes, work your way through the list and compare events to the printed text.

The Key Verse for today's lesson (Mark 14:55) is an excellent summary of the story. Help your class memorize it in the following way. Divide the class as it is seated into four groups and ask the groups to repeat a phrase after you. Group one gets "The chief priests and the whole Sanhedrin"; group two: "were looking for evidence against Jesus"; group three: "so that they could put him to death"; group four: "but they did not find any."

Ask the groups to stand in sequence and repeat their phrases. Have them repeat this stand-and-quote exercise three or four times. At the end say simply, "And that is the simple and sad truth of today's study."

## INTO LIFE

Ask your class to react to each of these "Lessons to Be Learned from Jesus Under Trial." Reactions may be agreement or disagreement, explanation, or editing to "correct." "Lessons": (1) Expect people to lie when they do not like the truth. (2) There is a time to be silent and a time to speak. (3) Some truths simply must be affirmed. (4) Personal humiliation may be necessary to preserve integrity. (5) Unanimity of judgment does not determine truth. (6) Truth is always the best defense. (7) Character is best demonstrated in hard circumstances.

Note to your class that people still make false accusations against the Son and the Father. Such accusations are heard in expressions such as, "If God is truly good, then he would not . . . " Or, "God abandoned me when I needed him most." Or, "Jesus was merely a good person who understood much about the happy life."

Ask the class to identify other such "accusations," and then suggest that they keep an "Accusations Alert" for the coming week, listening carefully for those who have false ideas about Jesus and his work. Close with a prayer to have a godly discernment in this regard.

# Evil and Innocent

Mark 14:53-65; 15:1-3 pictures a startling contrast between evil and innocence. For each of the elements noted, identify the evil party to the left and the innocent party to the right.

EVIL                                                                                                          INNOCENT

Who concealed their work in the dark of night?

Who predetermined the guilt of the one being judged?

Who looked for false witnesses?

Who refused to accept a true statement?

Who dramatically influenced the outcome by saying, "I am"?

Who became angrily violent?

# "Guilty as Charged"

Jesus did admit to three matters in the trials Mark records. Write below each of the following what Jesus admitted to.

*Mark 14:61b, 62a*                    *Mark 14:62b*                    *Mark 15:2*

1                    2                    3

# Acting As Jesus Did

Placed in situations where one is falsely accused and mistreated usually elicits one's worst behavior. In the scenes described in today's text Jesus is seen at his best. What behaviors do you see in Jesus that you find most admirable? The first one is given to get you started.

_____ Holding one's peace is preferable to losing one's cool.

_____

_____

_____

_____

Use the lines to the left to initial those behaviors you will commit to improving in your own lifestyle.

# TRIUMPH

**LESSON 4**

## WHY TEACH THIS LESSON?

Perhaps in 1 Corinthians 15 the apostle Paul, by the Spirit, wrote the best rationale for teaching today's lesson. If the resurrection triumph is not true, why believe anything about God? Why make any effort to win anyone over to the good news if the very foundation of that good news is a fiction?

Some truths demand attention. Some events are totally surprising. Even when one has been forewarned (or "forepromised," as the case may be), some events startle. Jesus' resurrection is just such an event and truth. His followers struggled to believe it. But when they did, their lives were turned and activated.

Jesus' final word of commission (Mark 16:15, 16) had no incongruity to those who knew he was resurrected. All that Jesus called for was a logical and natural response. For if he did indeed rise from the dead and validate his claims of messiahship, everyone everywhere must know. The truth of this lesson becomes the driving force for personal holiness, godly service, and compassionate evangelism. Until your learners are totally convinced of Jesus' resurrection, do not expect them to live a resurrection lifestyle.

## INTRODUCTION

### A. THE OLD CURIOSITY SHOP

Our family turned the corner in anticipation. The London guidebook promised that "The Old Curiosity Shop" was not only a landmark medieval building, but also a great source for the interesting souvenirs that our children loved so much. The shop, we read, was built in 1567 and may have served as the inspiration for a novel of the nineteenth century. Then we saw it, a white two-story building with green trim and a red roof. We could hardly wait to explore its treasures. But when we got to it, we found the Shop was empty. It had a sign that said, "The Old Curiosity Shop immortalized by Charles Dickens," but the door was locked and the shelves were bare. No one was there. We instinctively knew what this meant: although the shop was a well-known tourist attraction, it had failed to be a viable business location.

Today's lesson is about eager visitors who also unexpectedly find an empty place. They are a small group of women who hurried to the tomb of Jesus at dawn to finish their task of preparing his body for burial. They were worried about the mechanics of accessing the tomb and were therefore surprised and terrified to find it open and empty. The body of Jesus was gone. What did this mean?

### B. LESSON BACKGROUND

The events that come just before today's text have been sobering, indeed. Jesus Christ, the King of the universe, had been put to death in an act of judicial murder. One of his closest disciples had betrayed him for a paltry thirty pieces of silver. His other disciples had deserted him. The death he suffered was one of the most cruel, agonizing, and humiliating possible. "He came to that which was his own, but his own did not receive him" (John 1:11).

DEVOTIONAL READING:
MATTHEW 28:16-20

BACKGROUND SCRIPTURE:
MARK 16

PRINTED TEXT:
MARK 16:1-16

Jun
26

### LESSON AIMS

After participating in this lesson, each student will be able to:

1. Recount the events surrounding the resurrection, including the various reactions, as recorded by Mark.

2. Express his or her own emotional response to the resurrection of Jesus.

3. State some specific plan to share with others his or her faith in the resurrection of Jesus.

### KEY VERSE

"Don't be alarmed," he said. "You are looking for Jesus the Nazarene, who was crucified. He has risen! He is not here. See the place where they laid him."

—Mark 16:6

Those who first seek Jesus are a group of loyal women followers. It is not a living Jesus they seek, however, but a dead one. A resurrection is the furthest thing from their minds. After (what we can suppose to be) a sleepless night or two, they are in for quite a shock!

## I. TRIP TO THE TOMB (MARK 16:1-4)

### A. WOMEN AND MISSION (vv. 1, 2)

**1, 2. When the Sabbath was over, Mary Magdalene, Mary the mother of James, and Salome bought spices so that they might go to anoint Jesus' body. Very early on the first day of the week, just after sunrise, they were on their way to the tomb**

*The Sabbath* had ended at sundown on Saturday night, but darkness prevented the women from visiting *the tomb* until Sunday dawn. These are women on a mission: they intend to finish a respectful preparation of Jesus' corpse, a process that had been rushed to prevent violation of the Sabbath on Friday afternoon. This should not be seen as anything other than an act of great devotion. They suppose the smell of *Jesus'* rotting *body* will be disgusting.

The women are a curious band, and Mark has mentioned them before (Mark 15:40; two of them in 15:47). *Salome* is the mother of James and John, the wife of Zebedee (see Matthew 4:21; 27:56). She is old, perhaps frail. Tradition records that *Mary Magdalene* had been a prostitute, although this is not confirmed in the New Testament. Jesus had delivered her from great spiritual oppression (Mark 16:9; Luke 8:2) and won her as a devoted follower.

*Mary the mother of James* (and Joses, see Mark 15:40) is not known to us, but seems to have been well known to Mark's earliest readers. There are several women named Mary in the Gospels, so it's easy to get confused. In any case, she, too, is remarkably committed, having witnessed the crucifixion and burial of Jesus. The women venture out in the early morning, probably as soon as they are able to buy some sweet *spices* with which to *anoint* the body of Jesus.

### B. QUESTION AND ANSWER (vv. 3, 4)

**3, 4. . . . and they asked each other, "Who will roll the stone away from the entrance of the tomb?"**

**But when they looked up, they saw that the stone, which was very large, had been rolled away.**

The women apparently have no careful plan. They don't think about how they will gain access to Jesus' body until they are already on the way. Belatedly they recall that *the tomb* had been sealed. This was done with a heavy disk-shaped *stone*, carved to fit tightly over the tomb. Rolling the stone back will require several strong men. The issue is resolved when they arrive on the scene: the massive stone already has been removed and the tomb is open.

## II. ENCOUNTER WITH AN ANGEL (MARK 16:5-8)

### A. ALARM (v. 5)

**5. As they entered the tomb, they saw a young man dressed in a white robe sitting on the right side, and they were alarmed.**

It would be easy for us to see these women as weak and easily frightened, but that would be inaccurate. Their devotion causes them to venture to *the tomb* itself, overcoming any fear of dead bodies. But they do not find a dead body. Instead, they are confronted by *a young man* who seems to be waiting for them.

Mark intends that we understand this person to be an angel, a messenger of God. Matthew 28:2-5 tells us specifically that this is an angel. The women are understandably *alarmed*.

## B. MESSAGE (vv. 6, 7)

6, 7. "Don't be alarmed," he said. "You are looking for Jesus the Nazarene, who was crucified. He has risen! He is not here. See the place where they laid him. But go, tell his disciples and Peter, 'He is going ahead of you into Galilee. There you will see him, just as he told you.'"

The angel explains everything in three little words: *He has risen!* Jesus is not dead. He is alive! His body is not returning to the dust. Rather, Jesus is on the move back to Galilee! He does not need to be anointed with spices to combat the stench of death. He emits the sweet aroma of life eternal! The women must tell *Peter* and the other *disciples.*

### LEARNING FROM TOMBS

We can learn a lot from tombs. The early inhabitants of Italy were the Etruscans, and almost all that we know of them comes from their tombs. The British have filled Westminster Abbey with tombs. Some of them include a carved image of the one buried there—lying horizontally as in death. When the Greeks carved images, they carved them vertically, as they were in life.

Under the Capuchin Church in Vienna are tombs of Austria's rulers. One holds the remains of Empress Maria Theresa (1717–1780) and her husband Francis Stephen of Lorraine (1708– 1765). An image on their double sarcophagus depicts them sitting up, as if they are just awakening on the morning of the resurrection. Is this a testament to their faith in the risen Christ and to their confidence in their own resurrections?

There is a story about a man walking in a country cemetery when he saw a stone that read, "Death Is Eternal." He was astounded that anyone would put such a line on a tombstone. He walked over to investigate and discovered that his view had been obscured by another tombstone. What it really said was, "Death Is Eternal Life." Until Jesus rose from the dead, our view of both death and life was partial and obscured. Now we can see the true nature of both more clearly.     —R. C. S.

## C. FEAR (v. 8)

8. Trembling and bewildered, the women went out and fled from the tomb. They said nothing to anyone, because they were afraid.

The result at this point is not understanding but continued fear. This fear results in saying *nothing to anyone.* But after they calm down a bit they speak freely (see Mark 16:10; Luke 24:9).

### THE OPEN AND EMPTY TOMB

The town of Delft in the Netherlands is famous for its fine china. Not only that, the town is notable for the tomb of William of Orange (1533–1584), the founder of the nation. Those willing to pay the small admission fee can go in and see his tomb today.

But if you can get to Jerusalem, there is no admission charge to see what some think to be the tomb of Jesus. Of course, there is a significant difference: the tomb of Jesus is open and empty! The fullness of the Christian religion depends on that empty tomb. Our forgiveness depends on it. The apostle Paul said that if Christ did not come back from the dead there is no forgiveness and we are still in our sins (1 Corinthians 15:17). Belief in the resurrection is vital (Romans 10:9).

No other tomb is so important to humanity as the empty tomb of Jesus. While a single nation may honor the tomb of William of Orange, people in all nations honor the fact that the tomb of Jesus is empty. He is eternal. He rose from the dead. He sent forth his disciples into all the world. He ascended to the Father. Now we, who know the tomb is empty, must go into our world and take the message everywhere as those first followers did.     —R. C. S.

### WHAT DO YOU THINK?

The women were looking for Jesus in the wrong place—he was not there! In what wrong places do people today look for Jesus (or any kind of spiritual refreshment)? How can we ensure that those who come to our church do, indeed, find him?

### WHAT DO YOU THINK?

Peter, of course, had denied Jesus during the trials. Yet it was Peter whom the angel specifically mentioned when he told the women to report to the disciples. What significance do you see in that? What lesson is there for us in this?

## III. TRUTH AND UNBELIEF (MARK 16:9-13)

### A. MARY MAGDALENE (v. 9)

*9. When Jesus rose early on the first day of the week, he appeared first to Mary Magdalene, out of whom he had driven seven demons.*

*Mary Magdalene* has shown her great loyalty to Jesus. She was last at the cross and first at the tomb. Jesus had transformed her life by releasing her from tremendous spiritual bondage. It is entirely fitting that Jesus chose her to be the *first* witness of more than just the empty tomb. She sees the risen Lord!

### B. OTHERS (vv. 10, 11)

*10, 11. She went and told those who had been with him and who were mourning and weeping. When they heard that Jesus was alive and that she had seen him, they did not believe it.*

However, when Mary Magdalene shares the truth of the risen Lord, she is rejected. There are two reasons for this rejection. First, a woman is not thought to be a credible witness in the ancient world. Some scholars maintain that a woman's testimony was not considered valid in ancient Jewish courts. This, however, does not seem to be the primary reason Mary's story is rejected. The main reason her story is not believed is simply that believing in the resurrection takes a lot of faith, more faith than the disciples have at this point.

### C. WALKERS ON THE ROAD (vv. 12, 13)

*12, 13. Afterward Jesus appeared in a different form to two of them while they were walking in the country. These returned and reported it to the rest; but they did not believe them either.*

A second story follows, one that is given fully in Luke 24:13-35. Jesus appears to two male disciples as they journey away from the city by foot. These men return *to the rest* who are still in the city, but their testimony is received just like Mary's story—it is not believed.

Truth is powerful, but it cannot overcome stubborn unbelief. Mark never tries to hide embarrassing details from us. The fact is that those who first experience the resurrection of Jesus are not believed by the larger group of disciples. This shows how difficult it is to accept that the crucified Jesus, stone cold dead on Friday, is alive and free from his tomb on Sunday. It should give us confidence in the testimony of the early church concerning the resurrection. They do not come to faith quickly or rashly, but slowly and carefully.

## IV. BELIEF AND UNBELIEF (MARK 16:14-16)

### A. CHASTISEMENT (v. 14)

*14. Later Jesus appeared to the Eleven as they were eating; he rebuked them for their lack of faith and their stubborn refusal to believe those who had seen him after he had risen.*

Mark seems to say that Jesus realizes that no "third party" messenger will be believed. Jesus has to go personally, so he miraculously appears to *the Eleven* chosen disciples while they are having a meal. He attacks the cause of *their lack of faith,* which is *their stubborn refusal to believe.* This defiant spiritual condition is a frequent theme in Mark's Gospel (see Mark 3:5; 6:52; 8:17). In Mark, the person with the unbelieving heart is spiritually unwilling to repent or to show faith. In the Old Testament, the hard heart always results in stubborn disobedience (see Zechariah 7:12).

The disciples have no choice but to believe now! By appearing to them personally, Jesus has removed every excuse they may have.

---

WHAT DO YOU THINK?

*Mary Magdalene had seen the risen Lord, but her testimony was rejected. What lesson is there in that for believers today who share their faith with friends and family members?*

---

WHAT DO YOU THINK?

*The disciples had followed the Lord, they wanted to do right, and they had ministered in many ways in the Lord's name. Yet they were guilty of stubborn unbelief! How could that be? How can we tell if we ourselves might be guilty of the same? What can we do to prevent or to cure a lack of faith?*

### THE MAN WHO CAME BACK FROM THE DEAD

A Christian from America was speaking in a village church in Hungary. After the service the leader of the congregation came to him and said, "Come over here. We want you to meet the man who came back from the dead."

There was a twinkle in the leader's eyes as he led the visitor to an elderly man seated near the back. He then told the man's story. The man had been in the hospital, seriously ill. He was pronounced dead. They were ready to carry him out when someone noticed the flicker of an eyelash. Emergency resuscitation procedures were begun and the man revived. He recovered from this illness and there he was in church, reasonably well and healthy.

Of course, they did not think that he really came back from the dead. They knew he had been near death. They knew he had the symptoms of death, but he was not actually dead. They also knew that there was once a man who really did come back from the dead. They had met that day to worship him. They met together on the first day of the week because it was on the first day of the week that he arose.

You may know someone who has had a near-death experience. You may know someone who had all the symptoms of death but was resuscitated. If you are a Christian, you also know someone who really died and who really came back from the dead. When the apostle Paul summarized the Christian faith, he named three essentials: Christ died, Christ was buried, Christ arose (1 Corinthians 15:3, 4). It was a real death and it was a real resurrection. Will we live this week with these facts directing our thoughts and actions?       —R. C. S.

Visual for lesson 4. *Use this magnificent image to remind your learners yet again of the central truth: he is risen!*

### B. CHARGE (vv. 15, 16)

**15, 16. He said to them, "Go into all the world and preach the good news to all creation. Whoever believes and is baptized will be saved, but whoever does not believe will be condemned."**

Jesus does not allow the disciples to rest in their newfound faith, however. They are to act: to *go* and *preach the good news* of his resurrection. Their target audience is as broad as possible: *all creation*. This does not mean to evangelize birds or flowers, but all people. The importance of this message is underscored by Jesus. If the hearers reject the message, they will be *condemned*. If they do believe and respond by submitting to baptism, they *will be saved*.

We may note that the text says nothing about the status of those who believe but are not *baptized*. Such persons are unknown in the early church. The idea that baptism is an optional or superfluous part of Christianity is never entertained in the first century.

### CONCLUSION

### A. THE EVIDENCE FOR THE RESURRECTION

*He has risen.* In those three little words rests the central truth of Christianity. Christ has risen and is victorious over death!

In the nineteenth and twentieth centuries, many Bible-believing scholars developed elaborate systems to defend the historic and factual reality of the resurrection of Jesus. Some main items mentioned are (1) the empty tomb, which had been guarded by professional soldiers, (2) the inability of Jesus' opponents to produce his body, and (3) the many witnesses to the resurrected Jesus, as many as five hundred at one time (1 Corinthians 15:6).

While all three of these are certainly true, they can be a difficult "sell" to many unbelievers today. Unbelievers can say that the first two are arguments built on a lack of evidence and are therefore very difficult to prove. The third can be dismissed by modern people who are convinced that most information or testimony

*DAILY BIBLE READINGS*

*Monday, June 20*—*Jesus' Tomb Is Sealed (Matthew 27: 62-66)*

*Tuesday, June 21*—*He Is Not Here (Matthew 28:1-6b)*

*Wednesday, June 22*—*He Has Been Raised (Mark 16:1-8)*

*Thursday, June 23*—*Jesus Appears to the Women (Matthew 28:6c-10)*

*Friday, June 24*—*Jesus Appears to Other Followers (Mark 16:9-13)*

*Saturday, June 25*—*I Am with You Always (Matthew 28: 16-20)*

*Sunday, June 26*—*Go into All the World (Mark 16:14-20)*

## PRAYER

*Mighty God, we frail human beings are terrified by death. It is a curtain we cannot pull back, a darkness we cannot light.*

*But you have shown us that death is not the end. You have proven that death holds no power over you. You have given us hope by allowing your Son, Jesus Christ, to die, and then raising him from the dead forevermore. May we live confidently in the strong belief that Jesus left an empty tomb because he came back to life, and that we, too, will share in his resurrection. In his holy name we pray, amen.*

from the ancient world is inaccurate or unreliable. To use these arguments sometimes puts us in the same position of the three women in today's lesson: we tell the truth, but they don't believe. The idea of resurrection was hard to believe in the first century (see Acts 17:32) and it is difficult today.

There is a fourth argument, however, that still resonates well in the twenty-first century: the willingness of the early Christians to sacrifice their lives for their belief in the resurrection. The book of Acts and the history of the early church are filled with accounts of people who suffered persecution and even death for preaching Jesus as crucified and risen.

Would you die for something that you doubted to be true? No normal person would. It just doesn't make sense to think that average people would be willing to become martyrs on behalf of a "risen Savior" if they knew his body was still in a tomb. When Jesus came alive, walked out, and left the tomb empty, he changed history. Not only that, he changed the lives of many individuals who were committed to him.

### B. THE SIGNIFICANCE OF THE RESURRECTION

Once we have believed that Jesus rose from the dead, what significance does this belief have? The women in our story were terrified and shook physically, and sometimes we, too, should be overwhelmed by the power of the resurrection. Let me suggest three important ways the resurrection affects our lives on a continuing basis.

First, the resurrection shows that God accepted Jesus' death as atonement for our sins. This is what turned away God's wrath. (See Romans 3:25; 1 John 2:2; 4:10.) Paul refers to Jesus as the one "delivered over to death for our sins and was raised to life for our justification" (Romans 4:25). Jesus' death and resurrection were one-time events; they need not be repeated. They give us the assurance of forgiveness and salvation if we place our faith in him.

Second, the resurrection of Jesus gives us hope for life after death. The longer we live, the more we encounter death. We experience the death of our friends, our grandparents, our parents, our spouses, even our sons and daughters. The tragic separation from those we love can drive us to despair. Furthermore, we realize our own deaths are inevitable. One author said that a religion that has nothing to say about death has nothing to say. Christianity has everything to say about death. Yes, death is real. Jesus really died! But, as the poet said,

> And death's not the end 'neath the cold black sod,
> 'Tis the inn by the road on the way to God.

Third, the resurrection means that Jesus is alive today and will come again as he promised. Jesus' resurrection and ascension in A.D. 30 means that he has conquered death! He wasn't like Lazarus, who rose only to die again. Jesus wasn't just alive for a few more days or years. He is still alive today, right now!

Think about what this says about Christians and Christianity. We don't just follow the teachings of Jesus from centuries ago like Confucians do with Confucius's teachings. Rather, we make Jesus the active Lord of our lives. We don't just pray the way he taught us like Muslims do with Muhammad. Instead, we pray to the throne of God, where Jesus sits at the right hand. We don't just follow his pathways of spiritual enlightenment like Buddhists follow the Buddha. On the contrary, we allow Jesus to change us through the transforming power of his Word and his Holy Spirit. We don't just admire his courage and integrity, as secularists do with their historical heroes. Rather, we actively look for Jesus to return in power and glory to take us to be with him forever.

## THOUGHT TO REMEMBER

*His tomb was empty because Jesus is alive!*

# Discovery Learning

*This page contains an alternative lesson plan emphasizing learning activities. Classes*
*desiring such student involvement will find these suggestions helpful. The next page*
*is a reproducible activity page to further enhance discovery learning.*

## LEARNING GOALS

After participating in this lesson, each student will be able to:

1. Recount the events surrounding the resurrection, including the various reactions, as recorded by Mark.

2. Express his or her own emotional response to the resurrection of Jesus.

3. State some specific plan to share with others his or her faith in the resurrection of Jesus.

## INTO THE LESSON

Hand each learner this list of Bible texts as they enter the classroom: 1 Kings 17:17-24; 2 Kings 4:32-37; 2 Kings 13:21; Mark 5:22-24, 35-43; Luke 7:11-16; John 11:32-44; Acts 9:36-42. Say nothing of the subject matter of these passages or of your intention.

As class begins, ask, "What do the Bible texts on the list I gave to you have in common?" If no one has checked the texts or knows them, give an opportunity to check and wait for a response. The correct response is that all of these texts speak of a person resurrected from the dead. Note that though the resurrections recorded in these texts demonstrate God's ability to restore life to a dead body, only the resurrection described in today's text makes the way for the resurrection of all the godly.

## INTO THE WORD

Divide your learners into four groups; label the groups: SOCIAL, EMOTIONAL, PRACTICAL, DOCTRINAL. Once the groups assemble, give a leader in each group one of the following direction cards:

SOCIAL—Look at today's text in Mark 16:1-16 and list the various social relationships and issues seen. For example: three women went to the tomb together, as mutual support at a difficult time (v. 1).

EMOTIONAL—Look at today's text, Mark 16:1-16, and list the various emotions described or implied in the events recorded. For example, the mourning of the followers of Jesus had been so deep as to lead to tears (v. 10).

PRACTICAL—Look at today's text, Mark 16:1-16, and describe the practical elements related to the events. For example, the stone was so large the women knew they could not move it (vv. 3, 4).

DOCTRINAL—Look at today's text, Mark 16:1-16, and list what you consider the key doctrines included.

An example is the connection between belief and baptism (v. 16).

Give the groups eight to ten minutes to make their decisions. Then have each group give its report. For reinforcement, write the answers into a four-column graphic on the chalkboard, with appropriate headings. Some possible comments for the four categories are, respectively: "Sometimes even close friends don't believe what their friends tell them" (vv. 11, 13, 14); "Sometimes those whom one loves need to be corrected firmly" (v. 14); "Dead bodies need attention quickly, for decay is quick and inevitable" (v. 1); "Jesus was killed, but he lives bodily anew" (v. 6).

Ending on the DOCTRINAL element will allow you to affirm, "The resurrection of Jesus is at the heart of Bible doctrine." Have a good reader cued to your saying this exact statement and ready to jump up and read 1 Corinthians 15:12-26 with emphasis.

Repeat verses 13 and 14 of that text to lead to the *Into Life* activity following.

## INTO LIFE

Give each learner a copy of a sheet headed **IF—THEN**. Some or all of the following stimulus-response items should be listed below the heading. Feel free to add more if-then statements of your own devising. (This activity is included in the student book.)

*If resurrection from the dead has never happened, then . . .*

*If Jesus had not risen from the dead, then . . .*

*If I did not believe in God's power to resurrect me from the dead, then . . .*

*If the current life is all there is, then I will . . .*

Some of the key verses in 1 Corinthians 15 should be part of every Christian's "quotable repertoire" for a life of hope and witness. Select one verse and suggest a technique to your class for committing it to memory in the coming week.

One example of a memory technique is copying the verse onto a small card and placing it in a strategic location. This location may be the bathroom mirror, the refrigerator door, the edge of the computer screen, or on a key chain. You could also suggest that the verse be personalized, such as verse 1 Corinthians 15:17: "If Christ be not raised, [my] faith is futile; [I am] still in [my] sins." Close with prayer.

# True or False

?.? ? ? ?

Affirmation statements are either true or false. In today's text in Mark 16:1-16, many decide that the affirmations made to them are false. They proceeded accordingly. Decide if each of these statements is true or false based on today's text.

_____ 1. The three women came early to Jesus' tomb to prepare his body.

_____ 2. The women's expressed concern had to do with fear of the guards.

_____ 3. The two Marys and Salome were too afraid to enter the open tomb.

_____ 4. The young man in the tomb knew why the women had come.

_____ 5. The heavenly visitor became the first to announce Jesus' resurrection.

_____ 6. Peter is named to be a recipient of the good news of Jesus' new life.

_____ 7. At first the women were too scared to tell anyone what they had seen and heard.

_____ 8. Mary Magdalene was privileged to be the first to see the risen Jesus.

_____ 9. The message that Jesus had risen was quickly and eagerly accepted by all.

_____ 10. One of Jesus' purposes for appearing to the Eleven as they ate was to rebuke and correct them for their slowness to believe.

_____ 11. Jesus' directive was to preach to the whole world, not Jews only.

_____ 12. Jesus connects belief, baptism, and salvation in his final teaching to the apostles.

# Removing the Stone

Each circle below represents a stone rolled over a tomb of the dead. On each one write the key idea of the Bible text given. Put your initials by each to indicate your personal confidence in its truth for your final tombstone.

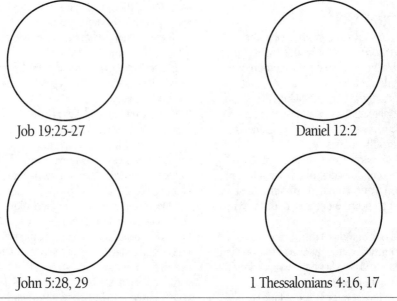

Job 19:25-27

Daniel 12:2

John 5:28, 29

1 Thessalonians 4:16, 17

# EXPERIENCING TRUE HAPPINESS

**LESSON 5**

## WHY TEACH THIS LESSON?

Charles Schulz's simple and classic bestseller, *Happiness Is a Warm Puppy* (San Francisco: Determined Productions, 1962), is one of many titles, humorous and philosophical, to try to capsulize the desire for bliss. A warm puppy in one's lap may indeed provide temporary joy and peace. But puppies bolt and run. And puppies often grow beyond lap size and change demeanor. True happiness must be found in something more than things.

Jesus capsulizes happiness best in his Beatitudes. He knows the "secret" of living the truly blessed life. People may still equate happiness and contentment with things such as profitable stocks, prestigious neighborhoods, and better health insurance—and many in your class still believe such temporal blessings are the key to being called blessed. This study allows you to understand and help your class members to understand the error of such a way of thinking. All need to learn that blessedness comes in spiritual behaviors and attributes.

## INTRODUCTION
### A. "ENJOY!"

The waiter brings the meals steaming hot from the kitchen and places them dramatically on the table. He looks around expectantly, hoping to see expressions of delight. Before he leaves, he pronounces the inevitable benediction: "Enjoy!"

Many seem to think that's how God should act. He should deliver all the pleasures of "the good life" on a silver platter and say, "Enjoy!" But the more that people try to find happiness in wealth, power, and sensual pleasures, the more they are tortured with inner unrest. Why has God failed to deliver the happiness they really want?

When Jesus preached the most famous sermon in history, he laid out the basis of true happiness. In the Beatitudes, the opening verses of the Sermon on the Mount, Jesus turned the usual ways of thinking upside down. Ignoring those who were complacent in their riches, Jesus commended those who knew their spiritual poverty. Spurning the proud and powerful, Jesus congratulated those who were gentle and merciful. Jesus emphasized character traits that have little value in the eyes of the world. But real happiness—eternal happiness—will be found only by those who believe in the values that Jesus taught.

### B. LESSON BACKGROUND

The Sermon on the Mount came perhaps midway in the second year of Jesus' ministry. After beginning in obscurity, Jesus gained a large following among the common people. Great multitudes came out to hear him and, if possible, to see a miracle. For the apostles and all his other followers, Jesus needed to explain what kind of people would be seen as heroes in the kingdom of God.

DEVOTIONAL READING:
LUKE 6:17-23
BACKGROUND SCRIPTURE:
MATTHEW 5:1-16
PRINTED TEXT:
MATTHEW 5:1-16

**Jul 3**

## LESSON AIMS

*After participating in this lesson, each student will be able to:*

*1. Describe the attitudes and blessings that bring true happiness to the followers of Jesus.*

*2. Explain how happiness is based not on what one possesses, but on how one's life reflects and glorifies God.*

*3. Suggest specific ways in which the Beatitudes can correct the distorted goals of contemporary culture.*

## KEY VERSE

*Blessed are those who hunger and thirst for righteousness, for they will be filled.* —Matthew 5:6

# I. CHRISTIAN CHARACTER (MATTHEW 5:1-12)

## A. To Be Lowly and to Mourn (vv. 1-4)

*1. Now when he saw the crowds, he went up on a mountainside and sat down. His disciples came to him,*

Jesus is at the height of his popularity. Large *crowds* gather to watch him heal the sick (Matthew 4:23-25). They are also attracted to Jesus because they are "amazed at his teaching, because he taught as one who had authority" (7:28, 29). Jesus speaks like a man who knows what he is talking about.

When Jesus goes up into a mountain, it could be any one of many possible locations in the hills of Galilee. The hilly location perhaps weeds out the people who are merely curious, and it provides a natural amphitheater for those who are willing to make the climb. As Jesus sits down to teach, he adopts the accepted posture of teachers in synagogues or schools (Luke 4:20). The parallel account in Luke 6:17-26 has Jesus standing. Putting together the accounts of Matthew and Luke, we see hints of a multi-day affair. Sometimes Jesus sits, sometimes he stands, depending on a variety of factors. The *disciples* include both the apostles and other followers who are serious about hearing the Master.

*2, 3. . . . and he began to teach them, saying:*

*"Blessed are the poor in spirit,*
*for theirs is the kingdom of heaven.*

It is important to catch the flavor of the word *blessed* in the Beatitudes. In the common language of the day (Greek), the word is used to describe people who are in an enviable position. Jesus is saying, in effect, "How fortunate are the poor in spirit." He is not feeling sorry for them as losers in the game of life; he is congratulating them as the ultimate winners.

Those who are poor in spirit are, in fact, better off than those who are arrogant and smug. People who recognize their own spiritual bankruptcy are much more likely to be ready to turn to God and receive salvation. Only those who humble themselves can enter the kingdom of Heaven—both now and in the life to come.

The church is the expression of God's kingdom on earth. After Jesus ascends, the earliest church will be made up of "not many . . . wise by human standards; not many . . . influential; not many . . . of noble birth" (1 Corinthians 1:26). The final expression of the kingdom is Heaven itself. Those who humble themselves will be exalted; they will have a home in Heaven. The best is yet to come!

*4. "Blessed are those who mourn,*
*for they will be comforted.*

Of all the Beatitudes, this one seems to be the most paradoxical. How can it be fortunate or happy for people to *mourn?* There are two senses in which mourning is good. First, the concept of mourning is found often in the Old Testament when people are expressing sorrow for sin (e.g., Ezra 10:6; Psalms 51:4; 119:136). Those who repent are obviously better off than those who do not. Second, people who are mourning in any kind of tragedy are more likely to learn deep truths than people who live happy but superficial lives. Maybe that is part of the reason why Solomon said, "It is better to go to a house of mourning than to go to a house of feasting" (Ecclesiastes 7:2).

God promises to comfort those who mourn. But the promise of "comfort" does not mean that God will make people "comfortable." It means, rather, that he will stand by them, support them, encourage them, console them (see Isaiah 40:1). Since this is the case, is it not better to mourn and have God near than to feast and have God absent? Is it not better for a nation to humble itself and repent than to abandon God and chase the elusive rainbow of prosperity and "quality of life"? (See also Isaiah 61:2, 3.)

*What Do You Think?*

*In what ways have you experienced the truth that those who mourn are blessed? What blessings have you received through mourning?*

## B. TO BE MEEK AND HUNGRY (vv. 5, 6)

5. *"Blessed are the meek,*
    *for they will inherit the earth.*

A sarcastic bumper sticker says "The meek shall inherit the earth—if that's OK with everyone else!" We should not, however, equate meekness with weakness. The word *meek* is used in Jesus' day to describe a trained elephant, a tamed stallion, or a reliable watchdog. These animals have strength, but their strength has been brought under control. Moses and Jesus are two of the most humble men in the Bible (see Numbers 12:3; Matthew 11:29; and 2 Corinthians 10:1). They are examples of strength that was yielded to the control of God.

Those who are meek are to be congratulated, for they will have great reward. In the new Heaven and the new earth (Revelation 21:1), when all things are made new, they will dwell in a place prepared for God's own people. They may never have owned a square foot of real estate on this old planet, but in the world to come they will inherit a mansion! (Compare Psalm 37:11.)

6. *"Blessed are those who hunger and thirst for righteousness,*
    *for they will be filled.*

In the physical sense, *hunger and thirst* are appetites that make us desire what is necessary for our very existence. By applying these words to the spiritual realm, Jesus applauds those who have a burning desire to be right with God. (See also Psalm 42:2.)

Righteousness—being seen as innocent in the eyes of God—is not very high on the list of priorities of worldly people. Their goals are wealth (how much can they get) and pleasure (how much can they get away with). Citizens of God's kingdom, on the other hand, long to be more godly than they already are. They long to live in a land where the tempter and his temptations are gone. They hunger for the day when the Lord's rebuilding project in their lives is brought to completion (Philippians 1:6).

John R. W. Stott sees a spiritual progression in these first four Beatitudes, with each step presupposing the one before. First, we must admit spiritual bankruptcy before God. Second, we must mourn over the cause of it—our sins. Third, we must yield humbly to the Master's control. Fourth, we must hunger for right standing with God. Seen in this light, we cannot pick our favorite Beatitudes and reject the others; the total package is what God desires in our lives.

## C. TO BE PURE AND GOOD (vv. 7-9)

7. *"Blessed are the merciful,*
    *for they will be shown mercy.*

In a society where people are conditioned to think they have evolved by "survival of the fittest," there seems to be little room for compassion. Big businesses swallow up little businesses; the strong demolish the weak. The world finds revenge sweet, but finds forgiveness tame by comparison.

Jesus commends those who try to reflect the *merciful* nature of God. If we have genuinely made the spiritual pilgrimage that began with admitting our own failure, we certainly will have pity for the failings of others. We will pray with conviction, "Forgive us our debts, as we also have forgiven our debtors" (Matthew 6:12). With the same measure by which we extend mercy to others, God's mercy will be extended to us (Mark 4:24). See also Matthew 18:21-35 and James 2:13.

8. *"Blessed are the pure in heart,*
    *for they will see God.*

Purity begins in the heart. If the heart is pure, right behavior will follow. If the heart is not pure, correct behavior is mere hypocrisy. Therefore, Jesus commends

### WHAT DO YOU THINK?

*If meekness is "strength . . . yielded to the control of God," then what examples of meekness have you seen demonstrated? What situations call for meekness more than others?*

### HOW TO SAY IT

*Colossians. Kuh-LOSH-unz.*
*Corinthians. Ko-RIN-thee-unz (th as in thin).*
*Ecclesiastes. Ik-LEEZ-ee-AS-teez.*
*Ephesians. Ee-FEE-zhunz.*
*Ezra. EZ-ruh.*
*Galatians. Guh-LAY-shunz.*
*Galilee. GAL-uh-lee.*
*Isaiah. Eye-ZAY-uh.*
*Judea. Joo-DEE-uh.*
*Philippians. Fih-LIP-ee-unz.*
*Sanhedrin. SAN-huh-drun or San-HEED-run.*

the people whose hearts are pure and good. Such a heart is a place where the seed of the gospel can take root and flourish (see Luke 8:15). Even though the world sees personal purity as a matter for scorn and mockery, those who are pure in heart will one day see God.

At the present time God is invisible to us (1 Timothy 6:16). Scripture promises, however, that in the life to come God's people will see his face (Revelation 22:4). We who long to see God must strive for holiness—to be pure in heart—for without this no one will see the Lord (Hebrews 12:14). See also Psalm 24:3, 4.

9. *"Blessed are the peacemakers, for they will be called sons of God.*

The Prince of peace commends those who are *peacemakers*. While the gospel will of necessity create division at times (Luke 14:26), believers should never seek conflict. Discord is a work of the flesh; peace is the fruit of the Spirit (Galatians 5:22). To the extent that it is within our control, we are to "live at peace with everyone" (Romans 12:18).

When believers love one another, they are recognized as true disciples of Jesus (John 13:35). When believers live in peace and work to promote peace, they will be recognized as children *of God.*

## D. TO BE PERSECUTED (vv. 10-12)

10. *"Blessed are those who are persecuted because of righteousness,*
    *for theirs is the kingdom of heaven.*

It is not by accident that the Beatitude on being *persecuted* follows the one on making peace, because making peace can be a risky business. The person who steps between warring parties may get shot at from both sides. In fact, all of the Beatitudes put the disciple of Jesus at odds with the world. Recognizing this fact, Jesus commends those whose distinctive difference will bring them persecution.

Not all persecution is undeserved, of course. Sometimes people bring opposition on themselves by their own folly. The one whom God honors is the person who, through no personal fault, suffers the world's wrath. When pursuing *righteousness* causes a person to be the target of the world's resentment, that persecution is honorably incurred. God will reward the Christian who suffers unjustly. See also 1 Peter 3:14.

WHAT DO YOU THINK?

*If we encounter opposition, how can we tell whether we have invited it by our own folly or if it is the kind of persecution for which Jesus says we are blessed?*

### AN UNUSUAL PERSPECTIVE ON PERSECUTION

During the Communist era in Eastern Europe, Christians often faced persecution. It included surveillance of their lives, interrogations, and sometimes beatings and imprisonment. The viewpoint of those suffering Christians is surprising: they understood that being a Christian always demands sacrifice. While Christians in the West saw prosperity as a sign of God's favor, Christians in Eastern Europe saw suffering in the same way. Suffering to them was proof that one was truly a disciple of Christ. It was something glorious, enabling one to grow in faith and enabling one to share in some way in the suffering of Jesus.

One minister in a former Communist country said, "When I entered the ministry I never expected that I would see a time when we were not persecuted." Those of us who live in the comfort and safety of the West so often complain and whine about some unwelcome experience and wonder if God has forsaken us. Such thoughts did not trouble those who served behind the Iron Curtain. They had no problem understanding the teaching of Jesus that persecution brings blessings. They saw them as unique blessings that might not be received in any other way.

Certainly no one goes out of his or her way to seek persecution; and everyone is glad when he or she does not have to face it. But persecution can bring a unique blessing to those who see it as Jesus did. —R. C. S.

11. *"Blessed are you when people insult you, persecute you and falsely say all kinds of evil against you because of me.*

In Jesus' eyes the Beatitude on persecution needs to be brought home more forcefully. Changing from "blessed are they" of verse 10, Jesus says, *Blessed are you when people insult you, . . . because of me.* Dedicated disciples should expect to be misunderstood, misrepresented, even reviled by the world. No matter how hard we try to live at peace with some people, sometimes those people refuse to live at peace with us.

Persecution is the inevitable result in the clash of opposite value systems. Those who prefer the darkness will instinctively lash out against the light. When we suffer at the hands of evil people, we can find consolation in the fact that we suffer for Jesus' sake. See also Matthew 10:22 and 1 Peter 4:14.

12. *"Rejoice and be glad, because great is your reward in heaven, for in the same way they persecuted the prophets who were before you.*

Dietrich Bonhoeffer, who was executed by the Nazis in 1945, said, "Suffering, then, is the badge of true discipleship . . . it is therefore not at all surprising that Christians should be called upon to suffer. In fact, it is a joy and token of God's grace." Just as the prophets were persecuted in the Old Testament, so will the disciples of Jesus be persecuted in the New Testament era. The apostles learned this lesson well, for when they were beaten and threatened by the Sanhedrin they rejoiced "because they had been counted worthy of suffering disgrace for the Name" (Acts 5:41).

## II. CHRISTIAN INFLUENCE (MATTHEW 5:13-16)

### A. SALT OF THE EARTH (v. 13)

13. *"You are the salt of the earth. But if the salt loses its saltiness, how can it be made salty again? It is no longer good for anything, except to be thrown out and trampled by men.*

*Salt* is a vital substance in the ancient world. It is flavoring to make food palatable; more importantly, it is a preservative to keep meat from putrefying. Just as a little salt can go a long way, even a few Christians can have tremendous influence for good. Christians are the moral disinfectant that keeps society from going bad.

But what if the salt becomes saltless? Salt from the Dead Sea area is not pure. If the place where it is stored gets wet, the sodium chloride can leach out, leaving only dust-flavored remains. Good for nothing, this "saltless salt" is *thrown out.*

Similarly, what if we Christians become indistinguishable from the people around us? What if we no longer mourn over sinfulness or hunger for righteousness? What if we are not pure? It is only as we live out the Beatitudes that we are the influence God intends us to be.

### A SUBSTITUTE FOR SALT

Many have been advised to reduce the amount of salt in their diets. This has led to the creation of salt substitutes. Most would agree that many of these substitutes really do not taste much like salt. People on a salt-free diet may adjust to them and use them, but most of us would find them unsatisfactory. The fact is, there just seems to be no substitute for salt. No other substance seems to be as versatile in adding flavor, preserving, and purifying.

Just as there is no substitute for table salt, there is no substitute for those who are spiritually the salt of the earth. Their influence—your influence—cannot be replaced by anything else. If we Christians do not season the world with the grace of Christ, it will not be seasoned.

You have an inescapable influence. You cannot avoid it. You can only determine if that influence will be for good or for bad, will lead people to Christ or will turn

### WHAT DO YOU THINK?

*If suffering is "the badge of true discipleship," then what of those Christians who never suffer for their faith? Which of us can truly say we have "suffered" for Jesus? What does this say of our faith?*

*[Use Acts 14:22 in your discussion.]*

### DAILY BIBLE READINGS

*Monday, June 27—Jesus Teaches About Discipleship (Luke 6:17-23)*

*Tuesday, June 28—Instructions on Living the Christian Life (Matthew 5:1-8)*

*Wednesday, June 29—More Instructions for True Disciples (Matthew 5:9-16)*

*Thursday, June 30—Love Your Enemies (Matthew 5:43-48)*

*Friday, July 1—Be Merciful (Luke 6:32-36)*

*Saturday, July 2—Do Not Judge (Matthew 7:1-5)*

*Sunday, July 3—On Judging Others (Luke 6:37-42)*

them away from Christ. It is a heavy responsibility, but Christ will help us. We need only yield ourselves to him in obedience and service. He will see to it that we become the salt for life—salt that preserves, that creates a thirst for God, and that heals the spiritual wounds of a broken world.    —R. C. S.

## B. Light of the World (vv. 14-16)

**14. "You are the light of the world. A city on a hill cannot be hidden.**

Like salt, just a small *light* can have a large impact. In the spiritual warfare against darkness, Christians shine as lights in *the world* (Philippians 2:15). Even a small light can do a great deal to dispel the darkness.

When Christians go about the business of being Christians, we cannot help but be noticed. Like *a city* that is set *on a hill,* with lights streaming from its windows at night, we cannot be overlooked. The light we project comes from Jesus (John 1:9; 8:12).

**15. "Neither do people light a lamp and put it under a bowl. Instead they put it on its stand, and it gives light to everyone in the house.**

It would be a total waste of perfectly good resources to hide the light *under a bowl.* In the same way, Christians are not intended to be invisible. We have *light* and truth that people in the world badly need. We should not be ashamed to let our friends and neighbors see what Christ is doing in our lives. See also Luke 8:16; 11:33.

**16. "In the same way, let your light shine before men, that they may see your good deeds and praise your Father in heaven."**

When we faithfully follow the teachings of Jesus, the world will notice the changes in our lives. We must be careful, however, that we do not do good works so that we will gain the praise of people (Matthew 6:1-4). If we do good works with the right attitude, the praise will go to God.

## CONCLUSION

Henry David Thoreau (1817–1862) claimed that most people lead lives of "quiet desperation." They want to be happy and successful, but seem to have lost their way. When life is all about self, it becomes stagnated and stale. When people lose sight of their Creator, they also lose sight of the road to happiness.

Long ago, Jesus taught principles that are still the key to true happiness. He taught that people should reflect the image of God in their lives and live for the praise of God. "Be perfect, therefore, as your heavenly Father is perfect" (Matthew 5:48). Then people will see our good works and give praise to God.

Jesus not only taught the Beatitudes, he also modeled them. He is the meek and lowly Savior (Matthew 11:29) who wept for the plight of sinful people (Luke 19:41). He hungered for God's Word and God's will (Matthew 4:4; 26:39). He showed mercy from a pure heart; He made peace between us and God by shedding his blood on the cross (Colossians 1:20). He endured persecution, even a cross, because he knew the joy that was set before him (Hebrews 12:2).

Jesus demonstrated the virtues that bring true happiness. He showed that satisfaction comes from giving, not from getting. He showed that contentment comes from "who you are" before God on the inside, not "what you have" on the outside.

Beyond contentment in this life there is final happiness, eternal bliss in Heaven. Perhaps this final lesson from Jesus is the most important of all. True happiness will finally be gained when we are able to look beyond our present trials and see the ultimate satisfaction that only God can give. When we hear the Savior say, "Well done" (Matthew 25:21), we will know what happiness really is.

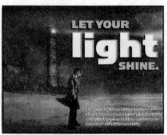

Visual for lesson 5. *This picture of a majestic lighthouse can stimulate a discussion on practical ways for Christians to act as "light."*

### What Do You Think?

*What is our church doing to equip the members to act as salt and light in the community? What more can we do?*

### Prayer

*Our Father in Heaven, forgive us for ignoring your truths and making our own futile attempts to gain happiness. Thank you for sending your Son, who taught us your truth and modeled the true life. Help us to be committed to following what he said and how he lived, as salt and light in the world. In Jesus' name, amen.*

### Thought to Remember

*It is a blessed and happy thing to be a follower of Jesus.*

# Discovery Learning

*This page contains an alternative lesson plan emphasizing learning activities. Classes desiring such student involvement will find these suggestions helpful. The next page is a reproducible activity page to further enhance discovery learning.*

## LEARNING GOALS

After participating in this lesson, each student will be able to:

1. Describe the attitudes and blessings that bring true happiness to the followers of Jesus.

2. Explain how happiness is based not on what one possesses, but on how one's life reflects and glorifies God.

3. Suggest specific ways in which the Beatitudes can correct the distorted goals of contemporary culture.

## INTO THE LESSON

As a class, create a list of the world's most "successful" people. Form several small groups, each of which is to serve as a selection committee for a "Top 10 People of the Year" award. Designate a different area for each group, such as business, sports, entertainment, and politics.

Have class members select the group they would like to be part of, and then allow about ten minutes for the groups to develop their lists. Have the groups share their results. Make the connection to the lesson by asking your learners to pretend to be someone on their list as they finish the following incomplete sentences. Write each of the three as a separate column across the top of the board:

*Happiness is . . .* [Try to define what happiness looks like in terms of money, fame, etc.]

*The road to happiness is . . .* [How do people achieve their dreams for happiness?]

*What I've learned about happiness is . . .* [This could foster discussion about life goals, about pursuing happiness the wrong way, that there is a price to pay to get happiness, that happiness can be lost easily, etc.]

(Do not write the thoughts in brackets on the board. These are provided to help you see the ideas that may surface regarding what many people understand about finding happiness and fulfillment in life.)

## INTO THE WORD

Say, "Jesus' view of true happiness is quite different from what is observed in contemporary culture and the media." Then discuss the meaning of *blessed* (from page 378), comparing and contrasting this idea with common understandings of happiness. Then start with the middle column entitled, *The road to happiness is . . .* This column that will list those whom the Beatitudes say are blessed (poor in spirit, those who mourn, the meek, those who hunger and thirst for righteousness, the merciful, the pure in heart, peacemakers, and those persecuted for Christ). Place these in the column one at a time, pausing to identify and cross out things that were written previously that this description contradicts. For example, when you write "pure in heart," you might cross out any comments that refer to inappropriate sexual relationships or lack of integrity in business as a means for finding happiness.

After you write each item in the middle column, follow by writing the description of their blessing in the *Happiness is . . .* column. For example, after writing "poor in spirit" in the middle column, you would then write "theirs is the kingdom of heaven" in this column. Again review and cross out any comments from the "Into the Lesson" exercise that this would contradict.

Finally, discuss personal "life lessons" about happiness. In what ways have your learners seen the truth of Jesus' words confirmed?

## INTO LIFE

Say, "While many would claim that they believe the words of Jesus to be true, their lives might contradict them. Each of us has times when our attention and energy are aimed at goals that represent contemporary culture more than the teaching of Jesus." Suggest to your learners that critical questions to consider include (1) What does your life say about what you really believe about true happiness? (2) How do you think your life would be different if the Beatitudes were truly your measure of success? (3) How would your church be different if everyone was committed to helping others live this way? (4) What would it take for that to happen?

Give each learner a blank index card. On this each should write at the top a Beatitude that he or she will seek to pursue this week; below that each should write a description of how he or she will pursue that Beatitude. On the back of the card, each should then write the opposite of the Beatitude; below that, have each write a description what living that way would be like. Encourage each to commit to reading this card (both sides) at least three times each day, asking for God's help in living with Jesus' words in mind.

# Jesus *vs.* Madison Avenue

On the chart below write several advertising slogans that promise happiness to the user of the product being advertised. Then contrast each one with one or more of the Beatitudes from Matthew 5:2-12. A couple of examples have been given to get you started.

| SLOGANS | BEATITUDES |
|---|---|
| "Have it your way." | Blessed are those who hunger and thirst after righteousness. |
| "Because I'm worth it." | Blessed are those who mourn. |

# Pursue the Blessing

In the box below write one of the Beatitudes, one that describes a character quality you will make a special effort to practice this week. Then write some specific ways you will attempt to do that.

Beatitude: _____

_____

*Actions I Will Take to Pursue It*                    *Barriers I Will Eliminate*

# PRACTICING GENUINE RIGHTEOUSNESS

**LESSON 6**

## WHY TEACH THIS LESSON?

Religious television has built-in temptations for its producers and participants. Looking holy and righteous for cameras and audiences—scripted facial expressions, words carefully planned for sound and impact, and edited deeds of service—all must be a real challenge to be avoided. But the same temptations exist for all Christians—to show a holy countenance and holy deed on cue; to arrive at the church's building, put a smile in place, and vocalize all the right words like a doll with a pull string; to sing at the worship team's downbeat; to lower the chin as the word *pray* echoes through the room; to pull the right currency from pocket or purse; to greet everyone with a firm handshake or a polite hug.

Hypocrisy is easy and gets easier and easier with practice. Sincerity is hard, but it also gets easier as it is lived. What adult disciple does not need to learn this grand truth? For his giving, what motives drive him? For her praying, what intentions mold her words? Today's text offers solid prescriptions.

## INTRODUCTION

### A. "HOLY, HOLY, HOLY"?

Simeon the Stylite was a holy man—a very, very holy man. He lived in Syria in the fifth century A.D., amazing the ancient world with his acts of holiness. At the age of thirty-three, he climbed on top of a six-foot wide pillar and did not come down for the next thirty-six years. He would stand for hours reciting Scripture or lifting his hands in prayer. People came by the thousands to watch what they called "this marvel of holiness."

Who is the most holy person you know? Is it a man who prays long and often? Is it a woman who sacrifices her meager income to give more to the church or to the poor? What is the true measure of the holy and righteous person? What is God's measure?

Jesus taught his followers to practice genuine righteousness. This kind of righteousness will not draw big crowds of admirers. It may not seem showy or impressive to the world, but it is far more pleasing to God. In this lesson we will examine how to practice righteousness—the lifestyle of the kingdom of Heaven.

### B. LESSON BACKGROUND

In the Beatitudes of Matthew 5:3-12, Jesus completely reversed the prevailing value systems of society. In the remainder of that chapter, he went on to correct the improper religious teachings of the day. "You have heard," Jesus said repeatedly, "But I tell you . . . " (vv. 21, 22, 27, 28, 33, 34, 38, 39, 43, 44). There were always surprises when Jesus taught.

Jesus insisted that his followers must do better than the teachers of the law and Pharisees had done (Matthew 5:20). The teachers of the law and Pharisees

DEVOTIONAL READING:
**LUKE 11:5-13**

BACKGROUND SCRIPTURE:
**MATTHEW 6:1-34**

PRINTED TEXT:
**MATTHEW 6:1-15**

**Jul 10**

### LESSON AIMS

After participating in this lesson, each student will be able to:

1. Identify what is wrong with acts of worship that are performed for others to see.

2. Describe the kinds of giving and praying that please God.

3. Decide what steps are necessary to bring one's own giving and praying into line with the teachings of Jesus.

### KEY VERSE

"Be careful not to do your 'acts of righteousness' before men, to be seen by them. If you do, you will have no reward from your Father in heaven."

—Matthew 6:1

were widely regarded as experts in carrying out God's laws, but in fact they had missed the point. They kept the externals of the laws, but Jesus insisted that his disciples start on the inside with the heart. When they did they would be ready to practice genuine righteousness—not for people, but for God.

## I. GUIDELINES FOR GIVING (MATTHEW 6:1-4)

### A. WRONG WAY TO GIVE (vv. 1, 2)

*1. "Be careful not to do your 'acts of righteousness' before men, to be seen by them. If you do, you will have no reward from your Father in heaven.*

The ancient Jews are frequently instructed in the importance of charitable gifts for poor people (Deuteronomy 15:11). People who have plenty are to share with people in need (e.g., Acts 9:36; 10:2; 24:17; 2 Corinthians 9:6, 7). Handicapped people would lie beside the public thoroughfares, waiting for someone to take pity and give them money (Acts 3:2). In a day with no welfare department or charitable foundations, this one-on-one approach to giving is vital.

It is easy, however, to do the right thing in the wrong way. A very righteous person may innocently think that personal giving should be a good example for others to follow. Such a person may think of himself or herself as simply modeling the godly life. Eventually, however, a person's real reason for public *acts of righteousness* may be so that he or she can *be seen by* others. People may praise such a person for his or her goodness, but that person will have no congratulations from God.

*2. "So when you give to the needy, do not announce it with trumpets, as the hypocrites do in the synagogues and on the streets, to be honored by men. I tell you the truth, they have received their reward in full.*

If a very righteous person decides that his or her giving is a good model for less righteous people to follow, then it stands to reason that such a person should call attention to what is being done. (After all, if very righteous deeds go unnoticed, how will others learn?) So the pompous Pharisee perhaps rationalizes to himself that it is appropriate to make ostentatious displays when inviting beggars to receive his generosity.

Jesus ridicules such trumpet-blowers as *hypocrites*. A hypocrite is a pretender. People who pretend to be religious but seek the glory of other people are phonies in God's eyes. They are nothing but playactors. When they receive the applause of people, they already have all the *reward* they will ever get.

### B. RIGHT WAY TO GIVE (vv. 3, 4)

*3. "But when you give to the needy, do not let your left hand know what your right hand is doing,*

Common courtesy should tell the donors that a gift to a *needy* person should be given quietly. If nothing else, this respects and protects the recipient's dignity. This kind of giving also helps to protect the giver's own character and integrity.

By saying that the *left hand* should not *know* what the *right hand is doing*, Jesus means that the gift should be given without attracting attention. We do not need an audience when we give. We should not even be our own audience, taking smug satisfaction in our righteous act. The audience is not others, nor self—the audience is God.

*4. . . . so that your giving may be in secret. Then your Father, who sees what is done in secret, will reward you."*

There is a certain tension in a Christian keeping his or her charitable giving secret, because Jesus earlier said, "Let your light shine before men, that they may see your good deeds and praise your Father in heaven" (Matthew 5:16). It would

WHAT DO YOU THINK?

*What measures can the church take to preserve the dignity of recipients of church benevolence funds?*

appear that we are tempted to hide what we ought to show, and to show what we ought to hide. The goal is always to do the right thing without any regard for human praise. God sees what we do in secret and does not need us to call it to his attention. He will not fail to reward us.

## II. GUIDELINES FOR PRAYING (MATTHEW 6:5-8)

### A. WRONG WAY TO PRAY (v. 5)

5. "And when you pray, do not be like the hypocrites, for they love to pray standing in the synagogues and on the street corners to be seen by men. I tell you the truth, they have received their reward in full.

Just as there is a wrong way to give charitably, there is also a wrong way to pray. In Bible times, many different prayer postures are acceptable (see Numbers 16:22; 1 Samuel 1:26; 2 Samuel 7:18; 2 Chronicles 6:13). The problem with *the hypocrites* is not their *standing* posture in prayer. Rather, the problem is their attitude. Sincere Jews usually stand *to pray* at the three daily times for prayer, sometimes stopping on a *street* corner to do so. There is nothing wrong with this procedure if their motives are good. However, hypocrites love to have people watch them being religious.

In Luke 20:47, a similar passage, Jesus accuses the hypocritical Pharisees of making long prayers for a pretense. They do the right things, but for the wrong reason—to be seen by people. They are playactors who think of life as a stage on which they can strut and show their stuff. As a result, the admiration of people will be their only reward.

### PRAYING IN SINCERITY

You can find odd and interesting place names all over the United States. Every state has them. In North Carolina, for example, you can find Friendship, Bridal Veil, Blowing Rock, Kill Devil Hills, and Sincerity. One supposes that people who pray in Sincerity are no more in earnest than those who pray in Raleigh or Charlotte. Wherever we live we should pray in sincerity.

If we are thinking of public prayers, sincerity means that we do not pray to be praised by people for the eloquence of our prayers nor for their length. Lee Carter Maynard once noted that when Jesus prayed in public he was very brief; when he prayed in private he prayed all night. Maynard said, "We usually reverse the process."

If we are thinking of private prayers, sincerity means that we do not pray simply out of habit, but rather pray from our hearts. Certainly we ought to have the habit of prayer. We need a definite time and place to pray. But when that time comes and we go to that place, our prayer must not be routine. To pray in sincerity means that we go beyond some memorized prayer repeated over and over.

Sincerity in prayer also means that we look for ways to enrich our prayer time. The remembered verses of a hymn may help. It may help us to read the prayers of others—not to repeat them, but to learn from them new depths of devotion. And, of course, sincerity means we truly believe God hears our prayers and responds to our prayers. We trust that he answers in his own way and in his own time.          —R. C. S.

### B. RIGHT WAY TO PRAY (vv. 6-8)

6. "But when you pray, go into your room, close the door and pray to your Father, who is unseen. Then your Father, who sees what is done in secret, will reward you.

Prayer can be spoken in public, of course. See Acts 1:24; 3:1; and 4:24-30. But prayer often is best done in private. To avoid the problem of wrong motives, Jesus tells his disciples to go to a *room* in the house where there are no windows through which others can see them. After they had shut the doors for complete

WHAT DO YOU THINK?

Jesus says our giving should be secret. But Paul publicly praised the Macedonian believers for their generous giving and told the Corinthians about it in an effort to motivate greater generosity from them (2 Corinthians 8:1-7). How would you resolve this tension?

WHAT DO YOU THINK?

Nearly every worship service has occasions when someone offers a prayer that everyone else can hear. What guidelines, from today's text and others, should such persons follow to be sure they are not falling into the same snare as the Pharisees whom Jesus rebuked?

privacy, they could then *pray to God in secret* (compare 2 Kings 4:33). Then they can say to God what they truly feel, instead of what sounds good to others. God will hear their prayers and *reward* them openly.

Interestingly, the prophet Daniel made a point of leaving the windows to his prayer room open in Daniel 6:10. But the wider context of that passage shows that he had a godly reason for doing so. We also can point out that public prayer can be done with a "closet mentality." Although there may be a large congregation present, it is still possible to make prayer a personal conversation with God. The more we can tune out everything but God, the more we have Jesus' attitude.

7. *"And when you pray, do not keep on babbling like pagans, for they think they will be heard because of their many words.*

Those who do not know God may use empty repetitions to make their prayers impressive, but true disciples do not. An incident in the Old Testament serves as a vivid example of this. At the famous contest on Mount Carmel, the prophets of Baal leaped on their altar and shouted to their god from early morning until noon (see 1 Kings 18:26). But there was no voice that answered.

Then Elijah prayed a brief, private prayer to God and fire fell from Heaven to consume his sacrifice. He was in public, but his prayer was in private. This is the kind of prayer that Jesus instructs his followers to pray.

We should also pause to point out that the phrase *their many words* doesn't mean that we can't be persistent in prayer (Luke 18:1-8). In the Garden of Gethsemane, Jesus repeats his own prayer (Matthew 26:39, 42, 44). It's all the pointless babble that we are to avoid.

8. *"Do not be like them, for your Father knows what you need before you ask him.*

Jesus expects his disciples, then and now, to be different. We do not need to try to impress God or even try to inform Him. God already *knows* our needs, even *before* we *ask* (see also Matthew 6:32).

Someone may ask, then, "What is the purpose of prayer? If God already knows what we will ask, why bother?" Perhaps part of the purpose of praying is to remind ourselves how much we depend on God. God wants us to ask him. If we do not take our requests to God, we are taking him for granted.

## III. A MODEL FOR PRAYER (MATTHEW 6:9-15)

### A. THINKING OF GOD (vv. 9, 10)

9. *"This, then, is how you should pray:*

*"'Our Father in heaven,*

*hallowed be your name,*

Jesus gives a sample prayer to show his disciples *how* to *pray*. However, if they do no more than memorize his prayer, then they will be no better than the pagans with their empty repetitions. Public recitation of this particular prayer can never take the place of heartfelt, private prayers.

Prayer must focus first on God: *your name*. All of our self-importance must melt away in the presence of the divine King. Only then are we ready to pray.

Amazingly, the grand Creator of the entire universe is pleased to relate to us as *our Father.* He accepts us as his children and gives us the right to address him intimately, "Abba, Father" (see Romans 8:15). Our Father reigns in Heaven, but hears our softest prayers on earth. Our earnest desire should be to see his name *hallowed*, that is, treated as a sacred and holy thing. See Ezekiel 36:23.

### A MODEL TO FOLLOW

Every aspiring artist studies the masters: Raphael and Rembrandt and Michelangelo. Every aspiring composer studies the masters: Beethoven and Brahms, Haydn and Handel. The Twelve noticed that there was something in the prayers of Jesus that they lacked. His prayers had more depth and breadth, and they wanted to pray like that. They were no strangers to prayer. They had prayed all their lives, but they saw in his prayers qualities that theirs did not have. So they said, "Lord, teach us to pray" (Luke 11:1).

In response to that request, he gave them a model by which they could form their own prayers. Is it wrong, then, to recite this prayer? Of course not. It is never wrong to quote Scripture. But the intent of Jesus was that they should learn from this to word their own prayers. The artist may start out copying some great work of art, but eventually composes his own painting. The composer studies closely the music of the masters, not in order to copy them, but that their work may inform, guide, and inspire her own composition. So, in public and in private, we compose our own prayers, using this model as a guide and as inspiration.

We pray remembering that we are children talking to our Father. We want our prayers to be the best that they can be, but we know that the Father accepts our poorest prayer efforts. He does not receive our prayers because of their eloquence, their nicety of expression, or their poetic qualities. He accepts them because he loves his children. —R. C. S.

"When you pray, go into your room, close the door and pray to your Father."
—Matthew 6:6

Visual for lesson 6. *Use this image as a starting point to discuss the nature of prayers that God finds acceptable.*

10. "'. . . your kingdom come,
    your will be done
        on earth as it is in heaven.*

Jesus teaches that before we pray for ourselves we should pray for the success of God's *will* and his *kingdom*. God's kingdom is more than just the territory over which he reigns. His kingdom is also his "kingship" over people's lives, beginning with our own.

When we pray *your will be done*, we are submitting to that will ourselves. How wonderful it would be if every man and woman were as quick to obey God as the angels *in Heaven* are! This is the kind of obedience seen in the total surrender of Jesus himself in the Garden of Gethsemane (Matthew 26:39; see also Hebrews 5:7, 8).

## B. THINKING OF SELF (vv. 11-13)

11. "*Give us today our daily bread.*

After giving the first priority to God and his kingship, it is appropriate next to address our own needs. It is right to ask God to provide the things necessary to sustain our lives. This acknowledges that God is the true source of every blessing.

*Bread* can be understood to refer to food in general. God is the ultimate source of our livelihood (Deuteronomy 8:18; James 1:17). But as we pray for bread we should remember that "man does not live on bread alone" (Matthew 4:4). We should also think about Jesus who is the bread of life who came down from Heaven to give us eternal life. Just as our bodies need physical food, our souls need spiritual food, or we grow weak and die.

12. "*Forgive us our debts,*
    *as we also have forgiven our debtors.*

When we pray we must confess our sins and ask for God's forgiveness (1 John 1:9). If we are sincere in our confession and repentance, we will personalize our prayers. If we are praying in secret as Jesus directed, we will naturally confess specific failures; otherwise we have not really admitted to having any sin.

In the same way that we want God to *forgive us* our shortcomings, we should also be ready to forgive the shortcomings of others. The Parable of the Unmerciful Servant in Matthew 18:21-35 helps us here. If God has forgiven us our enormous sin debt, how can we not forgive others in turn? In fact, if we pray the

*WHAT DO YOU THINK?*

*Does praying for our "daily" bread make it wrong to stock our pantries with several days' worth of provisions? Why, or why not?*

HOW TO SAY IT

Baal. BAY-ul.

Colossians. Kuh-LOSH-unz.

Corinthians. Ko-RIN-thee-unz (th as in thin).

Deuteronomy. Due-ter-AHN-uh-me.

Elijah. Ee-LYE-juh.

Ephesians. Ee-FEE-zhunz.

Ezekiel. Ee-ZEEK-ee-ul or Ee-ZEEK-yul.

Gethsemane. Geth-SEM-uh-nee (G as in get).

Pharisees. FAIR-ih-seez.

PRAYER

*Our Father, help us to make your name, your kingdom, and your will the top priorities in our lives. Forgive us for the times we have put our own holiness on display to receive the adulation of others. Teach us not to care so much about what people think and to devote ourselves wholly to pleasing you. In Jesus' name, amen.*

THOUGHT TO REMEMBER

*"If I were still trying to please men, I would not be a servant of Christ"* (Galatians 1:10).

model prayer of Jesus, then we are inviting God to forgive us only to the extent that we forgive others. This makes genuine prayer a sobering experience.

**13. "'And lead us not into temptation, but deliver us from the evil one.'**

God, of course, does not tempt people to sin (see James 1:13). We do not need to beg him to not do something that is already totally foreign to his nature. Some commentators think that what Jesus means is that we are to ask God to help us not to be led *into temptation* by Satan, as in John 17:15 and 2 Thessalonians 3:3. Other commentators think that our prayer is for God not to allow us to undergo the severe trials and testings of life, as in 2 Timothy 4:18.

## C. THINKING OF OTHERS (vv. 14, 15)

**14. "For if you forgive men when they sin against you, your heavenly Father will also forgive you.**

It is significant that when Jesus goes back to emphasize one part of the prayer, the part he chooses is about forgiving others for their wrongs *against* us. When we pray to God, Jesus expects us to get in tune with God. This means that our hearts should be willing to *forgive* people just as God forgives them. We should be encouraged to be more ready to forgive when we consider that God will then extend his forgiveness to us. See also Mark 11:25; Ephesians 4:32; and Colossians 3:13.

**15. "But if you do not forgive men their sins, your Father will not forgive your sins."**

On the other hand, if we are unwilling to *forgive* others, then it means that God's nature has not rubbed off on us. How could we dare to approach God and ask for what we refuse to give? (Again, see Matthew 18:21-35.) How can we repeatedly enter the throne room in prayer and yet learn nothing about being more like God? The warning of Jesus is severe: if we will *not forgive* others, God *will not forgive* us. Prayer, therefore, involves more than just the petitioner and God. True prayer also involves others and the way we behave toward them.

## CONCLUSION

Do you know how to spot counterfeit currency? Businesses that handle large amounts of cash always have to be on the lookout for fake money. Their cashiers are usually given training that enables them to spot the phony bills and reject them. For instance, a cashier may hold a bill up to the light to see if a hidden image (watermark) appears in one area while an embedded stripe appears in another. Being able to spot a counterfeit means saving their company a lot of trouble.

Jesus gave us instructions on how to spot religious phonies. We can hold them up to the light of his teaching and see if their lives are what they claim to be. We can see if the image of their Creator shows up in them. Members of religious cults continue to knock on doors in neighborhoods, and we must remain alert to the false gospels that they bring.

But the lesson today, from the lips of Jesus, is not so much about spotting a phony as it is about not being one. He gave warnings about the things that mark a hypocrite so that we, above all, could check ourselves.

Our challenge, then, is to learn to practice genuine righteousness without seeking the praise of people. Since at least some of our giving and praying is done in public, we will have to try all the harder to preserve a sense of privacy in what we do. In the final analysis, the secrecy of giving and the privacy of prayer are more matters of attitude than location. Whether public or private, our "acts of righteousness" must be carried out for the eyes and ears of God.

# Discovery Learning

*This page contains an alternative lesson plan emphasizing learning activities. Classes desiring such student involvement will find these suggestions helpful. The next page is a reproducible activity page to further enhance discovery learning.*

## LEARNING GOALS

After participating in this lesson, each student will be able to:

1. Identify what is wrong with acts of worship that are performed for others to see.

2. Describe the kinds of giving and praying that please God.

3. Decide what steps are necessary to bring one's own giving and praying into line with the teachings of Jesus.

## INTO THE LESSON

Begin class by asking, "What are some of the classic spiritual disciplines?" Expect answers to include the following: **solitude** (time spent alone for reflection and spiritual focus), **fasting** (abstaining from food, drink, etc.), **frugality** (abstaining from spending money on luxury items), **discreetness** (performing good deeds anonymously), **study** (time spent reading the Word of God, etc.), **prayer** (focused, intentional communication with God), and **journaling** (to focus thoughts on spiritual issues).

Remind your learners that this is only a partial list of the types of things that we can do to foster spiritual growth. While each discipline seems spiritual at first glance, each can be done in a way that does more harm than good. Say, "In today's lesson Jesus gives instructions for how to practice (and how not to practice) two disciplines: charitable giving and the practice of prayer."

## INTO THE WORD

Ask the class to consider the two cases of the lesson (charitable giving and the practice of prayer) in terms of the following four questions as you write them on the chalkboard: (1) What did the person do? (2) How did the person do it? (3) What was the motive for the actions? (4) What were the results of the actions?

You may find it helpful to divide the class into small groups to discuss the two cases. After ten minutes or so, call for conclusions. Responses will likely include the following.

**Case #1—charity:** What did the person do? *(gave charitable gifts for the poor)*; How did the person do it? *(called public attention to the charity)*; What was the motive for the actions? *(to receive human accolades)*; What were the results of his actions? *(received what was sought: the attention of people)*.

**Case #2—prayer:** What did the person do? *(prayed publicly)*; How did the person do it? *(prayed with fanfare and repetition)*; What was the motive for the actions? *(to receive human accolades)*; What were the results of the actions? *(received what was sought: the attention of people)*. You may add that, "In both cases, by receiving only what was sought, the person actually missed the greater blessing: the pleasure of God."

Ask, "If Jesus were teaching these two illustrations of charitable giving and prayer today, how do you think he would word them differently, based on what we see around us?" Expand the discussion by asking, "What other things do we Christians do that might be improper in God's eyes—things that promote attention to self rather than honoring God? What can we do to help ourselves and each other do these things with the right motives and in a way that truly honors God and prompts spiritual growth?" Allow time for discussion.

## INTO LIFE

Draw the attention of your learners to the Daily Disciplines exercise in the student book. (If members of the class do not have the book, they can still follow along with your discussion.) Learners should select two spiritual disciplines they believe will help them grow as they commit themselves to incorporating those disciplines into daily life for the next five weeks. (You can write on the board some of the disciplines from the "Into the Lesson" listing.) Today's passage specifically addresses prayer and charitable giving. Those would be good choices, or other disciplines can be selected.

Encourage each learner to establish a personal standard for each discipline (a certain amount of time, certain things they will do, etc.) and to keep a daily record of his or her practice of the disciplines. Emphasize that this is not a competition. The goal here is not to perform to another person's standard (or even performance at all). The goal is simply to incorporate helpful practices to create an environment that fosters spiritual growth.

Ask for ideas on how learners can practice these disciplines in ways that will foster, rather than inhibit, spiritual growth. Allow time as class ends for people to spend time alone in prayer, asking for God's help in this regard.

# Hidden Virtues

Jesus said our acts of righteousness were to be done for God's glory and not to be seen by others. In the grid below are hidden the names of no fewer than eight spiritual disciplines. See how many you can find.

```
S  F  R  U  G  A  L  I  T  Y  S  T  S  N  H  C
I  S  S  P  T  N  M  E  M  O  R  I  Z  I  N  G
T  O  S  R  W  H  E  A  N  C  R  M  D  O  E  O
F  L  A  A  A  E  E  T  N  F  O  B  Y  T  F
A  I  E  Y  A  G  E  E  I  B  N  H  B  G  G  S
S  T  G  E  O  C  T  O  M  N  Y  S  A  N  E  G
T  U  F  R  A  D  T  A  R  F  E  E  I  H  N  E
I  D  A  C  I  W  H  Y  A  R  E  L  S  I  E  D
N  E  A  N  C  I  C  S  T  I  A  E  V  N  H  C
G  I  N  R  H  E  H  T  T  N  H  I  E  W  O  W
O  U  O  D  R  U  S  R  R  U  G  N  S  T  C  N
E  O  O  C  N  I  T  U  A  E  D  O  T  S  T  E
I  O  E  A  O  A  O  C  P  A  R  Y  W  E  T  L
N  S  E  M  P  J  O  F  Q  B  N  W  E  O  R  E
```

# Right or Wrong?

*Read each of the situations below and decide right and wrong circumstances.*

**A.** During the church's annual stewardship campaign, Diane has been asked to tell how she, a single mom with a minimum wage job, is still able to give faithfully. She is hesitant to share, wondering if it wouldn't violate Matthew 6.

Under what circumstances would it be okay to share her story?

Under what circumstances would it be wrong to share her story?

**B.** Tom supports a Bible college that has announced a capital fund campaign to build a new ministry training center. If Tom gives $1,000 to fund the new building, a plaque with his name on it will be posted in a prominent location. He wonders how that fits with Matthew 6.

Under what circumstances would it be okay to participate in the program?

Under what circumstances would it be wrong to participate in the program?

# LEARNING TO LISTEN

## LESSON 7

## WHY TEACH THIS LESSON?

Every fall the small Tennessee town of Jonesborough welcomes more visitors than it has residents. What's the occasion? It's the National Storytelling Festival. Most of the visitors are listeners, not tellers. The delight of the oral story has drawn them from states near and far.

People have always enjoyed a good story. Jesus' good stories are no exception. But his stories are designed to teach rather than to entertain. He wants to elicit changed lives. His stories, widely familiar to adult churchgoers, may be dismissed by those adults as old and simple. But the parables of Jesus are ever new and fresh if they are carefully studied and pondered. Today's study presents an opportunity for you to enliven the stories of Jesus for your learners. As you do you may bring forth a renewed wonder at their depth and their life-enhancing value.

## INTRODUCTION

### A. "ONCE UPON A TIME . . . "

Everyone loves a good story. Children learn at an early age to perk up their ears at the magic words, "Once upon a time . . . " Stories can carry us to other times, other places, other worlds. Stories can be fun, but they can also carry important lessons.

Jesus told stories called "parables." Parables were Jesus' way of transporting his audience to another world—the kingdom of God. It is a world of hidden treasure and pearls of great price. It is a land of sprouting mustard seeds and of grain harvests in astonishing abundance. In this kingdom, beggars go to feasts and rich men go to Hades. It is a world where lost sheep and lost coins are found, where a prodigal son is welcomed home.

K. R. Snodgrass proposes that "parables are best defined as stories with two levels of meaning. . . . In effect, parables are imaginary gardens with real toads in them." Parables express moral or spiritual truths. The parables of Jesus are deceptively simple, but they are packed with an enormous amount of spiritual truth.

A parable may be a brief comparison ("the kingdom of Heaven is like a mustard seed") or a lengthy story ("a certain man had two sons"), but the parable somehow manages to bring a spiritual truth down to earth. Therefore, when parables are told, people need to learn to listen. They must learn to hear with their hearts, not just their ears, to understand the spiritual truths of God's kingdom.

Simon Kistemaker has suggested a helpful approach to interpreting parables. First, learn the life setting of the story. Second, note carefully the exact wording that is used, including how the parable is introduced and how it is applied. Third, seek the main lesson. Fourth, compare the teaching of the parable with other Scriptures. Fifth, determine how the parable meets the needs of the twenty-first century church.

When reading a parable, we should not try to see how creative we can be. It serves no purpose to invent special meanings for every detail. Many parables have one main truth. Some parables have two or three main truths. The person who learns to listen carefully to the parables of Jesus will be richly rewarded.

DEVOTIONAL READING:
MARK 4:10-20

BACKGROUND SCRIPTURE:
MATTHEW 13:1-23

PRINTED TEXT:
MATTHEW 13:9-17

LESSON AIMS

After participating in this lesson, each student will be able to:

1. Describe what parables are and why Jesus used them.

2. Explain why some people could not, or would not, understand the parables.

3. Commit himself or herself to taking the steps necessary to learn to listen to Jesus.

Jul
17

KEY VERSE

"He who has ears, let him hear." —*Matthew 13:9*

## B. LESSON BACKGROUND

Great crowds gathered on the shore beside the Sea of Galilee. Some of the people were eager disciples, some were hostile enemies, and some were curiosity seekers. In order to allow everyone to hear, Jesus got into a boat and spoke from a short way out into the sea (Matthew 13:1, 2). But the real problem was not just allowing people to hear; it was getting them to listen.

Jesus began his teaching with the Parable of the Sower (Matthew 13:3-8). Later in the same period of teaching, in the verses that follow the text of this lesson, Jesus explained what each part of the parable meant (see Matthew 13:18-23). In between this parable and its explanation, he talks about the issue of parables themselves.

## I. THOSE WHO HEAR (MATTHEW 13:9-12)

### A. CHALLENGE (v. 9)

9. "He who has ears, let him hear."

At the end of the Parable of the Sower, Jesus issues a challenge to his audience: whoever *has ears* is commanded *to hear*. Jesus' words go beyond the obvious fact that most everyone has ears and the sense of hearing. Some ears "hear," but do not really "listen." Whoever is willing to use his or her ears to hear and heed the word of Jesus is the subject of his command.

*Let him hear* does not mean "allow him to hear," as though someone might otherwise prevent a person from hearing. It is, rather, a command addressed to those having ears—hearing ears. Such people are under orders to listen attentively to the words of the Master.

Jesus knows that the important truths of eternal life cannot be taught to the crowd in complex, abstract terms. Thus he communicates in ways that common people can comprehend. Even with his use of down-to-earth stories, however, he cannot teach them if they choose not to listen. The prophet Ezekiel ran into this problem (see Ezekiel 33:30-32).

### B. QUESTION (v. 10)

10. *The disciples came to him and asked, "Why do you speak to the people in parables?"*

*The disciples* have been with Jesus long enough to recognize the change in Jesus' teaching. Using only *parables* (Matthew 13:34) has not been Jesus' custom to this point. Therefore they ask Jesus *why* he chooses to speak to the crowd in that way. All told, the parables of Jesus make up about one-third of his recorded teachings.

An example from 2 Samuel 11:1–12:14 shows the power of a parable. After David committed adultery with Bathsheba, he was slow to come to repentance. Therefore the Lord sent Nathan to tell David a parable about a poor man whose pet lamb had been taken by a greedy rich man. When David became incensed against the rich man of the story, Nathan replied, "You are the man!"

David then immediately recognized his sinful behavior. When a parable is told to someone with listening ears, that person can identify himself or herself in relation to the story.

### C. PROMISE (vv. 11, 12)

11. *He replied, "The knowledge of the secrets of the kingdom of heaven has been given to you, but not to them.*

Jesus explains that he speaks in parables because of the diverse nature of those who hear him. Some, including the disciples, are eager to accept the teachings of

WHAT DO YOU THINK?

How can you tell "who has ears" to hear? What is to be gained from noticing who is listening to the Master?

Jesus. For true seekers, each parable becomes an exciting moment when they can reach out and embrace *the secrets of the kingdom of heaven*. In these simple stories they can catch a glimpse of another world. Others in the crowd, however, do not want to believe. The teachings of Jesus serve only to strengthen their obstinacy. Like the sun that melts the wax but hardens the clay, Jesus' parables either break through to the hearts of the hearers or make them walk away in disgust. Thus the parables of Jesus can both reveal and conceal at the same time.

The verse before us has been understood very differently by sincere students of the Bible. Those who believe in "free will" have assigned to the people themselves the blame for their unbelief. Others, equally sincere, think that God in his sovereignty has given some people an open heart, but has not given a heart of belief to others. If taken by itself, this verse seems to affirm the second view.

In the overall context, however, Jesus calls for people to respond and holds them accountable for their choice. Also, it should not be forgotten that two chapters earlier Jesus had given an open invitation when he said, "Come to me, all you who are weary and burdened, and I will give you rest" (Matthew 11:28). Jesus draws everyone to him (John 12:32), but people can resist that drawing if they freely choose.

The promise of Jesus for those who do hear him is that they will know the secrets of the kingdom. These are not things that are necessarily complicated and difficult to understand, but are things that are not known until they are revealed. Part of the purpose of the parables is to reveal things in such a way that true seekers can understand them. Those who chose to follow Jesus will soon learn many more things about God and his kingdom.

What Matthew calls *the kingdom of heaven* is called the kingdom of God in parallel passages in Mark and Luke. The emphasis of this kingdom is not its location; the emphasis, rather, is the reigning "kingship" of God. People who submit to God's rule are part of his kingdom—both on this present earth and in the future Heaven.

**12. "Whoever has will be given more, and he will have an abundance. Whoever does not have, even what he has will be taken from him.**

What a blessing it is to be part of God's eternal kingdom! The idea expressed in this verse is so important that Jesus repeats it in Matthew 25:29 as part of the summary of the Parable of the Talents. See also Luke 8:18.

## II. THOSE WHO HEAR NOT (MATTHEW 13:13-15)

### A. UNNECESSARY FAILURE (v. 13)

**13. "This is why I speak to them in parables:**
  **'Though seeing, they do not see;**
    **though hearing, they do not hear or understand.'**

When Jesus speaks *in parables*, it brings to light the fact that although the people have eyes capable of normal sight, they *do not* really *see* God's truths at all. And although they have ears capable of receiving normal auditory input, they do not really absorb or *understand* what they are hearing. If Jesus tells them the will of God plainly, they will reject him out of hand. By using parables it is possible that the truth will get past their defenses and penetrate their hearts.

It should not be necessary for Jesus to use a roundabout approach to teach these people. They should be perfectly able to see and hear, but they are not. Their failure to open their hearts causes them to fail to understand God's message.

The parables of Jesus thus serve to separate people into their appropriate categories. First, there are the disciples, the people who have open hearts. They remain with Jesus and go on to learn the deeper truths about God and his kingdom.

*WHAT DO YOU THINK?*

*Jesus told parables so that those who were truly seeking the truth could understand it. Of course, that often meant they had to ask further questions to achieve such learning. How can we identify the true seekers of truth today, and how can we lead them to find it?*

*WHAT DO YOU THINK?*

*What can churches or individual Christians do today to get past people's defenses and share spiritual truth with them?*

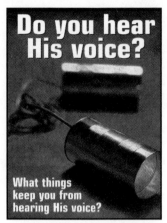

**Do you hear His voice?**

**What things keep you from hearing His voice?**

Visual for lesson 7. *Use this visual as you ask, "What things keep you from hearing his voice?"*

Then there are the people who are only curious. They soon go home, thinking they have heard only unimportant stories about careless farming practices.

Finally, there are the people who come out to detect false teachings for which they can accuse Jesus. They go home frustrated, since all they hear are harmless stories about everyday life. Soon enough, however, Jesus' enemies will understand that he is using parables against them (see Luke 20:19).

### HEARING AND DOING

There once was an executive who would not tolerate disagreement. He had a subordinate who often had to listen to what he, the boss, had to say. In the middle of a monologue, the boss would often pause, and it was obvious that he was waiting for the employee to agree with him.

The employee couldn't be dishonest and lie. Nor could he express disagreement if he wanted to keep his job. So he developed a habit of responding with, "I hear what you're saying." The boss took that to be agreement. Sometimes it was; often it was just a clever way to avoid a heated argument.

We cannot do that with our Lord. We cannot dismiss his words with, "I hear what you are saying." We who hear must do. To merely acknowledge that we have received the message is not enough. We must put it into action. James, the half-brother of our Lord, also has something to say about hearers and doers. He says that a person who hears but doesn't do is like a man who sees himself in a mirror and forgets at once what he looks like (James 1:23, 24).

When we hear God's wisdom on any subject, we should respond as did the young Samuel: "Speak, for your servant is listening" (1 Samuel 3:10). And we should say it with every intention of doing.    —R. C. S.

### B. FULFILLED PROPHECY (v. 14)

14. *"In them is fulfilled the prophecy of Isaiah:*
   *'You will be ever hearing but never understanding;*
   *you will be ever seeing but never perceiving.*

Long ago, the prophet *Isaiah* wrote about the kind of people Jesus is encountering in this narrative (see Isaiah 6:9). The quotation comes at the climax of the well-known vision of Isaiah in which he saw the Lord high and lifted up in his temple. Although Isaiah knew of his own unworthiness, he answered the Lord's call and said, "Here am I. Send me."

God told Isaiah to preach to his people, even though they would not accept the message. *"Be ever hearing,"* Isaiah is to tell them, *"but never understanding."* Even though they would refuse to listen, Isaiah was told to continue calling them to repentance until their cities finally lay wasted and desolate.

Jesus sees in Isaiah's words the parallel to his own situation. Thus the passage has both an immediate application in Isaiah's day and an ultimate fulfillment in Jesus' day. To be honest, should we admit that the words describe many people in our own day as well? Isaiah's words are so important that the apostle Paul repeats them in Acts 28:26, 27. Compare also Jesus' words in John 12:37-41.

### C. STUBBORN REFUSAL (v. 15)

15. *'For this people's heart has become calloused;*
   *they hardly hear with their ears,*
   *and they have closed their eyes.*
*Otherwise they might see with their eyes,*
   *hear with their ears,*
   *understand with their hearts*
*and turn, and I would heal them.'*

The prophecy of Isaiah continues with a very unflattering picture of the people to whom he was to preach, hundreds of years before Christ. There was a reason that *their ears* did not *hear* and their *eyes* did not *see:* it was because their hearts were dull and insensitive. Just as King David had been slow to repent following his sin with Bathsheba, Isaiah's original audience stubbornly refused to face up to their sinfulness and were slow to listen to God.

Like the people in Isaiah's time, many of the people in Jesus' day willfully close their eyes lest at any time they should *see.* They do not want to *hear* or *understand.* By their refusal to listen, they also signify that they do not want to be converted and that they do not want God to heal them. Perhaps they think they don't need any spiritual healing. Does any of this sound familiar?

The problem is on the part of the people, not on the part of God. God is not willing that any should perish, but that all should come to repentance (2 Peter 3:9). If only the people would listen and turn to Jesus, God would gladly forgive them. But even miraculous signs in abundance do not convince many (see John 12:37).

## III. THOSE WHO ARE BLESSED (MATTHEW 13:16, 17)
### A. BLESSING FOR YOU (v. 16)
16. "But blessed are your eyes because they see, and your ears because they hear.

It is truly a blessing for people to be in a position where they are listening to the Word of God! Jesus commends his disciples who have *eyes* that are open to *see* the truth. He congratulates those who have *ears* that are ready to listen to God's will and obey.

Those who open their hearts to Jesus will be taught many things in parables. Whenever it is needed, Jesus takes the time to explain the parables further to them. When people have open hearts and a receptive attitude, God will help them understand.

As followers of Jesus, we look forward to hearing him say to us on Judgment Day, "Well done, good and faithful servant" (see Matthew 25:21). If we expect to have the commendation of the Lord on that day, we must begin with open eyes and ears. Only after we have learned to listen and obey can we expect to hear Christ's words of approval.

### THE RIGHT FREQUENCY

Every radio transmitter has an assigned frequency. Certain frequencies are assigned to shortwave transmitters; others to police, fire, and other emergency services; and still others to commercial radio stations. In order to hear your favorite radio station, you have to tune your radio to the right frequency. If you turn the dial to another frequency, you will not hear what you want to hear or need to hear.

When someone ignores what another is saying, we say, "He tuned her out." We really do decide the things to which we will listen, don't we? We do this physically, and we do this spiritually. Physical hearing is a marvelous gift. Part of our stewardship is to use this gift wisely. But how much more important is "spiritual hearing"! If you keep your spiritual hearing tuned to the divine frequency, you will never be misinformed or led astray. However, if you move the dial of the heart to the devil's frequency, you are certain to be tempted; the longer you stay on that frequency, the more difficult it is to change it.

Our Lord knows what we need to hear. While on earth, Jesus had his own spiritual hearing tuned to the frequency of Heaven. He heard the voice of God. He never tuned his ears to the frequency of evil. We follow his example when we read the Word of God. We do this when we pray. We do this when we listen to Christian music, to sermons, to lessons.

### WHAT DO YOU THINK?

As in Isaiah's time and as in Jesus' time, so it is in our own time that people are reluctant to hear the message even though God is willing to forgive. Why is a message of hope and salvation so often rejected? What can we do about it?

### HOW TO SAY IT
Bathsheba. Bath-SHE-buh.
Ephesians. Ee-FEE-zhunz.
Ezekiel. Ee-ZEEK-ee-ul or Ee-ZEEK-yul.
Galilee. GAL-uh-lee.
Isaiah. Eye-ZAY-uh.
Messiah. Meh-SIGH-uh.
Nathan. NAY-thun (th as in thin).

*Father of Heaven and earth, help us to have open hearts to receive your truth. Help us cast off anything that would interfere with this communication. Forgive us when our eyes have been turned away and our ears have been tuned out. Teach us to listen and obey. In Jesus' name, amen.*

WHAT DO YOU THINK?

*In what ways are we especially blessed? How should we respond to such blessings?*

THOUGHT TO REMEMBER

*"Blessed are your eyes because they see, and your ears because they hear" (Matthew 13:16).*

We are blessed that we live in a time and place where Jesus' message can be heard. To deliberately close our ears to it suggests that we think we know better than God what is best for us. We need to say to ourselves, "Listen up!"   —R. C. S.

### B. ADVANTAGE OVER PROPHETS (v. 17)

**17. "For I tell you the truth, many prophets and righteous men longed to see what you see but did not see it, and to hear what you hear but did not hear it."**

The people who *hear* Jesus speak enjoy a special privilege: they hear things that previously had not been told, even to *prophets and righteous men.* In earlier times God had spoken in veiled prophecies about the messianic age, but he did not fully reveal his ultimate plan to humanity. But with the coming of Jesus Christ, God now reveals what "was not made known to men in other generations" (Ephesians 3:5).

Even the prophets "searched intently and with the greatest care" into the salvation that they foretold for coming generations (see 1 Peter 1:10-12). The prophets searched to learn what events would take place concerning the future sufferings and final glory of the coming Messiah. But God revealed to them that it was not for their own age that certain prophecies were given (e.g., Daniel 12:8, 9).

The ancient prophets were not alone in their yearning to know God's plan. Even the angels longed to look into such things. But neither Old Testament prophets nor angels were told fully the secrets about Jesus and the coming kingdom of God.

In a somewhat similar way to the first-century disciples, we are privileged to hear the gospel of Christ. We should count it a blessing to know the saving truth and we should live up to the responsibility that this blessing carries with it. God has placed in our hands the task of spreading the gospel to the whole world. If we are faithful to the Great Commission of Matthew 28:19, 20, then people of every tribe, tongue, and nation can share the blessing—if they have ears to hear.

### CONCLUSION

Mark Twain wrote an amusing book called *A Connecticut Yankee in King Arthur's Court.* The hero of the story goes back in time and amazes the people of King Arthur's realm by doing things as simple as lighting a match. There is much they cannot understand, because he comes from another world, a place far different from their own.

If a person really could go back in time a thousand years, imagine the difficulty he or she would have trying to explain what a computer is and how it works. Such a time traveler would be dealing with people who have never seen a typewriter, have no concept of electricity, and have never even seen a printed book. Imagine further that the people have little or no interest in even listening.

Jesus faced such a situation, only far more difficult. He actually did come from another world—God's eternal kingdom. His task was to explain the things of Heaven to people on earth. What made it even worse was that many of the people in his audience thought they already knew everything about religion. They closed their eyes and shut off their hearing. They had no interest in learning about God's world; therefore Jesus used parables to try to break through their callous hearts.

The parables of Jesus are timeless. His parables still resonate with us because the stories are so true to life. They illustrate the fact that the God of Heaven is also the God of planet Earth, and his principles are true in both worlds.

# Discovery Learning

*This page contains an alternative lesson plan emphasizing learning activities. Classes
desiring such student involvement will find these suggestions helpful. The next page
is a reproducible activity page to further enhance discovery learning.*

## LEARNING GOALS

After participating in this lesson, each student will be able to:

1. Describe what parables are and why Jesus used them.

2. Explain why some people could not, or would not, understand the parables.

3. Commit himself or herself to taking the steps necessary to learn to listen to Jesus.

## INTO THE LESSON

Begin the lesson by having some fun playing a game to introduce the concept of parables. Before class collect several common household items (toothbrush, fork, etc.). You could also include more unusual items, or even a newspaper or magazine headline from a well-known current event. Place each item in a separate paper bag, or wrap each like a Christmas present, and place them in the front of the class.

Next, divide the class into teams of 3-5 members each. Let each team select one of the wrapped items and present a short lesson about spiritual things using the object as an illustration. This impromptu game can provide much laughter. It will also help explain the format of parables, as ordinary objects or events are used to illustrate a parallel idea about life. This exercise will also increase appreciation for the creativity of Jesus' teaching, as he used very ordinary events and things to explain significant truths in memorable ways.

For the last item, have a small bag of seeds that you will open yourself. Use this as a bridge to share the parable of the sower.

## INTO THE WORD

Use Kistemaker's steps to interpreting parables (page 393) as an outline for discussing the Parable of the Sower.

1. *Life Setting.* Discuss methods of planting. You might want to have an experienced farmer or gardener from your class make a brief presentation on the process of sowing seed by hand and the importance of the soil.

2. *Exact Wording.* Review the specifics of where the seed fell, the composition of each of the soils, and the resulting harvest (or lack thereof). Compare each of the four soils (beside the road, rocky places, among the thorns, and good soil) and the results.

3. *Identify Main Lesson(s).* Have each member of the class work with a partner, trying to summarize the main lesson(s) of the parable in a single sentence. Discuss their conclusions. Write on the board some of the ideas and then work together to try to refine the sentence until the explanation is clear.

4. *Compare with Other Scriptures.* Ask, "How is this parable the same as, and how is it different from, other parables dealing with similar themes?" (For example, we can see a similarity to The Wise and Foolish Builders in Matthew 7:24-27, which illustrates the right response to Jesus' teachings for gaining a firm foundation that will endure through life and its difficulties. On the other hand, The Wheat and the Tares in Matthew 13:24-30 compares the results of good and bad plants growing alongside one another after sowing, with the nature of the soil not being an issue. Although also using sowing as an illustration, the Parable of the Sower, by contrast, is more concerned with the different qualities of soil (receptivity of hearts) involved.

5. *Determine Modern Application.* Consider each of the four soils and try to describe what type of person that would represent in today's society. What would their lives be like? How would you know if you were that person?

## INTO LIFE

Say, "The challenge is to truly 'hear' the parables." Then discuss the difference between just hearing the words and attentively heeding and responding to the message. Note the connection Jesus made between the ears and the heart. Say, "A heart that is hardened and closed to God's message will not listen. Such a person will never truly grasp what Jesus really meant by his teaching. It is only the open and receptive heart (fertile soil) that is truly able to listen and has the ability to truly understand."

Challenge each person to consider which category describes him or her: (1) a curious listener, hearing only interesting and confusing stories; (2) a judgmental listener, predisposed to refute and discredit Jesus, seeing these parables as distractions; (3) a disciple, hearing and eagerly discerning God's Word. Stress that the third type of person is the only one who will truly grasp and obey Jesus' teaching. Close by praying together for tender and receptive hearts.

# Soil Test

Consider each soil type from Jesus' Parable of the Sower. Determine what character traits or behaviors typify a person who is that soil type today. Frankly assess your own life for these traits or behaviors. Then suggest an "action plan" for each: a corrective for the behaviors in the first three types and a means to fortify the good soil character traits.

**SOIL TYPE**    *CHARACTER TRAITS & BEHAVIORS*    *ACTION PLAN*

Path

Rocky Ground

Thorns

Good Soil

# RECEIVING AND GIVING FORGIVENESS

### LESSON 8

## WHY TEACH THIS LESSON?

Clint Eastwood's Academy Award winning motion picture film of 1992, *Unforgiven* (Warner Brothers), was a strong depiction of the consequences of being unforgiving and unforgiven. Revenge, violence, death, and amorality follow a vicious evil precipitated by foolish words.

In today's text Jesus makes it clear that there are stern consequences for failing to forgive. Not a member of your class will escape those days when there are occasions needing forgiveness. Sin builds separation; separation builds resentments; resentments demand retribution . . . or grace and forgiveness.

The lessons of forgiveness in today's text offer the adult learner help at two points: (1) an understanding that God is gracious and forgiving, if he sees true repentance and godly intent in the sinner, and (2) a method for maintaining wholesome relationships with those who sin against him or her personally. Forgiveness is at the heart of both vertical and horizontal human relationships.

## INTRODUCTION

### A. "WITH MALICE TOWARD NONE"

At last the terrible Civil War of the United States was nearly over. Lincoln had won the election to serve a second term as president. He had the daunting task of bringing his nation back together. Many called for vengeance on the southern states. They thought that those states should pay, and pay dearly!

In his second Inaugural Address, delivered on March 4, 1865, Lincoln spoke words of surprising compassion toward those who had been his enemies: "with malice toward none" and "with charity for all" he called on the people "to bind up the nation's wounds, . . . to do all which may achieve and cherish a just and lasting peace." After Lincoln was assassinated, however, his program of "malice toward none" was not carried out. Forgiveness does not seem to be the human way.

Jesus had much to say about forgiveness. Because the Father forgives us, we should be willing to forgive one another (see also Ephesians 4:32). The Parable of the Unforgiving Servant shows us that forgiveness ought to go both ways: when we have received it, we should also give it. Forgiveness is a beautiful thing, but ingratitude is ugly to the core.

### B. LESSON BACKGROUND

Two specific lessons form the immediate background for the Parable of the Unforgiving Servant, which Jesus taught near the close of the final year of his ministry. The first lesson was about God's eagerness to seek and save his lost sheep (see Matthew 18:12-14). Like a shepherd who rejoices to restore one lost sheep to the ninety-nine that are safe in the fold, God is not willing to see even one of his little ones perish. God is not eager to judge and punish; God would far

DEVOTIONAL READING:
2 CORINTHIANS 2:5-11

BACKGROUND SCRIPTURE:
MATTHEW 18:21-35

PRINTED TEXT:
MATTHEW 18:21-35

LESSON AIMS

*After participating in this lesson, each student will be able to:*

*1. Relate the essential details in the Parable of the Unforgiving Servant.*

Jul
24

*2. Explain why receiving forgiveness from God requires passing along that forgiveness to others.*

*3. Commit himself or herself to identifying the people against whom grievances are held and determine to forgive them.*

KEY VERSE

*The servant's master took pity on him, canceled the debt and let him go.* —Matthew 18:27

*LESSON 8 NOTES*

rather accept a sinner's return. This first lesson established the fact that God loves to extend forgiveness.

The second lesson was about the steps that lead to repentance and reconciliation among people (see Matthew 18:15-17). Jesus taught that every effort should be made to bring about repentance and to offer forgiveness.

## I. QUESTION ABOUT FORGIVENESS (MATTHEW 18:21, 22)

### A. PETER'S SELF-ASSURED QUESTION (v. 21)

**21. Then Peter came to Jesus and asked, "Lord, how many times shall I forgive my brother when he sins against me? Up to seven times?"**

*Peter* has heard Jesus teach the principle of forgiveness as early as Matthew 6 in the Sermon on the Mount. At that time Jesus warned, "If you do not forgive men their sins, your Father will not forgive your sins" (Matthew 6:15). As Peter hears Jesus teach about forgiveness again (see Matthew 18:15-17), he mulls this over until a question begins to take shape. If, in fact, Peter does agree to forgive a person who has wronged him, what should he do if that same person wrongs him again? Will Jesus still want him to be forgiving?

With this in mind, Peter asks a question that seems to answer itself. At least the question includes Peter's answer, indicating what he thinks is obviously an extreme limit. Should he forgive the same person as many as *seven times?* Scripture often views seven as the "complete" number—see Leviticus 26:21; Deuteronomy 28:25; Psalm 79:12; and Proverbs 24:16—and Peter clearly thinks that number will be more than adequate as a limit to the times he should *forgive.*

It also seems apparent that Peter plans to keep track of the number of times he forgives. Once he reaches the necessary limit, he can turn off the compassion and turn on the revenge. His forgiveness will be "a limited time offer"!

### B. JESUS' SURPRISING ANSWER (v. 22)

**22. Jesus answered, "I tell you, not seven times, but seventy-seven times.**

Drawing on Genesis 4:24, Jesus shows Peter that what he thinks is a generous amount of forgiveness is far too small. Peter must be astonished at what Jesus states as the better number. *Seventy-seven times*—who could forgive that many times? Who could even keep track of that many times?

Jesus' point, of course, is not that 77 times is the point at which a person properly stops forgiving. He means that God expects us to keep on forgiving far beyond what we normally do. God himself has shown boundless forgiveness toward us, so he has every right to expect that we show that kind of forgiveness toward others.

### KEEPING SCORE

Once there was a lady who took a job where she expected she would be treated unfairly. So she brought along a little notebook and kept it with her at all times. Whenever she experienced what she perceived to be a slight, whenever she encountered anything that could possibly be interpreted as offensive, she wrote it down.

Soon she had a long list that seemed to her to confirm her initial expectations. Of course, many of the things on her list would have gone unnoticed if she had not written them down. Anything that could possibly be seen as offensive was assumed to be intentionally offensive. She was keeping score! If she had begun her job with a different attitude, she would have had very little to write down.

Are you this kind of person, always on the lookout for wrongful deeds done to you? Do you focus so intently on the negative that you interpret every word or deed in the worst possible light?

*WHAT DO YOU THINK?*

*Probably we all know people who "forgive" but do not forget. What is wrong with this approach? How can we be sure we don't fall into this pattern?*

*[First Corinthians 13 can be important to consider in your answer.]*

*WHAT DO YOU THINK?*

*Peter must have thought he was being very "righteous" in offering to forgive seven times, but Jesus thought otherwise! Have you ever made what you thought was a generous or righteous gesture, only to find out it was not appropriate or appreciated? How do you handle such a situation? What can you learn from it?*

If you are, consider this: God has forgiven us far more often than we will ever be called upon to forgive someone else. While it may be difficult to forget as well as to forgive, we certainly can put these things away in the back of our minds. We need not dwell on them, and we must not keep score.     —R. C. S.

## II. RECEIVING FORGIVENESS (MATTHEW 18:23-27)

### A. UNPAYABLE DEBT (vv. 23-25)

**23. "Therefore, the kingdom of heaven is like a king who wanted to settle accounts with his servants.**

Jesus then goes on to teach a parable to illustrate this principle of being ready to forgive far more often than we usually do. Like all of Jesus' parables, this story has a true-to-life tone with which the audience can easily identify. Life in God's *kingdom* will be like the situation of a certain *king* and *his servants*. These servants are actually the king's slaves, and the king is later called their "lord" or "master" (see vv. 25-27). They are not just his hired hands; they are his property.

The time comes for this king to take an inventory of what his servants owe him. He looks over his books to see what has been borrowed and what has been repaid. He takes action to collect old debts when the situation requires it.

**24. "As he began the settlement, a man who owed him ten thousand talents was brought to him.**

The king has not gone very far in figuring accounts with each of the servants when he discovers that one servant owes him *ten thousand talents*. A talent is a unit of monetary exchange worth six thousand denarii; a single denarius, for its part, is a day's wage for a laborer (see Matthew 20:1-15). So by multiplication we can see that what this servant owes his king is extreme indeed! It is far more than the servant can ever hope to repay.

Jesus' audience probably chuckles at the extreme predicament in which that servant finds himself. The poor fellow will not ever be able to repay that kind of money. The amount of money in the story is an obvious exaggeration or hyperbole; no earthly king would lend that kind of money to a mere servant. (See 1 Chronicles 29:3, 4 for a description of David's personal fortune.) But the principle of the parable is not an exaggeration; Jesus' hearers see it in real life all the time: a man borrows money, gets in over his head, and has no way to pay it back.

### HOW MUCH DO YOU OWE?

We are all familiar with debt. It is a part of life. Banking systems would collapse if no one borrowed money. Monetary debt touches all of life.

However, it is probable that you do not know the actual amount of your country's national debt. It is likely that you do not know the exact amount of the debt of your church. It is even possible that you do not know the precise amount of your own personal debt. Neither do we know the magnitude of our debt to God. We know that we have a huge sin debt. But it is possible—indeed, it is likely—that we have committed some sins unaware.

Our debt of sin is so great that it required the sacrifice of Jesus on the cross. The good news is that the debt is now paid. A hymn says, "The old account was settled long ago." Another hymn says, "Jesus paid it all!" No one is going to pay your personal debt for you. It's rare for an individual to pay a church's debt all by himself or herself. We must all participate. No country will come along and pay our national debt. It will be up to us. But the good news is that the sin debt we could never have paid has been paid—in full. "Jesus paid it all. All to him I owe."     —R. C. S.

**25. "Since he was not able to pay, the master ordered that he and his wife and his children and all that he had be sold to repay the debt.**

Visual for lesson 8. *Use this visual aid to start a discussion on how the cross relates to person-to-person forgiveness.*

When the king determines that he will not carry such a large debt any longer, he demands immediate payment. When the slave cannot *pay*, the king orders him and his whole family to *be sold*. It is a harsh decision, but the king has the legal right to reclaim at least a portion of his loss by whatever means he can.

Slavery to pay debts was common in the ancient world (see 2 Kings 4:1). But economic slavery was strictly and humanely regulated under the Old Testament laws (see Leviticus 25:39-55). Jesus is not approving slavery, of course, but his story tells what a king might do with a man who could not *repay* a *debt*. Jesus speaks in images that are understandable to the people of the day.

### B. UNDESERVED FORGIVENESS (vv. 26, 27)

**26. "The servant fell on his knees before him. 'Be patient with me,' he begged, 'and I will pay back everything.'**

*The servant* is distraught at the king's decree. He falls at the feet of the king in the Eastern posture of obeisance, showing his reverence for the king's power and position.

Again, Jesus' audience must chuckle as they hear the servant promise that if the king would just *be patient with* him, then he would repay the entire amount. A mere servant can never repay such an impossible debt! The servant asks for patience, but does he think his master should be patient for the numerous lifetimes it would take to repay that amount? The servant's promise is obviously empty; the servant's doom is certainly sealed.

**27. "The servant's master took pity on him, canceled the debt and let him go.**

Then the story takes a surprising twist. What kind of *master* is this who is so moved with compassion for the slave that he releases him from the hopeless predicament? To freely forgive the man such an incredible sum and ask nothing in return is startling, indeed! *The debt* is *canceled;* the man is free.

Such generosity rarely happens in the real world, but this story is about the kingdom of Heaven. God is the King in this kingdom, and it is entirely within his nature to show such mercy. When we hear this parable, at some point we begin to recognize not only God as the King, but ourselves as hopeless debtors. We realize that God has forgiven us a sin debt that we can never pay. For this we should be eternally grateful.

### III. WITHHOLDING FORGIVENESS (MATTHEW 18:28-30)

### A. SMALL DEBT (vv. 28, 29)

**28. "But when that servant went out, he found one of his fellow servants who owed him a hundred denarii. He grabbed him and began to choke him. 'Pay back what you owe me!' he demanded.**

No sooner has the slave been forgiven the huge debt than he goes out to collect a much smaller debt from *one of his fellow servants*. The debt of a hundred denarii is a hundred days' wages for an ordinary laborer. This is not "pocket change," but it is certainly miniscule when compared with the ten thousand talents of verse 24! Nevertheless, the servant grabs the other man by the throat, begins choking him, and insists on immediate payment. Even though the first slave has been shown a beautiful example of how to have a forgiving spirit, he apparently learned nothing from the experience.

Anyone hearing this parable immediately begins to feel the injustice of the situation. How can the forgiven slave show such ingratitude? Why couldn't he show some compassion for a much smaller debt?

**29. "His fellow servant fell to his knees and begged him, 'Be patient with me, and I will pay you back.'**

---

*WHAT DO YOU THINK?*

*Either the servant was lying or he was delusional! He could never repay that debt. When people make promises you know they cannot keep, how can you respond in a way that is in their best interest as well as protecting yourself from being stuck with their unfulfilled promises?*

*WHAT DO YOU THINK?*

*Sometimes people minimize the second servant's debt, interpreting it as almost pocket change. But it represented more than three months' earnings! How does recognizing this help you to understand what Jesus is demanding in his teaching on forgiveness?*

The reply of *his fellow servant* is the same as that spoken by the first servant to the king. Jesus intends that the crowd see that the plea for forgiveness is the same. The same result should be expected.

## B. IMPROPER PENALTY (v. 30)

30. *"But he refused. Instead, he went off and had the man thrown into prison until he could pay the debt.*

The unforgiving servant refuses to extend the kind of compassion he has been shown by the king. Instead, he takes his fellow slave and has him *thrown into* debtor's *prison*. The audience understands that a man thrown into prison has no way to earn money to *pay* off his debt. (His only hope is that his relatives and friends might care enough to contribute money to his release fund.) Knowing the harsh unfairness of debtor's prison makes their sense of injustice grow.

## IV. LESSON ABOUT FORGIVENESS (MATTHEW 18:31-35)

### A. SENSE OF INDIGNATION (vv. 31-34)

31. *"When the other servants saw what had happened, they were greatly distressed and went and told their master everything that had happened.*

When the rest of the master's *servants* find out *what* has *happened*, they are *distressed*. They know a miscarriage of justice when they see one. So they go to *their master* and report the whole story.

Like the servants in the story, we should realize that we are all servants of the same Master in Heaven. Unlike the situation in the story, however, no one needs to go and tell God when a fellow servant is being unfair. God already knows.

32. *"Then the master called the servant in. 'You wicked servant,' he said, 'I canceled all that debt of yours because you begged me to.*

The forgiving *master* is a generous man, but he also has a keen sense of what is fair and what is unfair. He summons *the servant* and calls him *wicked*. While the man can protest that he has not broken any laws, the master's accusation is correct. Because the master had forgiven him, the master has every right to expect that the slave would share this graciousness with his fellow slave.

We who serve the heavenly Master hope to hear him greet us one day with the words, "Well done, good and faithful servant!" What a devastating surprise it would be if we are summoned to his throne to hear him say, "You wicked servant!" We should pay special attention to this parable, therefore, to be sure we hear the words we want to hear on that day.

33. *'Shouldn't you have had mercy on your fellow servant just as I had on you?'*

Doing what is right is sometimes more than merely doing what is legal. What love demands is more than what law requires. When the servant was shown *mercy*, a profound sense of gratitude should have filled his heart. When he went out and attacked his *fellow servant*, he showed that he felt no gratitude at all. He felt no need to extend the master's forgiveness to others.

34. *"In anger his master turned him over to the jailers to be tortured, until he should pay back all he owed.*

The *master* has a right to be angry. His generosity has been treated with contempt. So he sends the slave *to be tortured* until he pays everything he owes. Even with contributions from relatives and friends—if the wretched slave still has any!—there is no way he can ever pay enough to escape his torment.

Jesus' parable no doubt stirs several emotions in the crowd. First, they may feel sympathy for the slave in the impossible predicament. Then they feel amazement at the master's compassion. Then comes anger at the slave's ingratitude. Finally, the crowd feels a sense of stern justice when the slave gets what he deserves.

### WHAT DO YOU THINK?

The "fellow servants" in this story "snitched" on the unmerciful servant. When is it right to report an offense, and when ought we to "mind our own business"?

[Psalm 82:3 and Proverbs 31:9 can help to direct your discussion.]

### HOME DAILY BIBLE READINGS

Monday, July 18—We Sin, But God Forgives (Daniel 9: 4-10)

Tuesday, July 19—God Does Forgive Our Sins (Psalm 32:1-5)

Wednesday, July 20—God Is a Forgiving God (Psalm 86:1-7)

Thursday, July 21—You Must Forgive (Luke 17:1-5)

Friday, July 22—Forgive the Offender (2 Corinthians 2:5-11)

Saturday, July 23—About Forgiveness (Matthew 18:21-27)

Sunday, July 24—The Unforgiving Servant (Matthew 18:28-35)

## B. CALL FOR A FORGIVING HEART (v. 35)

**35. "This is how my heavenly Father will treat each of you unless you forgive your brother from your heart."**

Jesus concludes his parable with a stern warning. Just as the indignant master turned the unforgiving servant over to be tortured, likewise shall the *heavenly Father* do to those who do not *forgive.* Jesus does not just recommend forgiveness as a nice thing to do; he says to do it or else!

Furthermore, when we forgive one another it must be more than mere words. Jesus insists that our forgiveness must come from the *heart.* Even if we have been seriously wronged by another, we must be ready to forgive. God has shown us how to forgive; now he demands that we follow his example when our fellow servant repents (Luke 17:3).

Finally, it is not enough to forgive in the abstract. It costs nothing to forgive vague groups of people for broad, generic offenses. Jesus requires us to extend forgiveness to our brother (a specific person) for the trespasses (specific wrongs) committed against us. Therefore, the best way to show that we have learned his lesson is for each of us to identify such people as we ought to forgive. Then we should take the appropriate, biblical steps toward reconciliation.

### THE HEART OF FORGIVENESS

At the heart of the word *forgiveness* is the little word *give.* Often we cannot forgive until we give up something. Sometimes it is our pride that we must give up. Sometimes it is our delusion that we are always right.

Sometimes we must *give in* so that we may forgive. We cannot always have our own way. We cannot always win. To hold on to power may make it impossible for us to forgive.

Sometimes we must *give over.* We cannot control the lives of others and we should not try. So we give people over to themselves and to God. Controlling persons find forgiveness very difficult.

Sometimes we must *give way.* We must allow others the freedom that God has already given them. That includes the freedom to make choices that may not always be the best choices. It includes the freedom to make mistakes.

But if we would be forgiving we must never *give out.* That is a natural inference of what Jesus is saying. We should not tire of forgiving others. What if God became tired of forgiving us? What if God set a time limit and we would have exhausted his forgiveness after one year or ten or twenty?

We may rest secure in the knowledge that God forgives us without limit upon our sincere repentance. When we forgive others, we, in a way, show them the nature of God. This is not a burden; it is a privilege.  —R. C. S.

## CONCLUSION

According to Alexander Pope (1688–1744), "To err is human, to forgive divine." People are going to make mistakes; they are going to let each other down. The great heart of God is ready, however, to forgive our trespasses and errors upon our repentance. Forgiveness is one of the most beautiful of all the divine traits. To say, "to forgive is divine" must not, however, mean that we think God ought to do all the forgiving. God expects his children to resemble their Father.

If forgiving is such a good thing, then why are we so reluctant to do it? Perhaps we should reword Pope's proverb: "To err is human; to refuse to forgive is very human, too!" Do we think that an offense against us is more outrageous than an offense against God? Do we fear that by forgiving the offender we let him or her off the hook too easily? Whatever the supposed reason, we need to learn the lesson from Jesus about receiving, then giving, forgiveness.

# Discovery Learning

*This page contains an alternative lesson plan emphasizing learning activities. Classes
desiring such student involvement will find these suggestions helpful. The next page
is a reproducible activity page to further enhance discovery learning.*

## LEARNING GOALS

After participating in this lesson, each student will be
able to:

1. Relate the essential details in the story of the unforgiving servant.

2. Explain why receiving forgiveness from God requires passing along that forgiveness to others.

3. Commit himself or herself to identifying the people
against whom grievances are held and determine to forgive them.

## INTO THE LESSON

Begin by taking a pen-and-paper survey of class members. You will be gathering information in a format similar to that used in the television game show, *Family Feud*.

Before class, prepare the surveys on letter-size paper
with the following categories (feel free to add additional
categories): Name a well-known case of financial mismanagement. Name an incident of someone not being
punished for wrongdoing. Name a well-known case of
criminal activity. Name an action or behavior that causes
great offense in personal relationships. Name a major
problem in personal relationships.

Collect the papers after five minutes. Discuss the results and list answers on the chalkboard for each of the
categories. Consider the topic of forgiveness by discussing the following questions. "If you were a judge,
for which of the crimes listed above would you tend to
punish most severely?" "Should court systems show
forgiveness, or is that only a person-to-person issue?
Why?" "For which offenses would you be most likely to
show mercy personally?" "Considering the personal offenses, which of those listed would be most difficult to
forgive? Why?"

## INTO THE WORD

Before class, select three individuals to read the quotations from within the parable that is part of today's
text. The quotations are in verses 26b, 28b (man with
large debt), verse 29b (man with small debt), and verses
32b, 33 (the king). Encourage participants to read their
parts with passion and enthusiasm.

Next, review the story by explaining its major elements: *Setting* (first-century kingdom with financial liability punishable by imprisonment); *Characters* (king,
servant with incredibly huge debt, servant with small

debt, fellow servants who worked for the king and observed the events); *Plot* (review the order of events, highlighting the elements of surprise); and *Big Idea* (the main
point[s] of the story). **Optional:** to explain the theme,
have class members work with a partner to summarize
the main point(s) of the story. Review their ideas and
help refine their statements. Your goal is to help them
convey the message of the story clearly and concisely.

Compare and contrast today's parable with Luke
7:36-50. You will note the similarities (two men were in
debt and unable to repay) as well as differences (in
Luke, both owed their debt to the same moneylender,
and both were forgiven). Allow several minutes to discuss the relationship of Luke 7:36-50 with that of the
parable from today's lesson.

## INTO LIFE

Next, split the class into small groups and give each
group the assignment of "rewriting" the parable in order
to help them see how this lesson may apply to modern,
real-life situations. Remind them that the *Big Idea* must
still be the same; this, in turn, demands that the *Plot* be
very similar. What would be different are the *Setting* and
*Characters*.

Suggest each group go through the following steps to
develop their retold parable. First, select a contemporary
setting (situation at the office, shop, school, home, etc.).
Next, identify the main characters, as appropriate for the
setting (supervisor at work and employees, parents and
children, etc.).

Next, describe what the offense was. That is, what is
the "debt" that is owed? Note that this does not have to
be financial, but could simply be a wrong committed
that has consequences for another person. The offenses
for each of those with "debts" should be very similar in
type, but very different in degree (two crimes of embezzlement, but of different amounts of money involved,
etc.). Allow time for each group to prepare and present
its version to the class.

Challenge class members to consider one situation
where they know they should forgive a person who has
wronged them. Distribute pieces of paper with the
phrase: "Forgiven People Forgive Others" as a reminder
of what God has done when forgiving us upon our repentance, and the opportunity (and challenge) that that
gives us to forgive others.

# "Survey Said . . . "

Complete the following survey. Then consider the questions cited below.

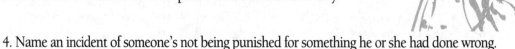

1. Name a well-known public case of extreme financial mismanagement.


2. What causes the majority of financial problems?


3. Name two or three well-known public cases of criminal activity.


4. Name an incident of someone's not being punished for something he or she had done wrong.


5. Name an action that causes the greatest offense in personal relationships.


6. What causes the major problems in personal relationships?



If you were a judge, for which of the crimes listed above would you tend to punish most severely? For which would you be most likely to show mercy?



Considering the personal offenses listed above, which would be most difficult to forgive? Why?


# Getting Personal

Is there someone who has offended you whom you have not forgiven? If so, complete the following.

Offender:

How I was hurt:

What I can do to move toward forgiveness and reconciliation:


When I will take the first step in doing so:

# MEETING HUMAN NEEDS

**LESSON 9**

## WHY TEACH THIS LESSON?

Sam Hurley grew up in the deprived and near lawless mountains of eastern Kentucky in the early twentieth century. His life knew physical need and emotional abuse, fear, and uncertainty. His surprising submission to the lordship of Christ made him a new creature. Volatility, vulgarity, and violence gave way to a new heart of concern, compassion, and child welfare.

Hurley's Mountain Mission School, one of the largest children's homes in America, continues to serve needy children and families to the present—all because one man understood Jesus' call to provide clothes for the naked, water for the thirsty, food for the hungry, nurture for the spiritually bereft.

Who knows but what there is another Sam Hurley in your class, one who needs the stimulus of the Spirit to meet needs in Christ's name? The affluence of Christians in the western world awaits the challenge of a cry from a prison, from a drought-stricken third world country, from a shattered inner city down the road. Today's text will allow you the privilege of sounding that cry.

## INTRODUCTION

### A. "ALL RISE!"

"All rise!" It is a familiar courtroom scene. The spectators suddenly stop their nervous chatter and stand up. The defendant, lawyers, and jurors come to attention. All eyes are fixed on the robed figure who strides importantly into the room. The judge takes a seat at an elevated desk, looking down on the proceedings. In this courtroom the judge is in complete control.

One day the command, "All rise!" will be given for the final time. On that day it will not be addressed to a few dozen spectators in some local court; it will be addressed to the whole world. The dead will rise from their graves; then the living saints will join them. Together they will meet the Lord in the air (see 1 Thessalonians 4:16, 17).

On the last great day of human history, the Lord Jesus will sit in judgment over all the earth. He will judge in behalf of the Father, and it is the Father's will that the Son exercise this judgment (see John 5:22, 27, 30). When Jesus considers the lives of people, one thing he will be looking for as evidence of faith in him is how they have treated their fellow humans. Have they cared about the needy? Have they done anything to meet human needs? In today's lesson, the Parable of the Sheep and the Goats, Jesus shows how important he thinks this is. In his eyes, when we do an act of kindness to one of the least of his brethren, we do it for him.

### B. LESSON BACKGROUND

Sometime during his final week—probably on Tuesday—Jesus taught in the temple and answered challenges by various religious leaders (see Matthew 21–23). Later, he left the temple and taught his disciples privately at the Mount of Olives. He told them what to expect in the future, both at the fall of Jerusalem (A.D. 70) and at the time of the second coming (see Matthew 24).

DEVOTIONAL READING:
LUKE 6:27-31
BACKGROUND SCRIPTURE:
MATTHEW 25:31-46
PRINTED TEXT:
MATTHEW 25:31-46

LESSON AIMS

After participating in this lesson, each student will be able to:

1. List some acts of mercy that the Lord expects to be done in his name.

2. Explain why meeting the needs of others is so important in the eyes of Jesus.

3. Decide what specific acts of mercy he or she will to do in the coming week.

Jul
31

KEY VERSE

"The King will reply, 'I tell you the truth, whatever you did for one of the least of these brothers of mine, you did for me.'"
—Matthew 25:40

*Lesson 9 Notes*

Then Jesus told three parables to show his disciples that they needed to be ready for his coming. The first was the Parable of the Ten Virgins. Five were foolish and five were wise (see Matthew 25:1-13). Some were ready when the bridegroom finally arrived; some were not. "Therefore keep watch," said Jesus, "because you do not know the day or the hour" (v. 13).

The second story was the Parable of the Talents (see Matthew 25:14-30). When a certain master went away "on a journey," he gave each of his servants a number of talents (money). Upon his return, he summoned the servants to find out what they had accomplished. The faithful and industrious were rewarded, but a "wicked, lazy" servant was cast into the outer darkness, where there would be weeping and gnashing of teeth.

The third parable was the climax of all that Jesus had been teaching about the end times. The Parable of the Sheep and the Goats is a dramatic picture of Judgment Day. Jesus sits as King on a glorious throne and separates the nations into two groups, just as a shepherd separates the sheep from the goats. What will be interesting for our study of this passage is the basis on which Jesus will evaluate and categorize people. We will take note of the importance of meeting human needs, and we will consider how the necessity of good deeds is in harmony with the Bible's teaching of salvation by grace.

## I. THE JUDGE (MATTHEW 25:31-33)

### A. JUDGE'S GLORY (v. 31)

*31. "When the Son of Man comes in his glory, and all the angels with him, he will sit on his throne in heavenly glory.*

*Son of Man* is Jesus' favorite self-designation. This description emphasizes how completely he identifies with the human race. He lived among us, faced our temptations, and felt our pain. He experienced firsthand what it was like to be hungry, thirsty, homeless, and ignored. The imagery of Son of Man in Daniel 7:13, 14 speaks to his qualifications to sit as our final judge.

No one knows the day when Jesus will come, but the fact that he will return is certain. Unlike his lowly entrance into this world as a baby at Bethlehem, at his second coming he will appear in all his brilliant majesty. The *"glory* of the Lord" that shone around the shepherds when Jesus was born will be but a faint candle compared with the shining grandeur that will surround him at that day.

Jesus will be accompanied by *all the angels* of Heaven at his second coming. They who praised him at his incarnation will rejoice to see his total victory over all evil. He will sit upon a splendid *throne*, surrounded by glory. This imagery is repeated in various ways in Zechariah 14:5; Matthew 16:27; 19:28; and Jude 14.

### B. JUDGE'S TASK (vv. 32, 33)

*32. "All the nations will be gathered before him, and he will separate the people one from another as a shepherd separates the sheep from the goats.*

In the dramatic scene Jesus describes, *all the nations* will be summoned to stand trial *before him*. People will not be able to go to the god of their choice; they will answer to Jesus. Certain nations will not be excused because of their remoteness; all will be present to answer to the Son of Man.

Then, just as a shepherd *separates* his *sheep from the goats,* Jesus will separate the righteous from the wicked. In the same way that a shepherd has no difficulty telling which is which, Jesus will be able to make a clear and correct judgment. As Abraham said of God in the Old Testament (Genesis 18:25), the Judge of all the earth will do right. See also Ezekiel 34:17, 20, 22.

*33. "He will put the sheep on his right and the goats on his left.*

*What Do You Think?*

Jesus says "all" nations will be gathered before him in judgment. What does this say about the imperative of missions? How would you answer those who say people who do not have an opportunity to accept the gospel cannot be judged as if they rejected it?

[You will undoubtedly find Romans 1:18-32 useful in your discussion.]

To be on the *right* hand is to be on the side of approval and acceptance (for instance, see Psalm 110:1 and Acts 7:55). In the scene described by Jesus, to be on the *left* side represents rejection. When the shepherd separates the *sheep* and *goats*, the sheep are put on the favored side.

It is interesting that Jesus describes only two groups: sheep and goats. There are no "almost-sheep" or "partly-goat" categories. When Jesus examines the hearts of people on Judgment Day, there will be no middle ground. We are either for him or against him (see Matthew 12:30; Mark 9:40). While we may see human behavior in shades of gray, Jesus will be able to pronounce judgment clearly and decisively. Each person will be either saved or lost.

## II. THE BLESSED (MATTHEW 25:34-40)

### A. APPROVAL FOR THE BLESSED (v. 34)

**34. "Then the King will say to those on his right, 'Come, you who are blessed by my Father; take your inheritance, the kingdom prepared for you since the creation of the world.**

Once the peoples of all nations have been separated and sent to their rightful places on one side or the other, King Jesus will announce his reward for those *on his right*. They are the sheep; they are the ones who have followed the good shepherd. They know the shepherd's voice, and he knows them by name (see John 10:2-4, 12-14). Jesus will call them to his side and confer blessings.

Even as God was creating "the heavens and the earth" (Genesis 1:1), he was already preparing a place for his faithful children to spend eternity (compare Luke 12:32). This not only tells us something about Heaven, it also tells us something about God. He has always wanted us to be with him in Heaven.

### B. DEEDS OF THE BLESSED (vv. 35, 36)

**35. 'For I was hungry and you gave me something to eat, I was thirsty and you gave me something to drink, I was a stranger and you invited me in,**

King Jesus lists the acts of mercy done to him by the righteous. They are the ones who *gave* him food when he *was hungry* and *something to drink* when he was *thirsty*. They gave him shelter when he needed it. The King does not overlook or forget any kindness they have shown.

Such acts are not usually considered as acts of worship or matters of religious devotion. For some people, in fact, giving a little help to needy people is nothing more than a way to get rid of them. But for people who really know God, meeting human needs can be the purest form of religion (see James 1:27). Jesus' parable shows us that meeting human needs is a significant act in the sight of God. See also Isaiah 58:7.

### A DRINK OF WATER

It has been over forty years since the movie *Ben-Hur* won the Academy Award for "Best Picture." The movie was an adaptation of the book written by Civil War General Lew Wallace (1827–1905). Many people do not realize that the subtitle of the book is *A Tale of the Christ*.

Two of the most compelling scenes in the movie focus on the giving of drinks of water. Early in the movie, the Romans are leading Judah Ben-Hur on a forced march. He has been denied food and water; he is terribly weak. A man steps forward to offer Ben-Hur a drink of water. We never see the man's face, but it is obvious that it is Jesus. Much later in the story, Ben-Hur has returned to Jerusalem. He follows along as Jesus is led through the streets of the city and out to Golgotha. In one of the cinema's most touching moments, Ben-Hur is able to give a drink of water to Jesus after he has fallen beneath the weight of the cross.

WHAT DO YOU THINK?

What significance do you see in the King's statement that the kingdom inherited by those on the right was "prepared for you since the creation of the world"?

WHAT DO YOU THINK?

Suppose a visitor to the class today said, "I belong to the Brothers of Fraternity lodge, and we do more to help the hungry and sick and homeless than your church does! Why should I join the church? It sounds to me like I've already done my part!" How would you respond?

## HOW TO SAY IT

Cana. KAY-nuh.

Ephesians. Ee-FEE-zhunz.

Ezekiel. Ee-ZEEK-ee-ul or Ee-ZEEK-yul.

Galatians. Guh-LAY-shunz.

Golgotha. GAHL-guh-thuh.

Isaiah. Eye-ZAY-uh.

Jerusalem. Juh-ROO-suh-lem.

Thessalonians. Thess-uh-LO-nee-unz (th as in thin).

Zechariah. Zek-uh-RYE-uh.

Lew Wallace wrote fiction, but the inclusion of the opportunity for Ben-Hur to return the kindness of Jesus may have been more than a brilliant literary device. It may have been General Wallace's gentle reminder to us that every opportunity to meet the needs of another is an opportunity to minister to Jesus by ministering to someone he loves. —T. A. C.

**36. '. . . I needed clothes and you clothed me, I was sick and you looked after me, I was in prison and you came to visit me.'**

The King continues to list the ways in which he was served. This much emphasis on service may well make us think Judgment Day will be merely a time for counting up good deeds and merit points. Such a view would contradict all the Scriptures emphasizing that we are saved by God's grace and Jesus' atoning death (e.g., Ephesians 1:7; 2:8, 9). The story of Ebenezer Scrooge is heartwarming to watch at Christmastime. But this tale shows us false doctrine when Scrooge is able to "redeem himself" by his own good works.

On the other hand, we should not think that a lack of good deeds will not matter to God. How shall this tension between grace and good works be resolved? In truth, there is both divine initiative and human response in salvation. Salvation by God's grace must be followed by appropriate good works (see Ephesians 2:10). Salvation based on faith in Jesus Christ must allow that faith to express itself through love (see Galatians 5:6). If a person claims to have saving faith but exhibits no good works, his or her so-called faith is dead (see James 2:26). We are not saved by works, but we are saved for works.

### C. SURPRISE OF THE BLESSED (vv. 37-40)

**37. "Then the righteous will answer him, 'Lord, when did we see you hungry and feed you, or thirsty and give you something to drink?**

There is a wonderful innocence in the question asked by the righteous. They are completely unaware of ever having done the acts of mercy for their Lord. When they gave food and drink to needy people, it was not with any thought of impressing the Master. Their acts of mercy were simply the natural outgrowth of hearts that knew the love of God.

**38, 39. 'When did we see you a stranger and invite you in, or needing clothes and clothe you? When did we see you sick or in prison and go to visit you?'**

The righteous continue to protest that they have done nothing for their Lord. When they provided shelter and clothing, it was simply for people in need, not for the Lord. When they went to care for the sick and the imprisoned, they had no idea they were serving the Master.

When the righteous see needy people, they do not make the usual excuses for doing nothing. They do not accuse the hungry of being lazy; they feed them. They do not let sickness keep them away; they visit them. They do not blame those in prison for causing their own predicament; they go to help them. In all of this they have no conscious thought of earning "merit" or impressing anyone.

**40. "The King will reply, 'I tell you the truth, whatever you did for one of the least of these brothers of mine, you did for me.'**

Because the King loves his people and identifies with them, anyone who helps them is helping the King. Even serving one of the least is not overlooked. No needy person is so insignificant that we can ignore his or her plight. When we give our time and resources to serve the needy, we are serving the Lord (see also Proverbs 19:17).

On an earlier occasion Jesus assured his disciples that even giving a cup of water in his name would not go unnoticed. He promised that whoever would do

## WHAT DO YOU THINK?

Aren't there some needy who are lazy or have brought their problems on themselves? How should we respond to their needs?

[Make sure to consider 2 Thessalonians 3:10 in your answer].

this "because you belong to Christ" would not lose his or her reward (see Mark 9:41). It is not the size of the deed but the state of the heart that matters.

## III. THE CURSED (MATTHEW 25:41-46)

### A. CONDEMNATION FOR THE CURSED (v. 41)

**41.** *"Then he will say to those on his left, 'Depart from me, you who are cursed, into the eternal fire prepared for the devil and his angels.*

The penalty for the wicked is stunningly severe. They are banished from the presence of their Master as those who are accursed. They are thrown into a *fire* that will burn for eternity.

The flames of Hell are the everlasting fire *prepared* in the beginning *for the devil* and his evil helpers. God does not want people to burn in Hell (see 2 Peter 3:9), but people who follow the devil will share his destiny. They will follow him into that same terrible place.

It should not be overlooked that two things are said to be prepared by God in this parable. The eternal kingdom has been prepared from the very beginning for God's children to inherit. Hell has been prepared for the devil *and his angels* (demons). See also Matthew 7:23; 2 Peter 2:4; Jude 7; and Revelation 20:10.

### B. FAILURES OF THE CURSED (vv. 42, 43)

**42, 43.** *'For I was hungry and you gave me nothing to eat, I was thirsty and you gave me nothing to drink, I was a stranger and you did not invite me in, I needed clothes and you did not clothe me, I was sick and in prison and you did not look after me.'*

The "goats" in Jesus' parable have totally failed to care about other people. Their complete lack of concern exposes the state of their hearts. Evil hearts and paucity of good deeds go hand in hand. Ignoring people who are *hungry, thirsty,* homeless, ill-clothed, *sick,* and imprisoned shows that the "goats" know nothing of the love of God.

#### TAKE DOWN THE SIGN?

A car loaded with college students missed a sharp curve on a narrow road and careened into a large tree, seriously injuring one young man. The other young men found themselves in the middle of nowhere—in desperate need of help. One of the students started running to find a house with a phone. To his astonishment, the first house he found had a sign in the yard: Doctor's Office.

The doctor answered the door himself, but explained that he was retired and no longer practiced his profession. The young man angrily responded, "Doctor, if you aren't going to practice medicine, please take down your sign!"

Does the church of Jesus Christ need to take down her signs? We may be very good at planning and executing impressive worship services, but are we busy representing the compassion of Christ to "the least, the last, and the lost"? Do we remember that Jesus seemed to be very comfortable with the poor, the hungry, the sick, and social outcasts?

Have you visited someone in prison, worked in a soup kitchen, or opened your home to someone in need? We often justify our lack of concern for the less fortunate by saying their poor decisions put them in adverse circumstances. Perhaps we should remember that Jesus is the one who looks beyond our situations to see our need. Are your eyes and heart open to "the least of these"? —T. A. C.

### C. PROTEST OF THE CURSED (vv. 44-46)

**44.** *"They also will answer, 'Lord, when did we see you hungry or thirsty or a stranger or needing clothes or sick or in prison, and did not help you?'*

"As ye have done it unto one of the least of these my brethren, ye have done it unto me."
—Matthew 25:40

Visual for lesson 9. *Use this visual to ask, "Who does God want you to minister to today?"*

## PRAYER

*Our kind and compassionate Father, thank you for caring about our needs. Help us to become more aware of the needs of people in our world, and help us to have a more compassionate heart. Lead us to someone whom we can serve in your name. And as we do, make us realize that the most compassionate thing we can do is to offer the gospel of eternal life. In Jesus' name, amen.*

## WHAT DO YOU THINK?

*Many people, even among believers, question the existence of Hell. "How could a loving God consign people to eternal torment?" they reason. How would you respond?*

When the wicked are bewildered and ignorant about why the *Lord* is disgusted with them, they show how little they understand God. They admit, in effect, that they have ignored the needs of their fellow humans.

The wicked attempt to defend themselves by implying that if they had known a needy person was actually the Lord, then they would have helped him. They perhaps assume that helping a needy person who is not the Lord is irrelevant and unnecessary. Just before his conversion, Saul of Tarsus learned that persecuting Christians was the same as persecuting Christ (see Acts 9:5).

**45. "He will reply, 'I tell you the truth, whatever you did not do for one of the least of these, you did not do for me.'"**

The judgment of the Master leaves no doubt about what the problem is: If they do not care about people, then they do not care about him. Since all human beings are created in God's image and reflect something of his nature, anyone who fails to help them is failing God. If even *the least of these* is slighted, God takes it personally. Anyone who loves the Father will love his children, too. See 1 John 4:20.

**46. "Then they will go away to eternal punishment, but the righteous to eternal life."**

Jesus describes eternity in only two categories: *eternal punishment* or *eternal life* (see Daniel 12:2; John 5:29). There is no "in between" place such as a "purgatory" where half-goats go to get their sins burned away before eventually entering Heaven. The endless punishment of the wicked will be a place where the fire is not quenched and the worm does not die (see Mark 9:48). Hell is an important topic to Jesus in Scripture. See Matthew 5:22, 29, 30; 10:28; 23:33; 25:30; and Luke 16:23-26.

While the wicked go away into everlasting punishment, *the righteous* will enter the bliss of eternal life. They will know full well that they have not earned it. All their deeds of mercy for unfortunate people were simply the natural outgrowth of having the Spirit of God in their lives. See you there?

## CONCLUSION

As it has been wisely observed, "Good deeds are the fruit, not the root, of the tree of salvation." We dare not think that good deeds produce salvation; instead, it is salvation that produces good deeds. When our faith is real and our hearts are in tune with God, we will naturally reach out to share God's love. On the other hand, if we claim to walk with Jesus but have no concern for the needy, something is seriously wrong. There is a mismatch between profession and action.

Jesus truly cared about meeting human needs. Even though he came primarily to meet spiritual needs, he took time to meet physical needs as well. The miracles prove it. Look at how he changed water into wine for the wedding at Cana (see John 2:1-11) or when he multiplied loaves and fish to feed the five thousand (see John 6:5-11). The marvel of the great miracles must not cause us to overlook the motive of simple compassion (Matthew 9:36; 14:14; 15:32; and 20:34). A loving heart cannot help but be moved by human needs.

Jesus said that a tree could be known by its fruit. Bad trees produce bad fruit; good trees produce good fruit (see Matthew 7:16-20). The way we live our lives—specifically the way we treat people in need—is a clear indication of the state of our hearts. Bad, worthless trees are cut down (Luke 13:9).

The challenge of the Parable of the Sheep and the Goats is not just to force ourselves to do more deeds of mercy. The challenge, rather, is to have our hearts so much in tune with God that we naturally try to relieve suffering. If we are sincerely motivated by God's Spirit, then whenever we see a need we will reach out in love to help meet it. It will be a natural outgrowth of our Christian love.

## THOUGHT TO REMEMBER

*"For we must all appear before the judgment seat of Christ"* (2 Corinthians 5:10).

# Discovery Learning

*This page contains an alternative lesson plan emphasizing learning activities. Classes desiring such student involvement will find these suggestions helpful. The next page is a reproducible activity page to further enhance discovery learning.*

## LEARNING GOALS

After participating in this lesson, each student will be able to:

1. List some acts of mercy that the Lord expects to be done in his name.

2. Explain why meeting the needs of others is so important in the eyes of Jesus.

3. Decide what specific acts of mercy he or she will to do in the coming week.

## INTO THE LESSON

Before class, arrange the chairs in two groups, with a sign posted telling the men to sit on one side and the women on the other. Play a brief game to introduce today's lesson. Tell the class that you are going to ask two questions that you want them to discuss privately within their groups and predict how the other group will answer. (It will be interesting to see who best understands how members of the opposite sex think!)

State each of the questions one at a time, allowing a few minutes for the group to discuss and write down their answers to each. (1) When getting ready for company, the five most important things that have to be done are . . . (2) If unexpected company showed up at my door, I would be most embarrassed if . . .

Make a transition to today's parable by saying, "I was just using a fun way to get you thinking about preparing for company, because that's related to today's lesson. In modern society, people prepare for the arrival of guests much more precisely than in the times of Jesus (or in many parts of the world today). Without telephone or e-mail, advance notice of a visit would have been rarer. When transportation was by foot or animal, it was much more difficult to predict arrival times than it is today. Hosts might look for guests during an extended period of time or might simply have guests arrive unexpectedly at the door."

Next, say, "The guest arriving in today's parable is more important than any person for whom we may be cleaning our home. The guest whose arrival we are anticipating is Jesus himself. It is a clean life that he expects when he arrives."

## INTO THE WORD

Begin by providing a brief overview of Matthew 25. Note that the parable you will examine in this lesson is actually one of three related parables. You can demonstrate this by presenting verbally each of the first two parables, and then concisely summarizing the main point of each. Demonstrate the logical way Jesus developed his argument by saying the following:

"First, the Parable of the Ten Virgins in Matthew 25:1-13 tells us to be ready and waiting for the return of Jesus. Jesus, the Son of Man, is our bridegroom. Our love for him and anticipation of his return should prompt us to prepare wisely for his return. For those who are ready there will be great reward; for those who are not ready, there is judgment.

"Second, the Parable of the Talents in Matthew 25:14-30 tells us that when Jesus returns there will be judgment. An important basis of that judgment will be the way that those waiting for him have used the resources he provided to accomplish his business in his absence. Preparing for the return of Jesus involves wisdom and diligence. This fact sets the stage for the parable we will examine more closely in today's lesson.

"Today's lesson involves a third parable, which we call the Parable of the Sheep and the Goats from Matthew 25:31-46. Here we will see that an important basis of the final judgment will be how we have used the Master's resources to meet human needs. Our true motives will be publicly revealed on that Judgment Day, showing whether we have truly been serving Jesus or merely serving ourselves."

As you move to discussing the lesson verse by verse, make sure to highlight that an important aspect of "the business of the kingdom" is providing for the needy, in the name of Jesus.

## INTO LIFE

Move to application by asking, "Who would be the hungry, thirsty, and strangers in our society today?" Allow discussion. (Just two possible answers are elderly shut-ins and the homeless.)

Prior to class, research local organizations that minister to various needs. Provide contact information for members to begin the process of getting involved. If your church has a working relationship established with one of these ministries, this may be a great opportunity to have a representative from that organization come and speak to your class. Ask him or her to emphasize ways for people to get involved.

# The Least of These

Read Matthew 25:31-46. Then consider the kinds of people that Jesus, the Judge in his parable, identified with in the way people gave or did not give help. For each one cite an individual or group of people who is in a similar situation to the people Jesus mentioned. Then tell what you or your church is doing to help them. What more could you do?

| GROUP | CONTEMPORARY EXAMPLE | CURRENT MINISTRY | WHAT MORE CAN BE DONE? |
|---|---|---|---|
| Hungry | | | |
| Thirsty | | | |
| Stranger | | | |
| Needing Clothes | | | |
| Sick | | | |
| In Prison | | | |

# Did You Ever?

Look over the list below. Put a check (✔) next to each item that matches an act you or your family has performed.

___ Provided a meal for someone because of a sickness or hospitalization in the family.

___ Gave away clothing so someone else could wear it.

___ Helped load or unload a truck or trailer for someone who was moving.

___ Provided a place to sleep for someone who was traveling.

___ Helped someone get a job.

___ Provided help for someone with an addiction.

Are any of these comparable to the actions for which Jesus commended His "sheep"? Why, or why not?

# CALLED TO A MISSION

## WHY TEACH THIS LESSON?

The recent popularity of Rick Warren's books and program for *The Purpose-Driven Life* (Grand Rapids: Zondervan, 2002) is testimony to a felt need of great proportions. Everyone wants purpose. Everyone needs significance.

Jesus' ownership of Isaiah's statement of the Messiah's purpose in today's lesson clearly identifies him as Messiah. But Isaiah's statement must not be limited to the Messiah. The elements of the "job description" in Isaiah 61:1, 2 can be rightly taken by all who would do God's will. The compassionate, others-driven lifestyle of the Messiah must be the lifestyle of every servant of God.

Your class members need to identify with Jesus' purpose even as he identified with Isaiah's prophecy. The faulty view, widely held, is that certain tasks related to the gospel are the duties and responsibility of the "professionals." God's view is that each of his children is responsible for the poor, the brokenhearted, the captives; each is duty bound to proclaim God's grace and judgment, to comfort and provide for those in need. Today's study gives you opportunity to help your learners make that vital connection and, in doing so, re-establish their true life purpose.

## INTRODUCTION

### A. "YOU'LL NEVER COME HOME AGAIN!"

My older brother helped me pack the car as I left home to go to college. He said, "Look around, because you'll never come home again." I thought he didn't know what he was talking about. But he was right. Things had changed when I returned two weeks later. The family dynamics were different from what I was used to as I was growing up. I was no longer the "kid," but rather someone out on his own. The way I viewed people and the way they viewed me had changed.

### B. LESSON BACKGROUND

Today's lesson puts us in Jesus' first year of public ministry—his so-called "year of inauguration." We will see Jesus returning to his hometown of Nazareth, the city in Galilee where Joseph and Mary lived before they were married (Luke 1:26-28). Jesus, of course, was born in Bethlehem.

Except for the record of Luke 2:41-52, Jesus lived the first thirty years of his life in relative obscurity. Joseph was a carpenter, and Jesus himself was also known for the same occupation (Mark 6:3). A Jewish rabbi of the second century A.D. said, "Anyone who does not teach his or her child a trade it is as though the child has been taught to be a thief." As Jesus began his ministry, the hometown folks naturally still thought of him by his occupation to that point.

Not only was Jesus known primarily by his occupation at this somewhat early point in his ministry, he also carried a stigma of his hometown. Just like certain cities today can have a reputation—for example, San Francisco with its vocal homosexual population—Nazareth was not known to be a particularly pious town. One of Jesus' early disciples, Nathanael, asked the question, "Nazareth! Can anything good come form there?" (John 1:46).

DEVOTIONAL READING:
MATTHEW 13:53-58

BACKGROUND SCRIPTURE:
LUKE 4:14-30

PRINTED TEXT:
LUKE 4:16-24, 28-30

### LEARNING AIMS

After participating in this lesson, each student will be able to:

1. Explain how Jesus described his call to ministry as fulfillment of prophecy.

2. Recognize contemporary ministries that continue Jesus' ministry of compassion.

3. Become an active participant in Jesus' continuing ministry.

Aug
7

### KEY VERSES

"The Spirit of the Lord is on me, because he has anointed me to preach good news to the poor. He has sent me to proclaim freedom for the prisoners and recovery of sight for the blind, to release the oppressed, to proclaim the year of the Lord's favor."
—Luke 4:18, 19

Yet from there Jesus will speak, and his audience will listen intently. They will initially speak well of this man they had watched grow up, but they will quickly turn into a mob intent on his murder. They will have missed the lesson that Jesus sought to teach them that day. The text will show how God has a concern for everyone. The Lord is abundantly able to meet the needs of all people. We will also see that each person has a responsibility to respond in faith to the offer that Jesus makes.

## I. JESUS COMES HOME (LUKE 4:16, 17)

### A. WORSHIPING ON THE SABBATH (v. 16)

*16. He went to Nazareth, where he had been brought up, and on the Sabbath day he went into the synagogue, as was his custom. And he stood up to read.*

Jesus is returning to his hometown of *Nazareth,* a fact that sets an interesting "stage" for what follows. Part of this stage is *the synagogue,* which carries the idea of an "assembly place." The synagogue has a variety of usages, depending on location. Most importantly, it is a place of religious instruction, the usage with which we are most familiar (Acts 15:21).

We learn something about the character of Jesus in this verse. Jesus is a man with regular habits and customs. And it is *his custom* to go to the synagogue. He is regular in his worship, prayer, and study. How much more so should his followers be today! Jesus is not slack in his worship; neither should his disciples be remiss in their attendance. It is no small wonder that the Hebrew writer said, "Let us not give up meeting together, as some are in the habit of doing, but let us encourage one another—and all the more as you see the Day approaching" (Hebrews 10:25).

### B. READING FROM THE SCRIPTURE (v. 17)

*17. The scroll of the prophet Isaiah was handed to him. Unrolling it, he found the place where it is written:*

The text that Jesus reads in *the scroll of the prophet Isaiah* is from Isaiah 61:1, 2, most likely from the Greek translation of the Hebrew Scriptures, called the Septuagint. We can wonder how much trouble Jesus has in finding just the right passage he wants to read. Scrolls are cumbersome, the book of Isaiah is quite long, and there are no chapter and verse divisions as we have today! But Jesus knows exactly what he wants to read.

## II. JESUS FULFILLS PROPHECY (LUKE 4:18-21)

### A. HOLY SPIRIT–INSPIRED MINISTRY (vv. 18, 19)

*18, 19. "The Spirit of the Lord is on me,*
*because he has anointed me*
*to preach good news to the poor.*
*He has sent me to proclaim freedom for the prisoners*
*and recovery of sight for the blind,*
*to release the oppressed,*
*to proclaim the year of the Lord's favor."*

Paul tells us that "when the time had fully come, God sent his Son, born of a woman, born under law" (Galatians 4:4). God had been working throughout the Old Testament to make the conditions favorable for the Messiah to be born at the best possible time. From as early as Genesis 3:15 when God spoke to Adam and Eve, to the promise made to Abraham in Genesis 12:1-3, and throughout God's dealings with the Jews, he was preparing a people and a world to receive his Son, Jesus.

The Holy *Spirit* is an important part of Jesus' ministry. When Jesus was baptized, the Holy Spirit descended as a dove upon him (Luke 3:21, 22). In Luke 4:1 we are told that Jesus was "full of the Holy Spirit," and that it was the Spirit who led him into the wilderness to be tempted by the devil. Accompanied with the testimony of the Father—both at Jesus' baptism and his transfiguration—that Jesus is his Son, there can be little doubt that Jesus is full of the Holy Spirit, prepared and empowered to do the work of God.

The two verses before us clearly lay out the nature of Jesus' ministry. He is to (1) *preach good news to the poor,* (2) *proclaim freedom for the prisoners,* (3) *help recover sight for the blind,* (4) *release the oppressed,* and (5) *proclaim the year of the Lord's favor.* The gospel is "the power of God for the salvation of everyone who believes"—to the Jew and to the Gentile (see Romans 1:16). God does not show favoritism in bestowing these blessings (Acts 10:34).

The first item in the list should remind us that Jesus said, "Blessed are the poor in spirit, for theirs is the kingdom of heaven" (Matthew 5:3). Once we recognize our spiritual poverty, we can make ourselves dependent upon God for our salvation. We cannot save ourselves. God, being rich in mercy and grace, provides salvation for us through Jesus.

Jesus is the one who sees the great need of people who are "harassed and helpless, like sheep without a shepherd" (see Matthew 9:36). People today likewise have a great number of "stresses" and "stressors" in their lives. Depression always seems to be on the rise, and people continue to search for answers, security, and hope. Jesus offers these things in abundance. To those who are brokenhearted and bruised Jesus comes with a message of hope and forgiveness. To those who are blind he returns sight. Yes, Jesus physically healed the blind (see Mark 10:46-52), but more importantly he also gave new "vision" to those blinded by the darkness of sin. As the old song says, "The whole world was lost in the darkness of sin; the Light of the world is Jesus"!

Sin holds people captive. It is a yoke of slavery that we cannot break by our own power. Yet Jesus sets the prisoner of sin free!

### FULFILLING OUR MISSION

What are you called upon to do at your job? Are you an accountant, reconciling financial records and keeping up with tax laws? Are you a mom, doing laundry, cooking meals, and taking care of kids all day long? Perhaps you are a teacher, imparting knowledge and wisdom to classrooms full of eager students.

Tim McCarthy was a man just doing his job—fulfilling his mission. He was on duty outside the Ambassador Hotel in Washington, DC, on a cloudy afternoon in March 1981. Suddenly, gunfire rang out. McCarthy reacted instinctively and did what he had been trained to do. He turned toward the sound of the gunfire and spread himself out to make the largest possible obstruction. Tim McCarthy was a Secret Service agent, and his mission was to protect the President of the United States. On that terrible day, Tim McCarthy was wounded protecting Ronald Reagan. Television sets across the world replayed his reaction to that first shot.

How many of us are doing exactly what we're supposed to do for God? God may not write out an exact, individualized job description and mail it to us. But Matthew 28:19, 20 gives us a clear idea of what the church's main task is. Most of us have an idea of how we can best serve him in that capacity. Do we make excuses? Do we procrastinate? Do we say that others could do it better? Do we simply resist?

Every Christian should be working toward a level of maturity that leads him or her to act instinctively to answer God's call. Jesus knew his mission, and we must know ours.
—T. A. C.

## WHAT DO YOU THINK?

Consider each aspect of what Isaiah said was the mission of the Messiah—and thus of his church. How are we doing in each area? Suggest some ministry we are involved in or could be involved in to fulfill each aspect.

Be Compassionate to One Another.

Visual for lesson 10. *Compassion has many expressions. Use this visual to help your learners think of people who need help.*

## HOW TO SAY IT

*Abraham.* AY-bruh-ham.

*Bethlehem.* BETH-lih-hem.

*Cana.* KAY-nuh.

*Capernaum.* Kuh-PER-nay-um.

*Elijah.* Ee-LYE-juh.

*Elisha.* E-LYE-shuh.

*Galilee.* GAL-uh-lee.

*Gentiles.* JEN-tiles.

*Messiah.* Meh-SIGH-uh.

*Naaman.* NAY-uh-mun.

*Nathanael.* Nuh-THAN-yull (th as in thin).

*Nazareth.* NAZ-uh-reth.

*Septuagint.* Sep-TOO-ih-jent.

*synagogue.* SIN-uh-gog.

*Zarephath.* ZAIR-uh-fath.

## DAILY BIBLE READINGS

*Monday, Aug. 1—The Year of the Lord's Favor (Leviticus 25:8-12)*

*Tuesday, Aug. 2—Elijah Revives the Widow's Son (1 Kings 17:17-24)*

*Wednesday, Aug. 3—Jesus Is Rejected in Nazareth (Matthew 13:54-58)*

*Thursday, Aug. 4—Jesus Teaches in His Hometown (Mark 6:1-6)*

*Friday, Aug. 5—Jesus Reads Isaiah's Words (Luke 4:14-19)*

*Saturday, Aug. 6—Today This Scripture Has Been Fulfilled (Luke 4:20-24)*

*Sunday, Aug. 7—All in the Synagogue Were Enraged (Luke 4:25-30)*

### B. JESUS' DRAMATIC PROCLAMATION (vv. 20, 21)

**20. Then he rolled up the scroll, gave it back to the attendant and sat down. The eyes of everyone in the synagogue were fastened on him,**

Have you ever sat through a sermon or a lesson that so fascinated you that you no longer paid attention to the time? Did it seem as if time just flew by because you were so intent on what you were hearing or reading at the time? It is likely that these people have heard this passage read from Isaiah before, but now something is very different! Is it in the way Jesus speaks that captures their attention? Is it in the pronunciation or the elocution? Does he emphasize certain words as he reads the passage from Isaiah? We are not told.

One thing is certain, however: his reading completely captivates his audience. They apparently want more and are hanging on his every word. There probably is absolute silence as they wait to hear what Jesus has to say about this passage.

This is not the first time that the teaching of Jesus makes an impact on people. There are many rabbis (teachers) in the Jerusalem temple and the synagogues, yet there is something about Jesus and his words that puts him in a different class altogether. Some clues can be found from Mark 1:22: "The people were amazed at his teaching, because he taught them as one who had authority, not as the teachers of the law." The Jewish rabbis quote the scholars who came before them as a basis for their teaching. Jesus needs no such help. His word stands on its own authority. It sounds very different to those who listen, as we see next.

**21. . . . and he began by saying to them, "Today this scripture is fulfilled in your hearing."**

Imagine being an eyewitness to a fulfillment of prophecy! How did Simeon feel when he held the Christ-child in his arms, knowing that God had promised that he wouldn't see death until his eyes beheld the coming of the Messiah? (See Luke 2:26-32.) Imagine being present on the Day of Pentecost (Acts 2).

This audience in Nazareth has just heard Jesus read a prophecy that Isaiah made over seven hundred years before. As Jesus sits down, everyone continues to look at him. He then calmly informs them that they are witnessing prophecy being *fulfilled* at that very minute. The one whom Isaiah refers to is seated in their presence. They can see, touch, and speak to the one upon whom the Holy Spirit had descended. He is the one who will do the things mentioned in the ancient prophecy. What a privilege it is to be there at that very hour!

### LEAVING A LEGACY

Alfred Nobel (1833–1896) had the opportunity to read his own obituary! His brother Ludvig died in 1888, and a newspaper mistakenly printed Alfred's obituary instead. Alfred Nobel had made his mark on the world up to that point by inventing dynamite. The obituary read, "The merchant of death is dead." The newspaper's mistake changed the Swedish chemist's life. He realized that that was not the kind of legacy he wanted to leave.

You probably will not have the opportunity to read your own obituary, but you can still ask yourself this question: When I am gone, what will people think my mission in life had been? Alfred Nobel apparently asked himself that kind of question, and he did not like the answer. He had become very wealthy, and he decided to use his wealth to encourage people to make the world a better place. Today the Nobel Peace Prize is one of the world's most prestigious awards. His awards also honor people in many areas of the arts and sciences. Alfred Nobel succeeded in changing his legacy. Today, if you ask people about Nobel, they know about his awards. Very few people know how his great wealth was attained.

So the question remains: When you are gone, what will people think your mission in life had been? Will they know that you were a servant of Jesus Christ? What evidence would they have seen to draw that conclusion? Perhaps you, like Alfred Nobel, need to do some things to change your legacy. When we look at Jesus, we see a total focus on his mission. Perhaps we could use a bit of that focus ourselves. Thinking of the kind of legacy we may leave can help.          —T. A. C.

## III. JESUS IS REJECTED (LUKE 4:22-24, 28-30)

### A. CROWD WONDERS (v. 22)

**22. All spoke well of him and were amazed at the gracious words that came from his lips. "Isn't this Joseph's son?" they asked.**

Although they speak *well of him,* many apparently do not sense the privilege they have at this moment in time. Their ears have heard the *words* Jesus read, but their minds have not caught up to the significance of those words. They must be wondering how these things can be, and who is Jesus to say that he is the fulfillment of this prophecy. Their question is, *Isn't this Joseph's son?* In other words they are saying, "We know this boy! We've watched him grow up! He's not anything more special than any other resident of Nazareth, is he?" (See also John 6:42.)

Jesus was reared in the home of Joseph, but Jesus is not that man's biological son. What those gathered need to be convinced of is the fact that Jesus is God's Son! This will prove to be a very difficult truth for the residents of Nazareth to accept. It is difficult even for the half-brothers of Jesus to accept him as the Messiah. They don't do so until after the resurrection. (See John 7:5; Acts 1:14.)

### B. CROWD IS WARNED (vv. 23, 24)

**23. Jesus said to them, "Surely you will quote this proverb to me: 'Physician, heal yourself! Do here in your hometown what we have heard that you did in Capernaum.'"**

The growing reputation of Jesus in other places as a miracle worker has not escaped the notice of the residents of Nazareth. They have no doubt heard about water being changed into wine at a wedding feast of Cana of Galilee (John 2:1-11). They are familiar with the healing of an official's son *in Capernaum* (John 4:46-54). Jesus anticipates that those gathered will now want to see their hometown son do something miraculous for them.

Yet Jesus will not do many miracles in Nazareth for one simple reason: there is a lack of faith. In Mark 6:5, 6 we are told regarding a later visit there that, "He could not do any miracles there, except lay his hands on a few sick people and heal them. And he was amazed at their lack of faith."

**24. "I tell you the truth," he continued, "no prophet is accepted in his hometown."**

Jesus recognizes that "familiarity breeds contempt." There is an arrogance among the residents of Nazareth that says, "Who does this man think he is?" They are convinced that they are just as good as Jesus and are not willing to accept the claims that he is making.

A teacher may have no difficulties being accepted by others, but may not be respected by his or her own family members. A preacher who establishes a reputation for credibility and wisdom in congregations far from home may not be *accepted* in the same way back in his home church. There is a great truth contained in this simple proverb: sometimes you have to get away from the *hometown* folks to be accepted. It is certainly true in Jesus' case!

### B. CROWD WANTS MURDER (vv. 28-30)

**28. All the people in the synagogue were furious when they heard this.**

In verses 25-27 (not in today's text), Jesus gives illustrations of God's dealings with Gentiles vs. his dealings with his chosen people, the Jews. Jesus men-

WHAT DO YOU THINK?

The people of Nazareth could not accept Jesus as anyone more than an ordinary human— "Joseph's son," as they put it. Many today have the same problem. How can we convince skeptical people that Jesus is more than an ordinary human, that he is the Son of God?

WHAT DO YOU THINK?

The people of Nazareth were prevented from accepting Jesus by their own pride. What obstacles prevent people from accepting Jesus today? How can we overcome these obstacles?

PRAYER

*Father, it's easy for us to criticize the people of Nazareth until we pause to think how much we have been like them at times. Jesus is in our midst today, but how often we treat him casually or with contempt by our thoughts and actions. Deliver us ever more closely into the arms of Christ this day! In Jesus' name, amen.*

tions how Elijah went to the widow from Zarephath (and not to the people of Israel) to make sure she had provisions during the years of famine. He also mentions how it was Naaman the Syrian whom Elisha provided healing from leprosy, and not the many lepers that were in Israel. This enrages those *in the synagogue.*

How quickly they go from being fascinated by what Jesus is teaching into a murderous rage against him! Jesus has seen through their unbelief and will not perform a miracle for them. He has rightly said that a prophet is not honored among his own people. The illustrations from the miraculous work of Elijah and Elisha demonstrate that fact. God works where there is faith!

There is nothing that requires God to work among people who reject him. The apostle John tells us that "He came to that which was his own, but his own did not receive him. Yet to all who received him, to those who believed in his name, he gave the right to become children of God" (John 1:11, 12).

**29. They got up, drove him out of the town, and took him to the brow of the hill on which the town was built, in order to throw him down the cliff.**

The public ministry of Jesus is barely several months old and already people are trying to kill him—people in his hometown! Some today mistakenly think that the only time anyone ever tried to kill Jesus was when he was crucified. Yet Jesus experienced opposition and murderous intent from the beginning of his ministry. In John 5:18 we read of the Jews seeking to kill him because he not only healed on the Sabbath but he also called God his Father, "making himself equal with God." In John 8:59 we see the crowds picking up stones to throw at Jesus because of what he was teaching.

Opposition is not a rare thing for Christ. He knows from the very beginning of his ministry that there will be those who will reject him and seek to kill him. He also knows that he will rise from the dead when they do kill him! (See John 2:19-22.)

The actions of the residents of Nazareth show how far from faith they are. They want to *throw him* off a *cliff!* They aren't interested in discussing, learning, or asking questions. Perhaps they want to be amazed or entertained apart from coming to faith in him as the Savior of the world. The purpose of miracles is to confirm the message and the messenger as being from God. Miracles are not used as entertainment or conversation starters. They have an intended purpose in their day. See John 14:11.

**30. But he walked right through the crowd and went on his way.**

Is it with a piercing look that Jesus stops *the crowd* from carrying out their intent? Does he wave his hand and the crowds part so he can leave them on that hill? We are not told. The point is not how Jesus escaped and went about his business, but rather that he can just walk away—one man against a mob! Jesus is in control of his ministry and his timetable from the beginning. Others will not exert their will over him. He has goals in mind to accomplish and will not allow anything to keep him from doing what he intends. The same is true of Jesus today!

WHAT DO YOU THINK?

*The people were angry with Jesus, to the point of violence. Jesus responded by simply walking away. What makes it so hard to remain calm and walk away from a hostile environment?*

## CONCLUSION

Jesus did not reject the people of Nazareth; it was they who rejected him. He was in their midst; it was they who "drove him out."

We must realize that the same thing can happen today. We can choose either to accept his good news and carry it to others or to reject him and leave him no place in our hearts and lives. There is no middle ground, as ignoring him is the same as rejecting him. What's your choice?

THOUGHT TO REMEMBER

*"Whoever rejects the Son will not see life, for God's wrath remains on him" (John 3:36).*

# Discovery Learning

*This page contains an alternative lesson plan emphasizing learning activities. Classes
desiring such student involvement will find these suggestions helpful. The next page
is a reproducible activity page to further enhance discovery learning.*

## LEARNING GOALS

After participating in this lesson, each student will be able to:

1. Explain how Jesus described his call to ministry as fulfillment of prophecy.

2. Recognize contemporary ministries that continue Jesus' ministry of compassion.

3. Become an active participant in Jesus' continuing ministry.

## INTO THE LESSON

Begin the lesson by asking your learners to consider the motivations people have. Say, "If we did a survey of your neighbors, coworkers, and family members, what would they say is the purpose of their life?" Another way to ask this is, "What is the primary motivation for the things that people do?"

You probably will get answers about pleasure, family life, accumulating wealth, preparing for retirement (and freedom), etc. Write answers on the chalkboard as they are suggested.

After a few minutes, point out that a person's behavior often contradicts what is said about the main purpose for living. Discuss this question: "How can you tell what really motivates a person?" (*Answers might include how people spend their time, the ways they spend their money, and the things that entertain and excite them.*)

Next, ask class members to consider what would happen if they evaluated their own lives the same way. Ask, "Considering the categories of time, treasure, and pleasure, what is the primary motivating force or agenda for your life?"

Point out that today's lesson features Jesus teaching a group of people who would express their agenda for life in religious terms, possibly a lot like the members of your class. They were in attendance at the synagogue when Jesus was teaching, and they highly valued their Jewish heritage and beliefs.

Next say, "As you consider today's lesson text, it will be evident that the agenda of Jesus was very different from that of those who were listening to him teach. This difference will raise the following critical questions: What is the agenda of Jesus? What is the agenda for your life? What would have to change for you to align your agenda with Jesus' agenda? Are you willing to put aside your agenda and commit yourself to following Jesus and his agenda for life?" (It will be helpful to write these questions on the board as you present them.)

## INTO THE WORD

Before class begins, select an empty chair in the front row and "mark it off" so nobody sits there. After discussing the questions in the "Into the Lesson" segment, pass out small slips of blank paper and ask your learners to write the name of a respected member of your church or community.

Next, collect the papers and read aloud the names that are written. Select one of the names and place the paper on the empty chair. Say, "As I read the following text, pretend that this person is sitting in this chair and will be teaching class." Then read Luke 4:14-21 aloud. Ask the class what would happen if the person you selected made the claim that Jesus did. Remind the class that Jesus claimed to be the fulfillment of ancient promises from God. Ask, "How would knowing the person well affect the way you would respond to that claim? What would make the claims of Jesus different?" (*Ability to support the claim by being able to perform miracles.*) Also ask, "What does the passage say about Jesus' agenda for his life?" (*Emphasis on fulfilling the commission of the Father, with a repeated focus on ministry to others with great need.*)

Now read aloud Jesus' response in Luke 4:23-27. Ask, "What is the significance of the Old Testament stories that Jesus included?" (*They were examples of God's message and miracles being received by Gentiles but not by Jews.*) "Why would this anger Jesus' audience?" (*Jesus confronted them with a history of rejecting God's message while claiming to be his people.*)

Read the rest of the story in Luke 4:28-30. Discuss other times Jesus faced opposition, as noted in the verse-by-verse commentary.

## INTO LIFE

Review the ideas shared during the beginning of the lesson. Ask, "How would the personal agendas of people have to change if the teaching of Jesus were to be accepted and followed?" Challenge class members to daily consider the agenda that is being demonstrated by their time, treasures, and pleasures in the week ahead. Consider steps that could be taken to commit themselves to the agenda of Jesus.

# Facing Opposition, Part 1

Luke 4:14-29 tells of a time when Jesus faced opposition—but it wasn't the only time. Read the following Scripture passages and summarize the cause for opposition Jesus faced. Then tell how Jesus responded to the opposition.

| | CAUSE FOR OPPOSITION | JESUS' RESPONSE |
|---|---|---|
| Luke 5:27-32 | | |
| Luke 6:1-5 | | |
| Luke 6:6-11 | | |
| Luke 7:36-50 | | |
| Luke 13:10-17 | | |
| Luke 16:1-15 | | |
| Luke 20:20-26 | | |
| John 5:1-10, 16-18 | | |
| John 7:25-31 | | |
| John 8:48-59 | | |

# Facing Opposition, Part 2

What opposition have you faced as a believer? How did you respond?

Compare your response with those of Jesus, above. What changes do you need to make in the way you respond to opposition?

# HEALING THE INCURABLE

**LESSON 11**

## WHY TEACH THIS LESSON?

Sooner or later every adult has a "Jairus crisis." Sooner or later every man and woman has Luke's unnamed woman's moment of desperation. Luke describes both in today's text. An individual at the end of his or her possibility turns to the one who knows no impossibility, or else turns to despair. Both the ruler of the synagogue and the anemic woman were wise enough in faith to turn to Jesus.

That is the wisdom every child of God needs to pray for: wisdom to know one's inability, wisdom to know God's complete ability. Certain conditions are beyond the science of the time and place. Physically, in the early twenty-first century that may be aneurysms or cancers or Alzheimer's. Spiritually, in any century, that is sin. The latter is the condition of greater consequence because it is eternal. And the latter is the condition with only one possibility: grace and forgiveness. But that one possibility is real and available in the same person Jairus and the woman sought and found—Jesus. Does everyone in your class know that? Is there anyone in your class that has the same desperation?

## INTRODUCTION

### A. SEE THE SPECIALIST

Have you ever had to see a specialist? You went to see your regular physician, and, for whatever reason, he or she sent you on to a specialist—someone better trained or with more experience for your situation. When the need is critical, you want the very best help.

Jesus is the ultimate specialist! He specializes in the critical needs of the body and of the soul. As one needs confidence in a physician's knowledge and skills to treat our needs, so our text challenges us to put our faith in Christ, even in the darkest hours. When no one else can help, Jesus still can!

### B. LESSON BACKGROUND

Today's lesson finds Jesus late in the second year of his public ministry. His popularity is very high. Before we reach the point of today's lesson, we notice that crowds seek him relentlessly (Luke 8:4, 19). But opposition presents itself as well (Luke 8:37). And yet as Jesus deals with both enthusiastic and hostile crowds, he never loses sight of the individual. That's how we see Jesus in today's lesson: taking time to minister to individuals as crowds swirl about. Matthew 9:18-26 and Mark 5:21-34 offer us parallel accounts.

## I. FATHER'S URGENT REQUEST (LUKE 8:40-42)

### A. JESUS' RETURN (v. 40)

**40. Now when Jesus returned, a crowd welcomed him, for they were all expecting him.**

Jesus has just *returned* from the region of the Gadarenes (or Gerasenes) where he had cast out the legion of demons from the man who was living in the tombs. This region (on the eastern side of the Sea of Galilee) has more of a Gentile population than Galilee or Judea. Jesus' occasional trips to these largely Gentile areas

DEVOTIONAL READING:
MATTHEW 9:18-26
BACKGROUND SCRIPTURE:
LUKE 8:40-56
PRINTED TEXT:
LUKE 8:40-56

LEARNING AIMS

After participating in this lesson, each student will be able to:

1. Explain the role of faith in the miracles performed by Jesus in the accounts of the hemorrhaging woman and Jairus's daughter.

2. Identify situations in his or her life that call for healing and wholeness.

3. Demonstrate faith in Jesus Christ when facing those situations.

Aug
14

KEY VERSE

He said to her, "Daughter, your faith has healed you. Go in peace." —Luke 8:48

*LESSON 11 NOTES*

demonstrate that his ministry is for all people, even as the gospel is the power of God to everyone who believes—both Jew and Greek (Romans 1:16).

This is a time in Christ's ministry when the crowds make it difficult for Jesus to have any solitary moments or time he can spend solely with the Twelve preparing them for future ministry. Wherever Jesus goes, there seems to be *a crowd* pressing against him for an opportunity to hear him speak or to receive a miracle. Now that Jesus is back in Galilee, the crowds again swarm around him. They are glad to have him back.

### B. JAIRUS'S REQUEST (v. 41)

**41. Then a man named Jairus, a ruler of the synagogue, came and fell at Jesus' feet, pleading with him to come to his house**

Not only is the average citizen excited to have Jesus back in Capernaum, Jesus' arrival also catches the notice of *Jairus.* As *a ruler of the synagogue,* he oversees the day-to-day operations of all that happens there. He is an important official. It is unusual for someone of prominence to come and fall at another's *feet* in Jesus' day. It is more typical for someone to come and bow.

Even the idea of bowing would itself suggest an attitude of humility in the presence of someone greater than you. This is the heart of submission. No one is immune from great personal needs. As important as Jairus may be in the eyes of the community—or even his own eyes—he still recognizes that he has a need that he is unable to meet on his own. So he humbly comes before Jesus, pleading with him to come into his house.

*WHAT DO YOU THINK?*

*How can we help people recognize that Jesus is the answer to their deepest need?*

#### A HUMBLE HERO

John Bradley was a funeral director from Appleton, Wisconsin. His children knew he had done something special in World War II, but Bradley would not speak of the event that made him famous. He was nearing the end of his life when he finally consented to tell his son James about the events of February 23, 1945.

Bradley was a Navy medical corpsman at the battle on Iwo Jima. He was on Mount Suribachi when a flag was to be raised to signal the capture of the highest point on the island. Joe Rosenthal photographed Bradley and several others hoisting Old Glory. That photograph became famous. When John Bradley came home, people wanted to make him a hero. He refused, thinking instead of the nearly seven thousand Americans who died on Iwo Jima. He said, "The real heroes of Iwo Jima are the guys who didn't come back." Such humility!

Jairus was a man of credentials as well. He was a synagogue ruler, but he humbled himself to come to Jesus and ask for help. Humility—once considered a foundation of character—is now often seen as a sign of weakness. But Jairus had a desperate need. He also had a proper attitude. We, too, have desperate needs. Do we have the proper attitude? If pride is your problem, remember the cross. The Son of God—the King of Heaven—humbled himself to bear our sins. How can your pride remain?          —T. A. C.

### C. JAIRUS'S DILEMMA (v. 42)

**42. . . . because his only daughter, a girl of about twelve, was dying.**

**As Jesus was on his way, the crowds almost crushed him.**

What motivates Jairus's urgent request of Jesus is now apparent: *his only daughter,* perhaps his only child, is sick and is becoming steadily worse. Any loving father will do whatever he can to save the life of his little girl, and one can almost see Jairus pushing his way through the crowds that are pressing in on Jesus. When the need is most urgent, you will go to extreme measures to have that need met (compare Luke 5:19). It is apparently not easy for him to get close to Christ. Muscling and elbowing his way through the crowd undoubtedly draws dirty looks. But Jairus is focused. He does not stop until he has the Lord's attention and can make his plea on his daughter's behalf.

## II. WOMAN'S URGENT NEED (LUKE 8:43-48)

### A. WEAKENED BY ILLNESS (v. 43)

**43. And a woman was there who had been subject to bleeding for twelve years, but no one could heal her.**

The story now becomes more complex. While on his way to perform one miracle, the Lord is "interrupted" and performs another. Picture Jairus and Jesus leading this mass of humanity through narrow, rough streets. Unbeknownst to everyone else, *a woman* with a great need also is seeking out Jesus.

Being *subject to bleeding* is what we would call "hemorrhaging." This is likely a condition associated with gynecological problems. This situation is difficult enough as a permanent physical ailment, but there is another ramification: this woman is ceremonially unclean. Leviticus 15:19-33 gives regulations concerning a woman's monthly cycle. A woman is considered "unclean" for as long as she continues to bleed. During this time she is to be excluded from religious activities, and those whom she touches are unclean as well. (See Numbers 19:22.)

It is an interesting coincidence that Jesus is on his way to help a sick twelve-year-old girl. Now this woman, who has been ill in her own right *for twelve years,* desires to be healed as well. Luke, a physician himself according to Colossians 4:14, tells us that she has spent all her money on physicians. Mark adds something to our understanding when he says, "She had suffered a great deal under the care of many doctors and had spent all she had, yet instead of getting better she grew worse" (Mark 5:26). We may smile as we wonder why Luke the physician leaves that part out!

### B. EMBOLDENED BY DESPERATION (v. 44)

**44. She came up behind him and touched the edge of his cloak, and immediately her bleeding stopped.**

Imagine jostling against dozens of people who surround the person you wish to meet. There is the roar of the crowd, a crowd impelled by its own desire to press ever closer to hear and see what the person at the center of attention may say. A woman weakened by sickness will have great difficulty managing to get through all of those people in order to have her need met.

Yet, somehow, perhaps finding the right angle to get her arm out far enough, she manages to touch the hem of Jesus' *cloak.* When she does, a miracle takes place!

So often with sicknesses there is a recovery period from the time the diagnosis is made to the time a procedure is performed or medications are given. It takes time for the desired results to occur. Such is not the case here. The supernatural results are instant, perfect, and complete.

She is now free from her disease. She is no longer under a cloud of being unclean, where she will have to be excluded from participation in religious services and even careful about who or what she touches. These are the results she has desperately hoped for, and her faith is what set Jesus' healing power in motion.

### C. DISCOVERED BY INQUIRY (vv. 45-47)

**45. "Who touched me?" Jesus asked.**

**When they all denied it, Peter said, "Master, the people are crowding and pressing against you."**

---

## WHAT DO YOU THINK?

We imagine Jairus abandoning social etiquette as he pushes his way through the crowd to Jesus. For what would you abandon social etiquette or risk upsetting people? Why are we not more bold to rescue people from eternal damnation?

## HOW TO SAY IT

Colossians. Kuh-LOSH-unz.
Corinthians. Ko-RIN-thee-unz (th as in thin).
Gadarenes. GAD-uh-reens.
Galilee. GAL-uh-lee.
Gentiles. JEN-tiles.
Gerasenes. GUR-uh-seenz.
Gethsemane. Geth-SEM-uh-nee (G as in get).
Jairus. JYE-rus or JAY-ih-rus.
Judea. Joo-DEE-uh.
Lazarus. LAZ-uh-rus.
Thessalonians. Thess-uh-LO-nee-unz (th as in thin).

Is Jesus aware of what is going on around him? Does he have power over the ability to heal and to withhold healing? Or is he a source of power that anyone can just "plug in to"? One thing is sure: he certainly knows that power has gone out from him. So he stops and asks the question, *Who touched me?* Typically, it is *Peter* who has something to say when no one steps forward. Peter in effect says, "Lord, are you serious? You see all these people *pressing* around you and yet you ask who touched you? How can you even ask such a question?"

*WHAT DO YOU THINK?*

*Peter thought the Lord's question was beyond belief. When have you felt the Lord's requirements were "beyond belief"? How do you come to terms with it and accept it in faith and submission even when it does not seem rational?*

At first glance, it does seem like a foolish question. Yet Jesus seems determined to have his question answered. The phrase *When they all denied it* seems to imply that even the woman who received healing said at first, "Not me!" or at least she tried to be inconspicuous.

**46. But Jesus said, "Someone touched me; I know that power has gone out from me."**

Jesus responds to Peter and others who are listening that the touch is not some inadvertent or accidental contact. Something happened when the hem of Jesus' garment was *touched.* Jesus knows that *power has gone out* of him. Jesus is indicating that he knows *someone* had a distinct purpose for touching him. He wants that person to speak up. The reason why will be clear in the next two verses.

**47. Then the woman, seeing that she could not go unnoticed, came trembling and fell at his feet. In the presence of all the people, she told why she had touched him and how she had been instantly healed.**

The joy this woman felt at her instant, miraculous healing is now changed to fear. She had sought to obtain this benefit from Christ without any notice—now she is caught! Perhaps she makes her admission as Jesus' piercing yet gentle eyes go from person to person, finally landing on her. Jesus' purpose is not to humiliate her or to retract the healing. Rather, it is to allow her the high privilege of offering a testimony of faith to the crowd of *people* who press in.

Are you able to picture her now choking back the tears as she recalls to Jesus and to others who are listening the story of her suffering? No doubt this touches even the most callous of hearts who hear her desperate story. She describes how she had come to believe that Jesus was her last hope. Perhaps her tears from fear of discovery turn to tears of joy as she is able to say with confidence that her body is whole and healthy again, and that it is Jesus who has provided this blessing to her. The crowds hear her testify that for twelve long, difficult years she has suffered; but with one touch of Jesus' garment the suffering has come to an end. Her body is free from the sickness, and her heart is made glad again.

## D. HEALED BY FAITH (v. 48)

**48. Then he said to her, "Daughter, your faith has healed you. Go in peace."**

Before the woman touched Jesus' garment, he was on his way to attend to Jairus's daughter. Now having heard this woman's testimony of faith, he sends her home and uses the word *daughter* as a term of endearment for her. No doubt this woman is a child of God, who has put her complete faith and trust in God as the only one who can lift her physical agony and spiritual separation.

*WHAT DO YOU THINK?*

*The woman's faith had ministered to both her spiritual and physical conditions. To what extent do our ministries lead people to such wholeness? How can we improve?*

Imagine the joy she experiences after twelve long years of misery—to finally have *peace.* Only Jesus could have provided that for her. And Jesus credits the woman's *faith.* The Bible teaches that without faith it is impossible to please God (Hebrews 11:6). The woman has faith, and she confesses it to others as well.

### TOO HIGH A PRICE

Two old prospectors wandered the desert for many years, searching for a silver mine. They had spent a long time in the desert, and their attitude toward matters of life and death was rather casual. That changed one afternoon when one of the prospectors disturbed a rattlesnake. He would not show any fear in the presence of his friend, so he cavalierly said he could kiss the rattler before the snake could strike. He bent forward to plant his lips on the snake and was promptly bitten. The "kiss" had been successful! The snake's fangs struck both his upper and lower lips.

The prospector panicked and sent his friend to town to get a doctor. The other prospector found the doctor, but he could not accompany the prospector back into the desert. He told him he could save his friend's life by using his own lips to suck the poison out of the wounds. As the friend rode back, he thought about what he would have to do to save his friend's life. When he finally arrived back at his friend's side, the natural question was, "What did the doc say?" The old prospector took off his hat and somberly answered, "He said you're gonna die!"

What a corny story! But it has a point: Are there times when we consider "the price of healing" to be too high? We are God's representatives in the world. We are, in the words of a missionary doctor, God's hands to heal. You may not be a physician, but you are God's messenger of healing to a world that has been poisoned and is dying. And the great physician still makes house calls!      —T. A. C.

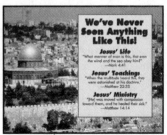

Visual for lessons 2 and 11.
*Display this poster again to review the quarter and to tie in today's lesson with the overall theme.*

## II. JESUS' TIMELY RESPONSES (LUKE 8:49-56)

### A. SAD NEWS (v. 49)

**49. While Jesus was still speaking, someone came from the house of Jairus, the synagogue ruler. "Your daughter is dead," he said. "Don't bother the teacher any more."**

From the joy of the woman who was healed comes now the devastating news that the little girl has died. What further need is there for Jesus to come? This messenger thinks that all hope is gone and that preparations now need to be made for the funeral and burial. The great excitement and joy of the crowd must turn to silence as the news spreads about the death of this young girl. *Jairus* is no doubt devastated by the announcement. Perhaps there is even some anger about the delay of Jesus caused by this woman (compare John 11:21). Jairus now probably believes he will never again see his *daughter* alive.

### B. ENCOURAGING WORDS (v. 50)

**50. Hearing this, Jesus said to Jairus, "Don't be afraid; just believe, and she will be healed."**

Jesus' response may seem somewhat mysterious. Just moments before, a woman confessed her faith to Jesus after having been made whole herself. But that woman is still alive, and Jairus's daughter lies dead. How can there be any hope? The healing of the woman's issue of blood after twelve years of suffering should be reason to *believe* that Jesus can do something about the death of Jairus's daughter.

The faith that saved the woman is the type of faith that *Jairus* now needs. When Lazarus dies a bit later, Jesus will tell Martha that her brother will rise again (John 11:23). Martha will state her faith that she expects Lazarus to rise on the last day. Before he raises Lazarus, Jesus will respond, "I am the resurrection and the life. He who believes in me will live, even though he dies" (John 11:25).

### C. ASTONISHING MIRACLE (vv. 51-56)

**51. When he arrived at the house of Jairus, he did not let anyone go in with him except Peter, John and James, and the child's father and mother.**

Jesus has twelve apostles, but on several occasions he allows only three of them to witness something special. These three apostles—*Peter* and *James* and *John*—have been called "the inner circle." They are now the only apostles allowed to see the raising of Jairus's daughter. They are the only apostles allowed to

WHAT DO YOU THINK?

*Jairus's worst fears had come to pass. But Jesus challenged him to rise above his fear on the wings of faith. How do we not be afraid but "just believe" when we face distressing circumstances? Tell of a time when your faith carried you above your fear in a difficult situation.*

## DAILY BIBLE READINGS

**Monday, Aug. 8**—*A Centurion's Servant Is Healed (Luke 7:1-10)*

**Tuesday, Aug. 9**—*A Girl Restored, A Woman Healed (Matthew 9:18-26)*

**Wednesday, Aug. 10**—*Two Blind Men Healed by Faith (Matthew 9:27-31)*

**Thursday, Aug. 11**—*A Hemorrhaging Woman Is Healed (Mark 5:24b-34)*

**Friday, Aug. 12**—*A Girl Is Restored to Life (Mark 5:35-43)*

**Saturday, Aug. 13**—*A Sick Woman Is Healed (Luke 8: 40-48)*

**Sunday, Aug. 14**—*Jairus's Daughter Is Alive (Luke 8:49-56)*

## PRAYER

*Father, may we never cease to be amazed at the one who died for our sins. Help us to share our amazement with others. In Jesus' name, amen.*

## THOUGHT TO REMEMBER

*Seek spiritual healing above all else.*

see the transfiguration. And while eight of the apostles are left near the gate of the Garden of Gethsemane, Peter, James, and John are the ones Jesus takes a bit farther into the garden before he falls in sorrowful prayer (Matthew 26:36).

**52, 53. Meanwhile, all the people were wailing and mourning for her. "Stop wailing," Jesus said. "She is not dead but asleep."**

*They laughed at him, knowing that she was dead.*

When Jesus and his inner circle arrive at the home of Jairus, the place is already filled with mourners (Matthew 9:23; Mark 5:38). While it certainly isn't unusual for there to be mourning at the passing of a loved one, what makes this unusual to us is that in the first century some are paid to mourn! To have people making a loud commotion at her passing shows just how loved the deceased person is. What demonstrates that the "carrying on" of these people is something less than sincere is the fact that they so quickly go from *wailing* to laughing when Jesus says the child is *asleep*. They know a lifeless body when they see one. Yet Jesus indicates that this condition is a temporary one, something these mourners cannot yet comprehend.

Jesus introduces the word *asleep* to indicate physical death. And it is appropriate. As one expects the body to awaken from a nap or a night of sleep, so, too, may a believer expect his or her body to rise to renewed life after physical death. God is able to restore life to the body again. Death will not have the last word; it is a temporary situation that God will reverse. Jesus uses the term *asleep* at the death of Lazarus in John 11:1-14. Paul uses the term in 1 Corinthians 15:51 as well as 1 Thessalonians 4:13.

**54, 55. But he took her by the hand and said, "My child, get up!" Her spirit returned, and at once she stood up. Then Jesus told them to give her something to eat**

Jesus does not take the time to explain his figurative meaning of sleep for physical death to those mourners. He simply takes the child *by the hand* and calls *her spirit* back into her body and *she* revives. Seven people including the daughter are in the room when Jesus calls her back to life (Mark 5:40). The God who created all life in the first place is more than able to restore life.

**56. Her parents were astonished, but he ordered them not to tell anyone what had happened.**

The *astonished* reaction of her parents is certainly understandable. They, too, know that she was dead, but now can see that she is full of life. Shocked and stunned would certainly be apt ways of describing them. Yet Jesus makes a surprising command of them: do not *tell anyone!*

How can they hide the fact that their daughter who was dead is now very much alive? Are they able to keep her locked in her room? Obviously the Lord would not command such a thing. But he is telling them not to broadcast the news to everyone they meet, as hard as that will be. Their natural inclination is to tell everyone. The Lord does not come primarily to heal the sick and raise the dead. Rather, he comes to seek and save the lost. That's where he wants attention given to his ministry.

## CONCLUSION

Jesus is truly amazing. He taught with great authority. He commanded demons and they obeyed. He healed the sick and raised the dead. With God all things are possible!

But Jesus is more than a great teacher, an authority over demons, and a healer of physical disease. Jesus is the one who voluntarily leaves his throne of glory to walk among sinners and die at their hands. His death pays the price for our sins. His resurrection proves, once again, who he really is. Now that's amazing!

# Discovery Learning

*This page contains an alternative lesson plan emphasizing learning activities. Classes*
*desiring such student involvement will find these suggestions helpful. The next page*
*is a reproducible activity page to further enhance discovery learning.*

## LEARNING GOALS

After this lesson each student will be able to:

1. Explain the role of faith in the miracles performed by Jesus in the accounts of the hemorrhaging woman and Jairus's daughter.

2. Identify situations in his or her life that call for healing and wholeness.

3. Demonstrate faith in Jesus Christ when facing those situations.

## INTO THE LESSON

Bring to class several headlines (current or historical) of famous people who have faced great difficulties in life. The difficulties should be ones that were not a result of their actions (criminal charges, etc.). Rather, they should be ones that they are powerless to change on their own (illness, etc.). The people you select could include politicians, entertainers, or religious leaders. Also bring articles describing the stories of "ordinary" people facing similar situations (these are people who are not famous, or are famous only because of their tragedy).

As you mention several of these situations to the class, note how tragedy comes to everyone, regardless of social class, wealth, or fame. Social status, wealth, fame, etc. often cannot "solve" a crisis. Say, "In today's lesson we will see two people facing terrible situations that they were powerless to overcome. We will see their responses and watch what happened when they had an encounter with Jesus."

## INTO THE WORD

Next, say, "As you consider this story, watch closely for three things: the setting, the response of the powerless, and the result." Distribute copies of the reproducible activity "The Powerless meet the Powerful One" from the next page.

*The Setting.* Read Luke 8:40-56 aloud. Ask class members to compare and contrast Jairus with the sick woman. You can let them work with a partner to make lists of similarities and differences. (*Differences may include: male/female; upper-class socially/unclean outcast from society; influential position in society/ordinary person; loved one was sick/facing illness personally. A similarity would be that both faced situations over which they were entirely powerless.*)

Read aloud the portions of the passage that demonstrate that these people were really sick or deceased (*eye-*

witnesses, the doctors who tried to heal the woman, the mourners who mocked Jesus when he said the girl wasn't dead, etc.). Remind them of the conclusions from the "Into the Lesson" section: situations over which everyone is powerless do not differentiate based on issues such as social class or wealth.

*The Responses of the Powerless.* Say, "Look again at the passage and focus on the faith responses of Jairus and the woman. What were those responses?" (*The woman responded in faith with humility as she silently touched Jesus' robe, then fell at his feet; Jairus demonstrated faith with humility in coming publicly to Jesus and asking for help, thus opening himself up to ridicule from the religious leaders who opposed Jesus.*)

*The Result.* Say, "Look closely at the descriptions of the woman's healing. Luke, a doctor himself, describes these events in ways that leave no doubt that it was truly a miracle performed by Jesus. The little girl came back to life in front of her own parents."

## INTO LIFE

Make a transition to application by saying, "Today's passage clearly demonstrates the power of God over disease and even death. But Jesus commanded the parents not to tell anyone what had happened. Why would Jesus do this?" (*He demonstrates that the ultimate focus is not on the healing, but on the way it confirms the person and message of Jesus*).

Continue by noting that, "Although the lesson clearly demonstrates the power of God over disease and death, Paul describes a personal situation where God chose not to heal, to allow a greater purpose to be accomplished through suffering (see 2 Corinthians 12:7-10). Physical death is a temporary situation that will be reversed someday by God. This should provide great hope for those who believe in Jesus Christ, providing comfort and encouragement, as well as a challenge to live life with eternity in view."

Ask class members to estimate how often they pray for spiritual healing in comparison with prayers for physical healing. The answer may be surprising! Allow time for them to pray for those who are facing difficult situations. Encourage prayers for the ability to trust God. Challenge class members to offer at least one prayer for spiritual issues for every prayer that involves physical needs.

# The Powerless Meet the Powerful One

Luke 8:40-56 tells of two powerless victims who met the powerful victor. Use the chart below to summarize their stories.

| | *JAIRUS* | *WOMAN WITH HEMORRHAGE* |
|---|---|---|
| The Setting | | |
| The Response of the Powerless | | |
| The Result | | |

# Power for Today

List below some contemporary situations that people are powerless to overcome. How can you help introduce people who face these situations to Jesus?

1.

2.

3.

4.

# BEING A GOOD NEIGHBOR

**LESSON 12**

DEVOTIONAL READING:
MATTHEW 22:34-40

BACKGROUND SCRIPTURE:
LUKE 10:25-37

PRINTED TEXT:
LUKE 10:25-37

## WHY TEACH THIS LESSON?

The expert in the law (Luke 10:25) asked a question universally asked: "How can I live forever?" Observation reveals that every person dies. Yet, God "has also set eternity in the hearts of men" (Ecclesiastes 3:11). As the writer of Ecclesiastes notes, all people readily ponder the ups and downs of everyday life. A certain sameness of patterns and options faces every generation. But that same writer concludes that people "cannot fathom what God has done from beginning to end"; no person fully comprehends eternity and his or her place in it. So the question is asked, "How can I live forever?"

Interestingly, Jesus turns his answer to the here and now with a simple story about helping a neighbor in need. Time and eternity are inextricably tied together for each person. So the old question remains for each: "What on earth are you doing for Heaven's sake?" Today's lesson will help your learners to make the connection between the deep theological question to the practical deed of service.

## INTRODUCTION

### A. TOO BUSY TO HELP!

"I can't help people because I am too busy, and besides, it can be dangerous." What a statement! We no longer stop and help people stranded alongside the road because of the potential risk involved. We might like to lend a helping hand to an elderly person, but we just have so many other commitments.

Of course we love the Lord and would do anything for him, but finding the time to help people is just too hard anymore. After all, I have my problems as well, and I don't ask anyone to help me! So why should anyone expect that I would help them? And how about all those government social programs that I support with my taxes? Can't they "help" like they're supposed to?

Does any of this sound familiar? Are we too busy, too self-involved, too wary of possible dangers, too much given to rationalizing that we no longer see the needs around us? Have we forgotten that as we show acts of kindness to people, we are doing it as unto the Lord? Remember what Jesus said: "The King will reply, 'I tell you the truth, whatever you did for one of the least of these brothers of mine, you did for me'" (Matthew 25:40).

### B. LESSON BACKGROUND

Today's text reminds us of the importance of loving God and loving others. The very familiar story of the Good Samaritan encourages us to see the needs of others, take the time to become personally involved, and demonstrate our love for God through love for others. As Jesus spoke these words, he was modeling the very principles he was advocating.

## I. WHAT MUST I DO? (LUKE 10:25-28)

### A. KNOWING WHAT TO DO (vv. 25-27)

25. On one occasion an expert in the law stood up to test Jesus. "Teacher," he asked, "what must I do to inherit eternal life?"

LEARNING AIMS

After participating in this lesson, each student will be able to:

1. Explain the meaning of the Parable of the Good Samaritan in light of the historical context in which it was taught.

2. Compare himself or herself with the main characters in the story, determining whom they most resemble.

3. Commit to sacrificially meeting the needs of a specific person.

KEY VERSE

He answered: "'Love the Lord your God with all your heart and with all your soul and with all your strength and with all your mind'; and, 'Love your neighbor as yourself.'" —Luke 10:27

Aug
21

LESSON 12 NOTES

WHAT DO YOU THINK?

How do you decide whether or not to answer a question when the person asking is not sincere? Tell of an experience either way, if you can.

[Amos 5:13; Matthew 27:12-14; and 1 Peter 3:15 can enrich your discussion.]

WHAT DO YOU THINK?

Why do you suppose Jesus answered the lawyer's question with a question? When would you find it appropriate to respond that way?

An expert in religious law attempts to trap Jesus. He wants to see if he can ask a question so difficult that Jesus will become confused or say something that would put him in trouble with the religious authorities. Instead, the lawyer stumbles across life's most important question: *What must I do to inherit eternal life?*

This lawyer is not the only person in the pages of Scripture to ask this essential question. In Mark 10:17 a young man asks, "Good teacher, what must I do to inherit eternal life?" A jailer in Philippi asks Paul and Silas the question, "Sirs, what must I do to be saved?" (Acts 16:30). Knowing and then following the answer to this question is the difference between eternal life and eternal damnation.

26. "*What is written in the Law?*" he replied. "*How do you read it?*"

Jesus answers the lawyer's question with a question of his own. In effect, the Lord says to him, "What do you think is the answer to your own question?"

The lawyer seems to come to Jesus with an agenda. He's convinced that he does indeed know the answer, but he wants to find out if Jesus agrees with him! In the next verse, the lawyer will proceed to give Jesus his best understanding of how to be saved.

27. He answered: "'*Love the Lord your God with all your heart and with all your soul and with all your strength and with all your mind'; and, 'Love your neighbor as yourself.'*"

The lawyer goes to the Old Testament for his answer. First, he makes reference to Deuteronomy 6:4, 5. These verses are called the *shema*, which means "to hear." Paraphrased, these verses say to *love* God with everything you have—*heart, soul*, and all your *strength*. With every part of our beings we are to love God. We cannot be divided in our affections—saying one thing but doing another. It is hypocrisy to say we love God and then proceed to disobey him. If we love God in our heart, it will be demonstrated by how we live and the things that we do.

The second part of the lawyer's answer is originally found in Leviticus 19:18: "Do not seek revenge or bear a grudge against one of your people, but *love your neighbor as yourself*. I am the Lord." The lawyer's answer could be summed up simply as, "Love God and then love others."

B. DOING WHAT YOU KNOW (v. 28)

28. "*You have answered correctly,*" Jesus replied. "*Do this and you will live.*"

To paraphrase a response from a TV game show, Jesus tells the lawyer, "Good answer!" Jesus does not disagree with the lawyer in the least bit. He tells him that he is exactly right. If he loves God and others, he *will live*.

It is interesting to note that Jesus comes back to these two concepts again in his teaching. During the final week of the Lord's ministry, another lawyer will seek to test him by asking what is the greatest commandment. Jesus will quote Deuteronomy 6:4, 5 as the greatest commandment and Leviticus 19:18 as the second greatest (see Matthew 22:34-40). The apostle Paul picks up on this theme at least twice. In Romans 13:8 he says, "He who loves his fellowman has fulfilled the law." And in Galatians 5:14 Paul writes, "The entire law is summed up in a single command: 'Love your neighbor as yourself.'"

Replying to the lawyer's Old Testament frame of reference, Jesus commends him for getting it exactly right: If he wants to be saved, he needs to love God and then love others. When the Holy Spirit is given on the Day of Pentecost, the answer will need to be expanded (see Acts 2:37-39).

II. WHO IS MY NEIGHBOR? (LUKE 10:29-35)

A. QUESTION ASKED (v. 29)

29. But he wanted to justify himself, so he asked Jesus, "And who is my neighbor?"

The lawyer is not quite satisfied. He may be feeling more than a little bit uncomfortable. Jesus has affirmed that loving God and then loving others are keys salvation. How well has the lawyer done these two things? Perhaps he is selective in his love, but he doesn't want to look bad in front of Jesus or others who ay be listening to this conversation. He apparently wants to make himself look good as possible, not having any doubt or suspicion cast upon him.

Thus he attempts *to justify himself,* that is, to make himself appear completely ee from wrongdoing in regard to loving God or his neighbor. After all, he is lking about how to be saved, and he certainly wouldn't want to put himself in light that would make him appear lost! So he asks the question, *Who is my ighbor?*

That, too, is an important question. Whom should we help? Whom should e love? Are my neighbors only those who live next door to me? Are they also he people I see at work whom I know and like? Certainly strangers are not my eighbors, are they? Should we be "nice" only to people who are nice and help-l (neighborly) to us? The lawyer probably feels like he has done at least that uch, thus he is safe. Yet Jesus will seize on his question and seek to open his es (and ours) as to who a neighbor really is!

### . STORY TOLD (vv. 30-35)

*0. In reply Jesus said: "A man was going down from Jerusalem to Jericho, when e fell into the hands of robbers. They stripped him of his clothes, beat him and ent away, leaving him half dead.*

This is the beginning of what is called the Parable of the Good Samaritan. sus offers several specifics in this story, including an interesting point of Bible ography. Jericho is approximately twenty miles northeast of Jerusalem. Typilly, when we speak of directions we'll say we're going "up" when we mean orth, and going "down" when we mean south.

The text says the man was going down *from Jerusalem to Jericho.* The Scriptures re consistent in noting that one always goes "up" to Jerusalem, and "down" hen departing from that city. The reason for this is that Jerusalem is built on a ill. It does not matter from what direction you approach the city—you are going go up to get there. The reverse is naturally true as well: you always go *down* as ou leave the city.

As this man made his way from Jerusalem to Jericho, he was attacked. Traveling alone by foot or by donkey in the open countryside is dangerous. What happened was much more than just having a wallet stolen. The thieves took his lothing along with whatever valuables he may have possessed. They *beat him* up nd left him *half dead.* The thieves may have intended to murder him. Perhaps ey assumed that he was indeed dead as he lay there unconscious.

The thieves had a mentality that still is with us today. It's a mind-set of what's yours is ours and we'll take it because we're stronger." This man was asy prey. Life was of no value to the thieves. They cared only for what they could et from him. If he died, that was no concern of theirs. Obviously, this is not a odly attitude! This is about as far away from love and concern as you can get!

The injured man presents the issue that Jesus wants to address. Here is a man ith a tremendous need. His personal possessions are gone, he is beaten and loodied, and perhaps he will die without the intervention from a "neighbor." Vho will rescue this man and love him as he does his own self?

*1, 32. "A priest happened to be going down the same road, and when he saw the an, he passed by on the other side. So too, a Levite, when he came to the place nd saw him, passed by on the other side.*

### WHAT DO YOU THINK?

From trying to trap Jesus, the lawyer finds himself on the verge of being trapped. He needs to "justify himself." What difficulties have you seen arise as a result of someone's trying to justify himself or herself? What should one do instead?

### HOW TO SAY IT

Assyrian. Uh-SEAR-e-un.

denarii. dih-NAIR-ee or dih-NAIR-eye.

Deuteronomy. Due-ter-AHN-uh-me.

Ezekiel. Ee-ZEEK-ee-ul or Ee-ZEEK-yul.

Ezra. EZ-ruh.

Jericho. JAIR-ih-co.

Jerusalem. Juh-ROO-suh-lem.

Levite. LEE-vite.

Leviticus. Leh-VIT-ih-kus.

Nehemiah. NEE-huh-MY-uh.

Samaritans. Suh-MARE-uh-tunz.

shema (Hebrew). shih-MAH.

When needs take place within the church today, our first inclination is often to "call the preacher." If he's not available, we call for an elder or a deacon! It is just typical to expect that these men of God will be the first to offer help and assistance in a time of need. That may be our expectation, but as Jesus tells the story we will have our expectation challenged.

After the thieves made their getaway, *a priest* came by and later *a Levite*. The priest served in the temple, where he offered sacrifices. A Levite likewise had duties in the temple services—see Ezekiel 44:10-14. Both certainly had read Leviticus 19:18 many times, but they had not made the personal application of what they had read. Why did they not stop and render assistance to the man?

There is a possible answer to this question: they may have been so concerned about "serving God" that they were unwilling to help this man in need. Temple service demands that those who officiate be clean from any sort of defilement. If the priest and Levite became unclean, they would be disqualified from serving in the temple until they were again considered clean. One thing that makes an individual unclean is coming into contact with a dead body (see Leviticus 21:11; Numbers 5:2; 9:6; 19:11, 13).

However, the priest was going *down* on that road, in other words away from the temple in Jerusalem. He should have been less concerned about ceremonial defilement if his service in the temple had concluded. Yet he walked *by on the other side* as if to say, "There is no way I will become defiled by you." The Levite likewise offered no assistance to the man. How callous could so-called "men of God" be not to at least investigate if the distressed man were alive or dead?

While the thieves had the attitude of "what's yours is ours and we'll take it," the priest and the Levite had the attitude of, "what's ours is ours, and we'll keep it." They saw a man with problems but had no concern for him. They obviously cannot see any connection between love for God and love for others.

33. *"But a Samaritan, as he traveled, came where the man was; and when he saw him, he took pity on him.*

Jesus has a way of introducing unexpected elements into his teaching. This story is no exception. The word *Samaritan* would definitely make the listeners pay special attention. And when the word *pity* is used in association with the Samaritan, that certainly causes even greater surprise. The reason for the shock would be the hatred and distrust that Jews and Samaritans have for each other. In John 4:9 we are given the note that "Jews do not associate with Samaritans."

We know that racial and religious tensions are severe in our era. But racial and religious problems have existed for many centuries, and the divisions they caused were just as severe (or more so) in other times. After the Assyrian conquest of northern Israel in 722 B.C., the Jews remaining in that land intermarried with people from other nations. Thus their descendants were not "pure blood" Jews. These Samaritans wanted to help rebuild the temple after the Babylonian captivity ended in 538 B.C., but the Jews refused their help (Ezra 4:1-5; Nehemiah 2:10, 19; 4:1-8).

What is striking, then, is that this Samaritan looked beyond racial and religious differences, *saw* a *man* with a tremendous need, and knew he had the ability to help. And he didn't just have the resources to help, he also had the willingness to actually do something. He didn't just wring his hands and say, "My, what a shame; someone really should do something." Rather, he stopped, got involved, and helped his neighbor—a man whom he had never met. The following verses describe the ways he helped.

34. *"He went to him and bandaged his wounds, pouring on oil and wine. Then he put the man on his own donkey, took him to an inn and took care of him.*

*WHAT DO YOU THINK?*

*What makes us reluctant to help someone in need? What can break down barriers to make us willing to help?*

The priest and Levite were unwilling to touch this stripped and beaten man, nd they went by on the other side of the road. The Samaritan demonstrated his ove and concern by "getting his hands dirty" and treating the man's injuries. He sed his own resources—*oil and wine*—to help clean the man's *wounds*. He banaged the cuts.

The Samaritan has invested his time, resources, and also his comfort. But the elp doesn't stop there. He put the injured man on his beast and took him *to an n* for recuperation. This Samaritan had started his day like any other day. He as traveling on his business. But his business suddenly took second place to ne more immediate and urgent needs of an injured man. He sacrifices much for person whom he had never seen until that day. But he does even more.

5. *"The next day he took out two silver coins and gave them to the innkeeper. .ook after him,' he said, 'and when I return, I will reimburse you for any extra xpense you may have.'*

It is one thing to sacrifice a little time, another thing to sacrifice a little comfort, ut now this Samaritan has sacrificed money! He has already used his oil and ine on the man's wounds, but now he is putting a significant amount of finan- ial resources into the man's care as well. *Two silver coins* in the original language , two denarii, or two days' wages. We are not talking about just a couple of pen- ies or dollars!

The Samaritan then does still more: he makes a legally binding agreement to ay *extra*, if need be. The injured man was someone he had never met, and he ould have said, "That's all I'm able to do right now."

This Samaritan is rightly described as a man having concern, compassion, and ove for people. His attitude can be described as, "What's mine is yours, and I'll hare it." This is far different from the robbers who stole and the priest and Levite rho would not get involved. The Samaritan demonstrated by his actions the ompassion that lived in his heart.

### GET MAD—IN A GOOD WAY

Can anger cause you to do something good? We usually think of anger in nega- tive terms, as an emotion that causes us to lose control and do things we later re- gret. There is no mention of anger in Jesus' Parable of the Good Samaritan. Yet when one reads it one cannot help but be angry at the thieves who left the man dying and at the "religious" people who passed him by without helping.

When Chrysler Corporation Chairman Lee Iacocca addressed a college graduat- ing class in 1983, he reportedly told them to get mad at things that were wrong in the world—mad enough to do something to change things. He wanted the gradu- ates to get mad about the state of things. The United States of America was born when several dozen patriots got mad enough to sign the Declaration of Indepen- dence. The U.S. put a man on the moon because Sputnik made the country mad at being number two in the space race. Getting mad in a constructive way is good for the soul.

Righteous anger is a valid emotion and a powerful motivator. It moves people to join causes that make the world a better place by combating abortion, hunger, illiteracy, poverty, injustice, and other societal ills. When we add the compassion of the good Samaritan to our justifiable anger, there will be no stopping the work of Christ!       —T. A. C.

## I. GO AND DO LIKEWISE! (LUKE 10:36, 37)

### A. WHAT DO YOU THINK? (v. 36)

6. *"Which of these three do you think was a neighbor to the man who fell into the ands of robbers?"*

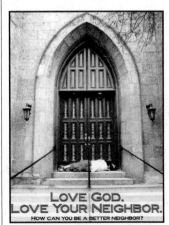

Visual for lesson 12. *Use this image to introduce the question,* "Who will experience God's love through me?"

## WHAT DO YOU THINK?

*To whom are we being good neighbors? Who has a "neighbor" who is not being helped? How can we do better?*

The lawyer is probably wishing he had never asked the question, "Who is my neighbor?" Jesus' question provides a tremendous opportunity to expose the hypocrisy and unsympathetic attitude of the religious leaders. It also demonstrates that love reaches across cultural boundaries. We learn that our *neighbor* is whomever we have occasion to help. A neighbor is not only someone who lives in geographical proximity to us, but rather anyone who needs our assistance.

### B. DO WHAT YOU THINK! (v. 37)

**37. The expert in the law replied, "The one who had mercy on him."**
**Jesus told him, "Go and do likewise."**

It is to his credit that *the expert in the law* does not try to slip out of the question by "blaming the victim." This would be something like, "Well, that beaten man should have known better than to be on a road that is well traveled by robbers."

Instead, the lawyer answers forthrightly. It is apparent that the priest and the Levite were not neighbors to the injured man. It is only the Samaritan who demonstrated the qualities of a good neighbor that we should display. Jesus challenges the lawyer—and he also speaks to our generation—when he says, *Go and do likewise.* Each day we will encounter neighbors whom we can assist. We must look beyond those people we know well and see others that still need the help we can supply.

## PRAYER

*Father, we confess that we have not always been your hands and feet in our love for others. Convict our hearts that we will be a "good Samaritan" to someone today. In Jesus' name, amen.*

### "LET THEM UP EASY"

On April 9, 1865, soldiers of the Confederacy waited outside the house that was the site of Lee's surrender to Grant. While they waited, they probably wondered about the terms of the surrender. The American Civil War had been a bitter contest, and it would have been easy for the victorious army to demand harsh terms of their vanquished foe.

President Abraham Lincoln already had thought about what would happen when the war was over and the nation needed to heal. He realized that this had been a war among neighbors, and it would need to be followed by a peace among neighbors. "Let them up easy" is a famous phrase attributed to Lincoln after the fall of Richmond. Lincoln's understanding of "neighbors" helped heal a nation.

There are various facets to the Parable of the Good Samaritan. At its heart, however, it is an illustration of being a godly neighbor. What kind of neighbor are you? "Neighbor" is not limited to the person or family next door. It means anyone who is in need. How do you respond to those in need? How do you respond to someone who has wronged you and is now in need? Your answer to those questions may reveal far more about your Christian character than the number of church services you attend!        —T. A. C.

## CONCLUSION

John wrote, "If anyone says, 'I love God,' yet hates his brother, he is a liar. For anyone who does not love his brother, whom he has seen, cannot love God, whom he has not seen. And he has given us this command: Whoever loves God must also love his brother" (1 John 4:20, 21). The lawyer wanted to know how to be saved. In his mind he knew the correct answer: Love God and love others.

Unfortunately, the lawyer had much to learn about loving his neighbor. The old chorus says, "And they'll know we are Christians by our love." Our faith in God our Savior is demonstrated as we love our neighbors. We must be willing to help those neighbors we find in need.

## THOUGHT TO REMEMBER

*Put hands and feet to your love.*

# Discovery Learning

*This page contains an alternative lesson plan emphasizing learning activities. Classes desiring such student involvement will find these suggestions helpful. The next page is a reproducible activity page to further enhance discovery learning.*

## EARNING GOALS

After participating in this lesson, each student will be ble to:

1. Explain the meaning of the Parable of the Good amaritan in light of the historical context in which it as taught.

2. Compare himself or herself with the main characters in the story, determining whom they most resemble.

3. Commit to sacrificially meeting the needs of a specific person.

## NTO THE LESSON

Bring several newspapers and current news magazines to class. Place them around the room on chairs before class members arrive. This may prompt conversations about current events as people arrive.

Begin by asking your learners to find examples of people in need from the articles and pictures. Cut them out and affix them to the wall or poster board. The eading should read *Needs in the World Today*. Say, Today's lesson will consider a very familiar and straightforward story: the Parable of the Good Samaritan. A major focus today will be on how the lesson applies, as e hear Jesus' answer to the question, 'Who is my eighbor?'"

## NTO THE WORD

Begin by reading Luke 10:25-29 aloud to review the background and context for this parable. Using three oster boards, write on top of the first, "Reaction #1"; he second, "Reaction #2"; and the third, "Reaction 3"; place them on the wall beside the collection of articles and pictures you have posted.

One by one, discuss the reaction of each of the three main characters in the parable (priest, Levite, and amaritan), asking the following questions for each: Who is this? How did he react? Why do you think he responded this way? What does this reveal about his ove for another? What does this reveal about his love or God?"

Next, write responses to the following additional uestions on the corresponding poster board: "What people today would correspond to the characters in the arable? That is, if Jesus were telling this story today, hat characters could he have used?" For the first two haracters, some suggestions may include a preacher,

missionary, or elder in place of the priest; in place of the Levite may be a deacon, a leader in a parachurch organization, or a Christian author.

After placing several suggestions on the board, ask, "What reason could each of these give for doing nothing to help someone they see in need?" For the part of the Samaritan, ask the class to list people today who would be considered outcasts. Again, write the ideas on the poster board.

Next, ask someone to come up and retell the story while walking across the room and selecting items from the lists on the poster board. For example, the story might sound like this:

> A family was homeless, with the mother hospitalized, after their house burned. A minister heard about it, but was too busy preparing his sermon to help. The chairman of the missionary society at the church thought it was more important to attend a committee meeting, so he didn't help either. A man/woman from *[fill in with an appropriate description of a "despised" group]* went to the hospital, volunteered to house the children, and brought money saved for vacation to buy meals.

Repeat this process several times. Each time before a person retells the story in modern terms, ask, "Who is my neighbor?" After the story is retold each time, stop and ask the class, "Who was a neighbor to the one in need?"

This process should help emphasize the way Jesus showed that the lawyer was actually asking the wrong question. The lawyer asked the question, "Who is my neighbor?" (Luke 10:29). Jesus showed him that the real question should be, "To whom can I be a neighbor?"

## INTO LIFE

Next, have class members identify situations where they have been confronted with people in need over the last year. Ask them to consider how they responded. Say, "If Jesus were telling the story with you as one of the characters, who would you be?"

Discuss specific ways members of the class can become more effective at seeing and sensitively meeting the needs of others. Also discuss the importance of doing this in Jesus' name. Pray as a class for the right heart and courage to act when seeing others in need.

# Be a Neighbor

The lawyer asked Jesus, "Who is my neighbor?" The parable Jesus told in response made it clear that the lawyer had asked the wrong question. The proper question—for him and for us—is. "To whom can I be a neighbor?"

Use each letter of the word *neighbor* to identify someone in your community who needs someone like you to be a neighbor. Each word may begin with, end with, or merely contain one of the letters of *neighbor*. One example has been done to get you started.

**N**

JOBLESS CHURCH MEMBER

**I**

**G**

**H**

**B**

**O**

**R**

# "Go and Do Likewise"

Choose one of the persons identified above. Consider one or more specific means to be a neighbor—that is to render help. Write your plan below.

Person: _____

Help Needed: _____

_____

Tangible Way to Help: _____

_____

When? _____

_____

# ACCEPTING THE INVITATION

**LESSON 13**

## WHY TEACH THIS LESSON?

How does one decide a "yes" or a "no" to the various invitations that come
his or her way? Excuses can always be fabricated to justify a "no." But the wise
decision maker considers only one criterion: does this opportunity within the invitation allow me to grow toward God or to grow away from him? Does attendance at a wedding give me an opportunity to bless another? Does the offer of a
new job provide an occasion of witness and service or only one of greed and self-
importance?

Adult learners are faced daily with invitations, most of minor consequence but
some of eternal consequence. Today's study provides a key to making the wise,
eternal response.

## INTRODUCTION

### A. "I MUST BE IN THE FRONT ROW!"

You may remember the television commercial from the 1980s featuring sports
celebrity Bob Uecker. He would enter a stadium and declare, "I must be in the
front row!" Next, you saw him way up in the "cheap seats." In this spoof, Uecker
thought he was more of an honored celebrity than he actually was. He felt in his
pretended arrogance that he deserved the place of honor.

Today's text will illustrate the importance of humility in a way that modern
celebrities rarely do. Make no mistake: we, too, can be guilty of assuming that we
are more important than others and deserve great recognition. Yet Jesus taught
that the first shall be last and the last shall be first. As we learn humility, we may
also learn discipleship.

### B. LESSON BACKGROUND

Luke 14 finds Jesus well on his way to Jerusalem and the crucifixion that
awaits (compare Luke 13:22). It is a time for more teaching and more miracles as
opposition steadily rises (13:31). The time is short, and Jesus has much left to
say and do. Today's lesson finds him at "the house of a prominent Pharisee" for a
Sabbath day meal (14:1a). There's an old saying: "Keep your friends close and
your enemies even closer." The Pharisees intend to do just that (14:1b)!

## WHERE SHOULD I SIT? (LUKE 14:7-11)

### A. PROUD ARE HUMBLED (vv. 7-9)

*When he noticed how the guests picked the places of honor at the table, he told
them this parable:*

People are selecting their *places* for the banquet just ahead. One wonders what
goes through the Lord's mind as he observes them. Does he shake his head or
even roll his eyes as he sees people posture for recognition? Does it grieve him to
observe how they step across one another in an attempt to appear more important than their counterparts? Perhaps he sighs as he recognizes that in order for
his disciples to be effective they will have to change their way of thinking and develop a genuine humility in their hearts and lives.

DEVOTIONAL READING:
1 PETER 5:3-10
BACKGROUND SCRIPTURE:
LUKE 14:7-24
PRINTED TEXT:
LUKE 14:7-11, 15-27

### LEARNING AIMS

After participating in this lesson, each student will be able to:

1. Explain the lesson from
Jesus' parables in Luke 14.

2. Understand the relationship between humility and being
a disciple of Jesus.

3. Accept the call of Jesus to
follow him humbly, gratefully,
and wholeheartedly.

### KEY VERSE

"Then the master told his servant, 'Go out to the roads and
country lanes and make
them come in, so that my
house will be full.'"
—Luke 14:23

Aug
28

LESSON 13 NOTES

## WHAT DO YOU THINK?

*How do people today posture for position, seeking to make themselves appear important in the eyes of others?*

*[Caution: Keep this discussion focused on issues—not people. Finger-pointing at people present or just known to those in your class will not be helpful.]*

Jesus thus tells a *parable* that illustrates the folly of pomposity. It is fairly easy to see how we find ourselves with the same attitudes at times.

**8. "When someone invites you to a wedding feast, do not take the place of honor, for a person more distinguished than you may have been invited.**

Imagine that you've heard that an important official is coming to town for an event followed by a meal. Somehow you assume that he will want you to be seated next to him at the head table. You put on your best clothes and proceed to make your way to the front. Moments later his security detail comes and forcibly removes you from the building! This scenario is both frightening and humiliating.

Jesus teaches that we should not assume that we are the most honored guest or the most important person in any situation. How embarrassing it would be to have someone of an even higher status show up unexpectedly. The next verse illustrates the type of embarrassment that can come when we assume that we are more important than what we truly are.

**9. "If so, the host who invited both of you will come and say to you, 'Give this man your seat.' Then, humiliated, you will have to take the least important place.**

One can picture that uncomfortable, awkward moment! Someone has assumed a place at the head table and sits down as if it were reserved for him. Unfortunately, someone comes along, taps him on the shoulder, and says, "I'm sorry, you're going to have to move. This is not *your seat.* You'll have to find another table, and I think there's one in the back!"

To the snickering of the other invited guests, this once self-important person shrinks back to the less-honored seat. Such a foolish error! Arrogance is his downfall. Had he not assumed a certain level of importance, such humiliation would have been avoided. Next, Jesus suggests a strategy to save a person from this type of shame.

### B. HUMBLE ARE PROMOTED (vv. 10, 11)

**10. "But when you are invited, take the lowest place, so that when your host comes, he will say to you, 'Friend, move up to a better place.' Then you will be honored in the presence of all your fellow guests.**

Go back to the previous illustration of the official coming to town. You've come into the convention hall and have seated yourself in the farthest corner of the building, perhaps more distant from the official than anyone else.

Next, you see him stand and begin peering through the crowd. Perhaps he asks for assistance in finding you! When he finally sees you, he smiles and begins waving to you and motioning for you to come up front. He's expecting you to sit with him. In full view of all, you make your way to the front where you are now seated in a place of high honor. You started at the back and found your way up front! How much better this is than to assume a *place* at the front, only to be sent to the back in shame.

Jesus tells us to not make false assumptions about personal importance. Start by sitting in the back and being thankful for even being asked to come in the first place. Then the one who invited you may give you a great honor by escorting you from the back table up to the head table. That would be tremendous, so much better than having to be told to move because someone more important than you needs that good seat.

All through this parable the application to servanthood and humility is seen. It is a high honor to be a disciple of the Lord. As the servant does the bidding of the master, so also should we view ourselves as servants of Christ. One should not assume that he or she is indispensable or favored more than another servant. Rather, God's servants should do the assigned work gratefully. There remains a

## HOW TO SAY IT

*Ephesians. Ee-FEE-zhunz.*

*Pharisees. FAIR-ih-seez.*

ay when the Lord shall judge the work of his servants. Those who have served
aithfully shall hear the words, "Well done."

**1. "For everyone who exalts himself will be humbled, and he who humbles him-
lf will be exalted."**

Jesus now provides the key point of the parable. Disaster comes when we
aink we are more important than we are (see Proverbs 16:18). Those who exalt
nemselves—presuming that they are more important than others or are deserv-
ng of special treatment—will be surprised to find themselves *humbled,* that is,
rought down lower or humiliated.

Yet Jesus also teaches that there is a counterpart to this. Those who do not
nake such false assumptions, who faithfully serve without desire of recognition,
nd who have an attitude of lowliness *will be exalted.* It is better to start low and
e promoted, than to assume you're starting high and get demoted!

The Lord's disciples must understand that pride and arrogance are counter-
roductive to the tasks that the Lord has given (compare Mark 10:35-37). If an
ttitude of pride and feelings of superiority exist, this will negatively affect our
itness and productivity in kingdom work. Many times we are too good at point-
ng out the shortcomings of others in an attempt to make ourselves look good.
here's truth in that old saying that when we point our finger at someone then
nere are three more pointing right back at us! We recognize that there is a job for
ach disciple. The Lord will evaluate the work (Romans 14:4). The task for the
Christian is to be concerned with his or her own work, not that of others.

## I. INEXCUSABLE EXCUSES (LUKE 14:15-24)

### A. INVITATION (vv. 15-17)

**5. When one of those at the table with him heard this, he said to Jesus, "Blessed
; the man who will eat at the feast in the kingdom of God."**

Those who are assembled with Jesus understand that it is a high privilege to
e invited into the Lord's kingdom and enjoy fellowship with him. It will indeed
e a high privilege to be in the presence of the Lord as it is to be called into his
ervice.

**6, 17. Jesus replied: "A certain man was preparing a great banquet and invited
nany guests. At the time of the banquet he sent his servant to tell those who had
een invited, 'Come, for everything is now ready.'**

In the first-century culture, an invitation is a significant thing. It is a social
lunder to receive an invitation, then fail to honor it when the time comes. If
omeone goes to the trouble of *preparing* a meal, it is expected that the one who
; *invited* will honor the invitation at the appropriate time. This *certain man* has
repared a sumptuous feast and is ready for his *guests.* He even goes to the addi-
ional trouble of sending a *servant* out to remind people that it is time for them to
rrive and enjoy the meal. All they have to do is show up!

### B. PROPERTY INSPECTION EXCUSE (v. 18)

**8. "But they all alike began to make excuses. The first said, 'I have just bought a
ield, and I must go and see it. Please excuse me.'**

As the servant goes out to remind people of the dinner to which they were in-
ited, he begins to hear one excuse after another. Employers often hear excuses
bout why an employee is late or doesn't complete a job. Teachers often get ex-
uses for why a student is absent or why assignments are not completed. We are
uick *to make excuses,* but not so quick to accept responsibility for our actions!
xcuses will not hold water with God. He has been very gracious to invite us into
is kingdom, even as the man said in verse 15. Yet many who are invited to the

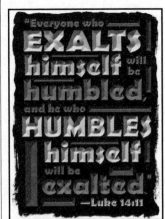

Visual for lesson 13. *Display
this poster and have it read aloud
as you begin your study of the
question above.*

Lord's kingdom make one poor excuse after another as to why they just cannot honor the invitation.

Think about the first excuse: *I have just bought a field.* Would this property disappear in the time that it will take to go and enjoy the meal the man has prepared? Would that much really be lost? It seems that the person's priorities are somewhat misguided. To this man, checking out his newly acquired land is more important than the fellowship he would enjoy with the friend who has invited him to dinner.

### C. YOKE OF OXEN EXCUSE (v. 19)

*19. "Another said, 'I have just bought five yoke of oxen, and I'm on my way to try them out. Please excuse me.'*

Likewise, this second individual has something more pressing on his mind, something of a higher priority to him than his friend's banquet. He chooses to go and work with his new *oxen* to see how productive they will be for him. One wonders if that really is such a pressing need right then. It also suggests that the man would rather spend time with his oxen than with his friend—someone who has gone to time and expense to prepare a banquet and invite him to attend.

### D. NEW WIFE EXCUSE (v. 20)

*20. "Still another said, 'I just got married, so I can't come.'*

The third man also has other things on his mind, namely enjoying time with his new bride. It is very possible that this banquet is a "men only" event, so she is probably not invited. Single men often lament that their married buddies no longer have time to "hang out with the guys." This newlywed's priorities have changed. He, too, declines to honor the invitation to dinner.

This man, however, has the rest of his life to spend with his new wife! Will one evening away from her really be such a burden to honor a friend? Misplaced priorities will keep people from experiencing the blessings of a relationship with God (see Matthew 6:33).

God is not fooled by the excuses that we make. The Lord is most definitely aware that people are telling him that other things or other people are more important to them than he is. God deserves to be in first place, and he expects it.

### E. INVITATION BROADENED (vv. 21-23)

*21. "The servant came back and reported this to his master. Then the owner of the house became angry and ordered his servant, 'Go out quickly into the streets and alleys of the town and bring in the poor, the crippled, the blind and the lame.'*

*The owner of the house* has gone to considerable trouble and expense. The meal was declared "ready," and there is no one to enjoy it! He is both offended and angered at the lack of regard that his invited guests have shown him. So now he changes his thinking and tells his servant to find anyone he can and *bring* them in.

Those who are included in this new invitation are not the high and noble—the ones who had turned him down. Rather, these are on the lower end of society's ladder. The servant is sent to the places where the homeless and the beggars are to be found. Among these there will be those who are dirty, sick, *lame*, and *blind*. These are not the ones who normally find themselves invited to "society events." But now they are invited to come and share in the prepared feast.

## THE UNEXPECTED INVITATION

Every U.S. president knows that his selection of cabinet officers may determine the success or failure of his administration. In 1862 Abraham Lincoln had to ap-

**WHAT DO YOU THINK?**

*What excuses do people offer for not getting more involved in church ministries? What priorities do these excuses reveal? What is the difference between an excuse and a reason, if any?*

point a new Secretary of War, a position of great importance during the American Civil War.

Lincoln extended an invitation to an old political enemy: Edwin M. Stanton (1814–1869). Stanton had snubbed Lincoln earlier, calling him a "gawky, long-armed ape" during the McCormick-Manny legal case of 1855. Stanton had publicly expressed his doubts about Lincoln's ability to serve as president.

Imagine how Stanton must have felt when Lincoln asked him to serve in the most crucial cabinet office in his administration! Imagine what others thought about Lincoln for extending that invitation. Many undoubtedly thought it was political suicide. Yet, when Lincoln died on the morning of April 15, 1865, it was Stanton who wept and said, "Now he belongs to the ages."

Some people have a difficult time understanding God's invitation to be part of his kingdom. That invitation, offered to his enemies, is extended by the power of grace available through the cross and empty tomb. The invitation is God's—not ours. We do not determine the invitation list; it is God who extends the invitation to all. We only decide if we shall accept it or not.      —T. A. C.

2, 23. "'Sir,' the servant said, 'what you ordered has been done, but there is ill room.'

"Then the master told his servant, 'Go out to the roads and country lanes and ake them come in, so that my house will be full.

This man will not be satisfied until his banquet room is *full*. That phrase *make em come in* is stronger than to merely invite. His so-called friends had spurned he invitation. Now others are told to come and enjoy a meal.

It would seem that Jesus is making clear what he taught in the previous para-le. The ones who were humbled had the opportunity to be exalted. And the nes who thought themselves to be too important and too busy are now being isdained. The next verse makes this clearer still.

### THE PLACE OF NO EXCLUSIONS

The Tomb of the Unknowns in Arlington National Cemetery is one of America's most "sacred" sites. It houses remains of service members from World Wars I and II and Korea. In 1999 it was announced that there probably would be no more remains interred there. It would be nice to think that it meant there would be no more wars. But there was a different reason: the U.S. armed services were now to use DNA samples for identification. Americans will still be killed in wars, but their remains always will be identifiable, thanks to modern technology.

In some respects, America has been defined by the Tomb of the Unknowns. The remains there, "known but to God," may have been the bodies of officers or enlisted, black or white, rich or poor, educated or illiterate. None of that matters. America is not a nation of kings and peasants, gentry and serfs, aristocrats and riffraff. The Tomb of the Unknowns does not reflect station in life at time of death.

When you look at your congregation on Sunday morning, what kind of people do you see? Mostly of one race? Mostly middle class? If the lack of diversity is intentional, something is very wrong! The church is not a body in which station in life should matter. The invitation to God's great banquet is extended to all.   —T. A. C.

### INVITATION REVOKED (v. 24)

4. "'I tell you, not one of those men who were invited will get a taste of my anquet.'"

The original group, first invited to share in the man's banquet, are now "unin-ited." They had their chance but lost it because other things had become more mportant to them. They turned down the gracious invitation. They now have no ne to blame but themselves for losing their places. The friendships are (we may

DAILY BIBLE READINGS

**Monday, Aug. 22**—*Bear with One Another in Love (Ephesians 4:1-6)*

**Tuesday, Aug. 23**—*Imitate Christ's Humility (Philippians 2:1-8)*

**Wednesday, Aug. 24**—*Clothe Yourself with Humility (1 Peter 5:3-10)*

**Thursday, Aug. 25**—*Parable of the Wedding Banquet (Matthew 22:1-10)*

**Friday, Aug. 26**—*Jesus Heals the Man with Dropsy (Luke 14:1-6)*

**Saturday, Aug. 27**—*Humility and Hospitality (Luke 14: 7-14)*

**Sunday, Aug. 28**—*Parable of the Great Dinner (Luke 14: 15-24)*

PRAYER

*Father, show us our crosses this week. Give us strength to carry them. In Jesus' name, amen.*

safely assume) permanently damaged! By their own choices, the "uninvited" have lost a relationship with someone who cared for them.

## III. GOD FIRST! (LUKE 14:25-27)

### A. FIRST IN LOVE (vv. 25, 26)

**25, 26. Large crowds were traveling with Jesus, and turning to them he said: "If anyone comes to me and does not hate his father and mother, his wife and children, his brothers and sisters—yes, even his own life—he cannot be my disciple.**

Jesus' ministry continues to experience great growth and excitement. People both observe and receive great miracles that he performs. They must enjoy watching him debate with the religious leaders and humiliate them for their arrogance and sinful attitudes (Luke 13:17). Yet Jesus now has a word for the people who are following him. They, too, have to make sure that they have the right priorities.

A person can be materialistic whether as a millionaire or as one beneath the poverty level. It is possible to put many things in a place of higher prominence than a relationship with the Lord. Some do it with entertainment, sports, leisure, or business dealings. Some even put their earthly family as a higher priority than their heavenly Father.

But doesn't the idea of "hating" one's own family members, and even one's *own life*, seem extreme? Doesn't Exodus 20:12 teach that we are to honor our father and mother? Are we not told that in 1 Timothy 5:8 that if we don't take care of the needs of our family we are worse than an unbeliever? Is verse 26 a contradiction to Ephesians 5:25 that tells us the importance of husbands loving their wives as Christ loved the church?

Jesus grabs the audience's attention by using that strong word *hate!* He uses it to illustrate the importance of having God first in one's life—a higher priority than any other thing or person. Our relationship with God must be such a passion that by comparison it would appear that we do hate everything else. Obviously, Jesus does not intend hate to be taken in an absolute sense. In a relative sense, our love for God must be greater than even that of our beloved family.

### B. FIRST IN SACRIFICE (v. 27)

**27. "And anyone who does not carry his cross and follow me cannot be my disciple."**

We sing songs about the old rugged *cross* and ask, "Must Jesus Bear the Cross Alone?" In the first century the cross is not beautiful or something in which people glory. Before Jesus' death and resurrection, no one would have worn a cross as jewelry. There is only one reason a person ever takes up a cross: to die upon it. As Jesus will be made to *carry* his own cross, so also is there a task for us. Jesus will not refuse his cross, but because of his devotion to his Father's will and because of his love for us, he will be nailed to that cross for our sins.

No one will die for a cause in which he or she does not believe. All of the bold statements of what we would do for Christ are empty if he is not actually first in our lives. Do we believe someone who says, "I'd die for Jesus," but won't do small things that serve and honor the Lord?

## CONCLUSION

The answer to the songwriter's question, "Must Jesus bear the cross alone, And all the world go free?" is this: "No; there's a cross for ev'ryone, And there's a cross for me" (Thomas Shepherd, 1665–1739). Those who are self-important and believe they deserve the very best have not made God their priority. Many reject the Lord's invitation to his kingdom because other things are more important. Humility and sacrifice are what the Lord seeks.

# Discovery Learning

*This page contains an alternative lesson plan emphasizing learning activities. Classes*
*desiring such student involvement will find these suggestions helpful. The next page*
*is a reproducible activity page to further enhance discovery learning.*

## LEARNING GOALS

After participating in this lesson, each student will be able to:

1. Explain the lesson from Jesus' parables in Luke 14.

2. Understand the relationship between humility and being a disciple of Jesus.

3. Accept the call of Jesus to follow him humbly, gratefully, and wholeheartedly.

## INTO THE LESSON

Before class, prepare invitations for a formal dinner party, leaving the significant details blank. For example: You are cordially invited to a party hosted by [name of host] to celebrate [occasion of celebration] on [time and date] at [location of party]. RSVP." Begin class by putting your learners into small groups. Have each group plan an imaginary party by filling in the blanks of the invitations. They should also comment on other details of the party, such as appropriate attire, entertainment, and menu.

After a few minutes, ask each group to read its invitation and describe the event they have planned. Say, Having these settings in mind sets the stage for understanding the two parables of Jesus we will examine, both of which occur in a banquet context."

## INTO THE WORD

*Banquet Attendance Etiquette.* Read Luke 14:7-11 aloud. Review the parable several times by describing the story in the context of the imaginary events that have been planned by your small groups. (For example, "While at the Lincoln Center, a guest took a seat next to the President of the United States, at which point security ushered him to a small adjoining room where he could only observe the event on closed-circuit TV.") After repeating this for several of the situations created by your class members, ask, "What lessons do we learn about pride and humility?" Conclude this discussion by reading aloud the summary in Luke 14:11.

*Banquet Invitation Etiquette.* Say, "So far we have learned something about banquet 'attendance etiquette,' but there's also something to learn about 'invitation etiquette.'" Then pass out small slips of paper (several to each learner) with the following phrase written on the top: "I'm sorry, but I will not be able to attend because . . ."

Inform your learners that you are now having a "Lame Excuse" contest. You want them to write the reason they could express to the host for not attending the event to which they have been invited. Remind them of the important galas that they previously had created. Say, "I will be looking for the lamest excuses based on how humorous or ridiculous they are." (You could even offer prizes!)

After a few minutes of small-group discussions, you can either have class members read aloud their lame excuses or you can collect them to read several aloud yourself. After reading these (and laughing together), ask, "How would you feel if you were the host who received such responses from the guests you had invited?" Next, read aloud Luke 14:15-20. After each excuse is given in the parable itself, pause to discuss how well it would do in your "Lame Excuse" contest.

Discuss what the excuses in the text might sound like today. Begin by saying, "Jesus extends an invitation for everyone to follow him. His offer of forgiveness and grace is free. However, people often respond by providing lame excuses. These show pride rather than humility. These excuses may indicate preoccupation with money, or success, or many other things. Ultimately, however, this attitude reflects a pride that says, 'I don't need Jesus.' It is an insult to him and his gracious offer. So how do any of our excuses really sound to him?"

Conclude this part of the discussion by reading aloud Luke 14:21-24. After you reach the end of verse 23, pause and tell your learners that you want everyone to join in as you read verse 24 aloud together, then do so. For dramatic effect, you can go around the room and have each person read verse 24 aloud separately.

## INTO LIFE

Distribute "invitations" that read as follows: "You are cordially invited by Jesus Christ to participate in a celebration of forgiveness and freedom beginning today and lasting for all eternity. RSVP." (Make these up ahead of time, preferably using some kind of "fancy" font as commonly found in word processing software.)

Encourage students to use the invitation as a bookmark or post it on the refrigerator. This is to remind them to consider daily their response to this invitation. Close with a prayer for this.

# Lame Excuse Contest

What are some of the lamest excuses you've ever heard? These can be excuses for not completing some task ("The dog ate my homework."), for not showing up for an appointment ("Four o'clock on the third? I thought it was three o'clock on the fourth."), or for not accepting an assignment or invitation ("I have to wash my hair").

List as many as you can think of. Then choose the worst excuse on the list. Compare with others in your class to see who came up with the lamest excuse of all!

?

Now read Luke 14:15-27. List the lame excuses from this parable. How do they compare with your own lame excuses above? Is there a new contest winner?

? ?

# No Excuses

Perhaps you have noticed a need, but you have done nothing to correct it. Or perhaps you've been invited to serve in some ministry, but so far you have declined. Write it below.

!

Why have you refused? Are you just making excuses? Is it time to say yes? Pray about this issue. Then write below what you plan to do.

! !